Human Resource Management in a Business Context

3rd edition

John Kew and John Stredwick

Chartered Institute of Personnel and Development

Published by the Chartered Institute of Personnel and Development
151 The Broadway, London SW19 1JQ

This edition first published 2016

Designed and typeset by Exeter Premedia Services, India
Printed in Great Britain

British Library Cataloguing in Publication Data
A catalogue of this publication is available from the British Library

ISBN 9781843984047
eBook ISBN 9781843984511

Chartered Institute of Personnel and Development

151 The Broadway, London SW19 1JQ
Tel: 020 8612 6200
Email: cipd@cipd.co.uk
Website: www.cipd.co.uk
Incorporated by Royal Charter.
Registered Charity No. 1079797

Contents

List of figures and tables

Preface

It has been accepted for many years that human resource management does not operate in a vacuum. To be effective, it needs to be deeply embedded in the business environment of the organisation. It is essential that human resources contribute to the organisation's business strategy that both reacts to changes in the environment and identifies future changes that provide opportunities for operational success in a harshly competitive world. Worldwide the economic balance of power is changing, especially with the growing power and influence of China.

An understanding of the business environment continues to be vital for all business and human resource students who wish to gain a wider understanding of both the context in which business decisions are taken and the major influences on those decisions. As the context becomes more turbulent and unpredictable, it becomes even more important to grasp the complexity of the many issues presented and the strategic options that can be followed.

Human Resource Management in a Business Context includes:

- updates on crucial political, economic and legal areas, including the European Union, international institutions and globalisation, and regulatory developments
- in-depth coverage of the causes and implications of the recent world financial crisis, and of swiftly changing demographic trends
- a discussion of the internal business environment which identifies a variety of management issues and evaluates the forces shaping the HRM agenda in response to those issues, including an analysis of the best practice-best fit debate.

The book closely follows the CIPD Level 7 module *Human Resource Management in Context*, and it also covers the content of the CIPD Level 5 module *Business Issues and the Contexts of Human Resources*. It is also suitable for students at all levels whose syllabus includes a module in Business Environment, as it covers all subject areas normally included in such modules. The emphasis is very much on developing student knowledge and understanding, while the main aim has been to make the text accessible and to encourage students to follow up key issues by linking the text with up-to-date cases, activities and associated reading.

The distinctive feature of this book is the large number of practical activities and case studies which apply the theory to real-life situations. A large number of new case studies and activities have been written for this edition, including the advice service NHS111, the ethics of the Ebola epidemic, the collapse of the courier firm Citylink, and the crisis in the UK steel industry. There is also a longer seminar activity for each chapter, as well as a number of self-assessment questions. Feedback for all the activities is provided in the companion website at www.cipd.co.uk/olr which supports the book, along with a large number of additional activities.

The information contained on this site is available free of charge to tutors, but tutors will have to register to gain access to the material. Visit www.cipd.co.uk-tss-registration to complete the online registration form. The site contains links to general business sites and advice to lecturers who adopt the text on how to use the book as a planned series of lectures. PowerPoint presentations are available to accompany each chapter and there is suggested feedback for activities, as well as additional activities.

A summary of the book's contents is as follows:

Chapter 1 sets the scene for the whole book – the interaction between the environment, the organisation, HR and strategy. We explore models of environmental analysis and of organisational design, along with stakeholder theory.

Chapter 2 begins by summarising the development of management theory and examining the issues involved in management power, authority and legitimacy. This is followed by an examination of the contemporary analysis of human resource models and roles, and the key issues facing human resource practitioners. Specific consideration is given to the role of human resources in areas such as quality assurance and customer care.

Chapter 3 begins with an analysis of supply and demand, followed by a consideration of market structures, including Michael Porter's Five Forces model. We then move on to the application of microeconomic theory to the working of the labour market and a consideration of changes in the industrial and employment structure of the UK.

Chapter 4 analyses the evolution of government policy in social, economic and industrial fields, and the impact of government policy on organisations. As developments in the UK are heavily influenced by the actions of the EU, we are concerned with both UK and EU policy. We start with formal legislative procedures in the UK and the EU, and then go on to consider informal influences on the evolution of policy. We then consider recent developments in policy in the UK, including the causes and impact of the world financial crisis in 2007–8, and developments in UK government and economic policy since the crisis.

Chapter 5 examines a wide range of legal and regulatory aspects, starting with a summary of the UK legal system and the way that regulation has developed in fields of employment, health and safety, consumer and commercial law. The impact of regulation on particular sectors is discussed and the direction of regulation is debated, especially in relation to regulation of the financial sector.

Chapter 6 Since the end of the Second World War, the world economy has become more and more integrated. Partly this has been a deliberate, planned process. A number of international institutions were set up to regulate the world economy and to ensure that the world did not suffer from a recurrence of Great Depression of the 1930s. Other developments were only made possible as a result of technological developments in communications and transport, which enabled the growth of globalisation. We examine theories of globalisation.

The European Economic Community, the forerunner of the European Union, was set up partly to ensure that France and Germany could never again go to war with each other. Current EU issues are analysed, including the introduction of the euro and the subsequent Greek debt crisis (GREXIT), and the debates over a possible UK exit from the EU (BREXIT). We examine the impact of the EU and globalisation on HR practice in the UK.

Chapter 7 summarises the startling changes in demography in recent years, both in the UK and worldwide, discussing the major implications of an ageing population in the advanced economies and a still-rapidly-rising population growth in developing countries. This leads to a debate about the flow of migrants from one grouping to the other, exacerbated by war in Syria and Afghanistan. The influence on markets for goods and services and the challenges and opportunities in the employment field are considered in detail, together with government initiatives on key areas such as pensions and migration. This is followed by a focus on the major social trends and attitudes alongside changing social structure. The causes of major social problems, such as the increase in criminal behaviour, are debated and the implications for employment and labour markets are examined. How organisations can react to the changes and options available is considered.

Chapter 8 presents an analysis of technological change and its substantial influence on the business environment, particularly in the fields of information and communication technology, including the explosive growth of social media. The opportunities in the labour markets that technology offers, such as teleworking and online recruitment, are discussed, together with the benefits and difficulties associated with such technologies. The reasons why there is considerable resistance to technology in certain quarters are examined.

Chapter 9 examines the nature of ethics and different approaches which can be taken to ethical problems. It discusses professional and business ethics, values and codes of ethics. The second half of the chapter analyses corporate governance, corporate social responsibility (CSR) and sustainability, the role of businesses, HR and the government in promoting CSR, and the extent of compatibility between CSR and profit.

Chapter 10 analyses the nature of strategic management and identifies different models of strategy. It analyses the stages of strategic decision-making – analysis, choice and implementation. The last part of the chapter concentrates on strategic leadership and the nature and practice of change management.

Chapter 11 builds on the analysis elsewhere in the book, particularly in chapters 1 and 2, explores the links between HR, strategy and performance, and examines the best practice, best fit and resource-based models of HR strategy.

We would like to acknowledge the help and encouragement we have received from colleagues and friends in writing this new edition. A special word of thanks goes to Rod Smith, a long-standing colleague at Bedfordshire University, for his contribution to Chapter 2, and to the staff at the CIPD library. Continuing thanks are extended to our families for their encouragement, support and forbearance over an extended period.

CIPD qualifications map

The content of the CIPD module is covered as follows:

Number	Learning outcome	*Human Resource Management in a Business Context* chapters
Understand, analyse and critically evaluate		
1	Contemporary organisations and their principal environments	Chapter 1 – Human Resource Management in Context

Chapter 9 – Ethics, Social Responsibility and Sustainability |
| 2 | The managerial and business environment within which HR professionals work | Chapter 2 – The Managerial Context of Human Resources |
| 3 | How organisational and HR strategies are shaped by and developed in response to internal and external environmental factors | Chapter 10 – Strategic Management

Chapter 11 – HR, Strategy and Performance |
| 4 | The market and competitive environments of organisations and how organisational leaders and the HR function respond to them | Chapter 3 – The Competitive Environment

Chapter 4 – Government Policy |
| 5 | Globalisation and international forces and how they shape and impact on organisational and HR strategies and HR practices | Chapter 6 – The World Economy |
| 6 | Demographic, social and technological trends and how they shape and impact on organisational and HR strategies and HR practices | Chapter 7 – Demographic and Social Trends

Chapter 8 – Technology |
| 7 | Government policy and legal regulation and how these shape and impact on organisational and HR strategies and HR practices | Chapter 4 – Government Policy

Chapter 5 – Regulation |

The content of the CIPD module is covered as follows:

Number	Learning outcome	*Human Resource Management in a Business Context* chapters
Understand		
1	Key contemporary issues affecting the HR function within public, private and third sector organisations	Chapter 1 – Human Resource Management in Context Chapter 2 – The Managerial Context of Human Resources Chapter 11 – HR, Strategy and Performance
2	The main external contextual factors impacting on organisations and the HR function	Chapter 3 – The Competitive Environment Chapter 4 – Government Policy Chapter 5 – Regulation Chapter 6 – The World Economy Chapter 7 – Demographic and Social Trends Chapter 8 – Technology Chapter 9 – Ethics, Social Responsibility and Sustainability
3	The role of HR in the managing of contemporary business issues and external contexts	Chapter 2 – The Managerial Context of Human Resources Chapter 10 – Strategic Management Chapter 11 – HR, Strategy and Performance
4	How organisational and HR strategies and practices are shaped and developed	Chapter 10 – Strategic Management
5	How to identify and respond to short-term changes in the business and external contexts	Chapter 1 - Human Resource Management in Context Chapter 10 – Strategic Management

Links to the CIPD HR Profession Map

CHAPTER 1

CORE PROFESSIONAL AREA: INSIGHTS, STRATEGY AND SOLUTIONS

Develop insights and spot opportunities

- 1.1.4 Use a range of analytical tools, personal experience and management information to develop a deep understanding of what's happening in the organisation and externally
- 1.3.4 Spot opportunities and patterns within the total organisation, business and context and use these to develop new insights

Business knowledge

- 1.20.4 Relevant internal and external business commentary – relating to the organisation and its competitors
- 1.22.4 The sector in which the organisation operates and the other market factors that impact sustainable organisation performance
- 1.23.4 The immediate and prospective political, economic, social, technological, legal and environmental (PESTLE) issues that may impact your organisation and its competitors
- 1.24.4 The key sources of relevant external information that may impact the current and future health of the business
- 1.25.4 The rationale for current organisational structures and espoused values and behaviour frameworks

PROFESSIONAL AREA: ORGANISATION DESIGN

Set the context for design

- 3.3.2 Analyse data on organisation structure, accountabilities and spans of control to support business case development. Support in identification of criteria for change and crucial success factors

Assess current organisational design

- 3.5.4 Identify misalignment between current organisation and operations today, and the way it will need to operate in future to deliver organisation's strategy and goals
- 3.11.4 Test the feasibility of operating models and the extent to which they meet the design criteria

CORE PROFESSIONAL AREA: INSIGHTS, STRATEGY AND SOLUTIONS

Develop insights and spot opportunities

- 1.1.3 Use a range of analytical tools, personal experience and management information to build a rich picture of what's happening in the organisation

- 1.3.4   Spot opportunities and patterns within the total organisation, business and context and use these to develop new insights

Turn insight into strategy and solutions

- 1.6.2   Raise risks with managers that may affect the long-term reputation of the of the organisation

Deliver and embed solutions

- 1.7.2   Develop and implement HR solutions that address actions emanating from insights, either to mitigate critical risk or capitalise on opportunity
- 1.8.2   Support the implementation of change by working with managers to ensure they fully understand the rationale behind the change, the vision for the future, what needs to be done, and to surface the impact that the changes will have on the organisation and the people
- 1.9.2   Support the timely and efficient delivery and evaluation of planned 'one-off' HR programmes and projects within the organisation

Building capacity and capability

- 1.12.3 Implement appropriate processes to ensure that the organisation has the right people in sufficient numbers, in the right places and with the right experience and capabilities to deliver the goals of the organisation.

Organisational knowledge

- 1.25.2 Organisational structure and processes, decision-making processes, governance and any espoused values or behaviours
- 1.27.2 A sense of how things really work in the organisation and the barriers to change
- 1.34.2 How to deliver successful change programmes and the importance of engaging managers and employees in the change

PROFESSIONAL AREA: ORGANISATION DESIGN

Set the context for design

- 3.3.2   Analyse data on organisation structure, accountabilities and spans of control to support business case development. Support in identification of criteria for change and crucial success factors
- 3.4.2   Ensure that managers clearly understand the likely impact/investment that will be required to make change happen

PROFESSIONAL AREA: ORGANISATION DEVELOPMENT

- 4.8.2   Support the design and implementation of a cultural change programme
- 4.15.3 How to conduct a cultural audit and manage a cultural change programme
- 4.16.2 The key stages in change management and the importance of identifying supporters, blockers and fence-sitters

PROFESSIONAL AREA: EMPLOYEE ENGAGEMENT

- 8.14.3 The key drivers of employee engagement such as career growth and development opportunities, nature and challenge of the job, perceptions of organisational trust and integrity, relationship with line manager and pride in the organisation and product
- 8.15.3 Approaches to communicating successfully with a diverse mix of people

- 10.4.2 Strive to maintain continued service excellence during times of change, using existing processes and infrastructure. Lead the parallel-test of new approaches during implementation phase
- 10.7.2 Adopt a customer-centric approach by focusing on the life cycle model and diverse employee needs during the joining employment phase, the in-service phase and during delivery.

CHAPTER 3

CORE PROFESSIONAL AREA: INSIGHTS, STRATEGY AND SOLUTIONS

Business knowledge

- 1.21.4 The total organisation, commercial and value drivers and how they impact on HR solutions for the business
- 1.23.4 The immediate and prospective political, economic, social, technological, legal and environmental (PESTLE) issues that may impact your organisation and its competitors
- 1.24.4 The key sources of relevant external information that may impact on the current and future health of the business

PROFESSIONAL AREA: RESOURCE AND TALENT PLANNING

Workforce planning

- 5.2.4 Lead the analysis of current resource and talent levels, taking into account factors such as current and future demand, demographics, attrition, capability by discipline, geography, critical and scarce skills
- 5.7.4 Build resource planning around analysis of availability of HR talent (locally, regionally and internationally as appropriate)

Resourcing

- 5.19.4 Organisational needs for resourcing, organisational models to support resourcing, eg permanent, contractors, outsource, and the evolving global situation within the market for skills
- 5.21.4 How to create talent and succession strategies to meet current and future organisational requirements

PROFESSIONAL AREA: EMPLOYEE ENGAGEMENT

Employer brand

- 8.9.4 Lead the development and implementation of a clear employer brand proposition to attract and retain new and existing talent

Diversity of needs

- 8.14.4 The key drivers of employee engagement such as career growth and development opportunities, nature and challenge of the job, perceptions of organisational trust and integrity, relationship with line manager and pride in the organisation and product

CHAPTER 4

CHAPTER 5

CHAPTER 6

CORE PROFESSIONAL AREA: INSIGHTS, STRATEGY AND SOLUTIONS

Business knowledge

- 1.23.4 The immediate and prospective political, economic, social, technological, legal and environmental (PESTLE) issues that may have an impact on your organisation and its competitors
- 1.24.4 The key sources of relevant external information that may have an impact on the current and future health of the business

CORE PROFESSIONAL AREA: LEADING HR

Personal leadership

- 2.5.4 Build global mindset. Bring understanding and insight into HR management across any given county's society: its social structures, institutions and demographics, legal, regulatory and economic structure

PROFESSIONAL AREA: PERFORMANCE AND REWARD

International, expatriate and executive reward

- 7.20.4 Consider constituent parts and levels of the international reward package for expatriates across the organisation, ensuring that there is coherence in the overall offer and that they are aligned with the organisation's strategy and plans

Benchmarking

- 7.23.4 Understand the local and competitor landscape in terms of reward and understand the factors that determine their overall reward packages, eg critical and scarce skills, talent mobility

PROFESSIONAL AREA: EMPLOYEE ENGAGEMENT

Internal communications

- 8.15.4 Approaches to communicating successfully with global communities of people

CHAPTER 7

PROFESSIONAL AREA: PERFORMANCE AND REWARD

- 7.6.3 Keep abreast of legislative changes that have an impact on performance and reward. Train and coach managers to ensure policies are followed and risks identified. Conduct equal pay reviews to ensure compliance with legislation

PROFESSIONAL AREA: EMPLOYEE RELATIONS

Embed employee relations policy, strategy and practice

- 9.6.2 Give accurate and appropriate advice, training and support to managers who are managing difference and fair access to opportunities
- 9.6.3 Design policies and practices and lead implementation to promote diversity and ensure fair access of opportunities

CHAPTER 9

CORE PROFESSIONAL AREA: INSIGHTS, STRATEGY AND SOLUTIONS

Delivering situational HR solutions which stick

- 1.10.4 Lead in risk mitigation, governance and ethics strategies

CHAPTER 10

CORE PROFESSIONAL AREA: INSIGHTS, STRATEGY AND SOLUTIONS

Building a picture

- 1.3.4 Spot opportunities and patterns within the total organisation, business and context and use these to develop new insights

Developing actionable insight

- 1.4.4 Use your insights to challenge and shape executive thinking around the risks and benefits of decisions or planned strategy
- 1.5.4 Align key influencers around purpose and strategies and ensure accountability for delivery
- 1.8.4 Lead and champion the implementation of the most significant organisation change activities, such as reorganisations, mergers and acquisitions

Delivering situational HR solutions which stick

- 1.11.4 Assess and review the impact of solutions, stay alert to changes in context and make appropriate corrections to strategy and solutions

Building capacity and capability

- 1.16.4 Assess the organisation's culture and its ability to deliver competitive advantage in the short and long term
- 1.17.4 Shape the evolving culture of the whole organisation in anticipation of future challenges as well as in response to current challenges

Business knowledge

- 1.18.4 The vision and purpose of the organisation and how to build functional alignment (organisation design, strategy and plans) to this vision and purpose

Organisation knowledge

- 1.27.4 Deep understanding of how things really work in the organisation and the barriers to change

HR professional knowledge

- 1.32.4. How to lead and shape organisation transformational programmes

PROFESSIONAL AREA: ORGANISATION DESIGN

Assess current organisation design

- 3.6.4 Work with senior leaders to assess the impact of the overall organisation design on factors such as behaviour, attitudes, culture, systems and communication

PROFESSIONAL AREA: ORGANISATION DEVELOPMENT

OD strategy, planning and business case development

- 4.2.4 Ensure the consideration and integration of organisational values and behaviours in all organisational strategies, plans and programmes

Culture assessment and development

- 4.7.4   Look ahead and lead the development and ongoing management of a culture that supports the need to change, learn, let things go and improve in order to position the organisation appropriately to deliver the long-term goals
- 4.8.4   Lead and monitor the organisational cultural change programme to ensure that it leads to a sustained improvement in performance aligned to the organisation strategy and priorities

Change communications

- 4.11.4 Ensure senior stakeholders understand the rationale for change, are engaged, aligned and fully supportive of the solution

Culture change

- 4.15.4 How to manage a cultural change programme, integrating it into all organisational priorities

PROFESSIONAL AREA: EMPLOYEE ENGAGEMENT

Employer brand

- 8.11.4 Lead processes to identify, articulate and reinforce the organisation's core values and behavioural expectations. Influence leadership at all levels to behave in a manner that is consistent with the values and behavioural expectations.

CHAPTER 11

CORE PROFESSIONAL AREA: INSIGHTS, STRATEGY AND SOLUTIONS

Delivering situational HR solutions which stick

- 1.7.4   Lead design of HR solutions that address actions emanating from insights, either to mitigate critical risk or capitalise on opportunity
- 1.9.4   Sponsor and evaluate delivery of major, planned, new, high-impact HR programmes and projects across the organisation

HR professional knowledge

- 1.32.4 What external HR (business and academic) thought leaders and benchmark organisations are doing in a variety of areas and considers how lessons may apply to own organisation
- 1.33.4 How to develop organisation and HR strategies and operating plans
- 1.34.4 How to lead and shape organisation culture. Can access and respond to the need for organisation agility

Professional leadership

- 2.4.4   Articulate and communicate the HR value proposition to the organisation and externally

Leading others

- 2.7.4   Maintain a long-term view of the organisation's direction, shaping and aligning the HR strategy in light of this
- 2.9.4   Lead a cohesive and influential HR function/practice, building HR capability in business, context and organisation knowledge to drive sustainable business performance

Leading issues: HR function design and service delivery

- 2.10.4 Design a fit-for-purpose HR function based on a long-term view on where the organisation is headed
- 2.11.4 Design an adaptable HR function that can quickly shift/adopt different situational HR strategies

HR service delivery models

- 2.24.4 Models and options for running the HR function (eg centralised, decentralised, account management, shared services, outsourced, integrated service delivery) and the risks and opportunities associated with these.

Source: *The CIPD Profession Map: Our Professional Standards V2.4.* January 2015. London: CIPD. Available at: http://www.cipd.co.uk/binaries/the-cipd-profession-map_2015.pdf

Walkthrough of textbook features and online resources

LEARNING OUTCOMES

When you have completed this chapter, you should be able to understand, explain and critically evaluate:

- the main theories of management, both traditional and contemporary
- the difference between power and influence and assess their suitability to a variety of management situations
- the use of conflict-handling styles in the process of managing conflict, including methods of operating repair situations

CHAPTER OBJECTIVES

At the beginning of each chapter a bulleted set of chapter objectives summarises what you expect to learn from the chapter, helping you to track your progress.

CASE STUDY 2.2

BUSINESS PARTNERS AT ELIOR GROUP, GENERAL MOTORS, BRITISH AEROSPACE AND PRUDENTIAL INSURANCE

Elior, a 5,400-employee European contract catering group, introduced business partnering in 2008 which provided benefits for both HR and business managers. HR professionals gained insights into business concerns while business managers appreciated the importance of a more scientific approach to people issues.

At Prudential Insurance, the HR business partner works in a business unit as a consultant, drawing down help from centres of excellence while a service centre deals with HR administration issues. As an example, one partner works in the marketing and innovation function running the people management side of a major change initiative to improve how to deal with customer complaints. Having

CASE STUDIES

A range of case studies from different countries illustrate how key ideas and theories are operating in practice around the globe, with accompanying questions or activities.

KEY LEARNING POINTS

Throughout this chapter, the implications for human resource practitioners have been emphasised. In short, HR practitioners need to:

- understand the management systems and identity the power structure so they are able to use their influence selectively and effectively to improve organisational performance
- be regarded as an expert in handling conflict so people issues can be addressed fully and appropriately and resolved in the interests of the great majority of stakeholders
- be aware of the options available for the structure of the human resources function and be able to recommend the best option which is appropriate to the organisational context
- use their influence to improve employee understanding of the importance of systems of customer care and quality assurance and ensure that employees respond accordingly

KEY LEARNING POINTS

At the end of each chapter, a bulleted list of the key learning points summarises the chapter and pulls out the most important points for you to remember.

REVIEW QUESTIONS

1 What did Fayol consider to be the main principles of effective management?
2 What is the Butterfly Effect?
3 According to Macmillan, what is the distinction between power and influence?
4 What is 'satisficing', according to Drucker?
5 What are the benefits of operating a 'business partner' HR system?
6 Identify the main important sources of management power, according to Morgan.
7 What are the crucial differences between a collaborative management style and an avoidance style?
8 What is the difference between emotional and transactional engagement?

REVIEW QUESTIONS

Review questions at the end of each chapter will test your understanding of the chapter and highlight any areas of development before you move on to the next chapter.

?   REFLECTIVE ACTIVITY 2.1

What indicators of power do you notice in your department or division of your organisation? Is it a high-status department/division? Is this confirmed by the indicators? Record your analysis and reflections in your self-development diary.

REFLECTIVE ACTIVITIES

In each chapter, a number of questions and activities will get you to reflect on what you have just read and encourage you to explore important concepts and issues in greater depth.

EXPLORE FURTHER

This chapter covers a very wide range of subjects, so the list of additional reading can be extensive. Here is a short selection:

Theories of management

COLE, G. (2010) *Management theory and practice*. 6th edition. London: Cengage Learning.

MINTZBERG, H. (2009) *Managing*. Harlow: FT Prentice Hall.

Power in organisations

GRAY, C. (2013) A very short, fairly interesting and reasonably cheap book about studying organisations, 3rd ed. London: Sage.

JERMIER, J., KNIGHTS, D. and NORD, W. (1994) *Resistance and power in organisations*. London: Routledge.

EXPLORE FURTHER

Explore Further boxes contain suggestions for further reading and useful websites, encouraging you to delve further into areas of particular interest.

SEMINAR ACTIVITY 4.1

ECONOMIC DEVELOPMENT IN INDIA AND CHINA

Between 1985 and 1995, GNP growth in the developing world averaged 6% a year, more than twice that of the developed world (World Bank 2000). This suggests that the developing world will soon catch up with the developed world. Unfortunately, this hopeful forecast ignores two key factors. One is the rapid rate of population growth in the developing world.

Secondly, the developing country figures are distorted by the outstanding success of the two most populous countries, India and China, In the period 1985–95, India's GNP per head rose by 3.2% per year and China's by an impressive (although possibly unreliable) 8.3%. Stripping out India and China from the figures, the rest of the developing world actually had a GNP per head which fell by nearly 1%.

SEMINAR ACTIVITIES

Each chapter ends with a longer activity, suitable for use in seminars, with questions.

ONLINE RESOURCES FOR TUTORS

- PowerPoint slides – design your programme around these ready-made lectures.
- Lecturer's guide – including guidance on the activities and questions in the text.
- Additional case studies – these can be used as a classroom activity, for personal reflection and individual learning, or as the basis for assignments.
- Additional activities – for you to use with students in seminars or lectures.

ONLINE RESOURCES FOR STUDENTS

- Annotated web-links – click through to a wealth of up to date information online.
- Activity feedback – track your learning with guidance on all in-text activities.

EBOOK BUNDLING

CIPD have partnered with BitLit to offer print and eBook bundling. BitLit has built a free eBook bundling app called Shelfie for iOS and Android that allows you to get a highly discounted eBook if you own a print edition of one of our titles.

Visit **www.bitlit.com/how-it-works/**

CHAPTER 1

Human Resource Management in Context

LEARNING OUTCOMES

When you have completed this chapter, you should be able to understand, explain and critically evaluate:

- the distinction between the general and the task environment
- the relationships between the environment, organisations, and strategy
- the STEEPLE model of environmental analysis
- the difference between placid, dynamic and turbulent environments, and their impact on organisations
- the identification of key environmental factors
- the use of SWOT analysis
- models of organisational structure – bureaucracy, divisionalisation, matrix organisations, networks and virtual organisations
- the use and limitations of strategic alliances
- the advantages and disadvantages of HR outsourcing and shared service centres
- stakeholder analysis
- E-V-R analysis.

VIETNAM, IRAQ AND AFGHANISTAN

CASE STUDY 1.1

In the early 1960s, the US intervened in the civil war in Vietnam. The North Vietnamese, under the political leadership of Ho Chi Minh, and the military leadership of Vo Nguyen Giap, had driven the French colonial government out of Vietnam in the 1950s, and the country had been divided in two – North Vietnam, under communist control, and South Vietnam, with a pro-Western government. The Northerners and their South Vietnamese communist allies, the Vietcong, had started a guerrilla civil war

in the south against the South Vietnamese government.

The Americans had overwhelming military superiority, and won every pitched battle between the two sides, including the North's biggest attack, the Tet Offensive in 1968, when Vietcong soldiers infiltrated into the South Vietnamese capital, Saigon, and even penetrated the US embassy.

Even so, in the end it was the North Vietnamese and the Vietcong who won the war. The Americans lost over 50,000 dead (compared with more than a million Vietnamese dead), and in 1975 they finally pulled out of Saigon. The next day, April 30 1975, the North Vietnamese army took the presidential palace in Saigon, and the unified communist republic of Vietnam was born.

Why did the Americans lose? Firstly, the North Vietnamese understood that ultimately the war was political, not military. If they could pin down the Americans for long enough, public opinion in the US would turn against the war and the loss of American life, and political pressure at home, would force the Americans to pull out. Ho Chi Minh also had a clear aim: to unify Vietnam under the communist banner. The Americans did not. Were they supporting the South Vietnamese government, fighting the Vietcong, seeking to defeat North Vietnam, or to stop the advance of world communism? An example of their ambivalence was the decision not to invade North Vietnam with a ground force, but to bomb the country, including its capital, Hanoi.

Secondly, the Americans had no clear strategy for fighting a guerrilla war. Their strategy was based on their overwhelming advantage in firepower, but this was of little use when every Vietnamese could be a potential guerrilla fighter. A typical example of this was the way the Americans could do nothing to prevent the infiltration of fighters and equipment into Saigon in 1968. The 'overkill' approach used by the Americans also caused hundreds of thousands of civilian casualties, which helped to turn public opinion in the US, and throughout the West, against the war.

In 2001, after the Al Qaida attacks on New York and Washington on September 11, a US-led coalition invaded Afghanistan, ostensibly to capture the Al Qaida leader Osama bin Laden, who was based there. Afghanistan looms over nineteenth century British military history. In 1842, in the First Anglo-Afghan War, a British army was wiped out almost to a man, after conquering the country

with little difficulty. In the Second Anglo-Afghan war of 1878–80, the British learnt the lesson that it was very easy to intervene militarily in Afghanistan, but very difficult to withdraw. The British army went in with overwhelming military force, won the war, imposed political terms, and then quickly withdrew without attempting an occupation. The Russian intervention in the 1980s followed much the pattern of the 1840s. After suffering heavy losses from guerrilla action, they were forced into a humiliating withdrawal.

The American-led invasion followed much the same pattern. The Taliban government was quickly overthrown, although Osama bin Laden evaded capture. However, the Taliban then led a long and very effective guerrilla war, which tied down thousands of US and British troops. The war became increasingly intelligence-led, as the guerrillas merged into the civilian population. The Americans also developed the tactic of using pilotless drone aircraft to attack Taliban bases, both in Afghanistan and in Pakistan. Failures of intelligence led to many cases of innocent civilians being killed in drone raids.

In 2003, a US-led coalition invaded Iraq. Again, there was a backdrop to the action. In 1990, Iraq, under Saddam Hussein, had invaded and occupied its neighbour Kuwait. A massive, widely-based but US-led, coalition had expelled him from Kuwait in a brilliant military campaign. This operation had unequivocal limited objectives – to liberate Kuwait – and commanded a high level of world support. The 2003 war was different. This time, the Americans had much less world support, did not have the unequivocal endorsement of the UN, and were unable to make it clear to the world exactly why the invasion was happening. Was it to depose Saddam Hussein (regime change)? Was it because Saddam was alleged (incorrectly) to possess chemical and biological weapons (the so-called 'weapons of mass destruction')? Was it to protect ethnic and religious elements in the Iraqi population who had been persecuted by Saddam – the Kurds in the north, and the Shi'ites in the south? Was it to fight world terrorism and in particular Al Qaida? Was it a desire on the part of the US president, George Bush Jr, to complete the job which his father George Bush Sr had started as president in 1991? Or, as many observers cynically suggested, was it to seize control of Iraq's huge reserves of oil?

The Americans believed that they would be welcomed as liberators, and for a brief period there was relief among many Iraqis at the overthrow of Saddam, particularly among the Kurds, but also to some extent among the Shia in the British-occupied southern part of the country. However, the Americans had underestimated the underlying religious and political divisions in the country. Iraq was an artificial country, invented after the First World War from the wreckage of the Turkish empire. The Shia had close links with their co-religionists in Iran, while the Kurds had much more in common with the Kurdish minority in eastern Turkey than with the rest of Iraq.

Although the Shia were the majority in the country, the Saddam government had been dominated by the Sunni minority,

who were strong in Baghdad and central Iraq. The Sunni population was generally hostile to the Americans because they had overthrown Saddam, and they quickly started a guerrilla campaign against the Americans. The Shia sought revenge on the Sunni, while Al Qaida, who had previously had no influence in Iraq, took advantage of the chaos to move into the country.

The Americans were again involved in a guerrilla war, just as in Vietnam, and again they reacted in a heavy-handed fashion, launching punitive operations against guerrilla-controlled towns, and making little effort to reconstruct the country or to win hearts and minds. American casualties rose into the thousands, and Iraqi casualties into the hundreds of thousands.

Again, just as in Vietnam, the war was increasingly unpopular in the US, and the guerrillas realised that in order to win, all they had to do was to outlast the Americans. In 2009, the US announced that its troops would cease to play a combat role, although 150,000 US troops remained in the country.

The Middle East continued to be volatile. Few foresaw the Arab Spring in 2011, the Syrian civil war, and the rise of so-called Islamic State, which rapidly occupied vast swathes of territory in Iraq and Syria.

What has an account of wars in Vietnam, Afghanistan and Iraq got to do with business? What lessons can we learn from the wars that are relevant to business environment and strategy? A surprising amount.

- *The need for clear objectives.* If a business does not know what it wants to achieve, any amount of strategic planning is irrelevant. There is a clear contrast between the totally clear objectives of Ho Chi Minh and Vo Nguyen Giap, and the confused objectives of the Americans in both Vietnam and Iraq.
- *An understanding of the environment.* The guerrillas in both Iraq and Vietnam were totally at ease in their local environments. The Americans, on the other hand, did not understand the motivation of their enemies in Vietnam, or the complex political environment in Iraq. The Vietnamese also understood and exploited the political environment in the US.
- *Understand the competition.* The Americans did not understand the strengths and motivations of their enemies in either Vietnam or Iraq.
- *An understanding of one's own resources.* The Vietnamese made the most of their limited military resources, while the Americans were hamstrung when the enemy in both Vietnam and Iraq neutralised their key resource, their overwhelming firepower.

- *The importance of organisational structure.* The difference in structure is epitomised by Robert McNamara, the US Secretary of Defense in the mid-1960s, and one of the main architects of US strategy in Vietnam (Jackson 2009). As a young man, McNamara was involved in planning the US bombing offensive on Germany, an example of detailed logistical planning. After 1945 he rose to be president of the Ford Motor Company. Ford was a classic huge, bureaucratic, hierarchical US corporation which had given its name to a scientific approach to organisational structure ('Fordism'). The US Army under McNamara in Vietnam was equally rigid and bureaucratic. In contrast, the Vietcong was organised on a highly flexible cell basis, and thus able to react much more quickly to changing tactical situations.
- *The importance of HR.* The North Vietnamese and Vietcong were highly motivated. The US Army, on the other hand, was largely a conscript army, most of whom did not want to be in Vietnam. To make matters worse, there were extensive exemptions from conscription (the draft), which made those who could not avoid the draft even more bitter about their fate. The alienation of the rank and file US soldier expressed itself in a contempt for the Vietnamese, and also in occasional atrocities against civilians.
- *The importance of values and culture.* The communist beliefs of the Vietnamese gave them a motivation and a will to win that the Americans could not match. At a tactical level, the gung-ho, macho culture of the US Marine Corps made them ideal for spearheading the invasion of Iraq, but totally unsuitable for any campaign to win hearts and minds.
- *The importance of stakeholders.* Businesses, like countries, have external stakeholders – third parties who can affect their actions. In Iraq, the key external stakeholders are Iran, with considerable influence over the Iraqi Shi'ites, and Turkey, the sworn enemy of the Kurds. In addition, a key stakeholder was US public opinion, which eventually turned strongly against both wars. The views of stakeholders must be taken into account in strategic management.
- *The importance of intelligence.* This is particularly crucial in a guerrilla war, where it is hard to identify who is the enemy, and who is an innocent civilian. In business, intelligence-gathering involves general techniques such as environmental scanning, as well as function-specific techniques such as wage surveys.
- *The importance of competences.* The key competence of the US Marine Corps was to be a killing machine, whereas totally different competences were needed for an army of occupation. Similarly, very different competences are needed to operate a drone over Afghanistan from a base in the US. War becomes a computer game.
- *The importance of an exit strategy.* Businesses, like armies, need to know how to abandon a strategy at minimum cost. The Americans in Vietnam were forced to make a humiliating exit, while they have been heavily criticised over Afghanistan and Iraq for their seeming failure to have a clear exit strategy.
- *The recognition and importance of risk.* In war, just as in business, any strategy is high-risk. You may well lose. The Americans had to accept their defeat in Vietnam, and the installation of a communist government, and made a crucial mistake in purging the Iraqi army, which made it vulnerable to Islamic State.
- *The danger of threats*, such as Islamic State, appearing from out of a clear blue sky, what Kim and Mauborgne (2004) call the 'blue ocean'.

All these themes will be explored later in this book.

1.1 HRM IN CONTEXT

The theme of this chapter, and indeed of the book as a whole, is the interaction between human resource management, the environment and the organisation. The theoretical underpinning for this approach is the best fit or contingency model of human resource strategy, particularly associated in the UK with John Purcell (Boxall and Purcell 2008). This model argues that there is no one model of human resource strategy which suits all circumstances. Instead, different strategies are appropriate in different environmental and organisational settings.

You should bear in mind that the best fit model is not the only model of HR strategy. Other models include the best practice model, which argues that there is one approach to HR strategy, the high performance workplace model, which is suitable in nearly all organisational and environmental settings; and the resource-based model, which argues that resources, particularly human capital and core competencies, are much more important for HR strategy than the environment. All these models will be explored in much more depth in Chapter 11.

The next sections will explore in more detail the relationships between the environment, the organisation and HR strategy. This will also be explored at greater length in Chapter 11.

1.2 WHAT IS THE ENVIRONMENT?

At its simplest, the environment is anything outside an organisation which may affect an organisation's present or future activities. Thus the environment is situational – it is unique to each organisation. As a result, we must always bear in mind the interaction between a particular organisation, and its particular environment.

It is useful to think of the environment on two levels. One is the general environment (also known as the societal environment, the far environment or the macro environment). The other is the task environment (or the specific environment, the near environment or the micro environment).

Forces in the general environment have a major impact at the level of the industry. These forces include national culture, including historical background, ideologies and values; scientific and technological developments; the level of education; legal and political processes; demographic factors; available resources, the international environment; and the general economic, social and industrial structure of the country.

The task environment covers the forces relevant to an individual organisation within an industry. These include customers, suppliers, competitors, regulators, the local labour market, and specific technologies.

The distinction between general and task environments is not a static one. Elements in the general environment are continually breaking through to the task environment, and impacting on individual organisations.

A different but complementary approach is to see the organisation as an open system, which interacts in two main ways with its task environment. It takes in resources from the environment, converts them into goods and/or services, and returns outputs to the environment in order to satisfy some need (see Figure 1.1).

Figure 1.1 A systems model of the organisation and its environment

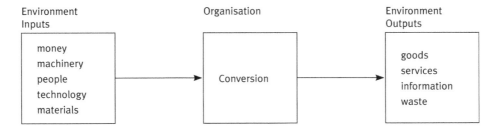

In order to function effectively in such a system, the organisation must fully understand both its input and its output environments.

A more complex variation is to add a third element – that of regulations which control the conversion process. The three elements (inputs, outputs and regulations) provide the organisation with both opportunities and constraints. All three elements are also subject to the influences of the general environment.

? REFLECTIVE ACTIVITY 1.1

The systems approach

Identify inputs, outputs, regulators and the conversion process in:

- a manufacturer of baked beans
- a trade union
- your own organisation.

1.3 ORGANISATIONS AND STRATEGY

The simple systems model used above takes us only so far. It treats the organisation as a 'black box' and does not analyse what goes on inside the organisation. We now have to build further elements into our model – HR, strategy and organisational structure.

In Case Study 1.1 we identified that the environment had an impact on HR. The political environment in the US, where the country was only 20 years away from the Second World War, led the US to rely on a conscript rather than a volunteer army to fight the Vietnam war. At the same time, HR had an impact on the environment – the alienation created by the draft affected the way in which the rank and file soldiers fought the war.

This gives us a two-way model of the relationship between the environment and HR, as shown in Figure 1.2.

Figure 1.2 The environment and HR

The next stage is to distinguish between HR strategy and HR practice. Here we assume that HR practice flows from HR strategy.

Figure 1.3 HR strategy and HR practice

The next stage is to put HR strategy in the context of the organisation's overall strategy. Here we see HR strategy as an integral part of overall strategy.

Figure 1.4 HR strategy and overall strategy

Finally, we need to add the organisation.

The great organisational theorist of the 1960s, Alfred Chandler, argued that 'structure follows strategy' (Chandler 1962). A more nuanced approach would suggest that there is a two-way flow between strategy and organisational structure, and similarly, that there is a two-way relationship between the environment, and both structure and strategy, although the stronger flow would go from environment to structure and strategy, rather than the other way.

An example of strategy following structure was discussed in the *Harvard Business Review* (Slywotsky and Nadler 2004). The French producer of industrial gases, Air Liquide, was producing gases in small plants at customers' factories. An unrelated company reorganisation suddenly gave the on-site teams involved greater autonomy. They seized the new opportunities, developing new lines of business, which now make up 25% of Air Liquide's revenue, compared to 7% previously.

Figure 1.5 The environment, strategy and structure

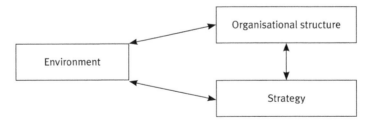

Putting everything together, we arrive at the comprehensive model shown in Figure 1.6.

1.4 ANALYSING THE ENVIRONMENT

Most organisations will not have much of a problem in analysing their task environment. They know who their customers, suppliers, competitors, etc are. Analysing the general environment is rather more complex. The first step will probably be to brainstorm a list of various environmental factors which seem to have an impact on the organisation. This is a start, but to progress further, it will be necessary to classify these influences.

One widely used tool for classification is PEST analysis and its derivatives. PEST analysis breaks down environmental influences into four categories:

Figure 1.6 The comprehensive model

- *Political/legal*: Taxation policy, European Union directives, trade regulations, geopolitical factors like the 'war on terror', government stability, employment law, contract law, competition law, etc.
- *Economic*: Business cycles, economic growth, interest rates, supply and demand factors, competition factors, public spending, money supply, inflation, unemployment, disposable income
- *Socio-cultural*: Demographic trends, income distribution. Social mobility, lifestyle, attitudes to work and leisure, levels of education
- *Technological*: Research and development, new inventions or innovations, speed of technology transfer, rates of obsolescence, development of systems.

PEST analysis was widely used during the 1980s and early 1990s. By the mid-1990s, it was becoming more common to talk of PESTLE analysis. Political and Legal were split from each other, and an extra factor, Environment, was added. This reflected a growing awareness of environmental factors, and the first concerns about global warming.

By the early 2000s, PESTLE had evolved into STEEPLE, with the addition of Ethics, reflecting the development of concern for corporate social responsibility and business ethics.

The classification currently used is thus:

S   Social
T   Technological
E   Economic
E   Environmental
P   Political
L   Legal
E   Ethical

The STEEPLE model forms the structure of this book. We will be examining each of the STEEPLE elements in turn (although not in this order), and we will conclude by bringing everything together in an analysis of strategy formation.

The next stage in a STEEPLE analysis would be to identify what impact each identified factor would have on the organisation.

1.4.1 WHY DO WE NEED TO UNDERSTAND AND MANAGE THE ENVIRONMENT?

Organisations have a choice in how they manage their relationships with their environment. They can sit back and wait for the environment to change, without attempting to predict its behaviour, and then react to changes as they happen. Here they are being reactive – constantly fire-fighting immediate problems. Or they can identify and foresee changes in the environment, and plan their responses before these changes happen. They are being proactive – planning for the future. A few organisations are in the fortunate position of being able to go even further and manage the environment in their own interests – at different times since 1900, Ford, IBM, Sony, McDonalds and Microsoft have done this.

The nature of the environment is also significant. Some organisations have static or placid environments, where it is reasonable to suppose that the future will be a continuation of the past. For example, this was true of many UK nationalised industries before privatisation. An organisation in this happy situation can afford to limit its analysis of its environment to past history. However, such an organisation is likely to be caught totally unawares if the nature of its environment does change rapidly. For example, many airlines in continental Europe were either owned by, or heavily protected by, their home governments. This cosy relationship was totally disrupted by the events of 11 September 2001, with the resultant rapid collapse of two national airlines, Swissair and Sabena; while to add insult to injury, American airlines received massive subsidies from the US government.

Other organisations face turbulent environments, either because the environment is dynamic or in a state of rapid change, for example the pharmaceutical industry or the defence industry; or because the environment is complex, and thus difficult to analyse, for example a multinational company with interests in many countries or industries. Turbulent environments are uncertain.

Igor Ansoff (1987) argued that the extent to which an environment is turbulent depends on:

- changeability of the market environment
- speed of change
- intensity of competition
- fertility of technology
- discrimination by customers
- pressure from government and influence groups.

In order to cope with a turbulent environment, the organisation must be aggressively ready to change.

CASE STUDY 1.2

THE COLLAPSE OF CITY LINK

The parcel delivery industry sounds simple – you collect a parcel from a warehouse or delivery centre, and deliver it to a customer. The reality is much more complex. The industry is segmented in terms of customers. The service offered can be: B2B – business to business, historically the major part of the market; B2C – business to consumer, rapidly growing in importance with the growth of online retailing; or C2C – consumer to consumer – getting a parcel for Christmas from your granny.

The industry is also segmented in terms of the service offered. This can be: courier – top of the market, offering same day delivery; premium express parcels – next day guaranteed delivery; and non-premium parcels – non-guaranteed, two to three day delivery.

The industry is a large one, with the express parcels segment estimated to be worth £5.8bn in 2010, and it is growing slowly, with a decline in the B2B segment more than compensated by a growth in B2C.

The market is dominated by about ten major players. The biggest is Parcelforce, part of Royal Mail; followed by DHL, part of the German Post Office Deutsche Post, which concentres on B2B; and Yodel, sold off by DHL in 2010, which specialises in B2C. The rest of the market is taken by a number of companies, each with around an 8–10% market share: UPS and FedEx, which are part of huge American corporations; TNT, which is Dutch-owned, although originally Australian; DPD, owned by the French Post Office, La Poste; Hermes, which is German-owned; and City Link, the subject of this case study.

City Link has had a chequered history. Founded in 1969, it was taken over by the pest control company Rentokil in 2006, but incurred heavy losses, including £26m in 2012. It was sold for £1 to the venture capital company Better Capital in 2013, which invested £40m in the business. On Christmas Eve 2014, Better Capital put City Link into liquidation.

What went wrong at City Link? Some of its problems were undoubtedly due to internal managerial mistakes, but a lot is to do with the turbulent external environment facing the industry. City Link was part of the premium express segment of the industry, which has come under increasing pressure since the start of the economic downturn in 2008. Online retailers increasingly expect to get a premium service from their delivery company, while only paying a standard price. Retailers are themselves under pressure, as online customers increasingly expect free but quick delivery of their purchases. It is the delivery companies who pay for the free deliveries, as competition forces down their prices. City Link was particularly exposed here, as it was the only one of the leading players in the market that was not part of a much bigger group. These market pressures were made

worse as Amazon, the biggest player in online retailing, increasingly began to make its own deliveries, rather than using a carrier.

The industry is also facing rapid technological advances. Increasingly customers expect to be able to be able to track their parcels online. This means that the carriers have been forced to make heavy investments in IT.

The B2C market, the most rapidly growing segment, is expensive to service. It involves large numbers of small deliveries, which are complex to schedule, and often means several attempts at delivery, when people are out at the time of the delivery. New developments are attempting to tackle these problems.

Increasingly, retailers are developing click and collect services, where purchases are delivered from a central warehouse to a local store, from which they are collected by the customer. Just as with self service tills in supermarkets, the customer is doing for free something that the retailer used to pay for. Another growing trend is the use of 'lifestyle couriers', where goods are delivered to a central depot, and then taken to the final customer by self-employed lifestyle couriers using their own cars, frequently women with young families, who fit in deliveries around their own lifestyle.

Finally, the B2C market is highly seasonal. Demand doubles in the two weeks before Christmas. This puts enormous pressure on systems and staff. For Christmas 2014, City Link took on 1200 extra drivers, 400 extra vehicles, and 450 extra warehouse staff, most of whom would not get paid as the company collapsed.

Source: BBC News 2013a, City Link 2014a, City Link 2014b, Cobweb Information (2013), Network Research 2013, Barrett and Shubber 2015.

A CATASTROPHIC ENVIRONMENT – ARMENIA IN THE EARLY 1990s

Sometimes an individual, an organisation or a country faces an environment which can only be described as catastrophic. This was true of Armenia in the early 1990s. Modern Armenia, in the Caucasus, has only existed as an independent state since 1991, but both the causes of its crisis in the early 1990s, and some of the solutions, date back to the early twentieth century. At the outbreak of the First World War, Armenia was in two parts: Eastern Armenia, which was part of the Russian Empire, and Western Armenia, which was part of the Turkish Empire. During the War, from 1915 onwards, Turkey carried out extensive pogroms against the Western Armenian population, resulting in 1.5 million dead, and the effective extinction of Armenian culture in Western Armenia. The remnants of the population emigrated to Eastern Armenia, Russia or, most importantly, the US, forming the worldwide Armenian diaspora, which is much bigger than the population of Armenia itself.

In 1921, Armenia became a republic within the USSR, and another of the defining events took place. On the borders of Armenia and Azerbaijan is an area known as Nagorno Karabakh, mainly inhabited by Armenians. However, the area was awarded by Stalin to Azerbaijan.

By the late 1980s, events in the Caucasus were moving towards catastrophe for Armenia. In 1988, guerrilla warfare broke out in Nagorno Karabakh between Armenian Karabakh nationalists and the Azerbaijan SSR. Also in 1988, there was a devastating earthquake in Northern Armenia, killing 25,000 and leaving hundreds of thousands homeless. This was a crushing blow for a country with a population of only 4 million. The earthquake also forced the closure of

Armenia's only nuclear power station, which supplied 40% of the country's energy, for checks and strengthening.

In 1991, with the break-up of the Soviet Union, Armenia became independent, but its troubles continued to mount. The USSR did not only break up politically, it also broke up as an integrated planned economy. This had two major effects for Armenia – its heavy industry lost its markets elsewhere in the USSR, and was unable to compete on a world scale. This led to massive unemployment. At the same time, supplies of gas to Armenia from Kazakhstan were disrupted, and contacts had to be renegotiated. With the loss of nuclear power, this now meant that 70% of Armenia's energy supplies had vanished. The country was subject to power cuts for 22 hours a day, and had to deplete its already small supplies of woodland for fuel for heating. At the same time, the war in Nagorno Karabakh escalated into an all-out war between Armenia and Azerbaijan in 1992.

The potential was there for Armenia to become a failed state as desperate as Somalia or Haiti. However, this did not happen. Armenians are proud of their heritage and culture, and rallied round to cope with the shortages. By 1994, the nuclear power station was back in operation, and the gas contracts renegotiated. A ceasefire was agreed in the Karabakh war in 1994, although a cold war stand-off between Armenia and Azerbaijan has continued until the present. Economic production was redirected towards agriculture, and a start was made on reafforestation. Russia and the Armenian diaspora provided massive aid for the earthquake victims, while the diaspora invested heavily in rebuilding Armenia's infrastructure – the Armenian-American hedge fund billionaire Kerk Kerkorian, for example, has paid for much of the modernisation of Armenia's road system. Finally, a quarter of Armenia's population emigrated in the 1990s, reducing short-term pressure on resources, but building up longer-term social problems, as those who emigrated were predominantly young men with skills which could be utilised in the US or Russia.

1.4.2 ENVIRONMENTAL SCANNING

Environmental scanning is defined by Choo (2001) as 'the acquisition and use of information about events, trends and relationships in an organisation's external environment, the knowledge of which would assist management in planning the organisation's future course of action'. Scanning can be as simple as reading the business press, or as complex as a market research survey. The more uncertain the environment, the more likely an organisation is to scan. Choo quotes a number of studies which suggest that scanning tends to improve organisational performance.

Choo puts forward a two-dimensional model of environmental scanning based on the two dimensions of environmental analysability (can we analyse what is happening in the environment) and organisational intrusiveness (do we intrude actively into the environment to collect information). His model is illustrated in Figure 1.7.

Figure 1.7 Models of environmental scanning

		Organisational intrusiveness	
		Passive	Active
Assumption about environment	Unanalysable	Undirected viewing	Enacting
	Analysable	Conditioned viewing	Searching

Source: adapted from Choo (2001)

Undirected viewing depends on casual information often obtained informally from personal contacts. Information builds up in an unstructured way, and may or may not reach a critical mass where it triggers a reaction from the organisation. It is cheap, but runs the risk that the organisation may be taken by surprise by events which could have been predicted.

Conditioned viewing organisations believe that the environment can be analysed, but put little effort into doing so. Sources of information which are used are those generally available in the industry. This runs the risk that disruptive new changes in the environment (new technologies for example) will not be spotted.

Enacting organisations actively seek information which they can use for experimentation and testing the environment. For example, an organisation might introduce a new product based on its own gut feelings rather than market research, and watch to see what happens. This is consistent with the view put forward by Schlesinger, Kiefer and Brown in a *Harvard Business Review* article in 2012, which advocates the use of small-scale, loss-limited experiments as the best way to cope with an unpredictable environment (Schlesinger, Kiefer and Brown 2012), and with James Quinn's logical incrementalism approach to strategic management, again based on small experimental steps (Quinn 1980), which is discussed further in Chapter 10.

In the searching mode, information seeking is broad, open, and based on a willingness to revise or update existing knowledge. The emphasis is on rigorous, systematic analysis. An example quoted by Choo is the US technology company Motorola, which is one of the few US companies which systematically monitors technology developments in Japan.

However good an organisation's environmental scanning, three issues must constantly be borne in mind. Firstly, it is easy to be overwhelmed by an excessive amount of information about the environment, leading to 'paralysis by analysis'. Secondly, the most serious threats are those which are 'over the horizon' and so most difficult to spot. Similarly, the best opportunities are those which nobody else has spotted, and which are difficult to pick up with environmental scanning – what Kim and Mauborgne call 'Blue Ocean Strategy' opportunities (Kim and Mauborgne 2004). Day and Schoemaker suggest techniques for picking up these peripheral trends (Day and Schoemaker 2005). If all firms in an industry use the same environmental scanning approaches, they are likely to concentrate on the same obvious opportunities. The result will be intense competition for these overcrowded 'mountain-tops' (Gavetti 2011).

Finally, if the environment facing an organisation is dynamic, the organisation will need to have procedures for sensing future environmental changes, and contingency plans for dealing with a range of possible changes. This involves the technique known as scenario building. This increases managerial awareness by examining what-if situations – if x happens, what will its impact be on us, and what can we do about it? The technique was first developed by Shell in the early 1970s, when it correctly forecast the 1973 oil crisis, and so was ready to deal with it (Cornelius, Van de Putte and Romani 2005). Schwartz (2003) argues that although most scenarios will be wrong, the mere fact of having been through the scenario-building process will make managers more able to cope with change.

CASE STUDY 1.4

CISCO AND SCENARIO-BUILDING

In 2010 the large US Internet company Cisco carried out a scenario-building exercise entitled *The Evolving Internet* to forecast the state of the Internet in 2025. How would the Internet evolve from 2010's two billion users and $3tr revenue?

Cisco started by outlining five premises or assumptions:

- Most growth will be outside the advanced economies
- Global governance of the Internet will not change
- New users will relate to the Internet in different ways from current users
- The QWERTY keyboard will not be the primary interface with the Internet
- Ways of paying for the Internet will become more varied.

They then identified areas or axes of uncertainty:

- Will broadband network build-out be extensive or more limited?
- Will technological progress be incremental or based on breakthroughs?
- Will demand growth be unbridled or constrained?

From these premises and axes of uncertainty they developed four scenarios for the Internet in 2025:

- **Fluid frontiers**. The Internet becomes pervasive. Global entrepreneurship and competition ensures that a wide range of needs and demands are met
- **Insecure growth**. Cyber attacks such as that (allegedly) by the North Korean government on Sony Pictures in 2014 (Wakefield 2014) become relentless. A secure Internet does emerge, but it is expensive
- **Short of the promise**. Prolonged economic stagnation slows the growth

of the Internet, and new technological breakthroughs do not occur

- **Bursting at the seams**. The Internet becomes a victim of its own success,

as Internet capacity fails to keep pace with demand.

Source: Cisco (2010)

An organisation with a complex environment may need to break down the complexity, so that environmental analysis is decentralised to product groups or countries within the organisation.

The most difficult situation of all, of course, is where the environment is both dynamic and complex. Here the organisation may have to recognise that it cannot predict its environment, and what is important is to foster a culture in the organisation that welcomes and is able to cope with radical change. The organisation must learn to live with chaos. One definition of a learning organisation is an organisation which has developed systematic procedures to ensure that it can learn from its environment.

? REFLECTIVE ACTIVITY 1.2

Turbulent environments

In what ways have the environments of local authorities become more turbulent in recent years?

1.4.3 ANALYSING THE ENVIRONMENT

Johnson et al (2011) propose a five-stage model in analysing the environment, as follows:

Stage 1   Audit of environmental influences
Stage 2   Assessment of nature of the environment
Stage 3   Identification of key environmental factors
Stage 4   Identification of the competitive position
Stage 5   Identification of the principal opportunities and threats.

Stage 1 involves the preparation of a STEEPLE analysis. Stage 2 builds on the placid/dynamic/turbulent classification of environments discussed in section 1.4.2. Stage 3 involves a more sophisticated analysis which may include:

- identifying a smaller number of key environmental influences – for example, for the NHS these might be demographic trends (ageing population), technological developments in health care, and implementation of government policy (public-private partnerships)
- identifying long-term drivers of change – for example, the increasing globalisation of markets for some products, eg consumer electronics, cars and pharmaceuticals.

The key principle here is that not all environmental influences are equally important. The analysis in Stage 3 involves identifying those that are most important.

Stage 4 (identifying the organisation's competitive position) will be tackled in Chapter Three, using techniques such as Porter's Five Forces (Porter 1980).

Stage 5 (identifying principal opportunities and threats, involves another well-known technique, SWOT analysis.

SWOT stands for:
Strengths
Weaknesses
Opportunities
Threats

Strengths and weaknesses are inward-looking, and particularly concerned with the resources of the organisation. Opportunities and threats are outward-looking and involve the analysis of environmental factors. The organisation should ensure that its strengths (or core competencies) are appropriate in order to exploit opportunities or to counter threats.

The CIPD suggests that opportunities and threats (the external environment) will emerge through a STEEPLE analysis, while strengths and weaknesses (the internal environment) can be analysed through a PRIMO-F framework:

- People – what do they do, do they have the appropriate skills?
- Resources – does the organisation have the right and adequate resources?
- Innovation – what new ideas are important to us?
- Marketing – how do they know what the organisation does?
- Operations – how is all this managed?
- Finance – prices, costs and investments. (CIPD 2010)

However, the use of such a framework could encourage 'smokestack' thinking. Analysis of strengths and weaknesses requires that a holistic view is taken of the organisation as a whole.

Both opportunities and threats can be analysed using matrices. Opportunities can be assessed according to their attractiveness and the organisation's probability of success.

Figure 1.8 An attractiveness/probability of success matrix

		Probability of success	
		High	Low
Attractiveness	High	1	2
	Low	3	4

Opportunities in cell 1 offer the greatest scope, and organisations should concentrate on these. Cell 4 represents opportunities which in practice can be ignored. Cells 2 and 3 may be worth investigating further.

Threats can be assessed on the basis of their seriousness and their probability of occurrence (as shown in Figure 1.9).

Figure 1.9 An impact/probability of success matrix

		Impact	
		High	Low
Probability of occurrence	High	1	2
	Low	3	4

A threat which has a high probability of happening, and the likelihood of a considerable impact on the organisation (cell 1), will be a key factor which must be a driver of the organisation's strategy, and for which detailed contingency plans must be prepared. At the other extreme (cell 4), a threat which has little likelihood of happening, and little impact if it does happen, can be largely ignored. The threats in cells 2 and 3 should be carefully monitored in case they become critical.

It should be remembered that opportunities and threats are rarely mutually exclusive. Many factors can be both – indeed, the Chinese characters for 'threat' and 'opportunity' are identical (Nathan 2000). For example, the technological development of EFTPOS (Electronic Funds Transfer at Point of Sale) money transfer systems (using debit and credit cards) can be a threat to small retailers, as their use by competitors may give the latter a competitive edge, but can also be an opportunity, because they lessen the amount of cash likely to be in tills, and so make the shop less attractive to thieves.

?   REFLECTIVE ACTIVITY 1.3

The hospital

How would you classify the following factors on a probability/seriousness matrix for a Hospital Trust? What contingency planning should the Trust make?

- a serious accident on the local railway line, casing scores of deaths and injuries
- an ageing local population
- a leakage of radioactive material at a nuclear power station 200 miles downwind away.

PEST AND SWOT: PRACTICAL APPLICATIONS

CASE STUDY 1.5

Logica: Planning for the future through PEST

Logica is an innovative IT services organisation. Logica's services aim to add value for clients through, for example, improving efficiency and productivity or reducing waste. As part of its business planning, it carried out a PEST analysis, and identified the following key drivers:

Political

Recent public sector budget cuts by the UK government and increased university fees are affecting the education sector. The increasing cost of becoming a student may restrict the social mobility of talented individuals and they may then need to consider alternative routes to gaining qualifications and experience.

Logica has therefore introduced an apprenticeship programme to develop an alternative source of skilled talent, and has launched a sponsored degree programme with the University of Winchester.

Economic

The global economic recession has affected how most firms conduct business, and some might choose to outsource functions to reduce costs, rather than employing people with specialist skills. This has created increased demand for outsourced services such as those Logica offers. For example, Logica was selected by BAE Systems, the global defence and security company, to provide a Human Resources outsourcing service for its employees within the UK.

Social

The UK has an ageing and increasingly diverse society, with people from many different backgrounds and cultures. Diversity is therefore a focus of Logica's HR strategy.

Technological

The speed of technological advances means that existing electronic equipment, IT processes and systems will quickly become dated. Logica has embraced recent advances in technology to offer its clients the most advanced and sustainable services possible. An example of this is the use of 'cloud' technology. This eliminates the need for firms to buy software for every staff member or support a server to store company data and pay for staff to maintain it.

Source: Times 100 Business Case Studies (2013)

Note: In May 2012 Canada's CGI Group agreed to buy Logica in a £1.7bn cash deal, and in 2013, Logica was rebranded as CGI.

Hewden: planning through SWOT analysis

Hewden is a leading company in the construction plant hire business, which employs 1400 people. It has a customer-focused culture. Its CEO is hands-on, and strongly drives the company's core values, which include the following:

- We care – about our colleagues and our customers
- We communicate – we believe in straight talk
- We are all accountable
- We trust and empower.

It identified its key strengths, weaknesses, opportunities and threats:

Strengths

- Strong brand and reputation

- Market leading training and development opportunities, particularly for graduates
- Flat organisational structure, which means that the CEO and other senior managers can be involved as coaches and mentors
- Dedicated workforce and high number of long-serving professionals
- Core fleet guarantee that any core plant equipment ordered before midday is delivered to the customer the next day. If this guarantee is not met, the customer receives £100 credit.

Weaknesses

- Its operating system needed updating. Depots had localised ways of working, and the system was reactive rather than proactive. The company invested in a new Microsoft AX ERP operating system which largely overcame these weaknesses but which required an intensive change management programme to ensure the acceptability of the new system
- The company's workforce is ageing as many employees are approaching retirement age. This called for efficient workforce planning.

Opportunities

- The use of social media to improve communication channels. Hewden uses LinkedIn, a social media site for business professionals. This has improved links with customers and has helped with recruitment
- Other uses of new media include a Hewden Smartphone app designed to make plant hire easier.

Threats

- The quality of Hewden's training programmes means its competitors are keen to recruit its employees. Hewden holds on to its staff through its progressive development programmes and its fun culture
- The recent recession. Hewden turned this potential threat into an

opportunity by recruiting high quality graduates and non-graduates, who were not getting the opportunities elsewhere.

Hewden has used a SWOT analysis to help it plan for the future in an

increasingly competitive and difficult market. The results of the analysis were used to plan and drive change.

Sources: Hewden web site; Times 100 Business Case Studies (2014a)

1.5 SWOT AND STRATEGY

Weihrich (1982) argues that SWOT is misnamed. He suggests renaming it TOWS. His argument is that SWOT implies that strengths and weaknesses come first, but that this is mistaken. The only logical starting point for analysis is with opportunities and threats. They are outside the organisation, largely beyond its control, and must be managed using the organisation's strengths and weaknesses. He thus argues that SWOT should be used as a contingency model.

Four combinations of opportunities, threats, strengths and weaknesses are possible, and each suggests a possible strategy.

- Strengths-opportunities (maxi-maxi). The organisation should pursue strategies which make most use of its strengths to capitalise on opportunities.
- Strengths-threats (maxi-mini). The organisation should use its strengths to minimise or neutralise threats.
- Weaknesses-opportunities (mini-maxi). Make the most of any new opportunities to overcome weaknesses.
- Weaknesses-threats (mini-mini). This combination calls for a defensive strategy, to minimise internal weaknesses and avoid external threats.

1.5.1 CRITICISMS OF SWOT

As an analytical technique, SWOT has many strengths. It is simple, easy to understand and (at least at a superficial level) easy to use, and it does encourage managers to think about both the internal and external aspects of their business.

However, both Hill and Westbrook (1997) and Koch (2000) are very critical about how SWOT is used. Hill and Westbrook surveyed 50 companies and found that 20 carried out SWOT analysis. What they had in common was the generation of long lists, general descriptions, failure to prioritise, and no attempt to verify the points which were made. Most damning of all, no company actually used the results in later strategic analysis.

Koch takes a more analytical approach. He argues that the main weaknesses are:

- it generates strategies based on the past or present, not on the future
- it cannot ensure the necessary rigour
- in practice it is rarely deployed below corporate level, although the strategic positions of Strategic Business Units (SBUs) will vary
- the company needs to know (but will not know) the relevant performance levels of all of its competitors
- it also needs to know (but does not know) future performance levels for competitors; it requires benchtracking rather than benchmarking of competitors
- SWOT is rarely modified for different strategies – something that may be a strength for one strategy will be a weakness for another
- it is too broad
- it is too vague.

All this suggests that SWOT is well past its sell-by date. However, Koch does suggest ways in which the technique can be made more effective:

- The boundaries and structure of the market, and anticipated changes, should be clearly defined.
- All changes in the environment capable of influencing future performance should be included.
- The corporate environment, structure, form, scope and intensity of competition should be properly examined and presented.
- There should clear reference to anticipated changes in the environment.
- There should be clear reference to future objectives and strategies.
- There should be a SWOT for each SBU.
- There should be a SWOT for each proposed strategy.
- The SWOT should be constantly updated.

To summarise, SWOT must be made a forward-looking technique in order to be effective. A good analogy is with the due diligence process carried out when a company is contemplating a takeover. At its best, this is rigorous and ruthless subjecting all elements of the potential target to forensic analysis.

Bridgepoint, a European private equity company, assembles a team of six managers to carry out a due diligence, each of whom represents one of four viewpoints. One is the prosecutor, who plays the role of devil's advocate. The second is the less-experienced manager, whose involvement is a key part of his or her training. The third is a senior managing director, who no longer has any hierarchical function at the company and who therefore cannot be undermined by corporate politics. The final members of the panel are managing directors who still have operational roles. The team's goal is to provide a thorough, balanced, and unbiased examination of the acquisition candidate (Cullinan et al 2004). A similar approach should be taken to SWOT.

In essence, SWOT is a simple framework and a potentially valuable tool which is often badly used by managers as an alternative to undertaking the grind of detailed internal and external analysis.

1.6 MODELS OF ORGANISATIONAL STRUCTURE

In this section we concentrate on the organisation, and examine different models of organisational structure and their attendant strengths and weaknesses.

1.6.1 BUREAUCRACY

Formalisation of the bureaucratic form of organisation dates back to the sociologist Max Weber's work on government departments in the 1890s (Weber 1964) and the form reached its peak in the US of the 1950s and 1960s.

Weber identified three central principles of bureaucratic organisation:

- specialisation
- hierarchy
- impersonal rationality.

Specialisation

Labour tasks are highly divided, and workers are recruited with specific skills to carry out specific roles. Tasks are functionally separated, and organised into rigid departments ('smokestack management'). Movement from department to department would be unusual. Some departments, such as production, would carry out the core tasks of the organisation, while others, such as finance or HR, would provide technical or physical support for the core activities. This was identified by Fayol as the distinction between line and staff activities. (Fayol 1916/1949). Parallels with Frederick Taylor's minute definition of tasks and Henry Ford's Model T production line should be obvious (Taylor 1947).

Hierarchy

Along with a rigid definition of tasks came a rigid definition of power and authority. The result was a hierarchical structure, with only those higher in the organisational hierarchy able to give instructions to those lower down. Promotion up the hierarchy was possible on the basis of either merit or seniority.

Impersonal rationality

In a bureaucracy, power belongs to the office, not to the office holder. Power was based on rules, which provided precedents for action. Behaviour was rational, based on logical principles, not on individual whim or prejudice. Remember that it was not long before Weber that reforms were enacted in the UK to eliminate corruption and nepotism in the civil service and the army. Impersonal rationality at least in theory made corruption and nepotism impossible. Impersonal rules also form the basis for our present-day anti-discrimination legislation – the right to be judged on your own merit, not on your sex, gender, skin colour, nationality, religion, disability or sexual orientation.

As a form of organisation, bureaucracy had many strengths:

- It provided predictable and secure career paths for those who worked in them – the civil service 'job for life'.
- Rules provided a number of protections. They guaranteed fair treatment within the rules, and avoided the arbitrary exercise of power, and they protected civil liberties, because everyone was subject to the rules.

However, there were also weaknesses:

- The rules could become so complex that the worker or the client of the organisation could feel helpless, confused, and trapped. See, for example, Franz Kafka's *The Trial* (Kafka 1956), or the labyrinthine regulations surrounding present day Tax Credits.
- Minute definition and sub-division of tasks could produce an alienated workforce, particularly as the hierarchical structure did not easily permit worker empowerment.
- Rigid adherence to rules could produce a 'jobsworth' mentality – 'no, you can't do X, it's not in the rules' (Clegg, Kornberger and Pitsis 2008). Perhaps most crucially, its very rigidity, which is in some ways its greatest strength, is also its greatest weakness. A pure bureaucracy can only operate successfully in a placid environment, and it becomes progressively less able to cope effectively as the environment becomes more turbulent.

Despite the weaknesses of the model, there are still strong bureaucratic elements in virtually all organisational forms today.

1.6.2 DIVISIONALISATION OR M-FORM

This is a development of the bureaucratic organisation. As the organisation becomes larger, it becomes more difficult to manage everything from the centre. As a result, some decision-making is decentralised. The divisionalised organisation sets up a number of separate product, market or geographic divisions, each responsible for operational decisions, which will usually include production, marketing, and some elements of HR (although US companies are more reluctant to delegate HR to divisions). Each division will thus be a mini-bureaucracy, competing against the other divisions. Strategic decisions will be taken at headquarters, including, crucially, investment decisions and allocation of capital, and setting and monitoring of targets (Boxall and Purcell 2008).

Divisionalisation was effectively invented by Alfred Sloan at General Motors in the 1920s. Here the motive was not so much to give more autonomy to operating divisions – Chevrolet, Buick or Cadillac – but to centralise authority over subsidiaries which had previously been independent businesses (Hales 2001). The divisional structure is particularly common among multinational corporations, with divisions usually organised on a country or regional basis.

The divisional form is more flexible than pure bureaucracy, but as noted above, there is a tendency for the divisions themselves to become highly bureaucratised, which then limits their flexibility. There is also a tendency for US or UK divisional organisations to impose mainly short-term targets on their operating divisions – in contrast to the longer-term goals favoured by the Japanese.

A more extreme form of divisionalisation operates through Strategic Business Units (SBUs). The typical SBU is smaller than the classic division, and based on a niche product, service or unit. Specialist services, like IT or training, will often themselves be supplied by SBUs, which are profit centres in their own right. These may not just provide services within the organisation, but compete for outside business. An extreme example of this was the internal market in the BBC under John Birt in the 1990s. Here, under a programme called Producer Choice, programme makers were given budgets which they could spend either on in-house facilities or on external contractors. If the in-house facilities could not attract enough work, they were closed (Hales 2001). The intention was to increase efficiency, but the internal market process was so expensive that any benefits were more than cancelled out. Producer Choice was abandoned by the next Director-General of the BBC, Greg Dyke.

1.6.3 THE MATRIX ORGANISATION

The matrix model of organisation was first developed in the US aerospace industry in the 1960s. Here the organisation is involved in a series of short or medium term projects, each of which has a finite life. Each project will require the services of a number of functional specialists, drawn from functional departments. Who is going to control these functional specialists – their departmental manager or the project manager? The solution offered in a matrix organisation is that he or she will be answerable to both the departmental and the project manager.

Figure 1.10 A matrix organisational structure

Production specialist U will report to his functional manager, the production manager, but while he is working on project A, he will be answerable to the project manager in charge of project A. He will also be working on project A alongside his colleague from marketing, V.

The matrix structure has a number of advantages:

● Communication within the organisation is improved, and as a result decisions can be made more speedily and effectively.

● Use of human and capital resources becomes more flexible.

- The use of project teams increases motivation, job satisfaction and personal development.

However, there can also be disadvantages:

- As each individual is answerable to at least two bosses, there can be problems of loyalty, and feelings of insecurity.
- Power struggles are likely over decision making and the allocation of resources between the functional and project managers.
- Although communication and decision making should be improved, decisions may be more difficult to make as decision-making authority is diffused.
- The structure is particularly threatening to functional managers, who can see their power base eroded.

1.6.4 THE NETWORK ORGANISATION OR N FORM

The network organisation is a less formal version of the matrix organisation. The aim is to build up networks and connections between different parts of the organisation, in order to break down rigid departmental smokestacks, and to ensure the faster diffusion of ideas throughout the organisation. The N-form entails combination of knowledge rather than its division, which is the basic principle in the M-form. Other attributes of the N-form are: temporary constellations of people, the importance of personnel at lower levels, lateral communication, a catalytic role for top management, and strategies aimed at focusing (Hedlund 1994).

This can be done in several ways. Unilever, for example, works hard to build up lateral relationships between managers in different divisions. Career development is carefully planned on a multiple spiral, with managers progressing between functions, divisions and countries (Boxall and Purcell 2008, p264).

Another approach is to use network managers, with several roles:

- boundary-spanners between levels and functions
- initiators of networks
- co-ordinators of information transfer
- conveyors of corporate vision downwards and advocates of decentralised initiatives upwards (Child 2005, p255).

A third approach is to use communities of practice. These are informal networks of people with common interests within an organisation (and often pulling in people from outside the organisation). Often run on the Internet or a company intranet, they enable quick informal communication of information and knowledge. All students know that you learn at least as much from your fellow students as from formal tuition, and communities of practice operate on the same principle of social learning (Clegg, Kornberger and Pitsis, 2008). CIPD professional communities (a form of community of practice) had 171,529 participants on 24 January 2015, taking part in 31,009 discussions, although it was not clear how many of these were currently active (www.cipd.co.uk/communities, accessed on 24 January 2015).

One key element in ensuring the success of any N form organisation is culture. As Whittington and Mayer (2000), said, 'N form works best with Eastern appreciation of the tacit, the embedded and the ambiguous, rather than the explicit, tightly specified knowledge systems of the West.'

Networks can operate outside as well as inside the organisation. Hansen and von Oetinger (2001) identified the concept of the T-shaped manager, with the vertical part of the T representing the manager's role within the organisation, and the horizontal part of the T the role of networking outside the organisation.

The key resource in an N-form organisation is knowledge. Bettis (1991) argues that with the development of N-form the M-form organisation is now an 'organisational fossil'. In the M-form Chandler argued that 'structure follows strategy'. In the N-form, structure *is* strategy (Purcell 2005).

?   REFLECTIVE ACTIVITY 1.4

Organisational structures

Tarmac Quarry Materials

Tarmac Quarry Materials is one of three companies within Tarmac Building Products, part of Lafarge Tarmac. It produces ready mixed concrete, asphalt, aggregates, lime, cement and contracting services. There are three business units within the company – Concrete, aggregates and asphalt; National Contracting; and Buxton Lime and Cement. Each business unit has the following functions: operations, commercial, technical, safety, health and environment, recycling, and estates and geology. The Head Office supplies support functions – HR, finance, marketing, procurement and IT.

The company sees operations as its key function. The operational structure is very hierarchical, with seven levels (more than the whole Catholic Church!) – Executive Director, Regional Operations Director, District Manager, Zone Manager, Unit Manager, Section Leader and Operator. Recruitment is mainly at two levels – apprentices join as operators, while graduates start by shadowing section leaders.

Finance is a central function because standards of reporting and accounting need to be the same across all parts of Tarmac. This is so that the business has a clear and accurate picture of its performance.

HR provides expertise in:

● managing change and facilitating training and development
● recruitment, selection and employee relations
● pensions and benefits
● communicating with employees.

An HR manager's role is to ensure that business managers apply HR policies and procedures consistently through all business units. This helps to develop partnerships across different teams, which supports corporate aims and objectives.

Source: Times 100 Business Case Studies (2012)

Capco

Capco is a leading international provider of consulting, managed services and technology solutions for the financial services industry. This requires its employees to be creative in order to provide tailored solutions to demanding clients who are facing large competitive and environmental pressures. Values of respect, integrity, commitment, excellence and knowledge define how the company works with its clients and reflect the behaviours Capco expects from its employees.

The organisational structure is flat, with wide spans of control. Communication channels are clear and effective. Within this overall flat structure, Capco works through matrix teams, a common form of structure for project-based work. The team is made up of individuals with specialist skills, such as marketing, HR, or sometimes specialist technical skills, who work together on a specific project. Once the project has been completed members of the team move on to another project with a different group of employees.

This structure creates a highly motivated and empowered workforce with everyone having access to advice and coaching. There is little bureaucracy, and all UK staff have open access to the UK Chief Executive Officer who sits in the middle of the office. Capco's culture celebrates individuality, integrity and openness in the work environment.

Idea generation for its financial services clients is developed through Capco's 'rocket teams'. The teams are small, with three to four people. The terms of reference of the rocket teams ensure that all ideas are considered and no ideas are blocked. There are clear parallels here with the skunkworks concept developed by the Lockheed Aircraft company during world war two (Economist 2008).

Capco believes in open lines of communication. Its local and regional offices host regular forums to disseminate information about developments in the business, as well as giving employees an opportunity to socialise. Consultants can often be based remotely on a client site and miss the day-to-day interactions of a team or connection with the firm. In order to keep in touch with other staff, despite working in different locations and on different projects, an internal social networking site was created called CapInTouch (a type of community of practice)

Source: Times 100 Business Case Studies (2014b)

Questions

1   What do you think are the strengths and weaknesses of the organisational structures of Tarmac and Capco?

2   How far do you think that the organisational structure is dictated by the environment in which each company operates?

3   Find out more about the skunkworks concept by searching the Internet under 'skunkworks'.

CASE STUDY 1.6

THE LEARNING AND SKILLS COUNCIL

The Learning and Skills Council was set up in 2001 to plan and fund programmes in further education colleges. Its organisational structure was extremely flat. A central head office set overall policy, while operational delivery was carried out through 47 semi-autonomous local Learning and Skills Councils, whose heads all reported direct to the chief executive. In addition, there were seven national directors who also reported to the chief executive. After 2003, the

structure was made more hierarchical. The national directors were reduced from seven to four, and a new level of nine regional directors were appointed to manage the local LSCs.

An independent staff survey in 2005 showed that engagement had increased by 14% since 2003 and confidence in management decision-making had risen by 26%. The council has also seen improvements in areas such as leadership, line management and communication. It was assumed that these improvements were the direct result of the changes in structure. However, any improvements may well have been short-lived. The LSC made a

quarter of its staff redundant in September 2005, and the organisation was abolished in 2008!

Source: Hope (2005)

1.6.5 VIRTUAL ORGANISATIONS

In a virtual organisation, physical assets – buildings, machinery, etc – are replaced by computer networks. Warner and Witzel (2003, Chapter 1) identify six characteristics of virtual organisations:

- *Lack of physical structure.* They have fewer physical assets, and ultimately might exist solely in cyberspace.
- *Reliance on communications technology.* Virtual organisations use communication networks supported by the Internet.
- *Mobile work.* Members of teams no longer have to be in physical contact. They can work anywhere, and communicate through ICT.
- *Hybrid forms.* Some virtual organisations are brought together for short-term projects, like producing a film or a book. Others are longer term, like a virtual supply chain.
- *Boundaryless and inclusive.* Virtual organisations often closely involve suppliers (through partnership sourcing) or customers (through customer relationship management). The fashion accessories company Topsy Tail, for example, had revenues of $80m in 1998, but only three employees. It outsources everything, and never touches its product (Child 2005).
- *Flexible and responsive.*

Perhaps the best example of a virtual organisation is Dell Computer Corporation. The key to Dell's business model is its direct sales strategy, which relies on demand pull. A computer is only produced against a firm customer order. The company therefore has no finished goods inventory or warehouses. It operates with half the staff and one-tenth the inventory of its competitors. On average it carries six days' work in progress stock, all held against firm orders. In 2000, 50% of orders were received online (Gillespie 2000). The ordering system permits the customer to write their own specification (mass customisation). In theory, each computer sold is unique. When it receives an order, it sends electronic orders for components to its suppliers worldwide. These components are then assembled in a Dell factory and despatched direct to the customer. In some cases the process is totally virtual – for example, when Dell receives an order for a computer monitor, it is despatched direct to the customer from a supplier like Sony (Child 2005).

1.6.6 STRATEGIC ALLIANCES

Strategic alliances are medium- to long-term co-operative relationships between firms which involve joint working. Wakeam defines five criteria:

- critical to the success of a core business goal or objective
- critical to the development or maintenance of a core competency or other source of competitive advantage
- blocks a competitive threat
- creates or maintains strategic choices for the firm
- mitigates a significant risk to the business (Wakeam 2003).

An alliance meeting any one of these criteria is strategic and should be managed accordingly. They can variously be called alliances, partnerships or joint ventures. They have become increasingly common. Between 1996 and 2001, US companies formed 57,000 alliances (Dyer, Kale and Singh 2004). The average US corporation manages more than 30 alliances, while many have several hundred. By 2001, they already accounted for up to 15% of the market value of the typical US company. However, it has been estimated that 60% have been outright failures (Parkhe 2001).

Alliances can take many legal and contractual forms. These are illustrated and discussed in Child 2005, pp 223–5. Contractor and Lorange (1998) identify six main objectives for alliances:

- reduction of risk
- achievement of economies of scale
- technology exchange
- countering competition
- overcoming government trade or investment barriers
- vertical quasi-integration advantages – linking the complementary contributions of partners in a value chain.

Dussauge and Garrette (1999) identified six different types, three between non-competing firms, and three between competing forms.

Non-competing

- International expansion joint ventures. Until the late 1990s, Western firms seeking to invest in China could only do so through a joint venture with a local firm.
- Vertical partnerships, between firms at different stages in the same value chain. For example Intel and Hewlett-Packard set up a joint venture to develop a new microprocessor.
- Cross-industry agreements: American Airlines and SNCF (French Railways) set up a joint venture to develop a computerised railway ticketing system.

Competing

- Shared supply alliances. These are common in the car industry.
- Quasi-concentration alliances, designed to counter competition. An example is Airbus Industrie, formed between competing European aircraft manufacturers to counter the threat from Boeing.
- Complementary alliances, designed to reduce risk and achieve synergy. These are common in the pharmaceutical industry. For example, in 1996, Pfizer used its superior marketing expertise to collaborate in the marketing of Lipitor, a cholesterol-reducing drug developed by a rival company, Warner-Lambert. By 1999, Lipitor had achieved sales of $3bn a year (Dyer, Kale and Singh, 2004).

Why do so many alliances fail? Many reasons have been put forward:

- *Communication problems.* A US–UK joint venture had to appear before a crucial British government hearing. The US firm asked the UK one to 'table' several key points at the meeting. To the horror of the Americans, the British firm brought up these very issues at the hearing, leading to disaster. The Americans had forgotten that 'to table' in UK English means to 'place on the table', whereas in US English it means 'hide under the table'.
- *Culture clashes.* In the 1990s, Siemens, Toshiba and IBM were working together to develop a new memory chip. Siemens reps were horrified when the Toshiba scientists appeared to go to sleep in meetings – a common practice among Japanese when the discussion does not directly concern them. The Japanese found it difficult to work in mixed-nationality groups speaking English. The Americans felt the Germans planned too much and the Japanese would not take decisions (Parkhe 2001).

- *Diverging strategic directions.* Alliances which might have made perfect strategic sense at the time may diverge over a longer period.
- *Failure to protect strategic knowledge.* In the early 1980s, Macintosh used Microsoft to develop software applications for the Apple Mac. As a result, Microsoft acquired crucial knowledge about Apple's mouse-based Graphical User Interface, which it then used to develop the Windows operating system. Eventually Apple brought an unsuccessful law suit against Microsoft to try to protect its intellectual property (Norman 2001).
- *Uneven benefits.* In 2001, Coca-Cola and Procter & Gamble formed a $4bn joint venture that would control more than 40 brands contributed by the parent companies. However, the markets felt that P&G would get more out of the alliance than Coke. P&G's share price immediately rose 2%, while Coca-Cola's fell 6%. Predictably, the alliance lasted only six months (Dyer, Kale and Singh 2004). The same thing may well happen with the Internet search technology joint venture announced by Microsoft and Yahoo in July 2009, intended as a defensive alliance against the market leader, Google. Here the share price disparity has been even more marked. Microsoft shares rose 2%, while Yahoo's fell 15%. Both sides moved fast to defend the alliance. Steve Ballmer, CEO of Microsoft, described the Yahoo share price fall as 'sort of unbelievable', while Tim Morse, Yahoo's chief finance officer, said, 'It's a perfect fit for our strategy' (Waters and Menn, 2009). The market's scepticism seems to have been justified. In the third quarter of 2011, Yahoo reported a fall in revenue of 5%, and attributed this to the Search Alliance with Microsoft (Crum 2011).
- *If either partner misunderstands the other's expectation of the alliance, it is likely to fall apart.* For example, if one partner believes the other is looking for revenue generation to achieve a core business goal, when in reality the objective is to keep a strategic option open, the alliance is not likely to survive.
- *Exit problems.* Daimler Benz had a long-standing alliance with ABB called Adtranz. The alliance had been losing money, and after Daimler-Benz merged with Chrysler, an ex-Chrysler executive suggested putting it into liquidation. The Daimler reaction was horror – 'You don't understand. This is Europe. Bankruptcy is not good over here.' Eventually ABB was bought out. In another example, Suzuki wanted to make redundancies at a joint venture in Spain. The result was riots outside the Japanese embassy in Madrid (Inkpen and Ross 2001).

? REFLECTIVE ACTIVITY 1.5

Successful and unsuccessful alliances – Galanz and Swissair

Galanz

Guangdong Galanz is the global leader in microwave manufacture, producing over 18 million units in 2004, 40% of the global market. It is one of the largest home appliance manufacturers in China, employing 20,000 people and with 2004 revenues exceeding $1bn.

This is a far cry from the first incarnation of the company, as the Guizhou Down Product Factory, a township enterprise set up by Quingde Leung in 1978, when the Chinese government set up its first Special Enterprise Zones in Guangdong in southern China. The company washed and processed goose feathers for clothing companies such as Yves St Laurent. By 1992, the company had sales of $19m, and ranked in the top 100 village and township enterprises in China.

However, Leung was worried that intense competition would kill the textiles business, and he took the momentous decision to diversify into microwaves, at that time a luxury item in China.

He changed the name of the company to the Galanz Group of Guangdong, recruited experts from a radio factory in Shanghai, and licensed microwave technology from Toshiba. In 1993, the company produced a trial run of 10,000 microwaves, and persuaded the Shanghai No 1 Department Store to stock them.

In 1994 Chinese government policy changed, and township enterprises were required to sell two-thirds of each enterprise to management. The result was a broad base of middle managers with a stake in the company's success.

Galanz was faced with fierce competition from the market leader SMC. However, ironically, SMC was crippled by its partnership agreement with the huge American white goods manufacturer Whirlpool. Whirlpool put in its own management team, and required that all major decisions were cleared first through regional headquarters in Hong Kong and ultimately through corporate headquarters in Michigan. By 1995 Galanz had a 25% share of the Chinese market, passing SMC, and by 1998 this had grown to half the market. Clearly further growth in the domestic market would be difficult.

In 1997, one result of the Asian financial crisis was that South Korean microwave manufacturers, including Samsung and LG, were accused of dumping microwaves on the European market. European manufacturers felt that they were unable to compete.

In a novel deal, Galanz offered to make their microwaves in China for half the European cost. European manufacturers shipped their whole production lines to Guangdong, where they could take advantage of Galanz's lower labour costs and efficient supply chain. The microwaves would then be exported back to Europe to be sold under the European companies' brand names. Galanz also secured permission from its partners to use their production facilities to produce Galanz branded goods in China. Galanz signed up 200 European partners, and its microwave production grew from one million in 1996 to 12 million in 2001.

The deal was a win-win. The European partners obtained product at a much lower cost than they could have produced themselves, while Galanz was able to expand and become a global presence without having to make heavy capital investments itself.

Source: Sull (2005)

Swissair

In the 1990s, Swissair was one of the most successful and respected airlines in the world, noted for its high quality, which permitted it to charge high prices. It was popularly known as the 'flying bank' because of its financial strength. In 1998 it made a profit of SFr400m (around £200m). Yet by 2000, the company was losing SFr2.9bn, and in October 2001 it went into receivership.

What went wrong? The immediate cause of the collapse was the world crisis in the airline industry following the terrorist attacks on 11 September 2001, but a more fundamental cause was Swissair's failed alliance strategy.

Until the late 1980s, the European airline industry was dominated by national carriers with effective monopolies in their home markets. This kept competition low, and prices and profits high. However, the first steps towards liberalisation of the world airline industry came in 1988. This represented a threat to Swissair, with its small home market. In 1993, talks (codenamed Alcazar) were opened between Swissair, SAS (Scandinavian Airlines), KLM (the Netherlands) and Austrian Airlines. A new company was proposed, with Swissair, SAS and KLM each holding 30%, and Austrian 10%. However, Swiss public opinion was hostile to the idea of Swissair losing its name, and the talks broke down.

In 1994, Swissair hired McKinsey to develop a new strategy, known as the Hunter Strategy. Three options were put forward:

- Go it alone. Given the small size of the Swiss home market, this was not seen as viable.
- Develop a new business alliance (in effect a repeat of the Alcazar strategy). This was seen as high risk, but the most politically acceptable.
- Ally with one of the large European airlines (BA, Lufthansa or Air France). This was seen as the safest option, but politically unacceptable, as Swissair would inevitably be a very junior partner.

As a first step, in 1994 Swissair acquired a 49.5% stake in the Belgian airline Sabena, which had only made a profit once in its 75 year history. Meanwhile, the world aviation industry was changing rapidly. In 1996, BA, American Airlines, Cathay Pacific and Qantas formed a new global alliance called Oneworld. Two other alliances followed – Skyteam, led by Air France, and Star, including United Airlines, Lufthansa and SAS.

Swissair decided to go for a strategy of forming a fourth alliance. It acquired minority stakes in the Polish airline LOT, the French company Air Littoral, the Italian airlines Air Europe and Volare, and South African Airways (SAA), in addition to its existing holding in Sabena and Austrian Airlines. None of the partners, with the possible exception of SAA, was known as a strong airline.

Swissair already had long-standing alliance relationships with Delta and Singapore Airlines, both strong companies. However, Delta decided to join Skyteam in 1999, while Singapore Airlines joined Star. In 2000, an aggressive attempt to increase Swissair's stake in Austrian led to that airline also defecting to Star. Meanwhile, the European market was increasingly being penetrated by the low-cost airlines Ryanair and easyJet. The latter set up a hub in Geneva, directly threatening Swissair on its home ground.

By mid-July 2001, Swissair had debts of SFr7.8bn, six times the value of its equity, and its share price was a fifth of its peak in 1998. Given this weakness, 9/11 was merely the last straw. Both Swissair and its partner Sabena were doomed. Swissair's assets were transferred to a successor airline, Swiss, which was taken over by Lufthansa in 2005.

Source: Ruigrok (2004)

Question

Why do you think that Galanz was successful in its alliances, and Swissair unsuccessful?

1.7 STRUCTURAL CHOICE

Goold and Campbell (2002) propose nine design tests against which choice of structure can be evaluated:

1 The market-advantage test. If co-ordination between two steps in a production process is important to market advantage, they should be placed in the same structural unit.

2 The parenting-advantage test. If the centre aims to promote synergy, integration specialisms should be placed at the centre.

3 The people test. The structure must fit the skills of the people available.

4 The feasibility test. The structure must fit legal, stakeholder and other constraints.

5 The specialised culture test. A structure scores poorly if it breaks up important specialist cultures.

6 The difficult links test. Does the structure set up links between parts of the organisation that are important but bound to be strained?

7   The redundant hierarchy test. Too many layers of management cause undue blockages and expense.

8   The accountability test. There should be clear lines of accountability, often a problem with matrix organisations.

9   The flexibility test. Is the structure flexible enough to cope with future change?

1.7.1 DOES STRUCTURE FOLLOW STRATEGY?

Alfred Chandler, one of the pioneers of strategic management, argued strongly that structure follows strategy. He quotes the example of Du Pont, which at the end of the First World War undertook a diversification strategy, which initially was unsuccessful, mainly because the company kept its old functional structure, which was unable to cope with increased diversity. Once Du Pont switched to a divisional structure, its strategy thrived (Chandler 1962).

Hall and Saias (1980) argue that the causality can go the other way – strategy can follow structure. A decentralised multidivisional structure can quickly take up new diversification strategies, but finds it much more difficult to follow a strategy which is dependent on knowledge-sharing.

Amburgey and Dacin (1994) found that structure followed strategy, but only most of the time. Finally, Mintzberg (1998) concluded that 'structure follows strategy as the left foot follows the right', ie that the two are linked, and neither consistently leads the other.

?   REFLECTIVE ACTIVITY 1.6

Henry Mintzberg and organisational structure

Henry Mintzberg has put forward a number of hypotheses about how situational factors affect the structure and functioning of organisations:

1   The older the organisation, the more formalised its behaviour.

2   The larger the organisation, the more formalised its behaviour.

3   The larger the organisation, the more elaborate its structure.

4   The more dynamic an organisation's environment, the more organic its structure.

5   The more complex an organisation's environment, the more centralised its structure.

6   The more diversified an organisation's markets, the greater the propensity to split into market-based units or divisions.

7   Extreme hostility in the environment drives any organisation to centralise its structure temporarily.

Source: Mintzberg (1998)

Question

From your knowledge of your own organisation, or any other organisations with which you are familiar, how far do you think these hypotheses are valid?

1.8 HR OUTSOURCING

Outsourcing can be a key element of a partnership strategy. One popular candidate for outsourcing is HR. HR outsourcing can cover a wide spectrum of activities, from a small business using a local personnel freelancer to handle its HR on a part-time basis, to a joint venture formed between a multinational company and an HR services company to handle all of the former's HR function. Here we are more concerned with the latter end of the spectrum, where control over significant elements of the outsourcer's HR function is outsourced to a partner organisation.

A 2009 CIPD survey found that 29% of organisations sampled were using HR outsourcing, with 64% increasing their use of outsourcing in the previous five years, and only 11% reducing it (CIPD 2009b). The top drivers for HR outsourcing were access to skills and knowledge not available within the organisation (71%), improving quality (64%), and cost reduction (61%). Outsourcers seem to have achieved these objectives. Ninety-one per cent claimed to have accessed knowledge and skills, 83% to have improved quality, and 90% to have reduced costs.

The most common functions to have been outsourced were legal, payroll, pensions, training and recruitment. Least likely to have been outsourced were resource planning, appraisal, strategy and policy. There seems to be a clear trend to outsource operational parts of the HR function, and to keep more strategic elements in-house.

Also interesting are reasons given for not using HR outsourcing, even when the organisation involved outsources other significant functions. The three most commonly given reasons for not outsourcing HR were:

- effective, well-resourced HR team within the organisation (52%)
- remain unconvinced of the benefits of HR outsourcing (35%)
- already use effective shared service model (24%).

Shared service centres are a common alternative to HR outsourcing which will be discussed below.

In practice, HR outsourcing does not always go smoothly. BP, for example, was the first major company to sign a large HR outsourcing deal, with Exult in 1998. Exult was a start-up, inexperienced organisation, and the early days of the contract were chaotic. BP's human resources employees were reluctant to cooperate with the transition, knowing they were eliminating their own jobs, and initially, the corporation's HR costs went up instead of down (Rafter 2005). Exult was taken over by Hewitt in 2004, and the deal ran into further trouble. By 2006, Hewitt was losing $166m, citing problems in HR outsourcing, while BP took back expatriate administration in-house, and also gave two years' notice that it intended to end the contract with Hewitt. However, in February 2009, it signed a new contract, extending the scope of the contract worldwide (rather than just the UK and US), but taking most aspects of recruitment back in-house (Pickard 2009b).

Another of the major HR outsourcing deals was BT's with Accenture. Initially, in 2000, the two companies set up a joint venture to run BP's HR function, but Accenture then bought out BT's share. Again, there were problems with the contract, mainly put down to a lack of effective communication. Some BT line managers were not even aware that HR had been outsourced, and were surprised to receive bills from Accenture when they requested extra services. After extensive negotiations, the outsourcing contract was renewed for 10 years in 2005, at a cost of £306m (Pickard 2004b, hrmguide 2005).

In 2006, Cable and Wireless, another of Accenture's clients, announced that it was not renewing its five-year contract, originally placed with the BT-Accenture joint venture. The main reason given was that Cable and Wireless had drastically downsized following the dot-com crash in 2001, from 57,000 staff to 14,000, and as a result could more easily do its own HR in-house. However, Ian Muir, the international HR director, admitted that some valuable tacit knowledge had been lost through outsourcing (Pickard 2006).

An alternative to HR outsourcing is a shared service centre. This involves the use of a call centre to give HR advice to line managers, and, often, individual employees (Marchington and Wilkinson 2008). Three models are common:

- an in-house function
- an in-house function which also offers services on the open market to other organisations seeking to outsource their HR
- a specialist unit offering HR services for a number of employers in a network. (This model is common among schools and in the NHS. An NHS example is discussed by Marchington and Wilkinson (2008, pp197–8)).

? REFLECTIVE ACTIVITY 1.7

Managing an HR outsourcing contract

You are responsible for managing an HR outsourcing contract in your organisation. What steps do you need to take to ensure that this contract is managed effectively?

? REFLECTIVE ACTIVITY 1.8

Semco

Semco is a Brazilian manufacturing company, based in Sao Paulo, and owned by Ricardo Semler. It is run like no other company. Its basic rule is that there are no rules.

- Workers make decisions.
- Management sets its own salaries and bonuses.
- Everyone has access to the company books.
- Shopfloor workers set their own productivity targets and work flexi-time.
- Workers negotiate with management the level of profit-sharing, and then decide among themselves who gets it.
- Before anyone is hired or promoted to a management position, they are interviewed, evaluated and approved by all the people who will work for them.
- Every six months, Semco managers are appraised by all their subordinates, and the results are published for all to see.
- Workers have the option of taking 75% of their basic pay, and receiving a supplement taking it up to 125%, but only if the company has a good year.
- Workers are encouraged to set up their own satellite companies to supply Semco.
- When a job opening occurs, a Semco employee who meets 70% of its requirements is given preference over an outsider.
- Semco doesn't have an organisation chart. Only the respect of the led creates a leader.
- Ricardo Semler takes two months' holiday a year, leaves no contact number, and does not himself contact the company. When he had a serious car accident in 2005, spending months in intensive care with a broken neck, the company maintained its 25% plus growth rate, and ran seamlessly without him.

● The guiding rule on everything is common sense.

Semco is one of Latin America's fastest-growing companies, acknowledged to be the best in Brazil to work for, and has a waiting list of thousands of applicants wanting to join it.

Question

Would you feel comfortable working for Semco?

Sources: Semler (1993); Fisher (2005)

1.9 STAKEHOLDERS

Stakeholders are 'those individuals or groups who depend on the organisation to fulfil their own goals and on whom, in turn, the organisation depends' (Johnson and Scholes 1997). Stakeholders can be inside the organisation, like shareholders or employees, or outside, like customers or suppliers. In some cases, the relationship is legal, as with statutory regulatory bodies or lenders, or moral, as with the local community, or a mixture of the two, as with employees (to meet the requirements of the contract of employment and to respect legal employment rights (legal), and to fulfil the expectations of the psychological contract (moral)). In the case of the public sector, there are no shareholders, but a wide range of client stakeholders.

Note that the CIPD has a narrower definition of stakeholder. It includes only those parties who have a legal or financial relationship with the organisation. All others are defined as 'other interested parties' – the CIPD specifically mentions the media and the local community (CIPD (2003b, pp6, 30). However, this narrow definition ignores the moral and ethical dimensions of stakeholder theory. For example, a local community may have no legal claim on a company that routinely but legally pollutes its environment, but few would deny its moral claim on the company.

Stakeholder theory states that organisations have responsibilities to a wide range of stakeholders. This can be contrasted with the stockholder theory of corporate governance, which states that the organisation's only responsibility is to its shareholders (stockholders in American). Stockholder theory has been defended from several different angles. One is the agency approach associated with Milton Friedman. He argues that managers are legally the agents of the organisation's owners (its shareholders), and under agency law are thus legally obliged to serve only their interests, as long as they keep within the law (Friedman 1962). It is interesting that by 1970 Friedman had modified his hardline view, stressing a need to conform to the 'basic rules of society', including those 'embodied in ethical custom' (Friedman 1970a).

Another perspective is the logical argument put forward by John Argenti, who argues that it is logically impossible for an organisation to pursue multiple objectives – ie it cannot simultaneously serve the interests of a range of stakeholders. In times of prosperity, the organisation might be able to deal out rewards in such a way as to keep all the stakeholders quiet, but in hard times, shareholders will take priority, if only because in the last resort, shareholders can sack the board of directors (Argenti 1993).

Not all stakeholders are equal. Some are much more important to the organisation than others. The relative importance of stakeholders can be analysed using stakeholder mapping (Johnson and Scholes 1997, pp197–203). Stakeholder mapping classifies stakeholders by the power which they have over the organisation, and the degree of interest which they have in it. These can be plotted on a two-by-two matrix.

Figure 1.11 Stakeholder mapping

Level of interest

	Low	High
Low **Power** **High**	A Don't bother C Satisfy	B Inform D Crucial

Source: Adapted from Johnson and Scholes (1997)

Stakeholders of type A can effectively be ignored. They are not interested in the organisation, and have little power to affect it anyway. Conversely, type D are critical, and their interests must be taken into account at all times. Type B are interested in the organisation, but do not have the power to affect it significantly. They need to be kept informed, particularly as they may in turn be able to influence other stakeholders. Type C are passive stakeholders. They have great potential to influence the organisation, but at present little interest in doing so. They need to be kept quiet, so that they do not suddenly take an adverse interest in the organisation, and shift into type D.

The implication is that stakeholders have to be actively managed. They can be crucial in mobilising support for the organisation, or if things go badly, they can cripple it.

CASE STUDY 1.7

STAKEHOLDER ENGAGEMENT: ANGLIAN WATER

In June 2008 a rabbit got into a water tank at Pitsford Reservoir in Northamptonshire, owned by Anglian Water, and caused an outbreak of cryptosporidium. The company immediately issued a 'Boil Water' notice to 108,000 households, which remained in force for ten days (*Northamptonshire Telegraph*, 2008).

Fortunately, Anglian Water's crisis management plan included a stakeholder pack which contained contact details for all key stakeholders, including politicians, regulators, media, business customers and vulnerable customers. The plan also had individual responsibilities assigned to roles along with written responses pre-prepared for different events to ensure response time wasn't lost to drafting press releases or statements.

Customers received several letters and were able to get updates from local media three times a day. Mobile units were also sent out into the two main towns to maintain full visibility and reassure the general public. Another priority was to get messages and help through to the most vulnerable customers, including the young, elderly and those that needed direct assistance. In the Pitsford area they had 300 registered vulnerable customers. During the incident this increased to 3,000. Other vulnerable groups were non-English speaking residents. To target these customers the company published information in a number of languages. They also used police contacts to identify the minority groups' community leaders and target specialist media (BITC).

After the incident, a report to the Drinking Water Inspectorate analysed Anglian Water's response in detail. By comparison with a similar incident the year before at Mythe in Gloucestershire, Anglian Water came out very well. The major information source in Pitsford was the water company (76%), whereas in Mythe, the water company was the major source for only 57%. In Pitsford, 97% received water advice, compared with 67% in Mythe, and 34% in Pitsford felt very informed, compared with 16% in Mythe (Rundblad et al 2011).

1.10 CONNECTIONS BETWEEN THE ENVIRONMENT, STRATEGY AND ORGANISATIONAL DESIGN

In this section, we will examine Thompson's model of E-V-R congruence.

1.10.1 E-V-R CONGRUENCE

Thompson (2005) developed the concept of E-V-R Congruence as a measure of how well an organisation is attuned to its environment. He develops the idea of SWOT analysis to incorporate values. In his model E represents the environment (the opportunities and threats part of a SWOT analysis), while R represents resources and V values, both of which are traditionally subsumed within the strengths and weaknesses sections of a SWOT. To Thompson, resources would be physical, while values represent the human strengths and weaknesses of the organisation, specifically its leadership and culture, as well as the underlying values which it holds.

More important than the mere idea of E-V-R is the concept of congruence. An organisation will achieve congruence when its environment, resources and values are mutually reinforcing. Its strategic position will be strong. A congruent organisation is illustrated in Figure 1.12.

Figure 1.12 The congruent organisation

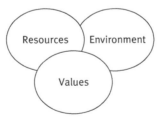

Thompson then identifies types of organisations where the three elements are not congruent.

Figure 1.13 The unconsciously competent organisation

Here the values of the organisation are out of line with its environment and resources, but because environment and resources are still aligned, the organisation still works, at least on a superficial level. This type of organisation is likely to be complacent, and runs the risk of serious trouble if its environment and resources start to drift out of line. The strategic imperative here is for a change in leadership style and a redefinition of values and culture.

Figure 1.14 The consciously incompetent organisation

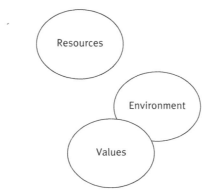

Here the organisation is aware that there is a resource mismatch, but tends to see it as a series of short-term problems. The organisation will tend to be reactive and to fight fires, while unable to take a long-term strategic view of resources.

Figure 1.15 Strategic drift

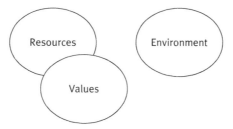

Here the organisation has lost touch with its environment, perhaps because of complacency, perhaps because of failure to scan the environment effectively. It must either find a way to change its environment, or to bring its resources and values back in line with changes in the environment

Figure 1.16 The lost organisation

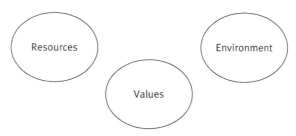

Unless this organisation takes swift and drastic action to reachieve congruence, in the long run it is doomed.

? REFLECTIVE ACTIVITY 1.9

The National Trust and E-V-R

The National Trust has as its core aim to 'look after special places, for ever, for everyone'. It is the largest private landowner in Britain, owning 640,000 acres, mostly rented out to tenants on commercial terms. It also owns 600 miles of Britain's coastlines, guaranteeing free public access to the coast, and around 300 houses and gardens, which are open free to members, and at a small charge to others. In 2005–6, there were 13.7 million visits to NT properties, of which 2.9 million, or around 20%, were paying visits, while the rest were visits by members (National Trust 2006).

Clearly the National Trust estate is a hugely valuable asset, which on an open market valuation would be worth billions of pounds. However, remember the words 'for ever' in the core purpose. The Trust is legally prohibited from selling property, and the result is that in many ways the estate must be seen as a liability rather than an asset, which must be maintained at ever-growing expense (Legg 2005).

More conventional physical resources include National Trust gift shops at most sites, and also extensive catering facilities (which earned £25m in 2005–6, twice as much as admissions).

A key resource of the Trust is its membership. This has increased from 152,000 in 1971 to 3.4 million in 2006. Over the same period income has risen from £2.4m to £337m (Clover 2003). The Trust made a healthy surplus of around £20m a year, or about 6% of turnover. By 2014, membership had risen to 4.1 million, and income to £460, but the Trust was running a small deficit of £7m (National Trust 2014) In addition, the National Trust has 6,000 staff, many of them highly qualified in conservation, property management or gardening, and tens of thousands of active volunteers.

However, the membership is overwhelmingly white, middle aged and middle class, with little penetration in the inner cities, and it is thought that most members join solely to get free access to Trust properties. The activists, the volunteers, who to visitors are the public face of the NT, are older and more middle class than the membership – seen by many as representatives of the 'green welly' county set.

By the 1990s, the National Trust, though growing rapidly, was seen as increasingly out of touch – reactionary, elitist and part of the Establishment, not interested in promoting social inclusion. Operation Neptune, a populist campaign begun in the 1960s to improve access to the coastline, had run out of steam.

Just as it was out of touch with modern urban society, it also antagonised many of its county-based members by getting involved in the hunting dispute. In 1997 it banned stag hunting on its property, and was split over fox hunting, with each side accusing the other of dirty tricks. Part of the problem was the Trust's system of governance. It was controlled by a 52-member council, mostly nominated by interest groups like the RSPB and the Open Space Society, which met only four times a year. The council was widely seen as a self-perpetuating old boy network (Houlder 2003). The system also gave great power to the chairman, who controlled proxy votes which he could use at his discretion. The pro-hunting lobby complained that the proxy voting system was frequently used against them.

A turning point came with the appointment of a new director-general, Fiona Reynolds, in 2001. She had previously headed the Cabinet Office's women's unit, was close to New Labour, and talked of shedding the Trust's 'remote and elitist' image. She appointed Lord Blakenham, sometime chairman of the Financial Times and the RSPB, to review the National Trust's system of governance.

Blakenham reported in April 2003. He recommended that in future the governing body should be a 12-member Board of Trustees (effectively a board of directors). The Council would remain and would in effect become a supervisory board on the German model. The proxy voting system should be replaced by postal voting. The Board of Trustees formally took control in 2005. The Blakenham report seems to have turned the tide. The national ban on foxhunting has also helped, defusing the main internal bone of contention. Reynolds has increased the educational role of the Trust, expanded family memberships, bringing younger people into membership, and has spearheaded a move into the inner cities, preserving back to back working class houses in Birmingham, and John Lennon's and Paul McCartney's boyhood homes in Liverpool (Proby 2005).

In 2007, the National Trust published a new strategy document, covering the period to 2012 and beyond. This demonstrates an extension of the new thinking in the Trust. The key future role of the Trust was to be an environmental education group, engaging with government and society in a quest to find ways of tackling climate change. Fiona Reynolds stressed that this represented a return to the original aims of the Trust's founders, which emphasised social philanthropy and mutual benefit. As Reynolds said, 'This is going back to our roots. We are a cause. It's a profound moment of recognition' (Vidal 2007). Whether she could carry the more diehard and reactionary elements among the Trust's volunteers was another issue.

In 2010, the Trust published a new 10-year strategy document, Going Local, which it described as 'our cultural revolution'. Out would go centralisation, elitism, rules, and a 'do not touch' culture. In would come empowerment to local managers, closer links with local communities, and a hands-on approach to visitor experiences (National Trust 2010). As the document says, 'We must challenge the perception that we are some sort of exclusive club for connoisseurs.' A blog on the campaigning website Corrupt the Brand put forward some differing views on the strategy:

- 'We've been a properties and places organisation; we need to be a people and activities organisation...'
- 'Seaton Delaval Hall [one of the grandest of the National Trust properties] "is basically going to be a huge great village hall, that happens to have been designed by Vanbrugh" [Sir John Vanbrugh was one of the most famous architects of the early 18th century]'. (Corrupt the Brand 2012)

Research in 2011 suggested that although several of the changes proposed by the strategy are well received, not all of them are accepted unreservedly. Although the Trust is keen to change its offer, these alterations could prove unpopular with traditional visitors (Tipler 2011).

By 2012, the National Trust seemed to have taken on a more campaigning stance. In February, along with the Council for the Preservation of Rural England and the Royal Society for the Protection of Birds, it criticised government proposals for reform of the planning system, saying that the proposals were likely to have little or no positive impact on economic growth, and could undermine public wellbeing (National Trust 2012a). In August it was announced that Dame Helen Ghosh, formerly permanent secretary at the Home Office, would replace Fiona Reynolds as Director General (National Trust 2012a). It will be interesting to see whether this will lead to a change in Reynolds's populist policies.

Question

How do you think that the National Trust rates in terms of E-V-R convergence?

KEY LEARNING POINTS

- The general environment consists of factors which have an impact at an industry-wide level, while the task environment is primarily concerned with the immediate environment which impacts on an individual organisation within an industry.
- Organisations can be seen as open systems which interact with their environments.
- The STEEPLE model lists and classifies the major general environmental factors which impact on organisations.
- The main point of STEEPLE analysis is to identify key environmental drivers.
- Opportunities and threats to the organisation can be classified according to probability of success and attractiveness; and probability of occurrence and impact respectively.
- There are a wide range of different organisational structures, including bureaucracy, divisionalisation, matrix, network and virtual.
- Strategic alliances are of growing importance.
- Stakeholder theory states that organisations have responsibilities to a wide range of stakeholders.

REVIEW QUESTIONS

1 What do you think are the main differences between the general and the task environments?

2 What do you understand by the best fit model of HR?

3 Why did Weihrich suggest that SWOT analysis should be renamed TOWS analysis? What criticisms have been made of the SWOT/TOWS approach?

4 Give examples where structure follows strategy.

5 What do you think are the main strengths and weaknesses of the bureaucratic form of organisation?

6 Can you see any disadvantages of the network form of organisation?

7 Why can strategic alliances fail?

8 Do you agree with the proposition that HR outsourcing is most suitable for very small or very large organisations?

9 Why do stakeholders require active management?

EXPLORE FURTHER

Further Reading

Mick Marchington and Adrian Wilkinson's book, *Human Resource Management at Work* 4th edition (2008), covers much of the material discussed in this chapter, particularly in Part 1 in general, and Chapter 4 in particular.

Useful websites

A key website to assist your study is the CIPD site (www.cipd.co.uk). If you are not a member of the CIPD, you will only be able to access part of the site, but you will have access to the latest HR news, and to *Factsheets* on a range of HR topics. If you are a member, you will have access to a much wider range of materials, including the Library, Company Profiles, Employment Law at Work, and, most usefully, online journals. CIPD provides direct access to about 350 journals, including *The Economist*, the *Harvard Business Review* and *HR Magazine*, and also gives you entry to the EBSCO database, which provides access to 3,000 journals, including all the leading HRM and HRD journals, as well as the American equivalent of *The Economist, BusinessWeek*. The CIPD members' site also gives you access to the archive of *People Management*. A useful source of business case studies is The Times 100 Business Case Studies, available at http://businesscasestudies.co.uk. Although mainly descriptive, they provide useful examples of the practical application of theoretical concepts.

Audio and video material

The CIPD produces monthly podcasts on a range of HR-related issues, where experts discuss or debate key issues. Many of these are relevant to the subject matter of this book (although not of this chapter).

A wealth of video material is available on the Internet, much of it on YouTube. A lot of this is poor quality, but high quality material is produced by the *Harvard Business Review*, and also by the Chartered Institute of Management Accountants. Videos relevant to this chapter include:

How to perform a SWOT analysis: a whiteboard video (5 minutes). www.mystrategicplan.com/resources/how-to-perform-a-swot-analysis-a-whiteboard-video

Environmental scanning (4 minutes)

www.youtube.com/watch?v=LNo3WRRHlwc

CIMA E3 Lecture 3 – Environmental Analysis (6 minutes)

www.youtube.com/watch?v=7uA3Z7i69bO&feature=bf_next&list=UUdMKlWhxld2ffqbQUb6ozg

CIMA E3 Lecture 4 – External Environment (9 minutes)

www.youtube.com/watch?v=XUhmoWk9yLA&list=VVdbMKlWhxld2ffqbQUbGOzg&index=7&feature=plcp

CIMA E3 Lecture 11 – Organisational Structure (7 minutes)

www.youtube.com/watch?v=KfAR9vTaZiE&feature=related

ACTIVITY HOLIDAYS

The holiday industry

The holiday industry is in a state of flux. The mainstay of the industry, the foreign package holiday – two weeks in the sun, with everything (flight, accommodation, food, transfers and so on) provided by the tour operator – is in slow decline. In the 1980s, package holidays had 60% of the market, but in 2005 this had fallen to 45% (*Daily Telegraph* 2006). In 2001 20.6 million package holidays were sold, and this had fallen to 19m in 2006.

Looking more closely at market segments, the bottom of the package holiday market is relatively stable, although not very profitable. The top end is growing rapidly, and has better profit margins. The segment which is really coming under pressure is the mainstream mid-market sector, which is in the most rapid decline, and where the competition is fiercest, with wafer-thin margins.

The package holiday market as a whole is coming under increasing threat from the short break market, built around the budget airlines, particularly Ryanair and easyJet. Increasingly people take a number of short, often city-based, breaks, booking both their flight and their accommodation through the Internet. The other major growth area is the specialist package holiday segment, loosely described as activity holidays, about which more later.

At the same time as the traditional package holiday was declining, the method of selling them has been changing. In 1999, 61% of package holidays were booked through a High Street travel agent, but by 2003, this has fallen to 49%. At the same time, the number of booking made direct with a tour operator, or through the Internet, both rose.

The trend is even more stark when we look at all holidays, rather than just package holidays. In 2004, travel agents and the Internet each had a one-third share of bookings, with the other third shared between family and friends and direct booking with a tour operator (*Marketing* 2004).

Until 2007, there were four major players in the UK overseas travel industry. All were vertically integrated, operating retail travel agents as well as tour operations and an airline. The market leader, Thomson, was owned by the German company TUI, while Thomas Cook had majority German ownership. First Choice and My Travel were UK plcs.

Different companies have adopted different strategies to cope with changes in the market. Thomson has concentrated on marketing different segments of its packages, rather than the complete traditional package holiday. If the customer wants to buy just a flight, or just accommodation, that is fine with Thomson. First Choice has gone for market segmentation. It is concentrating on two major segments, the bottom of the package market, and the much more upmarket specialist (particularly activity) segment. In early 2007, it put its mainstream package operations up for sale, with both My Travel and Thomas Cook interested. However, these two companies decided to merge instead, leaving My Travel out in the cold. In response, in the spring of 2007, First Choice and Thomson/TUI agreed to merge, while My Travel merged with Thomas Cook.

The activity holiday market

An activity holiday is broadly defined as a holiday in which some form of physical exertion is the main reason for the holiday. It covers a wide range of activities, including skiing, boating, golf, walking, cycling, fishing and birdwatching, as well as multi-activity, which combines two or more activities.

Unlike mainstream package holidays, activity holidays are growing rapidly. Twenty-four per cent of the population claim to have taken an overseas activity holiday in the past five years, and a further 20% say they are likely to in the future. Numbers of holidays sold (including UK holidays) were expected almost to double between 2001 and 2010, from around 5 million a year to around 10 million, with the value of holidays sold also doubling from around £4.5bn to around £9bn or around 17% of all holidays (Keynote 2006). At an average cost of nearly £1000, activity holidays are also significantly more expensive than other packages, and much more profitable. In 2006 the operating profit of First Choice's activity holiday division made up half of all group profits (First Choice 2007). However, the sector, like the rest of the holiday industry, was badly hit by the recession from 2008 onwards. The number of foreign activity holidays fell from 4.9 million in 2009 to 4.5 million in 2013, while their value rose slowly from £4.99bn in 2009 to £5.17bn in 2013, which meant a slight fall in real terms (Keynote 2014).

This Seminar Activity will concentrate on two types of activity holiday, walking/trekking and multi-activity. Walking holidays are the most popular activity holiday, with 10% of the population claiming to have taken a walking holiday in the past five years, while 9.5% claim to have taken a multi-activity holiday.

However, the consumer profiles for the two types of holiday are different. Walking holidays are almost exactly split between male and female, and are more popular with the ABC1 social groups (broadly the middle class), people who live in the South, the Midlands and Wales, and single people. People are more likely to take a walking holiday as

they get older, with penetration among the 45–54 age-group (11.4%) and 55–64 (10.8%) higher than the penetration for the population as a whole (10%). Multi-activity holidays are favoured by men (70%) and the under-35s, but again have a bias towards ABC1s, the South and the single. Perhaps people who enjoy activity holidays when they are young switch towards walking holidays as they get older.

Companies

This Activity will look at four companies in the walking/multi-activity segments of the market. One (Exodus) is owned by TUI, one (Explore) is owned by the upmarket holiday group Cox and King's, and two by member organisations (HF Holidays by the Holiday Fellowship and Ramblers Holidays by the Ramblers Association).

Exodus

Exodus is one of two leading companies in the 'soft adventure' sector. It provides walking-trekking holidays combined with sightseeing, white water rafting, sailing and other activities. Founded in 1973, it was taken over by First Choice in 2002. The number of bookings is unknown, but is believed to be in the region of 30,000 a year. Most holidays are outside Europe, including many in exotic locations, operated in liaison with indigenous specialist companies/guides.

Explore Worldwide

Founded in 1981, Explore uses a similar business model to Exodus. The average price of holidays is around £1000 plus. Holidays are usually offered on a bed and breakfast basis, with extensive use of local agents to guide tours. Explore was taken over by Holidaybreak in 2000, and forms about half of Holidaybreak's Adventure Travel division. The division had a turnover of £76m in 2006, and operating profit of £5.6m (Holidaybreak 2007). By 2013, turnover for the division had fallen to £70m (Whyte 2013). Holidaybreak was acquired by the upmarket India-based tour operator Cox and King's in 2011. The average age of Explore clients is in their early 40s. About 30,000 holidays are sold each year, and 45% are repeat bookings. Like Exodus, most bookings are made direct, but the company also sells through local travel agents in Australia, Canada and the US.

HF Holidays

This is the oldest of the companies surveyed, and also the biggest. Founded in 1913, and owned by the Holiday Fellowship, it has over 50,000 guests, over half in the UK. The company runs 17 country house hotels. It is noted for its 'English House party style of warm hospitality' (HF Holidays 2007), and has a very high degree of client loyalty. It claims that at least 80% of customers come back again the next year. It explicitly aims at the 'grey' market, and has the oldest client base of the companies surveyed.

Ramblers Holidays

Ramblers Holidays was founded by the Ramblers Association in 1946, and covenants its net profits to a charitable trust which supports environmental projects. Originally purely a walking company, in recent years it has expanded the proportion of sightseeing on many of its holidays, and also runs a range of holidays concentrating on birds or flowers. More than half of holidays are in Europe, but the proportion of long-haul (and more expensive) holidays has been increasing. In 2006 it introduced 'cruise and walk' holidays. It recently acquired Countrywide Holidays to increase its UK holiday coverage, and also offers a range of holidays aimed at the under-40s. Holidays are led by a volunteer leader from the UK, but on long-haul holidays, a local agency/guide is also used. In 2001 17,000 holidays were sold, and in 2004

turnover was £14m, giving a pre-tax profit of £1.1m. By 2010 turnover had risen to £15.6m, but profit was down to £424,000. In 2013 turnover was down to £14.6m, but profit slightly up at £545,000 (Keynote 2014). Details are not available of the average age of clients, but from personal experience this seems to be mid-50s.

The recession appears to be accelerating the trend towards activity holidays, appealing as they do to an older and more affluent sector of the community. In particular, the 'active retired', many of whom retired early, seem to be largely unaffected by the recession.

Questions

1. Compile a STEEPLE analysis for the activity holiday industry.

2. Compile a SWOT analysis for Ramblers Holidays.

3. On long-haul holidays, Ramblers Holidays always uses a UK-based leader, directly appointed by Ramblers (although often a volunteer), as well as a local guide, employed by their local partner organisation. Explore usually only uses a local guide. What do you think are the HR implications of this difference in policy?

4. How far do you feel that a tour operator like Ramblers or Explore is a virtual organisation?

5. What do you think has been the impact on Ramblers of the implementation of legislation against age discrimination? What about the impact on Club 18–30?

The Managerial Context of Human Resources

LEARNING OUTCOMES

When you have completed this chapter, you should be able to understand, explain and critically evaluate:

- the main theories of management, both traditional and contemporary
- the difference between power and influence and assess their suitability to a variety of management situations
- the use of conflict-handling styles in the process of managing conflict, including methods of operating repair situations
- the determinants of an effective customer care regime
- the difference between the group dynamics and the open systems approach to managing change and integrate this knowledge into your 'toolbox' of skills for effective change management
- the four stages of quality management and put forward proposals to implement each stage successfully
- the ability of human resources to improve organisational performance
- the various models of human resources, identifying which is appropriate for differing employment contexts
- the various approaches to change management
- in all the above areas, the role of human resources to contribute towards successful prevention and resolution of identified problems.

2.1 INTRODUCTION

The majority of the context of this book concerns the effect and influences of the **external** environment on the role and function of human resources. This chapter deals with the effects **internal** to the organisation, and offers a brief résumé of the roles that human resources can play in meeting organisational needs. It starts by providing a summary of the theoretical approach to management, both classical and contemporary. The nature of power and conflict in organisations is then analysed. This is followed by an analysis of how different roles and structures of human resources can adjust to and provide effective service to managerial requirements. Finally, an examination is made of the specific human resource contribution to organisational change, quality assurance and customer care.

2.2 THEORIES OF MANAGEMENT

2.2.1 RATIONAL GOAL MODELS

These were the earliest models set out by three principal theorists in the early twentieth century. **Frederick Taylor** (1947) carried out his research at the Ford Motor Company on manufacturing management, while **Max Weber's** (1925) models of bureaucracy emerged from 30 years' studying large complex organisations, especially those under government control.

Their key findings relating to operating organisations efficiently overlapped to a large degree, for example:

- Rationality and scientific methods should be used to study work and experiment with human activity. Staff, for example, should be selected on merit, judged by a rational selection process.
- Jobs should be fractionised with extensive division of labour to allow individual employees to become highly specialised in jobs which were easy to learn.
- Systems and procedures of management (both in the factory and in the office) should clearly be written down with instructions as to how they should be followed.
- There should be separation of those who plan the work (set out in a clearly ranked managerial hierarchy) and those who actually carry out the work.
- It must be recognised that employees will tend towards economic self-interest in the way that they approach the work situation.

The third theorist, **Henri Fayol** (1949), concentrated on the art of management, identifying core management tasks (such as planning, organisation of work, control and co-ordination) and setting out principles of effective management that can apply in all organisations. These included:

- unity of command, with orders coming from one source only and clarity of organisation structure
- consistency of purpose, usually associated with centralised control (although he did recognise there were some circumstances where decentralisation could be appropriate)
- a widespread sense of order with a place for everything (supplies, plant and machinery, clean working conditions) and a place for everything, including fixed times for breaks and a well-understood organisation chart
- the operation of 'equity', where management operated not just within the law but within the spirit of the law, treating employees both fairly and kindly
- long-term employment at all levels, leading to a sense of order and stability, rather than a constant change of personnel.

In their day, these three models represented a great step forward and often proved highly successful in practice, such as Taylor's changes in work practices at Bethlehem Steel, where, in one example, he reduced the number of workers needed in physical labour from 500 to 140, and the huge increase in productivity his ideas brought at Ford through the implementation of piece-work and other motivational schemes. Aspects of the work of all three writers have some resonance today for human resource practitioners who support equitable and rational selection processes, and clear communication of management procedures from mission statements to fair sick pay schemes.

However, the overall approaches of so-called 'rational goal models' have major defects in the light of changes in society in the late twentieth and early twenty-first century:

- The main context of the studies on which these models were based has been very large organisations with dominant positions in their sectors who wish to enhance their dominance and eliminate potential competitors. The growth of regulatory environments, which began in the early part of the twentieth century in America but which became much more developed from the 1970s, aimed to prevent monopoly and create healthy competition. There have been many examples of governments legislating to break up organisations with dominant positions, through privatisation of monopolist utilities or through industrial reorganisation. There are therefore fewer organisations to whom the theories immediately apply.

- Establishing a prescribed system of work makes it much more difficult to react to changes in the marketplace. For example, the rapid technological changes in ICT and telecommunications have condemned companies who lack nimbleness in a quick-changing competitive environment to decline and often complete disappearance. Examples here are GEC-Marconi in the UK and Nortel in Canada.
- The lack of employee empowerment and the discouragement of flexibility had negative effects on employee commitment, innovation and engagement.

2.2.2 HUMAN RELATIONS MODELS

Although the needs of the employee at work had been considered by early psychologists, the field of human relations study grew through the disquiet felt by some researchers of the work organisation in large industrial organisations in the 1920s and its effect upon employees. The leading exponent here was Elton Mayo (1933), who carried out a series of experiments at the Hawthorne works consisting of measuring productivity and employee satisfaction when changing the physical environment and work systems of the employees.

The results indicated that productivity rose every time changes were made, even if these appeared to be negative, such as reducing the light sources and cutting down on rest breaks. The experiments demonstrated that favourable social relations and situations were a much greater influence on performance than physical conditions. Taylor's claim of overriding employee economic self-interest was rejected. Expressions of encouragement worked better than management coercion and the influence of the peer group was high, emphasising the importance of informal groups within the workplace. It was recognised, therefore, that the group dynamics and social make-up of an organisation were an extremely important force in determining a successful organisation. From this stemmed growing awareness of the concepts of participation, greater trust, teamworking and openness – concepts that were supported by the growing personnel profession.

The practical implications of these two schools of thought (rational goals and human relations) were radically different and, for much of the latter half of the twentieth century, caused confusion among management as to which should be implemented in practice. Towards the end of the century, a number of theories were put forward to synthesise existing theories and to produce more practical advice regarding the conflict.

2.2.3 CONTEMPORARY MANAGEMENT THEORIES

Contingency theory

In simple terms, this theory states that there is no best practice in management and that using rational goal concepts can work in one environment and human relations concepts in another (Fielder 1967). What came to be regarded as much more influential was a two-prong process. First, the organisation's design and its subsystems (including its working processes and employee relations) must fit with its environment. So the Weber-style bureaucratic design matched with the Tayloristic style of management control may work in a prison or a nuclear-power station, where systems of control are absolutely vital, but a human relations style is much more appropriate in an advertising agency, where creativity and new ideas are paramount. Second, the quality and style of leadership are key to the successful implementation of the systems of management in place.

The contingency theory allows for predicting the characteristics of the appropriate situations for effectiveness. Three situational components determine the favourableness or situational control:

1   Group atmosphere – referring to the degree of mutual trust, respect and confidence between the leader and the subordinates.

2   Task structure – referring to the extent to which group tasks are clear and structured.

3   Leader position power – referring to the power inherent in the leader's position itself.

When there is a good leader–member relation, a highly structured task and high leader position power, the situation is considered a favourable situation.

Chaos and complexity theories

For many years, mathematicians and scientists had been finding that not all of nature's phenomena can be explained simply. For example, Edward Lorenz, a meteorologist from the Massachusetts Institute of Technology (MIT), was experimenting with computational models of the atmosphere and, in the process of his experimentation, he discovered one of chaos theory's fundamental principles – the Butterfly Effect. The Butterfly Effect is named for its assertion that a butterfly flapping its wings in Tokyo can affect weather patterns in Chicago. More scientifically, the Butterfly Effect proves that forces governing weather formation are unstable.

Chaos theory was adapted to management theory by Peters (1987) to identify that events can rarely be controlled, especially in a global economy. Chaos theory posits that systems naturally become more complex and, as they do so, they become more volatile and must expend more energy to maintain that complexity and therefore need a bigger structure to maintain stability. This trend continues until the system breaks down completely. It takes an effective management system to identify what is happening and try to prevent it. This theory has received additional credence from the recent credit crunch, where the complexity of financial instruments created by hedge funds and merchant banks arising principally from collateralisation of the US mortgage market created a bubble effect which eventually collapsed. The lack of a competent management system which allowed this to happen existed both in the banks, where top management did not understand the financial instruments, and in the regulatory system, which was both slow to act and badly structured (see Chapter 5).

Complexity is an interdisciplinary field which has emerged from the work of scientists associated with the Santa Fe Institute in the United States, such as Murray Gell-Mann, Stuart Kauffman and John Holland, and also scientists based in Europe, such as Ilya Prigogine and Brian Goodwin. Complexity theory leads us to view organisations as complex evolving systems which exist on the edge of order and chaos. It challenges the notion of striving for equilibrium and suggests instead that systems survive and thrive when they are pushed away from equilibrium.

A number of managing innovations are commonly associated with working effectively within a complex environment. This is shown in Case Study 2.1.

INTEGRATING COMPLEXITY THEORY AT HUMBERSIDE TRAINING AND EDUCATION COUNCIL (TEC)

Training and Enterprise Councils were established by the Government to promote local economic development. Within its region, a TEC would seek to ensure a programme of appropriate training for business and encourage organisations to take advantage of training opportunities made available. In 1998, Humberside TEC had 150 staff and a budget of £30m.

For some time, its chief executive, Peter Fryer, had been studying complex adaptive systems and their implications for employing organisations and he made a conscious decision to explore how the principles of complexity theory could be integrated into the running of the TEC. Using this perspective, he took out of the organisation many of the traditional approaches to management, such as rules, hierarchy charts, budgets, appraisals, job descriptions and, importantly, those posts relating to checking and supervising.

In their place, he introduced a culture which treated all its staff as responsible adults and who were trusted to act in the best interests of the business. Within these parameters, staff were free to take whatever decisions they felt were appropriate. The purpose of this approach was to recognise that the real business of the organisation took place at the interface between the staff member and the client or stakeholder. Therefore, the more staff who were available at this interface and were able to take decisions on behalf of the TEC, the better the standards of service would become. As employees developed a sense of ownership of their contribution

to the TEC, it became more effective and efficient, as was demonstrated by various independent benchmarking studies. The approach also encouraged employees to be more creative, to feel a valued part of the organisation and consequently to work smarter.

The effect of this was to disperse the leadership throughout the organisation, with the chief executive taking up a 'holding' style of leadership. This style entailed:

- helping determine the broad framework of the organisation and communicating it so that employees knew the parameters within which they were free to take decisions
- identifying and feeding back both the internal and external emergent patterns in the environment.

This created the space within which possibilities could be explored by all employees, risks taken and mistakes made and built on by recognising the new opportunities which were not previously apparent. It also nurtured the culture of responsibility and accountability.

Examples of the practical implications are as follows:

- *Learn continuously* – the TEC as a system needed to respond to and form its environment. Learning was seen as integral to the job and mistakes are valued as learning opportunities. The only form which is completed by everybody each month to be passed to the managing director was one which asks what people have learned. This communicates the message that learning is highly valued.

- *Make processes ongoing* – the TEC was a self-organising system where learning, planning and evaluating are an ongoing process. Structures should follow, not lead and systems and processes should be based on the best people in the organisation rather than the one or two people who might abuse the system. Many TEC policies were changed to trust people to use their judgement and take responsibility. For example, the expenses policy that any reasonable expenses incurred on TEC business will be reimbursed.
- One of the TEC's most powerful interventions was the formation of a steering group comprising people from the HR team and people from the IT team. The aim of this group was to implement IT in a way that encourages and increases learning. There was the realisation in the TEC that IT can be implemented in a number of ways on a continuum from controlling to empowering and it therefore seemed important to challenge assumptions about IT. These two groups of people differ quite markedly in their language and assumptions and priorities. The steering group gives them a common agenda and frequent opportunities to work together.
- Another example of creating space for *collaborative learning* was the process of developing and introducing 360-degree appraisal. This was undertaken by a group of volunteers who approached the task as an action research project. Every member of the group both contributed to the development and also piloted the system on themselves. The resulting system was a paperless appraisal system in which the appraisee was responsible for their own appraisal. Appraisal was now moving away from being a tool to 'know' or 'measure'

employees and thus to better govern them and towards being a vehicle for learning, which was in the hands of the job-holder.

To help staff cope with this new freedom and responsibility, a substantial self-development support programme was introduced which emphasised the development of thinking and learning skills and developing self-confidence.

An important part of this approach was the annual stakeholder study, which was conducted independently through face-to-face interviews with a representative group of over 70 stakeholders. The study looked at both the progress towards meeting the aims of the TEC and also how well it was living its stated values. The report was published each year in an unabridged version, however critical it was, and formed the basis of the following year's TEC plans in an open and responsive fashion.

Some years later, the TECs were replaced by Learning and Skills Councils and Peter Fryer, before his departure, said:

> This approach to running the TEC has been incredibly successful in terms of levels of customer service and staff satisfaction. We have started to extend this style of leadership to all those in the community that interact with the TEC, through approaches such as contracting for outcomes. However, a word of caution: no matter how many times I tell this story and no matter how many caveats I put on it, it always sounds as though we knew where we were going and that we had some grand plan for becoming a learning organisation. But we didn't, and for those of you who have experienced complexity you will know that we couldn't have, because complexity just doesn't work that way.

Sources: University of Hull Business School (2007); Storr (2009)

2.3 POWER, POLITICS AND THE SEARCH FOR MANAGERIAL LEGITIMACY

2.3.1 INTRODUCTION

Power is the ability to do something, the capacity for producing an effect. The possession and exercise of power is, clearly, an essential aspect of management. Managers usually have to achieve results in situations where there are a number of forces both for and against the aims they are pursuing and/or the manner in which they are being pursued. Consequently, an understanding of the nature of power, and skill in its acquisition and use, are important attributes of effective managers.

The political nature of organisations is increasingly recognised by managers and the need for such recognition is well expressed by Burns (quoted in Pugh et al 1971, pp46–7):

> For a proper understanding of organisational functioning, it is necessary to conceive of organisations as the simultaneous working of at least three social systems. The first of these is the formal authority system derived from the aims of the organisation, its technology and its attempt to cope with its environment. This is the overt system in terms of which all discussion about decision-making normally takes place. But organisations are also cooperative systems of people who have career aspirations and a career structure, and who compete for advancement. Thus decisions taken within the overt structure inevitably affect the differential career prospects of the members, who will therefore evaluate them in terms of the career structure as well as the formal system, and will react accordingly. This leads to a third system of relationships which is part of an organisation – its political system. Every organisation is the scene of political activity in which individuals and departments compete and cooperate for power. Again all decisions in the overt system are evaluated for their relative impact on the power structure as well as for their contribution to the achievements of the organisation.

Political activity within organisations is often regarded as inappropriate behaviour. On the other hand, organisations of all kinds actively promote the development of leadership that is regarded as a key quality in managers. And yet, leadership has to do with the exercise of power and influence; it is the process of influencing others, and the use of power is one means by which leaders gain the support of those they lead.

2.3.2 POWER AND INFLUENCE

Macmillan (1978) draws a useful distinction between power and influence. He defines influence as the capacity to control and modify the perceptions of others, whereas power is defined as the capacity to restructure actual situations. Power and influence, in combination, determine political capability. Macmillan defines politics as the process that takes place when one or more 'actors' attempt to structure a situation so that their individual goals are promoted. An actor can be an individual, a group, an organisation or a nation.

In relation to their own staff, with whom, in the main, they would not be in competition, effective managers will normally use their influencing skills, rather than overt power, to persuade staff of the merits of proposed courses of action. The exercise of influence and power can be considered in terms of a continuum in which a manager may move from, for example, a neutral style to a more overt use of power. The following illustrates, in very simple terms, such a progression:

- 'This is something for your unit, Bill.' – neutral drawing of attention.
- 'This is the situation and I suggest you do so and so. . .' – reference to the needs of the situation.

- 'As your superior I am telling you to do this.' – influence sought by reference to formal authority.
- 'I'm moving you on to another section.' – the manager has demonstrated their power to restructure the actual situation.

Effective managers seldom need to move to the 'power' end of this continuum with their own staff and colleagues.

In other circumstances, however, overt use of power may be the more important factor in achieving desired results. For example, if several competing developers are bidding for the same plot of building land, the successful bidder will be the one who has the necessary purchasing power to outbid the rivals. In such circumstances power rather than influence is the dominant element in determining the political capabilities of the parties involved.

Thus, the exercise of power and influence has an internal and an external dimension.

2.3.3 BUSINESS AS A POLITICAL INSTITUTION

In discussing business as a political institution, Drucker (1981) points to the development, in a pluralist society, of all institutions as political institutions defined by their 'constituencies'. This makes it essential, in Drucker's view, for managers to think politically. He elaborates on this as follows:

> In a political system there are far too many constituencies to optimise. One must try to determine the one area in which optimisation is required but in all other areas – their number in a political system is always large – one tries to satisfice, that is, to find a solution in which enough of the constituencies can acquiesce. One tries to find a solution that will not create opposition, rather than one that would generate support. Satisficing is what politicians mean when they talk of an 'acceptable compromise'. Not for nothing is politics known as 'the art of the possible', rather than the art of the desirable. (Drucker 1981)

It is through the exercise of power and influence, then, that individuals and groups seek to persuade, induce or coerce others into following certain courses of action.

Power does not function in isolation. It provides a base, a springboard from which to act, but there are a number of preconditions that need to be satisfied before its potential can be realised. Fundamentally, power involves the ownership or control of resources, and the influence of such resources is governed by the degree of dependence that others have on them and the extent to which alternative resources are available.

Changes in the organisation, such as new technology, mergers and redundancies, can reduce the power of some parts of the organisation and reduce the power of others. So, power relationships can change, and these changes are dependent upon changes in the environment in which the organisation operates. The parallels with evolutionary psychology are unmistakeable. In summary, organisations are collections of linked coalitions whose relative power determines the decisions taken in the organisation relative to the environment facing the organisation.

2.3.4 INDICATORS OF POWER

Johnson and Scholes (1988), drawing on Pfeffer (1981), suggest that power may be assessed by looking for indications of it. They identify the following four factors as useful power indicators (Johnson and Scholes 1988):

1 *Status of individual or group.* This may be indicated by position within the organisation, salary levels and reputation within and/or outside the organisation.

2 *Claim on resources.* The proportion of the organisation's resources claimed by a group can be a useful indicator of the group's power. If, in addition, the increase or decrease

of this proportion is known, this will indicate a parallel increase or decrease in the group's power. A comparison with the claim on resources of similar groups in other organisations can give a further indication of the relative power base of the individual or group concerned.

3 *Representation in powerful positions.* The functional areas of an organisation that are represented or not represented at board level provide a useful indicator of the influence of different functions on the major decisions of the organisation. The relative power of accounting, engineering or marketing, for example, may be the result of the functional origins of the organisation's founders or key decision-makers, and will inevitably affect the strategic orientation of the organisation.

4 *Symbols of power.* These are very varied and will be displayed both by those with formal power and by those whose power is derived from more informal sources. The demonstration of easy access to senior people, for example, can be an indicator of power.

? REFLECTIVE ACTIVITY 2.1

What indicators of power do you notice in your department or division of your organisation? Is it a high-status department/division? Is this confirmed by the indicators? Record your analysis and reflections in your self-development diary.

2.3.5 SOURCES OF MANAGEMENT LEGITIMACY

Morgan (1986) has identified the following power bases within the organisation which are among the most important sources of management power:

- The formal authority exercised by the owner/manager.
- Authority set out under legislation. This covers a very wide area including duty of care to employees, where employers can enforce health and safety rules, obligations under old master–servant common law which still apply (such as manager's right to enforce confidentiality of critical details – production methods, list of customers, etc) and duties to shareholders under public limited companies legislation.
- Authority as established by the formal organisation chart.
- Delegated authority, such as authority to spend under delegated budgets or instigate capital expenditure within prescribed limits.
- Authority through possessing vital knowledge or skills. For example, human resource practitioners may possess authority because of their skills in negotiating or their ability to win tribunals. IT staff may be the only employees able to fully understand aspects of the company's networking system. Research and development staff may have crucial knowledge of patented inventions. Certain production/maintenance staff may be the only employees who know how to carry out major alterations on vital production equipment.
- Political power (or connection power) can be exercised through the development of networks, both inside the organisation (inter-divisional networks) or external (customers, suppliers, lobbying, legal).
- Charismatic power, usually exercised at the top, is the simple but rare ability to convince all they meet that they know the correct answers and should be listened to.
- Reward power is that power exercised by managers who have the authority to give rewards that are valued by employees – bonuses, salary increases, benefits or other forms of recognition.

- Crisis power is the ability to manage under considerable uncertainty, such as prevails constantly in money markets or which occurs occasionally in other businesses, where instant decisions by those confident enough to grasp the opportunity are unquestioned.
- Countervailing power can be operated by specialists who can step in to oppose policies because of their special knowledge or authority. For example, the regulators, such as OFT, can step in to halt a merger or the tax authority to question dubious financial transactions. Internally, the auditors can do the same (but rarely do) but accountants can attempt to prevent excess spending or the HR manager to prevent an instant unfair dismissal. In the 1970s in the UK, the greatest countervailing power was exercised by the trade unions and this still applies today in isolated areas, such as London Underground.

? REFLECTIVE ACTIVITY 2.2

What are the sources of power in your department or division of your organisation? How has this changed over time? Are the sources becoming more important? Or less? Record your analysis and reflections in your self-development diary.

2.3.6 POWER ACTIVITIES

We saw earlier that there is always competition for limited resources and that individuals have to create political strategies in order to pursue personal goals. This pursuit will inevitably involve political action with others, which will itself involve some assessment of their power bases.

Hunt (1979) recommends acquiring the expertise likely to be required by the organisation ahead of others, rather than joining a department whose status and influence appear to be in decline, and assessing and adopting the values, attitudes and behaviour of those with power. He suggests that managers should get results that are regarded as important by those who hold power and establish social contacts with powerful individuals.

In a similar vein, Schein (quoted by Dixon 1978) identifies a range of tactics typically used by managers in pursuing their objectives. The following are examples of these behaviours:

1 *Presenting a conservative image.* According to Schein, enthusiasm can be interpreted as threatening behaviour in some organisations. He suggests that important proposals should be phrased as nothing more than modest adjustments to the status quo. He argues that many controversial projects have started in a small way – perhaps as pilot schemes – and then linking them to some existing non-controversial programme. Radical changes can then be viewed as a normal development of current activities.

2 *Strike while the iron is hot.* Schein suggests that a manager should capitalise immediately on any success by bringing forward another project the manager wishes to progress.

3 *Instituting research.* Some projects are likely to face stiff opposition. Emotional subjects such as equal opportunities fall into this category. Research can provide hard data which conservative colleagues will find much more difficult to argue against.

Schein quotes the way in which such data are typically presented: 'Well here's the evidence. I don't necessarily believe all of it but we can't just ignore it, can we?'

Schein claims that these are all legitimate activities if they help the manager achieve their objectives. However, this sounds suspiciously like the ends justifying the means, and we each have our own views about that. It is difficult to generalise about what is acceptable behaviour in any particular situation, and we each have to reconcile conflicting pressures in coming to terms with the situation.

2.4 HANDLING CONFLICT

2.4.1 INTRODUCTION

Handling conflict is concerned with managing the differences between individuals and groups of individuals. In business, as in all activities, conflict is inevitable as the needs and objectives of business stakeholders vary. Examples of conflict are:

- conflict between the organisation and employees (and their unions) over the size of the pay increase or allowances
- conflict between the organisation and its suppliers over terms and conditions of the suppliers' contracts on price, quality and delivery schedules
- conflict between the organisation and its shareholders over the amount of profit to be distributed as dividends
- conflict between line management and human resources over the control and operation of the performance management system
- conflict between the production department and quality assurance (QA) over the interpretation of the operation of the QA system.

Other examples can involve conflicts with customers, with banks and the tax office.

Conflict can come about because of the need to change the way the organisation operates. It also has to be recognised that much of the conflict arises from a competitive environment. In both of these cases, it can be the general viewpoint that one side has to win and the other to lose. For example, the current conflict between Google and the newspaper industry is seen by the newspaper industry as one that will only be resolved with one of them gaining so much power over the other that one side will be fatally wounded (probably the newspaper industry).

One of the signs of a well-managed organisation is the ability to resolve conflicts peacefully and amicably while ensuring that participants do not badly lose face.

2.4.2 CONFLICT-HANDLING STYLE

A number of conflict style inventories have been in active use since the 1960s. Most of them are based on the managerial grid developed by Robert R. Blake and Jane Mouton (1964) in their Managerial Grid Model. The Blake and Mouton model uses two axes. 'Concern for people' is plotted using the vertical axis and 'Concern for task' along the horizontal axis. Each axis has a numerical scale of 1 to 9. These axes interact so as to diagram five different styles of management. This grid posits the interaction of task versus relationship and shows that according to how people value these, there are five basic ways of interacting with others.

In the model shown in Figure 2.1, the two axes are:

- courage of one's convictions
- consideration for others.

So, to be assertive, you need high courage of your convictions and high consideration of others.

Figure 2.1 Conflict-handling style (based on Blake and Mouton)

(Adapted from Thomas 1976)

Courage of your convictions

This refers to your ability to set an objective and pursue it. It implies single-mindedness – sometimes bloody-mindedness and ruthlessness. We can usefully think of the idea of having a *bottom line* to help us understand this concept. A bottom line is the line we will not retreat beyond, even under pressure. We will walk away rather than retreat. For example, imagine that you are a union negotiator dealing with the human resources (HR) director of a company for the annual pay review. This director offers you his sixth final offer. What do you do? You reject it, of course, and wait for his seventh final offer. Clearly he doesn't have a bottom line and so he will continue to retreat.

Consideration for others

This means trying to understand the objectives of the other person. By considering the other person's objectives, it may be possible to satisfy one's own objectives – meet your bottom line – and meet theirs at the same time. This is the cherished win–win position.
   Combinations of these two dimensions give us the following five styles:

1 A *confrontational (aggressive) style* of conflict-handling, involving, for example, demanding apologies from others and redress of perceived 'wrongs', tends to be adopted by people who are high in concern for their own needs and low in concern for others' needs.

2 An *avoidance style*, which means refusing to acknowledge that a problem exists, while reducing interaction with the other person(s) as far as possible, results from low concern with both one's own and other people's needs. It does give the opportunity to gain time, however, and can be utilised in a situation where neutrality is important.

3 An *accommodation style*, apologising and conceding the issue to the other person regardless of the 'rights and wrongs' of the matter, goes with a low concern with one's own needs and a high concern with others' needs. It does ensure that peace is kept for the time being.

   These three conflict-handling styles are all, in their different ways, undesirable, tending to reinforce the conflict and create more ill-feeling, to prolong it below the surface or to encourage further aggression in others. The remaining two styles are both more effective than these:

4   A *compromising style* is next best; this approach means bargaining, explicitly or implicitly, with the other person until a compromise is reached; though this is often a reasonable approach, there is the well-known danger that the actual compromise agreed on will be 'the worst of all worlds' and only be a temporary solution.

5   A *collaborative (assertive) style*, then, is the optimal. It involves an approach that treats the need to repair the relationship as a problem which the parties need to solve together. More guidance on how to implement this style is given in section 2.4.3.

2.4.3 COLLABORATIVE STYLE

- Aggressiveness and submissiveness (avoiding and accommodating) get you nowhere. Don't use them.
- Ensure that you jointly identify what differences exist and analyse the cause of those differences.
- Be honest and relevant; stick to facts, not personalities.
- Consider the alternative solutions and work through the implications together, seeing which alternative is closest to each side.
- Each side should know its bottom line and stick to it, which is the point that each side will not cross. That bottom line should be honestly expressed so there is no misunderstanding.
- It is usually wiser to have an adjournment when a sticking point is reached to allow reflection from both sides and allow the points made to sink in. In most circumstances, a return to the meeting brings new ideas for a solution.
- When a solution is agreed, make sure there is no misunderstanding by going over it again and making sure it is correctly recorded.
- Ensure agreement is reached on how the preferred solution is implemented (although a certain vagueness in places is allowable – without this, no European Union agreement would ever be made).

This type of collaborative bargaining is often called *'integrated bargaining'*, where a solution is often win–win. The opposite approach, confrontational bargaining, is called *'distributive bargaining'*, where a win–lose result emerges.

2.4.4 REPAIR TECHNIQUES

Edgar Schein (1980) is one authority on organisational behaviour who has looked at the question of how to repair relationships after breakdown. It is clear from his discussion that the main requirement, as so often in face-to-face work, is to come to terms with your own psychological blockages. Being afraid that unpleasant events will be repeated often prevents people from starting to build bridges. For instance, you may be afraid that when you make an overture – a friendly or helpful remark – to someone else, they will snub you. Alternatively, you may find it easier to blame others than to work out how to renegotiate your relationship with them. These are some suggestions for overcoming one's own psychological barriers to bridge-building:

- Look for new elements in the situation that you may not have noticed before: for one thing, the other people in the situation may have changed in significant ways. Other people tend to be more flexible and adaptive than our assumptions about them allow; our impressions become straitjackets or self-fulfilling prophecies. The confrontation itself is likely to have affected them in some way: often, it is true, people become more rigid after such an experience, but some may wish to change even if they lack the skill to do so.

- Look to superordinate goals around which a new set of relationships can be built. If you needed to keep in touch with this person before, you still need to even though you have quarrelled.
- Force yourself to see what happened from the other person's point of view. A friend or sympathetic colleague can often help to make this process less painful than it would otherwise be.
- A colleague who is a good listener can also be very helpful if your blockage is emotional – hurt or anger. Talking it through, if necessary over and over, blunts the edges of emotions which otherwise may prevent you from being skilled in handling the repair interaction. Allowing some time to pass also helps in this because emotions tend to recede over time.

When you have handled yourself, you are ready to handle the situation, using, as recommended above, a collaborative approach. To succeed you should:

- Set up a meeting that is explicitly for the purpose of making the repair. This approach, which can be thought of as confronting the problem, is more likely to succeed than either evading it or attempting to build bridges in the course of other business. The best way to set up the meeting is to telephone the person with whom your relationship has broken down – or intercept them in the corridor – and say something along the lines of, 'Look, Andrew, do you think we should get together to sort out why we are at loggerheads like this? I do, because it's affecting my work, and making me miserable – I very much dislike being on bad terms with colleagues.' You may need to persist to get agreement to the meeting, but usually you can get it in the end, because the other party is aware that it is unreasonable to refuse. It is important not to be dragged into discussing the cause of the dispute itself at this stage, because your objective is to get agreement to the meeting, this agreement itself being the first stage in the bridge-building process. An intermediary may be used to set up the meeting if someone really suitable is available but this is less satisfactory because it reduces the amount of repair achieved by this first overture.
- In the meeting, allow the other person to express their negative emotions about what has happened, while keeping close control of your own. If you detect that they are in the grip of emotion that is not being expressed at the start, encourage them to bring it into the open. This may be painful for you, but is an essential first step in the bridge-building process. Make it clear that you are listening to and understanding what they say, though you do not necessarily accept that they are right.
- Make it clear that you do not intend the repair process to lead to further loss of face for either party.
- Treat the repair as a problem to solve jointly rather than a self-abasement: your objective is to reach agreement on a new basis for the relationship but your offer is not unconditional. You are trying to explore differences creatively and locate some common ground but you do need to protect yourself from any attempt by the other person to exploit your overture, perhaps to gain, unfairly, the point on which you differed before. If their position was unjustified before, it remains so now, even if you do want to apologise for having lost your temper. You will need to be articulate and assertive to clarify what you are and are not conceding.

? REFLECTIVE ACTIVITY 2.3

Think of a situation that needs repair. Using the techniques described in this section, start this process. Record your reflections over time as you try to make this repair in your self-development diary.

Feedback on Reflective Activity 2.3

Actively reflecting on how to improve situations involving conflict is an excellent way of planning how to retrieve the situation. You should find that doing this exercise will make you more effective and confident.

2.5 FORCES SHAPING HUMAN RESOURCE MANAGEMENT AT WORK

In the course of this book we are examining the way that external effects influence the role and practices of human resources in practical terms. You will see many examples in each of the forthcoming chapters, but here are some brief extracts:

- *Social* – how demographic changes influence the need for human resources to engage in initiatives in flexible working and to widen the pool of recruitment.
- *Technological* – how technological developments have provided scope for new ways of working – in call centres and distance/teleworking.
- *Economic* – how economic cycles influence both the internal and external labour market and how human resources need to move swiftly to anticipate and utilise such changes.
- *Environmental* – how the growing international emphasis on environmental issues provides opportunities for human resources to lead in areas such as engagement with the community and secondment.
- *Political* – how developments in Europe have influenced the migratory pattern and employment regulation with the associated need for human resources to ensure advantages are gained from such changes.
- *Legal* – human resources need to respond to changes in the UK regulatory climate through ensuring organisations understand fully the implications of such changes and implement appropriate policies and procedures.
- *Ecological* – the growing support for socially responsible organisations provides the opportunity for human resources to take the lead in areas such as ethical behaviour codes towards employees, customers, the community and in business transactions.

We have already seen earlier the responses that human resources make to some of the internal effects, such as internal structure, power, conflict and change. The remainder of the chapter deals with the way that human resources can be structured and the effect it can have.

2.6 MODELS AND ROLES OF THE HUMAN RESOURCE FUNCTION

Given that human resources can make a contribution to organisational performance – and there is a healthy debate how this can be effected – the next question relates to the models and roles of the human resource function that can effectively and cost-efficiently organise this contribution.

This next section, therefore, briefly examines the changing employment relationships before setting out the various models and roles of the human resource function as revealed by the last 30 years of research.

2.6.1 THE HUMAN RESOURCE EQUATION – MODELS OF THE EMPLOYMENT CONTRACT

The *traditional employment contract* was simple. In return for a wage or salary, the employee carried out the work indicated to the required standards. However, a subsidiary, unwritten contract has also been present in most employment contracts that is more difficult to pin down and often deals with unexpected and unforeseeable changes in the nature of the work concerned. This is often referred to as the *psychological contract*, first explained by Schein (1980) and discussed by many writers since (Herriot 1998; Conway and Briner 2005). This form of contract deals with the expectations that employees and employers have of their relationship, especially how each expects to be treated by the other.

In the *traditional* form, the format was for the employer to offer a secure and dependable income, a degree of job security, a safe environment and a possible opportunity for advancement, while the employee carried out the work indicated in the contract, followed the prescribed rules and standards and showed long-term loyalty. Although this contract never applied to large numbers of employees (temporary, low-paid and unskilled) and varied considerably by sector of employment, for the good majority to whom it applied, it reflected a dependable, foreseeable environment.

Since around the early 1980s, however, there has been a recognisable change in the nature of this contract which reflects the rapidly changing employment market and the unpredictability and volatility of the organisational context. This has led to a restating of the psychological contract. Employment for life is not the expected norm (police, prison and fire services excepted). There has developed a growing intensification of work in many sectors where employees are expected to work much longer hours and take on much more varied and flexible responsibilities beyond their apparent contractual duties, called 'going beyond contract'. In return, employers offer the opportunity to gain experience, learn extra skills and competencies and, in many cases, additional variable pay and bonuses. This has been identified as a change from a *relational* contract to a *transactional* contract, moving from an emotional commitment to one that can be regarded as a simple economic exchange (Taylor 2008).

In theory, this change in the psychological contract should have led to much lower levels of job satisfaction and equally low degrees of satisfaction with the state of the psychological contract. However, research by Guest and Conway (2002) in the late 1990s and early 2000s has found evidence to the contrary. In general, employees have expressed a reasonable (if varied) degree of satisfaction, both with their jobs and with their psychological contract. This may have been because, over the period 1995–2008, the UK enjoyed a steady period of economic growth with a healthy labour market, which meant that most employees unhappy with their employment could move on if they chose to do so, rather than remaining dissatisfied.

With a tight labour market and a shortage of key skills, employers have reacted by attempting to be much more attractive to key employees by setting out to develop an employer brand and becoming an 'employer of choice'. This has been achieved not just by increasing the salary rates but also by improving the employees' work–life balance, entering into extensive recognition initiatives which regularly support special employee achievements in the workplace and by introducing attractive benefits, such as flexible hours, the ability to work at home and systems of flexible benefits.

2.6.2 MODELS OF THE HUMAN RESOURCE FUNCTION

There are a number of examples of models illustrating the varying roles and styles for the operation of HR departments and practitioners, and here are three of them.

Karen Legge (1978) identified three HR practitioners ('personnel' in those days) who were seeking to develop their power within the organisation. The first of these is the *conformist innovator*, the person who works with the conventional organisational objectives and identifies with them, and comes up with initiatives that help the organisation towards achieving those objectives through cost saving, productivity increases and reducing conflict. The *deviant innovator*, on the other hand, stands somewhat aside from the conventional organisation aims and adopts an independent professional stance. The initiatives they recommend tend to be unconventional and their adoption will depend on their individual status and conviction, with the results somewhat unpredictable. Subject areas here could, today, involve proposals on work–life balance, empowerment or knowledge management. Their innovative ideas, which may face considerable opposition, can provide results which lead to the organisation obtaining clear competitive advantages. The third role is that of *problem-solver*, a more conventional role, one that looks to provide day-to-day assistance to the line management.

Storey's (1992) analysis set up a grid which contrasts on one axis how far the work undertaken is strategic or merely tactical and, on the other axis, the degree to which the human resource manager intervenes in the management process. This is shown in Figure 2.2.

Figure 2.2 HR interventions

	STRATEGIC	
I N T E R V E N T I O N A R Y	CHANGEMAKERS	ADVISORS
	REGULATORS	HANDMAIDEN
	TACTICAL	N O N - I N T E R V E N T I O N A R Y

(Adapted from Storey 1992)

Working clockwise, human resource specialists who fall into the *advisor* category are those who focus on strategic issues but are not themselves responsible for carrying out the actions they recommend. *Handmaidens* are those who also have little part in implementing policy but they only operate at a tactical level, dealing with administration and the provision of welfare, training and basic recruitment. *Regulators* are, again, involved only in tactical issues but they are more interventionary, trying to ensure that the human resources policy is carried out properly in co-operation with line managers. The *changemakers*, on the other hand, are both strategic and interventionary, concerned less with administration and more with the broader view of people management in their organisations. A changemaker is expected to assess the organisation's needs, reach appropriate conclusions and then drive the required changes to completion. This is regarded, Storey indicates, as the proper role for an effective and senior human resource specialist.

Ulrich (1998) followed a similar tack but developed the model so that the x-axis measures the degree to which the HR practitioner manages the process and, on the other hand, manages the people involved, as shown in Figure 2.3.

Figure 2.3 Role of HR

	STRATEGIC		
MANAGEMENT OF PROCESSES	CHANGE AGENT	BUSINESS PARTNER	MANAGEMENT OF PEOPLE
	ADMINISTRATIVE/ FUNCTIONAL EXPERT	EMPLOYEE ADVOCATE OR CHAMPION	
	TACTICAL		

(Adapted from Ulrich 1998, Ulrich and Brockbank 2009)

The *administrative/functional expert* manages the processes on a day-to-day basis, ensuring that policies on, for example, grievances, discipline, equal opportunities and incentive arrangements work effectively. This is not a role to be derided because it is generally vital to the organisation's smooth running. Recognition, however, does not come easily from this role as it is only really noticed when things go wrong. These activities have, in recent years, been prime candidates for outsourcing or some form of shared services system, which was detailed in Chapter 1.

The *employee advocate/champion* acts as a voice for employees on a day-to-day basis, working for an improvement in their position, their contribution and their engagement with the organisation. This role is intended, by improving their engagement, to improve their overall performance. In Ulrich's revised (2009) version, the role has been strengthened with an additional dimension of *human capital developer*, who works to develop employees as assets through extending their skills and developing their career.

The *change agent* works from a strategic viewpoint, attempting to ensure that employees go along with business changes, making sure that visions and values are translated into action and reality.

The *business partner* works with line management to ensure board strategy is developed and put into effect, identifying areas where action is required and instituting remedial initiatives. Line managers use them as consultants to debate issues in their area, such as salary and incentive issues and difficult disciplinary cases.

The concept of the business partner has found substantial support in recent years, adopted by a huge range of companies. It is interpreted in different ways but the central precept is the close relationships with business units, helping to solve practical problems and delivering real value to the organisation. Four examples are shown in Case Study 2.2.

CASE STUDY 2.2

BUSINESS PARTNERS AT ELIOR GROUP, GENERAL MOTORS, BRITISH AEROSPACE AND PRUDENTIAL INSURANCE

Elior, a 5,400-employee European contract catering group, introduced business partnering in 2008 which provided benefits for both HR and business managers. HR professionals gained insights into business concerns while business managers appreciated the importance of a more scientific approach to people issues. Senior HR specialists could spend more time on strategic issues, such as succession planning and performance management, while line management have much greater control over performance management. A key difficulty involved in setting up the scheme was a lack of formal meetings for exchanging views and understanding between business partners where good practice could be exchanged.

In 2003, Vauxhall Motors at Ellesmere Port (part of General Motors) reorganised the HR departments, with HR staff either outsourced to specialist or routine roles or assigned to a business-focused role. The latter staff were trained to understand all aspects of the business and given a desk in the unit's open-plan offices next to the car production lines. They engage in day-to-day operations, such as assisting managers in performance management, identifying training needs, coaching and discussing the facts and figures about people in their unit, their promotions, potential, disabilities and concerns. The main purpose is to develop close relationships with line managers and help to solve business issues through their knowledge of people management.

At Prudential Insurance, the HR business partner works in a business unit as a consultant, drawing down help from centres of excellence while a service centre deals with HR administration issues. As an example, one partner works in the marketing and innovation function running the people management side of a major change initiative to improve how to deal with customer complaints. Having worked out with the unit manager what needs to be achieved, the partner pulls together an HR team for the project, uses the recommendations of the specialist HR group and co-ordinates the delivery of the project. This needs skills in relationship-building and a good understanding of the business.

A feature throughout cases is the need for flexibility as explained by John Whelan, HR Director, BAE Systems:

Our HR teams have become used to seeing the business boundary as flexible and reaching out to partner organisations. From organisation design to promoting effective partnering behaviours and gain-sharing, we seek to find win-wins and deliver greater value to the customer and ultimately the taxpayer. Increasingly, our HR leads are working within the partnering structure and learning to balance the interests of the parties and optimise the overall output. This is a delicate balancing act requiring sophisticated commercial and relationships skills

Sources: Hennessy (2009); Pickard (2004a), CIPD (2013a), Whelan (2015)

A survey by Roffey Park in 2009 found that 58% of respondents judged the change to a business partner system to be successful, while only 10% found it unsuccessful. It was most likely to become successful where the organisational culture had a higher level of sociability with high scores for focusing on people, building relationships and a concern for colleagues and where there was also a good degree of 'solidarity' (a strong focus on working together to deliver shared objectives) (Griffin et al 2009).

Boroughs (2015) found even greater success in his survey of 40 US companies where 90% considered that the HR function was more efficient and commercially focused, compared to 10 years previously, chiefly due to introducing the Ulrich model. However, a weakness concerned talent management services (recruitment, performance and reward) where satisfaction ratings which were less than half the ratings for HR operations.

Purcell and Ahlstrand (1994) incorporate a number of Ulrich model features but use a more holistic approach to HR direction and objectives. They set out the nine core activities that HRM departments should engage in to become fully influential in an organisation. They believe these to be applicable to most, but not all, medium to large organisations, but it will depend on the nature of the business and the way the organisation is directed. Some are indisputable, such as human resource planning and developing essential human resource policies; others are more debatable:

- *Corporate culture and communications* – organisations are bound together internally, not just by common ownership or by everything being included on the balance sheet. Culture, 'the ways we do things around here', is difficult to define but easy to identify, especially when it is articulated well and often. It is normally up to the chief executive to set out or redefine the principal aspects, the philosophy, the set of values and the essential style of management, but it is human resources that must be responsible for championing and disseminating these cultural aspects around the organisation in an effective fashion.

- *Human resource planning in strategic management* – developing a human resource plan which emerges from the strategic plan is the second core activity. This is clearly a core activity but one where the link is not always made as tightly as it should be.

- *Essential policy formulation and monitoring* – established policies and procedures remain an essential feature of an effective organisation and policies regarding the way people should act and be treated are no exception. Standards need to be set and monitored for compliance. The recognised difficulty here is striking the happy medium between a rigid bureaucratic set of procedures that deal with every eventuality but restrict innovation and empowerment and a set of vague guidelines that have many interpretations and are largely ignored.

- *'Cabinet Office' services* – this is a more unusual observation and based on the need for the chief executive to have advice from a trusted senior subordinate, one that is not linked to a major department, such as finance or sales, which would be liable to defend their own territory and not be regarded as independent. The advice would be principally concerning the implications for staff in general, succession planning for senior executives, but would also include the cultural development issues and some specific investigations set in place through issues raised by non-executive directors. This is a considerable source of power and influence for human resources and emerged from their personal relationship, not from their specific position.

- *Senior management development and career planning* – this is another undisputed, important role, even when longer-term planning is more difficult to undertake. It is linked with the succession planning process and with the need to develop managers with wide experience, so there is flexibility in place for strategic moves into new or existing marketplaces.

- *External advocacy – internal advice* – as human resources develop a close relationship with the chief executive, their 'cabinet' responsibilities may stretch to representing the organisation in the corridors of power. This is not just on local matters, such as trade association committees, but some political lobbying on crucial issues such as government legislation or interpretation of European directives. The internal advice is feeding matters such as this back to the executives in the organisation.

- *Information co-ordination* – this involves helping large organisations to co-ordinate necessary information across the group on pay, bargaining and general personnel statistics, such as headcount, turnover and absenteeism.
- *Internal consultancy and mediation services* – included in this role are aspects of organisational design and learning. The introduction of competencies would be an example here.
- *Human resources for small units* – an extension of the internal consultancy to part of the larger group that have little or no human resource presence.

Purcell and Ahlstrand recognise that this list does not indicate a comprehensive attention to all human resource matters. Training, health and safety, recruitment and pay issues do not come to the fore on their own. In fact:

> Our research shows that the role and authority of corporate HR departments is becoming more ambiguous and uncertain. ... Much of the activity identified ... places a premium on political and interpersonal skills and 'corridor power'. In this situation, the authority of corporate human resources staff comes more from their own expertise and style than from a clearly defined role and function. It has often been noted that human resource managers need to be adept at handling ambiguity. (Purcell and Ahlstrand 1994, p113)

In Chapter 10, the role of human resources in improving organisational performance is examined further.

2.6.3 RESOURCE-BASED VIEW OF THE ORGANISATION

Alongside these investigations, theories have been developed regarding the nature of human resources whereby they can be regarded as uniquely valuable to the organisation because they are a collection of assets (skills, competencies, experience) that are much more difficult to imitate or replicate, unlike other conventional assets such as land or capital. This is associated with the 'resource-based view' (RBV) of the organisation, where competitive advantage is associated with four key attributes – value, rarity, a lack of substitutes and the difficulty of imitation:

- Human resources are seen to be *valuable*; looking at employees of football teams, for example, the very skilled ones are certainly seen to be extremely valuable and some senior executives transfer to new organisations with an upfront payment. The cost of replacing employees who leave organisations is often high, especially if they are experienced and are seen by customers as important. As explained by Boxall and Purcell (2008):

> [Organisations]... can never entirely capture what individual... [employees]... know. Some of what we know – including many of our best skills – cannot be reduced to writing or to formulas. When we leave the firm, we take this knowledge with us. When whole teams leave... the effects can be devastating. (p83)

- *Rarity* is associated with value as there will always be a labour group which is in short supply: IT staff in the 1980s and 1990s, nurses and teachers in the early 2000s, plumbers most of the time. Organisations that have a steady supply of skills in short supply will have a competitive advantage.
- It is possible to *substitute for labour*, through automated call centres and production lines, but those organisations that possess skilled employees where such substitution is impossible (most service organisations, consultancies, etc.) should be able to gain an advantage. It has been argued that the UK's competitive advantage has been maintained because of our very large service sector, whereas Germany's large

manufacturing sector has been constantly chipped away by international competition and automation.

- Similarly, it is difficult to *imitate* the skilled work of employees. Cheaper versions of services can be available (self-service in restaurants) but the market for high-quality service by skilled employees is normally in a state of constant growth.

Having recognised the importance of people as a resource, it provides encouragement to employers to identify and then improve the quality of their 'human capital'. In terms of identification, the CIPD (Brown 2003) put forward a proposal in the form of a framework so organisations could report on the way they:

- acquire and retain staff, explaining how the firm sources its supply, the composition of the workforce in terms of diversity and employment relationships and its retention policies
- develop staff, including details of skill levels and development strategies
- motivate, involve and communicate with employees
- account for the value created by employees, including how they manage the bank of employee knowledge and the methods of determining team and individual performance.

2.6.4 HUMAN RESOURCES AND LEADERSHIP STYLES

The role of developing leadership skills is sometimes downplayed in UK writing, but it is very strong in American versions of successful HRM ambitions. Rucci (1997) has set out six key requirements for HR departments to add value to the organisation and ensure its own survival:

1 *Create change* – HR should move away from the control, standardisation and compliance model and encourage the development of an organisational capability of flexibility, speed and risk-taking. This will mean eliminating unnecessary rules and giving greater emphasis to individual judgement and accountability for line managers.

2 *Develop principled leaders* – top executives who ground themselves in a base of moral or ethical principles are few and far between, but it is they who lead organisations to sustained long-term success. HR needs to set in motion systems to develop such talent, especially leaders who have the courage of their convictions and an unwillingness to compromise on ethical issues.

3 *Promote economic literacy* – too much specialisation has led to many managers not having the breadth of outlook to understand the 'big picture' within the organisation. HR should give more emphasis to ensuring managers learn all the skills and knowledge so they can contribute advice on big policy decisions.

4 *Centre on the customer* – HR should help to create boundaryless organisations where the customers' viewpoint seriously influences policy decisions and ensure that customer-directed activity is central in performance reviews, promotion criteria and reward decisions.

5 *Maximise services/minimise staff* – HR needs to focus on its internal customers, identifying where it adds value and driving down its costs.

6 *Steward the values* – HR's role should not just be the organisation's conscience or the 'values police'. It should ensure that the values are understood and ensure that the progress is monitored and measured by embedding them in all HR activities – selection, training, performance management and reward.

The CIPD (2012a) has identified an HR leadership approach which contains four key activities:

1   *Understanding the business model at depth* by knowing where value is created and destroyed across the complete value chain, revealing the improvement points around people and performance which drive value and identifying the opportunities to drive revenue and reduce costs through more effective use of employees.

2   *Generating insight and impact through evidence and data* to support initiatives – data that has been mined for insight, inspiration and impact, especially data in key areas such as employee engagement.

3   *Actively seeking opportunities for HR to connect and collaborate* with stakeholders, using curiosity, purpose and impact, often by stepping outside the HR boundary but always putting HR at the heart of business strategy.

4   *Leading with integrity, consideration and challenge*, including facing the emotional and ethical consequences of business decisions. This often involves serving all stakeholders rather than power structures, especially in the public sector.

Bersin (2015) has identified the trend of moving HR back to a more local role in the business, focused on effectiveness and outcomes, rather than process and efficiency. Local HR staff, often with business experience and working through networks, have a better understanding of precise jobs, management styles and culture of the local team and share best practice by using common IT tools and methodologies.

These different prescriptions reflect the nature of HR programmes entered into by progressive and successful companies. An example in practice is set out in Case Study 2.3.

 HR PLANS FOR TOMORROW AT NATIONAL GRID

CASE STUDY 2.3

National Grid, responsible for the transmission and distribution of electricity and gas across the UK, has recently placed more focus on talent, capability and driving a performance culture to meet the growing challenges of providing a secure and affordable supply of energy in a low carbon environment.

The talent pipeline for engineers has presented a specific problem in recent years with fewer and fewer young people choosing engineering-type subjects at A level, especially physics. As well as the conventional contacts with schools with extensive work experience programmes, open houses and free learning resources, National Grid has initiated Careers Lab, rolled out across 600 secondary schools where lesson plans for 11–16 year olds are delivered by employees in concert with teachers, and which is starting to

have an effect in encouraging more interest from both sexes in engineering careers.

This is linked to strenuous efforts to create and develop mixed teams which has produced 'different thought processes, different conversations and better quality decisions' according to Mike Wescott, HR Director.

Much research has been carried out into National Grid's employee value proposition (EVP), to identify what makes the company different, which can then be sold to potential applicants. In their case, the main feature has appeared to be working on large, exciting long-term projects and also dealing with power emergencies.

Linking with the community is also seen as vital, encouraging staff to be part of their local communities. One in five staff have chosen to volunteer and opportunities are matched to individual development needs through the use of an external brokerage company. Encouraging innovation has also been increasingly encouraged (it is an important part of the recently agreed regulatory regime with Ofgem) so employees are given incentives to produce new ideas, many of which emerge from employees' informal discussions and social networking over subjects such as energy usage and reducing costs.

Source: Shaylor (2015)

2.6.5 HR AND EMPLOYEE ENGAGEMENT

The concept of engagement centres on the degree to which employees 'buy into' the company culture, strategy and values. Few people would argue that engaged employees are far more likely to be productive and to employ the correct competencies to help achieve organisational success. The clearest example we have all seen is when we, as a customer, have faced employees who could not care much about our needs or expectations and provide us with appalling service. They are therefore not engaged in their jobs. Measuring the level of employee engagement and then taking initiatives to maintain and improve this level are therefore seen as key HR strategies.

The subject was considered so important by the Government that a substantial report on the subject was commissioned in 2009 (the Macleod Report). This confirmed the association of engagement with performance and the fact that:

> Engagement, going to the heart of the workplace relationship between employer and employee, can be a key to unlocking productivity and transforming the working lives of many people for whom Monday morning is an especially low part of the week. (Macleod and Clarke 2009, p2)

Measuring engagement

Engagement is usually measured by forms of staff surveys which ask detailed questions concerning employee attitudes to areas such as:

- understanding of organisational purpose
- commitment to key competencies, such as customer satisfaction, quality improvement, etc
- satisfaction in the job they carry out
- satisfaction with the rewards
- plans on staying or leaving the organisation
- willingness to go the extra mile
- willingness to put forward new ideas and to accept changes in their job and the organisation
- pride in working for the organisation
- agreeing to promote their organisation to their friends and recommend people to work for the organisation
- views on 'fairness' within the organisation
- degree of trust in senior management and their own manager
- belief that the organisation is a 'happy' or 'fun' place to work
- belief that the organisation cares about its employees
- belief that the organisation is serious about equal opportunities and diversity.

For some organisations, these surveys are complex and detailed because management believe the results to be critical to the success of the organisation. Nationwide Building Society, for example, describes the survey as 'their genome project, mapping the DNA of the organisation'. Two data modellers, the 'insight team', are dedicated to the outcomes, searching for correlations. Their research has found that, if employees are 2% more satisfied, that translates into customers being more satisfied and buying more – and vice versa with dissatisfied employees. Nationwide customers like staff with longevity, so it is important for the organisation to find out what it is that makes staff stay and why they leave. One of the key outcomes of the surveys is that staff who strongly share the values are more likely to stay (Syedain 2009). At Marks & Spencer, survey results show that stores with high engagement scores have high mystery shopper and sales against target scores and lower absence (Arkin 2011).

Most research into retaining staff demonstrates that the employee's relationship with their immediate manager is one of the most important predictors of their length of service. The features of 'engaging' managers has been set out by the Institute for Employment Studies, summarised in Case Study 2.4.

CASE STUDY 2.4

MANAGERS AND ENGAGEMENT

The Institute for Employment Studies has studied aspects of engagement for some years and their 2009 report examined how managers who inspire and engage their teams to perform well behave in their dealings with staff. Twenty-five managers, found to rate highly on engagement, were chosen from seven organisations and these managers were interviewed, together with their teams. They had varied responsibilities, from 4 to 5,000 staff.

The research discovered that the engaging managers had a lot of characteristics in common, but personality was not one of them. Some were energetic extroverts, others were quiet, even shy – some were intensely practical, while others were creative and innovative, or liked intellectual challenge. Most had been with their organisations for some time, but others were more recent recruits. Their behaviour towards their teams, however, was very consistent. The interest they took in

people as individuals, and in developing and nurturing their teams, did not prevent them from tackling difficult issues such as breaking bad news and managing poor performance. The consensus was that honesty and openness was important, along with empathy and a demonstration that the manager had an understanding of their possible impact on staff.

Something else they shared was a focus on performance and an expectation that their teams would deliver to a high standard. The recession was biting when they carried out our research, and some of the private sector companies they visited were suffering, but the engaging managers recognised the need to maintain their engaging behaviours in bad times as well as good. The general feeling among engaged teams was that they were happy and enjoyed their work and there was a good atmosphere compared with other teams.

Source: Robinson and Hayday (2009)

The level of engagement is usually measured by way of staff surveys, but these do not always show the whole picture, as research by Gourlay et al (2012) has shown, because engagement may be transactional or emotional:

- Emotionally engaged employees are employees who enjoy the work they are doing, have high levels of wellbeing and enjoy working with their manager and co-workers. They also tend to have high levels of performance. They are truly 'engaged' to the organisation.

- Transactional engagement, on the other hand, is shaped by employees' concern to earn a living, to meet minimal expectations of the employer and their co-workers. They tend to respond positively to surveys but may not be high-performers. In other words, their responses to surveys can be misleading and, because they often display lower levels of organisational identification, they are more likely to display deviant behaviours and to leave the organisation when their personal or economic circumstances change.

Further, evidence was found that work intensification (ie greater pressure on employees to get results) may drive up transactional engagement at the expense of emotional engagement. So it is in the interests of organisations to take initiatives to improve emotional engagement rather than relying on statistical results from staff surveys which may disguise the true picture.

Improving engagement in practice usually involves the understanding what matters to employees and then delivering it to them, as shown in Case Study 2.5

CASE STUDY 2.5

INTEGRATING ENGAGEMENT WITH TALENT MANAGEMENT AT VIRTUSA

Virtusa, employing 9000 staff world-wide, 86% of whom are under 30, provides enterprise IT services, cloud computing and software development, chiefly from its Indian hub but with a growing presence in the UK. The company is 20 years old and as agile as its employee base in a highly competitive market place. It has long understood that improving its employee proposition is the key to long-term success.

The company has introduced a set of highly visible values and a talent management programme (backed by a platform called Career Compass), where the aim is to develop 70% of its talent internally. It recognises that employees' needs differ across the employment spectrum so it has to create a variety of processes and procedures to recognise all talent, especially hidden IT skills, and then create imaginative and attractive development opportunities built around the individual needs, making substantial use of the employees' own inputs.

Use is made of traditional coaching and competency development but also more esoteric processes, such as career monitoring dashboards. The aim is to design a holistic solution for all covering day one to the day they may leave. The company also tries to ensure that staff find work that is fulfilling, that they are passionate about and which matches their aptitudes and competencies.

Considerable use is made of employee feedback via a portal that measures their 'Employee delight Index' from which emerges programmes and deliverables that meet employees' wants. On top of a complex flexibility over shift patterns, sabbaticals and tuition reimbursement, they have created a well-used internal social media network to allow improved communication and collaboration. All of which has gone some way in mirroring their core business, namely transforming clients' business outcomes, to achieve the same for employees so that millennial team members thrive in the organisation.

Source: *People Management* (2015)

2.7 CUSTOMER CARE

Customers are the lifeblood of any organisation. If they do not receive satisfactory and even pleasurable experiences, they will go elsewhere. The purpose of customer care, therefore, is to ensure that customers' needs and expectations are met or exceeded so that they remain committed to that organisation. An American survey by Infoquest (2002) found that a totally satisfied customer contributes 17 times as much revenue to a company as a dissatisfied customer, but a totally dissatisfied customer decreases revenue by a factor of 30. So with twice as many satisfied customers as dissatisfied, a business will still be doing little better than standing still. Other surveys have shown that a 1% increase in customer satisfaction translates into a 3% market value increase, and that companies with higher regarded customer care systems increase their sales per annum twice as fast as organisations where customer care is poorly regarded (Fraterman 2009).

2.7.1 STRATEGIC APPROACH TO CUSTOMER CARE

Driving an effective customer care approach through the organisation requires a strategy that incorporates all aspects of the company's operations. Marketing must find out what products and services will meet customer needs and design and development departments must produce them in ways that provide sufficient choice and at acceptable prices. Production must produce goods that have very high quality levels backed up by guarantees that will satisfy customers. Distribution must ensure they are available for customers within acceptable deadlines. Even more important, employees throughout the organisation must buy in to the concept that customers must be treated fairly, speedily and with attention to detail. Without the thorough commitment by staff and the built-in desire to 'go the extra mile', gaps will develop in the process through which customers will fall. So any strategic plan will have the employees at its centre.

The strategic plan will need to establish a set of *standards* and *measures* which will identify critical success factors in customer service. These will include:

- *measures of immediate customer dissatisfaction*, such as volume and value of goods returned within seven days or a month, number of service contracts cancelled within seven days, number of time-limited contracts which are not renewed
- *number and type of customer complaints*, identified by product and sales area
- *metrics associated with surveys of customer satisfaction* – many organisations, for example, ask customers to respond immediately after buying goods or services. For example, the national double glazing companies usually provide customers with a short questionnaire to fill in when the products are installed relating to their sales and installation experience. Other companies will circulate questionnaires to a selection of customers on service contracts on a periodic basis
- *measures of on-time production and delivery* compared with contracted times
- *quality and speed of response* to customer contact in terms of sales achieved, problem-solving and returning customers
- *for call-centres, specific metrics on call-handling*
- *metrics from mystery shoppers* – although the implementation of mystery shopping schemes was first regarded with suspicion by employees, there has been remarkable acceptance of the process, especially as most reporting systems do not identify specific employees but measure the general ambience of customer relations.

2.7.2 CUSTOMER CARE – THE EMPLOYEE DIMENSION

To thoroughly involve employees, the following areas need to be included in any customer care training programme:

- *Training employees in products and services*, so that all employees, not just sales, can be in a position to deal with customers' needs.
- *Specific training for sales staff*, especially retail staff, to ensure that sales made benefit both the organisation and the customer. Customers need to leave the sales environment feeling confident that they have not been persuaded to purchase by clever sales

techniques. This may lead to short-term sales increase but ultimately will lead to poor customer relations and, in the worst cases, litigation. An important issue here is the danger of mis-selling. The Office of Fair Trading (OFT) has carried out two major investigations in this area. The first, in the 1990s, was into pensions mis-selling, and the second, in 2003, into the selling of extended warranties. In the first case, heavy fines were imposed on a number of companies involved and, in the second, the OFT imposed a number of conditions under which the financial service could be sold, both to ensure customers received better protection in the future.

- *A clear understanding of the standards established* in customer care and the processes operated. This is not always straightforward. Although guidelines are usually established in, say, when and how contracts can be changed or cancelled, it may be necessary to go outside of these guidelines as a means to solve difficult problems. The authority for such action used to be restricted to senior management, but some companies with sophisticated customer care systems have delegated authority to low levels to allow problems to be solved swiftly. They have found that this often wins back customers who do not have to wait to talk to a manager and whose anxiety or anger over the issue is quickly assuaged.

- *Specific training for service staff* in areas where the quality of service is the essential feature of the sale, such as in hotel and catering operations and in-flight service. The switch to call centre handling of sales and service operation since the mid-1990s has meant that specialised staff training is required in dealing with customers over the phone, although anecdotal experience leads most people to doubt that such training has taken place in many cases. In recent years, the specialised customer care in the health service has been the subject of comprehensive training, although results, again, still appear to be mixed.

- *Training in communication and problem-solving* – the development of the competency frameworks in organisations, where emphasis is placed on the necessary enhancement of skills in communication and problem-solving, is closely related to customer care and not just restricted to immediate customer-facing staff. The ability to identify where contracts have gone wrong (problem-solving) and for staff to effectively communicate with each other to ensure problems are immediately solved and to prevent them happening again is crucial to the process of improving customer care.

- *Providing incentives for efficient customer care* – there is a growing trend for incentive schemes to contain a strong element of measuring and rewarding customer care performance, rather than simply using output or quantity measures. Often this change has been made because, under previous schemes, employees have acted to raise output at all costs without considering the consequences of poor quality, delivery times or unacceptable service quality. Examples here include the Sainsbury's store-based team incentive, which is wholly based on the CSI (customer satisfaction index) (IRS 2003), the DaimlerChrysler Aftersales Managers scheme,* where CSI scores represent 20% of the managers' bonus, and AOS Heating, a small plumbing firm based in Cheshunt, where the bonus for the plumbers is entirely based on the customer ratings.*

- *Recognition of employee action* – as an additional reward for demonstrating the required employee behaviours, many organisations have instituted a formal system of recognition for excellent customer care. For example, Claridge's Hotel in London has a 'Pot of Gold' recognition scheme where an employee who has demonstrated 'service perfection' in the course of a day's work (a core value in the organisation) can be nominated by a fellow employee to take part in a 'lucky dip' from a pot of gold envelopes in the HR director's office. The reward can vary from an extra day of holiday or a facial treatment in the hotel's spa to an all-expenses paid night in the hotel's top suite, which would normally cost over £4,000 (IRS 2004).

*author's research

The aim of an integrated policy is to develop a customer care culture within the organisation where employees put the requirements of the customer first and behave in line with this belief.

Two examples are shown of customer care initiatives in Case study 2.6, one in the private sector and one, more surprising, in the public sector.

CASE STUDY 2.6

HOW DAMART TURNED INTERNAL CHALLENGES INTO AWARD-WINNING SERVICE AND SUCCESS

Over the last fifty years, Damart has grown from a small, French family business into a trusted global clothing brand. The company's popular thermal garments have been to both the Arctic Circle and the summit of Everest, but are perhaps best known in the senior home shopping market.

Damart employs around 700 people in the UK alone – more at peak trading times – and turns over £110m per year. Satisfying so many customers is an intensive process, needing widespread colleague engagement. But when Damart achieved the Institute's ServiceMark accreditation in 2013, and won the award for Employee Engagement Strategy of the Year at the Institute of Customer Service's UK Customer Satisfaction Awards 2014, it set the seal on how much colleagues are valued and how they are empowered to act for the benefit of customers.

Engagement challenges

Head of HR Helen Taylor explains: 'We went through quite a difficult time. In 2008 we brought in a new warehouse management system that challenged our business. In terms of the amount of change involved, we learnt that we needed to improve employee engagement around change management.'

The implementation brought specific challenges to parcel dispatch and affected customer service for a considerable amount of time. In addition, the change process had an unexpected impact on team members' working patterns which continued to have an impact on Damart for a further six months. Colleague engagement was put under further pressure by the financial crisis, as a collective redundancy process – aimed at improving flexibility – took its toll on morale.

Damart recognised that it needed to do more to put its customers back at the heart of its business – something that could only be achieved through active engagement with colleagues. Following that difficult time, the company started to build employee engagement around change management, making sure the company was customer focused in its approach to changes, and invested heavily in service improvements which customers told them they wanted.

A framework for change

The ServiceMark accreditation process uncovered the depth of the disparity between Damart's external reputation and its own staff engagement. While the UK Customer Satisfaction Index element rated the company at a world-class 90%, the internal ServCheck self-assessment returned just 57%. This was no surprise to Damart as their colleagues had been through significant changes.

More specifically, ServCheck revealed engagement was lowest among operational colleagues, while team members at the distribution centre sometimes felt less informed due to their physical location being five miles from head office. The findings gave Damart a structure to work with and the company set about adopting a more inclusive approach, empowering colleagues in all departments to propose changes on customers' behalf.

Customer service challenge meetings took place every two weeks, where a cross-section of colleagues told management about issues which impacted on customers. Directors' surgeries also took place regularly where employees came to talk to a Director about what was going on in the business and ask any questions or share ideas. Roles were created in business teams dedicated to improving the customer experience.

Staff engagement soared, and in December 2013 Damart succeeded in achieving ServiceMark accreditation. Meanwhile, improvements in process – and suggestions from staff, as part of their new FirstImpressions service training programme – had begun to make a noticeable difference to customer service, morale, and the company's bottom line.

Among other changes, customers' letters and emails were dealt with more quickly, colleagues were formally trained in responding to customers, and customer-facing website text improved. Damart introduced new payment and delivery options as well as further website improvements to help customer choices.

At the same time that customer satisfaction improved, colleague turnover fell by 28%, and there were 13% fewer absences.

Overall, Helen believes the outcomes of ServiceMark were, if anything, more valuable than the accreditation itself: 'The accreditation is one thing, but it's the engagement you get from everybody, and the hard work, that makes such a difference. Winning the award wasn't the end; everything is still happening – that open culture, with colleagues generating ideas and listening to what our customers really need. Our challenge now is to keep all those things happening... because they work.'

Source: Bell (2015)

MODern Housing Solutions (MHS) is a dedicated venture company between Enterprise plc and Carillion plc constructed specifically to deliver the Housing Prime Contract, valued at £700m over seven years, which maintains 43,000 units for service families' accommodation in England and Wales.

Re-enlistment rates have been found to be highly correlated to satisfaction with living accommodation of service families, so ensuring families have decent, habitable and stress-free accommodation, regardless of rank, is vital to the future human resource plans for the defence forces. In previous years, the reputation for quality maintenance has not always been high, both in terms of work carried out and, in particular, the level of response. A key initiative in this contract has been the development of a dedicated customer care centre incorporating a 24-hour freephone helpdesk.

The customer care centre, which needed the highest level of security accreditation, was established in Liverpool with state-of-the-art telephony equipment which received, on average, 7,000 calls per week. According to Enterprise, after two years of operation, the service level has been running consistently above KPI requirements (such as 95% of calls answered within two minutes), with customer satisfaction rates showing substantial improvements.

However, the National Audit Office showed a mixed view of customer satisfaction. When the new contract began in 2006, there was a higher than expected level of demand for repairs, which the helpdesk and other systems could not cope with. Many families remain dissatisfied with the service, in particular with the understanding shown by helpdesk operators of the nature of the maintenance problems. Survey respondents reported that only 42% of problems were rectified at the first visit and, in cases where the respondent felt the helpdesk had not understood their problem, it fell to 13%. Having said this, however, families were generally satisfied with the manner in which the work was carried out and confirmed that there had been an upward trend in the contractor's performance against KPIs.

Sources: Enterprise (2009); National Audit Office (2009)

2.8 QUALITY MANAGEMENT

2.8.1 THE IMPORTANCE OF QUALITY MANAGEMENT

Quality management has moved on a long way from the traditional view that a quality product just meets the technical specification and that customers have to accept and pay for the product or the service if the company can show it has met that specification. Today, successful companies are those that aim to produce products and services that exceed customers' expectations and reach success in that aim. Meeting the specification is just one step on the road to high quality.

In many industries, quality failures can be catastrophic. The failure in preventing fire spreading was one (among other) quality faults that caused the deaths of 189 people in the Piper Alpha North Sea oil rig disaster in 1989; the failure in signalling quality was a major cause of the Paddington rail crash in 1999, killing 30 people; and, worldwide, other, larger disasters at Bhopal in India (Union Carbide) and Chernobyl caused multiple deaths and untold misery for thousands.

Quality remains a subjective subject. Organisations, such as Ferrari, the Ritz Hotel and Cartier, whose entire business is geared to producing products and services at the highest possible level, will not be so concerned with cutting costs, only with ensuring nothing ever goes wrong. Other organisations, such as McDonald's or Tesco, will seek to provide good-value (generally meaning cheap) products and services associated with a pleasant experience, with the costs being firmly under control. Both examples concern organisations that are totally focused on quality. Slack et al (2007) call the first example the *transcendent* approach and the second the *value-based* approach.

2.8.2 HIERARCHY OF QUALITY MANAGEMENT

It is possible to identify five developments in quality systems, as shown in Figure 2.4.

Level 5 – Inspection

Inspection systems have been in place for centuries, with records available of the inspection that took place during the building of the Egyptian Pyramids more than 4,000 years ago. Inspection is generally an after-the-event activity concerned with identifying faults, removing defective items from the process and either reworking or scrapping them. Without inspection, faulty goods would proceed to the retailer and eventually the customer, where rejection would take place. Solving the problem at that stage would be much more costly and damages the company's reputation.

Inspection systems, however, have their difficulties:

- Having an inspector at the end of each process is expensive in labour cost and the work can be extremely tedious (although it is possible to replace human inspection with automated processes).
- Inspection may remove the immediate problem but it does not always attack the symptom of the problems.

- Operatives may not be too concerned with the quality of their work knowing that an inspector will pick up any faults in the process. Inspection is linked closely with Tayloristic principles of fractionalising work, which presents the inherent difficulties of reducing the value of the work and, hence, the operative's regard for it.

Figure 2.4 Quality management analysis

Level 4 – Quality control (QC)

QC is a step up from inspection in that it makes use of more scientific and statistical data in examining quality issues. This makes use of sampling techniques, relating both to the inputs (supplies, materials) and the outputs at different stages in the manufacturing process. Statistical results are compared with predictive charts and control limits. An obvious example of its use is in the water industry, where water is sampled and tested for numerous hazards before it is released into the water supply. The operations are normally controlled by a quality department which consists of training and qualified personnel. The benefit of quality control is that the problems are identified at an early stage in a thorough, scientific way. For example, the sampling of braking components before they are released on the assembly line will save the quality problems later of rejecting full braking units, in terms of both cost and time.

Difficulties still remain, however, especially the separation of quality management from the manufacturing process and the difficulties of ensuring that samples are representative.

Level 3 – Quality assurance (QA) systems

QA systems are quality systems that are subject to external verification. The most comprehensive and well known are the ISO 9000 series (International standards, launched in 1987) and European Foundation for Quality Management standards (EFQM), launched in 1999, which have both built on less complex systems introduced from the 1960s. They were initially introduced in industries where failure of the products would cause severe problems, including loss of life, such as guided weapons and the aircraft industry as a response to customers (especially governments) demanding complete assurance on the quality of the product.

At the heart of these standards is the initiating by the organisation of a comprehensive system of quality management throughout the organisation. This includes comprehensive identification of the correct manufacturing methods (no shortcuts allowed by employees!), methods of identifying customer satisfaction, full recording of all data and training of all employees concerned. The QA systems can apply to all organisations (manufacturing, service, government and not-for profit). Systems need to be agreed with the external agencies, who will make periodic unscheduled visits to ensure the quality processes are being followed. If there are gaps found by the external agencies, the accreditation can be withdrawn.

There is no doubt that quality assurance accreditation has improved the overall quality in organisations that have adopted the accreditation process. This has occurred both because of the comprehensive approach required and the discipline imposed throughout the organisation and also because all employees do become aware of the catastrophic effect that the removal of the accreditation would have on the organisation's reputation and act accordingly. The system encourages a regular rethink of processes and acting to meet feedback from customers. The accreditation can be used in marketing. Increasingly, large government and private contracts are offered only to organisations that have the appropriate accreditation.

Criticism of the QA systems essentially concerns the bureaucratic approach required. For example, every time a new process or material is introduced, this has to be reported to the accrediting body. The external verification procedures are also seen as draconian at times. The processes are costly. Too much emphasis is placed on following the quality manual, rather than using a sensible and flexible approach. As the manual constantly changes, some employees find it difficult to keep up with the changes. Finally, from an employee viewpoint, QA accreditation can be seen as a management imposition and employees may do no more than they have to, to follow the rules (Hill 1991).

Level 2 – Business process re-engineering (BPR)

BPR is the process of systematically examining every stage of production/service to ensure that value is added for the benefit of the customer at each stage of the value chain. It has arisen chiefly from the work of Porter (1985) and Hammer and Champy (1993), whose emphasis on getting ahead of the competition laid a strong emphasis on building quality into the product or service through a radical rethink of every process. In practice, this has meant speeding up decision-making, becoming much more responsive to the customer, allowing new ideas to shape internal processes and empowering employees.

This process incorporates many of the facets of QA accreditation (in fact, they can operate side by side) but there is a much greater emphasis on employees taking hold of quality issues themselves. In a number of radical solutions, such as at Vauxhall in Luton, employees agreed to the elimination of all inspection jobs because the attention they now gave to quality made inspection redundant (Stredwick 1997).

However, in the process of reducing bureaucracy and becoming more flexible, it has also led to de-layering management, reducing the number of employees (except in customer-facing areas) and, evidence indicates, placing more stress on employees at all levels. Although shown to be effective in many cases in improving quality, it is much criticised for its top–down and secretive approach, which leads to cost saving at the expense of employees.

Level 1 – Total quality management (TQM)

TQM is a strategic approach to quality that incorporates most, if not all, of the facets described at the lower levels. It attempts to take the best of the QA systems and BPR and incorporate them into a model of 'best practice'. It therefore expresses itself as culturally based and has a big emphasis on employee involvement. The key ideas were introduced to Japan by the Americans as the occupying force immediately after the Second World War as part of the process of resuscitating their manufacturing industry (Needle 2004). The main initiators of the concept were Deming (1986) and Juran (1988).

In organisational terms, it integrates the company systems with those of suppliers and, in a business-to-business environment, major customers as well. For example, the 'just in time' system operating with suppliers will be integrated with supply sample testing and production schedules. Strong attempts are made to eliminate all costs associated with control and failure and an emphasis is put on 'right first time' and 'right every time'.

There are the following associations with employee involvement:

- Key values, such as 'customer awareness', 'teamworking' and 'continuous improvement' are cascaded down the organisation through training, performance management and regular communication.
- TQM statements regularly emphasise teamworking, creative thinking and empowerment.
- Initiatives on improving quality are encouraged through concepts such as 'quality circles' and 'recognition schemes'. All of these initiatives support teams to work together to achieve improved quality. These are especially focused on preventing problems, rather than solving them.
- An important aspect of training includes multi-skilling, so employees understand the quality requirements on a number of jobs so they can cover for absence, vacancies and where sections have any additional pressures. This is in response to research which has indicated that, to nobody's surprise, poor quality is associated with lack of employee expertise.
- Another training aspect is better understanding of statistical and recording methods so employees understand what is actually happening in their department.
- Communication is enhanced with regular feedback on quality performance and employee recognition awards.

An effectively run TQM system will produce better benefits than the other systems set out in Figure 2.4 on their own. Despite this, not all TQM systems have been an unqualified success. Difficulties faced have included:

- Employees still regard TQM as a form of management control, which can work to stultify individual initiative and increase the stress faced by employees, especially where quality standards are not met.
- TQM is associated with a high-trust environment, especially where serious attempts at empowerment are made. Therefore, when employees made suggestions that are not taken up, or where employees are blamed for not implementing initiatives effectively, it can reduce that degree of trust and lead to cynicism.
- At times, the whole TQM approach is seen as a marketing device, unrelated to the reality of the situation.
- It can also remain a high-cost bureaucratic process, by its very nature.

2.9 HUMAN RESOURCE MANAGEMENT AND THE CHANGE AGENDA

2.9.1 THEORIES OF CHANGE MANAGEMENT

There are essentially two main groups of theories that underpin models of change management. They all have their respective benefits and they focus in principle on individuals, group and organisation-wide issues.

These two groups represent the major schools of thought concerning change management theory. They are:

1 the individual perspective school

2 the group dynamics school.

The individual perspective school

This, as its name suggests, focuses on the individual as the principal unit of change. It also has two major camps within the school: the 'behaviourists' and the 'gestalt-field' psychologists. The behaviourists believe behaviour is the result of an individual's interaction with their environment. The gestalt-field psychologists believe that an individual's behaviour is the product of their environment and their own reason. The behaviourists advocate that behaviour is learned and that the individual is a passive recipient of external and objective data. In addition, they hold that individuals respond to the manipulation of reward-enforcing stimuli. Behaviour that is rewarded will tend to be repeated. The behaviourist approach is very close to that of the classical school of management, which presented humans as cogs in a machine responding to the external stimuli being provided.

The gestalt-field psychologists claim that learning is a process of gaining or changing insights, outlooks, expectations or thought patterns. The group takes into account not only the behaviours or actions, but also the responses that these elicit.

In applying these theories to change, the behaviourists seek to achieve change by modifying the external stimuli acting upon the individual, as opposed to the proponents of the gestalt-field, who seek to help individuals or organisations change their understanding of themselves. In turn this leads to changes in behaviour. In simple terms, behaviourism is a 'carrot and stick' approach to achieving change. For example, systems of rewards and sanctions are very visible in sales environments, such as call centres and recruitment agencies.

Both of these approaches have had some influence in management of change. This approach, not surprisingly, has many characteristics of the human relations school of management, largely brought about through the work of Maslow (1943), which stresses the need for both internal and external stimuli in order to influence human behaviour. The human relations school, in understanding the role of the individual, also draws attention to the roles of social groups in organisations, as does the group dynamics school.

Pavlov and his dogs – Pavlov, a Russian psychologist, is possibly the most well-known behaviourist. In a famous experiment, Pavlov used a group of dogs. He rang a bell and then immediately produced food for the dogs. After a time, the dogs began to associate the ringing of the bell with the provision of food and began to salivate when they heard it. Once this stage had been reached, Pavlov rang the bell but did not provide food. The dogs still salivated on hearing the bell. Their behaviour had been changed.

Kurt Lewin and field theory – Kurt Lewin (1958) is a major figure in change management. He made major contributions in the areas of force-field analysis (a method of identifying and measuring resistance to change), group dynamics, organisational development, action research and field-gestalt psychology.

Hall and Lindzey (1978, p386) summarised the central features of Kurt Lewin's force-field theory as follows:

> Behaviour is a function of the field that exists at the time the behaviour occurs. Analysis begins with the situation as a whole from which are differentiated the component parts, and the concrete person in a concrete situation can be represented mathematically.

It is not only in the area of organisations that you see the application of these theories. Until the end of the 1980s, the therapy regime in mental hospitals used the 'carrot and stick' approach of the behaviourists. Since then, mental health therapy has adopted a development approach, more representative of the gestalt-field approach.

A detailed critique of Lewin's force-field theory is set out in Chapter 10.

The group dynamics school

Group dynamics is the field of study within the social sciences that focuses on the nature of groups. In management, we call them teams, but the terms are interchangeable. The main theme of the school is that the influence of the group or team may become very strong indeed and overwhelm the individual's actions and tendencies. So the group may well change the behaviour of the individual. This, effectively, also forms the basis of group therapy. There is particular interest in group dynamics at the moment because of the rise of online interaction made possible by the Internet.

Since the late 1970s in the UK, there has been great interest in 'teambuilding', which can involve a variety of activities from departmental 'away days' (days spent away from the workplace) to full-blown outward bound activity sessions run by ex-military types. The Leadership Trust in the UK is an excellent example of this.

Kurt Lewin is commonly identified as the founder of the movement to study groups scientifically. He coined the term group dynamics to describe the way groups and individuals act and react to changing circumstances.

William Schutz (1966) looked at interpersonal relations from the perspective of three dimensions: inclusion, control and affection (now called openness). This became the basis for a theory of group behaviour that sees groups as resolving issues in each of these stages in order to be able to develop to the next stage. Conversely, a group may also devolve to an earlier stage if unable to resolve outstanding issues in a particular stage. Schutz developed a psychometric instrument – fundamental interpersonal relations organisation (FIRO) – to incorporate these ideas.

Wilfred Bion (1961) studied group dynamics from a psychoanalytic perspective. Many of his findings were reported in his published books, especially *Experiences in Groups*. The Tavistock Institute has further developed and applied the theory and practices developed by Bion.

Bruce Tuckman (1965) proposed the four-stage model called Tuckman's stages for a group. Tuckman's model states that the ideal group decision-making process should occur in four stages:

1 *forming* (being polite to others and pretending to get on with them)
2 *storming* (dropping the pretence of politeness and focusing on the issues, even if emotions rise)
3 *norming* (getting used to each other and developing trust and productivity)
4 *performing* (working in a group to a common goal on a highly efficient and co-operative basis).

Later, Tuckman added an *ending* stage, recognising that the work of a group may come to an end and the group disbanded.

It should be noted that this model refers to the overall pattern of the group, but of course individuals within a group work in different ways. If distrust persists, a group may never even get to the norming stage.

The school's primary emphasis is on bringing organisational change about through teams and work groups rather than individuals. Lewin suggested that the rationale behind this is that because people in organisations work in groups, individual behaviours must be modified or changed in the light of the prevailing group practice and norms.

He went on to suggest that group behaviour is an intricate set of symbolic interactions and facets which not only affect group structure, but also modify individual behaviour. He argued that individual behaviour is a function of the group environment.

To enable change, according to the group dynamics school, the focus must be at group level and should concentrate on influencing and changing the group's norms, roles and values. Therefore, it is useless to concentrate on the behaviour of individuals (French and

Bell 1984). In this context, norms are the rules or standards that define what people should do, roles are patterns of behaviour that individuals are expected to conform to, and values are the ideas and beliefs that individuals hold about what is right and wrong.

The group dynamics school has proved to be very influential in developing the theory and practice of change management. Mullins (2007) remarked that 'this can be seen by the very fact it is now usual for organisations to view themselves as comprising groups and teams, rather than merely a collection of individuals'.

French and Bell (1984) pointed out:

> The most important single group of interventions in OD are team building activities, the goals of which are the improved and increased effectiveness of various teams within the organisation. The team building meeting has the goal of improving team effectiveness through better management of task demands, relationship demands and group processes. The team analyses its way of doing things and attempts to develop strategies to improve its operation.

Here, norms, roles and values are examined, challenged and changed. Despite the emphasis many place on groups within organisations, others argue that the correct change management approach should be one that focuses on the organisation as a whole.

2.9.2 MANAGING INDIVIDUAL CHANGE

The DREC model – how individuals cope with change

Elisabeth Kübler-Ross (1969) was a psychiatrist and the author of the ground-breaking book *On Death and Dying*, where she first discussed what is now known as the Kübler-Ross model.

She proposed the now famous 'Five Stages of Grief' as a pattern of phases, most or all of which people tend to go through, in sequence, after being faced with the tragedy of their own impending death. The five stages of grief, in sequential order, are denial, anger, bargaining, depression and acceptance. The five stages have since been adopted by many as applying to the survivors of bereavement and, subsequently, to survivors of all change situations.

The 'Five Stages of Grief' model has become known in management circles as the 'Coping Cycle'. In this section, we use an adapted version of this model, known as DREC (denial, resistance, exploration and commitment). The model is shown in Figure 2.5.

The stages of the cycle are as follows:

- **Denial** – initially, the individual concerned will refuse to accept that the change affects them. The immediate response is to say 'Not me!' At this stage of the cycle, the individual is still firmly attached to the past and the change is seen as something external. The best response is to give specific instructions to the individual, to tell them what to do next.
- **Resistance** – after a period of time, the individual will accept that the change will take place, but not now. The individual is still attached to the past, but not as strongly as before, and is beginning to internalise the need for change. The correct response to this is to ask the individual what they are going to do next.
- **Exploration** – by this stage, the individual has accepted the need for change and is beginning to explore options. They are now looking to the future and everything seems possible. But there are dangers. The individual will wish to experiment with everything, become overloaded and achieve nothing. Focus is needed and this is provided by telling the individual to choose their focus.
- **Commitment** – at this stage, the individual is fully committed to the change, has internalised it, has a clear focus and gets on with it. Individuals clearly face towards the

future. They have internalised the change, need no telling, just asking to learn what they will do next.

There is one more danger: it takes time for individuals to work through the cycle. They cannot be hurried. Any attempts to rush them through the cycle may result in a cosmetic change from denial to commitment, but when individuals experience pressure or failure, they revert back to denial. When this happens, it is known as the Tarzan swing, because it represents Tarzan making two giant swings in quick succession.

Figure 2.5 The DREC model

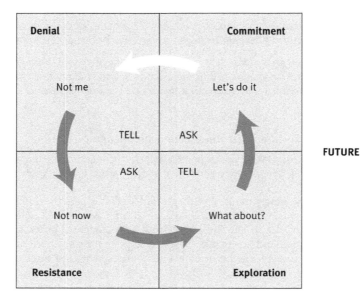

2.9.3 HUMAN RESOURCES: THE CHANGE AGENT

Earlier in this chapter, the various models of human resources were identified and most of them emphasised that human resources has a key role as a change agent, especially the Ulrich model. There are numerous areas when this role can be played, such as:

- helping the organisation to adjust to changes in the external environment, both in the immediate term with legislative changes and with the longer term, such as changes in ethical behaviour and in advancing corporate social responsibility (see Chapter 9)
- leading negotiating teams in persuading unions to change working practices and become more flexible and efficient to meet the changing competitive environment
- involvement with mergers and acquisitions where, in this most sensitive area, changes may need to be taken quickly and, perhaps painfully, in the employee area; survivors need to be quickly turned round to ensure they contribute to the long-term benefit of the merged organisation
- initiating changes in the organisation's culture, such as introducing a new behavioural environment or an enhanced competency framework

- introducing innovations in reward, such as greater emphasis on performance-oriented rewards, moving away from job- or service-related payments – here, the creation of a robust and fair performance management system becomes crucial and this involves a substantial change programme for management and employees to ensure it works appropriately
- organising research into the degree of employee engagement through employee surveys and producing proposals aiming to increase the engagement metrics
- working with the board and consultants to create and develop an employee brand, using the defined organisational culture and building up an integrated system of recruitment and selection, learning and development, employee relations and reward and recognition which enhances that brand.

Kotter has integrated much of the role of change agent into his 8-step change model.

Kotter's (1996) 8-step change model

Step 1: Create urgency

For change to happen, it helps if the whole company really wants it. It is essential to develop a sense of urgency around the need for change which will help spark the initial motivation to get things moving.

This isn't simply a matter of showing people poor sales statistics or talking about increased competition. An honest and convincing dialogue about what's happening in the marketplace and with your competition is required. If many people start talking about the change you propose, the urgency can spread quickly.

Step 2: Form a powerful coalition

Convince people that change is necessary. This often takes strong leadership and visible support from key people within your organisation.

Effective change leaders throughout your organisation need to be found – they don't necessarily follow the traditional company hierarchy. To lead change, a coalition is needed to bring together team of influential people whose power comes from a variety of sources, including job title, status, expertise, and political importance. Once formed, this 'change coalition' needs to work as a team, continuing to build urgency and momentum around the need for change.

Step 3: Create a vision for change

When the urgency for change is first considered, there will probably be many great ideas and solutions floating around. Link these concepts to an overall vision that people can grasp easily and remember.

A clear vision can help everyone understand why they are being asked to do something. When people see for themselves what's trying to be achieved, then the directives they are given tend to make more sense.

Step 4: Communicate the vision

What happens with the vision after it has been created will determine its success. It needs to be talked about and used daily to make decisions and solve problems. When it is kept fresh on everyone's minds, they'll remember it and respond to it.

It's also important to 'walk the talk'. What is done by HR and other management is far more important – and believable – than what they say. Demonstrate the kind of behaviour that is wanted from others.

Step 5: Remove obstacles

Put in place the structure for change, and continually check for barriers to it. Removing obstacles can empower the people you need to execute the vision, and it can help the change move forward. This includes identifying and hiring change leaders, revamping organisational structures, job descriptions, performance and pay to reflect the changes, recognising and rewarding people who make change happen and remove barriers, especially where key employees may create centres of resistance.

Step 6: Create short-term wins

Nothing motivates more than success. Give your company a taste of victory early in the change process. Within a short time frame (this could be a month or a year, depending on the type of change), some quick wins are wanted that the staff can see. Without this, critics and negative thinkers might hurt the progress.

Create short-term targets – not just one long-term goal. Each smaller target must be achievable, with little room for failure. The change team may have to work very hard to come up with these targets, but each 'win' that is produced can further motivate the entire staff.

Step 7: Build on the change

Kotter argues that many change projects fail because victory is declared too early. Real change runs deep. Quick wins are only the beginning of what needs to be done to achieve long-term change.

Launching one new product using a new system is great. But if ten products can be launched, that means the new system is working. To reach that tenth success, it is necessary to keep looking for improvements.

Step 8: Anchor the changes in corporate culture

Finally, to make any change stick, it should become part of the core of the organisation. The corporate culture often determines what gets done, so the values behind the vision must show in day-to-day work.

Make continuous efforts to ensure that the change is seen in every aspect of the organisation. This will help give that change a solid place in your organisation's culture.

It's also important that the company's leaders continue to support the change. This includes existing staff and new leaders who are brought in. If the support of these people is lost, then the whole project could be in jeopardy. Back all this up with talking about progress every chance management has, communicating stories about successes throughout the organisation.

A further review of the role of human resources in change is found in Chapter 10.

KEY LEARNING POINTS

Throughout this chapter, the implications for human resource practitioners have been emphasised. In short, HR practitioners need to:

- understand the management systems and identity the power structure so they are able to use their influence selectively and effectively to improve organisational performance
- be regarded as an expert in handling conflict so people issues can be addressed fully and appropriately and resolved in the interests of the great majority of stakeholders
- be aware of the options available for the structure of the human resources function and be able to recommend the best option which is appropriate to the organisational context
- use their influence to improve employee understanding of the importance of systems of customer care and quality assurance and ensure that employees respond accordingly
- act in the best interests of the organisation in facilitating organisational change, ensuring that employees willingly support the required changes.

REVIEW QUESTIONS

1 What did Fayol consider to be the main principles of effective management?

2 What is the Butterfly Effect?

3 According to Macmillan, what is the distinction between power and influence?

4 What is 'satisficing', according to Drucker?

5 What are the benefits of operating a 'business partner' HR system?

6 Identify the main important sources of management power, according to Morgan.

7 What are the crucial differences between a collaborative management style and an avoidance style?

8 What is the difference between emotional and transactional engagement?

9 What are the four key attributes of human resources that are associated with the resource-based view of the organisation, according to Boxall and Purcell?

10 Identify the main stages in the DREC model relating to change.

EXPLORE FURTHER

This chapter covers a very wide range of subjects, so the list of additional reading can be extensive. Here is a short selection:

Theories of management

COLE, G. (2010) *Management theory and practice*. 6th edition. London: Cengage Learning.

MINTZBERG, H. (2009) *Managing*. Harlow: FT Prentice Hall.

Power in organisations

GRAY, C. (2013) A very short, fairly interesting and reasonably cheap book about studying organisations, 3rd ed. London: Sage.

JERMIER, J., KNIGHTS, D. and NORD, W. (1994) *Resistance and power in organisations*. London: Routledge.

PFEFFER, J. (1992) *Managing with power*. Boston, MA: Harvard Business School Press.

Handling conflict

CIPD (2015) Conflict management: a shift in direction. Research Report, March.

NICOTERA, A. (1995) *Conflict and organisations*. New York: State University of New York.

RAHIM, A. (2001) *Managing conflict in organisations*. New York: Quorum Books.

Models of the human resource function

CIPD (2015) *Changing HR operating models: a collection of thought pieces*. CIPD Research Reports.

DANIELS, K. (ed.) (2008) *Strategic human resource management*. London: Chartered Institute of Personnel and Development.

MARCHINGTON, M. and WILKINSON, A. (2008) *Human resource management at work*. London: Chartered Institute of Personnel and Development.

Best practice

CIPD (2015) *From best to good practice HR*. Research Report, October.

Engagement

HOLBECHE, L. and MATTHEWS, G. (2012) *Engaged: unleashing your organisation's potential through employee engagement*. New York: Wiley and Sons.

Customer care

COOK, S. (2008) *Customer care excellence*. 5th edition. London: Kogan Page.

JOHNS, T. (1994) *Perfect customer care*. New York: Arrow Books.

Quality management

BESTERFIELD, D. et al (2003) *Total quality management*. New York: Prentice Hall.

MAUCH, P. (2009) *Quality management: theory and practice*. London: CRC Press.

Management of change

CAMERON, E. and GREEN, M. (2015*Making sense of change management*. 4th ed. London: Kogan Page

CIPD (2015) *Leading transformational change: closing the gap between theory and practice*. Research Report, September.

HUGHES, M. (2006) *Change management*. 9th edition. London: Chartered Institute of Personnel and Development.

SEMINAR ACTIVITY 2.2

FIELD-GESTALT EXERCISES

Introduction

These are a series of exercises that you, as a student, can use to manage your own change. They are based on exercises used by life coaches, but they employ standard techniques such as critical incident techniques and gestalt. Students can work on these individually and then compare their results in small groups to aid the learning process. The group's most interesting examples can be shared with the whole class.

Rules for winning

This is an essential system to enable you to build on what you already do well, so that you can do even better. It uses the critical incident technique:

1   Recall a time when you succeeded in achieving something.

2   How did you manage to achieve the successful result? Use the following questions:

    ○   What worked for you? – list the answers and write them down.
    ○   What can you learn about yourself from these results? – write it down.
    ○   What got in the way? – write it down.
    ○   What can you learn from that? – write it down, in positive form.
    ○   How will you overcome that difficulty next time? – write it down.

3 Rules for winning are personal to each individual and help you to identify positively how you as an individual overcome a given situation and achieve required objectives.

Golden moments

This uses ideas from gestalt psychology. Fundamentally, it asks you what you are feeling, seeing, sensing – but **not** thinking – in given situations.

1 Identify your bottom line, that is, the line you will not retreat beyond. It could be such things as trying to right injustice where you see it, not being treated as a doormat, standing up to unreasonable fellow students you share a flat with, and so on.

2 Think of times when you exemplified your bottom line.

3 List times in your life when you achieved your objective – what did it feel like? (These last two experiences are the golden moments.)

These moments are personal to you and help you to affirm positively that you can achieve your objectives and stick to your bottom line.

The lifeline

1 Graph the highs and lows of your life on a chart as shown in Figure 2.6.

2 Label the highs and lows with life events, such as changing schools, a new job, father dying, and so on. For the purposes of the exercise, we are interested in the business-related highs and lows of the lifeline, and the messages these send to us.

3 Code the business-related highs and lows of the lifeline in this way:

Figure 2.6 Example of a lifeline chart

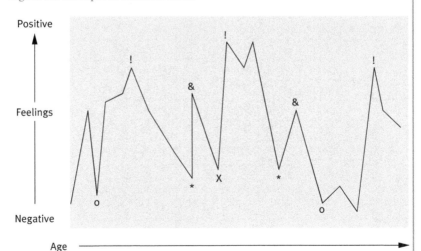

! I took a great risk

* I played it safe.

o Someone else made a major decision I thought should be mine.

+ I made one of my best decisions.

x I felt I had no control.

& I was in control.

What does this now tell you about yourself?

CHAPTER 3

The Competitive Environment

LEARNING OUTCOMES

When you have completed this chapter, you should be able to understand, explain and critically evaluate:

- the fundamental economic problem of scarcity and choice, and the ways in which this problem is tackled by market and mixed economies
- determinants of supply and demand
- the main types of market structure, including perfect and monopolistic competition, monopoly and oligopoly, and their implications for price and output
- pricing strategy
- Michael Porter's Five Forces model of competitive structure
- portfolio approaches to SBU analysis, including the Boston Matrix and the Shell Directional Policy Matrix
- the working of the labour market – wage determination and employment levels; perfect competition and monopsony models of the labour market
- changes in the industrial and employment structure in the UK
- the feminisation of the workforce
- the growth of flexible forms of organisation and flexible working
- the nature and importance of the psychological contract
- the changing nature and role of trade unions
- HR responses to changes in the competitive environment.

3.1 ECONOMIC SYSTEMS

Different types of societies have organised their economies in different ways, but all have to produce answers to the same questions, whatever their economic system.

? REFLECTIVE ACTIVITY 3.1

Scarcity and choice

Economists often say that economics is about scarcity and choice. What do you think they mean by this? What problems are caused by the conflict of scarcity and choice?

Three main models have emerged:

- the command economy
- the market economy
- the mixed economy.

Of these we will consider the market and mixed economies in some depth. The pure command economy we can dismiss quite quickly, as it no longer exists in any real sense, except perhaps in North Korea. Here all economic decisions are made by the state, or rather by a central planning authority acting on the state's behalf, which decides what will be produced, by whom and who gets it. However, a command mentality was powerful in Western economies at least until the 1970s. In the UK, large sectors of the economy were controlled by the state through nationalised industries, which did not always make the best decisions on the allocation of resources. For example, the advanced gas cooled reactor (AGR) nuclear power programme cost over £50bn to build, but when British Energy was privatised in 1996, the AGRs were sold for £1.9bn, but only after the state agreed to underwrite liabilities for future decommissioning costs (Kay 2003, pp91–3).

Nor was the private sector much different. The 1960s and 1970s were the heyday of detailed quantitative corporate planning, which in many companies bore a close resemblance to the Soviet Union's Five Year Plans. A classic example, also discussed by Kay, was General Electric. When Jack Welch took over as CEO in 1981, he inherited what the US Defense Department described as 'the world's most effective strategic planning system'. Welch promptly dismantled the whole elaborate planning system, and in its place brought in systematic decentralisation of decision making (Kay 2003, pp96–7).

3.1.1 THE MARKET ECONOMY

Here economic decisions are taken on the basis of prices. There are no central planners, and decisions are taken by millions of individual consumers and producers. Producers produce only what they can sell to consumers, workers sell their services to producers and receive income, which they use to buy goods and services from the producers. In the last resort it is thus the consumers who decide what is produced (consumer sovereignty), and the economy is a closed two-player system.

Our core economic problems are thus answered as follows:

- What is going to be produced? – anything which consumers are prepared to buy (demand, in the jargon)
- How is it going to be produced? – in the most efficient way. If a producer is not efficient, he will be driven out of business by an efficient one
- Who is going to get it? – anyone who is prepared to pay for it

---

?   REFLECTIVE ACTIVITY 3.2

Market economies

1   What would you say are the strengths and weaknesses of the market system?

2   Can you think of any examples of pure market economies?

The basic principles of the market economy were laid down by Adam Smith in his *Wealth of Nations* in 1776.

Figure 3.1 Flows in the market economy

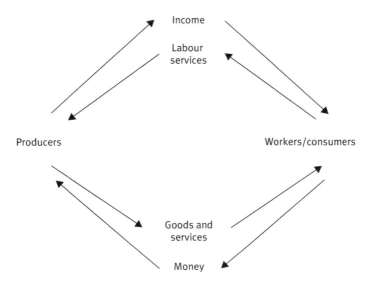

When the quantity of any commodity which is brought to market falls short of the effectual demand, all those who are willing to pay... cannot be supplied with the quantity which they want... Some of them will be willing to give more. A competition will begin among them, and the market price will rise...

By pursuing their own self-interest, producers and consumers would inadvertently produce an optimum result for society. 'It is not from the benevolence of the butcher, the brewer, or the baker that we expect our dinner, but from their regard to their own self-interest.

However, Smith also realised that there were risks that the market economy could be perverted:

People of the same trade seldom meet together, even for merriment and diversion, but the conversation ends in a conspiracy against the public, or in some contrivance to raise prices. (all quotes from Smith 1776, 1982).

Belief in the efficacy of capitalism and the free market peaked in the 1990s, following the reunification of Germany in 1990, and the collapse of communism and the Soviet Union in 1991. However, disillusionment soon set in. Russia demonstrated that without a strong state and the rule of law, capitalism would corrupt and be corrupted. Russia sank into 'crony capitalism' where super-rich oligarchs who had benefitted from rigged privatisations came to control the state. It required the rise of a strong totalitarian leader in Vladimir Putin to curb the power of the oligarchs (Gelman 2011). In the West, disillusionment came later, as failure to regulate world financial markets effectively led to the pressures which eventually caused the world crash in 2007–8. At the same time, rewards went disproportionately to those at the top. Between 2000 and 2009, the ratio between the pay of a FTSE 100 company CEO and average earnings rose from 69 times to 149 times (Rosselson 2012).

One of the leading critics of the free market system is the economist and political thinker Will Hutton, whose book *The State We're In: Why Britain is in Crisis and How to Overcome It* (1995), with its advocacy of an economy based on stakeholding was a key influence on the early years of New Labour. His latest book, *How Good We Can Be: Ending the Mercenary Society and Building a Great Country* (2015), criticises the short-termism of British industry. Terrified of losing their jobs, or of their companies being taken over, managers put short-term profits above everything else, with the result that too little is spent on investment in new equipment, on innovation or on training. He advocates a capitalist system more like that in Germany, where businesses take more of a long-term view, workers have a say in policy through the supervisory board system, and disparities in pay between the top and the bottom are smaller. The UK is also particularly vulnerable to takeovers. Between 1998 and 2005, the value of all Japanese mergers and acquisitions amounted to 2.5% of that country's gross domestic product, and US deals to some 10.7%. Over the same period, the comparable figure in the UK was 21.8% of GDP (Ford 2014).

An example of what Hutton criticises came with the attempted takeover of the Anglo-Swedish pharmaceuticals giant AstraZeneca by its US rival Pfizer in the summer of 2014. It was widely felt that the main motive behind Pfizer's bid was to minimise its own tax bill. Through a system called tax inversion, it could register itself in the UK if it took over AstraZeneca, and so pay less corporation tax in the UK than it would in the US. Political opposition to the bid in the UK was strong, and eventually Pfizer backed down. The US then moved to block the tax inversion loophole (Hirschler and Berkrot 2014).

A moral criticism of capitalism is made by Eve Poole in her book *Capitalism's Toxic Assumptions* (2015) which forms the basis of Reflective Activity 3.3.

?   REFLECTIVE ACTIVITY 3.3

Capitalism's toxic assumptions

In her book *Capitalism's Toxic Assumptions* (2015), the ethicist and theologian Eve Poole makes seven basic criticisms of capitalism's toxic assumptions:

1　Capitalism is based on competition, a male perspective (fight or flight), whereas a female perspective (nurturing and befriending) would stress co-operation

2　Markets are assumed to be self-regulating (the 'invisible hand')

3　An over-emphasis on utility, which leads to a neglect of ethics

4　Agency theory, which suggests that everyone is motivated by self-interest, and which leads to an unhealthy 'us and them' perspective in organisations

5　The idea that the market price is always the fair price

6　The concept of shareholder value, which argues that companies should be run in the sole interests of their shareholders

7　Limited liability, which provides shareholders with too much protection

Critically examine each of Poole's toxic assumptions.

3.1.2 MIXED ECONOMIES

In practice all economies are mixed to a greater or lesser extent. Command elements commonly include:

- a framework of law – the law of contract, company law
- publicly provided social goods like defence, police, education, welfare and health

- publicly owned industries – the BBC in the UK, Amtrak in the US, Electricité de France in France
- state regulation of the level of economic activity
- control of economic behaviour – employment law, anti-trust law, anti-discrimination law, etc
- often the use of taxation to redistribute income as well as to raise revenue for public services

It is interesting that some of these elements were recognised by Adam Smith. He argued for a state system of education, nearly a century before it was introduced in the UK in 1870, and he also advocated a progressive taxation system: 'It is not very unreasonable that the rich should contribute to the public expense, not only in proportion to their revenue, but something more than in that proportion' (Smith 1776, 1982).

Indeed, the state is essential to the efficient working of a capitalist economy. As President Obama said in a campaign speech in July 2012, 'Look, if you've been successful, you did not get there on your own... If you were successful, somebody along the line gave you some help.' He cited great teachers, government research, and roads and bridges as examples, echoing the work of the liberal sociologist Leonard Hobhouse (1864–1929), who argued that government investment, funded by taxation, was a fundamental requirement for effective capitalism, and that capitalism required the interaction of society, social capital and the entrepreneur. It is perhaps significant that Obama's argument was immediately condemned by Fox News as 'socialism'. (Hutton 2012). It is significant that many of the most important technological innovations of the twentieth century, including jet aircraft, the computer and the internet, were promoted and financed through state intervention.

Throughout the rest of this chapter, we will be analysing the working of the mixed economy, with particular reference to the UK.

CASE STUDY 3.1

MARKETS IN THE NHS

In an article in *The Guardian* in 2007, a Sheffield GP, Paul Hodgkin, discussed the different types of market operating in the NHS.

- *The market economy.* This is the model which underpins the concept of patient choice, where informed consumers choose between different providers, thus driving up quality. Unfortunately, there are at least two snags. Firstly, in the public sector, markets are zero sum. As spending is capped, more spent on one procedure means less on another. Secondly, consumers (patients) are not informed, and they are not attempting to 'buy' a desirable good. No-one in their right mind would positively desire a major operation! The patient

is by definition anxious, and frequently not in a fit state to take an informed decision.

- *The barter economy.* This most clearly operates between the NHS and social services. Partnerships here are only possible given local give and take and mutual obligations – 'do me a favour today with patient X, and next month I'll do the same for you'.
- *The centrally planned economy.* Evidence-based medicine, treatment dictated by the National Institute for Health and Clinical Excellence, targets, star ratings, inspections and so on.
- *The gift economy.* This has always existed throughout the public sector, and is part of the public service ethos – giving more than is strictly required

under contract, for the good of the patient. Hodgkin sees this as being eroded in the NHS, as new contracts become much more restrictive and time-based. A classic example of the gift economy which Hodgkin does not mention was identified in the NHS many decades ago – the totally free and voluntary UK blood donor scheme (Hodgkin 2007).

The Thatcher, Blair and Cameron governments brought in many aspects of the market economy – competition, targets, outsourcing. The result is that the NHS has become fragmented, with some parts competing against each other, and other parts fighting off outsourcing to the private sector. This has led to the development of a defensive, frightened, blame culture, which is the opposite of the open, candid, learning culture that the NHS needs.

One example is the controversy over the NHS 111 patient advice service. The Labour government set up NHS Direct, a national phone-based advice service, run directly by the NHS, which built up a good reputation. NHS Direct operated on the basis of two call handlers to one nurse. As a result, qualified medical advice was readily available (BBC 2013b).

NHS Direct was replaced by the Coalition government with NHS 111, also phone-based, but run through 46 different local centres, for which organisations had to make tender bids. Unlike NHS Direct, which was just an advice service, NHS 111 could request ambulances to take patients to Accident and Emergency. A quarter of the contracts were won by NHS Direct, some by local ambulance trusts, and the rest by the private sector, including 12 won by the private healthcare company Harmoni

(Lawrence 2013). One advantage of the new decentralised service should be increased local knowledge, but set against this are the diseconomies of scale caused by duplication. NHS 111 typically operated on the basis on 15 call handlers to one nurse. Rather than advice from a health professional, the handlers relied on problem-solving computerised algorithms. This was cheaper. NHS Direct typically cost £20 a call, while the NHS 111 contracts were typically tendered at £7.50–8.50 (BBC 2013b).

Throughout 2012 and 2013 there were growing complaints about the poor quality of the service, and in the summer of 2013, NHS Direct announced that it was pulling out of the contracts which it had been awarded, saying that it was losing too much money on them, as it had had tried to maintain its old staffing levels, with high levels of nurse input (Ramesh 2013; Wilby 2013).

Problems with NHS 111 continued during 2014, and became acute during the winter crisis of 2014–15, when the NHS Accident and Emergency service faced being overwhelmed. Dr Clifford Mann, President of the College of Emergency Medicine, blamed this partly on the computer software used. This was risk-averse, and frequently defaulted to sending the patient to A&E as the safest, even if not the best, option (Turner et al 2012; Pym 2014).

One lesson that can be drawn from this Case is that fragmentation of the NHS will often throw up unexpected costs. NHS 111 is cheaper to operate than NHS Direct, but it has the unintended consequence of increasing the cost of A&E when it sends the latter unnecessary patients.

3.2 MARKET STRUCTURES

Economists classify market structures by the number of firms within the market (and to a lesser extent the number of purchasers).

The main classifications are:

- perfect competition
- monopolistic competition
- monopoly
- oligopoly

There are also two other less commonly found firms

- monopsony
- bilateral monopoly

3.2.1 PERFECT COMPETITION

This is a market where no one producer has an advantage over any other producer. There are many producers, none of whom has a sufficient share of the market to be able to influence the market price. They are known as price takers. Similarly, there are a large number of buyers, who are also price takers. The price in the market is set by supply and demand.

Demand measures the amount of the good or service which buyers are willing to buy at a given price (note not the amount they need – demand is based on willingness to pay). Broadly speaking the lower the price the greater the quantity which buyers will demand. This enables us to plot a demand curve – in practice plotted as a straight line.

Figure 3.2 A typical demand curve

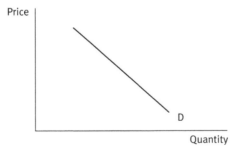

If the price rises, the quantity which buyers are prepared to buy will fall. This is known as a fall in quantity demanded. On the other hand, some external event may mean that buyers are prepared to buy more of the product at all prices – perhaps their incomes have increased. This is known as a rise in demand, and is illustrated on our diagram by a shift of the demand curve to the right. Similarly, a fall in demand is shown by a shift of the curve to the left.

Figure 3.3 An increase in demand

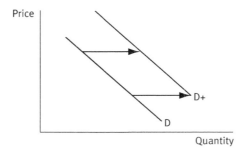

The same principles apply to supply. Broadly speaking, the quantity of a good which producers are prepared to supply is higher the higher the price, producing a supply curve. Again a movement along this line is known as a change in quantity supplied, a shift to of the curve rightwards or leftwards is known as an increase or decrease in supply.

Figure 3.4 The supply curve

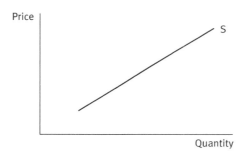

If we put together the supply curve and the demand curve, we get Figure 3.5. This shows that there is one unique combination of price and quantity where the two lines intersect (point E). This sets the price that will be charged in that market, and the quantity which will be bought and sold, and crucially this is an outcome which is equally acceptable to both buyers and sellers.

Figure 3.5 Supply, demand and equilibrium

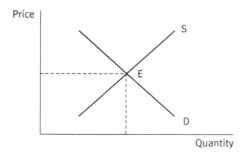

Oil prices

In 1973, OPEC quadrupled the world price of oil overnight. The result was a severe bout of stagflation for the world economy – simultaneous rising inflation and unemployment. In 1990–1, the oil price again rose rapidly in the build-up to the first Gulf War. However, after the war, oil prices quickly fell back, and by the late 1990s were at their lowest level for many years. In 2003, oil prices again rose rapidly in the build-up to the second Gulf war, but this time, after a brief fall in the immediate aftermath of the war, they have continued to rise, and on 2 January 2008 reached $100 a barrel, five times their low in the late 1990s. Despite this, world inflation stayed relatively low, and economic growth stayed high. Oil prices eventually peaked at around $150 a barrel, before collapsing after the onset of the world recession in mid-2008. After falling to around $35 they then recovered to stabilise at around $70 in mid-2009, although by 2011–12 they had risen again to around $100. In the autumn and winter of 2014–15, the price then collapsed again, from over $100 to around $45, recovering slowly in the spring of 2015 but falling again to $40 at the end of 2015.

Questions

1   Why were oil prices so high from the war in 2003 to mid-2008?

2   Why did the increase in the price of oil after 2003 not lead to stagflation, as in the mid-1970s?

3   Why have oil prices risen since the start of the recession, although many economies have not recovered to their 2008 levels?

4   What have been the consequences of the oil price collapse in 2014–15?

The product sold in a perfectly competitive market is assumed to be identical – thus there is no reason to favour one seller over another on grounds of quality or special features or service. It is also assumed that all players in the market are extremely well informed, and capable of reacting very quickly to any changes. There is thus no point in advertising – all products are identical and buyers know them to be identical. Buyers will react very quickly to any change in price, while sellers will very rapidly copy any innovation introduced by one of their rivals. Entry to the market is also completely free – anyone can enter or leave the market at any time.

Because of the nature of the market, there is no incentive for any one seller to cut his price – remember he can sell as much as he likes at the current market price. Conversely, if he raises his price even a fraction above the market level, he will sell nothing, because there is no incentive for his customers to stay loyal.

Economists freely admit that perfect competition is extremely unlikely to exist in the real world – its assumptions are too restrictive. Why spend so much space describing it, you may say? The reason is that it is a classic example of an economic model – it is a stylised attempt to explain behaviour, rather than a prescription for managers who want to make sound decisions. Models simplify the real world, and cut it down to its bare essentials, and on the basis of these bare essentials they make logical predictions. Thus the essence of the perfect competition model is to say that if the real world was like this, certain predictions would logically follow from it.

One consequence of the model is that it would lead to an efficient use of resources in the economy. Market forces would push production costs down to the minimum, and ensure that the most efficient production methods are used. Any firm which did not use them would be forced out of business. Profits would also be forced down to the minimum level required to keep firms in business. Any firm which made more profits than the minimum in the short term would be unable to sustain this position in the long term. Unfortunately this also writes economic progress out of the model. There is no incentive to innovate or develop new products, because any advantage will be immediately wiped out through perfect knowledge.

It is also possible to apply the perfect competition model to labour markets. The lower the wage, the higher the number of workers which will be demanded by employers, while the higher the wage the greater the incentive to work in that industry. The only difference is that people's labour services are being sold, rather than, say, apples. Again, the result will be a market equilibrium – exactly the number of workers who are prepared to work for the equilibrium wage will be employed. The labour market will be examined in more detail later in this Chapter.

3.2.2 MONOPOLISTIC COMPETITION

Rather more likely is that many firms will compete in a market, but each will sell a slightly different product. This type of market is classified as monopolistic competition. As the product is differentiated, the firms in the market have slightly more freedom in setting their prices. They can decide to charge a slightly higher price and sell a slightly lower volume of goods, and vice versa. To a small extent they are price makers. They can build up customer loyalty, and loyal customers will be prepared to pay a higher price for what they perceive as higher quality, or a closer match with their precise requirements, either in the product itself, or in the services which surround its delivery. Each firm is thus seeking to obtain a mini-monopoly for its product.

Note that a real difference in product is not necessary – what is required is that consumers perceive there to be a difference. Firms in monopolistic competition frequently advertise in order to differentiate their product, while firms in perfect competition do not, as they can sell all they wish anyway.

3.2.3 MONOPOLY

Theoretically, a firm has a monopoly if it is the only firm supplying a market – ie it has 100% of the market. This is very rare in practice, particularly if one defines a market widely. The Royal Mail had until recently a monopoly in the UK for delivery of letters of a certain weight, but we also need to include close substitutes for letters in our definition of this market. Once we do this, it is clear that the Royal Mail faced competition in information transfer from a host of organisations and services, including e-mail, faxes and courier services. Virtually the only organisation with anything approaching a world-wide monopoly is Microsoft, whose operating systems have about 90% of the PC market. Even here, in practice the monopoly is weakened by software piracy, with some estimates saying that half of all software in the UK is illegally copied.

In practice economists tend to define monopoly functionally – a firm is in a monopoly position if it is able to control the market price of the product it produces. This depends on the size of the firm relative to that of other firms in the industry. If firms in the industry tend to be large, the market leader may need to have perhaps half the market in order to dominate, but in an industry characterised by very small firms, 20% of the market may be enough.

Because it has some control over price, a monopoly can manipulate the price and the quantity which it produces in order to maximise its own profit. Thus price will tend to be higher and quantity produced lower than in a competitive market. This does not necessarily mean that a monopoly will make an excessive profit. If no one wants to buy the product sold by the monopoly, there will be no excessive profit. Being the only producer of horse-drawn hansom cabs is not the best short cut to a fortune!

However, monopoly does have a tendency to excess profit, as well as other disadvantages. It encourages inefficiency in management and production, as there is no competition to force efficiency, and, most crucially, monopoly leads to a misallocation of resources in the economy as a whole. This would tend to suggest that monopoly will not be in best interests of consumers, and therefore should be at a minimum be controlled, at best banned. This is broadly the approach taken by anti-trust legislation in the US.

In practice things are not so simple. Often monopolists can gain significant cost advantages (economies of scale) purely because they are big, and the end result might be both higher profits for the monopolist, and a lower price for the consumer. As we will see later, this argument is put forward by supermarkets in the UK. This argument (the natural monopoly argument) has been put forward to oppose the break-up of British Rail at privatisation. Similarly, it may be judged desirable for a company to have a monopoly in the UK market, if the result is that it is big enough to compete efficiently on the world market. As a an example, the Monopolies Commission in the 1970s and 1980s was prepared to tolerate both British Airways's dominant position in the UK market, and its takeover of competitors like British Caledonian and Dan-Air.

There is also a view that monopolies and monopoly profits may well be a necessary part of the competitive process (Schumpeter 1976). Entrepreneurs are continually trying to exploit new opportunities. If they do so, they will achieve a temporary monopoly. Unless this monopoly arises from the sole ownership of a resource for which there is no substitute, the monopoly will be temporary because other firms will recognise the opportunity and enter the market, or they will devise substitute products. Schumpeter called this process 'creative destruction'.

Profits may thus be true monopoly profits, based on ability to restrict entry to the industry; windfall profits, based on short-term fluctuations in the environment and which in different circumstances could be windfall losses, or entrepreneurial profits, based on superior foresight or management, exploiting opportunities which were open to all. This view is supported by the law on patents. Anyone may invent a new process or product, but the reward for doing so is to be granted a temporary monopoly by the state, in return for the entrepreneurial risk and research and development expenses which have been incurred. Patent protection is the driving force behind industries like pharmaceuticals.

Following this view, the key element in assessing monopoly power is not market share but barriers to entry. This has led to the development of the concept of contestable markets (Lipsey and Chrystal 1999). Markets are contestable if entry is easy, entrants can compete on equal terms with incumbents, and they are not deterred by the threat of retaliatory price cutting by incumbents. The threat of entry to the market can be as effective as actual entry.

3.2.4 OLIGOPOLY

An oligopoly exists when a few large producers control a market between them. The number of firms may vary between two (a duopoly) and about a dozen, and the products can be homogeneous or diversified. Oligopolies are also known as complex monopolies, and it is the latter term which is used by the UK competition authorities. In all cases, the firms in the industry are interdependent. The performance of each firm depends not only on its own actions, but also on the actions of the other firms in the industry. Thus, for example, before an oligopoly takes the decision to raise its prices, it must decide whether the other firms are likely to follow, or to keep their prices down and aggressively push to increase their market shares.

Oligopoly is extremely common in the UK. Indeed, think of any major consumer good or service, and it will almost certainly be supplied by oligopoly firms – cars, petrol, banks, cigarettes, soap powder, instant coffee, chocolate, baked beans, etc.

One way of measuring oligopoly is by calculation of the Five Firm Concentration ratio. This is simply the share of the market in percentage terms held by the five largest firms. The higher this figure, the higher the degree of oligopoly.

Table 3.1 UK concentration ratios 2004

Industry	Concentration ratio
Five most concentrated	
Sugar	99%
Tobacco	99%
Gas distribution	82%
Oils and fats	88%
Confectionery	81%
Five least concentrated	
Metal forging	4%
Plastic products	4%
Furniture	5%
Construction	5%
Structural metal products	6%

Source: National Statistics Economic Trends: Concentration Ratios (2004)

Remember that these figures only cover UK producers. As a result of globalisation, all manufacturers are subject to greater and greater international competition, and of the industries listed in Table 3.1 only in tobacco can the UK be considered world class. Real oligopoly power is higher in services, where there is less chance of competition from imports. In the case of food production and retailing we have a bilateral oligopoly. Many branded goods are produced by oligopolies, and then sold through oligopolies.

Firms in an oligopoly market have a choice between a number of broad types of behaviour.

Collusion

One possible outcome is that the firms in the industry join together and collectively behave as if they were a monopolist. They can then collectively exploit any monopoly profits which are available. An extreme form of this type of behaviour is a cartel or price ring like OPEC (the Organisation of Petroleum Exporting Countries). Unfortunately from the point of view of potential cartel members, in most countries cartels and other forms of collusive behaviour are illegal. Cartels also tend to be unstable. They must have some mechanism for dividing up production and market quotas among their members, and this is fraught with difficulty. There is also a great temptation for individual members to cheat on their quotas. The cartel may be undercut by new producers (as with UK oil in the 1970s or fracking in the US in the 2010s), or new substitutes may be developed (as happened to a limited extent after the oil price hikes of 1973 and 1979).

Price war

An opposite possibility may be a price war, with the aim of driving the competition out of business, and eventually emerging with a single firm monopoly, which can then be exploited. The enormous risk, of course, is that you might lose, and yourself be forced out of business. In nearly all cases, the stakes are simply too high, and the risks too great. Indeed, in many cases it is only the market leader which can afford the risk of a price war, and it is the market leader which has the least need of one. In practice, most apparent price wars are extremely limited, and are used by the market leader as a sharp shock to the rest of the industry to stay in line. There are also risks in winning a price war. Driving a weak competitor out of business may just create a vacuum which can be filled by a much more formidable rival. A parallel would be the decision taken by the US to disband the Iraqi army after victory in the Iraq war in 2003. This left a military and political power vacuum which was quickly filled by sectarian militia groups, by Al-Qaida, and eventually by Islamic State.

Non-price competition

Rather than risk an all-out price war, firms will frequently engage in non-price competition – they will compete on everything except price. This might include competitions, quality, individual features, BOGOF (buy one get one free – for a limited period). The aim is not to drive the competition out of business, but to gain a marginal increase in market share. All participants understand the rules of the game, and know very well that the war is limited not total. Another possible form of non-price competition is complexity. In the old days, there was one mortgage rate, charged by all mortgage lenders on all mortgages. Now there are a multiplicity of different types of mortgage, each with its own terms and conditions, with the result that it is almost impossible to compare rates. The same thing has happened with utility pricing.

 OLIGOPOLY AND THE CUT-PRICE AIRLINE INDUSTRY

CASE STUDY 3.2

The cut-price airline industry has developed in the UK since the mid-1990s, on the lines pioneered in the US by South West Airlines. It is based on providing a no-frills service at low cost. It is dominated by two firms, Ryanair and easyJet, who between them control half the total European low cost market. Both Ryanair and easyJet are constantly engaged in sniping at each other, with each claiming that it has the lowest fares, and that the other is inefficient, incompetent or worse. There appears to be every sign of a constant price war, with both companies sometimes in effect offering free flights, and offers of twice the fare back if a customer can find the same flight cheaper elsewhere. However, appearances can be deceptive. Until 2003, the main target of Ryanair's knocking copy was its *bête noire*, the Irish state airline Aer Lingus (which it unsuccessfully tried to take over in 2007), while easyJet's prime target was British Airways, and particularly its low cost subsidiary Go. Neither has the serious intention of driving the other out of business. Direct competition between them (in the sense of flights to and from the same airport) is limited. On a strict definition, Ryanair and easyJet are direct competitors on only one route, London Stansted to Rome Ciampino. As a result, the 'price guarantee' is almost meaningless. The price war is aimed much more at deterring new entrants to the industry (both Ryanair and easyJet have taken over one of their main competitors, Buzz in the case of Ryanair and Go in the case of easyJet), and to squeeze better terms out of airports (who gain from a big throughput of passengers).

Price leadership

Here one firm within the industry is regarded unofficially as the price leader. If the leader changes its prices, the other firms in the industry are likely to follow suit. In order to be legal, it is essential that there is no collusion between the firms.

Game theory

Here the firm makes assumptions about the nature of the environment and the behaviour of competitors. Game theory is a huge area, but two simple strategies which can be followed are *maximax*, where the firm assumes that the best possible combination of circumstances will happen, and chooses the strategy which will maximise its position in this favourable set of circumstances, and *maximin*, where the firm assumes that the worst will happen, and chooses the best (or least bad) strategy on these pessimistic assumptions.

3.2.5 MONOPSONY AND BILATERAL MONOPOLY

Monopsony is a market form where there is a monopoly buyer. Normally the monopsonist is the government or one of its agencies. For example, for all practical purposes the NHS is a monopsony buyer of pharmaceuticals in the UK. If we have a market where a monopoly is selling to a monopsony, we have a bilateral monopoly. This applies where the NHS buys a particular patented drug from one pharmaceutical company. Monopsony will be important in our later discussion of the labour market (as well as the buyer version of oligopoly, known as oligopsony!).

 THE CANCER DRUGS FUND

CASE STUDY 3.3

Healthcare in the UK is a classic example of a bilateral monopoly. On one side is the NHS, the monopsony purchaser of drugs in the UK, on the other side the pharmaceutical companies, each of which is a monopoly seller of a particular drug. The price of each drug will be decided by the bargaining power of the two sides.

The bargaining power of the NHS is increased by the National Institute of Health and Care Excellence (NICE). NICE authorises the use of drugs by the NHS, on the basis of their cost-effectiveness. This is measured in terms of Quality-Adjusted Life Years (QALYs) – the extra length of quality life which use of the drug provides. Drugs which cost less than £20,000 per QALY are approved, while those which cost between £20,000 and £30,000 per QALY may be approved. Drugs which cost more than £30,000 per QSLY will not normally be approved (NICE

2013). If a drug is not approved, NICE will negotiate with the drug company to obtain a price reduction. If this negotiation brings the cost within the £30,000 limit, the drug is then likely to be approved.

There is a particular problem with some cancer drugs, which are extremely expensive, but which provide only a few extra months of life. To appease the cancer lobby, the Coalition government set up the Cancer Drugs Fund, with a budget of £200m and a brief to purchase cancer drugs which had been rejected by NICE. By 2014 the budget had grown to £280m.

The Cancer Drugs Fund ensured that NICE would not be able to negotiate down the price of these drugs. It alters the bargaining power between the NHS and the pharmaceutical companies. Not surprisingly it is defended by the drug company lobby group, the Association of the British Pharmaceutical Industry.

It has been calculated that the £280m spent on the Fund has provided a benefit of 5,600 QALYs, a cost of £50,000 per QALY, way above the NICE upper limit. If the money had been spent elsewhere in the NHS, it would have provided a benefit of 21,645 QALYs. This raises an ethical issue – is it fair that cancer patients should have access to a resource which is not available to those with other illnesses? (McKie 2015). A study in February 2015 suggested that the NICE £30,000 limit was itself too high. A spending of £10m on a drug with a benefit of £20,000 per QALY

would produce a gain of 200 years of quality life, but there would be a loss of 270 QALYs elsewhere in the NHS, making a net loss of 70 QALYs (Boseley 2015a).

In mid-January 2015 NHS England announced that the Fund would exceed its 2014–15 allocation by £100m. In response, the size of the Fund for 2015–16 was increased to £340m, but approval was withdrawn for 25 of the least cost-effective treatments, leaving 62 treatments approved. This would save £80m a year. Patients currently receiving the unapproved drugs would continue to receive them. (Triggle 2015).

3.3 STRATEGIC RESPONSES

A later chapter on developing and implementing strategy will consider this issue in greater depth, but here we will consider strategic response in more general terms. Basically, an organisation can make only two responses if it is in an industry where it does not have monopoly or oligopoly power, and so is not in a position to manage its competition and its environment. It can opt for low price, or it can opt for differentiation. In the supermarket industry, Aldi and Lidl have opted for low price, albeit at the cost of low perceived quality, and have seized a niche in the market by doing so. Differentiation could include high quality, innovation or specialisation. The seminar activity at the end of this chapter examines other strategies adopted in the supermarket industry.

A firm in an oligopoly market has more freedom of manoeuvre, but it is constrained by the need to consider how its competitors will react to a change in its tactics. If it increases its price, and its competitors follow, the chances are that all firms in the industry will increase their profits, although if there is a suspicion of collusion, the competition authorities may intervene. However, if our firm increases its price, and the competition does not follow, our firm will lose sales, and almost certainly lose profit, while the competition will gain. A monopoly has a simpler decision to make. In principle it can choose whatever combination of price and quantity produced and sold which will maximise its profits, although in practice its ability to do this is constrained by the ability of new firms to enter the market (contestability).

3.3.1 PRICING STRATEGY

A fundamental distinction in economics is between price takers (who have no control over the price which they can charge) and price makers (who have some degree of control over their prices). As we have seen above, price takers are characteristic of perfect competition, while price makers have some degree of monopoly power. If we argue that perfect competition does not exist in the real world, all sellers are to some degree price makers, with the level of their control over prices dependent on their degree of monopoly power.

However, the degree of control over price depends not just on the position of the seller, but also on the perceptions of the buyer. Nagle and Holden (2002) identify nine factors that influence how price sensitive a buyer is likely to be:

1   *Reference price effect*: price sensitivity for a given product increases the higher the product's price relative to alternatives.

2   *Difficult comparison effect*: price sensitivity decreases when it is difficult to compare the product with alternatives.

3   *Switching costs effect*: the higher the investment a buyer must make to switch suppliers, the less price sensitive the buyer will be (for example, older consumers and utility prices).

4   *Price-quality effect*: buyers are less sensitive to price the more that higher prices signal higher quality.

5   *Expenditure effect*: The higher the percentage of budget accounted for by the purchase, the more price sensitive the buyer will be.

6   *End-benefit effect*: the smaller the given component's share of the total cost of the end benefit, the less sensitive the buyer will be to the component's price (think cigarettes and matches for a smoker).

7   *Shared cost effect*: the smaller the proportion of purchase price buyers must pay for themselves, the less price sensitive they will be.

8   *Fairness effect*: buyers are more price sensitive when the price is higher than they perceive as 'fair'.

9   *Framing effect*: buyers are more price sensitive when they perceive the price as a loss rather than a foregone gain.

3.3.2 ALTERNATIVE PRICING STRATEGIES

Different pricing strategies are appropriate in different circumstances. Here we examine some of the more popular.

- *Premium pricing.* Used where there is a unique brand and a substantial competitive advantage – top end cruises or first class air travel.
- *Economy pricing.* The opposite of premium pricing, a no frills low price. This is typical of budget airlines and of many supermarkets (see EDLP in Case Study 3.4).
- *Promotional pricing.* Money off vouchers, sales or BOGOFs (see Case Study 3.4 again).
- *Optional product pricing.* Charging more for optional extras. The budget airline Ryanair is a past master at this, even charging extra for things which few would see as optional, like buying a ticket!
- *Captive product pricing.* Where products have complements, charging a premium price for the complement as the consumer has no choice. The classic example was razors and razor blades, but the same is true of computer printers and toners/ink cartridges.
- *Penetration pricing.* The price charged for a new product is set artificially low in order to gain market share, and once this is achieved, the price is increased. This strategy was used by satellite TV companies in the UK.
- *Skimming.* A company charges a higher price for a new product because it has a substantial but short-term competitive advantage. It skims the cream off the market before competitors move in. New product pricing strategies were discussed by Joel Dean in a classic *HBR* article (Dean 1950, 1976).
- *Price discrimination.* Charging different consumers different prices for the same product. A classic example – the pricing strategy of the budget airlines – is discussed in Case Study 3.5. In order for price discrimination to work it is essential that the seller must be able to prevent arbitrage – the development of a secondary market in which the product or service can be resold. In the case of the airlines, tickets are non-transferable.

SUPERMARKET PRICING STRATEGY

CASE STUDY 3.4

Supermarkets in the UK are in intense competition with each other, and pricing strategy is one element of this competition. They have a choice of three basic strategies:

- Everyday Low Pricing (EDLP), where low prices are consistently maintained
- promotion pricing, where the general level of price is higher, but there is a rolling programme of special offer promotions, often BOGOFs (buy one, get one free)
- combination pricing, combining both EDLP and promotions.

Historically, the main proponents of EDLP have been Asda and Morrison, while Sainsbury led on promotions, and Tesco on the mixed strategy.

A survey by the Institute of Grocery in 2003 found that 60% of shoppers preferred EDLP, while 40% preferred promotions. EDLP was particularly favoured by lower income shoppers, and those in the north of England. BOGOFs were more favoured by larger households, shoppers who were not working, and those in the south-east. However, even those who favoured EDLP felt that it took much of the interest out of shopping. As Joanne Denney-Finch, the chief executive of the IGD, put it, 'It

is...clear that promotions are not just about reducing the overall cost of shopping, but are liked because they bring variety and excitement to what can be a routine task'. It is probably significant that the most successful supermarket of the 2000s, Tesco, consistently followed a mixed strategy (Food and Drink Europe 2003).

Attitudes may have changed with the onset of the recession. EDLP seems to have become much more popular with shoppers. All the major retailers now emphasise low prices, and price matching with their competitors, particularly with Tesco. This is true of Waitrose, which traditionally has emphasised quality rather than price, and of Budgens, which has relied heavily on fortnightly promotions backed by heavy local distribution of flier leaflets. Both now deliberately price match with Tesco on many products.

It should also be borne in mind that consumers may not be as price sensitive as supermarkets assume. A study in Florida found that fewer than half of supermarket shoppers knew the price of the article which they had just selected. Most under-estimated the price, and 20% could not even guess at the price (Skapinker 2004).

EASYJET AND DYNAMIC PRICING

CASE STUDY 3.5

The classic way to price a product is to charge each consumer exactly the same price. Tesco and Sainsbury do not haggle with their customers – a price is published and the customer takes it or leaves it. However, supermarkets do reduce prices as goods approach their sell-by date, or perishable goods are unlikely to keep until the next day. This is an example of dynamic pricing or yield management – if the alternative is to

throw the good away, any price for it is better than nothing.

A much more sophisticated use of the dynamic pricing model is common in the airline industry. Taking advantage of its computerised reservations system, and the deregulation of airlines in the US in the late 1970s, American Airlines introduced dynamic pricing in the early 1980s, charging different customers different fares, depending on when they booked their flight. This is much easier to do online than in the physical market, as the costs involved in changing prices are much lower. American is alleged to make up to $500m a year through its dynamic pricing system. It changes half a million prices each day, an enormous number, as it only carries 50,000 passengers a day (McAfee and te Velde 2005). The model is widely used by the low-cost airlines in the UK, and has been copied by full-cost carriers like British Airways. The result is that theoretically each passenger on a particular flight might have paid a different fare, although they are all consuming the same product – a flight from A to B.

The economic theory underlying dynamic pricing is price discrimination – the idea that different consumers will place a different value on the same product, and that if possible the seller will strive to extract as much of this value as possible from each customer (Weiss and Mehrotra 2001).

The classic model for dynamic airline pricing is that the price will start low for a flight which is several weeks or even months ahead. This will attract the tourist or leisure market, where customers are not prepared to pay a premium price, but are prepared to book some time ahead of the flight. As the date of the flight approaches, the price will rise, attracting business travellers, who are less price sensitive, and who may well have to fly at relatively short notice. As the date of the flight approaches, the price will fall if there are still large number of seats unsold, or will rise if the plane is nearly full.

To test the model, I plotted the prices charged by easyJet on one particular flight, flight 211 from London Stansted to Glasgow, departing on 3 July 2007 at 11.25am. I checked the price being charged on the easyJet website once a day from 3 June 2007 until the day of take-off on 3 July (easyJet 2007).

The results confirmed the classic model. The price on 3 June was £4.99, and remained at this level until 13 June, when easyJet started its summer sale, and the price fell to £2.99. It stayed at that price until 20 June, when it rose to £7.99, but it was back to £2.99 on the next two days. It then started a steady rise – £7.99 on 23 June, £11.99 on 24 June, and £16.99 on 27 June. The price remained at £16.99 until 1 July, when it rose to £30.99, and then to £38.99 on July 2 and 3.

I repeated this exercise in May–June 2015, plotting prices for flight 201 from London Stansted to Glasgow at 08.10 am from 11 May to take-off on 11 June (easyJet 2015). Two differences stand out. Firstly, the final price was much higher than in 2007, at £63.99, an increase of 63% on 2007, much more than the CPI inflation rate of 23%. Secondly, there was much less fluctuation in price, and no bargains. The lowest price recorded was £29.49, on 12 May and 20 May. The price was either £35.99 or £36.99 for 15 days, until it started to rise past £40 on 1 June.

Stelios Haji-Ioannou, the founder of easyJet, is a passionate advocate of dynamic pricing, and he has applied the concept in at least two other of his many ventures, easyCinema and easyInternetcafe. However, both of these projects were failures. Part of the problem was a general lack of demand for the products, but there was also a fundamental flaw in the dynamic pricing model as applied to these products. Although the supply conditions were appropriate for value management, this was not true of demand conditions. In the case of the airline, price discrimination is possible, because different customers do value a flight differently, but this does not really apply to a cinema seat or an hour in an internet café (*Economist* 2003a).

> ## ❓ REFLECTIVE ACTIVITY 3.5
>
> **The Serengeti National Park – an example of price discrimination**
>
> The Serengeti National Park in northern Tanzania is generally regarded as the finest game reserve in Africa. With an area of 15,000 square kilometres it is three-quarters the size of Wales, it is estimated to contain two million wildebeest, half a million zebra, and 3,000 lions (Briggs 2009). The park effectively continues over the Kenyan border as the Maasai Mara National Park, and it straddles one of the major road routes between Tanzania and Kenya.
>
> Entry charges to the National Park vary enormously depending on nationality. Citizens of the five East African Community countries (Tanzania, Kenya, Uganda, Rwanda and Burundi), pay 1,500 Tanzanian shillings a day (approximately $1 at summer 2012 exchange rates), while foreigners pay $50 a day (Tanzania National Parks 2009).
>
> Questions
>
> 1 Can the enormous differential in entry charges be justified?
>
> 2 Why not let Tanzanian citizens into the Park for nothing?

3.4 COMPETITIVE STRUCTURE

3.4.1 MICHAEL PORTER'S FIVE FORCES MODEL

The economic theory of market structure, distinguishing perfect and monopolistic competition, monopoly and oligopoly, provides a powerful but inevitably simplified model. The real industrial world is much more complex. One important model which attempts to match this complexity is Michael Porter's Five Forces model of competitive rivalry (Porter 1980).

According to the model, the structure of competition in an industry can be described in terms of five major forces. These are:

- the threat of entry of new firms
- the power of buyers
- the power of suppliers
- the power of substitutes
- the intensity of rivalry among existing forms.

Each of the five forces is itself determined by a number of different factors. When the five forces are completely analysed, this determines how attractive the industry is to firms within it, and those who might wish to enter it.

Unlike economic models, the value of this model lies not in its predictive ability, but in the way in which it provides a checklist whereby particular firms can clearly analyse and define their own position in relation to their own industry. It is a tool which can be used as the first stage of strategic analysis.

The threat of entry

The threat of entry of new firms to an industry depends on the extent of barriers to entry. These include:

- *Economies of scale*
  Some industries have very high economies of scale – unit costs of output fall considerably as output increases, as in the car industry or the aircraft industry. Others have very low economies of scale, for example estate agency. A new firm seeking to enter an industry with big economies of scale must either buy a high market share on entry or suffer a cost disadvantage. Economies of scale are measured by the concept of Minimum Efficient Scale (MES), or the market share which is necessary to compete at minimum unit cost. It is also possible to calculate the cost penalty incurred by producing at below this volume. However, note first that globalisation has meant increasingly that what is significant is not share of the UK market, but share of a world market, and secondly, that lean production and flexible manufacturing techniques like Just in Time have somewhat reduced the importance of economies of scale.

- *Capital requirements*
  Capital-intensive industries like the car industry have a very high cost of entry, while an on-line consultancy operating from home has a very low cost of entry.

- *Access to distribution channels*
  A new entrant must establish its own distribution channels. For example, it is difficult to persuade supermarkets to stock new products in competition with existing brands. Reforms in the tied house system, and the spread of the concept of guest beers, have made it easier for small real ale brewers to gain a foothold in the beer market.

- *Absolute cost advantages*
  Established firms in an industry frequently gain from a learning curve effect, which gives them a cost advantage over new entrants. In other cases incumbents may use a technology or process which is protected by patents.

- *Expected retaliation*
  The likely reaction of existing firms is key. If incumbents are expected to retaliate to defend their markets, entry becomes more difficult.

- *Government policy*
  In some cases, the government might restrict entry (commercial television and radio). In other cases, government policy might open up a market to competition (the telephone directory enquiries service).

- *Differentiation*
  If existing operators have established a strong brand image for their products or services, this effectively deters new entrants. Existing operators often produce a wide range of brands to plug all possible niches in the market.

- *Switching costs for buyers*
  If it is very expensive for buyers to switch to a new supplier, this will deter new entrants to the market. For example, if you have a gas central heating system, it is very expensive for you to switch to electricity, but very cheap to switch to a new gas supplier.

The power of buyers

Buyer power will depend on:

- *Concentration of buyers*
  If there is only a small number of buyers, buyer power will be high, particularly if the volume purchases of the buyers are high. For example, although cola drinks are sold through a multiplicity of outlets, high volume sales are dependent on the big

supermarket chains, and even Coca Cola does not have the muscle to dictate terms to them.

- *Alternative sources of supply*
  If the buyer is able to shop around, this will increase his power. This may come about because deregulation of markets has produced new competitors. For example, when the gas industry was privatised and deregulated, consumers became able to buy gas from a large number of possible suppliers, not just British Gas. Similarly, the ending of pre-entry trade union closed shops has helped buyers of labour such as the newspaper industry.

- *Component cost as a percentage of total cost*
  If materials form a high percentage of the total cost of a finished product, there is a greater incentive for buyers to shop around. Thus the provision of power to a steel works forms a high percentage of cost, while the provision of paper clips to a management consultancy forms a very low percentage.

- *Possibility of backward integration*
  If there is a risk that the buyer may be in a position to set up his own supply operation, this increases the buyer's power.

Power relationships between buyers and suppliers can be changed as a result of deliberate strategic decisions. For example, car manufacturers since the 1980s have followed a deliberate strategy of reducing the number of their suppliers. Suppliers have gained bigger orders and greater security, but at the cost of strict adherence to quality and JIT requirements.

Power of sellers

Seller power will depend on:

- *Number of suppliers*
  The smaller the number of suppliers, the greater their power, as in any other monopoly or oligopoly situation.

- *Switching costs*
  If switching costs to another supplier are high, this will increase seller power, particularly in a situation where the product supplied is highly specialised, and the supplier is integrated into the production process, for example in a JIT environment.

- *Brand power*
  If the supplier's brand is powerful, this will give him more bargaining power. For example, Heinz or Kelloggs, who do not produce own brands, can exercise influence over supermarkets, who have to stock the brand leader.

- *Possibility of forward integration*
  If there is a risk that the seller may be in a position to set up his own distribution operation, this increases the seller's power.

- *Dependence on customer*
  If the supplier is not dependent on selling a high volume of output to a particular customer, and his individual customers are generally small, this will increase seller power.

Threat of substitutes

The threat of substitution can take many forms. There could be technological substitution of one product for another – the fax for the letter, then the email for the fax. In the last resort all goods are substitutes for each other, because they are all competing for consumer spending. This is particularly true of non-essential goods, where there is the ultimate substitute of doing without.

Key questions that need to be addressed are:

- *Relative price and performance of substitutes*
  If substitutes are available that offer similar performance at comparable prices, the threat of substitution is very strong and limits are put on the ability to charge high prices – for example brands of pet food.

- *Switching costs*
  The cheaper it is for consumers to switch to other products, the higher the threat of substitutes. Switching costs for pet food appear to be zero, as long as the pet is prepared to eat the substitute!

- *Buyers' willingness to substitute*
  If an article is both low-cost and an infrequent purchase, little effort is likely to be put into shopping around. No-one shops around for the best value box of matches.

Competitive rivalry

Competitive rivalry is to some extent a function of the other factors. However, there are other special factors:

- *Industry growth*
  If the industry is growing rapidly, there is plenty in the cake for everyone so competition does not need to be intense. As an industry moves into the maturity phase of its life cycle, competition will become more intense.

- *High fixed costs*
  This is likely to lead to a high break-even point, and the likelihood of price wars in times of depression to maintain turnover. In the steel wars of the late 1990s the US and the EU each accused the other of dumping steel on export markets.

- *Volatile demand*
  This is likely to lead to intermittent over-capacity, with resultant price wars – steel again.

- *Product differentiation*
  The more homogeneous the product, the more intense the rivalry – steel yet again.

- *Extra capacity in large increments*
  The competitor making such an addition is likely to create at least short-term over-capacity. For example in the late 1980s, the Japanese car firms Nissan, Toyota and Honda all built new car assembly plants in the UK.

- *Balance of firms*
  If the number of firms is large and/or firms are of a similar size, the risks of aggression may appear acceptable, and rivalry will be intense, although probably not lethal. Conversely, a clear market leader can enforce discipline in the industry.

- *High exit barriers*
  If there are high exit barriers, excess capacity is likely to persist and rivalry to be intense. This would apply, for example, if there were high pollution clean-up costs associated with decommissioning a plant.

Bear in mind when using Five Forces that it is an analytical technique, which can tell you where you are now, probably why you are there, but not how to get where you want to get. There is also a danger is carrying out more and more detailed analysis – paralysis by analysis!

3.5 CRITICISMS OF FIVE FORCES

It must be remembered that Porter takes an economist's approach to his analysis. As a result, his model is over-simplified, and makes some basic assumptions. In particular, it is a static analysis. It assumes that change will be slow, and that as a result, the firm can take a planned approach to strategy once it has carried out its Five Forces analysis. This view is challenged by more recent writers on strategic management, who advocate a much more experimental emergent approach to strategic management (see Chapter 10).

The Five Forces analysis was a product of its time. Porter was writing before the economy was transformed by globalisation and the Internet. In a comprehensive critique of Five Forces, Larry Downes (1997) identified three new forces which had to be taken into account:

- *Digitalisation:* The development of the Internet means that all players now have instant access to enormous amounts of information. As a result, change has become much more rapid than in the late 1970s, and the environment much more unpredictable. As a result, new competitors can appear extremely quickly, and from outside the conventional definition of an industry. Examples would be the way in which the bookselling industry has been transformed by the rise of Amazon, and the travel agency industry by the rise of online bookings.
- *Globalisation:* Businesses now operate on a global scale, and customers, using the Internet, can shop around and compare prices on a global scale. A Five Forces analysis must now take account of global as well as of national trends
- *Deregulation*: In the UK, the US and the EU, many industries have been radically deregulated since Porter wrote about the Five Forces. Again, the effect is to make the environment more dynamic, complex and unpredictable. An example is the explosive growth of low-cost airlines like Ryanair and easyJet, and the effect which they have had on the environment facing full cost airlines like British Airways.

Remember, though, that just as Porter was a product of his time, so was Downes. He was writing in 1997, approaching the peak of the dot-com boom. Since the dot.com crash in 2000, views on the future of the Internet are perhaps less gung-ho than in 1997.

One study examined Dutch retailing between 1982 and 2000, in an attempt to evaluate whether Five Forces-style competitive analysis or Blue Ocean-type innovation was more effective. To their surprise they found evidence that a Blue Ocean strategy was sustainable. They suggested that a blended strategy might be optimal (Burke, van Stel and Thurik 2010, p28).

Sarah Coles re-examined Five Forces in 2009 (Coles 2009). Her main criticisms are that Five Forces

- does not consider the role of the government, corporate social responsibility or business ethics
- provides a snapshot of the competitive position, rather than a dynamic picture
- doesn't explain how to define an industry
- doesn't consider internal factors such as company history or culture
- can become a tick-box exercise

Other criticisms have been made of the model:

- Not only does it ignore the general influence of government, it also does not consider the importance of regulation as a restraining factor on the corporation. It is also very much a private sector model, and so much less relevant to the public and not for profit sectors – a reflection of its US origins perhaps.

- It assumes that competition is a zero-sum game – if one side wins, the other loses. This ignores the more recent development of co-operative strategies such as strategic alliances or joint ventures.
- It stresses efficiency at the cost of effectiveness, and so may discourage innovation. Sumantra Ghoshal (2000) has developed this point. He argues that an excessive preoccupation with competition and market forces, by stressing efficiency at the cost of effectiveness, will discourage innovation.
- The internet has revolutionised access to information. This has fundamentally altered the relationship between buyers and sellers (Dalken 2014)

Porter's response (Porter 2008) follows logically from his background as a classically trained economist. He says 'in essence, the job of the strategist is to understand and cope with competition'. Given this concern with competition, factors such as the government, regulation, and ethics are not relevant, although they may be key for other aspects of strategy-making. He says that government is not a sixth force, but an influence, albeit an important one, on the five competitive forces.

He argues that what he calls complements (reflected in strategic alliances) are already built into the model, and are important only to the extent that they affect the five forces. He recognises that industry structure and the five forces should not be static, but again he argues that change can be built into the model.

He recognises that it is possible to define the boundaries of the industry incorrectly, but argues that even if industry boundaries are drawn incorrectly, five forces analysis will still reveal important competitive threats.

Finally, Porter identifies common pitfalls in Five Forces analysis:

- defining the industry too broadly or too narrowly
- making lists instead of engaging in rigorous analysis
- paying equal attention to all of the forces rather than digging deeply into the most important ones
- using static analysis that ignores industry trends
- confusing cyclical or transient changes with true structural changes
- using the framework to declare an industry attractive or unattractive rather than using it to guide strategic choice.

In conclusion, I would feel that Five Forces is still a necessary technique, although it is not a sufficient one. As one of a range of analytical tools, it is invaluable.

 A FIVE FORCES ANALYSIS OF RYANAIR

CASE STUDY 3.6

Ryanair is one of two firms (with easyJet) that dominates the budget airline industry in the UK. A Five Forces analysis of Ryanair would be as follows:

Power of suppliers

Two main suppliers are of particular importance to Ryanair. One is Boeing, because Ryanair only operates one type of plane, the Boeing 737. This would suggest that Boeing has considerable power. However, Ryanair has power as a big purchaser, and also takes advantage of fluctuations in the market for aircraft. It tends to place big orders at times of global low demand for aircraft, and can thus extract very good terms from Boeing. It has also flirted with the Chinese aircraft manufacturer Comac, which is developing a rival to the Boeing 737. However, switching to another supplier would lead to high pilot retraining costs for Ryanair.

The other important suppliers are operators of airports. Ryanair is notorious for using secondary airports, which are desperate for Ryanair's business, and as a result they offer the company very favourable terms.

Power of buyers

Ryanair's buyers (customers) have high but individual bargaining power because switching to another airline is simple and free. In addition, there appears to be little if any brand loyalty to Ryanair. Here Ryanair may have been its own worst enemy. Historically its attitude to customers verged on contempt, which hardly inspires customer loyalty.

Availability of substitutes

In theory, easyJet is a direct substitute for Ryanair, but, as noted in Case Study 3.2, there is little direct competition between the two airlines. There are few other substitutes. High speed rail competes with airlines over short distances, but this only really applies to routes such as London to Manchester, Paris or Brussels.

Threat of entry

It is very easy to set up a new small airline, but an airline the size of Ryanair has huge economies of scale, which would not be available to a new entrant. The only serious risk would be if a rival European low-cost airline, such as German Wings, the low-cost subsidiary of Lufthansa, decided to enter the UK market.

Competitive rivalry

Rivalry with other airlines is intense, but, as with most oligopoly industries, unlikely to be lethal.

Sources: Milmo (2011); Dudovskiy (2012)

3.6 COMPETITOR ANALYSIS

Porter's Five Forces is a valuable technique, but as it is industry-wide, it does not necessarily tell a firm a great deal about its direct competitors. Here it is useful to identify strategic groups. These are organisations within an industry or sector with similar strategic characteristics, following similar strategies or competing on similar bases. In grocery retailing, for example, Johnson et al (2011) identify supermarkets, corner shops and convenience stores as different strategic groups. They suggest two key characteristics of strategic groups – the scope of an organisation's activities (product range, geographical coverage) and resource commitment (brands, marketing spend, etc.).

The strategic group concept is valuable in three ways:

- understanding competition
- analysis of strategic opportunities
- analysis of mobility barriers

3.6.1 PORTFOLIO ANALYSIS

In the 1970s and early 1980s, strategic emphasis was on organisations building up a balanced portfolio of activities, or Strategic Business Units (SBUs). Several techniques were developed to assist with analysis of portfolios of SBUs.

3.6.2 BOSTON MATRIX

This technique was developed in the 1970s by the Boston Consulting Group, and plots SBUs according to their rate of market growth and their market share.

Figure 3.6 The Boston Matrix

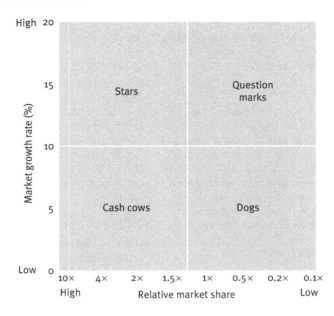

Market growth rate is arbitrarily divided into high growth and low growth, ranging between 0 and 20% per annum. Market share is assessed as share relative to that of the largest competitor, with a high of ten times the nearest rival, and a low of one-tenth. SBUs are plotted on the matrix, with their precise position within a cell depending on their exact market share and market growth rate.

The significance of the Boston Matrix is that an SBU's position on the matrix has an impact on its profits and its cash flow. One of the main selling points of the technique is the colourful names attached to the various cells (Joyce and Woods 1996).

- *Dogs:* They have a weak market share in a low-growth market. They generate a very low profit or even a loss, and also may well have negative cash flow. They absorb management resources, and the organisation must decide whether they are worth keeping in the long term, closed down or sold off.
- *Stars:* They have a high market share in a high growth market. Production will be at relatively low cost because of economies of scale, and profits are likely to be sound. However, because the market is growing rapidly, heavy investment will be needed to sustain market share. Cash flow is therefore likely to be at best neutral.
- *Question marks*: They have a low market share in a high growth market. This means that like the stars they need heavy investment, but as they are not the market leader they cannot fully exploit economies of scale. Cash flow is likely to be negative, but profits may well be positive. Management has to take hard decisions – either close down (on the assumption that the question mark may turn into a dog) or sit it out (on the assumption that it will turn into a cash cow).

- *Cash cows*: They have high market share in a low growth mature market. In the short and medium term this is an ideal position. Because the product is a market leader, it will be low cost, and it does not need heavy investment to cope with market growth. It is therefore likely to produce both profits and positive cash flow, which can be milked, but which will not last for ever.

Two further types have also been identified off the bottom of the matrix. These are *war horses* (high market share and negative growth – a cash cow on its last legs), and *dodos* (low market share and negative growth – dead dogs!)

The strategic implications are that an organisation should aim for a balanced portfolio of SBUs, which should include products which can evolve through the sequence of question mark – star – cash cow. Some organisations, particularly at the height of the popularity of conglomerates in the 1980s, became extremely successful by identifying and exploiting cash cows. One such was Hanson Group, whose strategy was to purchase cash cow products/companies (Imperial Tobacco in cigarettes, London Brick in bricks, Ever Ready in batteries), put in the minimum level of new investment, and exploit the cash-generating potential of the products.

The ideal types identified in the Boston Matrix also have implications for HR practice. The dog business will be mainly concerned with redundancy and redeployment. Star businesses are growing rapidly, so the HR priorities are recruitment and flexibility. Question marks ideally should be converted into stars, which will require a willingness to embrace change, and an emphasis on training and development. Cash cows place an emphasis on efficiency and effectiveness, and on customer service, which will require an emphasis on training, motivation and reward (Christy and Christy 2009).

There are, however, some weaknesses in the Boston Matrix approach. One is that there is no clear-cut way to define markets. If the market is defined too narrowly, the organisation will over-state its market strength, and so tend to ignore 'over the horizon' competitors, who may be quietly building up their strength in a related market. Possibly more serious is that the matrix ignores any synergy factors. Synergy is defined as the way in which the whole organisation is greater than the sum of its parts. SBUs are not totally self-contained – they often provide each other with benefits, such as sharing production processes or distribution channels, or being part of a balanced catalogue of products. As a result, if an organisation decides to kill off a dog product, this may have adverse impacts on its other products.

A final weakness is that it assumes a simple relationship between market leadership and profitability. This ignores the way in which many organisations have prospered long-term by exploiting small niche markets. Despite these weaknesses, however, the Boston Matrix has been used successfully by a number of companies, including Black and Decker Europe, although alongside other techniques (Walker 1990).

3.6.3 SHELL DIRECTIONAL POLICY MATRIX

This technique, developed by the Shell Chemical Company, meets some of the criticisms of the Boston Matrix. Rather than using market share as a variable, it uses the enterprise's competitive capabilities, assessed as weak, average or strong. This can take into account factors such as managerial skill, possession of appropriate technology and competencies, etc., as well as market share. Market growth rate is replaced by prospects for sector profitability, which again can include other factors. Finally, the analysis is made more discriminating by being based on a 3×3 matrix rather than the Boston Matrix's 2×2.

Figure 3.7 The Shell Directional Policy Matrix

Prospects for sector profitability

		Unattractive	Average	Attractive
Enterprise's competitive capabilities	Weak	Disinvest	Phased withdrawal	Double or quits
	Average	Phased withdrawal	Custodial growth	Try harder
	Strong	Cash generation	Growth leader	Leader

? REFLECTIVE ACTIVITY 3.6

Killing the dog

The board at Gamma Manufacturing was deeply divided. Under discussion was Product X, which had been a source of argument within the company for years past. The finance director wanted Product X dropped. He argued that it had absorbed considerable development funds over the years, but had never fulfilled its original promise. It tied up valuable production capacity in the factory, and wasted a lot of management time. 'It's a dog,' he said. 'We should put it out of its misery now.'

The marketing director disagreed. She argued that a lot of time, energy and money had been put into the product, and it would be a shame to waste all this just at the point when it might be about to take off. She also made the point that it filled a hole in the product mix. With some customers, it was important to be able to offer a complete product line, including Product X. 'If we haven't got X, I can name at least two big customers who will go straight to the competition,' she said.

Question

If you were the managing director, how would you evaluate the arguments put forward by the finance and marketing directors?

3.7 THE WORKING OF THE LABOUR MARKET

The same supply and demand analysis which we discussed earlier in relation to goods can be applied to labour, although, as we will see, there are some important differences.

3.7.1 DEMAND FOR LABOUR

Demand for labour is a derived demand. No employer will demand workers purely because he enjoys employing them. They are demanded because the output which they will produce is valuable to the employer. Demand for labour is thus derived from the demand for the goods or services which they produce.

To understand the demand for labour, we have to consider the law of diminishing returns. This states that marginal output (the addition to total output resulting from the employment of one more worker) will fall as more and more units of labour are combined with a fixed quantity of other factors of production (land and capital). The classic example is an allotment of, say one acre, which has a fixed quantity of gardening tools. One worker will grow very little on the plot, as he has to handle all the tools. Two workers are likely to produce more than twice as much as one worker, because they can specialise (one may be best at digging, the other at weeding). There are increasing returns to scale. Adding a third worker may well add more again. But employing a fourth worker causes co-ordination problems, particularly if there are only three spades available. The fourth worker adds less to total output than the other three. There are diminishing returns. Things get even worse with five workers. A typical situation is illustrated in Table 3.2.

Table 3.2 Diminishing returns to scale

Labour input (workers)	Total output product (units)	Marginal physical product (units)	Price of product (£)	Marginal revenue (£)	Wage rate (£)
1	8	8	10	80	70
2	17	9	10	90	70
3	25	8	10	80	70
4	32	7	10	70	70
5	38	6	10	60	70
6	43	5	10	50	70
7	47	4	10	40	70

At a wage rate of £70, it is just worth employing the fourth worker, but not the fifth, because this would lose the firm £10. If the wage rate rises to £80, it is only worth employing three workers, while if it falls to £60, it becomes worth employing five workers. Plotting this on a graph gives us the familiar downward-sloping demand curve. Demand thus equals marginal revenue product.

Figure 3.8 The demand curve for labour

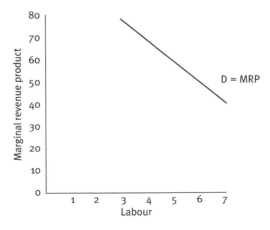

The demand curve for labour can shift to the left or right if the marginal revenue product of a given quantity of labour changes. The curve will shift to the right (an increase in demand for labour) if either marginal physical product increases (a rise in productivity per worker) or the price of the product increases.

3.7.2 THE SUPPLY OF LABOUR

From the point of view of an individual worker, as wage rates rise, the average worker is prepared to work more hours per week. The extra money earned, and the purchases of goods and services which it represents, is more attractive than extra hours spent in bed. Workers substitute work for leisure as wages increase. However, beyond a point, high wages do not tempt a worker to put more hours in. It is more attractive to work fewer hours and spend more time on leisure. This is known as the income effect. At high levels of income, the positive substitution effect of a wage increase is more than offset by the negative income effect. The result is an individual supply curve like that shown in Figure 3.9.

Figure 3.9 The supply curve for an individual worker

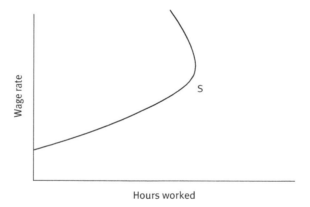

The supply of labour to a firm depends on assumptions which we make about the type of labour market facing the firm. If we assume that the labour market is perfectly competitive, there are many firms hiring many individual workers. In these conditions, an individual firm can hire an extra worker at the existing wage rate. In other words, the supply curve for labour facing that firm is perfectly elastic, as shown in Figure 3.10.

Figure 3.10 Supply of labour to a firm in perfect competition

However, things are very different if we assume that the employing firm has some monopoly power (ie that it is a monopsonist, or a monopoly purchaser of labour). The supply curve facing this firm will be upward-sloping, which means that to employ more workers, it needs to offer a higher wage. The cost of employing an extra worker (the marginal cost) will be higher than the wage rate the firm has to pay the extra worker. This is because it has to pay the higher wage to all its other employees as well. This is illustrated in Table 3.3 and Figure 3.11.

Table 3.3 Labour costs facing a monopsonist employer

Units of labour supplied	Cost per unit £	Total cost £	Marginal cost £
0		0	
1	20	20	20
2	40	80	60
3	60	180	100
4	80	320	140

Figure 3.11 Supply curve and marginal cost curve of labour facing a monopsonist employer

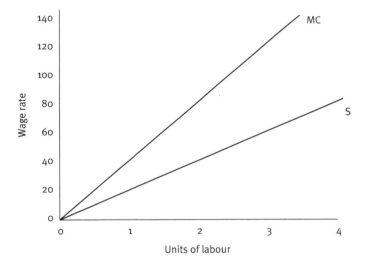

3.7.3 WAGE DETERMINATION

Putting together our demand and supply models helps us explain how wages are determined.

Firstly, assume that there is a perfectly competitive market for labour. Supply and demand would be as shown in Figure 3.12.

Figure 3.12 Employment and wage rates, perfectly competitive market

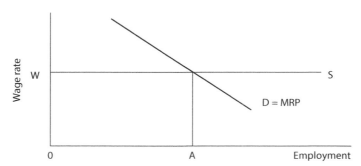

The wage rate, W, is set by the industry as a whole. The firm will employ OA workers at this wage rate.

As you would expect, the situation with a monopsony employer is more complex. Here the number of workers who will be employed is dependent on the firm's marginal cost curve (MC) not its demand curve (see Figure 3.13).

Figure 3.13 Wage determination under monopsony

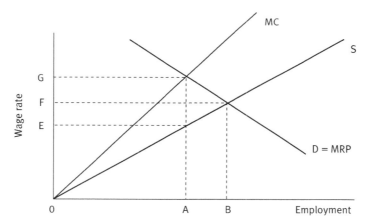

A monopsonist will only recruit labour if the marginal revenue product of that labour is equal to its marginal cost (ie point OA). However, it does not have to pay a wage OG. The wage rate depends on the supply curve, not the MC curve. It will therefore pay only OE.

If the market were perfectly competitive, OB workers would be employed, and they would be paid a wage OF. A monopsonist drives down both wages and employment compared with a perfectly competitive market.

3.7.4 WAGE DETERMINATION WITH TRADE UNIONS

The aim of a trade union in a labour market is to increase the bargaining power of labour. Rather than being an individual selling his or her labour to a monopoly employer, the union member becomes a part of a monopoly supplier of labour.

What the union does is to fix a minimum price for labour. The result is to kink the supply curve for labour, as shown in Figure 3.14.

Figure 3.14 Trade unions in a competitive market

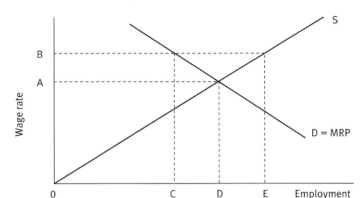

Here the union has set a floor for wages at OB. At this wage, the firm will employ OC workers. If there had been no union, the wage rate would have been lower, but employment would have been higher, at OD. At wage rate OB, OF workers would have chosen to work, but only OC can do so. As a result, there will be unemployment equal to CD.

The situation is totally different if the labour market is monopsonistic, as shown in Figure 3.15.

Figure 3.15 Trade unions in a monopsonistic market

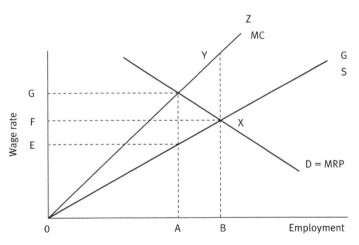

The union sets a floor wage of OF. The result is that the supply curve is now FXG, while the marginal cost curve is FXYZ. The result is that not only is the wage rate higher, at OF rather than OE, but the level of employment has also increased, from OA to OB – the total opposite of the perfect competition case. Workers are better off and more are employed, and the only loser is the employer, who will lose some of his monopoly profits.

It can be argued that unions are not only good for workers, they are also good for employers. This is because unions can exert discipline over their members. If an employer wishes to introduce change, and it is not unionised, it will need to negotiate individually with all workers, which will be expensive and potentially disruptive. On the other hand, if it can persuade the union to support the change, its introduction will be much easier. This is the reasoning which underpins the TUC's New Unionism project, and the moves towards social partnership, which are discussed later in this chapter.

For an extensive discussion of wage determination see Anderton (2006, pp461–515, or for a more scholarly approach, Manning (2003).

CASE STUDY 3.7

IMPACTS OF THE NATIONAL MINIMUM WAGE AND THE LIVING WAGE

The National Minimum Wage (NMW) was one of the major labour market reforms of the first New Labour government, introduced in April 1999 at a rate of £3.60 an hour. The rate is set annually by the Low Pay Commission, an independent body with three employer representatives, three workers and three independents.

Successive increases saw it rise to £5.80 in October 2009. This represented an increase of over 60% in nominal terms, and over 30% in real terms (after adjusting for changes in the retail price index). The NMW has risen faster than average earnings. Between 1999 and 2007 it rose from 47 to 52% of median earnings. The increase in 2009 was minimal (only 7p an hour) but this has to be set against a fall in the Retail Price Index and a very small increase in average earnings. The NMW rose only slowly during the recession, and by 2014 was £6.50 an hour.

It is clear that the NMW has had an impact on wages. When it was first introduced, it raised the pay of between 5 and 6% of workers (1.2 to 1.3 million workers) by about 15% on average. The effect was much more marked for women, 8.5% of whom gained in 1999, compared with 3.2% of men.

The effect on employment is much less clear-cut. As we found earlier in relation to trade unions, there are two conflicting theoretical perspectives. Just like a trade union, the NMW sets a floor to wages. One perspective is the classical (perfect competition) model, which argues that the result will be a fall in employment. The other is the monopsony (imperfect competition) model, which argues that employment will increase, as a result of a squeeze on employers' profits.

The former view was taken by the Conservative Party in the 1990s. In 1991, the then Employment Secretary, Michael Howard, argued that a minimum wage would cost two million jobs. This would be caused both by the classical theory model, and by a knock-on effect, where higher paid workers demanded compensation in order to maintain their wage differential over the low paid, which would have the effect of increasing inflation and interest rates in the economy as a whole. The monopsonist view was taken by the Labour party, following a long socialist tradition dating back to the first call for a minimum wage by the Fabian Society in 1906.

In practice the effect of the NMW on employment has been complex. In some cases, the monopsonist model has applied, and both wages and employment have risen. In other cases, marginal firms have gone out of business as a result of the NMW, leading to a fall in employment. In cases where there is a large number of small employers, such as the care home sector, the market approximates more to the perfect competition than to the monopsony model, and there has been a small fall in employment.

In some cases the NMW has led to an increase in training, aimed at increasing the productivity of workers to compensate for the higher wage. There has also been some evasion of the NMW. One study suggested that 20% of workers who should have been paid at the minimum wage were actually paid below it in 2000.

The above effects seem to broadly cancel each other out, and the overall impact on employment has been minimal. As a result, there is now a political consensus on the NMW, and since the 2005 General Election, the Conservative party has pledged to keep it. Indeed, the Conservative Mayor of London, Boris Johnson, is a leading advocate of not just the minimum wage, but also the living wage.

Finally, the NMW has to be put in a wider context. Firstly, it is part of a wider package of welfare to work measures introduced by Labour, including the working families tax credit. Secondly, many of the poorest householders do not benefit from the NMW because they have no-one in employment – pensioners, the disabled, many single parents, and so on. Thirdly, many recipients of the minimum wage are second wage earners in a family where the primary wage earner is paid considerably more than the minimum wage.

Attention is now switching to the living wage. This is a wage rate which is calculated as the amount which is needed to provide a low but acceptable standard of living. While the minimum wage in 2014–15 was £6.50 an hour, the living wage was £7.85 outside London, and £9.15 in London (to reflect the higher cost of living in London).

Unlike the minimum wage, the living wage is voluntary, and by 2014, 18 companies from the FTSE 100 had signed up to it. KPMG, one of the leading advocates of the concept, found that 5.28 million UK workers are being paid less than the living wage.

Pro-living wage campaigners argue that workers who are paid the living wage have better morale, making them more loyal and more productive. Barclays found that its catering-staff retention increased from 54% to 77% following the introduction of the living wage, and its

retention rate for cleaning staff rose from 35% to 92%.

KPMG, which adopted the concept in 2006 for its catering, cleaning and postroom staff, says the annual costs of providing such services are £1m a year below the level when the project started. Higher wages were offset by reductions in recruitment costs, increased skills and productivity.

More than 80% of living wage employers believe that the living wage has enhanced the quality of the work of their staff, while absenteeism has fallen by approximately 25%. Two thirds of employers reported a significant impact on recruitment and retention within their organisation. Seventy per cent of employers felt that the living wage had increased consumer awareness of their organisation's commitment to be an ethical employer.

A living wage also saves money for the Exchequer. Many workers paid below the living wage are dependent on in-work benefits such as working families tax credits. Tax credits in the UK cost £11bn a year, in effect a subsidy to low-paying companies, and more than ten times as much as the cost of benefit fraud. The Low Pay Commission estimated its 12p an hour increase in the NMW in October 2013 would increase tax revenues by £110m and reduce benefit expenditure by £73m, suggesting a larger increase of about 50p an hour could save the exchequer about £750m a year. Research from the trade union Unite suggests that raising the minimum wage to the living wage level would create 30,000 new jobs, as extra spending spread through the economy.

Those who are more sceptical about the living wage point out that it is easy for organisations such as banks or accountancy companies, with large payrolls, but very few low-paid workers, to adopt the living wage. It is probably significant that until the autumn of 2015, none of the major UK retailers has signed up to the living wage. The first to adopt the living wage was Lidl, which estimated that the cost would be £9m a year. They were quickly followed by Morrison's.

In his July 2015 Budget, the Conservative Chancellor of the Exchequer, George Osborne, announced a new 'National Living Wage', of £7.20 an hour from April 2016, but only for workers over 25, increasing to £9.35 by 2020. Workers under 25 would receive the (lower) National Minimum Wage. Osborne's proposal has been criticised on several grounds – it is lower than the living wage as defined by the Living Wage Foundation, it does not include a higher rate for London, where living costs are much higher, and it introduces a further distortion into the labour market by an artificial distinction at age 25. Employers may be tempted to recruit the under-25s, because they are cheaper, but they could then run the risk of falling foul of age discrimination law. In addition, Osborne also announced a reduction in tax credits, which in many cases will more than wipe out any gains in income from the National Living Wage.

Sources: Metcalf (2007); Draca and Dickens (2008); Greater London Authority (2011); *Economist* (2014c); Living Wage Foundation (2014); Giles (2014); Meadway (2015); Pooler (2015); Pratley (2015a); D'Arcy and Kelly (2015)

❓ REFLECTIVE ACTIVITY 3.7

The lemon

In 1970 the economist Akerlof discussed the case of the used car market as an example of imperfect information (Akerlof 1970). In the used car market, sellers have much better information than buyers. In particular, sellers know whether there is something wrong with the car they are selling – whether it is a lemon. Because the buyer knows that some cars being sold are lemons, but not which ones, the price in the market will be an average of the values of good cars and of lemons. If a particular car is a good one, the buyer will get a better deal than the seller. The opposite happens with a lemon. As a result, owners of lemons will be willing to sell, but owners of good cars won't. As a result, the proportion of lemons in the market will increase, the more suspicious buyers will be, and the more prices will be pushed down. The whole used car market will spiral downwards.

It is in the interests of potential sellers of good cars to do something to improve information in the market, and so to get better prices. There are many ways of doing this. One is to offer warranties on used cars, as is done by Ford through its dealers, for example. Another is to encourage buyers to get the car checked by an independent third party, like the AA.

From the point of view of the buyer, it is essential to know the reputation of the seller. Large, established main dealers of the major car brands are likely to have a better reputation than the back-street garage or cars sold through small ads in newspapers.

The lemon problem is really a modern application of Gresham's law, which dates from the sixteenth century. This law, 'bad money drives out good', was invented by Sir Thomas Gresham, treasurer to Queen Elizabeth I. Governments at the time were notorious for debasing the currency – mixing cheaper material into the gold and silver used to make coins. The government made a profit on this, as the coin cost less to make than its face value. If you had two coins, one of which you knew to be good (of full gold content), and the other to be debased, you would hoard the good one, and spend the bad one – bad money drives out good. Unfortunately, everyone else would know that only bad coins would stay in circulation, and as a result prices would go up. Gresham advised Elizabeth to avoid inflation by resisting the temptation to debase the currency.

1   Do you think the lemon model is relevant to wage determination?

2   Find out how eBay, the online auction site, gets round the problem that buyers know very little about the reputation of sellers on the site.

3.8 TRENDS IN EMPLOYMENT

3.8.1 CHANGES IN THE INDUSTRIAL STRUCTURE

In 1951, manufacturing accounted for a third of GDP and nearly 40% of employment. By 2001 employment in manufacturing had fallen to 14% of the workforce, although as the size of the workforce had increased considerably, the number working in manufacturing had only fallen from 8.7 to 3.7 million. Part of the reason for this fall is the shift of manufacturing jobs to eastern Europe and the Far East, a consequence of globalisation. Another reason is peculiar to the UK – the chronic over-valuation of the pound since the late 1970s, which made UK manufacturing uncompetitive, and which triggered recessions in the early 1980s and early 1990s. The trend continues – before the recession of 2008 there was much talk of an over-strong pound and a two-speed economy – booming services and recessionary manufacturing. By 2008, the number of manufacturing jobs was down to 2.8 million (10% of the workforce), a fall of nearly a million in seven years, and by 2015, it was down to 8% of the workforce and 10% of GDP (Clancy 2009; Department for Business, Innovation and Skills 2015). Where manufacturing has survived, the nature of work within it has changed, from skilled and semi-skilled manual work to much more knowledge-based and less manual work. Between 1978 and 2013, employment in manufacturing fell by 60%, in mining and quarrying by 80%, and in agriculture, forestry and fishing by 30% (CIPD 2013d; Holmes and Mayhew 2012)).

Services of all kinds have boomed, and have grown from about half of employment in 1966 to 83% in 2008. (Clancy 2009). In 2015, knowledge intensive services account for 34% of UK output and 29% of total employment, while health and social care account for 13% of employment (Department for Business, Innovation and Skills 2015).

There have also been changes in the occupational level of the workforce. The share of manual workers in the workforce fell from 64% in 1952 to 38% in 1991, with the biggest proportionate fall among unskilled manual workers, whose percentage has fallen by nearly two-thirds. Skilled manual workers have fallen from 25% of the workforce in 1951 to 12% in 2001, while the managerial professional and technical workforce has risen from 12% in 1951 to nearly 40% in 2001, and relatively poorly paid service sector jobs have also increased.

The public sector workforce stood at around 5.7 million in mid–2013, and made up just under 20% of total employment, lower than at any point in at least the last 40 years. Falls in privatised public corporations and the armed forces have been matched by growths in education and the NHS. The NHS and public education workforces have grown steadily over the last 50 years, both in size and as a proportion of the public sector workforce. This reflects a combination of sustained growth during times of buoyant growth in public spending levels and the fact that they were relatively protected from workforce cuts while other areas were making cuts (eg in the early 1990s and early 2010s). Together, these two functions made up 23% of the public sector workforce in 1961, 42% in 1991 and around 57% in 2013 (Cribb, Disney and Sibieta 2014).

The proportion of those in employment aged over 50 grew from 21% in 1992 to 29% in 2013, while those aged under 25 fell from 18 to 12%. The number of over-50s in employment rose by 3 million, while the number of under-25s fell by 800,000 (CIPD 2013d).

The above trends are typical of most of western Europe, although the proportion of workers in manufacturing is higher in Germany and Italy, and the proportion working in services higher in the Netherlands (Gallie 2000).

3.8.2 THE IMPACT OF THE RECESSION ON HR

Clearly one of the major impacts of the recession on HR has been the level of redundancies which have been imposed. Between Quarter 1 of 2008 (effectively the start of the recession), and Quarter 4 of 2011 the number of people in employment had fallen by 463,000, at a time when the size of the potential workforce rose by 614,000. The fall in the number of employees was even greater, at 650,000, as the number of self-employed went up by nearly a quarter of a million. Redundancies were running at half a million a year. The number of people working part-time because they could not find full-time work had doubled from 0.67 million to 1.34 million, while two-thirds of those who were made redundant and found a new job suffered a pay penalty of 28%. On average, the cost to an employer of making a redundancy is £13,000, suggesting that redundancies since 2008 will have cost UK employers around £35bn (Philpott 2012).

Ben Willmott and Cary Cooper discussed the HR implications of redundancy in a CIPD Podcast in 2009 (CIPD 2009e). Willmott argued that the increased risk of redundancy would lead to increasing work intensity, stress conflict and bullying in the workplace, while Cooper argued that survivors of redundancy would be likely to turn to unproductive presenteeism in an effort to preserve their jobs from the next round of redundancy. Both agreed that the good practice built up in HR over recent years could be at risk as management becomes even more obsessed with the bottom line.

A major study on HR in recession was carried out for the Irish Labour Relations Commission, reporting in January 2011 (Roche et al 2011). Ireland is significant because it went into recession before the UK, and has suffered more severely. Virtually all firms surveyed had implemented general HR retrenchment programmes, comprising pay freezes, recruitment freezes, curbs on overtime, short-time working, redundancies and more rigorous work regimes, including more rigorous management of performance and disciplinary issues. This approach was generally allied with an emphasis on improved communication with both employees and unions – perhaps made easier by the longstanding Irish agreements on social partnership between employers, the government and the unions (see Chapter 4) – and an emphasis on maintaining employee engagement and commitment.

An interesting, though perhaps atypical, example is the estate agent Sherry Fitzgerald (Roche et al 2011, pp27–29). Property bore the brunt of the Irish recession, with the volume of transactions down by 40%. The initial reaction of the firm was to opt for salary cuts, weighted towards the better paid, employment protection and job security. Recruitment was frozen, and career breaks, reduced working weeks and redeployment were offered to staff. However, as the recession deepened, 31 compulsory redundancies became inevitable, and a second round of salary cuts followed in 2009. Interestingly, the cut this time was across the board with no protection for those on the lowest salaries. This arose from staff feedback that insulating any groups from the pay cuts was unfair. HRD was maintained but spend was reduced, and employee engagement was identified as an area of future activity. The HR function was seen as central to the response. It was seen as operating in a partnership role with senior managers. It led the communication efforts, and maintained an open-door policy for all staff.

Senior managers felt that the company had experienced no significant fall in morale, and 'staff in general appeared to have formed the view that changes introduced in pay and conditions were unavoidable, appropriate and fair' (Roche et al 2011, p29).

REDUNDANCY — COSTS AND ALTERNATIVES

Costs of redundancy

Redundancies are a fact of life in a recession, such as that experienced in the UK from 2008 onwards. In the February 2009 edition of *Impact*, the CIPD research journal, John Philpott discussed the cost of redundancy (Philpott 2009a). Although redundancies can sometimes be inevitable, employers should always remember that there are significant costs associated with them. Philpott calculated the following average costs for a redundancy:

- Redundancy payments: Any employee made redundant after two years' service is entitled to statutory redundancy pay. Many employers pay more. The average redundancy payment in autumn 2008 was £10,575.
- Hiring costs: After the recession ends, it is likely that new workers will have to be hired. The average cost of recruitment in 2008 was £4,667.
- Training costs: New hires will have to be trained, at an average 2008 cost of £1,133.

Survivor syndrome

1 There is likely to be a decline in morale among those left employed (survivors). The CIPD *Employee Outlook: Job seeking in a recession* Summer 2009 (CIPD 2009a), found that seven out of ten employees whose organisations had made redundancies reported a fall in morale, while 27% said they were personally less motivated in their jobs. On the other hand, half of employees feel under increased pressure to perform after redundancies. The cost of a fall in morale was calculated by multiplying the reduction in output of survivors, by their average earnings.

2 Increased turnover as a result of redundancies. This measures the cost of additional hiring and training costs if turnover increases as a result of redundancies. However, this effect may be small during a recession, when there are few other jobs to go to, although turnover may shoot up once the recession is over and alternative jobs become available. A CIPD survey in August 2009 found that 22% were so unhappy with the way that redundancies had been handled that they were planning to change jobs as soon as the labour market improved (Churchard 2009a).

If we ignore survivor syndrome costs as being indirect and very difficult to quantify, we are still left with an average figure per redundancy (on CIPD figures) of between £10,575 (where redundant workers are not subsequently replaced) and £16,375 (where re-hires need training). Put another way, it costs roughly six months' wages (at the average wage) to make a worker redundant.

Alternatives to redundancy

Most employers have some idea that redundancies cost money, and most also feel a sense of responsibility to minimise suffering to their workforce. Hence a search for alternatives to redundancy discussed by John Philpott in a follow-up to his *Impact* article quoted above (Philpott 2009b).

One possibility is to use voluntary rather than compulsory redundancy. This has the advantage that it is likely to be more attractive to employees, and so may marginally reduce survivor syndrome costs, but its direct costs are the same as compulsory redundancy, and there is the added disadvantage that as the employer does not choose who is made redundant, the organisation might inadvertently lose key workers. Much the same is true of early retirement, where there is again a loss of control, as well as additional pension costs.

Philpott identified six common alternatives to redundancy, and their rate of use by employers.

Use of main alternatives to redundancy 2009 (%)

Recruitment freeze	50
Termination of temporary contracts	44
Flexible working	19
Cutting bonuses	17
Short-time working	15
Cutting pay	7

Recruitment freeze: This reduces the headcount through natural wastage, and has the advantage of being cheap, but like voluntary redundancy, the wrong people may be leaving. The recruitment freeze may need to be combined with redeployment to ensure that key tasks are covered.

Terminating temporary contracts: This is attractive, as temporary workers can be terminated without redundancy pay, but the effect for the temporary worker is the same as a redundancy – he or she is out of a job.

Flexible working: This may be desirable in its own right, but is not usually an alternative on its own to redundancy.

Cutting bonuses: This is usually simple and straightforward, as there is rarely a contractual right to a bonus. However, by definition, it is only possible if a bonus is already being paid.

Short-time working: A number of possibilities are available here:

- *Lay-offs*: Here the worker is told to stay at home for a specified period of time, during which time they are likely to be unpaid, or paid at a reduced rate. If the lay-off is without pay, employers are required to pay statutory guarantee pay of £21.50 a day for a maximum of five days in a three-month period.
- *Short-time working*: Here hours are reduced (for example a four-day week), usually with a commensurate pay reduction.
- *Sabbaticals*: This is in effect a form of lay-off, where employees are offered an extended period of (usually) unpaid leave while retaining all their employment rights.

Unless there is a specific right written into the contract of employment, all of the above are dependent on the agreement of the employee. If they are introduced without agreement, this is breach of contract

Pay cuts: Again, these will need to be agreed. However, they are cost–effective. If one reckons that a redundancy costs half a year's pay, a 5% pay cut for ten workers is the equivalent of one redundancy, and can be sold to the workforce as a fair way of spreading the pain, particularly if managers take a bigger pay cut than workers.

Philpott calculated the savings from the various alternatives to redundancy. He found a recruitment freeze and terminating temporary workers to be the most cost-effective. Other measures save less than redundancy, but they have the advantages of retaining talent, and of having less impact on survivor morale.

? REFLECTIVE ACTIVITY 3.8

Alternatives to redundancy

Xilinx 2001

Xilinx is a medium-sized US semi-conductor company with about 2,600 employees. In 2001, it was hit hard by the collapse of the dot.com boom, with its revenues falling by 50% in six months. Other firms in the industry reacted by introducing redundancy programmes, but the Xilinx management wanted to avoid this if possible. They understood the cyclical nature of the industry, and the need to hold on to skilled staff ready for the upturn.

In 2001, they implemented a programme of pay cuts, ranging from zero for the lowest-paid workers to 20% for the CEO, and a two-week shutdown. Employees were given the choice of taking the shut-down without pay, using paid leave entitlement, or 'borrowing' future leave entitlement if they had not accrued enough leave to cover the shutdown. The CEO announced that lay-offs would only be considered as a last resort.

As the market continued to deteriorate, employees agreed to take an additional 7.5% pay cut, with the choice of taking stock options in lieu of pay. However, the events of 9/11 then hit the industry, and even further measures were needed. After extensive consultations throughout the company, two additional programmes were agreed:

- Voluntary redundancy and early retirement, taken up by 82 employees.
- A one-year sabbatical leave, with two months' pay, an education bonus of $10,000, and/or a bonus of $10,000 for working as an executive on loan to a local non-profit organisation. The employee could return with no loss of benefits, seniority or stock options. This was taken up by 41 employees.

In 2002, the market recovered, and the pay cuts were restored. By 2003, Xilinx had increased its market share from 30 to 52%, and it was making profits which exceeded that of its three major competitors combined (Cascio and Wynn 2004) .

Honda and British Airways 2009

Both Honda and British Airways were hard hit by the 2009 recession, and both took imaginative measures to cope. Honda decided that it had to reduce production at its Swindon car factory from a planned 218,000 vehicles to 113,000, which in effect made half its 4,700 staff surplus to requirements. The first step was a voluntary redundancy programme, taken up by 1,300 workers.

However, the company still felt that it had 490 more workers than it needed, but it did not want to lose them as they would be needed when the economy picked up. Two major programmes were agreed with the union, Unite. One was a four-month shutdown, ending in June 2009. Staff got full pay for the first two months of the shutdown and 60% for the second two months. The second was a pay cut, of 3% for employees, and 5% for managers, for ten months from June 2009 to April 2010, with six extra days of paid leave. In Japan, pay cuts of 10 and 15% respectively had been agreed. The pay cut was agreed to by 89% of Honda employees, and the Unite regional officer Jim D'Avila said, 'In true solidarity the workers at Honda are standing together during difficult times to protect hundreds of jobs.' In addition, some of the surplus workers were found jobs in Honda's nearby suppliers. (Pidd, 2009; Stewart 2009; Churchard 2009b).

In June 2009, British Airways was reported as asking staff to work for a month for free. Willy Walsh, the CEO, set an example by foregoing his pay for July, a total of £61,000. However, there were media reports that undue pressure was being put on workers to agree to the proposal, and cabin crew and ground staff were reported to be considering industrial action. BA then widened the proposal to a range of options including unpaid leave and a temporary switch to part-time work as well as unpaid work, while making it clear that employees who took up the unpaid work option would still receive allowances and shift pay.

In the end the take-up for the company's proposals was small. Total take-up was 8,000, or 20% of the company's workforce, while the unpaid work option was only accepted by 800 workers, or 2% (*People Management* 2009a; Churchard 2009c; McCarthy 2009).

Question

Why do you think the programmes at Xilinx and Honda were successful, while that at BA was a relative failure?

3.8.3 THE FEMINISATION OF THE WORKFORCE

Male participation rates (the proportion of the population of working age who are in employment) have fallen steadily since 1951 (and indeed since 1911). They were 88% in 1951 and had fallen to 71% in 1998 (Gallie 2000). The fall is explained by early retirement, and greater levels of sickness incapacity. However, by 2008, this had risen to 78%, mainly because of an increased participation rate among the over-50s (Kent 2009). Female rates over the same period have risen from 33 to 70% in 2008. As a result the share of women in the labour force has risen from 30 to 48%. All of the gain in female employment has come about as a result of an increased participation on the labour force of married women. The single participation rate has fallen from 73% in 1991 to 64% in 1991, while the married women participation rate has risen from 22 to 53%. It is difficult to remember that in the early 1950s women in occupations like the civil service were routinely expected to resign when they married! The overall percentage working part-time has risen from 23.6% in 1992, to 25.5% in 2008. This increase has been driven by men, who are more likely to work part-time in 2008 than in 1992, while women are less likely to do so. Overall, 42% of women in employment were working part-time, compared with 11.6% of men (Kent 2009).

Women are under-represented in the higher professions, managers and administrators, and manual work, while they are over-represented in lower professionals and technicians (primarily education and the NHS), clerical work, and sales and personal service.

Why has the work force become feminised? Giddens (2006) puts forward three main reasons.

- *Demographic trends.* The birth rate has declined, and women are having children at a later age. As a result, they work for longer before they have children. As families are smaller, it is easier for them to return to work after having children. Domestic housework has also become much less labour-intensive, and men are at last tending to take a greater share of it. Women spend nearly three hours a day on housework, but men spend one hour 40 minutes (ONS 2005).
- *Financial pressures.* Single mothers often have little choice but to work, and increasingly this is being encouraged by the working of the welfare support system. Even two-parent families often find they need two incomes to maintain their desired standard of living.
- *Personal fulfilment.* The women's movement in the 1960s and 1970s increased women's self-esteem, and a desire among women for more independence.

A fourth reason could be that women workers are particularly attractive to employers, because they are much more likely to want to work part-time. In 2004, there were 5.2 million women in the UK in part-time employment, as against only 1.2 million men. Part-time workers are much more flexible than full-time ones, and this gives a considerable advantage to employers.

The reasons for women taking part-time work in 2004 are shown in Table 3.4.

Table 3.4 Reasons for women taking part-time work (2004)

Reason	%
In education or training	3
Disabled	2
Caring for children or other family member	36
Found no full-time job	7
Did not want full-time job	19
Other	34

Manning and Petrolongo (2005)

CASE STUDY 3.9

THE FEMINISATION OF MANAGEMENT

The National Management Salary Survey has been carried out by the Chartered Management Institute and Remuneration Economics for 36 years. The 2005 and 2006 surveys throw interesting light on the feminisation of management.

The 2005 report found that women made up 35.7% of managers and directors, up from 31% the year before. Women were a majority of managers under the age of 29, although female representation fell rapidly after that age. Between 35 and 39, women made up only a third of managers, and only 11% of those aged 50 or more (CMI 2006). Women received more rapid promotion than men, however. The average female team leader was 37, the average male team leader 42. For department heads, the corresponding ages were 40 and 43 (CMI 2007).

For ten years up to 2005, the pay gap between male and female managers had narrowed. The gap was 13.6% of earnings in 2003, and had narrowed to 11.8% in 2005, but in 2006, it rose to 12.2%. In 2007–8, female salaries went up marginally more than male, 6.8% versus 6.6%. At this rate, pay equality for managers would be reached in 2195! (CMI 2009). The only sector with anything approaching wage equality was the public sector and charities, where the gap was only 0.7% in 2006. In HR the gap was 40%, with female managers earning on average £35,198, and males £47,502 (Carvel 2007).

The picture had changed little by 2014. Although women made up 69% of entry-level managers, this had fallen to 30% at senior management level. The managerial pay gap in 2014 was only 6% at age 20–25, but this had widened to 34% for the over-45s (CMI 2014).

3.9 WORK ORGANISATION

3.9.1 THE FLEXIBLE ORGANISATION

The idea of the flexible firm was first identified by Atkinson (1984), and the concept was refined by Handy (1991). Atkinson identified four types of flexibility:

- *numerical flexibility*, achieved by altering working hours or altering the number of workers employed through part-time working, etc
- *functional flexibility*, achieved by training workers to perform a wider range of tasks (multiskilling) and breaking down barriers to deploying workers on different tasks (demarcation)
- *distancing*, replacing employees with sub-contractors
- *pay flexibility*, switching from centralised collective bargaining and rigid pay scales to individually negotiated pay and benefits.

The result is a segmentation of the workforce into core and peripheral workers. Core workers are those key workers who are central to the organisation's core functions. They will be long-term employees, possibly with guaranteed employment, and highly trained. They will be committed to the organisation, and the organisation will be committed to them. Peripheral workers will be those performing non-core services, often as sub-contractors. They will be hired and fired as required, and will serve as a buffer protecting the core workforce from fluctuations.

Handy developed the core-peripheral concept into his Shamrock concept. This type of organisation has three interlocking leaves consisting of three distinct groups of workers who are treated differently and have different expectations – specialist core workers; a contractual fringe, who may or may not work exclusively for the organisation, and who are paid a fee based on results rather than a wage based on time taken; and a flexible workforce, who are likely to be employed on a temporary or casual basis.

Remember, however, that what Atkinson and Handy are discussing is a theoretical model of organisations. Although many organisations have moved towards this kind of structure, many have not. As with other new management techniques, British management tends to be conservative and reluctant to adopt new ideas (Marchington and Wilkinson 2008).

One theoretical justification for increasing the flexibility of the labour market is that the more competitive the labour market is, the more efficiently it should operate (on the analogy of perfect competition). This has led to moves to deregulate the labour market, and to Margaret Thatcher's attacks on the trade unions in the 1980s. However, as we have seen above, the working of the labour market is extremely complex, and the results of deregulation in another important sector of the economy, the finance industry, have been disastrous, as we will see in Chapter 4.

A recent report, by the venture capitalist Adrian Beecroft, examined whether changes in employment law would make the labour market more flexible. One change which he recommended was to relax the laws on unfair dismissal by introducing the concept of Compensated No Fault Dismissal. Here an employee could be dismissed at any time, even in circumstances which would at present constitute unfair dismissal, as long as compensation was paid equal to that which would have applied in the case of redundancy. (Beecroft 2011). This is akin to the concept of Dismissal at Will which applies in many US states.

Beecroft produced no hard evidence to back his proposal, and reaction generally was lukewarm. The Government had already increased the qualifying period for unfair dismissal from one year to two, in April 2012, and in response to Beecroft it announced a very short consultation period on the introduction of Compensated No Fault Dismissal, but only for micro companies (those with up to 10 employees). The CIPD in its response was dismissive – 'we do not believe that a deregulation drive will lead to employers creating more jobs and thus stimulating economic growth'. They pointed out that the UK already had the third least regulated labour market in the OECD. They also said, 'the encouragement that [it] would give to bad practice would also tend to suggest to many that the typical micro business was a 'rogue employer' and so make it harder for them to recruit' (CIPD 2012b). The Liberal Democrat Vince Cable, Secretary of State for Business, Innovation and Skills, issued a ministerial statement when the report was published which said 'at a time when workers are proving to be flexible in difficult economic conditions, it would almost certainly be counter-productive to increase fear of dismissal' (Cable 2012). His rejection of the proposal was confirmed by his Conservative successor as business secretary, Sajid Javid, in May 2015 (BBC 2015a).

Allied to the concept of flexible organisations is that of flexible working. While the flexible organisation primarily benefits the employer, flexible working primarily (although not exclusively) benefits the employee. The Family Friendly Working Hours Taskforce, reporting in March 2010, found a compelling business case for flexible working (CIPD 2010):

- falling absenteeism and higher retention leads to a reduction in costs
- increased productivity
- increased ability to recruit from a wider talent pool
- greater loyalty amongst staff.

Changes in social structure have increased pressure on people in work.

- In the 1950s and even into the 1960s, women routinely gave up work on marriage, and so were at home to care for children. People married young, and had children young, with most families being completed by the age of 30. At the time when children were dependent, many parents also had an extended family to draw on and relatively young grandparents, who probably lived nearby.
- In the 1990s and 2000s, over half of all married women were in work, whether or not they had children, and families had come to expect and need two incomes. The age of marriage had risen, and many women had not had their first child by 30. The extended family had broken down, and by the time the family needed support, grandparents were too old, did not live locally, and increasingly needed care themselves.
- The increase in the rate of marriage breakdown meant that increasing numbers of single parents with children, usually women, needed to work to support their families, but had no external support networks to draw on. In 1991, 20% of dependent children lived in single-parent families.
- Millions of women in their 50s have to care for an elderly dependent parent.
- An increased desire on the part of employers as well as employees for a more flexible workforce.

An Institute of Management survey in 2001 highlighted the extent of the problem (*Professional Manager*, 2001):

- 46% of female managers have children
- 26% care for others such as elderly parents
- 27% cite family commitments as a career barrier (up from 17% in 1992).

In 2003, 9% of males and 33% of females had at some time given up work to care for somebody (*Social Trends* 2004).

In addition, people without caring responsibilities also feel that they are entitled to a life outside work. One in five people take work home almost every day, and one in ten work more than 48 hours a week (CIPD 2003b).

There are some legal requirements on employers to meet the needs of their employees for work–life balance. These are mainly concerned with the right to time off to cope with one-off situations or emergencies, and full details are given in the *CIPD Factsheet, Work–life balance* cited above. In addition, from 2003, (under the Employment Act 2002), employees with children under six (18 if disabled) can request a change in their hours, time or place or work. The employer must consider such a request, and can refuse it, but only after following a detailed procedure and basing their decision on specified business grounds. This was extended in 2007 to employees with children under 17, as a result of the Work and Families Act 2006 (CIPD 2009e), and in 2014 to all employees with at least 26 weeks continuous employment. In return, the procedures for considering a request were simplified, but must be reasonable (CIPD 2015a).

Any other employee can ask for flexible arrangements, and many employers have granted this. CIPD research in 2014 (Zheltoukhova 2014) showed that 90% of organisations were offering some form of flexible working, with the most popular being:

Part-time working	74%
Flexi-time	41%
Career breaks/sabbaticals	38%
Job share	36%
Study leave	35%
Phased retirement	30%
Term-time working	25%

The highest levels of provision were in large organisations and the public sector, the lowest in SMEs and the private sector. In 44% of organisations, flexible working was open to all employees, while in 62%, flexible working was considered upon employees' requests.

Managers with experience of flexible working tend to be very positive about its benefits (Institute of Leadership and Management 2013):

Enhances staff well-being	85%
Encourages high-potential women to return after maternity leave	79%
Easier to retain staff	78%
Greater level of commitment and motivation	65%
Matching of workforce to organisational needs	64%
Better able to meet customer needs	62%

However, in some organisations there are still barriers to flexible working. Almost a third of managers have heard colleagues make derogatory remarks about flexible workers, almost half say flexible working can cause resentment within teams, and a third say they have had to undertake extra work because a colleague is working flexibly.

? REFLECTIVE ACTIVITY 3.9

Flexible working

1 Our discussion above has been in terms of flexible working hours or time off. What other family-friendly arrangements could employers offer?

2   What business case could you put to your employers to persuade them to adopt family-friendly policies?

3   What skills and characteristics do you think that both employees and managers need to make a success of flexible working?

4   Among your workforce are two workers – Anne, who is a single parent with a daughter aged four, who has asked to work school hours only, and Peter, who is the sole family carer for his elderly mother, who has Alzheimer's disease. He has asked to work a 30-hour week, instead of the normal 35, and to leave work one hour early, in order to get home before his daytime carer leaves. What response would you make to each worker?

? REFLECTIVE ACTIVITY 3.10

Zero hours contracts

Most forms of flexible working are universally popular, but this is not true of zero hours contracts, which remain controversial.

What is a zero hours contract?

The government definition is 'an employment contract in which the employer does not guarantee the individual any work, and the individual is not obliged to accept any work offered'. This means that there is no mutuality of obligation, and that the individual on such a contract is a 'worker' not an 'employee'. This means they have no right to redundancy pay, maternity and paternity leave, sick leave, and protection from unfair dismissal (Wakeling 2014). In practice, zero hours workers can often feel under threat if they refuse work, with their future hours being reduced, a practice known as 'zero down' (Pennycook et al 2013). Until 2015, some zero hours contracts were exclusive, meaning that the worker was not allowed to work for anyone else, even if no work was offered. This was abolished by the Small Business, Enterprise and Employment Act (CIPD 2015d).

Why do employers use them?

There are three primary reasons for the use of zero hours contracts:

- where the work is highly erratic and unpredictable, for example in the tourism industry
- evading employment rights
- meeting the wishes of some employees for a flexible relationship – for example students and those near or past retirement age.

How many people are on zero hours contracts?

Basically, nobody knows! The latest official figures from the Office for National Statistics estimate around 700,000, or about 2.3% of those in employment, but as many people are on more than one zero hours contract, the total number of contracts is much higher, at around 1.8 million (Fullfact 2015). The CIPD thinks the number is higher, at just over a million in 2013 (CIPD 2013e). Nobody disputes that the number is growing rapidly (Green 2015).

Where are zero hours contracts most common?

They are most common in the care and hospitality industries (60% of care workers), but a surprisingly high proportion (43%) are in the manager, professional, associate and technical employment categories. Zero hours contracts are very common in further and higher education (Brinkley 2013).

Do workers like zero hours contracts?

Many zero hours workers (38%) would like to work more hours, but 52% would not. Almost half say they are satisfied with having no minimum contracted hours, with a quarter saying they are dissatisfied. Just under a third are looking for a new job, compared with a quarter of all employees. On job satisfaction and work–life balance, findings are very comparable with those of all employees. The real downside of zero hours contracts is insecurity, with no hope of ever getting a mortgage (CIPD 2013e).

Is there exploitation?

Undoubtedly, in a minority of cases. One highly publicised example is the sporting goods retailer Sports Direct. The Labour Party claims that 17,000 of its 20,000 employees are not guaranteed regular hours, a fifth of all zero hours contracts in retailing, and that Sports Direct cannot claim that its level of work is unpredictable or erratic. Zero hours employees at Sports Direct were excluded from a £160m share bonus paid to 2,000 'permanent' workers in 2013. When Labour lost the 2015 election, shares in Sports Direct shares shot up by 5%, leaving its majority shareholder, Mike Ashley, the controversial owner of Newcastle United football club, £96m better off! (BBC 2014b; Neville, 2015; Butler 2015a; Craven 2015).

Questions

1   Should zero hours contracts be made illegal?

2   The Unite trade union carried out a survey of 5,000 of its members in 2013 and found that 22% were on zero hours contracts (Unite 2013). It concluded from this that the figure for the UK as a whole was 5.5 million. What is wrong with Unite's calculations?

3.10 THE PSYCHOLOGICAL CONTRACT

All employees have a legal contract of employment, but for the employee this is usually presented as a 'take it or leave it' situation. The employee has to accept it or leave. The psychological contract is different. It is implicit rather than explicit, individual rather than collective, tacit rather than written (although elements of it may be incorporated into a social partnership agreement with a trade union) (CIPD 2003a). There are dangers in making it too explicit, as organisational and environmental changes may make it impossible to deliver on an explicit contract (Briner and Conway 2001). It can be defined as 'the perceptions of the two parties...of their mutual obligations towards each other' (Guest and Conway 2002). By its very nature, the psychological contract is dependent on trust between the employer and the employee.

Ian Wilson identified eight elements in his 'new social contract' (Wilson 2000):

- a vision and sense of shared purpose
- inspiring leadership
- empowerment
- customisation of work
- a climate of equity, respect and due process
- reduced volatility in employment patterns
- increasing employability
- good on-site amenities and services.

Wilson's elements link with the view of the psychological contract that it has changed from an 'employment security' contract to an 'employability' contract. This reflects the shift from the monolithic to the flexible organisation which we discussed earlier. Under the employment security contract, the employee offered time and loyalty in return for security of employment and the possibility of promotion (Kimberly and Craig 2001).

As redundancy and downsizing became more common, employers could no longer guarantee their side of the bargain, and gradually it was replaced by the employability contract – employees would still offer time and loyalty, but in return the employer would ensure that they received the work experience and training that would enable them to get another job elsewhere. This has been described as the 'new deal' at work and as producing a 'free agent' mentality among workers.

If this model is correct (and there is some doubt about this – the 'old' psychological contract often still exists, and where it has gone, it has not necessarily been replaced by an employability contract), loyalty may not be enough to keep the free agent employee on board. The organisation may have to offer more, including possibly empowerment. If workers are to be trusted, they expect trust back from the organisation.

Rousseau (2004) distinguished between relational contracts, based on give and take and on trust in the employer, and transactional contracts, which are more short-term in approach and concentrate on pay and conditions. The CIPD (2005) points to a suggestion that there has been a shift in recent years from relational to transactional, as trust in employers has declined, but refutes this, saying that employee commitment is broadly stable.

Other implications of the new psychological contract suggested by the CIPD include:

- *process fairness*: employers need to put in processes which ensure that employees see the way in which decisions are made as being fair
- *communications*: communication mechanisms have to be set up to ensure that employers are aware of the employee 'voice' (this is reflected in the EU information and Consultation Directive)
- *management style*: employees expect to know what is going on – management style needs to change from 'top-down' to 'bottom-up'
- *managing expectations*: managers must be seen to be fair, honest and open
- *measuring employee attitudes*: managers need to know what their employees are thinking
- *the decline of collective bargaining* has increased the importance of individual relationships between employers and employees (CIPD 2014a).

The employability and free agent approaches in many ways put a lot of pressure on employees. They are forced to take responsibility for their own future in a way which, while attractive to many, does not suit everyone. Many people want security rather than opportunity. Those who really crave opportunity may well have shifted to self employment already (the self-employment rate in the UK is currently at least 12% of the workforce – Philpott 2009b). Increasingly, employers have to offer something else as part of their side of the psychological contract. This is work-life balance, a recognition that workers have other interests and responsibilities outside work.

3.11 WORKFORCE PLANNING

Like much in our current world, workforce planning was a product of the Second World War. In 1942 the government drew up the first Manpower Budget to ensure there was enough labour to meet the needs of war production, and was shocked to discover that there was a shortfall of one million workers. This led to a realisation that the recruitment, retention and training of workers needed to be planned (Turner 2010). Like classic strategic planning, workforce planning (or manpower planning, as it was then called), reached its peak of popularity (and complexity) in the 1960s, but then became discredited as the environment became more turbulent from the 1970s onwards. However, the recession from 2008 onwards has led to a resurgence of interest in workforce planning as a key tool in managed downsizing, but as a bottom-up tool with heavy input from line management, rather than the top-down approach of classic manpower planning.

The CIPD defines workforce planning as 'a core process of human resource management that is shaped by the organisational strategy and ensures the right number of people with the right skills, in the right place at the right time to deliver short- and long-term organisational objectives' (CIPD 2010). As the CIPD's Angela Baron wrote: 'the public sector in particular is looking at how it can ensure that the current round of cuts fall in the right places and do not minimise their ability to provide core services efficiently and effectively. The private sector is looking for innovative ways to keep costs under control while maintaining engagement and holding onto their best talent' (Baron 2010).

The importance of effective workforce planning was starkly illustrated in July 2012 when the CEO of the world's biggest security company G4S, Nick Buckles, was forced to admit to a Commons Select Committee that his company's planning for the Olympic Games had been a 'humiliating shambles'. G4S had been contracted to supply 10,000 security guards for the Olympics, but was forced to admit two weeks before the games started that it would miss its target by thousands of workers, leaving a security gap which had to be hurriedly plugged by the calling up of an additional 3,500 members of the armed forces (BBC 2012a).

? REFLECTIVE ACTIVITY 3.11

Teachers and workforce planning

Intuitively you would think it would be easy to plan the supply of teachers. After all, you know how many children are born each year and where they are born, because all births have to be registered. Then you just project four years ahead (for primary schools) and 11 years (for secondaries), and you know how many children will be entering each level of school in each year. Adding up the years gives you a total school population. Divide this by your planned pupil-teacher ratio, and you know exactly how many teachers you need in each year.

Unfortunately, of course, it doesn't work like that. Over the period 1946–2001, there was a shortage of teachers (an excess demand) for all but ten years, reaching a peak of 80,000 in the early 1990s. There was a surplus (excess supply) for ten years from the mid-1970s to the mid-1980s, peaking at about 15,000 (Dolton 2005).

Question

Why is it so difficult to plan the supply of teachers?

3.12 TRADE UNIONS

So far in this section on work organisation we have concentrated on the position of individuals. We conclude by analysing the collective – the role and position of trade unions.

Trade union membership peaked in 1979, at more than 13 million. Since then it nearly halved, to around 7.5 million in the late 1990s. The rate of decline has since slowed, helped by legislation on union recognition in 1999, to 6.5 million in 2013. The nature of trade union membership has also changed. Overall union density (the proportion of workers who are union members) has fallen from 54% in 1979 to 26% in 2013 (23% for men), but for women it has only fallen from 37 to 28%.

Density is also affected by age. Increasingly, trade union members are older workers. Density is higher among full-time workers than among part-time workers. Density among professional and associate professional workers and personal service workers is higher than among manual workers. Density in the public sector is 55%, while in the private sector it is only 15%. Membership in the private sector has been rising slowly since 2010, but this may be mostly technical. The heavily unionised further education sector, for example, has been re-classified from public to private sector.

In 1979 the typical union member was a male manual worker in heavy industry – a miner or a steel worker. By 2013, the typical union member was a female teacher or NHS worker.

There are still wage benefits in being a union member. The trade union wage premium (the difference in average gross hourly earnings between members and non-members) was 20% in the public sector in 2013, compared with 7% in the private sector, although both these figures are well down since 1995, by 10% in the public sector and 8% in the private sector (all figures from Department for Business, Innovation and Skills/National Statistics 2014).

Many reasons have been put forward for the decline in union membership. These include:

- the decline of traditional highly unionised sectors of industry
- the anti-trade union legislation of the Conservative governments between 1979 and 1997. (Latest proposals from the new Conservative government are that strike action will require a turnout of at least 50% of those entitled to vote, and, in essential public services, the support of at least 40% of those eligible to vote (Blackhurst 2015))
- the recessions of the early 1980s, 1990s and 2008–10
- the growth of a flexible workforce, which is more difficult to unionise
- the growth of pay review bodies in the public sector
- the spread of performance related pay and individualised HRM systems
- the fall in the size of firms
- defeat in highly publicised set-piece disputes like the miners' strike
- a general shift within society from collectivism to individualism. (Employees have become more self-sufficient, and see solidarity, if at all, through social media rather than unions (Blackhurst 2015)).

The response of the trade unions, led by the TUC, was to change their orientation. The traditional perspective taken by unions was a pluralist one – that management and unions have some common aims, but many more conflicting aims, within the employment relationship. Collective bargaining was seen as managing the balance between the interests of management and workers, and would frequently be adversarial. Many individual union leaders took a more radical Marxist perspective, and saw the management–labour relationship as an exploitative one.

In the early 1990s, unions in America had developed a different approach, known as New Unionism, based much more on a co-operative relationship, recognising that management and unions have basic agreement in wanting the employment relationship to work more smoothly, and that both sides benefit from a high-wage high-productivity environment. New Unionism also recognised that the approach of union members and potential members is an instrumental one – they want a union to protect their individual interests. They buy union membership like they buy a foreign holiday – they want value for their money.

In 1996, the TUC adopted New Unionism. The emphasis in future was to be on developing social partnerships with willing employers, and on stressing casework for individual members. (Barber 1998). To further New Unionism, the TUC set up an

Academy in 1998 to train union representatives. The typical Academy student was female and from an ethnic minority.

A recent study of trade unions in the finance sector showed that having a union rep onsite helps to improve job quality. This not only benefits the worker, but is also important for organisations looking to increase productivity, as it leads to lower absenteeism and turnover. (Lewis 2015). As Nita Clarke of the Involvement and Participation Association says (quoted by Blackhurst 2015) 'It's naive of employers to dance on the grave of the trade unions.'

CASE STUDY 3.10

SOCIAL PARTNERSHIP AT VERTEX

Vertex is an outsourced services company, part of United Utilities, formed in 1996 when North West Water merged with North West Electricity. In five years, it has moved from collective bargaining to union derecognition to non-union consultation to collective bargaining based on partnership.

The head of employee relations, Tony Stark, said: 'I'd had a bellyful of trade unions after working in the car industry and the docks in Liverpool.' However, he was to lead negotiations with Unison which led to partnership. Even when the union was derecognised, union officials were elected onto the company-wide employee consultation forum, and proved constructive partners.

After the passing of the Employee Relations Act, Unison applied for a ballot on recognition. Rather than fight the request, Vertex set up a working party with the union, which produced agreement on recognition and social partnership. The company and the union put in a successful bid to the DTI's Partnership Fund, which aims to make organisations aware of best practice in partnership. This funded six months of workshops, facilitated by Ruskin College.

The partnership has produced tangible results, including a pay progression agreement, which has helped the company to achieve a retention rate much higher than that prevalent in the call centre industry. The partnership has also helped the company to win contracts with the public sector (Walsh 2001).

Legislation introduced by the Labour government supported the New Unionism approach. Under the Employment Relations Act 1999, all workers have the right to be accompanied by a fellow worker or union official to disciplinary proceedings. The Employment Act 2002 set out the statutory rights of union learning representatives, who have a key role in helping to promote learning and development within organisations which recognise unions. (CIPD 2004a).

Perhaps most important, the 1999 Act introduced a statutory right to union recognition through ballot, as long as 50% of workers vote in favour of recognition, and at least 40% of those eligible to vote are in favour. This ensures that a small minority of the workforce cannot force through recognition.

Crucial recognition agreements were those with Honda and Sheerness Steel in 2001. Honda is a classic example of the 'good' company which feels that because it is a good company, unions are not needed (Clement 2001), while Sheerness Steel was the scene of a bitter derecognition dispute in 1992 between the ISTC and the then owners, CoSteel (Gall 2001).

?   REFLECTIVE ACTIVITY 3.12

Union recognition

What do you think are the advantages and disadvantages to employers of recognising trade unions?

Attitudes to trade unions are no longer as polarised as they were in the 1970s. In 2014, the European Commission, in one of its regular Eurobarometer surveys on public opinion in the European Union, asked respondents throughout the Union about their perceptions of the term 'trade union'. The term had positive connotations for 51% across the EU 28, with 39% expressing negative connotations. This was a significant change since 2009, when 63% were positive, and 30% negative. The UK was one of only two countries (the other being Sweden) where perceptions of trade unions had grown more positive since 2009, up from 54 to 57%.

The survey also broke down figures for socio-economic groups across the EU. Attitudes were more positive than average for those born after 1980, those who studied past the age of 20, managers, white collar workers and manual workers. Attitudes were less positive than average for those born before 1946, those who left school at 15 or younger, and the self-employed (European Commission 2014).

3.13 HR RESPONSES TO CHANGES IN THE COMPETITIVE ENVIRONMENT

We illustrate this section with a case study which analyses examples where environmental change had to be met with HR responses.

    TALENT MANAGEMENT

CASE STUDY 3.11

The CIPD defines 'talent' as 'those individuals who can make a difference to organisational performance, either through their immediate contribution or in the longer-term by demonstrating the highest levels of potential', while talent management is 'the systematic attraction, identification, development, engagement, retention and deployment of those individuals who are of particular value to an organisation' (CIPD 2009d). Capelli has a simpler definition of talent management – 'a matter of anticipating the need for human capital and then setting out a plan to meet it' (Capelli 2008).

Capelli argues that talent management, at least in the US, is in a mess. One approach is to do nothing internally, and to rely on hiring talent in from outside as needed. This poaching model is dependent on someone else developing the talent, and is ultimately self-defeating. The alternative approach harks back to the heyday of detailed quantitative strategic planning in the 1950s, when the environment was much more stable and benign. The problem with this approach is that all plans fail in a turbulent environment, and the organisation will end up with either a surplus or a deficit of talent. A deficit is not so serious, as the shortfall can always be met by hiring in. A surplus means that talented and qualified individuals have no role to perform. An example he quotes is that of Unilever India, which found itself with 1,400 well-trained managers in 2004, 27% up on 2000, despite the fact that its demand for managers had fallen after the 2001 recession.

Capelli's approach is to apply the just in time principles of supply chain management to talent management:

- Aim to under-shoot in internal talent development, and to buy-in any shortfall.
- Break up development programmes into smaller segments. Rather than recruiting graduates once a year, for example, plan for two intakes instead. Break down a development programme into smaller modules, so that needs can be re-assessed at the end of each module. Concentrate on general management rather than functional skills in the early modules.
- Share the cost of development with trainees. Common in the UK, this is apparently rarer in the US.
- Keep in touch with leavers. Deloitte, for example, informs former employees of important developments in the firm.
- Involve the employee in talent management. Rather than relying on detailed succession plans, throw promotion posts open to internal competition.

In a 2009 report, *Fighting back through talent innovation*, (McCartney 2009), the CIPD identified a number of strategies organisations can use to manage their talent through the recession:

- Build up the employer brand. This will make it easier to acquire talent when the economy turns.
- Acquire talent from other organisations. Some organisations are making talented individuals redundant, making more talent available on the market. Both Tesco and Standard Chartered are actively recruiting talent.
- Keep talent warm for the future. Interest potential future recruits in the

company, even if there are no vacancies at present.

- Increase your focus on talent performance, engagement and retention. It is vital that talented employees are fully engaged and motivated.
- Review the effectiveness of current talent management programmes.
- Maximise any available funding opportunities. Management is not the only type of talent. A flow of skilled workers is also vital. The government has increased funding for apprenticeships, and this has been exploited by the London Borough of Tower Hamlets and National Express.
- Encourage line managers to be less risk-averse and provide support for stretch assignments. Recruitment freezes force line managers to make better use of internal talent.
- Ask for innovative suggestions by talent pools. The talent is there – make best use of it.
- Experiential-based learning. On the job learning need not be expensive, and can give a quick pay-off.
- Set up a leadership exchange group and partner with other organisations. Talent management across firms on a partnership basis can provide a wider range of experiences. Consider seconding managers to a charity, for example.
- Build a sense of community. People in talent pools progress faster if they can learn, share ideas and network with each other, and if they know this is actively encouraged by the organisation.

In its Factsheet on talent management (2015c), the CIPD stresses that talent management is a key survival strategy in difficult economic conditions – 'it is crucially important that organisations not only respond to current talent challenges but actively scan the horizon, anticipate future challenges and opportunities and develop pipelines of talent for the future'.

- The fundamental economic problem is how to reconcile scarcity and choice. Market and mixed economies tackle these problems in slightly different ways.
- Market economies are underpinned by the concepts of supply and demand, and their interaction to create equilibrium.
- Perfect competition is an unrealistic but ideal model. Other models of the market are measured by their deviation from perfect competition.
- The extent of monopoly power can be measured either by market share or by the degree of contestability of the market in which they operate.
- Performance in oligopoly markets depends on an interaction between the firms operating in the market.
- Porter's Five Forces model is a powerful way of analysing the competitive forces operating in an industry.
- Portfolio analyses, including the Boston Matrix and the Shell Directional Policy Matrix, are valuable but must be used with care.
- The perfect competition and monopsony models are alternative ways of explaining the working of the labour market.
- Since the 1970s, manufacturing has declined rapidly in the UK, along with a growth in employment in services. This has helped to lead to an increasing feminisation of the UK workforce. Globalisation and computerisation have also led to the growth of flexible forms of work organisation.
- The labour force in the UK has increasingly been feminised, although inequality of opportunity between men and women still persists.
- The psychological contract has evolved from an emphasis on job security, to employability, and to work–life balance.
- Workforce planning has returned as a key tool in HR responses to the recession.
- Trade union membership in the UK has almost halved as a result of changes in social and industrial structure. The response of the unions has been to develop the concept of New Unionism.

REVIEW QUESTIONS

1 What would you say are the differences between a pure command economy and an economy with a command mentality?

2 What do you understand by the concept of dynamic pricing?

3 What are the differences between oligopoly and monopolistic competition?

4 Why is non-price competition a favoured strategy in an oligopolistic market?

5 What are the Five Forces identified by Porter in his model?

6 What criticisms have been made of the Five Forces Model?

7 Why might a firm decide not to drop a dog product, as identified in the Boston Matrix?

8 How well do you think that the perfect competition model of the labour market explains wages and employment?

9 Under what circumstances can trade union activity increase both wages and employment?

10 Why do you think that the share of manufacturing in the UK's GDP has fallen?

EXPLORE FURTHER

Further reading

The theoretical background to this chapter is covered in any good economics textbook, such as Lipsey and Chrystal's *Principles of Economics* (Oxford University Press), or Alain Anderson's *Economics* (Causeway Press/Pearson). Each edition of *Impact*, the CIPD's quarterly update in policy and research (available to members through the CIPD website), has an article by John Philpott, the CIPD's Chief Economist until 2012, on some aspect of the labour market. There is a useful guide from the CIPD and ACAS, *How to manage your workforce in a recession*, published in February 2009 (CIPD/ACAS 2009).

Useful websites

As a manager you need to be able to apply the theory to contemporary examples and situations. The best way to do this is to make sure that you regularly read *The Economist*, and at least one of the quality broadsheet newspapers – preferably two, one broadly liberal, like *The Guardian* or *The Independent*, and one broadly conservative, like *The Times* or *The Daily Telegraph*. *The Financial Times* is also very useful, and easier to read than you might think. All of these have their own websites, on which you can access their archives, but only the *Guardian* website (www.guardian.co.uk), which also includes *The Observer*, is free. You can access *The Economist* via the CIPD website. Most local libraries provide free access to the Thomson newspaper website, which includes all the newspapers mentioned above. Both our local libraries (Essex and Hertfordshire) provide this service. You should certainly check your own local library website.

The SHRM (the American equivalent of the CIPD) has a pamphlet in its Effective Practice Guidelines series, *Employment downsizing and its alternatives: strategies for long-term success* (2009), available at: http://www.shrm.org/about/foundation/Products/Documents/Downsizing%20EPG-%20Final.pdf

Audio and video material

The CIPD produced two excellent podcasts on redundancy in March 2009. The first (Podcast 29 Part 1) discusses managerial issues around redundancy, while the second (Podcast 29 Part 2) discusses practical and legal issues. Podcast 99 (March 2015) discusses family-friendly working, and Podcast 75 (May 2013) covers the right to request flexible working. The podcast *Dreams: creating the best workplace on earth* (December 2013) links with an article by Gareth Jones and Rob Goffee in the May 2013 issue of *Harvard Business Review*. Michael Porter has a *Harvard Business Review* video on youTube (available at: www.youtube.com/user/HarvardBusiness), *The five competitive forces that shape strategy*, which supports his *HBR* article with the same title (Porter 2008).

SUPERMARKETS: AN OLIGOPOLISTIC INDUSTRY

Introduction

The supermarket industry has come a long way since Sainsbury's opened the first self-service supermarket in the UK in 1951. Until the 1970s, the industry was fragmented, with a large number of supermarket groups mostly operating small stores, and over 100,000 independent grocery outlets of various types. Economies of scale were low, with deliveries being made direct by wholesalers or manufacturers to individual stores. Supermarkets were in town centres, and most people shopped regularly several times a week.

By the late 1970s, two leaders had emerged from the pack – Sainsbury's and Tesco. Sainsbury's was a private family company until 1973. It was concentrated in London and the south-east, with a mainly middle class clientele. Tesco was a much younger company, founded by Jack (later Lord) Cohen, who was responsible for the notorious slogan "pile 'em high, sell 'em cheap". In the late 1970s, Tesco began the slow and at times painful move upmarket that has continued ever since. The two firms were neck and neck in the market until 1995, when Tesco took the lead for the first time.

Tesco is now way out in front, with a market share which peaked at 32%. Sainsbury's and Asda, which was a northern-based also-ran until it was taken over by the biggest grocer in the world, Wal-Mart of the US, in June 1999, jostle for second place. In fourth place is Morrison's, which again was a long-established northern chain which came from nowhere to take over the struggling but larger Safeway group in 2004.

Between 2000 and 2006, total supermarket grocery sales rose by 26% in real terms, although there was a small fall in the total number of stores. Supermarkets had increased their share of grocery sales over this period from 67 to 72%. Convenience stores held their market share at 20%, while other grocery outlets, including specialist grocery stores, fell from 13 to 8% (Competition Commission 2007).

Superstores

In the late 1970s, the UK supermarket groups started to adopt the French concept of hypermarkets, huge out of town stores. In the UK they became known as superstores. A superstore was defined as a store with at least 25,000 square feet of selling space, at least 20 check-outs and selling at least 16,000 lines. In theory, a superstore can be located anywhere, but increasingly they came to be purpose-built buildings on green or brownfield sites either on the edge of towns or out of town, with their own extensive and normally free car parking. Increasingly, they also included a petrol station selling cut-price petrol, rapidly making the supermarket chains the biggest retailers of petrol in the UK. Evidence suggested that people were prepared to drive up to ten miles to visit a superstore. By 1993 there were 750 superstores, taking half of all grocery sales. Superstores yielded very high economies of scale. They were supplied from huge centralised depots, which minimised distribution costs, and the huge superstore buildings were very cheap to maintain. Increasingly the big groups used new technology to improve efficiency and lower costs. Electronic point of sale (EPOS) was used by all the big groups. This enabled the store to re-order automatically from the till, to minimise on warehousing, to maximise use of shelf space as less stock needed to be on the shelves, and to react almost instantaneously to changed circumstances. Tesco also exploited the data mining potential of its Clubcard, which recorded full details of every cardholder's shopping patterns, enabling the company to target each individual with personalised offers.

By the mid-1990s, the explosive growth period of superstores was over. Most of the best sites had gone, and the government was tightening up the planning controls on new development. The response of the supermarkets, particularly Tesco, was fourfold:

- *extended opening hours*: many of the larger stores are now open 24 hours a day, and only close (very reluctantly) on Christmas day
- *a move into e-commerce*, with grocery deliveries co-ordinated from the local store
- *a move back into town centres*: Tesco started to develop its Tesco Metro chain, and Sainsbury's started Sainsbury's Central. Both aimed particularly at lunchtime and commuter shoppers, selling a more restricted range of convenience goods
- *introduction of new services*, like pharmacies, film processing and in some cases dry cleaning.

Diversification

Another growth route for the supermarkets was diversification. Both Tesco and Sainsbury accelerated their movement into the convenience store market through takeovers. Tesco took over T&S Stores in 2004, acquiring 850 stores, and Sainsbury's took over Jacksons Stores (110 stores) (Wheatcroft 2004). Even the Co-op got into the act, taking over Alldays, doubling its number of convenience stores to over 2,300. At the end of 2006, Tesco owned 1,150

convenience stores, and Sainsbury's 287, together making up 3% of the national convenience stores total (Competition Commission 2007). The big groups also moved heavily into non-food sales, which in the mid-2000s made up more than 10% of their total sales (Hiscott, 2004). One pound in every eight spent in the UK went to Tesco. It sold more DVDs than HMV and more shampoo than Boots in 2004 (Purvis 2004). In the summer of 2004, it was reported that Asda had become the UK's biggest clothing retailer, overtaking Marks & Spencer. Sainsbury for a long time owned the DIY store Homebase.

Diversification has also been global, particularly by Tesco. They have moved into France, Hungary, Poland, Thailand, and China. Sainsbury's has made less good strategic decisions by opting for expansion in the US, a saturated market. Both Sainsbury's and Tesco ultimately failed in the US, at great cost. Asda has gone the other way. It has been expanded into by Wal-Mart, with its huge purchasing power, which gives Asda a bigger influence on the market than its market share would suggest.

Price wars

Supermarkets are notorious for their price wars. These are launched by all the groups at regular intervals with a fanfare of publicity. The reaction of customers to price wars tends, probably rightly, to be cynical. Market research in the summer of 1993, during a particularly intense period of price cutting, showed that more than half of shoppers regarded price cuts as gimmicks, 20% said they took no notice, and only 22% believed they were genuine. Price cuts always tend to be concentrated on Known Value Items (KVIs) – the 200 or so items, like tea, butter and coffee, where customers remember prices. The great bulk of the 20,000 lines stocked by the average superstore are not affected by price cuts. The analysts Smith New Court estimated that the 1993–4 price war would have saved on average 1.5p on a £100 shopping trolley. Remember also that in the main it is not the supermarkets who pay for the price cuts – it is the suppliers.

All the major supermarkets engage in below cost selling (selling goods below their cost price), representing up to 3% of total revenue. Below cost selling is concentrated on dry groceries, alcohol, and CDs, DVDs and books. The Competition Commission does not think that below cost selling is part of a predatory policy aimed at excluding rivals, but does think that it could unintentionally harm smaller grocery retailers and specialist stores. If it leads to these shops exiting the market, this could harm consumers (Competition Commission 2007).

After an investigation of the industry, the Office of Fair Trading in 2002 brought in a 'voluntary' code of practice governing how supermarkets treat their suppliers, particularly farmers. A review of the working of the Code of Practice in 2005 found that on the whole the supermarkets had complied with its terms (Competition Commission 2007), but in 2015 a survey of direct suppliers found that 34% said that Tesco rarely or never complied with the code, the worst result among the big supermarkets, although slightly better than in 2014. The best result was from Aldi, with 94% saying it consistently or mostly complied with the code (Butler 2015e).

Competition

In the mid-1990s, supermarkets appeared for the first time to be facing serious new competition from the entry into the market of discount stores from the continent, particularly Aldi and Netto, which had been very successful in Germany and the Netherlands. They stocked a very limited range, mainly of tertiary brands (brands which no-one had ever heard of), and at rock-bottom prices. Although much feared at the time, they seem only to have affected the bottom end of the market, particularly Kwik Save.

Supermarkets and the recession

Like the rest of the economy, supermarkets were hard hit by the recession that started in 2008, which coincided with a spike in food price inflation, to 13%. The first impact was a significant trading-down by consumers. In the summer of 2008, the 'hard discounter' Aldi was achieving annual sales growth of 17%, with a 25% increase in footfall, and a 17% increase in customers from the ABC1 social groups. By Christmas 2008, Aldi's growth rate was up to 25%. By contrast, Tesco's year on year growth, at 4.6%, was below the market average of 6.2% (Finch 2009a). The other big losers were the upmarket Waitrose and Marks & Spencer.

By the summer of 2009, the big retailers had recovered their nerve, and were hitting back hard against the hard discounters. Tesco launched its own 'discounter' range, and rebranded itself as 'Britain's biggest discounter'. Asda went for a 'round pound' promotion, selling hundreds of goods for £1. Sainsbury went for 'switch and save', showing the saving in switching from branded products to its own brands, while its advertising frontman, Jamie Oliver, showed how to feed a family for a fiver. Even Waitrose launched a new budget range called Essentials, which now accounts for 15% of its turnover.

The result was that the explosive growth of the hard discounters was stopped in its tracks. In the year to July 2009, Aldi's sales were up 8.3%, but this was beaten by Morrison at 9.5%, and virtually equalled by Asda, Sainsbury and Waitrose. The only group unable to show a strong come-back was the market leader, Tesco, with growth of just 4.5%. The result was a fall in its market share, down from a peak of 32% to just 30.6% (Finch 2009b). In August 2009, it announced that it was doubling the value of its Clubcard reward scheme, from 1 to 2%, in effect a further price cut of 1% on all purchases (Thomas 2009).

There was also significant further restructuring in the industry. One significant change to the structure of the market was the demise of Somerfield, taken over by the Co-op in March 2009. The Competition Commission required more than a hundred ex-Somerfield stores to be sold off, of which 22 were bought by Waitrose. The new Co-op had a market share of around 7%, putting it firmly in fifth place, well ahead of Waitrose and Aldi (*Retail Week* 2009). In 2010, Asda/Wal-Mart took over the UK operations of the Danish cut price retailer Netto, in an attempt to get a foothold in the convenience store sector of the market, previously dominated by Tesco, and to a lesser extent Sainsbury and the Co-op (*Independent* 2010).

The market was then stunned in January 2012 by a profit warning from Tesco, the first for 20 years. The company announced that sales were down by 2.3% for the six weeks to 7 January (covering the key Christmas and New Year trading period), while Sainsbury's grew by 2.3% and Morrison by 0.7% over the same period. Profit growth for 2012–13 would be 'minimal', compared with the 8–10% expected (Thompson 2012).

The shortfall in performance was blamed on the way in which Tesco had used its UK business as a cash cow to finance its expansion in the US and the Far East. Between 2007 and 2012, the average number of workers in a typical 40,000 square feet superstore fell from 275 to 226, with a resulting fall in customer service (Wood 2012). In the short term, Tesco was also hit by the failure of its Big Price Drop discounting campaign, financed largely by cutting the rewards paid on its Clubcard scheme (Moore 2012).

In April 2012 Tesco announced its Build a Better Tesco programme. Its key points were to recruit 20,000 more staff in the UK (cost £350m), improve training, revamp existing stores (£300m), and boost the online business (£200m). The future emphasis was based on opening more smaller Metro-style stores, and an

end to the hypermarket building programme, which would save £300–400m a year. Hypermarket sales were particularly hard-hit, as non-food sales were increasingly going online. Tesco was also hit by a downgrading of its credit rating by Moody's from A3 to Baa1 (Felsted 2012a, 2012b, 2012c).

By the summer of 2012 there was no clear evidence that the Build a Better Tesco programme was working. Underlying sales at Tesco were still falling, and sales were once again shifting both to the upmarket Waitrose and to the discounters Aldi and Lidl (*Guardian* 2012a: Felsted 2012d). On a positive note, Tesco dominated the rapidly growing online grocery business, with a 48% market share (Moore 2012). In December 2012 Tesco announced that it was withdrawing from the US, at a cost of £1.5bn.

The whole of the sector was also coming to realise that their rush into online trading had perhaps been a mistake. Figures released in early 2013 suggested that while it cost a supermarket around £20 to assemble and deliver an online order, the highest charge which it appeared the market could bear was £5. The result was that the three supermarkets which had gone heavily into online (Tesco, Asda and Sainsbury) were to a large extent cannibalising their own sales rather than gaining from each other, while the fourth, Morrison, was losing market share because it had not gone heavily online. None of the four was a clear winner from e-commerce (Pratley 2013).

Although the UK began a tentative recovery from recession by 2012, it became clear that this was not to benefit the Big Four. Consumers voted with their feet against the huge out-of-town superstores in which Tesco, in particular, had invested so much. They preferred to shop in-town and more often, which saved on petrol and food waste. At the same time, the electrical goods which filled the superstores were increasingly being bought online.

At the same time, the hard discounters Aldi and Lidl were rapidly gaining market share. Their share of the market rose to 9% in 2015, up from 5.4% in 2012, and Aldi, with 5.3%, overtook Waitrose to take sixth place in the market, with fifth-placed Co-op firmly in its sights (Butler 2015b). This is the highest share for the hard discounters since 1999, when Kwiksave and Netto were still trading. The Tesco share of the market was down to 29.4%.

It is easy to assume that Aldi and Lidl are small-time players who have come from nowhere. This is far from the truth. Both have operated in the UK for over 20 years, and between them they have 37% of the German market (Observer 2014). In 2015, Aldi leapfrogged Tesco to eighth place in the BrandZ global retail brands list, with an increase in brand value of 27%. Tesco slumped from sixth to twelfth, with a fall in brand value of 37%. Lidl came in at 20th (Gilbert 2015).

Although all the Big Four suffered in the mid-2010s, it was Tesco which suffered most. In 2013, it was implicated in the horsemeat scandal, when horsemeat was discovered in ready meals (Farrell 2015); in 2014 it was involved in an accounting scandal, when it was caught over-stating its profits by £263m (Butler 2015c); and in 2015 it recorded the worst-ever loss for a UK retailer of £6.4bn. UK sales fell by 3.6%, with the Tesco Express convenience stores the only part of the UK business to achieve positive growth in sales. Group operating profits were £1.4bn, compared with £3.3bn in 2014. Of this, more than half came from the Asian division, particularly Thailand. The UK margin was down to 1%. One-off charges included a £3.8bn write-down on property, £925m on 49 stores which had been planned but were now cancelled, £416m on redundancies, £570m write-down on stock, and a £630m write-down on its operations in China (Butler and Farrell 2015a 2015b; Butler 2015d).

Questions

1 Why do you think the competition authorities allowed Tesco to take over T&S Stores, even though Tesco had a market share over the 25% which would make it a monopoly under UK law?

2 In what ways does the behaviour of the supermarkets fit with the theory of oligopoly?

3 Carry out a Five Forces analysis of the UK supermarket industry as at summer 2015.

4 Tesco has a full-time equivalent UK workforce of 194,000. How can such a huge organisation keep track of its talent?

5 Why would a large supermarket chain be interested in local pay bargaining? Why would the union (USDAW) be opposed to this?

Government Policy

4.1 INTRODUCTION

In this chapter we will analyse the evolution of government policy in social, economic and industrial fields, and the impact of government policy on organisations. As developments in the UK are heavily influenced by the actions of the EU, we will be concerned with both UK and EU policy. We start with formal legislative procedures in the UK and the EU, and then go on to consider informal influences on the evolution of policy. We then consider recent developments in policy in the UK.

4.2 THE LEGISLATIVE PROCESS IN THE UK AND THE EU

4.2.1 THE UK

Most legislation originates in government departments and is directly sponsored by the government. Some legislation, particularly on matters of conscience, starts as a Private Members' Bill. Most of these fail. Normally they only pass with substantial cross-party support, and support, or at worst neutrality, from the government. Indeed, frequently the purpose of a Private Members' Bill is not actually to pass a new law, but to bring public attention to an issue which is important to an individual MP and those pressure groups which support him or her. In this section, we are only going to look at government Bills.

At least for Bills published relatively early in the life of a parliament, the general subject matter of the Bill will appear in the governing party's election manifesto – 'we intend to bring in legislation to put right the long-standing grievances concerning...' This is significant, because there is a constitutional convention that the House of Lords will not vote against any issue on which the Government has a manifesto mandate.

The next (optional) stage is a Green Paper. This is a consultative document setting out the case for the forthcoming legislation, and the pros and cons of various approaches to legislation. This does not commit the government to anything, but forms a basis for discussion with interested parties and pressure groups. After consultation on the Green Paper, the government may choose to:

- follow it up with a White Paper
- go straight to legislation
- drop the proposal.

A White Paper firms up on the proposal, but again does not commit the government on detail. A lengthy period of consultation may then follow.

The parliamentary session normally starts in November, with the Queen's Speech, where the Queen sets out the programme of legislation for the coming year – 'my government intends to introduce legislation on...' The Government will then publish a Bill, drafted by specialist parliamentary lawyers. The Bill then goes through a number of formal stages:

- First Reading – a formal presentation of the Bill to the Commons.
- Second Reading – a full debate on the principles of the Bill rather than the details.
- Committee Stage – the Bill is then scrutinised in detail by a Standing Committee of the Commons, consisting of between 15 and 20 MPs, with a government majority. The Bill will be debated and voted on clause by clause, and some provisions may be amended.
- Report Stage – the amended Bill goes back to the full Commons, where the government has an opportunity to reverse any amendments forced on it at the Committee Stage.
- Third Reading – this is formal, and not usually debated.
- The Bill then goes to the House of Lords, and repeats the same stages as in the Commons. The Lords can amend the Bill or reject it. If they reject it, this delays the Bill for one parliamentary session. Having passed through the Lords, the Bill goes back to the Commons, which can reject any amendments made by the Lords.
- Royal Assent – the Queen then agrees to the Bill, which becomes an Act. In theory the Queen could reject the Bill, but this has not been done for 300 years.

As a legal document, every word of an Act matters, and it is subject to interpretation by the courts.

4.2.2 THE EU

This is very different from the process in the UK. Initial proposals for legislation are drawn up by the Commission, and must be based on one of the EU Treaties (Rome, Maastricht, Amsterdam, Nice, etc.). Each Treaty has to be unanimously ratified by the member states. By contrast, in the UK the government has a free hand to legislate on anything that it chooses (including leaving the EU).

At this stage, the proposal is known as a draft framework law or a draft directive. The draft then goes out for consultation to the Council of Ministers, the European Parliament, and the Social Partners (the two employers' bodies Unice and CEEP, and the trade union body ETUC). The Commission then revises its proposals, which are then formally presented to the Council of Ministers, which will take a decision on unanimity or qualified majority voting, depending on the nature of the legislation. The European Parliament has the right to debate and to comment on the proposed directive, but until the Lisbon Treaty was adopted, no right to amend or reject it. Under the Lisbon Treaty (which replaced the ill-fated EU Constitution), the European Parliament has the right to reject or amend the proposal, but only by a majority of more than half of all MEPs (not just those who vote).

The law will be adopted if:

- both the Parliament and the Council of Ministers approve it (by either unanimity or qualified majority, depending on the type of legislation)
- the Council of Ministers approves the parliament's amendments. (If the Commission opposes an amendment, it must be approved by a unanimous vote of the Council of Ministers).

The directive then has to be implemented by member states – ie EU directives become law in the UK through a UK Act of Parliament. At the end of 2003, there were about 2,500 EU directives, and the compliance rate by member states ranged between 96 and 99% (Mulvey 2003). The number of directives will have increased considerably since 2003.

? REFLECTIVE ACTIVITY 4.1

UK and EU legislation

What are the differences in passing legislation between the UK and the EU? Which system do you think is more democratic?

4.2.3 INFORMAL INFLUENCES ON POLICY

Political parties

Traditionally the electoral system in the UK has ensured a predominantly two-party electoral system (plus regional and/or nationalist parties representing Scotland, Wales and Northern Ireland) – a broadly 'right wing' party in favour of maintaining the status quo (the Tories in the early nineteenth century, the Conservatives from the late nineteenth century onwards), and a broadly 'left-wing' party in favour of change (the Whigs in the early nineteenth century, the Liberals in the late nineteenth century, Labour from the 1920s). The two wings broadly represented different class interests – the right wing the 'haves' who resisted change (the ruling class, and later the middle class), and the left wing the 'have-nots', those seeking change (the working class). Thus ideology and social class were seen as underpinning the UK party system. In Reflective Activity 4.2 you will explore how far this is still true.

The influence of members of political parties, even MPs, over government policy-making is small, and probably getting smaller. MPs are subject to party discipline, and although they can and do vote against their own government on occasions, every MP knows that if he votes to bring down his own government, his party career will be finished. Even massive revolts are unlikely to change government policy, as can be shown by the Labour revolt on university fees, and on the Iraq war, where even the resignation of a leading Cabinet member, Robin Cook, had no influence on policy.

Party conferences can pass resolutions critical of government policy, but governments have never had to take much notice of these. Policy is nowadays decided much more by focus groups and think tanks. MPs do have the power to force an election for the post of party leader, and when the Conservatives ousted Margaret Thatcher and replaced her with John Major, the decision was taken solely by Conservative MPs. However, the

Conservative party now elects its leader through a complicated electoral college system, where MPs, peers, MEPS, and party members all have a weighted vote. In 2015 the Labour party shifted from an electoral college procedure to elect its leader to a one member one vote system, with votes also given to supporters of the party, who paid a small one-off fee for the right to vote. The result was the shock election of the veteran left-winger Jeremy Corbyn as party leader in September 2015.

CASE STUDY 4.1

EASYCOUNCIL

Conservative-controlled local authorities are providing evidence for a radical new approach to the provision of local services. Hammersmith and Fulham, for example, is raising the rents for its social housing to market levels, and has suggested an end to the 'tenure for life' held by social housing tenants. Essex has suggested that social security benefits should be set and administered locally.

The most radical changes are coming from Barnet council in north London, which includes Margaret Thatcher's old constituency of Finchley. The council has consciously modelled itself on the low-cost airlines easyjet and Ryanair. The key to the low cost airline business model is that you get what you pay for. *The Guardian* quotes the example of a Ryanair flight from Stansted to Perugia where the fare was £2.99, but once you add in online booking (£5 – cheaper than checking in at the airport), taxes, priority booking and two bags of luggage, the cost rose to £69.26. Ryanair argues that this extends customer choice, as customers choose the level of service they need, and pay accordingly.

Barnet is extending this model to local authority services. It is proposing a charge for 'jumping the queue' on planning applications. Recipients of adult social care will be given a personal budget, which they can spend how they wish, including perhaps a weekend in Eastbourne, rather than the council saying 'you need help with shopping, cleaning and meals on wheels' whether the clients wanted that package or not.

Another controversial proposal is to remove live-in wardens from sheltered

housing, and to replace them with mobile (and outsourced) wardens who can be summoned through alarm buttons. As the leader of Barnet council says, 'It is surprising how able even so called vulnerable people are. Helping people help themselves, that's the new Conservatism.' A council document, *Future Shape*, says the goals of the proposed reforms are 'facilitating self-help through behaviour change' and 'more services delivered by organisations other than the council'. Outsourcing services such as street cleaning, parking, planning and residential care is expected to save up to £15m a year.

The programmes of councils such as Barnet present a dilemma for the Conservative leadership. David Cameron has worked hard to change the image of the Tories as the 'nasty party', but at the same time, there is a considerable attraction for a Conservative government in having cuts administered locally, where they are less visible to the general public. Hammersmith and Fulham's 3% reduction in council tax has received more attention outside the borough than its spending cuts. Indeed, then the shadow Chancellor, George Osborne, said in a major speech in September 2009 that 'a Conservative government will have much to learn from Conservative local councils'. Charges for jumping the queue on NHS waiting lists, perhaps?

Labour has hit back with a 'John Lewis council' proposal – to run Lambeth council in London as a co-operative. Suggestions include:

- an 'active citizens' dividend' whereby those involved in community organisations would get a council tax rebate

- turning local services like primary schools into citizen-led mutuals
- turning council housing estates in co-operatives.

The early evidence from Barnet is not encouraging. In the financial year 2010–11 the council spent £1.5m to achieve savings of £1.4m. The policy is now known as 'One Barnet', and involves the outsourcing of 70% of the council's functions in two 10-year private sector contracts, worth a total of £1bn. The 10-year life of these contracts has severe implications for local democracy, as London Boroughs like Barnet operate on a four-year electoral cycle.

Sources: Mulholland (2009); Travers (2009); Burgess (2009); Booth (2009a); Booth (2009b); Booth (2009c); Booth (2010); Harris (2012)

Pressure groups

A pressure group is 'any group in society which, through political action, seeks to achieve changes which it regards as desirable or to prevent changes which it regards as undesirable' (Forman and Baldwin 1999, p128). They can broadly be classified into two main types:

- interest or sectional groups
- attitude or cause groups.

Interest groups are those pressure groups which have a common interest, and they exist to promote the interests of that group. Classic examples are trade unions and employers' associations, but interest groups also include professional bodies, The Royal British Legion and the AA, the last of which started as a members' organisation but later became a public company, and later still was acquired by a private equity group.

Attitude groups are those pressure groups whose members have attitudes or beliefs rather than material interests, and they seek to advance particular causes. Examples include the National Trust, Oxfam, Greenpeace, Liberty, the RSPB. Some pressure groups appear to be hybrids. The Countryside Alliance, for example, would see itself as an attitude group, while its opponents would see it as an interest group.

Pressure groups have a number of important functions:

- Intermediaries between the government and the public. The prime role of a pressure group is obviously to apply pressure on the government (or sometimes on other political bodies like the EU, the IMF or a foreign government). They channel and express public opinion on key issues. Some pressure groups use professional lobbying organisations to put forward their point of view to decision-makers. American gaming interests are alleged to have spent £100m in 2004 in support of the Gambling Bill which would have introduced Las Vegas-style 'super-casinos' to the UK (Mathiason 2004). For a detailed analysis of the tactics used by the lobbyists in this case, see Hencke (2004).
- Opponents and critics of government policy. Party discipline prevents governing party MPs from opposing government policy, while criticism from opposition parties tends to be ignored because everyone expects the Opposition to oppose. Pressure groups can provide detailed and (hopefully) constructive criticism of policy. Indeed, on some occasions pressure groups in effect write government policy for it.
- Agents of government. This is controversial. Increasingly, pressure groups which themselves provide services, particularly charities, receive government grants towards providing those services, which some feel may compromise their independence.
- Publicists, to promote an interest or defend a standpoint.

? REFLECTIVE ACTIVITY 4.2

Political parties and pressure groups

1 What arguments would you put forward if asked to support the proposition that ideology and class no longer underpin the present party system?

David Farnham argues that there are two crucial differences between a political party and a pressure group (Farnham 1999, p137):

(a) Parties try to win political control to use political power. Pressure groups seek to influence political decisions not to get in a position where they can make those decisions themselves.

(b) The political programmes of parties are broad-based, while pressure groups tend to concentrate on a single issue.

2 Given the above, would you say that the UK Independence Party (UKIP), which won the EU elections in 2014, but won only one seat in the 2015 General Election, is a political party or a pressure group? What about the Scottish National Party?

3 Make a list of the ways in which pressure groups can influence the government.

4.3 THE GOVERNMENT AND THE ECONOMY

4.3.1 SOME KEY DEFINITIONS

Before we can examine ways in which the government can manage the economy, we need to define some key concepts.

Gross Domestic Product

The most common method of measuring the output of an economy is Gross Domestic Product (GDP). This is the measure of the country's total annual output of goods and services. This is not the same as the sum of the outputs of all organisations in the economy, as this would involve double counting. For example, sales of cans of baked beans made by a supermarket are counted, but not sales of the tinplate for the cans made by a steelworks. When calculating GDP:

- indirect taxes and subsidies (like VAT) are normally ignored
- exports are included, because they form part of the output of the UK
- imports are excluded, because although they are consumed in the UK, they are part of the output of other countries.

John Maynard Keynes defined GDP (or Y) in terms of an equation as follows:

$$Y = C + G + I + X - M$$

where C is consumption, which is a function of disposable income (Y – T (taxation)), less savings, plus borrowing; G is government current spending, I is investment on long-term capital items by industry or the government (mainly dependent on interest rates and the prospect of making a financial return), X is exports (dependent on productivity and the exchange rate), and M is imports (dependent on exchange rates and the level of national income). To stress Keynes's understanding that demand is the main driver of GDP, he argued that Y = aggregate demand (Sexton and Fortura 2005). It follows that if any of the components of aggregate demand (C, G, I and (X – M)) fall, GDP will fall. This will be important in our later discussion of current economic policy.

An important distinction to make is between GDP and the standard of living or quality of life. Governments are concerned to achieve economic growth, defined as an increase in GDP over time. Individuals are much more concerned with their own standard of living or quality of life. The American politician Bobby Kennedy, campaigning for the US Presidency in 1968, graphically analysed the difference between GDP and quality of life: 'Our Gross National Product... counts air pollution and cigarette advertising, and ambulances to clear our highways of carnage... It counts napalm and counts nuclear warheads... Yet the gross national product does not allow for the health of our children, the quality of their education or the joy of their play... it measures everything in short, except that which makes life worthwhile.' (John F Kennedy Presidential Library and Museum, quoted in Rogers (2012)). The concept of quality of life is explored further in Chapter 9.

?   REFLECTIVE ACTIVITY 4.3

Standard of living

How might an individual's standard of living increase without there being an increase in GDP?

Business cycles

The economy tends to move in a series of ups and downs in the short term, although the long-term trend is for the size of GDP to grow. These fluctuations, over a 5–10 year period, are known as the business cycle. Governments attempt to dampen the effects of these cycles, but have not succeeded in abolishing them entirely. The top of a cycle is known as a peak, the bottom as a trough. In the period between a peak and a trough, economic growth may merely slow down, as in the period 2001–3, following the terrorist attacks of 11 September 2001, or GDP may actually fall. If GDP falls for two consecutive quarters, this is technically known as a recession, as the UK experienced in 1973–5, 1979–81, 1990–2 and 2008–9. If two recessions follow each in quick succession, as in 2008–9 and 2012, this is known as a double dip recession. The double dip recession in 2012 was later recalculated away as two quarters of zero growth, much to the relief of the Coalition Government. If a recession is both deep and long-lasting, it is known as a depression, as with the Great Depression of 1929–33 following the Wall Street Crash.

Unemployment

Unemployment is a surprisingly complex concept which has significant social as well as economic consequences. It is not even simple to define unemployment. A person can only be unemployed if he or she is out of work and seeking work. But what about someone who is:

- working part-time but would rather work full-time?
- on a zero-hours contract?
- apparently seeking work, but has totally unrealistic expectations about the sort of job which he or she could obtain?

There are two main ways of measuring unemployment:

- *To count those people who are claiming unemployment benefit (the claimant count).* This means that those who do not have work, and are seeking work, but who do not qualify for benefit, are excluded. On the other hand, some people who are not genuinely seeking work may be included.

- *To carry out a survey and ask people whether they are employed or unemployed.* This is carried out through the Labour Force Survey, using internationally agreed definitions provided by the International Labour Organisation (ILO). Here someone is classified as unemployed if they:
  - are out of work
  - have been seeking work within the last four weeks
  - are available to start work within two weeks.

The ILO method is now the government's preferred measure, but both are regularly published in the UK. The ILO figure comes out higher than the claimant count measure, mainly because it includes large numbers of women who are ineligible for unemployment benefit.

Inflation

Inflation is a general rise in the level of prices. In the UK it is measured in three ways:

- *RPI – the Retail Price Index.* This is calculated by measuring monthly changes in the price of a basket of goods which is meant to represent the spending pattern of the average family. This is the measure used to assess yearly increases in pensions and some state benefits.
- *RPIX – the Retail Price Index excluding mortgage interest.* Until November 2003 this was the government's preferred target measure, as it represents the underlying rate of inflation in the economy (mortgage interest rates depend on the general level of interest rates, set by the Bank of England).
- *CPI – the Consumer Price Index.* This is the agreed measure of inflation used throughout the European Union, and was adopted as the official inflation target in the UK in November 2003 (when it was known as the Harmonised Index of Consumer Prices – inevitably called hiccup!). It is now used to assess yearly increases in most state benefits excluding pensions.

Balance of payments

The balance of payments is a measure of flows of money into and out of the UK economy. It is extremely complex as it has a number of different components. The most commonly used elements are:

- *the balance of trade* – this measures imports and exports of goods
- *the balance of payments on current account* – this measures imports and exports of goods and services.

4.3.2 ECONOMIC OBJECTIVES

All governments, whatever their political complexion, are basically trying to achieve four main economic objectives:

- *Economic growth.* Since the 1990s this has increased by an average of around 2–2.5% a year, with some periods of falling GDP, and others when the growth rate in the short term has gone as high as 4%.
- *Full employment.* This does not mean that nobody is unemployed, but that there are in theory jobs available for those seeking them, at current wage rates. In practice, this means that full employment is achieved if the number out of work is matched by the number of unfilled vacancies.

- *Stable prices (or low inflation).* Again there is some dispute about the optimum level of inflation, but most economists would agree that it is around the Labour government's target of 2.5% on the RPI-X index in the late 1990s (restated as 2% on the CPI index in November 2003), and still in force in 2016.
- *Equilibrium in the balance of payments.* That is, that the value of goods and services exported should roughly equal the value imported. This has deteriorated in recent years, with the trade deficit around £120bn in 2014, although this is offset to some extent by a surplus on the balance on services, leading to a current account deficit of £93bn.

The New Labour government since 1997 had been more successful than most governments, at least until 2007, achieving full success on economic growth and inflation, and considerable success on full employment. The only blot on its record was a worsening balance of payments, but of course it was blown seriously off course by the onset of the credit crunch recession in 2008. The performance of the Coalition and Conservative governments since 2010 will be examined later in this chapter.

In addition, governments will have policies on other economic objectives. These might include:

- *Redistribution of income* – this is seen as a social objective in its own right, but its prime economic function is as a means to achieve economic growth. Traditionally the objective was to use the tax system to redistribute from the rich to the poor, but increasingly the distribution of income favours the rich.
- *Exchange rates* – the exchange value of the pound is seen as a political virility symbol, but it is primarily important as a means of managing the balance of payments. UK entry to the euro is of course a long-running contentious political issue.
- *The level of taxation and the level of government spending* – both in terms of their absolute level in the economy, and of the balance between them. The Coalition and Conservative governments from 2010 see eliminating the budget deficit as the most important economic objective. The deficit is discussed in more detail later.
- *Interest rates* – these are seen either as a means of controlling inflation or of managing growth.
- *Money supply* – in the 1980s this was seen as an objective in its own right, but is now seen as a means of achieving other objectives.
- *Privatisation (or nationalisation).* Linked with this is more general regulation or deregulation of the economy.

As you will see from the above list, economics is not value-free. Managing the economy inevitably has strong political and social, as well as economic elements.

4.3.3 THE TOOLS OF GOVERNMENT POLICY

A range of tools are available to the government in its objective of managing the economy.

Fiscal policy

This involves a manipulation of the level of taxation and/or government spending. The theory underpinning this was established by the economist John Maynard Keynes in the 1930s. If there is a persistent level of unemployment in the economy, he argued that this is fundamentally due to a lack of demand. In order to increase demand in the economy, the government can inject demand into it, either by increasing its own spending, which will directly lead to a higher demand for goods and services, or by cutting taxation, which will put more money into the hands of consumers, and so enable them to demand more goods and services. However, changes in taxation or public spending are subject to long time lags before they take effect, and increasingly Chancellors of the Exchequer have not seen fiscal policy as an appropriate tool for short-term management of the economy. Instead, they have taken the view that the level of spending and taxation are much more issues of political rather than demand management policy. Gordon Brown expressed this in his Golden Rule, which stated that over an economic cycle, the government should aim for a balanced budget, ie, the revenue raised through taxation should equal the amount spent on current goods and services. This policy does allow for some flexibility, ie for expenditure to exceed taxation during the trough phase of the cycle, as long as this is balanced by a surplus at the peak. However, the Golden Rule, and its accompanying more general policy, Prudence, were torn up when the full impact of the credit crunch became apparent in the autumn of 2008. In 2015, George Osborne brought in his Charter for Budget Responsibility, which requires public finances to be in overall budget surplus by 2019/20, and would legally force future governments to run an absolute budget surplus when the economy is expanding (Godley & Co 2015).

Monetary policy

Monetary policy was strongly in vogue during the 1980s, at the height of the power of Margaret Thatcher, and under the influence of the American economist Milton Friedman, who argued a direct causal link between the supply of money and the level of inflation. Policies were therefore implemented directly to control the supply of money. However, as the leading monetarist economist Sir Alan Budd, who was chief economic adviser to the Treasury between 1991 and 1997, says, 'I hope I can say without offending anyone that the experiment in seeking to control inflation by setting quantitative monetary targets did not match the hopes of its most enthusiastic supporters (among whom I am willing to count myself).' (Keegan 2004a). One of the main problems was not the existence of the link between money supply and inflation, but the difficulty in producing a watertight definition of money at a time of great technological change, including the explosive growth in the use of credit cards (which enable people to spend money they do not possess, and which does not exist until they spend it).

Monetary policy is now much simpler. It consists of control over interest rates, set by the independent Bank of England. The way in which this works will be explored in considerable detail in Section 4.3.5.

Competitiveness (supply-side) policy

Policy here is linked to the concept of NAIRU (the rate of unemployment which ensures a stable level of inflation). If the economy can be made more competitive, the rate of NAIRU should fall, and the economy will be able to operate at lower levels of inflation and unemployment. This involves deregulating the markets for both goods and services and for labour, through policies including privatisation and rigorous control of monopolies and cartels. It also involves a concerted drive to increase the rate of growth of productivity in the economy, by encouraging investment in research and development, and in the enhancement of worker skills. Again, this policy will be examined in depth in the following sections.

Exchange rate policy

It is possible to manipulate the exchange rate in order to achieve economic objectives. For example, if an exchange rate is set at a level below that justified by market forces, the currency will be under-valued. This will stimulate exports, which will be artificially lowered in price, and discourage imports, which will be artificially highly priced. An over-valued currency will have the opposite result. However, there are two major snags with this.

Manipulation of the exchange rate is only seriously possible if the exchange rate is fixed. However, since the 1970s, most currencies have floated, ie been subject to market forces. Even in a fixed exchange rate system, it is very difficult in the long term to maintain an exchange rate markedly different from that implied by market forces.

The other key issue in exchange rate policy is of course the euro. Should the UK join, or not? At the moment, the UK has an opt-out from Economic and Monetary Union, and thus from the euro. However, the UK is qualified to join EMU if it chooses. In 1997, the Chancellor of the Exchequer postponed a decision on entry, saying that the UK would consider joining only if five economic tests were met: These were:

- Are business cycles and economic structures compatible so that the UK can live with euro interest rates?
- Is there sufficient flexibility to deal with any problems which might arise?
- Will joining EMU create better conditions for firms making long-term decisions to invest in the UK?
- What impact will entry have on the competitive position of the City?
- Will joining the euro promote higher growth, stability, and a lasting increase in jobs?

If the government decided that these tests were met, it would recommend entry to the euro, but the final decision would be taken by a referendum. To no-one's surprise, the government decided in 2003 that the Five Tests had not been met, and as a result, any decision in favour of entry has been postponed indefinitely – to the great relief of virtually everybody in the UK as the crisis in the eurozone developed from 2010 onwards. This will be discussed more fully in Chapter 6.

CASE STUDY 4.2

INFLATION AND INTEREST RATES

The impact of inflation

We have already defined inflation as a general increase in the level of prices in the economy, measured in various ways – RPI, RPIX or CPI. In the last resort this is caused by excess demand in the economy, basically when the amount of goods and services which people want to buy is greater than the productive potential of the economy – 'too much money chasing too few goods'. The generally accepted view is that inflation is harmful, and it follows from this that low inflation is beneficial, for the following reasons.

- *Increased price competitiveness for UK goods.* The important factor here is relative inflation – in order for UK goods to be competitive, UK inflation must be rising at a slower rate than that of our international competitors. Of course, if UK inflation is very rapid, it is likely that the value of the pound will fall, but this itself could generate further inflation, as import prices will rise.

- *Distribution of income will be less distorted.* High inflation benefits borrowers, particularly those with outstanding mortgages, which fall in value in real terms as the value of their houses tend to rise. In addition, the gap in money terms between wage settlements obtained by strong unions as compared with weak ones tends to be greater in times of rapid inflation.

- *Reduced uncertainty.* The more rapid the rate of inflation, and particularly the more variable it is, the more unpredictable the environment becomes for business and individuals. As a result, investment will be discouraged, as firms do not want to take risks, and the result could be falling output and rising unemployment.

- *High inflation means high nominal interest rates.* This puts pressure on the cash flows of borrowers if their main source of income is interrupted, for example by unemployment.

?   REFLECTIVE ACTIVITY 4.4

Deflation

If the effects of high inflation are adverse, would it be better to have falling prices (deflation), as in 2008–9 and 2015?

4.3.4 THE LINK BETWEEN UNEMPLOYMENT AND INFLATION

In the late 1950s, Professor Phillips identified that over the previous hundred years there was an inverse relationship between the rate of change of money wages and the level of unemployment. In the short term this intuitively makes sense. If unemployment is low, workers can demand higher wages, and vice versa. As wage inflation is a very important component of general inflation, it could thus be argued that there was an inverse relationship between unemployment and inflation – if unemployment rose, inflation would fall, and vice versa. This implied that governments could in principle choose the trade-off between inflation and unemployment which best suited their overall objectives.

Unfortunately, almost as soon as Phillips identified the relationship, it ceased to apply. Throughout the 1970s, both inflation and unemployment rose steeply at the same time, giving rise to a phenomenon known as stagflation. Gradually over the 1980s, inflation was squeezed out of the system through strict control of the money supply, but only at the cost of continuing high levels of unemployment. Since 1992, unemployment has fallen considerably, while inflation has stabilised at the 2–3% level.

Clearly the simple concept of the Phillips curve no longer applies, but it has been replaced by the concept of NAIRU (or non-accelerating inflation rate of unemployment). This is the level of unemployment at which inflation will be stable. Nairu appears to have been about 7–8% in the 1970s, but to have fallen to around 3–4% (on the ILO measure) by the early 2000s. One prime objective of governments is to continue to improve the trade-off between inflation and unemployment by lowering the level of NAIRU. This can be done through making the labour market more competitive.

However, as the Bank of England says, 'The level of the NAIRU cannot be determined with any precision for the purposes of setting monetary policy... It is easier to construct plausible estimates after the event – ie once we have observed inflation – rather than in anticipation of it.' (Bank of England 2004a). NAIRU appears to be much lower in the UK and US, with largely deregulated labour markets, than in the eurozone, where labour markets are much more heavily regulated. Of course, there is a political and social, as well as an economic trade off here – which is preferable, a higher risk of unemployment in the eurozone, or the higher level of benefits which accompany unemployment there?

4.3.5 INTEREST RATES

An interest rate is simply the price of money. However, unfortunately the real world is more complicated. As an individual, you are almost certainly paying and receiving several different rates of interest – on your bank current account, on your building society account, your internet savings account, your mortgage, your credit card, your hire purchase agreement. Ultimately these come back to one rate, the official rate set by the Bank of England, and at which it will lend money to the banks and other financial institutions. This is set monthly by the Bank's Monetary Policy Committee.

If this official rate changes, the banks and building societies will change the rates for their own savers and borrowers. Equally importantly, an increase in interest rates affects expectations. If interest rates start to rise after a period when they have been static or falling, the expectation is that they will continue to rise in the near future. The Bank of England used this to great effect in 2004, when it made a series of quarter-point increases in interest rates, none of which was particularly serious on its own, but which had a big effect on expectations. A series of aggressive interest rate cuts in 2008–9 signalled the seriousness of the credit crunch crisis. The Bank of England interest rate has remained at 0.5% since 2009.

4.3.6 INTEREST RATES AND DEMAND

When interest rates are changed, demand can be affected in a number of ways.

- *Spending and saving.* An increase in interest rates makes saving more attractive and spending less attractive. Consumer spending is likely to fall. At the same time industrial investment will fall, as the margin between what an investment costs and the profit which it will produce becomes narrower.
- *Cashflow.* Higher interest rates mean higher mortgage rates – normally paid monthly, and higher rates of interest on savings – normally paid annually. The short-term effect on the cashflow of individuals is likely to be negative, reducing demand.
- *Asset prices.* A change in interest rates affects the price of stocks and shares. If interest rates go up, the price of stocks and shares tends to fall, as it becomes more attractive to hold cash. There will be a similar effect on house prices. An increase in interest rates thus marginally reduces individuals' wealth, again making them more reluctant to spend.
- *Exchange rates.* At the same time, the exchange rate is likely to rise marginally, as it becomes more attractive to hold pounds rather than other currencies. This makes export prices higher, which again reduces demand. At the same time, import prices become cheaper, which immediately reduces inflation (Bank of England 2004b).

An increase in interest rates thus clearly reduces demand in the economy, which will lower the rate of inflation. However, as with everything in economics, this is subject to time lags. Some effects are almost immediate, such as the impact on the exchange rate, some take a matter of weeks, such as the impact on mortgage and savings rates, while others are long-term, like the wealth effect of falling share prices. The Bank of England calculates that it takes up to two years for the full impact to work through the economy. In making its interest rate decisions, the Bank of England thus has to make estimates of the level of inflation two years hence. This produces the apparently perverse result that the Bank can sometimes cut interest rates at a time when current inflation is above target, or vice versa.

4.3.7 CENTRAL BANKS AND INTEREST RATES

The Bank of England

The Bank of England has been involved in setting interest rates for many years, and this system was formalised in the mid-1990s by the Ken and Eddie Show, when interest rates were set at a monthly meeting between the Chancellor, Kenneth Clarke, and the Governor of the Bank, Eddie George. However, in the last resort, the decision was the Chancellor's. This was changed in the first act of the incoming Labour government in May 1997. To great surprise, Gordon Brown announced the granting of operational independence to the Bank. In future, interest rate decisions would be taken monthly by the Monetary Policy Committee, chaired by the Governor, which consists of both Bank and government nominees (a total of nine members).

Interest rate decisions were to be taken in line with the government's inflation target, initially set as 2.5% on RPIX, subject to a margin of plus or minus 1%. The target was thus a symmetrical one, unlike the previous Conservative target, which was 2.5% or less.

Under the Bank of England Act 1998, the Bank's remit was to:

- maintain price stability and
- subject to that, to support the economic policy of the government, including its objectives for growth and employment.

In its remit for the Monetary Policy Committee, this was interpreted as 'The Government's central economic policy objective is to achieve high and stable levels of growth and employment. Price stability is a precondition for these high and stable levels of growth and employment, which will in turn help to create the conditions for price stability on a sustainable basis' (Bank of England, 2003).

In December 2003, the target inflation rate was changed to 2% on CPI, again plus or minus 1%. This was a slightly looser target, as 2% on CPI roughly equates to 3% on RPIX.

If inflation moved away from target by more than one percentage point in either direction, the Governor was required to send an open letter to the Chancellor, setting out:

- the reasons why inflation has missed the target
- what the Bank is doing about it
- the time span for remedial action
- how the remedial action meets the government's monetary policy objectives.

It is a measure of the success of the policy that such a letter was only required once before the onset of the world recession, when inflation became much more volatile. From 2010 to 2013 CPI inflation was above target, at 3.3, 4.5, 2.8, and 2.6. It fell below target in 2014, to 1.5%, and was around zero in 2015.

The European Central Bank

The ECB was set up in 1998, to manage Economic and Monetary Union, including setting interest rates for the eurozone. Interest rates are fixed on a monthly basis by the Executive Board of the ECB, which consists of six members appointed by the 17 eurozone countries, headed by the President of the ECB, Mario Draghi.

The ECB is totally independent, and sets its own inflation target. The prime objective of the ECB is to maintain price stability, originally defined as 2% or less on CPI. In 2003, this was slightly but significantly modified to 'close to 2 per cent over the medium term' (*Guardian* 2003a). This was slightly less deflationary. The objective was modified again in 2004, when the ECB said that, 'without prejudice to the objective of price stability', the eurosystem will also support the general economic policies in the Community', including 'a high level of employment' and 'sustainable and non-inflationary growth' (ECB 2004).

The Federal Reserve

The central bank of the US is the Federal Reserve Board, currently headed by Janet Yellan. It has no specific inflation target, but its remit is laid down by the Federal Reserve Act as to 'promote effectively the goals of maximum employment, stable prices and moderate long-term interest rates' (Federal Reserve 2004). Interest rates are set monthly by the Federal Open Market Committee.

?   REFLECTIVE ACTIVITY 4.5

The objectives of the Bank of England

The left-wing Labour shadow chancellor, John McDonnell, announced in September 2015 that he would change the remit on the Bank of England on interest rates from a primary aim of maintaining price stability to one that gives equal emphasis to jobs, investment and inequality (Rawnsley and Helm 2015).

What do you think would be the likely impact of such a change in policy?

4.4 THE CREDIT CRUNCH CRISIS OF 2008–9

In October 2008, the world financial system came within a whisker of complete meltdown. In September 2008, the US government had decided to allow the investment bank Lehman Brothers go bust, and in October the UK government nationalised Royal Bank of Scotland, and Bradford and Bingley, and forced Halifax Bank of Scotland into a shotgun takeover by Lloyds, funded by government money. Also in October, the US government nationalised the massive insurance group AIG. Meltdown was avoided, but the world moved rapidly into recession, with an almost complete shut-down of bank lending and rapidly rising unemployment.

What went wrong? The immediate seeds of the crisis were sown with the terrorist attacks of 11 September 2001. The US economy was already slowing before the attacks, and Alan Greenspan, the head of the US Federal Reserve, felt that decisive monetary action was needed to avoid outright recession. He quickly slashed US interest rates to an unprecedented 1%, and the Bank of England and the European Central Bank followed, although not to the same extent. US interest rates were held at this low level for several years.

With hindsight, it is clear that Greenspan went too far too fast. The economic impact of 9/11 proved to be short-lived, and by 2004, the US economy was back in boom. In normal circumstances, such a loose monetary policy would have rapidly led to a rise in inflation, but retail prices in the US, the UK and the eurozone were kept down by the boom in cheap imports from China. Instead, inflationary pressures built up on asset prices, particularly house prices.

There were also long-term trends which contributed to a build-up of pressure on the economic system. Real incomes for workers in the US had been stagnant or falling for decades, for all income groups except the very rich (Elliott 2012), and research by the Resolution Foundation showed that the same had been happening in the UK since 2001. The median male worker's real wage in 2011 was only 96% of that in 2001, while a male worker in the bottom 10% of the wage distribution received a real wage 94% of that in 2001. Even male workers in the top 10% had seen stagnant real wages. Average income of the top 0.1%, on the other hand, grew by 63% over the same period. The average household's income was only maintained through tax credits, through a second income if that was available, and, increasingly, through borrowing, which often took the form of equity withdrawal from the increased value of houses (Resolution Foundation 2012). The debt to income ratio of the average household rose from 95% in 1997 to 160% in 2008 (Lansley 2009b). As early as 2004, *The Economist* was already concerned about the danger from the credit explosion, reporting that household debt had passed £1tr (*Economist* 2004c).

The combination of stagnant real incomes, rising debt, and rising house prices produced a toxic mix. Mortgage lenders in the US started an aggressive lending programme, buoyed by the expectation that house prices would continue rising indefinitely. Many specialised in lending to so-called 'ninja' borrowers – no income, no job, no assets – in the so-called sub-prime market. In the UK the ex-building society Northern Rock followed a similar policy, lending on mortgages of 125% of the value of a property, financed by its own borrowing from the wholesale money markets. The money markets themselves became contaminated. In order to spread their risk, the US mortgage lenders packaged up their mortgages (a process known as securitisation), into so-called collateralised debt obligations – a package of mortgages sold as a bond to other institutions. By 2007, CDOs in the US were valued at $1.3tr, and this was only the tip of an enormous syndicated debt iceberg worth $14tr in the US, 7% of total US GDP. The securitised bundles were so complex that an individual bank found it almost impossible to assess the risk they were running.

Like any pyramid scheme, the whole thing only worked as long as house prices continued to rise. Unfortunately, as US interest rates began to rise again, the ninja borrowers were no longer able to meet their mortgage obligations. US house prices peaked in summer 2006, and fell 25% over the next year.

The first victim of the crisis was Northern Rock, which failed in September 2007, and was eventually nationalised by the UK government. In March 2008, the US government rescued the investment bank Bear Stearns, and in July it rescued the two major US mortgage providers, Fannie Mae and Freddie Mac. The crisis then reached its peak in September–October 2008.

An underlying contributory factor was the very loose supervision of financial institutions in the UK, and to a lesser extent in the US. As Vince Cable points out, the Financial Services Authority 'to the end remained supportive of Northern Rock's business model' (Cable 2009, p13).

The result of the bank crashes was that inter-bank lending totally dried up, as no bank could be sure how safe its fellow bank was. This was passed on to customers, who found it increasingly difficult to obtain loans. Many totally viable companies with temporary cashflow needs were forced into bankruptcy. Spending dried up, unemployment rose, and the economy spiralled downwards, rapidly moving into recession (two successive quarters of negative GDP). Mervyn King, the Governor of the Bank of England described this bank behaviour as individually understandable but collectively suicidal (Cable 2009, p57).

The UK government's reaction to the crisis was swift and decisive. HBOS and RBS were bailed out to the tune of £35bn, VAT was cut from 17.5 to 15%, interest rates quickly slashed to 0.5%, and a fiscal expansion package worth 1% of GDP introduced. The Bank of England also undertook a programme of quantitative easing, in effect printing more money. All these policies were generally applauded, except by the Conservative opposition, quickly followed by the US and endorsed by the G20. However, each policy had risks.

- The bail-out of the banks risked moral hazard, where in effect the banks were shielded from the effects of their folly.
- The VAT cut was widely seen as minimal and unlikely to stimulate spending.
- If interest rates were held down for too long, there was a risk that inflationary pressures could build up in the long term. The same was true of quantitative easing. However, as Keynes said, in the long run we are all dead.
- The fiscal stimulus, coupled with the bail out of the banks and a natural fall in tax receipts and rise in government spending due to unemployment, ran the risk of driving the government deficit to unacceptable levels. However, as the government pointed out, the UK deficit before the crisis was on the low side compared with the rest of the G7, and even after all the extra spending would still be relatively low by historical standards.

The crisis seems to have developed in a way uncannily like that suggested by Karl Marx in *Das Kapital* in the late nineteenth century. Marx predicted that the inherent conflict between capital and labour would manifest itself as companies' pursuit of profits and productivity naturally led them to need fewer and fewer workers, creating an 'industrial reserve army' of the poor and unemployed: 'Accumulation of wealth at one pole is, therefore, at the same time accumulation of misery.' (Marx 1867, 2004)

Marx also pointed out the paradox of over-production and under-consumption: The more people are relegated to poverty, the less they will be able to consume all the goods and services companies produce. When one company cuts costs to boost earnings, it's smart, but when they all do, they undermine the income formation and effective demand on which they rely for revenues and profits. As noted above, the fall in real wages predicted by Marx was concealed to some extent by the easy credit available in the early 2000s, but Marxists would see this as a cynical move by the capitalist class to protect their own interests (Magnus 2011).

In the US, the share of GDP going to profits in 2011 was 12.6%, the highest since 1950, while the share going to wages was 54.9%, the lowest since 1955 (*Wall Street Journal* 2011). The fall in the share of GDP going to wages is not as extreme in the UK, but the trend is similar. Wages took around 58% of GDP in the 1950s and 60s, and briefly peaked at 65% in 1975, at the height of trade union power. Between 1977 and 2008 the share going to wages fell from 59 to 53%, while the share going to profits rose from 25 to 29% (Elliott 2012).

After bottoming at 52% in 1996, after Margaret Thatcher had neutralised the countervailing power of the unions, the wage share rose slightly under the Labour governments after 1997, before falling to 53% in 2008 (Willow 2011; Weldon 2012). As Marx put it in *Kapital*: 'The ultimate reason for all real crises always remains the poverty and restricted consumption of the masses.'

For a concise and relatively impartial account of the crisis, see book by the then Liberal Democrat shadow chancellor, Vince Cable, *The Storm: the world economic crisis and what it means* (2009). Cable was Secretary of State for Business, Innovation and Skills in the Coalition Government from 2010 to 2015, but lost his seat in the Liberal Democrat rout in the 2015 General Election.

? REFLECTIVE ACTIVITY 4.6

Gordon Brown and the recession

The Conservative party blamed Gordon Brown for the recession in the UK in 2008–9. Is this fair?

4.5 THE UK ECONOMY SINCE 2010

By the middle of 2010 there were signs that the UK was moving into a sustained recovery from the recession. In Quarter 2 of 2010 the economic growth rate was 1.1%, and government net borrowing was falling slightly (Pettinger 2012a). The reduction in interest rates and the cut in VAT were having an impact.

After the UK General Election of May 2010 a Coalition Conservative/Liberal Democrat government was formed, with the primary economic objective of attacking the budget deficit. The deficit in 2009–10 was £167.4bn, about 11% of GDP, way above the generally accepted target of 3%. Total national debt was around 65% of GDP, again well above the generally accepted target of 40%, but well below the 180% of the late 1940s, and below that in Japan (194%), Italy (100%) and the US (75%) (Pettinger 2012a).

George Osborne, the Chancellor the Exchequer, set two targets for the budget deficit and the National Debt:

- To eliminate the structural budget deficit by 2014–15 (the structural deficit is that part of the deficit which persists even with full employment). The Government estimated that this was around 80–90% of 2009–10 borrowing.
- To reduce the National Debt as a percentage of GDP by 2015–16 (HM Treasury 2010).

The Labour party agreed that the deficit must be reduced, and had already published its own deficit reduction programme, but disagreed on two key issues:

- The speed of the reduction programme. They claimed that the Government's programme was much too rapid, and could lead to a further recession.
- How the deficit would be reduced. Two options were available – cutting government spending and increasing taxation. Both sides called for a balance between the two, but

the Government preferred cutting spending, while the Opposition favoured increasing taxation.

The conventional Keynesian approach to the deficit was to deal with the recession first, and leave the deficit to take care of itself. As the economy recovered from recession, tax receipts would rise, and payments such as unemployment benefit would fall, thus gradually reducing the deficit. Cutting the deficit during a recession would be self-defeating, as this would make the recession worse. To understand this, we need to go back to the Keynesian national income equation which we discussed in Section 4.3.1:

$$Y = C + I + G + X - M$$

Cutting government spending would reduce G, and thus by definition (other things being equal) reduce Y (national income). Increasing taxation would lower disposable income, a main component of consumption, which would reduce C, and hence again reduce national income.

The Keynesian approach was not without risk, however. There would be a time lag before the deficit began to fall, and in the short term stimulating the economy could increase the deficit.

The Government used two main arguments to justify its aggressive deficit reduction programme. One was the household analogy, beloved of Margaret Thatcher – just as a household in debt will rationally cut its spending in order to reduce its debt, so should the government. The fallacy in this argument is that what is rational for a household is not rational for a government. If a household cuts its spending, this has virtually no impact on other households, whereas if a government cuts its spending, this impacts on all other parts of the economy.

The second argument was a much better one. Back to the Keynesian equation again. Cutting government spending would free resources for the private sector. Lower government spending would mean less state borrowing, which would lower interest rates, and so encourage the private sector to invest. This would increase I, and so increase national income. Lower government spending should also increase exports, as again resources would be freed. Higher exports would again increase national income. Their ideal combination economic policy was tight fiscal policy combined with loose monetary policy.

The Coalition government started its deficit reduction programme very quickly. Value added tax was increased from 17.5 to 20% in January 2011, and plans announced for big cuts in government spending, concentrating on welfare payments and local government spending.

For two years the deficit reduction programme seemed to proceed well. The deficit in 2010–11 was down to £145bn, and in 2011–12 down to £111.9bn. The biggest cause of the drop was a fall in public sector net investment of around £20bn, partly as a result of cuts already planned by the previous Labour government, and partly as a result of coalition cuts, for example in the school rebuilding programme (Pettinger 2012b). However, the near onset of a double dip recession in the fourth quarter of 2011 started to push borrowing up again, and the deficit for 2012–13 was forecast to be £127bn, an increase of £15bn over 2011–12 (Pettinger 2012a).

The effect on economic growth was as the Keynesians had forecast. After inheriting a growth rate of 1.1% in quarter 2 of 2010, economic growth was negative by quarter 4, and anaemic throughout 2011. By 2012 the economy was desperately near to a double dip recession with two quarters of zero growth. Only in the third quarter of 2012 was there a significant bounce-back, to growth of 1%, helped by the boost given by the London Olympics. Total growth in the first two and half years of the coalition government had been little more than 1%, and the economy was still well below its peak in 2008 (unlike the US and Germany, both of which by 2012 had output higher than 2008, and China, whose economy by 2012 was half as big again as it was in 2008). If one takes account of four years of lost growth at the long-run average of 2.5% a year, the economy was something like 13% smaller than it should have been by 2012.

Private sector investment had not increased as the government had hoped. Small firms were unable to obtain bank funding, and the private sector was not prepared to invest purely because interest rates were extremely low. They calculated (probably correctly) that because aggregate demand was down, there was little prospect of selling the extra goods resulting from extra investment. They also built in the risk involved in new investment, particularly once the economy went into a double dip recession.

Pressure increased on George Osborne to change his deficit reduction policy and adopt a less deflationary Plan B. In June 2011, 52 signatories, including many leading UK economists, called for a Plan B (Stewart and Boffey 2011). In August George Osborne hit back, saying that 'the alternative of more spending and yet more borrowing... places those who advocate it "to the ludicrous outer fringe" of economics' (Osborne 2011). Among those advocating just such a policy were four winners of the Nobel Prize for Economics – Paul Krugman, Amartya Sen, Joseph Stiglitz and Christopher Pissandes (Chu 2011). In January 2012 the heads of eleven world economic bodies, including the IMF, the World Bank and the WTO, warned of the dangers of austerity (Elliott 2012). Osborne countered that he was right, and that the worsening situation in the UK was caused not by his policies, but by the eurozone crisis, which was driving our main trading partners into recession.

2012 represented the nadir of George Osborne's fortunes. He had narrowly missed a double dip recession, his 2012 Budget had been condemned as an 'omnishambles', and he was booed at the Olympic Games. While insisting that he was still following Plan A, he quietly cut back on the speed and intensity of his austerity drive. The result was that the country started on a slow recovery.

How successful was the Coalition government at running the economy? Here it is useful to compare the forecasts which the Office for Budget Responsibility, the body which monitors economic policy, made for 2014–15, against actual performance. Most importantly, the budget deficit should have been eliminated by 2014–15, but was actually £90bn, or 5.5% of GDP, half its peak size. The National Debt had been forecast to peak in 2013–14, and to have fallen to 67% of GDP in 2014–15. It was 80% in 2014–15, and still rising. The other major failure concerned the balance of payments. The balance of payments on current account was forecast to be 2% of GDP, but was actually 5.6%, or £93bn, the worst ever (OBR 2010, 2015).

On other measures, the government was more successful. Unemployment was on target, at 6%, and inflation, forecast at 2%, was at zero. GDP growth was 2.7%, exactly on target. GDP was bigger than before the crash, but not by much, and GDP per head in mid-2015 was lower than before the crash (due to the big increase in UK population since 2008) (Anthony 2015). In 2014–15, average household disposable income finally edged past its pre-crash peak, although for working age households it was still below the peak, while pensioner households were 10% above the previous peak (*The Week* 2015).

? REFLECTIVE ACTIVITY 4.7

The UK budget deficit

After the heavy and unexpected Labour defeat in the May 2015 general election, the senior Labour politician John Cruddas commissioned a public opinion poll to try to ascertain why Labour had lost. One question was as to whether 'we must live within our means, so cutting the deficit is the top priority'. There was overwhelming support for this, with 56% agreeing and only

16% disagreeing. Even among Labour voters, a third agreed with the question, while a third disagreed (Wintour 2015).

Do you agree with the statement?

?   REFLECTIVE ACTIVITY 4.8

The 2015 UK general election

In May 2015, the Conservative party unexpectedly won the UK general election with an overall majority of 12. Every opinion poll up to the election had forecast a hung parliament, with the Conservatives and Labour neck and neck. The most likely outcome seemed to be a Labour minority government, with SNP and possibly Liberal Democrat support.

Given the generally lack-lustre performance of the economy over the period of Coalition government from 2010 to 2015, why do you think that the Conservatives won the election?

?   REFLECTIVE ACTIVITY 4.9

Quantitative easing

One reaction of central banks around the world to the financial crisis of 2007–9 was to slash interest rates virtually to zero. Another was to try to stimulate demand by increasing the money supply, through a technique known as quantitative easing. This involved the central bank creating electronic money, which it used to buy government bonds from the financial system. The intention was that the commercial banks would use this money to increase their lending, so stimulating demand.

The technique was first used by the Bank of Japan in the early 1990s, by the Federal Reserve from 2008 and the Bank of England from 2009. The European Central Bank initially resisted the technique, fearing that it would increase inflation, but finally adopted quantitative easing in 2015 (BBC 2015). The Federal Reserve created $3tr and the Bank of England £75bn of new money, in each case around 20% of GDP. The policy helped to stabilise the financial system, may well have prevented further bank collapses, and stopped the crash getting even worse. It has been estimated that this was worth around 1.5 to 2% of GDP (Martin and Milas 2013). The Bank of England argued that by 2014, QE had increased UK GDP by a total of 3% of GDP, or £50bn (Monaghan 2014). To put this in perspective, compensation paid by the banks to purchasers of unnecessary Payment Protection Insurance totalled over £21bn by August 2015 (Financial Conduct Authority 2015).

There seems little evidence that quantitative easing had much effect on stimulating medium term economic growth. Despite having more cash in their balance sheets, the banks were reluctant to lend, particularly to small business, and at the same time business was reluctant to borrow to invest, although interest rates were at unprecedentedly low levels. This is consistent with the view of Keynes, that trying to stimulate demand during a recession through monetary techniques will be ineffective (Blyth 2012). Instead money leaked into the stock market, boosting the wealth of the already rich, and into property, increasing the risk of another property boom such as the one that precipitated the 2007–9 crash.

Questions

The new Labour leader, Jeremy Corbyn, and his shadow chancellor, John McDonnell, have proposed what they call People's Quantitative Easing. They propose the creation of a new National Investment Bank, which would issue debt which would then be bought by the Bank of England. The NIB would use the proceeds to invest in 'new, large-scale housing, energy, transport and digital projects: quantitative easing for people instead of banks' (quote from Corbyn). Why has Corbyn's proposal been criticised both by the Bank of England and by his rival for the Labour leadership, Yvette Cooper? Could the policy work?

You might find the following articles helpful:

ELLIOTT, L. (2015) Is Jeremy Corbyn's policy of 'quantitative easing for people' feasible? *The Guardian*. 14 August.

WEAVER, M. (2015) Economist defends 'Corbynomics' after Chris Leslie's criticism. *The Guardian*. 3 August.

YATES, T. (2015) Corbyn's QE for the people jeopardises the Bank of England's independence. *The Guardian*. 22 September.

4.6 PUBLIC OWNERSHIP, PRIVATISATION AND PFI/PPP

4.6.1 PUBLIC OWNERSHIP

When most people think of public ownership, they think of the nationalisations of the Labour government in the late 1940s. But public ownership goes back a lot further than that. The beginnings of a state system of welfare came with the Elizabethan Poor Law in the sixteenth century. The Post Office dates back to the seventeenth century, and developed telegraph services in the nineteenth (the precursor of British Telecom). The Metropolitan Police was founded in 1829, while a primitive system of policing through parish constables goes back hundreds of years before that. A state system of education dates from 1870, and in the 1840s Gladstone gave the state reserve powers to nationalise the railways if necessary. In the late nineteenth century, gas, electricity and water services were developed by local authorities ('municipal socialism').

During the First World War, the state obtained a controlling interest in what later became BP, in 1919 the Forestry Commission was set up to manage Britain's woodlands, and the BBC came into public ownership in the 1920s.

These early examples illustrate some of the driving forces behind public ownership:

- to ensure adequate coverage of services (Post Office, Poor Law, schools)
- to safeguard interests vital to the State (BP, Forestry Commission, BBC)
- to control natural monopolies (police).

The nationalisations of the 1940s added a further motive, a socialist desire to control the 'commanding heights' of the economy in the interests of the state. But even here things were not entirely straightforward. When the Bank of England was nationalised in 1946, it had been effectively under total state control for at least a hundred years. The nationalisations of water, gas and electricity involved taking over municipally-owned companies rather than private ones. The railways were in private hands, but had been subject to compulsory amalgamations in the 1920s. The NHS took over Poor Law hospitals, by this time under local authority control, as well as charity hospitals. The really socialist thing about the NHS was the concept of services free at the point of use, rather than ownership. Perhaps the only truly socialist nationalisation was the National Coal Board, which took over from the generally hated coal owners. Generally, the force behind the 1940s nationalisation could be seen equally as a desire to exercise effective centralised planning (Kay 2003).

In recent years, nationalisations have been rescues of failing businesses – Northern Rock and Bradford and Bingley during the financial crash, and Prestwick Airport by the Scottish government. In addition, the US government nationalised the insurance company AIG.

The nationalised industries had a mixed record of performance, but suffered from a number of systemic flaws:

- John Kay has argued that in order for any type of organisation to operate efficiently and effectively, it must be subject to 'disciplined pluralism'. Because there was no requirement to make a profit, there was little pressure to achieve greater efficiency, ie no discipline. And because the nationalised industries were monopolies, there was also no pluralism (Kay, quoted in Palmås 2005).
- Although day to day management was given to the public corporations who controlled the industry, there was a great temptation for governments of all hues to interfere, and government also strictly controlled the level of investment. Nationalised industries thus tended to be used as an instrument of macroeconomic policy, with their investment levels moved up or down depending on the state of unemployment or inflation.
- Nationalised industries were at their height in an era before most businesses, public or private, gave much attention to customer service. As a result, allied with the strength of trade unions, nationalised industries tended to be run in the interests of staff rather than the customer – television in the 1970s loved to expose 'jobsworths' in the nationalised industries and local government. On the other hand, public sector staff did tend to share a 'public service ethos', which in the case of the railways, for example, led to a high emphasis on safety, and a determination to 'muddle through'. Thus trains kept running during the terrible winter of 1963 in a way which in many cases they failed to do during the floods of 2007.

4.6.2 PRIVATISATION

The Thatcher/Major governments between 1979 and 1997 embarked on an extensive programme of privatisation, starting with British Telecom in 1982 and ending with British Rail in 1996. Most of the big privatisations were public offers of shares to the general public, while others, like the National Freight Corporation and National Bus, were trade sales.

The arguments for privatisation were partly financial and partly political. Privatisation raised very large sums of money for the Treasury, and so permitted tax cuts (memorably criticised by Harold Macmillan as 'selling the family silver'). It also reduced the role of the state (a key element in Thatcherism), which hopefully would give managers more autonomy to manage efficiently. By making the privatised businesses leaner and meaner, they would be better able to compete effectively in a globalised economy. Privatisation was also intended to stimulate personal share ownership. To ensure that the privatised companies did not exploit their monopoly positions, they were subject to detailed regulatory controls, particularly over pricing, which were intended to force efficiency.

However, just as with nationalisation, flaws in the model gradually become apparent. Firstly, there is no evidence that personal share ownership was significantly expanded. The small investors who bought shares in the privatised companies usually have no other equity investments, and most quickly sold out. Individual share ownership is now half what it was before the Thatcher privatisations (Jefferies 2015).

In most cases, prices to the consumer have been reduced, but it is impossible to say whether this is the result of privatisation. In the case of BT, for example, privatisation coincided with a period of rapid technological advance and globalisation in telecommunications. It appears more likely that it is intense competition which has transformed BT rather than privatisation. Privatised industries which are not subject to competition, like water and railways, have been much less successful.

There is also the problem that once an industry is privatised, the state loses effective control over it. One way to try to alleviate this was the system of golden shares – a single share, held by the state, which gave it veto powers over the ownership of the privatised company. For example, the state retained a golden share in the airport operator BAA, which capped a single shareholding at 15%. In other words, the state could veto any takeover of BAA. This was declared illegal by the European Court of Justice in 2003, as it was against EU rules on free movement of capital (Osborn 2003). The hostile takeover of BAA by the Spanish company Ferrovial duly followed in 2006. Other privatised industries which did not have a golden share, such as water and electricity distribution, are now effectively in the hands of French and German companies, including the state-owned Electricité de France and Deutsche Bahn. Surely if a key part of the economy is to be in public hands, those hands should be British rather than French or German!

A fourth problem is what happens when a privatised company fails. By definition, the services provided by a privatised company are vital, and it is important that there is continuity in their supply. An example of where this happened, Railtrack, is discussed in Section 4.7.1.

Finally, although often regarded with amused contempt, the nationalised industries had a fund of goodwill from the public. When things went wrong, as with train crashes under British Rail, these tended to be regarded as 'acts of God' rather than the fault of the company. The privatised companies have not been successful at building up a similar fund of goodwill. Thus the drought in Yorkshire in 1996 was widely, if unfairly, seen as the fault of the (privatised) Yorkshire Water (Kay 2002).

4.7 THE PUBLIC AND VOLUNTARY SECTORS

Broadly speaking, four types of organisation operate in the UK today: businesses, which produce goods and services with the aim of making a profit: the public sector, which supplies goods and services which cannot be supplied at a profit; public goods (where the whole of society benefits from a service such as public health, whether they pay for it or not); and natural monopolies. The voluntary sector meets the needs of its members (clubs, mutual organisations or professions), its clients (charities), or campaigns on issues (Greenpeace, RSPB).

Unfortunately, these distinctions are not as watertight as they were 30 years ago. Some public goods and natural monopolies are now supplied by privatised businesses, and the private and voluntary sectors provide some services, such as refuse collection and welfare services, on behalf of the public sector. Many public sector and voluntary bodies have commercial arms (like BBC Enterprises and CIPD Enterprises) which operate in competition with the private sector. One organisation, Railtrack, changed in a five-year period from being part of a nationalised industry (British Rail), to being a privately-owned company on privatisation, and then to a non profit-making trust (Network Rail), when Railtrack collapsed in 2001.

A growing trend is social enterprise. Social enterprises are profit-making, but plough their profits back into society, rather than primarily paying dividends to shareholders. Examples include Jamie Oliver's Fifteen restaurants, the *Big Issue* and Divine Chocolate. There are 62,000 social enterprises in the UK, with a combined turnover of £27bn (Harding 2004; Lucas 2009). Officially known as Community Interest Companies (CICs), they were recognised legally by the 2006 Companies Act. They have two main legal features:

- assets owned by the company are held in an asset lock which ensures that they are used for the good of the community, and protects the CIC from takeover
- there are limitations on dividend and interest payments to ensure that the primary focus remains on achieving benefit for the community (CIC Association 2012).

The three sectors also have more similarities than differences in how they are managed. They all:

- spend money
- need income to carry out their activities
- produce a product or service
- have consumers of their good or service (whether or not the consumers directly pay for this)
- need people to staff their operations
- use the same range of management services – accounting, IT, personnel, etc.

This all suggests a convergence. This view would be supported by the former Prime Minister, Tony Blair. His Third Way philosophy argues that what is important is not ownership (public or private), but how efficiently services are delivered, along with accountability.

Lawton and Rose (1994) distinguish four different cultures which they see as prevalent in the public sector:

- *Political culture*. Particularly prevalent in local government, where council officers are in almost day to day contact with the politicians to whom they are answerable. Also true in the sense that the whole of the public sector is ultimately politically directed.
- *Legal culture*. Public bodies are only permitted to do what is specifically allowed to them by statute. Any other action is *ultra vires* (beyond their powers), and is subject to judicial review. Private sector companies are in theory limited in their activities by their Articles Memorandum of Association, but the control is much less strict.
- *Administrative culture*. Concerned with rules, roles, and authority – the 1960s and 1970s caricature of the local authority 'jobsworth'.
- *Market culture*. Where public sector organisations are exposed to the market through competitive tendering, best value, contracting out, internal markets, etc.

They argue that the last of these, the market culture, is becoming predominant, and that as a result, running the public sector is becoming much more an issue of management, and much less an issue of administration.

The distinction between the sectors is becoming more and more blurred:

- Many local authority services which may previously have been free, are now charged for, and often contracted-out to the private sector (leisure centres, for example). This has involved the development and application of legal systems such as Tupe.
- Much of the long-term finance for the public sector is now provided by the private sector, through the Private Finance Initiative and public-private partnerships. This is particularly true in the NHS.
- There is a growing realisation that the private sector, almost as much as the public sector, operates in a political environment, and that the activities of the private sector are heavily constrained by the legal environment.
- The government is keen to increase the involvement of the voluntary sector in the delivery of public services, partly to move the debate away from a head-to-head clash between the public and private sectors (Ward 2000). Not for profit trusts are the government's preferred option for failing public services. They can borrow private cash without this counting as public borrowing, and they can also reinvest any surpluses into service improvement (Weaver 2001). The voluntary and social enterprise sector is

at the core of both David Cameron's Big Society and Ed Miliband's One Nation approaches.

CASE STUDY 4.3

MANAGING VOLUNTEERS

One major issue for the voluntary sector is how to manage staff, both paid and volunteers. Paid staff are likely to have a high commitment to the objectives of the organisation, and thus likely to be prepared to work for less than the current market wage, but in return want a high degree of autonomy. The psychological contract is highly important, and any move by management to alter the contract will lead to resentment, and perhaps staff moving to other organisations.

The issue is even more crucial with volunteers. By definition, volunteers can move to other organisations at any time. Volunteers want autonomy, the ability to put their knowledge and skills to best use, and a sense of being valued. They do not want to be seen as having a lower status compared with paid staff, and they do not want to be over-regulated.

Moreton (2006), suggests that the ideal management style for managing

volunteers is the Team Management style on the Blake and Mouton Management Grid. This has a high concern for production combined with a high concern for people. It is characterised by work accomplishment through committed people, and interdependence through a common stake in organisation purposes that leads to relationships of trust and respect.

All organisations need some degree of bureaucratic management systems, if only to conform with the law and regulation, but Moreton recommends that these should disguised so that volunteers are as far as possible unaware of them. He quotes the analogy of the swan, which appears graceful to the onlooker, but is actually paddling furiously under the surface.

Source: This Case Study is based on material kindly supplied by Stephen Moreton of the charity Attend, which is gratefully acknowledged.

4.7.1 PUBLIC INTEREST COMPANIES

The advent to power of the New Labour government in 1997 revived interest in a third way of delivering public services, which was neither a nationalised industry nor a privatised company. This was the Public Interest Company. These had three main characteristics:

- they do not normally have shareholders
- they are independent from the state
- they deliver a public service.

Legally the Public Interest Company is normally a company limited by guarantee. A typical PIC was a housing association, providing and managing social housing.

As Maltby points out, it has always been an over-simplification to see a simple dichotomy between privatised companies and nationalised industries. In fact there is a continuum of types (Maltby 2003). Going from pure public sector to pure private sector, we have:

- nationalised industries
- public plcs, where a company operates as though it is in the private sector, but is wholly owned by the state (a good example is the Post Office before its privatisation)

- public interest companies
- public private partnerships, including private finance initiative contracts
- regulated private companies – typically privatised companies
- private companies – ordinary plcs.

Public interest companies appealed to New Labour for two main reasons:

- they represented a Third Way between nationalisation (socialism) and privatisation (capitalism)
- they provided an opportunity to give formal influence to stakeholders.

As Palmås argued, PICs combined the management freedom, efficiency and innovativeness of the traditional plc, the public interest ethos of the public sector, and the stakeholder governance of mutuals and the voluntary sector (Palmås 2005).

Dwr Cymru Welsh Water is a leading example. Originally privatised, it has been owned and managed by Glas Cymru as a PIC since 2001. All financial surpluses are reinvested for the benefit of customers, and since 2001 it has returned £98m to customers as 'customer dividends'. It has also reduced its level of borrowing from 91% to 75%, so lowering its level of risk (Article 13 and CBI 2007).

An opportunity to experiment with the PIC model on a large scale came with the collapse of Railtrack in 2001. Railtrack had been set up as a result of rail privatisation in 1996, with responsibility for running the rail infrastructure (train services were provided by Train Operating Companies such as Virgin which rented track use from Railtrack).

At first Railtrack was very successful in financial terms, mainly because it laid off 65% of its staff and outsourced most of its maintenance. It was then hit by a series of accidents, culminating in the Hatfield crash of 2000, caused by a broken rail. In response to public pressure, Railtrack was forced to impose drastic speed restrictions on the network while rails were checked. As a result, Railtrack's profits were shattered, leading to a £534m loss in 2001. However, Railtrack then paid out a dividend of £137m.

Railtrack's fortunes continued to decline, and in October 2001, the company was put into administration. By this time its share price had dropped from a peak of £17 to 280p. Eventually, in the spring of 2002, the government effectively bought Railtrack at a price of 250p a share, and handed its management to a new PIC, Network Rail (Palmås 2005).

Network Rail's governance was in the hands of a large group of individuals representing major stakeholders, including 30 drawn from companies already heavily involved in rail, including Amey, Jarvis and London Underground, 34 public members drawn from a range of organisations ranging from Eurotunnel to the National Farmers Union, and 51 individual members selected by a membership panel, and who were mostly drawn from 'the great and the good' who frequently appear on the boards of quangos (*Guardian* 2003b).

There is an argument that Network Rail is effectively answerable to no one. In these circumstances, argues Jeremy Warner, 'the engineers are taking over', and 'all [they] want is a shiny new train set' (Warner 2003). However, because Network Rail did not have to distribute profit to shareholders, it was unlikely to be so obsessed in the short term as Railtrack.

4.8 THE PRIVATE FINANCE INITIATIVE AND PUBLIC PRIVATE PARTNERSHIPS

Public Private Partnership (PPP) refers to any financial collaboration between the public and private sectors. For example, in the 1980s, local authorities were forced to put many of their services out for tender to the private sector under the Compulsory Competitive Tendering system. The result today is that the council dustman has virtually disappeared.

Instead, they are employed by private waste disposal companies, although their job is still to collect people's rubbish.

Other examples include the use by schools of private security companies, or the way in which the BBC uses private production companies to produce many of its TV programmes. Some PPPS are really Public Voluntary Partnerships – the transfer of local authority social housing to housing corporations, for example, since 1989 (Ward 2000).

The Private Finance Initiative (PFI) is a specialised type of PPP. Set up by Norman Lamont in 1992 after the UK was forced out of the EU Exchange Rate Mechanism, it was seen as a way simultaneously to stimulate the economy and to hold down public spending. Say the NHS wants to build a new hospital. Under the old system, the capital cost of the hospital was financed by the state, and so increased public borrowing. Under PFI, the private sector provides the cash, which is repaid with interest once the new hospital opens. The NHS (and the government) avoids a high capital payment up front, but it is committed to monthly payments for the next 25–30 years, which will amount to much more than the hospital would have cost in the first place. Deals will include penalty clauses if the terms of the contract are not met – if the heating system fails, for example. The private sector company will gain a guaranteed flow of income for 25–30 years, but takes the risk if there are cost over-runs.

Many PFI deals went much further. Not only would the contractor in effect lease the hospital to the NHS, but the contract also included the provision of ancillary hospital services, typically catering, cleaning and security. This included the transfer of NHS jobs to the private sector, where they were subject to the EU Transfer of Undertakings (TUPE) regulations.

When New Labour came to power in 1997, it was at first thought that the days of PFI were numbered. Instead, the system was expanded. The opportunity for Gordon Brown to keep public sector capital spending off the public sector borrowing requirement was too good to miss. However, Labour did bring in some safeguards. The system of Compulsory Competitive Tendering for local authorities was changed to Best Value, where the local authority could continue to provide services in-house if it could establish that it provided as good value as outsourcing. PFI was also stopped for small projects, where the cost of the tendering process outweighed any financial savings, and for IT projects, where many contracts had proved expensive failures. It was also stressed that PFI could only be used where it did not come at the expense of employees' terms and conditions.

Several possible models for PFI/PPP were identified by the Institute for Public Policy Research in 2001. These were:

- *public sector default* – the public sector provides all services – broadly the position for police and fire services
- *private sector rescue* – the private sector acts as provider of last resort only if the public sector is seen to be under-performing – for example some failing local education authorities have been taken over by the private sector
- *level playing field* – equal treatment between different organisations seeking to deliver public services – broadly the position with local authority Best Value
- *public sector rescue* – the public sector acts as provider of last resort only if the private sector is seen to be under-performing – the replacement of Railtrack by Network Rail
- *private sector default* – the private sector provides all services – the building and operation of new prisons (IPPR 2001).

The Treasury stressed that one of the main benefits of PFI was that it transferred risk to the private sector. The public authority received the certainty that specified services would be delivered at the cost at which they were contracted In 2006 the Treasury estimated that PFI would total 10–15% of total investment in public services, and in the five-year pipeline were 200 projects worth £26bn.

Treasury research in 2006 also established that on the whole the public sector was satisfied with the results of PFI.

- 79% said service standards are delivered always or almost always.
- Overall performance of 96% of projects was at least satisfactory.
- 70% of public sector managers believe relationships with private sector partners are good or very good.

Only 20% of PFI projects are late, compared with 70% of non-PFI contracts, while 20% are over budget, compared with 73% of non-PFI projects (HM Treasury 2006).

However, there are many criticisms of PFI:

- They lock the public sector into contracts that are too long. It is very difficult to forecast demand for facilities as far ahead as 30 years. Schools, for example, are frequently surplus to requirements long before 30 years because of changes in local population. Government NHS policy is to shift significant portions of the work of hospitals into the community. This again puts in doubt 30-years contracts (Batty and Weaver 2006).
- A PFI contract may deliver on time, but this does not take into account the length of time required to finalise contracts – frequently a matter of years. The contracting process itself is also extremely expensive, and the contracts frequently too restrictive. The process also creates a 'contract culture', with endless arguments over exactly what the contract does and does not require.
- PFI threatens the public sector ethos. For example, when cleaners in hospitals were employed by the NHS, they were driven by a desire to produce the best possible service for the patients. When the same people are employed by the private sector under PFI, they are ultimately contract and profit driven – they are not permitted to go beyond the terms of the contract, because this will cost their employer money.
- Many PFI companies are moving into areas well away from their core expertise. The leading firms involved in educational administration are Jarvis and Atkins, both primarily civil engineering specialists, and VT Education, the service arm of defence and shipbuilding firm Vosper Thorneycroft. In a Fabian report, Colin Crouch argued that the main expertise of these companies lies in their experience in lobbying and negotiating large contracts with the government (Woodward, 2003).
- PFI drains public services of current spending power. At the end of 2006, £8bn worth of NHS hospital PFI schemes were operational or under construction in England. On these, the NHS would have to pay £37bn in debt payments over the next 30 years. It is estimated that 50% of NHS trusts with major PFI schemes in the mid-2000s were in financial difficulties, a much higher than the average across the NHS. Some, like South Tees and Queen Elizabeth Woolwich, both in substantial deficit, were paying 20% of their turnover to PFI partners (Hellowell 2006). In the case of Queen Elizabeth, the PFI deal cost £9m a year more than an equivalent hospital built with money borrowed directly from the government (Batty and Weaver 2006).
- In practice, risk is not completely transferred to the PFI partner. In 2004, the PFI contractor Jarvis was in severe financial difficulty following its involvement in the Potters Bar train crash, where it was responsible for track maintenance. At the time Jarvis was responsible for 14 PFI projects, all of which ground to a halt as the City sorted out a rescue package for Jarvis. Part of the problem appeared to be that Jarvis had been 'lowballing' – bidding too low in order to secure bargain basement PFI contracts, and then running into trouble when unexpected problems appeared. At the very least, Jarvis's failure led to delays and waste for its public sector partners; at worst,

contracts would have to be renegotiated with another partner, leading to higher costs than originally budgeted (Hirst 2005).

4.9 COMPETITIVENESS

In the 1970s, the UK was widely seen as a failed economy. It was subject to wide fluctuations in economic performance, and suffered from high inflation and unemployment. Taxation was high, the economy was heavily regulated, and trade unions were widely seen as too powerful. Some of these shortcomings were tackled by the Thatcher governments between 1979 and 1991, which lowered taxation, cut back on regulation and attacked the power of the trade unions. The result was an increase in the efficiency of the economy, although this was largely a function of the contraction of manufacturing. The manufacturers which survived were inevitably more efficient than those which had failed.

However, the impetus behind the reforms of the Thatcher governments was as much political as economic. Policy changed with the advent of the Major government in 1991. This was much less ideological. Policies were to be followed because they were effective, rather than because they were politically correct.

This approach was continued by New Labour in 1997, with an almost seamless transition from Ken Clarke to Gordon Brown as Chancellor of the Exchequer. Competitiveness became the watchword, and pragmatism the policy. The aim was to reform the British economy so that it could compete with the best in the world.

4.9.1 PRODUCTIVITY

Competitiveness has a large number of facets, from a tightening of anti-trust legislation to the promotion of a higher skills base in the UK, and stabilisation of macroeconomic policy. What ties them all together is the concept of productivity. As Paul Krugman, the Nobel prize-winning economist, has said, 'Productivity isn't everything, but in the long run it is almost everything.' (quoted in Giles 2015).

Productivity is a measure of how much the economy is producing per worker employed. This is dependent on both the efficiency of the worker and on the hours worked, so a better measure is probably output per worker hour. In 2002, productivity measured by output per worker was 39% below the US, 15% below France and 7% below Germany. However, France and Germany work fewer hours than the UK, and the US works more, so on the better measure, output per worker hour, the UK was 26% behind the US, 24% behind France and 11% behind Germany. This is known as the productivity gap (Philpott 2002b).

The 2002 figures represented a considerable improvement on the position in 1991, when the UK was 35% behind France on output per worker hour, and 30% behind Germany (Daneshkhu 2007a). The improvement continued after 2002, and by 2007, the UK was 18% behind the US and 20% behind France, although the gap with Germany had widened slightly, to 13% (Daneshkhu 2007b). Between 1995 and 2006, UK labour productivity growth was 2.1% per annum, France's 1.9%, Germany's 1.7%, and Italy's 0.4% (Giles 2007).

Productivity normally falls during a recession, but recovers within about 18 months (Meadway 2014). This happened in the rest of the G7, although productivity growth is slower than before the crash. By 2015, productivity in the G7 had risen by 5%, but in the UK it was still at pre-crash levels (Economist 2015c). Seven years of zero productivity growth means a loss of around 15% compared with the trend rate of increase of just over 2% a year. If the trend rate had been achieved, not only would people be better off, there would have been no need for further spending cuts (Giles 2015). Productivity performance in Germany and Italy has been equally dismal, but France, and particularly the US, have moved well ahead. GDP per hour in the UK is 17% below the G7 average (Valero and Roland 2015).

Why did the UK do so badly? A large part was due to how UK business reacted to the slump. In previous recessions, trade unions were stronger, and could resist wage cuts, although this meant more job losses. In 2007–9, the main impact fell on wages. Inevitably, as roughly the same number of workers were producing a smaller output, productivity fell. This effect seems to have persisted, and the UK is tending towards a 'low-road' economy, of low wages, low productivity and low skills, epitomised by zero-hours contracts, spiralling working tax credits and the Beecroft proposals aimed at making dismissal easier (see page) (Mayhew and Keep 2014).

As workers become cheaper, there is less incentive to invest in new capital equipment, even at very low interest rates. Overall investment is 14.5% of GDP – the lowest in the G20, and lower than it was before the crash. In the 1980s it was 25% of GDP (Meadway 2014).

Another factor reducing UK productivity is the existence of so-called 'zombie' companies, where an inefficient company is technically insolvent and would normally be liquidated by its bank. As a result of the recession, bank balance sheets were weak. Liquidating a zombie company would worsen the bank's balance sheet even further, by removing an asset, even a non-productive one (Giugliano 2015; Peston 2015a).

Finally, the restructuring of British industry from manufacturing to services makes it more difficult to sustain productivity. Manufacturing makes up only 10% of GDP, while services are 75%. Services like hairdressing and social care find it very difficult to increase their productivity (Elliott 2015c).

An increase in productivity depends on changes in a number of factors. These include:

- *Capital investment.* The more modern the equipment with which people work, the more efficient they will be. Historically, investment in the UK has been low, and increases in productivity have come more through the shut-down of the most inefficient plant rather than the building of new plant. A telling comparison with the US is that while the UK produces the same volume of manufacturing output with half the capacity of the 1970s, the US produces twice the output with the same capacity.
- *Economic stability.* One key factor which deters investment is economic instability. Investors need to be convinced that there will be a consistent demand for what they produce, and that inflation will be stable. De Grauwe has argued that a comprehensive and reliable welfare state is also necessary, although this does not seem to be required in the US (De Grauwe 2001).
- *Research and development.* The UK is excellent at scientific research but much less good at the applied R&D needed to convert this into practical products and processes. It is significant that the UK's only world-class industry, pharmaceuticals, is the heaviest investor in R&D.
- *IT and the internet.* During the dot.com boom of the late 1990s, the Internet was seen as the Holy Grail of productivity, and some US economists put forward the concept of a New Economic Paradigm, where the business cycle was abolished, and growth would continue indefinitely. This rosy view was shaken by the dot-com crash in early 2000, and shattered by the events of 11 September 2001. Of the dot.com companies, virtually only Amazon, e-Bay and a few business to business (B2B) companies are profitable.
- *Restrictive practices.* Restrictive practices by the trade unions were tackled by the Thatcher governments, so the main concern is restrictive practices by industry. The UK has anti-trust laws (covered in more detail in the chapter on regulation), but they are much less tough than in the US. One change here has been to make participation in price-fixing activities a criminal offence, subject to imprisonment – a measure in force in the US since 1890 (Lennan 2001).

- *Management.* The quality of management in the UK is widely perceived as being poor, despite the spread of management qualifications such as the MBA. As with the whole of UK industry, there are some very good examples of management practice, but a very long tail of poor performers. The average standard needs to be raised to be nearer the best. Two main failings are a short-termist approach, which discourages long-term investment and development, and a failure to introduce modern management practices such as Just in Time and continuous improvement. Many sectors of industry still experience high levels of stress and alienation, and many managers refuse to consider a partnership approach with their workers. There appears to be a good correlation between high performance workplaces and high productivity (Mayhew and Keep 2014).
- *Infrastructure.* The UK has the most congested roads in the EU. This adds to business costs and makes the operation of techniques such as JIT more difficult. It is significant that recovery from the Great Depression of 1929–33 was faster, partly due to heavy investment in infrastructure, particularly in housing, roads (the arterial road system) and electricity (the National Grid).
- *Flexibility.* Industry must become more flexible in order to optimise its use of resources. This involves being:
  - *Numerically flexible* – Working time must adjust to meet customer demand – 'the 24/7 society'. This involves the use of techniques such as annual hours
  - *Functionally flexible* – Skills levels must be improved, and these skills fully utilised
  - *Occupationally flexible* – Workers must become multi-skilled
  - *Wage flexible* – Reward must be used as an incentive to higher productivity
  - *Mindset flexible* – Diversity must be encouraged in order to tap all available talent, and organisations must be family-friendly in order to encourage diversity (Philpott 2002, Merrick 2001, Briner 2001). However, as noted above, excessive flexibility may support the drive towards a low-wage, low-productivity economy.
- *Skills.* These are discussed further in Case Study 4.4.

It is also important to remember that productivity per head is not the only driver of economic growth. As William Keegan pointed out in October 2004 (Keegan 2004b), superior economic growth in the US is largely caused by factors such as:

- a growing labour force, driven by high rates of immigration. this tends to lower the average age of the workforce, and also forces a high rate of investment to keep pace with the demand created by a growing population
- long hours and short holidays
- generally expansionary macroeconomic policies.

CASE STUDY 4.4

SKILLS POLICY

A key element in promoting productivity is the need to develop workforce skills. The UK has a higher proportion of low-skilled workers than other comparable economies. A whole series of initiatives have been introduced, ranging from NVQs to TECs, ILAs to LSCs. The result has been an alphabet soup, without a great deal of impact on the skills base. As usual, the UK pattern is one of excellence at the top, with very effective degree-level provision, a gap in the middle, where technician-level skills are poorly developed, and a long tail of functional illiteracy and innumeracy. However, it is becoming clear that workforce development is a dual responsibility, with the government responsible for developing the basic skills of numeracy, literacy and IT (as stressed in the Tomlinson Report on the reform of 14–19 education in October 2004), and industry being responsible for the development of workplace-specific skills.

In 2006, Lord Leitch identified the skills weaknesses of the UK (Leitch 2006). He discovered that only 85% of adults had basic literacy skills, and 79% basic numeracy. Only 69% of adults had gained at least a level 2 qualification (equivalent to five GCSEs at A*–C grade), and 29% had a higher education qualification (Level 4 or above). In order to be in the top 25% of OECD countries by 2020, these figures would have to be considerably improved:

- basic literacy up from 85 to 95%
- basic numeracy up from 79 to 95%
- level 2 qualifications up from 69 to 90%
- level 4 qualifications up from 29 to 40%
- apprenticeships to reach 500,000 a year in England.

The Leitch proposals were accepted in full by the government in July 2007 (Department for Innovation, Universities and Skills 2007). The Leitch review stressed that the emphasis in the skills strategy should be on adults, as 70% of the 2020 workforce was already beyond the compulsory education age in 2006.

As significant as the targets were the mechanisms by which Leitch felt they should be achieved. He stressed a demand-led approach, with employers and workers given funding to commission their own training. In the case of employers, funding would be channelled through the Train to Gain programme, which was forecast to rise from £440m in 2007–8 to £900m in 2010–11. Funding for individual training would come through a new scheme of Skills Accounts.

The Leitch proposals were broadly welcomed by interest groups. The TUC welcomed the proposal to create a statutory right to workplace training to level 2, but questioned the emphasis on an employer-led approach. It felt that a social partnership approach between both employers and employees would be more appropriate, and that more emphasis should be given to the role of Union Learning Representatives. It also questioned whether employers would actually take up their responsibility to lead on training (TUC 2008). The CBI welcomed the employer-led approach, and stressed the cost of low skills to business. Low basic skills cost a typical SME with 50 employees £165,000 a year, and the cost to the whole UK economy was £10bn a year (CBI 2005).

The CIPD pointed out that the government should not put all its efforts into improving basic and low skills. They stressed that the productivity gain from boosting basic skills is only 1%, whereas higher level skills would boost productivity by 4.4% (CIPD 2008).

The skills strategy produced some early successes. Between 2001 and 2007, the percentage of establishments with any staff who were not fully proficient fell from 23% to 15%, while the percentage of staff not fully competent fell from 9 to 6%. The number of vacancies caused by lack of skills fell from 25% in 2005 to 21% in 2007. The National Employers Skills Survey 2007 identified the main causes of skills gaps as lack of experience/newly recruited (68%), staff lacking motivation (28%), failure to train and develop staff (20%), and inability of the workforce to keep up with change (19%) (LSC 2008).

However, despite all the measures undertaken, levels of basic skills in the UK are still low. As the Chancellor, George Osborne, said in 2015: 'The level of skills in our country is unacceptable – we're one of only three OECD countries where the skills of our 16-to-24-year-olds are no better than our 55-to-65-year-olds.' (Elliott 2015b).

A cornerstone of UK skills policy is the Modern Apprenticeship programme. This was introduced in 1994, and later renamed Apprenticeships (except in Scotland). Apprenticeships can be at Intermediate level (equivalent to five GCSE passes), Advanced (equivalent to two A levels, or Higher (equivalent to a Foundation Degree). All must contain a knowledge-based element, a competence-based element, functional skills and Employment Rights and Responsibilities. The original intention was that Apprenticeships should concentrate on school leavers and those aged under 24, but in 2011–12, of 520,000 apprenticeships started, 230,000 were aged 25 plus, In 2011, only 6% of under 19s were on an apprenticeship programme, and in 2009 only 4% of employers employed apprentices. Seventy-one per cent of apprenticeship starters were existing employees. It appears that many large employers,

particularly retailers, were rebranding employees as apprentices, and gaining government funding for training which they would have provided anyway (Jones 2013). A study in Scotland in 2007 concluded that an apprenticeship in retail had no effect on the employee's wages, whereas in construction it led to a wage increase of 32% (Close the Gap 2007).

The Coalition and Conservative governments tackled two of the criticisms of the Apprenticeship programme. One was the introduction in 2013 of the trailblazer system whereby groups of employers would develop apprenticeship programmes for their sector which would be more relevant to the needs of employers. As of July 2015 there were 140 trailblazer groups (UK Government 2015a). The other was the proposal in the July 2015 Budget for a system of training levies, which would ensure that all employers in a sector paid for training in that sector (UK Government 2015b).

CASE STUDY 4.5

INVESTORS IN PEOPLE

Investors in People was introduced in October 1991. It is one of the key competitiveness-promoting initiatives which has been truly non-political, enthusiastically backed by both the Major and the Blair governments. By 2001, 25,000 organisations had qualified for the standard, employing 24% of the UK workforce.

Research carried out for IIP suggests that 73% of organisations awarded the standard more than 12 months ago feel that it has increased their productivity. However, there is a counter-view, put forward by Scott Taylor of the Open University, that IIP frequently has little impact on performance (Brown 2001), and this is supported by research from the Institute of Directors, where only 15% of 275 company directors felt that IIP had

increased profitability, and a quarter thought it had decreased productivity (Nelson 2001).

Arguments in support of Taylor's contention could include:

- Some organisations see IIP as a marketing exercise. The standard is treated as 'just another badge on the wall' rather than a development tool.
- Achievement and maintenance of the standard involves considerable amounts of management and worker time. These have to be offset before there can be any overall improvement in productivity.
- There is considerable emphasis on measurement of outputs. There is a risk that too much emphasis may be put on the targets rather than the processes. To many people,

governments since 1997 seem obsessed with targets, which can cause distortions. In one case, patients waiting for accident and emergency assessment were held in ambulances outside an A&E department, because there is a target for maximum waiting times in A&E, but the clock does not start ticking until the patient actually enters the building! (Bowcott, 2004)

More generally, IIP can only succeed where it is seen not as a box-ticking exercise, but as a fundamental change in values and attitudes. As with similar initiatives such as Total Quality Management, a belief in the virtues of development must be internalised in the organisation and become an integral part of its culture. Many organisations of course do this, and it is clear that in many cases IIP has been a total success.

4.10 HR ISSUES IN THE PUBLIC SECTOR

The final section of this chapter, on HR issues in the public sector, consists of Case Study 4.6, on recruitment of social workers.

CASE STUDY 4.6

BABY P, BLAME AND THE RECRUITMENT OF SOCIAL WORKERS

Child protection social work must be one of the most stressful jobs imaginable. Not only are interactions with difficult, evasive and often violent or abusive clients emotionally draining, but social workers know they are constantly walking a tightrope. If they make a mistake and, at worst, a child for whom they are responsible dies, they will be vilified by the tabloid press as murderers, while if they err on the side of caution, and take children too readily into care, they will be condemned by the same tabloid press as callous family-breakers. In addition, social work, like teaching, the police and the NHS, is a victim of the government's target culture for the public services, which has resulted in an increase in time-consuming bureaucracy (Hudson 2009; Kirkpatrick and Ackroyd 2003), as well as the public sector cuts implemented from 2010 onwards.

As a result, the level of unfilled posts in local authority social services departments is high. The national average for social work vacancies in June 2009 was 12%, while some authorities had much greater problems – Sandwell, in the West Midlands, had a vacancy rate of 39%, Waltham Forest in East London

34.9%, Hounslow in West London, 31%, and Essex county 28.1% (Bowcott 2009a). There is also some concern over the quality of social workers. Like teaching and nursing, social work is an all-graduate profession, with qualification through a Bachelor's degree in social work or a postgraduate qualification. A Commons Committee found that since 2003–4, the failure rate of students is only 2.62%, much lower than for other degree courses. The entry level of students is also lower than average. In 2006–7, nearly half the students admitted to social work degree courses had fewer than 240 points, which is the equivalent of three C grades at A level (Newman 2009). The social work qualification is a generic one. There are no specialist degrees in child protection.

Already suffering from severe recruitment problems, social work was then hit by the Baby P case. Baby P (Peter) was born in Haringey in March 2006. In December 2006, he was placed on the Haringey child protection register for physical abuse and neglect. Despite extensive contacts with social services, the NHS and the police, it was decided in July 2007 that the case did not meet the legal threshold for care proceedings. On 3 August 2007, Peter was taken to hospital but pronounced dead on arrival. In November 2008, his mother, stepfather and a lodger were found guilty of causing his death.

A review by Lord Laming declared Haringey's child protection services to be exceptionally inadequate. The council leader and cabinet member for children and young people resigned. The director of children's services was summarily dismissed on the direct instructions of Ed Balls, the children's secretary. Later Haringey dismissed a social worker and three managers. A hospital consultant who examined Peter just before his death but found no cause for concern was suspended, as was Peter's GP, who had seen him 14 times before his death. No action was taken against any of the police involved in the case (Batty 2009).

The reaction to the Baby P case was a classic case of a blame culture. The emphasis was on finding scapegoats, rather than learning from mistakes made. Predictably, many social workers moved to less demanding areas than childcare, and those remaining in post intervened more aggressively, to ensure that children in their care did not become the next Baby P. Fear became the driving force, rather than the welfare of the child (Syed 2015).

In May 2009, Ed Balls announced a series of measures designed to improve recruitment and retention. These included:

- a recruitment campaign designed to attract 500 social workers who have left the profession to rejoin it, supported by refresher training
- sponsoring 200 university places to encourage 'the highest-achieving graduates, from any disciplines' to take social work conversion courses
- improvement of supervision for newly-qualified social workers in their first post

- a new Master's degree in social work
- advanced social work status – at present the only progression route for social workers is to go into management; as with teaching, the proposal would provide for a practitioner progression route, as well as a managerial one
- simplification of the Integrated Children's System software system for recording social workers' interactions with children and families.

Balls said he expected these initiatives to cost £58m (Carvel 2009). However, in 2012, recruitment remained difficult, with research citing the demanding nature of children's social work, and its poor public image (Centre for Workforce Intelligence 2012).

Other measures which emerged later included:

- a national social work college, to give support, leadership and enhanced status to the profession (Brindle 2009)
- an advertising campaign to raise the image of social workers by highlighting success stories, featuring, among others, the Oscar-nominated actor Samantha Morton, who was herself in care as a child (Samuel 2009)
- Haringey has recruited 22 social workers from the US and Canada, after failing to recruit in the UK (Bowcott 2009b).

The government has so far refused to implement two of Lord Laming's key recommendations:

- ring-fencing of spending on child protection
- specialist undergraduate programmes in child protection (Carvel 2009).

Nothing, of course, has been done about one commentator described as the 'vicious reporting' of the tabloids (Sawford 2009).

- Legislation in the UK is normally initiated by the government, whereas in the EU it is initiated by the Commission. The role of Parliament is much greater in the UK than in the EU.
- Political parties and their members have some influence on policy formation, but this influence is tending to decrease.
- Pressure groups are of two main types, interest or sectional groups and attitude or cause groups. They have considerable influence both on the evolution of government policy and on its implementation.
- There are crucial differences between gross domestic product and standard of living or quality of life.
- All governments, of whatever political colour, are striving to achieve economic growth, full employment, stable prices, and equilibrium on the balance of payments.
- Policy instruments available to governments include fiscal policy, monetary policy, competitiveness policy and exchange rate policy.
- Interest rates in the UK are set by the Bank of England, subject to an inflation target set by the government.
- The inflation target in the UK is symmetrical, and therefore less restrictive than that of the European Central Bank.
- A drive to increase productivity and competitiveness is a key aim of both UK and EU economic policy, but does not lead to quick results.
- Despite their very different political systems, both India and China have been very effective at stimulating economic growth.

REVIEW QUESTIONS

1 What is the difference between a Green Paper and a White Paper?

2 Through what stages does a Bill pass in the UK before it becomes an Act?

3 What are the differences between an interest and an attitude pressure group?

4 What are the differences between RPI, RPIX and CPI? Which do you think is the best measure of inflation?

5 What are the Five Tests on whether the UK should join the euro?

6 What were the main causes of the Credit Crunch recession of 2008–9?

7 What is a Public Interest Company?

8 What is the difference between PFI and PPP?

9 Why has UK productivity 'flat-lined' since 2008?

10 What were the main recommendations of the Leitch Report?

EXPLORE FURTHER

Further reading

For the underlying economic theory, see Lipsey and Chrystal (recommended in Chapter 2). John Philpott, the CIPD's chief economist until 2012, produced an occasional series for the CIPD entitled *Perspectives*, which is invaluable, as are his articles in the CIPD's magazine *Impact*. For updating on economic events, serious newspapers such as the *Financial Times, The Times, The Guardian* and *The Economist* are essential.

Useful websites

For the evolution and application of policy, the Bank of England (www.bankofengland.co.uk) and the Department of Trade and Industry (www.dti.gov.uk) websites are useful. For current political party policy, you should check out the main party websites (www.conservatives.com, www.labour.org.uk, and www.libdems.org.uk), and for the reaction from the major political interest groups see the TUC (www.tuc.org.uk), CBI (www.cbi.org.uk) and CIPD (www.cipd.co.uk) websites. The BBC News website (www.bbc.co.uk/news) frequently has background articles on economic policy.

Audio and video material

Two videos are useful. One, by (Lord) Robert Skidelsky, the biographer of Keynes, on *A Keynesian Response to the Crisis*, 6 September 2012, puts the orthodox Keynesian point of view (www.youtube.com/watch?v=8RIEVY5T). The other, by Deanne Julius, an ex-member of the Bank of England's Monetary Policy Committee (A reduction of UK deficit targets seen as risky, 11 October 2012) is a more monetarist view (www.onenewspage.com/video/20121011/1079138/Reduction-of-Deficit-Targets-Seen.htm).

SEMINAR ACTIVITY 4.1

ECONOMIC DEVELOPMENT IN INDIA AND CHINA

Between 1985 and 1995, GNP growth in the developing world averaged 6% a year, more than twice that of the developed world (World Bank 2000). This suggests that the developing world will soon catch up with the developed world. Unfortunately, this hopeful forecast ignores two key factors. One is the rapid rate of population growth in the developing world. When this is stripped out, and growth converted to GNP per head, the growth rate per head in the developing world falls to 3.8%, while that of the developed world falls to 2.1%.

Secondly, the developing country figures are distorted by the outstanding success of the two most populous countries, India and China. In the period 1985–95, India's GNP per head rose by 3.2% per year and China's by an impressive (although possibly unreliable) 8.3%. Stripping out India and China from the figures, the rest of the developing world actually had a GNP per head which fell by nearly 1% a year. Since the 1990s, annual growth in both countries has accelerated, to 10% or more in China, and 8% in India.

China's success has been particularly remarkable. It took England 58 years to double its GDP after 1780, the US 47 years from 1839, Japan 34 years from 1885, and South Korea 11 years from 1966 (Meredith 2007). It took China nine years from 1978. It then doubled again by 1996, and doubled yet again by 2006 (Hutton 2007).

Why have India and China done so well? To some extent both countries are returning to their historic position in the world economy. At the time of the Roman Empire, China had 26% of the world's economy, and India had 33%. Even by 1820, China had 33%, India 16% (compared with western Europe at 24%, and the US at 2% (Smith 2007b). It was only in the nineteenth century that the Indian and Chinese economies collapsed. China's GDP per head in 1950 was only three-quarters of its 1820 value. By the early 1970s, China's share of world output was only 5%, and India's 3%, compared to western Europe's 26% and the US and Canada's 25%.

India and China have some distinct similarities in their economies. Both had their Year Zero in the 1940s, when their political and economic status was transformed – India's by independence in 1947, China's by the victory of Mao and the Communists in 1949. Both have huge populations, and a dominant agricultural sector, employing more than half of population. Both went through the same sequence of economic development, of emphasis on heavy industry and a planned economy, followed by agricultural reform, followed by export-led growth, with greater emphasis on the market (Goyal and Jha, 2004).

The main difference comes in their political systems. China has been a unitary state since the time of the first emperor (he of the terracotta warriors) in the second century BC. Throughout most of its history, India has been a cultural rather than a political entity, and has only been a single state under foreign conquerors, from the Mughals in the fifteenth and sixteenth centuries to the British in the eighteenth to twentieth

centuries. China is a one-party state with power centralised in the Communist party, India is a multi-party democracy. China is relatively homogeneous racially, with few religious or racial minorities, except for Muslims in the far west, while India is a heterogeneous state both racially and religiously, with a very large Muslim minority population (India has a bigger Muslim population than Pakistan), and significant numbers of Sikhs, Buddhists, Jains and Christians.

Both initially made economic mistakes, but both laid the foundations for their future success immediately after their respective Year Zeros. Mao took over a state where illiteracy was rife, with a male illiteracy rate of 70%, and female illiteracy up to 99% in rural areas. (Hutton 2007, p76). Mao immediately instituted a crash programme of primary education, and by the mid-1990s adult literacy was up to 80%. It is forecast that by 2025 there will be more English speakers in China than there are native English speakers in the rest of the world (Smith 2007b, p100). China's economic policy was eccentric and destructive until the 1970s. The Great Leap Forward between 1958 and 1961 tried to industrialise China through village communes, which predictably proved to be a failure, while the whole Chinese economy was torn apart by the Cultural Revolution between 1966 and 1976.

India after independence went for a moderate socialist economy similar to that constructed in the UK in the 1940s, with extensive nationalisation of key industries, and also, following the ideas of Gandhi, opted for economic self-sufficiency (autarky). Small industries were encouraged, and tariff barriers were high. The economy was also highly bureaucratic (known as the Permit Raj), and this discouraged entrepreneurialism. However, many small-to-medium-sized firms prospered under this benign and protectionist regime, and India developed skills in small-scale manufacture.

The first Prime Minister of India, Pandit Nehru, was also, like Mao, committed to education. His legacy was the foundation of a group of seven Indian Institutes of Technology, founded in 1947. Although small, these were excellent, rated in 2005 as the third best institutions of technology in the world, behind only MIT and the California Institute of Technology. Graduates from the IITs were later to develop the Indian software industry, as well as much of Silicon Valley.

China's switch to a high-growth economy began in 1978, when the veteran communist Deng Xiaoping came to power. Deng realised that results were more important than ideology. One of his sayings is: 'It doesn't matter whether a cat is black or white as long as it catches mice.' Deng dismantled the rural communes, giving land back to the peasants, which immediately led to a rise in agricultural output. He ensured that state enterprises were run by managers rather than party bureaucrats, and he set up Special Economic Zones, tax-free enclaves which welcomed foreign investment, initially from the Chinese diaspora in Hong King, Singapore and Taiwan, but later from the West, particularly the US. He cut tariffs on imports, and launched a huge programme of infrastructure investment, with tens of thousands of miles of motorway and dozens of new international airports being built. The combination of good infrastructure and plentiful, cheap but well-educated labour proved irresistible to foreign investors. By 2008, China made two-thirds of the world's photocopiers, shoes, toys and microwaves, half the DVD players, digital cameras and textiles, a third of the desktop computers, and a quarter of the mobile phones and TVs (Jacques 2009). China's manufactured exports have boomed, although there has been some criticism that the result is that goods are 'made in China', but not 'made by China' (Hutton 2007, p114). There are very few major Chinese-owned companies, and none which are truly world-class. However, the success of Chinese

companies like Galanz (see Case Study 1.6) suggests that this will soon change. In addition, as Hout and Ghemawat (2010) argue, increasingly China is insisting that one requirement for Western companies entering into joint ventures in China is that they transfer advanced technology know-how to their Chinese partners. They cite the case of the development of the Chinese high-speed rail system. In the early 2000s this was dominated by Alstom, Siemens and Kawasaki, and Chinese firms only manufactured simple components. In 2009 the Chinese government announced that in future the foreign rail companies must form joint ventures with the Chinese rail equipment companies CSR and CNR, and share their latest technologies.

China's industrial policy concentrated on developing clusters and exploiting external economies of scale, as suggested by Michael Porter (1990). The small town of Qiaotou (population 64,000) has 380 factories that manufacture 70% of the buttons used in China. Datang manufactures a third of the world's output of socks, and Shenzhou 40% of the world's neckties (Hessler 2010). On a larger scale, the city of Wuhan in Hubei province in central China is a world leader in optoelectronics, and produces 25% of the world's optical fibre. This is supported by 80 universities, and 100 high-tech research institutions. The city also has the fourth-biggest air hub in China, and a high-speed rail link to Beijing (1,200 kilometres in four hours) (Li 2012; Zhang 2012; Hao 2012). It is interesting that the main driver for investment in Wuhan is not the central government, but the city of Wuhan and the provincial government of Hubei.

Potentially the Chinese economy was at severe risk from the onset of world recession in 2008, because one of the first manifestations of the recession was a collapse in world trade. This hit China hard, as its economy was crucially dependent on exports of manufactured goods, particularly to the US. However, the Chinese government took quick and decisive action, putting a fiscal stimulus of 4 trillion yuan (about £400bn) into the economy, and switching production to the home market.

China's economy again came under pressure in 2012 as a result of the euro crisis and near recession in the UK. Growth slowed to around 7% (seen as the equivalent of a recession in China), and exports of manufactured goods slowed down again. The response of the Chinese government was to introduce another economic stimulus, this time of one trillion yuan, as usual mainly aimed at infrastructure investment, but also aimed at stimulating domestic consumer demand, for example through reducing tax for farmers (Sweeney and Chiang 2012). It is interesting to compare the various economic stimuli in China with the programmes of quantitative easing implemented in the UK and US. In the case of China, the money is spent, while in the UK and US quantitative easing has mainly been used to improve bank balance sheets rather than for real investment.

Simultaneously the Chinese government worked at a programme to rebalance the economy away from investment, manufacturing and exports towards services and consumption. This is the path typically taken by economies as they mature – initial break-neck growth based on manufacturing and heavy investment, then a transition to slower growth and domestic consumption. The difference with China is that it is trying to do this very quickly, and in the aftermath of a world recession.

The policy has had some success. In 2014 the Chinese growth rate was 7.4%, relatively low by Chinese standards, but consumption contributed more to this (3.8%) than investment (3.6%). For the first time for many years, exports contributed nothing, as the balance of payments was more or less in equilibrium. Consumption accounted for more than 50% of GDP, up from 39% in 2009 (Yueh 2015). Throughout 2015, the growth rate continued to fall, down to an annual 6.9% by July (lower than India at 7.2%), and China had a balance of payments deficit (Trading Economics 2015). This had severe repercussions on the world economy. As manufacturing slowed, Chinese imports of oil and raw materials fell, leading to a collapse in world commodity prices. The Chinese reacted by devaluing the yuan (Peston 2015b).

The Chinese government also faced a growing shortage of labour and the problems of an ageing population (see Seminar Activity 6). This led them to abandon the much-hated one child policy in October 2015, and replace it with a two-child policy (BBC 2015b).

For over 40 years, India bumbled along, with some economic growth, but not sufficient to cut rural poverty significantly what J K Galbraith described as 'functioning anarchy' (Smith 2007b, p172). Despite the success of the IITs, illiteracy, especially in rural areas, remained high, and India was also held back by its caste structure. Since independence, discrimination against *dalits* (untouchables) has been illegal, but in practice it persisted. Only 20% of rural residents are *dalits*, but they make up 38% of the very poor. A further 11% are *adavasis* (members of tribal groups), but they are even poorer, making up 48% of the very poor (Meredith 2007, p119).

India's point of change came in 1991, when the country faced a financial crisis. This led to reforms introduced by Manmohan Singh, the finance minister, and later Prime Minister of India. He liberalised external trade and deregulated the domestic economy, copying Deng's concept of Special Economic Zones. The growth rate accelerated, reaching 8% by 2000. India built on its strength in small- and medium-sized manufacturing, backed by highly skilled craftsmen.

Whereas China was the country of choice for mass production, India concentrated on short, highly specialised production runs. More importantly, India latched on to the boom in new technology in the 1990s. Not only did it scoop the market in call centres and business process outsourcing, by the 2000s taking a 48% share of the world market (Smith 2007, p132), but it also developed a world class software industry, centred on the southern city of Bangalore, where Infosys and Wipro are world class and rapidly growing software companies. The software for Apple's highly successful iPod was developed in India (and the product assembled in China) (Meredith 2007, p102). Services now account for more than half of India's GDP (Rudiger 2008). Older industry also started to flourish, led by the long-established conglomerate Tata, which now owns Corus (the ex-British Steel) as well as a range of Western companies including Tetley Tea. It subsequently bought Jaguar and Land Rover from Ford in 2008 for $2.3bn. In 2007, India became the world's 12th largest economy (De Vita 2009). India seemed to have weathered the world recession without too much damage, and expected economic growth soon to return to the pre-credit crunch figure of 9%.

India also had great institutional strengths – the English language (although China now teaches English from the primary school stage), a vibrant democracy, a free press, and universal acceptance of the rule of law. Hutton sees these soft attributes as key. However, like China, India has weaknesses. Its literacy rate lags well behind China, and its physical infrastructure is very weak. Its roads, with a few exceptions, are appalling, and anyone who has experienced Agra airport

will know that the same can be said for most of its airports.

Each of the 28 Indian states has its own border controls and regulations. Smith describes a lorry journey from Kolkata (Calcutta) to Mumbai (Bombay), a distance of 2150 kilometres), which took eight days, including 32 hours waiting at border toll booths (Smith 2007, p164). However, the latest Five Year Plan (2007–12) has earmarked $500bn for infrastructure improvement. The highest-performing, Goa, had a GDP per head in 2012 ten times of the poorest performer, Bihar (Narayanan 2014)

Like China, India also suffers from endemic corruption. In 2007, Andrew Wileman described an attempt to transport a bull elephant from Kerala to Bangalore in order to take part in a Hindu ceremony at one of the IT companies, Aditi. The 300 mile journey involved the payment of £250 in bribes at every state border to and from Bangalore, because 'elephant transportation papers were not in order'. He also tells the story of the auto-rickshaws in Delhi. Apparently there are 500,000 of these, but only 100,000 hold official licences. The other 400,000 stay in business by paying regular 'fines' to the traffic police (Wileman 2007).

The latest move to lessen the grip of the bureaucratic 'permit raj' came in September 2012 with the decision to allow foreign supermarket chains to enter India. However, being India, this was hedged with restrictions. The foreign chains had to form joint ventures, they were only allowed into cities with more than 1 million population (46 cities), and they must invest $100m over three years. The reforms are opposed by the nationalist opposition BJP party, traditionally the party of small shopkeepers, and by left-wing parties, including that which controls the state of West Bengal. This means that Kolkata, the capital of West Bengal and one of India's biggest cities, will be excluded (Jack 2012).

In 2012–3, the Indian economy collapsed, in a delayed reaction to the world financial crisis. The growth rate fell below 5%, and inflation soared. This led to the defeat of the Congress government of Manmohan Singh, and its replacement in May 2014 by a right-wing Hindu nationalist BJP government headed by Narendra Modi, the former Chief Minister of Gujarat, one of the more successful Indian states. Modi promised a liberalisation of the economy, and a war on corruption. Time will tell whether he is any more successful at this than Manmohan Singh, but by 2015 the Indian economy had recovered, with growth in the year to July 2015 at 7.2%, higher than China.

As a democracy, India is relatively slow to take decisions, and to make major shifts in policy. On the other hand, decisions in India have democratic legitimacy. China can take quick decisions, and tends to be better at taking long-term decisions, as its government is not answerable to an electorate, while decisions in India are shorter-term, and geared to the electoral cycle. As a result, China was better placed to make long-term investments in its education and health programmes, and to steamroller through its infrastructure improvements. Despite its centralised political system, China has been very effective at decentralising economic decision-making. It has given a great deal of economic autonomy to the growth areas of Shanghai, Quangdong and Hong Kong.

China has also been more effective at opening its economy to the West and at encouraging foreign direct investment through a stable exchange rate and low real interest rates. India has gained through the widespread use of English in its higher education system, which has led to the outsourcing of large numbers of service jobs from the West. China has

tended to gain from the outsourcing of manufacturing rather than service jobs. This has led to a big increase in Chinese exports, particularly to the US and Japan.

Both countries clearly have economic systems which are highly effective at generating economic growth. As an authoritarian stare, China has been able to be more single-minded in its pursuit of growth, and as a result has achieved a higher rate of growth. However, there are costs in the Chinese system. As the development economist Amartya Sen has pointed out, no democratic country has experienced a devastating famine, whereas authoritarian states like China have (Steele 2001).

It appears that a combination of authoritarian political control and a decentralised market-run economic system seems to be highly effective at producing economic growth, but with accompanying costs like loss of freedom, economic inequality and social disruption.

However, it is possible to over-hype the success of China (Hilton 2004). It took until 1993 before China's exports were back at the level they reached in 1928, before the Japanese invasion, and despite its vast population, China's GDP in 2000 was only a quarter that of Japan. It is a sign of the relative growth rates of the two countries that in 2011 China overtook Japan to become the world's second-biggest economy, although its GDP per head was still only a quarter of that of Japan (BBC 2011a).The dash for growth has also caused enormous environmental degradation. China has 16 of the world's 20 most polluted cities.

Question

Which do you think is more likely to sustain its economic growth in the long term, India or China?

There are three excellent books, all published in 2007, which provide background material for this Seminar Activity. Two are journalistic accounts of the economic rise of India and China. David Smith's *The Dragon and the Elephant; China, India and the new world order*, examines the issues from a UK perspective. Robyn Meredith's *The Elephant and the Dragon: The rise of India and China and what it means for all of us*, covers much the same ground from a US perspective.

Will Hutton's *The Writing on the Wall* takes a more analytical approach, concentrating on China, and is as much a critique of the West as it is of China. A further book, published in 2009, is Martin Jacques's *When China Rules the World,* which takes a mainly cultural perspective on the rise of China.

Regulation

5.1 INTRODUCTION

The *rule of law* that applies in democratic societies is one of the key features that differentiate democracy from dictatorship and tyranny. Legal decisions cannot be taken capriciously or for small special interest groups but for the long-term benefit of society as a whole. Laws, as determined by an elected parliament and interpreted by the independent judiciary, are fundamental to a well-governed and stable society.

The last time that this was tested was in March 1984 when Arthur Scargill led the miners' union into a national strike to try to improve working conditions in the mines and to prevent a massive programme of pit closures. He dismissed the legislation passed two years earlier requiring a ballot before strike action could go ahead, taking the view that 'bad laws should be ignored', just as the trade union movement had successfully done in 1972 against earlier Tory trade union legislation. In a defining moment of the Thatcher administration, the Government brought the full force of the establishment – police, army, public opinion – to restore the '*rule of law*', supporting the concept that laws passed in a proper democratic process must be obeyed by individuals and organisations. The view was widely promulgated that 'societies where the rule of law can be flouted with impunity cannot survive' and it was the almost unanimous support of this view across the UK that ultimately sealed the miners' fate.

The legal system, then, is at the heart of a democratic society. It sets out the rules within which people and organisations live and do business with each other; it reflects the current views on morality held by the majority of its citizens; it defines the punishments for breaking these rules; it establishes the nature of the contracts between the individual, the organisation and the state whereby the state is paid (through taxation) to protect the interests of all parties in a fair and impartial way. It allows everybody to plan their lives with the fair certainty of foreseeing what actions and behaviour are allowed and what is forbidden.

This chapter provides a general introduction to the structure of UK law, details some of the specific legislation that sets out a level playing field for business and the consumer, indicates the main protection for employees in the workplace, examines how law regulates particular sectors and labour markets and suggests ways that employers can respond to new legislation. There is a detailed examination of the role of government in regulating business activity, from health and safety to the size and compensation of bankers' bonuses.

Law is a complex subject and organisations and individuals regularly call on experts to advise them, so the outline provided in this chapter is primarily to raise awareness of the legal framework together with a good number of working examples.

5.2 LEGAL CONTOURS

5.2.1 LEGAL CONCEPTS

There is a clear *division of authority* between the judiciary and the executive, a factor that distinguishes true democracy from a dictatorship. Judges are independent and, once appointed, cannot be dismissed, except in extreme cases such as where they are convicted of corruption or another serious offence. If they take decisions that the Government does not like (and this is increasingly happening with the increased use of judicial review), the Government simply has to accept their decisions.

Precedent requires courts to follow decisions laid down in earlier cases where the facts are broadly similar. To give an example, in decisions made on unfair dismissal claims soon after the Industrial Relations Act was passed in 1972, higher courts confirmed the circumstances under which an employee could claim *constructive dismissal*, including the need for the individual to immediately resign and leave the employment once the incident had occurred. If a claim reaches a tribunal today and the claimant is delayed by a few weeks in leaving the employment after the incident occurred, the tribunal would be required to follow the precedent and throw out the claim.

When lawyers are advising on a case, then, they need to be well-read not just in the law itself, but in the way it has been interpreted by the courts as shown in the precedents involved. They need to read the '*obiter dictum*', which are the judge's recorded comments justifying their decisions. Faced by precedents which indicate that a case would be unsuccessful, a lawyer would either advise their client to withdraw or the lawyer would try their best to argue that the facts of the case were significantly different so the precedent did not apply.

That is not to say that precedents cannot be changed. One of the duties of the Court of Appeal is to examine precedents argued before them and judge whether such precedents are out of date for changing social times or preserve a system which is clearly unfair. In such cases, they may decide they need to be altered at the margins or completely reversed. A well-known example of reversal was the *Walker v Northumberland County Council* case (see Case Study 5.1).

CASE STUDY 5.1

CHANGING A PRECEDENT

John Walker was a social work manager who returned to work having had a mental breakdown brought on through an excessive workload. He requested a reduction in his duties and additional resources to allow him to cope with his responsibilities and serve the community. His employer did very little to help him and he subsequently suffered a further extended breakdown which ended his career. Prior to this case, the precedent had been that the employer had a clear duty of care in respect of preventing foreseeable physical illness but not mental illness brought on by stress. The Court of Appeal confirmed that this duty of care should be extended to foreseeable mental illness because there was no logical reason why it should be excluded from the scope of the Health and Safety at Work Act. Walker was awarded £175,000 in damages and this decision established a change in precedent. Consequently, employers have had to give much more careful consideration to the issue of foreseeable stress and subsequent mental illness among their staff.

Source: Walker v Northumberland County Council 1995 IRLR 35/95

In serious criminal cases (and, surprisingly, civil cases for libel or slander), the final decision is made by a jury – one is *judged by one's peers*. In jury trials, even the judge's advice can be overturned under the belief that it is a matter of whose word can be trusted and a jury of 12 people is the best way to test this.

5.2.2 TYPES OF LAW

The law is divided into two main divisions.

Civil law

The ground rules dealing with relationships between individuals and between an individual and an organisation are laid down under civil law. Where one side believes that the law has been broken, they will take the case up in the civil courts and aim to have the wrong righted and/or obtain compensation. The main areas under which civil cases are brought are *breach of contract* (where it is claimed that one party has broken the terms of a legally enforceable contract) and *torts*, which are civil wrongs independent of contract, such as negligence, nuisance or defamation (see Case Study 5.2).

CASE STUDY 5.2

EXAMPLE OF A TORT

Your next-door neighbour has allowed a tree to grow so large that parts are overhanging your small garden and take away most of your light. You have asked him politely to take some action but nothing happens. You therefore bring a case claiming *nuisance*. Before the case comes to court, a gale brings down a large branch which smashes your fence and greenhouse. You therefore add a further claim for *negligence* to the case.

The remedies you can obtain are:

- *compensation (damages)* – but only to the extent of your proven losses, plus costs you have expended

- *specific performance* – where the court instructs the plaintiff to carry out an action (see Case Study 5.3)
- *injunction* – where the court instructs the plaintiff to *not* carry out an action, such as demolishing a listed building.

CASE STUDY 5.3

SPECIFIC PERFORMANCE

You have successfully bid for an original painting at an auction but you learn subsequently that the owner decided to withdraw the painting for sale. You believe you have a valid contract and you successfully ask the court to instruct the owner to complete the contract and deliver the painting to you. You have set your heart on obtaining that unique painting and no alternative or compensation would satisfy you.

Criminal law

Here offences (crimes) are defined which society believes need punishing. The court case is a result of a police investigation and a case brought by the Crown Prosecution Service. Very occasionally, a private prosecution takes place, such as by the families of the victims of the Hillsborough stadium disaster in the 1990s. In general, however, these have a very low success rate and can be stopped by the Attorney General if they are not regarded as in the public interest.

Cases are divided into *indictable offences*, generally serious crimes – murder, rape, serious fraud – where conviction can result in imprisonment – and *summary offences* – parking, petty theft – which are less serious and where conviction brings a fine.

? REFLECTIVE ACTIVITY 5.1

In February 2010, Cotswold Geotechnical Holdings was charged with gross negligence manslaughter over the death of a geologist. He was taking small samples from a development site when the pit he was working in collapsed, killing him.

Look up the Corporate Manslaughter Act 2007 and trace the outcome of this case, which was the first such case brought under this legislation. The outcome will indicate under what other circumstances an organisation can commit a criminal offence.

5.2.3 FROM WHERE DOES THE LAW ORIGINATE?

We are so used to a flood of new legislation (statute law as explained in Chapter 4), emerging from parliament each year that it is a common fallacy to believe that this process is the only source of law. However, there are two other main sources.

Common law

Up until the nineteenth century, most law was 'common', which meant that it had come into effect through judges recognising custom and practice (and common sense) and this was spread around the country by judges on their circuits. These decisions made up the precedents. In most areas today, common law decisions have been incorporated into statute, but there are a number of fundamental common law concepts that remain, such as those relating to the law of contract and employee rights (see later in the chapter). There also remain some more isolated specific rights under common law, such as grazing rights held by New Forest Commoners.

Codes of practice

Although not technically law, formal codes have a strong influence on decisions taken by the courts. For example, an organisation facing a tribunal claim for unfair dismissal that has not followed closely the Acas Code on Disciplinary and Grievance Procedures is less likely to make a successful defence. Similarly, an employer facing an equal pay claim should ensure that the Equality and Human Rights Commission's Code on Equal Pay has been incorporated into their procedures.

It should also be noted that much of the statute law originates from the European Union, whose legislative processes were also set out in Chapter 4.

5.2.4 COURTS SYSTEM

In Figure 5.1, the courts system for England and Wales is set out (Scotland has had its own, somewhat different system for more than 500 years). Courts are distinguished through their regulation of civil or criminal law and whether they are courts of first instance or whether they hear appeals or both.

Figure 5.1 Court system in England and Wales

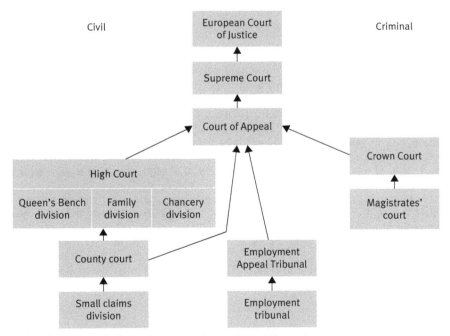

Note: the tribunal route indicates the process for employment law only.

5.2.5 CIVIL CASES

Claims start in the county court or, if the amount at issue is less than £10,000, the *Small claims division*. Speed, accessibility and informality are the keynotes here, with representation frowned upon and costs normally limited to the value of the summons. The judge acts alone as the arbitrator and the case can be dealt with using written evidence only. It provides an opportunity for businesses and individuals to claim small debts and torts to be examined and resolved. One day it may be resolving the overhanging tree dispute, the next, dealing with a claim from an ex-employee for unpaid overtime. From 2014, county courts were brought under centralised control, although they sit in a large number of cities and market towns with judges still going on 'circuits' to try to ensure a degree of consistency. Small claims courts are overseen by a registrar.

County courts deal with actions for less than £25,000 together with some others up to £50,000 by agreement with the parties, depending on their complexity (although this can vary depending on the nature of the claim). Additional subject areas at the county courts, apart from contract and tort cases, include probate disputes, bankruptcy, undefended divorce, consumer credit issues and some land questions. Around 1.5 million summonses a year are taken out at county courts, but only around 5–10% arrive in court and an even smaller percentage are actually defended.

Summonses valued at over £50,000 go directly to the High Court. This has three divisions which deal with cases of first instance and appeals from lesser courts. The *Queen's Bench* division is the busiest, with jurisdiction over high-value contract and tort cases, and a special commercial court dealing with banking, insurance and other financial services and technology cases. It also has an admiralty court to hear cases involving ships and aircraft, while it also hears some appeals from the county court and a comparatively small number of criminal appeals from Crown Courts. The *Family* division handles matrimonial cases, including wardship, adoption and custody claims. Finally, the *Chancery* division, the oldest court of all, has jurisdiction over high-value tax cases, trusts, partnership disputes, patent and copyright actions and land disputes.

5.2.6 CRIMINAL CASES

The *magistrates' courts* manage most of the criminal cases, determining around 98% of all crime. Motoring offences make up around half of their work (1.5 million cases). They handle all forms of petty crime with the maximum penalty that can be applied being a £5,000 fine or six months' prison sentence, although few prison sentences are awarded. It has special arrangements to handle juvenile cases. There are 330 magistrates' courts, with a total of 23,000 magistrates who hear the cases. They are a mixture of stipendiary (paid) officials and unpaid appointees. Stipendiary magistrates can sit alone. It is possible for those accused at a magistrates' court to decide to be heard in front of a jury at a Crown Court, usually in the hope that juries convict less often than hardened magistrates. Appeals (there are few) go generally to the Crown Court.

There are 77 *Crown Courts*, the most famous being the Central Criminal Court (Old Bailey). Cases are heard by juries, although the judge has a strong influence through control of the proceedings, interventions to clarify issues and the summing up. The number of Crown Court cases increased to a peak in 2010 but there was a small fall registered up to 2015.

From 2010, a number of serious cases may be heard by a judge sitting alone where jury tampering may be a serious threat.

5.2.7 HIGHER COURTS

The *Court of Appeal* hears both criminal and civil court appeals with three to five judges in attendance (out of a total of 38) and a majority decision prevailing with each judge's reasons published. Their judgments are extremely influential, much used to clarify the law and to set the ultimate precedent. Cases are sometimes referred to this court when new evidence has come to light that casts doubt on the validity of criminal convictions, cases that may have been held as long as 20 years or more ago. The appeal to the *Supreme Court* can only be on a legal issue and the decision is final, except where the case comes under European law, where much of employment law resides. If so, the case is heard by the *European Court of Justice* (see Chapter 6 for more details), which gives a ruling and then refers the case back to the UK court for implementation.

5.2.8 TRIBUNALS

The most well-known tribunals are those in employment areas, such as unfair dismissal and sex, race and disability discrimination. However, there are numerous tribunals set up by statute in other areas. There are rent tribunals, set up to help protect tenants from unscrupulous landlords, social security appeal tribunals, to provide an opportunity for citizens to question decisions made about their right to benefits, such as unemployment and sickness, and various tribunals related to appeals over taxation. They all have the same intention, which is to provide a formal yet accessible process for the aggrieved citizen to have their cases heard fairly, impartially and thoroughly by persons not involved in the original decision. The accessibility comes about through, first, some discouragement of legal representation, as with the small claims court, by generally not awarding costs, and second, by ensuring that help in the initial stages is provided by the tribunals themselves and by volunteer bodies such as the Citizens Advice Bureau.

In the employment area, the tribunals are bound by rules of evidence and precedent but the three-member tribunals are allowed to operate a much more informal and inquisitive approach than the higher courts. Appeals to the employment appeal tribunal and subsequent appeals to higher courts can only be on the basis of law. Examples of Employment Tribunal cases are detailed later in the chapter.

5.2.9 OMBUDSMEN

A final grouping of quasi-legal intent are the sets of ombudsmen, set up by legislation to investigate complaints of maladministration, mostly in the public arena. There are a number of commissioners (ombudsmen) in areas such as local government, the National Health Service and parliament whose reports have no precise legal standing but put pressure on the bodies concerned to rectify mistakes and improve their services. An example of a case where the work of the ombudsman led to substantial costs to the Government is set out in Case Study 5.4.

 PARLIAMENTARY OMBUDSMAN REPORT ON PENSION LOSSES

CASE STUDY 5.4

Between 1997 and 2005, 400 private sector pension schemes were closed with outstanding deficits. The main reason for the closures was the demise of the company or its financial inability to continue contributing to the scheme. The outcome was that 85,000 employees, ex-employees and pensioners did not receive the pensions they had been promised under the scheme. Some, indeed, lost all of their pension entitlement.

In 2005, the Parliamentary Ombudsman was asked to investigate the Department for Work and Pensions' (DWP) role in encouraging employees in this debacle. In March 2006, Commissioner Ann Abraham reported that the DWP had been guilty of maladministration. Its official guidance to employees was 'inaccurate, incomplete, unclear and inconsistent'. Much of the criticism was directed at government information leaflets which gave a misleading impression of the security of the schemes. They had not given sufficient warnings of the possibility of scheme closures and loss of pension rights.

The Government responded that they dismissed the report, pointing out that employees did not rely exclusively on these leaflets as a basis for their financial decisions. The minister responsible declared that the Government could not take on the heavy financial responsibility for the failure of private pension schemes. They were not obliged under legislation to take any further action and would not do so.

Pension campaigners then took the matter to the High Court and, in 2007, obtained a decision that the Government had wrongly rejected the ombudsman's findings. It confirmed that the DWP had committed maladministration in its advice on the schemes.

This put additional pressure on the Government, which was forced, in April 2007, to make concessions in terms of compensation to many of those who lost out. The Government agreed to cover 80% of the losses at a cost of around £2bn.

5.3 REGULATING BUSINESS AND PROTECTING THE CONSUMER

On a hot summer's day in 1930, a bottle of ginger beer was bought at the end of a walk by a young man for his lady friend. She gratefully drank up but, in finishing the opaque bottle, the remains of a decomposed snail appeared and, not surprisingly, she became very ill. On recovering, she wanted recompense for her unhappy experience but she could not sue the shopkeeper because she had no contract with him, nor could she sue her boyfriend because there was no consideration – the bottle was a gift. Nor did she have a contract with the manufacturer. However, a lengthy legal case was commenced which, two years later, appeared at the House of Lords (*Donaghue v Stevenson*), where the landmark decision was reached that manufacturers can be guilty of the tort of negligence.

Prior to the case, 'caveat emptor' (let the buyer beware) applied in all consumer purchases but *Donaghue v Stevenson* established that manufacturers have a duty of care to their customers not to be negligent and to avoid any acts or omissions which can be reasonably foreseen to kill, injure the consumer or member of the public or to damage property. Subsequent cases have clarified guidelines, such as drug manufacturers having a greater duty of care than newspaper publishers because the consequences of faulty goods are far more serious.

Donaghue v Stevenson was an important case and the outcome was a distinct improvement in the degree of protection for consumers. By the late 1960s, however, governments started to take a more supportive view for the consumer. There were a number of reasons for this:

- The growth of huge multinational corporations made it much more difficult for the view to be held that a contract was made between equal partners.
- Mergers and acquisitions were growing to the stage that some companies had control of substantial sectors of the marketplace and could dictate terms.
- There was a growth in practice of large organisations inserting 'small print' into contracts where special conditions were inserted and liabilities excluded to the detriment even of the observant consumer.
- Pressure had developed from consumer organisations, such as *Which?* magazine, which helped develop consumer awareness of shady practices and politicians appreciated they needed to take notice of this pressure.

- Britain decided to join the European Union in the early 1970s and some legislation was required to bring the UK in line with European law.
- Trading practices were changing in line with technological and monetary developments and there were gaps in the law in these areas.

The legislation can be divided into the macro area – to control and enhance competition generally – and in the micro area – where specific unfair business practices are made illegal.

5.3.1 CONTROLLING AND ENHANCING COMPETITION

Fair Trading Act 1973

It was considered essential that a watchdog with wide powers of investigation should exist to champion the consumer interest and provide independent advice to the Government. The Office of Fair Trading (OFT) took this role and its powers have been increased with subsequent legislation, including the Competition Act 1998 and the Enterprise Act 2002. In 2014, the OFT was abolished and its role in consumer credit was taken by the Financial Conduct Authority (FCA) with the remainder of its responsibilities passing to the Competition and Marketing Authority (CMA), the successor to the Competition Commission.

The FCA has the responsibility to investigate commercial activities which may appear to be against the interests of consumers and advise the Government if it believes action is necessary. The scope of activities investigated is wide, covering all sectors, businesses large and small, and dealing with contract terms, selling methods, packaging and promotion. Although its powers have limits, the fact that an investigation can take place and that it can seek orders from the Government to stop certain activities are, in practice, strong deterrents and have often changed the way business is carried out. In its early days, it investigated pyramid selling and ensured its abolition.

Restrictive Trade Practices Act 1976/Competition Act 1998

This legislation was passed to prevent the use of monopoly power either by individual companies or groups of companies colluding. A restrictive practice is defined as collusion on prices, terms of supply, manufacturing processes and any activity that is likely to have the effect of restricting, distorting or preventing competition. The CMA has the right to enter premises and demand documents and to enforce restrictions on movement or destruction of evidence. If an organisation refuses to co-operate, it can be penalised to the extent of 10% of turnover.

When a practice is found to exist, it can only be successfully justified by the argument that it:

- protects the public from injury
- is a counterweight to another monopoly (such as in negotiations with the Royal Mail)
- provides extensive benefits to exports.

Examples of investigations in recent years include extended warranties (see Case Study 5.5), operation of small pharmacies and the major chains, private dentistry, consumer IT services and estate agencies. It has also investigated some business methods, including doorstep selling and public sector procurement. A number of investigations were carried out in the 1980s and 1990s regarding price-fixing by colluding cement companies (see Chapter 3 for a discussion of the economic aspects of collusion), which eventually resulted in the cartel being broken up and cement prices substantially reduced.

COMPETITION COMMISSION REPORT ON EXTENDED WARRANTIES

In 2003, the Competition Commission (now the CMA) carried out an investigation into the £500m market in extended warranties, following on from a referral from the OFT, chiefly for electrical goods. They found that the bulk of warranties were purchased at the point of sale of the goods and could add 50% to the price of the product and were generally poor value. Bad practice reported included:

- Sales staff emphasised the risk of product failure.

- Customers were told that independent repairs were difficult to obtain and were expensive.
- The consumer was not encouraged to shop around.

It was also reported that self-regulation had not worked and that the large electrical retailers were exploiting their monopoly situation to the detriment of consumers.

Source: Competition Commission (2003)

The CMA reports to the Government, which can decide to refer the matter to the Competition Commission either for a decision or, in the case of an impending merger where the organisation will have 25% or more of the market, a fuller enquiry to decide if the merger is in the public interest and under what terms the merger would be allowed to progress. Full-scale investigations by the Commission in recent years have included one into the position of Nestlé (where it found it did not have excessive monopolistic power on coffee prices), video games (where it recommended the abolition of licence controls) and UK car prices (where it found that the exclusive dealership system operated against the public interest).

Investigations of potential wrong-doing, or the threat of referral to the CMA, have a huge impact on organisations or their future planning of possible mergers. A raid by the CMA or FCA on premises can cause the company's share price to drop 10% and many mergers have been decided by the policy of the CMA.

Two investigations in 2011 demonstrated the balance it needs to hold between encouraging effective competition and the consideration it must give to the changing business and technological environment. In the first case, the examination of local bus services, it found that there was a high level of concentration, large barriers to entry and operators avoiding competing with each other in one operator's 'core territory', leading to geographic market segregation; all such activities lead to harmful effects on consumers. A number of requirements to improve the competitive framework were set out by the Commission. On the other hand, it cleared a proposed merger of the travel and leisure interests of Thomas Cook and the Co-operative Group because, although it led to much more limited competition in the field of travel agents, the development of Internet travel and leisure compensated such a restriction in the marketplace.

In 2014, the OFT and the Competition Commission were merged into the Competition and Markets Authority (CMA).

A direct effect on the resourcing aspect of human resource management is shown in Case Study 5.6.

COLLUSION BY RECRUITMENT AGENCIES

In 2009, six recruiting agencies were fined £40m by the OFT for operating a cartel that fixed fees and boycotted a rival. The biggest company involved, Hays Recruitment, was fined £30m, equivalent to more than 2% of its turnover. The agencies, acting together as the Construction Recruitment Forum, met five times over two years to fix prices to allow higher profits. At the same time, they organised an effective boycott of contracts where a competitor, Parcs (which was not part of the cartel), was offering cheaper rates. Two other companies that took part in the cartel were offered immunity in return for providing evidence against the six companies.

Source: Mathiason (2009)

? REFLECTIVE ACTIVITY 5.2

The OFT carried out a survey of doorstep selling in response to complaints from the Citizens' Advice Bureau. Their report in 2004 recommended that legislation needs to be updated to combat the psychological tactics employed by many salespeople.

The study into the practice of selling goods and services on the doorstep and in the home, worth at least £2.4bn a year, found that a range of sales tactics and influencing techniques can lead consumers to make inappropriate purchases which they later regret. This highlights a gap in consumer protection. The current legislation gives consumers who are cold-called a seven-day period in which to cancel a contract. This protection does not apply to consumers who asked for the visit.

Buying in the home provides a unique setting for a business transaction – salespeople effectively have a captive audience. Nearly 40% of consumers have bought goods or services in the home. While 70% of those were satisfied, a significant minority of 30% experienced problems: at least 15,000 complaints a year are made to trading standards departments regarding doorstep sales. Most respondents to the OFT's consumer survey said they felt buying in the home was more pressurised than other settings.

The OFT recommends that the Government should extend the legislation to give cancellation rights to solicited visits as well as unsolicited. The OFT will also run a consumer education campaign in conjunction with interested groups to raise awareness of consumers' rights and alert them to the psychological techniques used and how to combat them.

Look up the Competition and Marketing Authority's website and examine two more of its recent investigations, the decisions it has made and the justification for those decisions.

5.3.2 CONSUMER PROTECTION

Economic theory would argue that rational behaviour by consumers makes their protection unnecessary. Poor-performing products would not survive and consumers simply walk away from poor service. To a large extent that is true, but the consumer is not always in a position to behave rationally. They may not have sufficient information about the product (hence the need for product description on the label), they may not have a choice of products if an uncontrolled monopoly exists and they may not be able to challenge a large and unscrupulous supplier. So a whole raft of legislation has been passed in recent years covering all business–consumer relationships and attempting to tighten up on legal loopholes. Much of the legislation encoded the common law in place and then extended it. Here is a brief summary of the key features, all of which have been incorporated in the **Consumer Rights Act of 2015:**

Trade Descriptions Act 1968/Consumer Protection Act 1987

These two Acts protect against traders who deliberately give false descriptions in the price, quality and nature of service. These are criminal offences and can result in fines and even imprisonment for repeated offences. The Act is policed by local government Trading Standards officials, who, incidentally, also assist the CMA in gathering information. Examples of cases include:

- advertisements showing massive price reductions when the prices had only been increased the day before – regulations now state that goods must have been at the pre-reduction price for 28 continuous days during the previous six months
- cars being advertised with 'one owner' which was a leasing company who had leased the car out for long periods to five different drivers
- prices being advertised but no indication that VAT is to be added.

 MISLEADING VALUATIONS

CASE STUDY 5.7

The Office of Fair Trading carried out an investigation in 2011 into the activities of the website Webuyanycar.com, following complaints from customers and consumer support groups. Consumers were given the impression that they would be paid the full online valuation if the company's inspection matched the condition of the car entered by the seller on the website. However, customers found that other factors reduced the original online valuation, including 'market conditions',

and that vehicle inspectors were set targets regarding the purchase price of vehicles, sometimes to reduce the online valuation by as much as 25%.

As a result of the investigation, the company gave undertakings to change their methods of operation in line with OFT requirements.

Source: www.oft.gov.uk press release (April 2011)

The Consumer Protection Act also places strict (but not absolute) liability on suppliers for damage and death/injury caused by defects in their products. There is no need to prove negligence or a contractual relationship, but there is a defence that the state of scientific and technical knowledge at the time the product was supplied was not sufficiently advanced for the defect to be recognised (the 'state of the act' defence).

Unfair Contract Terms Act 1977

Introduced to prevent 'small print' removing consumers' rights, generally without their knowledge, the Act has two parts. First, the seller cannot remove the liability for death or injury through negligence under any circumstances. Second, a trader cannot enforce a contract term that the courts hold to be unfair. For example, a coach company advertised a tour by luxury coach with videos, toilet, etc, but added in their small print that they reserved the right to substitute a coach of inferior quality. The courts held this to be unfair as it gave too much leeway to the coach company and most customers would not have picked up this particular item among the small print. The claimant was awarded compensation. Most decisions in this area are now dealt with by the CMA through an 'informal undertaking' agreed with the company. A 2007 example of this is set out in Case Study 5.8.

CASE STUDY 5.8

UNFAIR CONTRACT TERMS – CARPETRIGHT PLC

Carpetright had a series of clauses in their contracts which the OFT considered unfair. These included:

- All delivery dates were not legally binding.
- Time was not an essence of the contract.
- The fitter, not the company, was responsible for any liability arising from the work carried out.

- There was exclusion of liability if the consumer did not inform the company of the nature of the existing floor surface.
- There was a right to charge for cancellation of order without limit.

After consultations between the two parties, these were removed or altered by the company.

Source: OFT website (2007)

A number of well-publicised cases and the constant vigilance of consumer societies and other pressure groups have resulted in much greater honesty in communicating the real (and generally reasonable) contract terms by suppliers since this Act was passed.

Sale of Goods Act 1979/Supply of Goods and Services Act 1982

These Acts enable dissatisfied customers to take civil action against the supplier. The Acts require that:

- goods and services must match the description
- goods and services must be of merchantable quality – in appearance, finish and durability
- goods and services must be fit for the purpose
- services provided must be carried out with reasonable skill and within a reasonable time.

As the Act has been interpreted, the issue of reasonableness is key. A very cheap pair of canvas shoes is fit for purpose if they last six months, while a pair of expensive, hand-made leather shoes would not be fit if they wore out after four years' light wear. In essence, it has been for the court to decide what are the bounds of reasonableness and we shall see this again in the field of employment law.

If the product fails to meet the tests under the Act, the consumer has the remedy of the right to their money back, or receive a credit note, or for the goods to be replaced free of charge or the consumer can take the goods at a reduced price.

Consumer Credit Act 1974

This Act was introduced following the boom in hire purchase and credit agreements in the 1960s and 1970s, which led to high-pressure selling, especially in people's homes, and high rates of interest. The Act took two main directions. First, it aimed to clean up the industry by enforcing licensing of lenders for all credit activities, including credit cards.

The licensing involves an inspection regime and a requirement for effective staff training and proper funding of the business.

The second direction was to ensure that contracts were not oppressive. All credit contracts and all contracts signed outside of business premises have a seven-day 'cooling-off' period where the consumer can cancel without loss to either party. The terms of the credit can be altered by the courts if they regard the rate of interest as excessive. The consumer has the right to full details of the agreement before signing, including the annual rate of charge (calculated by means of the FCA's current formula), the full cost of the loan, the debtor's right to pay the loan off early and the terms under which they would do so. The Act does not apply to loans over an upper limit, currently £25,000, and only applies to consumer credit, not corporate credit.

Additional EU-wide consumer protection has been introduced for ordering on the web (**Electronic Commerce Regulations 2002**) and mail order (**Consumer Protection (Distance Selling) Regulations 2000**).

Consumer Contracts Regulations 2013

Arising from the EU Consumer Rights Directive 2011, these regulations seek to protect consumers through specifying clear pre-contract information that must be provided (such as total cost, delivery arrangements, etc.) and that the trader must clearly label the order button online to indicate that placing the order entails and obligation to pay. Cancellation rights have been increased to 14 days and other clauses cover the need to provide details in areas such as refunds, returning goods and help-line charges.

Consumer Rights Act 2015

This Act, which also arose from the EU Consumer Rights Directive 2011 has both codified all existing acts and improved consumer rights with respect to rights to reject goods or seek other remedies (replacement, repairs, etc.) with similar terms for services and digital content.

Later in the chapter we will look in more detail at the effect these laws and additional regulations have in specific sectors and industries.

5.3.3 EMPLOYMENT LAW

The regulation of employment relationships has changed beyond all recognition over the last 40 years. Originating from the individual 'master–servant' contract, the fundamental inequality of the parties to the relationship became clear by the mid-nineteenth century and a political party (the Labour Party) was set up essentially with the aim to rectify these inequalities through legislation by establishing employee rights and removing legal restraints on collective bargaining. It was clear that there was a major difference between a conflict over an employment contract, which can lead to unemployment and suffering abject poverty, and a difference over buying a pair of shoes. Moreover, the evidence of unscrupulous use of dominant employer power was widespread.

Although much progress was made in these areas in the early twentieth century, especially in the collective bargaining field, the stimulus to enacting more radical and extensive employee protection has come from the European Union. At the same time, the political consensus in recent times has been that the rights granted to trade unions in the collective bargaining field went too far. They have been reined in by Conservative Governments in the period between 1980 and 1997, and have been subject to further tightening by the Coalition Government (2010–2015). Further legislation is planned by the Conservative government that came to power in 2015.

A contract of employment arises directly out of contract law. A job must be offered and unconditionally accepted; there must be genuine agreement with no misunderstanding of the essential terms and conditions, such as the need to work night shift or the type of company car; the contract must be legal, with no illegal activities such as 'cash-in-hand';

there must be consideration, a wage or salary, as voluntary work is not enforceable; and only those over 13 can have an employment contract, with strict regulations relating to the employment of those under 18.

5.3.4 SOURCES OF THE EMPLOYMENT CONTRACT

The terms of an employment contract come from a surprising number of sources. It is not just the *express terms*, which are those specifically included in the contract (usually set out in the offer letter), such as salary, notice and holiday entitlement. Other sources are of equal importance:

- There are a number of *implied terms* originating from common law. These include the duty of the employee to co-operate with the employer in such areas as reasonable changes to the job, exercise due care in looking after the employer's goods and property, and show loyalty demonstrated by not disclosing confidential information. The employer also has duties, such as to exercise due care over the employee's health, safety and well-being (see Sections 5.3.8 and 5.3.9), to provide work, indemnify the employee if he or she incurs loss, expense or liability in carrying out the employer's instruction and to pay wages on time and correctly.
- Many contracts incorporate *collective terms* negotiated between the employer(s) and union(s) either at a local or national level. These may deal with issues such as overtime payment, holidays and disciplinary procedures.
- Contract terms are also incorporated through the *employee handbook*, which sets out rules and policies set out by the employer that the employee must sign up to.
- Many more unwritten contract terms reflect *employment laws* covering employee rights and benefits (see Section 5.3.6).

An additional complication is that the *contract terms do not need to be written down*. Rules relating to, say, employees swapping shifts, which have operated informally for some years (that is, through custom and practice) with the full knowledge of management, become part of the contract. In claims for unfair dismissal, the tribunal is very keen to establish whether terms written into contracts are those that actually operate in practice. For example, if an employee is dismissed for fighting (as clearly laid out in the employee handbook) but it comes to light that on the last two occasions when a similar incident occurred the employees were merely warned, the tribunal can take the view that custom and practice is that dismissal is not the normal punishment under the contract.

That is not to say that contractual terms cannot be changed by either party. An individual employee can request changes to his or her holiday arrangements which are different from the standard contractual terms. Or changes can be negotiated on a collective basis, usually through unions but sometimes through a works council. An employer can change shift arrangements and introduce different work practices and systems. In doing so, they should consult with the workforce, be able to justify the changes for business reasons and ensure they are published widely. They do not need to get every individual's signed agreement to the changes. An employee who continues to work under the changes is deemed to have accepted the changed contract.

A further complication is differentiating between the normal employee contract, called a *contract of service*, and the contract for the self-employed, who work under a *contract for services*. The legal implications are great in that a different tax regime applies (hence considerable interest by the Inland Revenue in this area) and the self-employed have none of the rights and benefits detailed in Section 5.3.5. Legal tussles have occurred in areas such as commission-only salespeople and those providing occasional but regular services, such as consultants. Although a complex area, the courts examine the degree of control and the nature of exclusivity of contract which can sometimes overcome the apparent clarity of the payment and tax arrangements.

Under the Employment Rights Act 1996, employers are required to give to each employee within two months a statement of certain contract terms under 16 headings, which includes details such as the date that continuous employment started, hours of work and holiday entitlement. This is called the 'principal statement' but, to repeat, it is not the actual contract of employment.

5.3.5 EMPLOYEE RIGHTS

The bulk of employment law since the 1970s has been enacted to improve the minimum level of benefits for employees and to protect them from potential employer abuse. There was some earlier legislation in this area, such as the prohibition of child labour and the nine-hour working day in the coal mines from the nineteenth century, but the recent legislation has taken the process much further and allowed employees to benefit extensively from the changes.

Employee protection has been enhanced in the following areas:

Protection from discrimination

Since the 1970s, groups seen as vulnerable in the employment field because of well-evidenced discrimination, harassment and bullying have been given legal protection. The various Acts make it unlawful to discriminate on the grounds of sex, ethnic origin, disability, age or religion. The Equality Acts of 2006 and 2010 created a common framework for all equal opportunity issues.

Discrimination has taken two forms:

- *Direct discrimination* – an instance here would be to advertise for a 'Girl Friday' or to use different criteria for selection for promotion. In the case of race discrimination, it may relate to an employer indicating to a recruitment agency that they do not want black casual workers; or an employer may turn down a deaf or partially sighted applicant specifically because of this disability. In each case, an individual or group is treated less favourably than another on the grounds of sex, race or disability. The employer has no defence even if they genuinely believe that what they are doing is right. The motives are irrelevant.
- *Indirect discrimination* – this occurs where the employer treats all applicants or employees the same but a practice, condition or policy adversely affects one sex or race more than another, or it affects the disabled more than the able-bodied or the elderly more than the young. The way it normally adversely affects that group is because the proportion of people from a particular group able to meet the condition or policy is considerably smaller. Moreover, the employer cannot objectively justify the practice, policy or condition. If the employer cannot convince the tribunal that the defence is genuine and substantial, the employer will lose the case. Tribunal cases where the applicant has won have included:
  - the requirement to restrict applicants geographically by residence to a specific area, which discriminated against ethnic minorities whose representation in that area was slight
  - recruiting only through word of mouth in an employment site dominated by white males
  - promoting internally when the workforce is unbalanced.

Legislation prohibits discrimination in pay and benefits between men and women, where work is 'like' or rated as similar under a job evaluation scheme. In addition, an employee can claim that their work is of 'equal value' to that of another employee of the opposite sex.

Harassment and bullying

Described as 'unwanted behaviour which a person finds intimidating, upsetting, embarrassing, humiliating or offensive', the courts have increasingly punished harassment and bullying, using both the concept of an employer's duty of care and discrimination legislation, supported by the EU Equal Treatment Directive (amended in 2000). This reflects the changing social attitudes in society where a predominantly male, white culture in workplaces, where power may be exercised over staff in a vulnerable position, is no longer acceptable in a modern state. It has been accepted by the courts that the judgement as to whether behaviour is acceptable or not comes from the subject(s) of the harassment. There can be additional compensation awarded for 'loss of feelings'.

No service requirement is necessary in any area of discrimination. Protection applies from day one of employment.

Protection from unfair dismissal

Since 1972, employees have been protected from arbitrary and unfair dismissal. From 2012, employees need two years' service to qualify for this protection, except in the case of trade union, equal opportunities or health and safety issues. To successfully defend a claim, the employer has to show that they have a justifiable reason (usually based on poor performance, conduct or redundancy) and that they have carried out the dismissal using the correct procedures. If they fail, the tribunal awards compensation up to a maximum of £78,335 (2015) or one year's pay. Occasionally, the tribunal can order the employer to reinstate the employee.

Acas has provided codes of practices in dealing with dismissal and redundancies which organisations need to observe to defend claims successfully. For example, where the offences are deemed to be misdemeanours (timekeeping, attendance, poor performance), warnings are required, whereas with gross misconduct (theft, violence), instant dismissal is permitted. Employees' rights, including that of a fair hearing, a colleague to help support their case and a fair appeal procedure, must be observed.

From 2013, a charge has been made for applications to a tribunal, currently £250 (2015) with an additional cost of £950 if the claim goes to a hearing and higher costs for more complex cases. This has led to a sharp reduction in tribunal applications, down around 70% by 2015. Concern has been expressed that many people who consider that they have been unfairly dismissed are put off making an application by the fees so justice is not done.

Similar protection is also afforded against dismissal due to pregnancy or for being a union activist (see Case Study 5.9).

CASE STUDY 5.9

DISMISSAL BECAUSE OF PREGNANCY

In *Hildreth v Perdu* (2006) UKEAT 0533/ 06, Hildreth, a finance manager, endured a campaign of harassment, intimidation, embarrassment and verbal abuse by the company owners after she had told them she was pregnant. They indicated strongly that they would not want to continue to employ her in a pregnant state. Her position had become so difficult that she resigned and successfully claimed constructive dismissal, receiving £8,000 in compensation.

Protection from working excessive hours

Arising from an EU directive and essentially a health and safety measure, the Working Time Regulations 1998 have had a controversial history. They have established that employees cannot be forced to work in excess of 48 hours a week, averaged over 17 weeks. Employees should have 11 consecutive hours of rest in any 24-hour period and a 24-hour rest in every seven-day period, plus a 20-minute break if the shift exceeds six hours. The Regulations also insist on the provision of 28 days' holiday.

The controversial aspect is that employers and employees can agree to 'opt out' of the Regulations so that they often apply as a voluntary measure.

Protection when being transferred

The Transfer of Undertakings (Protection of Employment) Regulations 1981 (known as TUPE) were introduced as a result of the EU Acquired Rights Directive. The philosophy here is that employees need to be protected when their organisation is sold to or merged with another organisation, or they are outsourced with their work. Prior to these Regulations, employees' terms could be fundamentally and unilaterally altered, with the employees having the choice to accept or leave.

Under the Regulations, all employment terms and conditions are protected (except pensions) and prior service is recognised. This does not stop the new employer having the right to change terms at a later date, but this right is limited by statute. Full consultation must take place with the employees being transferred.

Protection from deductions from pay

Under the Employment Rights Act 1996, employees have the right of an itemised pay statement and deductions can only be made with prior authorisation from the employee in writing.

5.3.6 EMPLOYEE RIGHTS AND BENEFITS

A summary of the minimum benefits introduced through legislation is set out in Table 5.1.

Table 5.1 Employee rights and benefits introduced through legislation

Minimum benefit	Legislation	Summary of key details
Minimum wage	National Living Wage (introduced 2016) National Minimum Wage Act 1998	Provides a minimum wage (£7.20 for employees aged 25 and over in 2016), includes bonuses and tips, with lower rates for employees under 25. Aims to eradicate exploitative pay in vulnerable sectors, such as home-workers and hospitality and will have a greater effect on female employees. It is expected to rise to around £9.35 by 2020.
Holidays	Working Time (Amendment) Regulations 2007	Minimum entitlement, including public holidays, is 28 days.
Maternity pay	Employment Rights Act 1996, amended by Employment Act 2002	Payable by employers for 39 weeks. Six-month qualifying period. Paid at 90% of average earnings for six weeks. Remaining weeks paid at £139.58 per week (2015) or 90% of employee's weekly earnings if this is lower.

Minimum benefit	Legislation	Summary of key details
Ante-natal care	As above	Right to paid time off during working hours for all ante-natal care and treatment
Maternity leave	As above	On top of paid maternity leave, an additional 26 weeks' unpaid maternity leave can be taken, with the right to the same job back upon return (see Case Study 5.10).
Paternity leave and pay	Employment Act 2002	Six-month qualifying period. Applicable to father of child, mother's husband or partner and be expected to have some responsibility for upbringing of child. Paid for two weeks at £139.58 per week (2016). Government plan to allow sharing of maternity/paternity leave through the 2013 Children and Families Bill.
Adoption leave	Employment Act 2002	One of the parents can take up to 26 weeks' unpaid leave when an adoption takes place. Six months' qualifying service.
Parental leave	Maternity and Parental Leave Regulations 1999	Parents with children under 5 (or disabled children under 18) can take up to 18 weeks' unpaid leave with the right to return to the same job. One year qualifying service. Shared parental leave is planned for 2015.
Time off for dependants	Employment Rights Act 1996	Reasonable unpaid time can be taken off to provide assistance when a dependant dies, falls ill, gives birth or is injured/assaulted, if there are any school problems or disruption to existing care arrangements. It is not applicable simply to provide normal care on a regular basis and only applies for an immediate crisis. In *Qua v John Ford Morrison Solicitors*, the employment appeal tribunal confirmed a fair dismissal when Qua took 17 different days off to look after her child who had medical problems.
Flexible working	Employment Act 2002/ Employment Rights Act 1996 Work and Families Act 2006	Provides the right of a parent of a child under 6 (18 if disabled) to apply for a change in working arrangements, including to work flexibly in order to care for the child.
Time off for public duties	Employment Rights Act 1996	Reasonable unpaid time can be taken off relating to work as a member of a local authority, health authority or similar.
Time off for trade union duties	TULRCA 1992	Officials of independent trade unions have right to time off with pay during working hours to carry out reasonable and relevant trade union duties and to undertake training, as specified by the Acas Code of Practice.
Statutory Sick Pay (SSP)	Social Security Contributions and Benefits Act 1992/Statutory Sick Pay Act 1994	Employers are responsible for payment of SSP for up to 28 weeks of sickness/injury in any single period of entitlement, payable at £88.45 per week (2015).

Minimum benefit	Legislation	Summary of key details
Redundancy consultation, time off and pay	TULRCA 1992	Consultation with employees/representatives must take place 45 days before redundancies take effect if 100 or more employees are redundant (30 days if between 20 and 99 employees) and adequate information must be provided by the employer. Redundancy pay entitlement at one week's pay (1.5 weeks at age 41 and over, 0.5 week from 18–21) for each year of service, up to 20 years. The maximum week's pay is £475 (2015). Reasonable time off with pay must be given to look for alternative work.

Notes: These benefits are correct at the time of writing but are subject to amendment, both in terms of the pay arrangements and in other details.

These are minimum benefits and employers can (and do) improve them by granting pay where there is no entitlement under the legislation, increasing the rates or enhancing the terms and conditions.

CASE STUDY 5.10

RIGHT TO RETURN TO SAME JOB

Blundell, a primary school teacher, was allocated a different class on her return from maternity leave. She claimed she should have returned to teach the same class in the same room. The Employment Appeals Tribunal held her job was to teach at the school, not to teach the same class. The terms and conditions of the job gave the school head discretion in allocating staff, and although staff could indicate a preference, they could not insist on a particular class. The school also pointed out that staff were rotated to different classes and the change in Blundell's class was due to this rotation. But the school lost on its procedure. They did not consult her because she was away on maternity leave (all other staff were consulted) and this was held to be sex discrimination.

Source: Blundell v St Andrew's Catholic Primary School UKEAT/0329/06

REFLECTIVE ACTIVITY 5.3

Should the rights and benefits set out in Table 5.1 be applicable in all organisations or should small employers be exempt from some of them? Set out arguments for and against such exemptions.

5.3.7 REGULATION OF CONTRACTS THROUGH COLLECTIVE BARGAINING

In the nineteenth century, government legislation was put in place to stamp out the infant trade unions, who were attempting to interfere with the employment contract. Over the last 200 years, as explained in Chapter 3, the pendulum has swung, first to provide a legal framework for union immunity so union activities are protected in tort, and then back the other way under Thatcherite reforms, where tight restrictions on this immunity were introduced to protect employers from arbitrary union power.

Under a variety of Acts in the period 1980–95, legal immunity is only available for unions in leading their members to break their contracts through strikes or other industrial actions when they:

- have a secret ballot before action is taken (with strict requirements as to notifying the employer, how the ballot should be carried out and who is entitled to vote)
- only take action against their own employer (so-called secondary action against suppliers or customers is not protected)
- carry out picketing only at their own place of work and in very small numbers (to prevent the dangerous and oppressive mass picketing which took place during the 1984 miners' strike)
- do not insist on a 'closed shop' – employees can join or not join a union as they wish
- ensure they elect their full-time officials on a regular basis under strict governance and follow their own rules on disciplining and expelling members.

After the 1997 election of a Labour Government, the pendulum swung somewhat back towards improving the regulation of relationships with the workforce, chiefly through organised labour. First, the statutory recognition procedures in the 1999 Employment Relations Act have served to support union members who wish to formally negotiate in the workplace (see Reflective Activity 5.4). Second, the European-initiated Information and Consultation Regulations 2004 gave rights to employees to be informed and consulted about the business for which they work. Third, the requirement for proper grievance and disciplinary procedures to be in place and operating fairly in all organisations was set out in the Employment Act 2008. Fourthly, an organisation cannot recruit agency staff to take the place of lawfully striking workers.

Legislation granted discretionary powers on employment tribunals to adjust awards by up to 25% if parties have failed unreasonably to comply with a relevant Code of Practice.

? REFLECTIVE ACTIVITY 5.4

Union recognition

An application was made to the Central Arbitration Committee in 2012 by the GMB union for the right for recognition for manual staff at Intersnack, Ltd. The union claimed that they already had 18 members out of the 110 staff and that they had organised a petition that showed a further 37 employees would be interested in joining the union and for the union to act on their behalf. The employer had responded to the request by stating that he had little evidence of interest in union recognition and that he was concerned that the involvement of a union would upset the existing relations with staff and the operation of a successful existing works council.

After fully investigating the union membership claims and considering the ballot that had taken place, CAC found that, 'given the level of union membership and support demonstrated by the petition, and in full consideration of the evidence made available, the panel is satisfied that, in accordance with paragraph 36(1)(b) of the schedule, a majority of the workers in the proposed bargaining unit would be likely to favour recognition of the union'. They therefore approved the union right for recognition for bargaining purposes.

Look up the website for the Central Arbitration Committee and examine a further two decisions that they have taken recently, including the parties involved, the background to the dispute over recognition and the justification for the decision.

5.3.8 HEALTH AND SAFETY REGULATION

The protection of employees in the workplace has been extended in recent years by a substantial collection of legislation emanating from both Europe and the UK. Regulation of health and safety in the UK is very extensive, with over 100 current pieces of legislation. Although there has been a steady decline in the number of deaths and serious accidents over the last decades, over 200 people are killed in accidents at work each year, including nearly 100 members of the public (HSE 2015). Not only is this a huge waste of human resources, but it is very costly for the economy. The main aim of the regulation, therefore, is to reduce the number of accidents and resultant ill-health and to ensure that a safety-conscious culture becomes widespread so that business can operate more efficiently.

5.3.9 ROLE OF HUMAN RESOURCES IN HEALTH AND SAFETY

In the majority of organisations where separate human resource departments exist, they either have responsibility for health, safety and welfare issues in that organisation or they play a major part in those activities. The main activities consist of:

- formulating policies and procedures
- monitoring policies and procedures
- advising management and employees on safety legislation
- designing, providing and recording health and safety training
- assisting in risk assessments
- identifying and dealing with occupational stress
- formulating initiatives that help create a healthy working environment.

Formulating policies and procedures

This activity is more than a formality required by law. It is essential that new employees understand how safety works within a new organisation and the policies and procedures will set out how the safety responsibilities are structured and the requirements from each employee. Specific references to areas (such as responsibility for checking lifting gear, or guards) should be clearly spelled out. The document should give a statement of management intent as to how safety issues will be treated in the workplace. Detailed procedures should be set out for dealing with emergencies, safety training, information arising from the investigations under COSHH, and procedures should be set out for all departments where hazards have been identified. Human resources should ensure that such documents are logical, readable and have been circulated correctly.

Monitoring policies and procedures

At regular intervals, all procedures need examining to see if they need updating to take account of new processes, materials and layouts. By attending management and safety meetings, human resources can ensure such necessary revisions can be identified and put into place.

Advising management and employees on safety legislation

The defining Act has been the Health and Safety at Work Act 1974 but HR practitioners should be aware of other legislation dealing with, for example, Control of Substances Hazardous to Health (1988), Reporting of Diseases and Dangerous Occurrences Regulations (1995) and those relating to manual handling and display screens. New regulations continue to emerge, especially from Europe, with different levels of importance and different implementation dates.

Designing, providing and recording health and safety training

Systematic training is essential if procedures are to operate properly. It should start with induction training to ensure that employees who are involved in any hazardous operation have instruction in key areas before they set foot on the work site. Safety instruction should be incorporated into any new processes or where new materials are introduced onto site. There is a legal requirement to recognise safety representatives and they have the right for time off for training.

Assisting in risk assessments

It is a legal duty for employers to assess and record health and safety risks for all of their operations. Much of this work involves attempting to balance the nature of the risks, their seriousness in terms of likely danger to employees and the cost of implementing protection from these risks.

Identifying and dealing with occupational stress

Stress has become one of the most serious health issues of recent years. A survey by the HSE (2014) estimated that stress accounted for over 10 million days lost, (43% of all days lost through illness) and cost nearly £10bn per year in the UK, over 2% of gross domestic product, close to £400 per employee per year. In a recent survey (Steadman et al 2015) 44% of employees found their work stressful or very stressful. Employees aged between 34 and 44 suffer the most, while the problems worsen the longer they stay in the same job. The National Institute for Health and Clinical Excellence (NICE) estimated that a firm with 1,000 employees could save £250,000 a year by tackling the causes of work-related stress (NICE 2009).

The causes of occupational stress are numerous. They are associated with perceptions of job insecurity, increase in work intensity, aggressive management styles, lack of effective workplace communication, overt or insidious bullying and harassment, faulty selection for promotion or transfer and lack of guidance and training (Cartwright and Cooper 1997). Employees may be exposed to situations which they find uncomfortable, such as continually dealing with customers, excessive computer work, repetitive or fragmented work or having to make regular public presentations. Probably the most common cause, however, is the constant fear of organisational change through restructuring, takeovers, mergers or business process re-engineering. A lack of control over their work, their environment or their career progression can also be stressful (Rick et al 1997).

When a work environment containing these cultural aspects is added to personal problems, such as divorce or separation, ill or dying relatives, difficult housing conditions or financial problems, it is not surprising that the employer will be faced with a good proportion of employees with stress-related problems.

Stress is manifested not only in high absence levels. Fatigue, increases in infections, backache and digestive illnesses are commonly found. Irritation, hostility, anxiety and a state of panic can arise in the workplace, with knock-on effects on working practices and relationships between employees. The end result may be that the employee is 'burnt out', unable to cope with pressures that previously had been regarded as challenging and stimulating. Employees may also turn to palliatives, such as alcohol or drugs.

The employer who neglects the problem of occupational stress may face legal action. The first legal breakthrough for an employee was John Walker, a social work manager with Northumberland County Council, who, having had a mental breakdown arising from his occupation, returned to his job but received no positive assistance from his employer to help him to cope successfully, as set out in Case Study 5.1.

Successive cases have included a primary school head who won £100,000 after suffering two nervous breakdowns allegedly caused by stress brought on by bullying and harassment, and an out-of-court settlement which was reached in 1998 between an NHS trust and the bereaved spouse of an employee who committed suicide. In a later case,

Birmingham City Council admitted liability for personal injury caused by stress where they moved a 39-year-old senior draughtsman to the post of a neighbourhood housing officer without sufficient training. The nature of the work was so different and the interpersonal demands so great that she had long periods of ill-health leading to early retirement on medical grounds. She was awarded £67,000 (Miller 1999).

Greater clarification as to the employer's responsibility in the case of psychiatric injury based on exposure to unacceptable levels of stress was given by the Court of Appeal in 2002 (*Sutherland v Hatton*). The court held that an employer was entitled to assume that an employee was able to withstand the normal pressures of the job and to take what the employee said about her own health at face value. It was only if there were indications which would lead a reasonable employer to realise that there was a problem that a duty to take action would arise. In terms of whether the injury to health was foreseeable, factors that should be taken into account include whether:

- the workload was abnormally heavy
- the work was particularly intellectually or emotionally demanding
- the demands were greater compared with similar employees.

If the only way of making the employee safe was to dismiss him or her, there would be no breach of duty by letting the employee continue if he or she was willing to do so (IRS 2002).

An organisation's responsibilities for stress reduction was shown in stark outline in 2008 when the HSE issued an improvement notice to United Lincolnshire NHS Trust for 'failing to identify the potential risks to the health and safety of its employees from exposure to work-related stress'. The issue in this case was the complete lack of a work-related stress policy or risk assessment (Scott 2009).

All of these cases show that employers need to carefully consider the way that the work demands affect their employees and ensure that they investigate each case, taking appropriate action to ameliorate potentially health-damaging situations. A further consideration is the level of employees' expectations on welfare provision. It is a sure sign of a sympathetic and caring employer who will make special provision for the personal and individual needs of employees.

?   REFLECTIVE ACTIVITY 5.6

You have been brought in as a consultant to carry out a review of the level of stress in an organisation. Having investigated safety and welfare statistics, and carried out an employee attitude survey, you report on the following indicators of stress:

- The absenteeism levels had risen from 6% to 9% over the last three years, of which 3% was reported as being caused by stress-related illnesses.
- The number of staff on long-term sick had increased from 8 to 14, with 6 incidents of stress or other mental problems.
- The level of reported accidents lrave had doubled from 12 to 24 over the same period.
- There had been three incidents of violence inside the site, two alcohol-induced. Five employees had been dismissed arising from these incidents. Two had resulted in claims to employment tribunals.
- The staff attitude survey showed that over 70% considered that they worked excess hours which caused stress 'occasionally' or 'regularly'.
- Twenty per cent of staff found that their relationships with their managers were 'poor' or 'very poor'.
- Thirty per cent believed that urgent improvements in their physical environment were required.

Formulating initiatives that help create a healthy working environment

All the research indicates that a healthy workforce will be a successful one and a higher-performing one, so being proactive in introducing and encouraging initiatives to support health programmes can make a substantial difference to organisational performance, as shown in Case Study 5.11.

CASE STUDY 5.11

IMPROVING HEALTH AND SAFETY TRAINING AT STADCO

The death of an employee in 2010 at Stadco, an automotive supplier employing 875 people in Wales and the west Midlands, caused a radical re-think of its strategy for engaging all employees in effective health and safety activities. Despite being cleared of any blame for the fatality, the board reflected on its responsibilities and embarked on innovative training to alter behaviours.

This involved affecting the heart more than the head, so the company turned to a theatre and a performance company to embed the message. Actors played out scenarios in front of an audience of staff and stopped in places to ask them what a character should do, which involved them in the decision-making process. This has led to a situation where staff are raising and discussing near-misses and having real conversations about what should be done to avoid the situation in future.

The approach has led to a reduction in accidents from 235 in 2011 to less than 100 in 2014. Further developments planned include peer-to-peer observations, which involve an employee from one factory watching how colleagues in another factory work and talking to them about their behaviour.

Source: Chynoweth (2014)

The most successful initiatives are those that are shown to be cost-effective as well as improving employee health, an example of which is shown in Case Study 5.12.

CASE STUDY 5.12

PHYSIOTHERAPY FOR NORTH EAST AMBULANCE SERVICE (NEAS) CREWS

Ambulance work is physically demanding, sometimes causing musculoskeletal injuries among staff. NEAS, employing 1,800 ambulance staff, found that the waiting time for an in-house physiotherapist first appointment was over three weeks and crew members were unable to work on full duties during this time, with average individual productivity levels dropping to 36%.

To counter these delays, NEAS hired a private contractor in February 2011 who provided an appointment within three days. The effect was immediate, according to Susan Kaszefko, HR Manager, with an 81% reduction in

> musculoskeletal absence and a saving in the first year of £532,926 from time that would have been lost in absence. The service cost only £39,563. A similar system for providing an MRI scan (currently with a waiting time of over two months) has also been introduced at a cost of £400 for a scan provided within a week.
>
> Source: Griffiths (2012)

A test of overall success is whether a safety-conscious culture pervades the organisation. This is shown through management operating systems and procedures, not just because of the legal requirements but because they see that it makes good business sense, both in terms of reducing costs arising from accidents and from establishing a caring relationship with the labour force.

5.4 IMPLICATIONS OF REGULATION

Earlier in this chapter, the roles of the Office of Fair Trading and the Competition Commission, and their successors, in disseminating, regulating and enforcing commercial and consumer legislation were set out (see Sections 5.3.1 and 5.3.2). Additional industry-specific regulation has been put in place over the last 20 years and this section will examine the operation of a selection of these regulators and the implications in the fields of privatised utilities, financial services, communications and areas of the public sector.

5.4.1 INDUSTRY REGULATORS – PRIVATISED UTILITIES

During the period 1980 to 1995, public utilities in the UK were privatised in what is now seen as a momentous and generally successful business revolution. The Labour Party ideology of nationalisation of key industries, which led to coal, steel, gas, electricity, railways and many others coming under state control in the post-war period until 1976, was replaced by the free trade and competition philosophy, promulgated by Milton Friedman (1970a). It had become clear that the philosophy of veering towards a centrally controlled interventionist state operation, which had operated for the previous 20 years in the Western economies, had failed to produce the economic success that had been promised. Managers in state-controlled industries complained of constant ministerial interference, starvation of investment and regular changes in strategic direction. At its peak, almost 10% of GDP came under government control. By 2002, after privatisation, this had been reduced to only 1%.

Historical studies (Martin and Parker 1997; Electricity Association 1998) have shown that labour productivity rose at an average of 15%, service provision improved substantially and prices generally fell, especially in telecommunications and electricity.

In Chapter 3 you will have read about the issues associated with the privatisation of state monopolies. The model for privatisation was essentially one of attempting to break up state monopolies, introducing a variety of methods to stimulate competition and to keep a measure of control through regulation in the interests of the consumer. Unbundling has involved separating out the potentially competitive areas (for example electricity generation, telecommunication value added services) from the monopoly part (for example transmission and distribution grids, telephone lines to homes). This picture has been repeated across Europe with only a handful of mostly Scandinavian governments owning the state telecommunications company, reinforced by EU directives requiring member states to establish independent regulatory agencies to provide a 'level playing field' for potential competitors (Pollack 1997; Curwen 1997). This policy has continued with EU accession states having to sign up to privatisation of their main utilities.

Regulators

In each sector privatised in the UK, a *regulator* has been appointed to oversee the operation of the business for the benefit of the consumer (business and private) and to try to ensure that the form of privatisation actually worked in practice. The main responsibilities of the regulator are:

- to set out the pricing model (with or without agreement from the participants)
- to establish and monitor service standards
- to encourage the working of a competitive market
- for products such as gas and electricity, to ensure stable sources of supply
- to prevent the exercise of any remnant of monopolistic power
- to ensure the industry meets social and environmental responsibilities.

The regulator is appointed by the Government but is independent of government control. Each industry has been faced by a specific business context and the model of regulation has constantly been changed as the nature of the competitive challenges within each sector has altered. For example, one of the major issues in the telecommunication industry has been the role of the dominant provider, BT, which originally controlled landlines into most UK homes. The challenge was to encourage competition to this control, achieved mainly through encouraging the development of cable and mobile phone systems and through complex agreements allowing other companies access to the landlines to provide alternative services and through acting as a mediator in resolving disputes between the parties, such as the dispute in 2004 over NTS discounts. The telecommunication industry has, in fact, moved from one monopoly provider in 1984 (BT) to over 100 providers by 2015, while the degree of competition in the power industry has extended so far that over 5 million customers switched their electricity supply amongst the 37 providers in 2014. In 2004, Ofgem fined Powergen £700,000 after the company stopped more than 20,000 domestic customers from switching to new gas/electricity contracts.

In another sector, the policy of the water industry regulator, Ofwat, has changed over recent years. At the time of privatising in the early 1990s, the water industry was allowed to make a substantial increase to tariffs to fund the substantial investment required to transform sewage treatment, reduce effluent discharge and thereby improve water quality around the UK coastline. However, in 2009, the regulator drafted a new five-year pricing regime which required water companies to cut prices by 0.2% per year and increase capital expenditure. In 2014, Ofwat encouraged further competition in the provision of water to businesses through sections of the 2014 Water Act.

As an example of its policing role, Ofwat imposed a penalty of £176m on Southern Water in 2014 reflecting the company's underperformance on discharging in the sewerage network since 2010, plus internal sewage flooding together with poor customer service and complaint handling. This penalty was implemented by forcing Southern Water to reduce prices by 8% for the period 2015–20, before inflation adjustment (Waterbriefing 2015).

The ability to set pricing models (unsuccessfully challenged in the courts in the mid-1990s by the gas industry) and to discipline players in the industry has given the regulator substantial power over operating companies. However, the need for establishing a fair pricing model has been reduced in recent years as more sophisticated markets have been introduced into gas and electricity, as mentioned earlier, allowing more providers to enter the market and create more competition, while natural competition has developed in the telecommunication industry.

5.4.2 INDUSTRY REGULATION – FINANCIAL SERVICES (FCA/PRA) AND COMMUNICATIONS (OFCOM)

A second strand of regulation covers two industries that the state regards as needing special forms of regulation, namely financial services and communications. These are industries which, generally, have not been government-owned (apart from the BBC and BT), but where there is a strong public interest. This interest is not just to preserve or encourage competition but to inspire confidence in the financial or communication systems, regulate ethical behaviour and to act as a watchdog over technical developments.

Ofcom, set up in 2003, covers activities previously controlled by, among others, the Broadcasting Standards Commission, Radio Authority, Oftel and the Independent Television Authority. In 2011, it took over the responsibilities for regulating the postal service from Postcom, which was abolished. It has a duty to 'balance the promotion of choice and competition with the duty to foster plurality, informed citizenship, protect viewers, listeners and customers and promote cultural diversity'. Its activities include:

- reform of public service broadcasting, the effects of digital television on the BBC's channel provision and the regular licence review
- policy on awarding of radio and television licences
- policy on television advertising under a single terrestrial commercial provider (ITV)
- advising the Government on foreign takeover of major communication players, such as national newspapers
- *protecting small players* – producing codes on the ability of independent programme producers to retain their programming rights
- *technology reviews* – advising on the digital switchover between 2007 and 2012
- *protecting public morals* – advising on television programme content in terms of sex and violence.

Financial Conduct Authority/Prudential Regulatory Authority

Regulating financial markets has, in recent years, been a key part of government economic activity. Understanding that confidence is at the heart of a country's financial system and, fearful of the 'meltdown' that could occur should this confidence suddenly evaporate, governments have established systems of financial supervision to try to avoid rogue activities. Up until 2013, much of this authority had been shared between the Bank of England and the Financial Services Authority, with a good part of the detailed supervision, investigation and enforcement taken up by the latter. Its main aims had been to:

- protect consumers through vetting firms and individual traders for honesty, competence and financial soundness
- promote public understanding of the financial system
- help to reduce financial crime, including money laundering and insider trading
- maintain confidence in the UK financial system by supervising exchanges, settlement houses and conducting market surveillance and monitoring transactions.

However, the financial crisis which began in 2007 and continued into 2013 – with little sign of abating – demonstrated that the FSA had signally failed to maintain the required level of financial supervision while financial confidence in the UK system had been severely shaken. As indicated in Chapter 4, the FSA had adopted a 'light touch' policy on banking regulation during the period 2000–07 so that it had been unable to forecast the financial crisis of 2007 or to handle it effectively. The FSA was accused of failing to apply enough regulation to bullish financial institutions in the boom years, a failure that contributed to the size of the crisis.

It also failed to give proper protection and redress on various fronts, including the mis-selling of endowments, payment protection insurance and allowing banks to apply sky-high overdraft charges and to sell risky investments to customers looking for safe savings products.

The Coalition Government announced in 2010 that the FSA would be broken up and two new bodies appointed:

- *Prudential Regulatory Authority (PRA)* – under the control of the Bank of England, chaired by its governor and responsible for the supervision of banking and other financial institutions.
  The aim was that financial policies would be better integrated between the micro and macro sides and that a tighter grip would be held over financial banking and financial institutions.
- *Financial Conduct Authority* – an independent regulatory body that promotes confidence in financial services and protects the consumer.
  The FCA inherited much of the powers of the FSA to investigate and, where necessary, fine organisations and individuals and restrict their activities.

A detailed example of disciplinary action taken by the FSA in 2012 is shown in Case Study 5.13.

 FSA DISCIPLINARY ACTION AGAINST PETER CUMMINGS 2012

CASE STUDY 5.13

Peter Cummings, ex-chief executive of the corporate division of HBOS bank, was fined £500,000 and banned from holding any senior position in a UK bank, building society, investment or insurance firm. This is the highest fine imposed by the FSA on a senior executive for management failings.

The FSA judged that between January 2006 and March 2008, Cummings failed to exercise due skill, care and diligence by pursuing an aggressive expansion strategy within the corporate division without suitable controls in place to manage the associated risks. Also, between April and December 2008, Cummings failed to take reasonable care to ensure that the corporate division adequately and prudently managed high-value transactions which showed signs of stress. They found that he was aware that there were significant issues with the corporate division's controls, including: weaknesses in management information; staff being incentivised to focus on revenue rather than risk; and a culture which saw risk management as a constraint on the business rather than an integral part of it. Under Cummings's direction, the division pursued an aggressive growth strategy, despite these known weaknesses in the control framework. This focus on growth peaked in 2007 and continued into 2008, despite Cummings being aware of concerns within HBOS about some of the markets in which the division operated and growing signs of problems in the economy. Rather than taking reasonable steps to mitigate potential risks, he directed his division to increase its market share as other lenders were pulling out of deals.

Source: FSA Website

Other examples of FSA action included:

- Fining BlackRock Investment Management (UK) Limited (BIM) £9,533,100 for failing to protect client money adequately by not putting trust letters in place for certain money market deposits, and for failing to take reasonable care to organise and control its affairs responsibly in relation to the identification and protection of client money.

Obtaining a successful prosecution of traders Christian and Angie Littlewood for insider trading, which led to custodial sentences and confiscation orders totalling over £3m. (Source: FSA website.)

- An example of action taken by the FCA in 2015 was the order to Dollar Financial, owner of payday lenders Money Shop and Payday UK, to refund £15.4m to 147,000 customers for handing out loans it knew they could not repay. (Source: FCA website.)

As a direct result of the financial crisis of 2007–10, the FSA issued a *Code of Practice on Remuneration Practices* in 2009 which applied to 26 large financial institutions – banks, building societies and investment firms. This code aims to discourage the payment of large cash bonuses for short-term gains, which has been considered as one of the major causes of the recent crisis because this encouraged substantial risk-taking.

The essential features of the code were:

- bonuses should be based on employees' long-term contributions to minimise the impact of volatility on awards
- profits should determine bonus pools, which should be adjusted to reflect current and future risk profiles
- a proportion of bonuses should be deferred to reflect the long-term aspects of financial performance
- firms should be able to explain how individual pay awards have been calculated
- the practice of agreeing 'guaranteed bonuses' for new employees should be discouraged and limited to a period of one year only.

This code was extended by the PRA from 2015 to make specific requirements for clawback over the following seven years of variable elements of payments (ie bonuses).

This code has been criticised by commentators on a number of counts:

- It is only a code and therefore non-binding, except on those organisations where the UK Government has a majority holding. Although the companies affected have signed up to the code, no action can be taken for any subsequent evasions. 'Toothless' is a word that has been often used.
- Restrictions on bonuses will affect the long-term position of the City of London as the top performers will move to unregulated companies in places such as the Gulf or Hong Kong although there is little evidence of this having an effect. In fact, a number of announcements were made in 2015–16 of bankers being re-located back to London from Switzerland.

This issue can be regarded as an important example of the difficulty of applying regulation in a global economy. Without international agreement, organisations and individuals may tend to migrate to those countries which have the most amenable forms of regulation.

The splitting up of the responsibilities of the FSA has also been criticised because it may not be easy to divide the 'prudential' aspects from the 'conduct' aspects. As Black and Hopper (2011) explain:

… for example the proposal that the FCA is to make provisions on internal controls for Conduct of Business rules, the PRA on internal controls for capital rules. However, in many firms the risk and compliance functions are merged. In practice, there is an enormous overlap between prudential and conduct regulation. For example, managing compliance with conduct requirements has significant overlap with operational risk management which is of increasing importance to prudential regulation; effective credit risk management and 'responsible lending' are intimately connected. There are real dangers of inconsistencies emerging in the internal control and risk management standards required by the two different regulators leading to costly and confusing requirements for firms with no proven beneficial impacts. (p8)

5.4.3 REGULATION AND THE PUBLIC SECTOR

For 30 years, the Audit Commission has carried out a different form of regulation in the public sector. It has been a true 'watchdog', carrying out investigations into the operations of local authorities, health services and government departments. It principally examined issues of efficiency and ethical behaviour, endeavouring to establish realisable targets, examples of best practice and to shame poor performers into change by publicising their faults. Although it had no executive power to change an organisation's policies or practices, the Government takes note of its findings when it takes decisions over funding, especially with local authorities. It has had a degree of success in leading public organisations to carefully examine their methods of operation and benchmark their performance against similar bodies.

However, in 2010, the Coalition Government announced that it would be substantially reduced in size (from 2,000 employees down to around 70) in order to save around £50m. Local authorities and other public sector bodies would be able to appoint their own auditors. This was a decision criticised by a House of Commons Select Committee:

The abolition of the Audit Commission will leave a substantial hole in the system of audit and inspection in local government and ministers must not assume that freedoms and market forces will automatically fill it. It is not clear to us that significant savings will result from abolition of the Audit Commission, at least in the short to medium term. (Communities and Local Government Committee Report 2011, pp24, 28)

5.4.4 REGULATION AND OTHER SECTORS

Although most business sectors operate without a specific regulator, they are touched by regulation in a number of ways:

- Their practices may be investigated by the FCA and CMA, such as the doorstep selling example explained in Section 5.3.
- A planned merger or takeover can be referred to the CMA to decide if it breaches the monopolies guidelines, such as was threatened in the 2003 battle over Safeway PLC.
- Their detailed operations can be constrained by UK or European law in areas such as labelling and packaging, information to consumers or environmental regulations.
- Planning laws have become increasingly intrusive, such as the government policy in 2000 to reject any further out-of-town shopping developments, including supermarkets, because of their effect on traffic growth and decline of the local high street.

5.4.5 CODES OF PRACTICE

Each of the regulators is authorised to produce codes of practice. Ofgem, for example, have produced a code of practice for the action that should be taken when a provider proposes to cut off a consumer's gas or electricity supply, and Ofcom has a Code of Advertising Practice. They do not in themselves have a force of law but they have strong influence on business behaviour. They help to raise standards throughout the industry, stopping organisations from indulging in dubious practices which, although not illegal, give the industry a bad name. Many organisations are happy to accept and influence the production of a code rather than having legal restrictions imposed on them.

?

? REFLECTIVE ACTIVITY 5.7

Benefits of a regulatory system

What are the benefits of a regulatory system, controlled by autonomous bodies, as opposed to a state-controlled system?

5.4.6 TRENDS TO WATCH

Governments of all shapes, EU and UK, find it difficult to restrain themselves from introducing legislation, so watch out for developments in the following areas:

- In the *employment law area*, the continuing extension of flexible working rights in the UK and a resolution of the long-standing debate on the rights of what the EU call 'atypical working', such as agency workers.
- In the *consumer protection area*, greater clarification and consistency on the roles of regulators, especially the FCA and the Competition and marketing Authority (CMA), with a more consistent approach across Europe.
- In the *financial area*, the European Union's continuing activity on regulating banks and other financial institutions.

5.5 HOW FAR SHOULD REGULATION EXTEND?

There have been two major debates centred on the extent and development of regulation in recent years. The first covers the *breadth* of the regulation – the degree to which regulation should be local, national or international. The second deals with the *depth* of the regulation – how tightly it should apply and in what detail. We shall deal with each of these in turn.

5.5.1 BREADTH OF REGULATION

Governments in the West have led the way in most areas of regulation, from creating and protecting individual employment rights to enhancing consumer power and protecting the environment. However, this action has been taken at a number of levels, as shown in environmental regulation in the UK (Brooks and Weatherston 2004).

At the local level, local authorities have a number of responsibilities, including food hygiene, pest control and noise pollution. At the national level, a number of enabling laws, such as the Environmental Protection Act 1990 and the Environment Act 1995, cover a wide area of environmental control, including waste disposal and recycling requirements, mostly enforced by the Environment Agency.

At the international level, the European Union has taken a number of initiatives through environment action programmes with mixed success to obtain compliance across the EU. Many attempts have been made by governments to agree to international environmental standards, the most well known being the Kyoto Protocol in 1997, which has had mixed take-up in the twenty-first century. There have been numerous attempts subsequently to gain worldwide approval to standards of greenhouse gas emissions and systems of carbon emission trading.

In the financial area, governments and central banks have made many attempts in recent years to produce effective regulation in the banking area but few have shown much success. For example, the overhaul of banking rules under Basel III was finally agreed in 2013 but the detailed implementation was much watered-down because of disagreement between nations on the measures necessary to regulate capital requirements. Similarly, no agreement has been reached on an overall EU system to encourage women on to boards of EU companies. However, a directive which covers the financing of mortgages across the EU was agreed in 2014 and becomes operational in 2016.

In January 2013 an agreement was reached at the EU Council of Ministers to limit bankers' bonuses to no more than base salary, or up to twice salary with the explicit approval of shareholders. This decision was widely criticised in some UK business circles because it would drive away the highest talent in banking to centres outside the EU such as Switzerland, Singapore and Hong Kong. The European Banking Authority recognized in 2015 that the regulations were ineffective as banks can circumvent them by simply increasing the base rate of their top bankers. The Chair of the EBA has recognised that countries have too many opportunities to bend regulations sent to them which undermines the supervision of banking and undermines the banking union (Enria 2015).

There are a number of benefits of operating at different levels:

- It involves all communities at whatever level to get involved in subjects that affect them.
- Without multi-level involvement, it would be difficult to get general support for regulatory action.
- A combination of experimental policies can be tried out in different countries (or within countries) to see which ones can work and to identify the main problems faced.
- It is recognised that international agreement is always problematic, so it is foolish to wait for a complete international solution before acting. Partial success is seen as better than no progress.
- The long-term aim of organisations and countries operating and competing on a level playing field is to be applauded and has been successful in some areas, such as agreements within the World Trade Organization.

There are also disadvantages of operating at different levels:

- The raft of regulation can be very confusing for companies trying to operate within the law.
- International companies may choose to locate to the less regulated environments. Most shipping companies, for example, operate with 'flags of convenience' in countries which have little enforcement on labour rights and minimum health and safety. Similar action has been threatened recently by hedge funds.
- Countries are likely to operate regulation to disadvantage international competitors. This can take the form of excessive health and safety requirements for imported goods or very large fines on foreign companies who have broken national rules. Examples include the US fines on BP exceeding £40bn for the Deepwater Horizon oil spill and the huge fines on international banks for Libor and other transgressions which banks hastily agreed to pay following the threats to take away their licences to operate in the United States. Similarly, the EU has attempted to operate anti-trust regulatory powers to reduce the dominance of Google (Stelzer 2014b; Duke and Pancevski 2015).
- There is little optimism that some countries, such as China, will accept international regulation and the slow progress allows them to continue to operate as accepted competitors without having to change their policies in fields such as ecological effects and human rights because there is not the willpower to penalise them.

5.5.2 DEPTH OF REGULATION

There is much debate as to the degree of regulation that is ideal for a society. The current trend is for government to steadily increase the intensity of regulation in all fields, this being their main thrust of legislation. Occasional attempts to reverse the tide, such as Margaret Thatcher's policies on privatisation and encouraging more competition in the financial and other sectors, though having a good degree of success, can be set against the huge amount of additional legislation in recent years in enhancing labour rights, controlling financial activities, increasing planning controls and protecting the environment.

Those who doubt the benefits of additional regulation put forward the following arguments:

- Regulation discourages entrepreneurial activity and therefore restricts job creation, especially in small organisations, which have to cope with an annual collection of laws with which they have to comply, despite having few resources to judge the degree and cost of compliance necessary. Support for this viewpoint from the Coalition Government led to a package of measures introduced in 2013 to cut unnecessary bureaucracy and reduce government regulation which exempted large numbers of low-risk organisations from safety inspections. These included shops, offices, pubs and clubs, unless they had an accident or poor safety track record.

- Regulation is expensive. There are large costs involved in obtaining agreement, especially on the international front, in terms of providing incentives for poorer countries and those less willing to comply, let alone the huge costs of endless international conferences. There are similar large costs in enforcing the regulations. It had been estimated that 50,000 UK staff were employed within financial organisations in 2007 to ensure compliance to regulation set out by the Bank of England and the FSA. It should be added that all this expense failed to prevent the financial crash of 2008–13, as the report on the collapse of HBOS found (Ahmed 2015).

- Some businesses argue that regulation goes too far. In the field of employment law, for example, much lobbying continues to take place to try to ensure the UK National Minimum Wage is kept as low as possible, and French employers have attempted, with some success, to reverse the legislation which introduced the 35-hour working week. The rapid increase in the financial regulation has been hotly opposed by many companies, although the opposition has been much quieter of late following the continuing financial crisis.

KEY LEARNING POINTS

- UK law can be divided into criminal and civil law and originates chiefly from legislation emanating from the European Union, the UK parliament and common law. Courts are bound by precedent.
- The last 30 years have seen a substantial increase in the volume and intensity of legislation to protect employees and consumers with increased regulation of business activity.
- The burden of this legislation has been borne by businesses, which need to adapt their operations to ensure compliance.
- A larger emphasis has been put on organisations carrying out safety audits and risk assessment to ensure accident prevention and a healthier workplace.
- Few sectors now manage to avoid a form of regulation, with a substantial presence in the privatised utilities and the financial and communications sectors, where regulators have considerable legal powers.
- Consumers are also protected through the regulation of markets to prevent the use of monopolistic powers by large organisations.

REVIEW QUESTIONS

1 What are the main roles of the Financial Conduct Authority (FCA)?

2 What actions should HR practitioners take to improve health and safety?

3 Set out the main influences on governments which have led to the enhancement of consumer rights through legislation from the 1960s onwards.

4 What are the main sources of the employment contract?

5 Describe the main roles of a regulator in the utilities sector.

6 Give six examples of legislation introduced in the UK to give protection to employees.

7 Trace the path of a tribunal application through the UK/European courts.

8 What is the meaning of the expression 'precedent' under UK law?

9 What are the six main elements in any employment contract?

10 What are the responsibilities of an employer concerning stress in the workplace?

EXPLORE FURTHER

Further reading

There are large numbers of legal textbooks available dealing with the English legal system. Some cover the whole picture, including criminal and civil law; others specialise in areas such as contract law, commercial law or employment law. It is worthwhile for the HR practitioner to have a general legal textbook on their shelves together with a specialist book on **employment law.** Current publications of the latter include:

CABRELLI, D. (2014) Employment Law. 4th edition. London: Pearson.

DANIELS, K. (2012) Employment law: an introduction for HR and business students. 3rd edition. London: CIPD.

LEWIS, D. and SARGEANT, M. (2013) Employment law: the essentials. 12th edition. London: CIPD.

SMITH, I. and BAKER, A. (2015) Employment Law. 4th edition. Oxford University Press.

In terms of legal issues relating to *discrimination*, good sources include:

CONNOLLY, M. (2011) Discrimination law. 2nd edition. London: Sweet &Maxwell.

SARGEANT, M (2013) Discrimination and the law. Abingdon: Routledge.

For **financial regulation**, a good introductory approach to this difficult and complex area is given in:

KATTEL, R. and KREGEL, J. (2015) Financial regulation in the European Union. Abingdon: Routledge.

MOOSA, I. (2015) *Good regulation, bad regulation: the anatomy of financial regulation*. Basingstoke: Palgrave Macmillan.

For **Consumer Law:**

TILLSON, J. (2014) *Consumer and commercial law*, 3rd edition. Harlow: Pearson Education.

SEMINAR ACTIVITY 5.1

RACE DISCRIMINATION

In 2004, Mahmood Siddiqui, aged 59, was awarded £180,000 from the Royal Mail arising from a four-year campaign of racial abuse at work. He was repeatedly sworn at, bullied and called a 'Paki' by colleagues at a sorting office in Harlow, Essex. On one occasion, one of them ignited a cigarette lighter in front of him and threatened to burn him. Others daubed offensive graffiti, including the messages 'Siddiqui hang him' and 'Paki scab lover'. His car was vandalised and threats were made to his wife and children.

Despite repeated complaints to his managers, the racial harassment continued with 'tacit support' from his boss. It was only some time later when a hidden camera was installed that the culprits were caught and disciplined. By then, Mr Siddiqui, the only non-white on the night shift, was suffering severe stress. Ill-health forced him to retire in 2002 after 12 years' service. The tribunal commented that 'throughout the case, the word "banter" was used. We consider this to have often been employed as a euphemism for racial abuse for which he alone was singled out'. His award consisted of £104,000 for loss of earnings, plus £20,000 for loss of interest and £8,000 legal costs together with £48,000 for personal injury and injury to feelings.

Questions

Consider the above summarised article and answer the following questions:

1. What action should the organisation have taken when the complaints were first made?

2. What specific steps should HR departments take to try to prevent such action occurring in their organisations?

The World Economy

LEARNING OUTCOMES

When you have completed this chapter, you should be able to understand, explain and critically evaluate:

- major international bodies which impact on the business environment of organisations (IMF, World Bank, WTO)
- the causes and extent of globalisation processes
- multinational and transnational organisations, and their HR systems
- major debates about the significance and desirability of globalisation
- the response of governmental organisation to globalisation processes
- the impact of globalisation on markets for goods and services
- the impact of globalisation on employment and labour markets
- globalisation and the recession
- Geert Hofstede's cultural dimensions
- management and HR styles in selected members of the G20
- the role and functions of the European Union and its major institutions
- debates about the evolution of the European Union (integration and enlargement)
- the eurozone crisis of 2010 onwards
- Brexit.

6.1 INTRODUCTION

Should Greece leave the euro? Is globalisation good or bad for the developing world? These are the kinds of issues that will be explored in this chapter on the international economy.

Since the end of the Second World War, the world economy has become more and more integrated. Partly this has been a deliberate, planned development. The International Monetary Fund, the World Bank and the General Agreement on Tariffs and Trade were set up to regulate the world economy, and to ensure that the world did not suffer from a recurrence of the Great Depression of the 1930s. The European Economic Community, the predecessor of the European Union, was set up partly to ensure that France and Germany could never again go to war with each other. Other developments were only made possible as a result of technological developments in communication and transport which enabled the growth of globalisation.

6.2 INTERNATIONAL FINANCIAL INSTITUTIONS

6.2.1 THE BRETTON WOODS CONFERENCE

In 1944, the wartime Western allies held a conference at Bretton Woods in New Hampshire which was to shape the economic future of the international economy. Their prime aim was to prevent a repetition of the competitive devaluations and protectionism which had followed the Wall Street crash in 1929, and which had made the ensuing Great Depression even more severe in its impact. The idea was to impose strict controls on the ability of each country to follow beggar-my-neighbour policies, and to force international economic co-operation.

Out of Bretton Woods came three great international institutions, the International Monetary Fund (the IMF), the International Bank for Reconstruction and Development (the World Bank), and the General Agreement on Tariffs and Trade (GATT).

6.2.2 THE IMF

The main plank of the IMF regime was a system of fixed exchange rates, which all member countries agreed to maintain. In practice this meant that each member state fixed the value of its currency in terms of the US dollar, while the US dollar itself was linked to gold. It was recognised that members might experience problems with their balance of payments in the short term (an excess of imports over exports). In such a situation, the IMF agreed to make hard currency available to them on a short-term basis, to allow the member a breathing space to adjust its economy. Only if the balance of payments problem was long-term was the member state permitted to devalue its currency. The system was financed by subscriptions from member countries, with by far the largest contribution coming from the US.

The system worked reasonably smoothly for nearly 30 years, although there were still balance of payments crises, and occasional devaluations (most notably in the UK, France, and Italy). Most lending was to developed countries, and the IMF had little involvement with the Third World. However, the world economic structure changed fundamentally in the early 1970s. Now it was the US which experienced a balance of payments crisis. The IMF system could not cope with this – the absolute stability of the dollar was fundamental. Eventually, President Nixon abandoned the fixed price link between the US dollar and gold – in effect devaluing the dollar. As a result, fixed exchange rates were abandoned, and have never been restored on a world level.

The floating exchange rate regime immediately removed the IMF's major role. It still carries out its role of alleviating short-term financial crises, but almost always with developing rather than developed economies – the Asian Tiger economies (Thailand, South Korea, Indonesia) in 1997, Russia in 1998, Brazil in 1999 and Argentina in 2001 – but the IMF also started to develop a wider role of encouraging structural reform in member states (often known as 'mission creep' – a typical example of an organisation broadening its original aims beyond all recognition). An early example of this was the loan to the UK in 1976, which was made conditional on the (Labour) government cutting public spending and adopting monetarist policies.

This process has now gone much further, and from the 1980s onwards the IMF has followed a policy of imposing Thatcherite, free-market neo-liberal conditions (particularly privatisation) on its support, particularly to Third World countries:

- Tanzania was forced to charge for hospital visits and school fees.
- Ecuador was forced to sell its water system to foreigners and to increase the price of cooking oil by 80%.
- Malawi was told to sell off its strategic reserves of maize, two years before the country was hit by famine.
- Guyana was told to privatise its sugar industry.

- Zambia was told to privatise its banks (Mathiason, 2003).

Should the IMF try to impose long-term neo-liberal reform in the Third World, rather than concentrating on lending money to countries in short-term financial difficulties?

There are three main arguments in favour of this policy.

- State-run sectors in Third World countries tend to be inefficient, corrupt, devourers of resources, and they discourage foreign investment. The state may also spend wastefully and not in the best long-term interests of its population – for instance by excess spending on arms.
- Moral hazard – the concept that because countries expect to be bailed out if they get into difficulties, they will be reckless in their behaviour, because they know they will never really be called to account for their actions. For example, Brazil has defaulted on its debts five times, and Venezuela nine times. In essence, this is the same argument that says that insurance companies should carry out very strict checks before they pay out on policies, in order to discourage fraudulent claims.
- Short-term intervention tends by definition to treat short-term symptoms rather than the long-term illness. The only way to tackle long-term problems is through long-term reform.

There are two counter-arguments:

- While the above may be true in the long-run, the short-term effect of privatisation and liberalisation is to increase poverty and inequality in the Third World.
- By concentrating on the long term rather than the short term, the IMF is moving into areas which should more appropriately be the responsibility of the World Bank (Stiglitz 2003).

The current consensus seems to be that the IMF should concentrate on macroeconomic factors such as budget deficits and inflation, rather than trying to micro-manage the economies of clients. Charles Wyplosz, professor of economics at the Institute of International Studies in Geneva, was quoted in *The Financial Times* in May 2004 as saying, 'when firemen come to your house to put out a blaze, you would not expect them to meddle in your marriage' (Swann 2004).

Ngaire Woods suggests three changes:

- The IMF should be the cornerstone of global monetary co-operation.
- The IMF should help countries mitigate or cushion shocks from the global economy.
- The IMF must command the confidence of all its members (Woods 2007).

The IMF is currently heavily involved, with the European Union and the European Central Bank (the Troika), in managing the Greek debt crisis, and has called for some write-off of Greek debt, on order to alleviate the impact of the cuts imposed by the EU and the ECB (the Greek crisis is discussed on more detail later in this chapter).

6.2.3 THE WORLD BANK

Like the IMF, the World Bank was set up at Bretton Woods, and nearly all countries in the world are members. Unlike the IMF, its main role is to provide access to capital for long-term development, particularly in the Third World. It does this partly through direct lending through a number of its own agencies, some of it interest-free, and partly by leveraging investment from the private sector.

It also has a wider social remit than the IMF. It emphasises social services, the environment and gender equality as well as economic growth. However, like the IMF it has been criticised for the neo-liberal conditions which it tends to attach to its loans, and also for over-lending to relatively advanced developing countries like Brazil and particularly China, which have sufficient clout to be able to borrow to finance their development on a commercial basis. The Bank is also a key component in the so-called Washington Consensus, not least because of the convention that its President is nominated by the US (Woods 2007).

One proposal that has been put forward is that the IMF and the World Bank should merge. There is clear overlap – in practice if not in theory – between the activities of the IMF and World Bank, although in principle their functions are distinct. A merger might therefore seem logical, and it might help to prevent mission creep. However, if the IMF had a dominant role in the merged organisation, its neo-liberal agenda might swamp the wider social and environmental principles of the World Bank.

6.3 INTERNATIONAL TRADE AND COMPARATIVE ADVANTAGE

Very few countries are self-sufficient, in the sense that they produce everything which they need within their own boundaries. Ever since the stone age, societies have traded with each other. The most obvious reason for a country to trade is to obtain something which it is incapable of producing for itself. For example, until the discovery of North Sea oil, the UK had to import oil. However, strictly speaking this only applies to extractive industries. Anything else could be made or grown, at a price. There is nothing to stop the UK growing its own bananas in greenhouses (except common sense!). It is a much more efficient use of resources for countries to concentrate on what they are best at producing, and to import other goods. For example, if we compare the UK and the Windward Islands, the UK has an *absolute advantage* in the production of pharmaceuticals, while the Windwards have an *absolute advantage* in the production of bananas. It therefore makes sense for the UK to specialise in pharmaceuticals, and to export these to the Windwards, while the Windwards should export bananas to the UK. (As we will see later when we look at the banana war, in Case Study 6.1, the real world is a lot more complicated than this simple example suggests.)

Even if one country is better at producing everything than another country, international trade will still benefit both sides. For example, let's stretch our banana example even further. Assume that the UK is four times as efficient as the Windwards at producing pharmaceuticals, but twice as efficient at producing bananas. In this case, the UK has a *comparative advantage* in the production of pharmaceuticals, and the Windwards a *comparative advantage* in bananas. Both sides would benefit if the UK specialised on pharmaceuticals, and the Windwards on bananas. The mathematics to prove this can be found in any textbook on international economics.

For comparative advantage to work, however, it is essential that there are no restrictions on trade between the countries involved, ie that there is *free trade*. For example, assume that the UK has a banana industry which is struggling to cope with competition from Windwards bananas, and then assume that the UK banana industry persuades the UK government to place either quotas (restrictions on quantity) or tariffs (taxation) on imports of Windwards bananas. People working in the UK banana industry would benefit, but everyone else in both economies would lose.

If you think that this example seems totally unrealistic, you are probably right, but bear in mind that Japan, for example, protects its rice growers with a 500% tariff on imported rice.

? REFLECTIVE ACTIVITY 6.1

Is comparative advantage good for you?

The theory of comparative advantage suggests that everyone gains from free trade. Why then do so many countries protect their own domestic industries?

6.4 THE WORLD TRADE ORGANIZATION (WTO)

After the Second World War, the Allies set up the General Agreement on Tariffs on Trade (GATT), whose remit was to encourage free trade, and prevent the destructive protectionism that had blighted the world economy in the 1930s. Its objectives were to:

- eliminate existing trade barriers
- deter the formation of new barriers
- eliminate all forms of trade discrimination.

In 1995, GATT was absorbed into a new body, the WTO, with wider objectives. Its membership now includes virtually the whole world, following the accession of China and Taiwan in the early 2000s. The WTO continues the process of liberalising world trade, but its powers also extend to trade in services as well as goods, and also the regulation of international property rights like patents and copyright. It also has the power to adjudicate on disputes between members, with the right to impose financial penalties.

CASE STUDY 6.1

THE BANANA WAR

The banana war was one of the most bitter trade disputes of the 1990s, and one of a number of disputes between the two dominant trading blocs, the EU and the US. The key to the dispute was the preference that the EU gave to bananas from ex-British and French colonies in Africa, the Pacific and the Caribbean (the APC countries). The EU argument was that without protection, the banana industries in these areas, particularly in the Caribbean, would collapse, devastating the local economies, and perhaps pushing producers to alternative less desirable crops like cannabis or coca. They pointed out that the WTO had an objective to assist developing and transition economies.

The US responded that the EU action was a gross breach of WTO rules. Three US companies – Chiquita, Dole and Del Monte – control two-thirds of world trade in bananas from their huge plantations in Central America (the APC has 4% of the world market).

Legally, the US had an unanswerable case, but it weakened its moral position by imposing punitive import tariffs in 1998 on a range of EU exports to the US in retaliation, before the WTO delivered its judgement. Worse, this was announced shortly after Chiquita gave a big donation to the ruling US Democratic Party.

The WTO ruled in favour of the US, and ordered the EU to abolish its protective quotas on APC bananas by 2005. The effects on the Caribbean have been predictably devastating. Between 1993 and 2000, two-thirds of the banana growers in the Windward Islands went out of business, while exports of bananas from St Vincent and the Grenadines fell from $120m to $50m (Ryle, 2002). By 2009, only 4,000 of the 24,000 Windward Island banana growers in 1993 were still in business. Between 1992 and 2007, UK banana imports almost doubled from 545,000 to 927,000, but the proportion imported from the Caribbean fell from 70 to less than 30% (Doward 2009).

6.4.1 THE WORKING OF THE WTO

The WTO (and its predecessor GATT) works in a series of long trade rounds, initiated at a major conference, and then negotiated and implemented over a long period. The Uruguay Round in the 1990s was primarily concerned with textiles, where the developing world had a comparative advantage, but where the developed countries maintained protection of their own textile industries. The developed Western countries agreed to eliminate protection, but only over a ten-year period, with most of the concessions coming in the last year! This tends to be the pattern – the West speaks the language of free trade, is keen to impose free trade on the developing world, but drags its heels when it comes to its own concessions.

Larry Elliott in *The Guardian* in 2004 drew a telling parallel with medieval Europe, where in theory all states owed spiritual allegiance to the papacy and the universal values of the Church, but in practice spent most of their time at war with each other (Elliott 2004).

6.4.2 THE DOHA ROUND

The Doha Round of trade negotiations was launched by the World Trade Organization in 2001, in the wake of the 9/11 terrorist attacks on New York and Washington. The negotiations were specifically designated as a 'development round', aimed at improving the economic position of developing countries, as a symbol of world solidarity against terrorism (*Economist* 2003b). Unfortunately, WTO negotiations are always difficult, as all agreements have to be unanimous. Unlike at the IMF, rich countries do not have disproportionate power.

Agricultural liberalisation was the crucial issue. When the first Doha meeting was called, it produced a pledge to improve market access for third world countries, to reduce trade-distorting domestic support, and to reduce export subsidies.

Reform was urgently needed. In 2001, assistance to rich country farmers amounted to $311bn, compared with $50bn in development aid. The EU paid subsidies of $913 a year to each EU cow, and $8 in aid to each sub-Saharan African. Comparable figures for Japan were $2,700 and $1.47 (Wolf 2005, p215). The EU was the world's largest exporter of skimmed milk powder, sold at half its cost of production, and of white sugar, sold at a quarter the cost of production (Wolf 2005, p216).

Stuart Harbinson, the WTO chairman for agriculture, proposed a package that would:

- end export subsidies in nine years
- reduce tariffs by 40–60%
- cut trade-distorting farm support by 60%.

It was calculated that these proposals would increase annual global income by $100bn, with 20% of the gain going to developing countries and 80% to rich countries through lower prices (De Jonquieres 2003).

The US and the Cairns Group of major agricultural exporters (including Australia and Canada) argued that the Harbinson proposals did not go far enough, while the EU and Japan claimed that they were too ambitious. India wanted to maintain its own tariffs to protect its farmers. The ACP (Africa, Caribbean and Pacific) group of developing countries sided with the EU, worried about losing their preferential access to EU markets (see Case Study 6.1, on the Banana War).

The key to the negotiations was the attitude of the EU. The European Commission proposed reform of the Common Agricultural Policy which by phasing out incentives for over-production, and switching to support based on rural development and protection of the environment, would reduce export subsidies, but would not make EU markets more open to imports. Meanwhile France and Germany had reached an agreement to maintain spending on the CAP until 2013. Under the terms of the negotiations, agreement was required by 31 March 2003, by which time the Iraq war had just broken out, relations between the US and France were at an all-time low and, ironically, Doha was the military headquarters for the war. Not surprisingly the 31 March deadline was missed.

Negotiations staggered on for another three years. In Geneva in August 2004, the WTO agreed that export subsidies should be abolished, but no starting date or timetable has been agreed. The final breakdown came over fundamental disagreement between the EU and the US. The US argued that the EU was not offering big enough reductions in tariffs, while the EU claimed that the US was not proposing a big enough reduction in subsidies. On 24 July 2006, the Doha Round was formally suspended, with no date set for a resumption (*Economist* 2006a).

Eventually negotiations were reopened. Agreement was nearly reached in 2008, but failed at the last minute due to one outstanding issue between the US and India. Unfortunately the Doha Round is based on the principle that 'nothing is agreed until everything is agreed' (McClanahan 2013). Negotiations were then put on hold during the Great Recession, eventually reopening in Bali in December 2013. Unusually, Bali actually achieved something. The main remaining cause of contention was India's insistence that it should be allowed to pay its farmers above market price in order to build up the country's reserve stockpiles of food. This was opposed by competitors such as Pakistan and Thailand, as well as the US. Eventually a compromise was reached, whereby India was allowed to continue its policy for four years, in return for an Indian pledge not to allow the policy to distort trade (McClanahan 2013).

6.4.3 WHAT DOES THE FAILURE OF DOHA TELL US?

The failure of the Doha Round reveals:

- the hypocrisy of the developed world, which is ready to impose trade liberalisation on the developing world, but not to make meaningful concessions itself
- the strength of the farm lobby in both the EU and the US, which prevented any agreement
- divisions among the developing countries and agricultural exporters, with diametrically opposing stances being taken by India, the Cairns Group and the ACP.

6.5 DEBT RELIEF

One of the most pressing problems of the world economy is the crushing burden of third world debt. The 52 most indebted countries, mostly in Africa, have debts of $375bn, most of it unpayable, but on which interest still has to be paid. In 1998, it cost these countries $23.4bn to service their debt, mostly owed to Western governments, the IMF or the World Bank. In many countries, debt repayment dwarfs welfare budgets. Mauritania pays $63m to service its debt, but only $51m on education, and $17m on health (Madeley 2001).

Much of the debt is a product of the cold war period, when the West was keen to tie the third world to its side, and much of the money was wasted, either going on armaments, or disappearing through corruption, by the likes of the late unlamented Presidents Amin and Mobutu.

Many arguments can be advanced for relieving at least some of this burden of debt. These range from: the moral, that debt is denying the inhabitants of these countries the human rights of decent education and health; the economic, that money being spent on debt repayment is not being spent on imports from the West; and the geopolitical, that poverty and discontent create an environment conducive to terrorism.

An international campaign for debt relief was launched in 1996 by the pressure group Jubilee 2000, which has produced some results. The IMF and the World Bank have set up the Heavily Indebted Poor Countries (HIPC) initiative to administer debt relief to the 52 poorest states; the G7 promised the cancellation of $110bn of debt, while the UK government agreed to hold debt repayments in a trust for poverty relief, to be released when each country agreed a poverty reduction plan (Madeley 2001).

However, progress has been limited. By the end of the Jubilee 2000 campaign in December 2000, only one country, Uganda, had debt cancelled, with reductions agreed for another 21, and in line with normal IMF/World Bank policy, stringent conditions were attached.

The Jubilee 2000 campaign was followed by the Make Poverty History campaign, which seemed to have reached success at the Gleneagles conference of the G8 in July 2005, chaired by Tony Blair. This pledged to double development assistance to Africa, including debt relief and aid, to $100bn a year by 2010. However, in April 2007, the Africa Progress Panel (APP), set up to review progress on the pledge, headed by Kofi Annan, the former UN secretary-general, reported that the G8 was only 10% of the way to reaching its target. The UK, alone of the G8, has met its commitments in full, but Bob Geldof, who is also a member of the APP, singled out Germany and Italy as countries which were significantly failing to meet their commitments. At the same time the OECD reported that after one-off packages of debt relief for Iraq and Nigeria were taken into account, aid flows from the West fell for the first time in a decade in 2006 (Elliott and Connolly 2007).

However, the issue of debt relief and aid is not straightforward. Boone (2005) argues that much aid is ineffective. Countries which received large aid flows did not do better at reducing child mortality than those which received small amounts of aid. Indeed, contrary to popular belief, little aid goes to finance social reform. Only 4% went to health, 12% to education and 6% to emergencies. Countries or regions which were most successful at reducing child mortality were Cuba, Sri Lanka and the Indian state of Kerala. These had very different political systems, but all had put a lot of effort into developing their infrastructure. As a result, aid was spent where it was needed, rather than being wasted on bureaucracy or corruption.

? REFLECTIVE ACTIVITY 6.2

Debt relief

Can you put forward any arguments against either the principle or the practice of debt relief for the Third World?

6.6 GLOBALISATION

Globalisation is an emotive word. It has inspired violent demonstrations all over the world, and also vehement defence. But what is globalisation? There is no single clear definition.

First, it is useful to look at what globalisation is not (Scholte 2000).

- *Internationalisation.* The world has always been international. There were trade links between the Roman and Chinese empires, for example.
- *Free trade.* Trade was at least as free in the late nineteenth century as it is now.
- *Westernisation.* Western culture was exported to much of the world as a result of the dominance of western empires in the late nineteenth and early twentieth centuries.
- *Universalisation.* Global lifestyles and ideas are nothing new. Islam spread across half the known Western world in 50 years in the sixth century, and later spread to countries as far apart as Nigeria and Indonesia.

John Gray sees its key features as free mobility of capital and free trade (Gray 1995). Ngaire Woods sees globalisation as much wider, and political and social as well as economic.

She distinguishes three elements (Woods 2000):

- *The expansion of markets.* Technological changes like the mobile phone and above all the Internet have speeded up communications to the extent that both financial and physical transactions can be carried out instantaneously, while improvements in transport permit goods to be shipped quickly and relatively cheaply anywhere in the world. (Think of the universal availability in the UK of asparagus from Peru and French beans from Kenya.) At the same time, governments throughout the world have been deregulating, and reducing their control over their economies, at the same time as the growth of e-commerce has started to erode their control of their tax base. The result has been the spread of transnational enterprises and global brands, leading to what Kenichi Ohmae, the Japanese management guru and one of the early proponents of globalisation, called 'the borderless world' (Ohmae 1990).

- *The knowledge economy also creates a borderless world.* Knowledge is not dependent on possession of natural resources, and can instantaneously be transmitted via the Internet. As Lester Thurow says, 'knowledge is the new basis for wealth' (Thurow 1999). Hence the outflow of call centre and data handling jobs from the UK to India.
- *The transformation of politics.* Free movement of capital has produced a world financial market which has the potential to swamp any single economy. At the same time, transnational issues have become of increasing importance – global warming, human rights, drugs, world poverty and immigration, terrorism. Increasingly, in order to have any influence, nation states have to join together in regional groupings. The European Union is the best known, but there are other important groupings like the North Atlantic Free Trade Area and ASEAN. Just as nation states are handing over power to regional groupings, they are also devolving power internally to regional entities – Scotland and Wales in the UK, Catalonia in Spain.
- *The emergence of new social and political movements.* A global (or American) culture has developed, with US corporations like McDonald's, CNN, Disney and Nike setting trends across the world. At the same time, counter-movements have developed, ranging from the anti-globalisation movement to militant Islam.

Globalisation is nothing new. An early example came with the Opium Wars in the 1840s, when Great Britain forced China to open its borders to imports of opium in order to finance the early Victorians' obsession with China tea. It has often been argued that the golden age of globalisation was the period 1880–1914, when the world economy was regulated by the universal use of the Gold Standard, there was almost universal free trade, and free movement of capital. Indeed, this period had one element of globalisation which does not apply today – free movement of people. Not only could an individual travel without a passport, there was also free movement of labour, and very little control on international migration – this is the period when the Statue of Liberty was erected in New York. One commentator even said in 1911 that a major war was now impossible, as the world had become so interdependent (Micklethwait and Wooldridge 2000).

Two dates mark the development of modern globalisation. One is 1973, and the first oil crisis. This led to two things – a realisation that the world economy was inextricably linked through its dependence on oil, and the collapse of the Bretton Woods system of fixed exchange rates, which ushered in a period when world financial markets became much more dominant.

The other is 1989. One factor here was the collapse of communism as a world ideology, and the triumph of the US in the Cold War – what the US political scientist Francis Fukuyama called 'the end of history' (Fukuyama 1992). The other, much less noted at the time, but equally important, was the final bursting of the Japanese 'bubble economy'. Throughout the 1980s, it seems that globalisation was likely to be Japanese rather than US-dominated. Japanese industrial techniques were sweeping the world, and most of the world's biggest corporations were Japanese rather than US. The economic collapse of Japan ensured that globalisation would be US-dominated economically, as well as politically and culturally.

6.6.1 DRIVERS OF GLOBALISATION

A number of drivers of globalisation have intensified in the last 20 years or so:

- *Technology*: The most important developments here are in information and communication technology (ICT), particularly the mobile phone and the Internet. These have transformed the way in which particular industries operate. An example is the insurance industry, which traditionally was staid and conservative, but has been transformed by the application of new technology, which has led to a wave of mergers.
- *Cultural homogenisation*: The universal availability of television, and the global audiences for international sporting events like the World Cup and the Olympic Games, combined with the explosion in overseas travel, has led to a homogenisation of international culture, which permits the development of global brands. However, global brands like McDonald's still have to be responsive to local cultural differences – no traditional beef Big Macs in India, for example. Two small but telling examples are that since the 2008 Olympics in Beijing, all public lavatories in China are labelled in English as well as Chinese, while in London, Harrods and John Lewis accept Chinese yuan over their counters.
- *Economies of scale*: Developments in manufacturing techniques have meant that the minimum efficient scale of operations in many industries has become a significant percentage of the available world market. The most extreme example is the aircraft industry, where the total world market is barely big enough to support two firms (Boeing and Airbus).
- *Deregulation*: Deregulation has been driven by bodies such as the WTO and the EU. It reduces the costs of cross-border trade, and so promotes the development of global companies.
- *Competition*: If one firm in an industry globalises, it will gain a competitive advantage. In order to stay in touch, its competitors will also be forced to globalise (Segal-Horn 2002).

 SAMSUNG – GLOBAL OR GLOBALISED?

CASE STUDY 6.2

Samsung (meaning 'three stars') is the biggest of the South Korean *chaebol* – the family-owned conglomerates that dominate South Korean industry. Founded by Lee Byung-Chul as a trading company and noodle maker in 1938, it moved into electronics in the late 1960s. Electronics now dominates the group, although it also has very big interests in such diverse areas as shipbuilding, construction and life insurance. It produces 20% of South Korea's exports, and its revenue equals 17% of South Korea's GDP. In the 1980s it built assembly or R&D facilities in Portugal, New York Tokyo and England. In 1996 it built another facility in Austin, Texas. By 2012 the Austin location was the largest foreign investment in Texas and one of the largest single foreign investments in the US.

Samsung Electronics is best known in the West for its televisions, its computers and above all its mobile phones. It is the world's largest manufacturer of TVs, and the world leader in consumer electronics. In 2007, it overtook Motorola to become the world number two in mobile phones, behind Nokia of Finland, which it passed to become number one in 2012. Since then it has contested the world lead with Apple. In the first quarter of 2015, it regained the lead from Apple, with both companies a long way ahead of the Chinese companies Lenovo-Motorola and Huawei.

In addition to its consumer products, Samsung has invested heavily in component manufacture. Despite its well-publicised legal battles with Apple over patents, it is the largest supplier of chips to Apple. Over the next ten years the group plans to invest $20bn in five fields in which it is a relative newcomer: solar panels, energy-saving LED lighting, medical devices, biotech drugs and batteries for electric cars.

Lee Byung-Chul ran the company until his death in 1987. When he was a young man, Korea was still a Japanese colony, and he was educated in Japan. He ran Samsung on Japanese lines – a long-term perspective, lifetime employment, rigid hierarchy, promotion on seniority. He was succeeded by his son Lee Kun-Hee, who saw the need to make the business more innovative. In 1993, he announced his New Management Initiative, which aimed to blend the best of Japanese and Western approaches to management. He introduced merit-based pay, accelerated promotion, opened recruitment to middle management outside the company, and sent promising young managers on overseas assignments to gain a wider global perspective. He also started to recruit non-Koreans to management positions, initially Korean-Americans, but in 1997, he set up an internal consulting group, the Global Strategy Group, staffed by non-Korean MBAs from leading Western global companies.

By 2015 there were some clouds on Samsung's horizon. Lee Kun-Hee suffered a severe stroke in 2014, and the group is now run by a committee headed by his son and heir apparent, Lee Jae-Yong. Little is known about him, but there are some doubts about his ability. On the other hand, he is seen as good-natured and approachable, unlike his authoritarian father, a management style that may be more suited to the twenty-first century. There is also a growing feeling that Samsung is a 'fast follower' – good at tweaking other firms' products, but not truly creative in the style of Apple.

The other cloud is the rise of China in electronics, particularly Lenovo, which has prospered since taking over IBM's PC business in 2005. Despite the success of the Global Strategy Group, Samsung's top management is still overwhelmingly Korean. Lenovo, on the other hand, has factories and research centres in Mexico, India, Japan and the USA, makes more than half of its sales outside China (a much bigger market than Korea), and has a top management which is a mixture of Asians, Americans and Europeans. While Samsung is undoubtedly a global company, it is Lenovo which is the globalised one.

Sources: Economist (2011); Khanna, Song and Lee (2011); Kim (2012); Kim (2015); Gibbs (2015)

? REFLECTIVE ACTIVITY 6.3

Why do people hate the WTO and globalisation?

Throughout the West, there is deep suspicion, on many cases verging on hatred, of the progress of globalisation in general, and the activities of the WTO in particular. Why do you think this is?

6.7 MULTINATIONAL AND TRANSNATIONAL CORPORATIONS

Multinational corporations (MNCs) are companies producing or distributing goods or services in two or more countries. A transnational corporation is an MNC with more than two-thirds of its activities outside its home country. Such companies can locate different activities in parts of the world where they reap the biggest comparative advantage. Thus Rupert Murdoch's News Corporation is controlled through holding companies in the

Cayman Islands, a notorious tax haven. The result is that News Corporation pays an average tax rate of 10%.

In another example, the fall in the costs of air transport has led to the centralisation of the world flower industry in the Netherlands. Flowers are flown in from Kenya or India one day, sold at auction and then flown to customers on Europe or the US the next day.

The best-known example of local advantage is low labour costs. This is most obvious in low-wage industries like textiles, but a high-tech example is that of the Brazilian manufacturer of regional jet airliners, Embraer. Its employment costs in 2002 were $26,000 per employee, as against $63,000 in the regional jet business of its major Canadian competitor, Bombardier (Ghemawat 2003).

Rollinson (2008) suggests a more complex model. The simplest form is the domestic organisation, which supplies only its home market in its country of origin. Next in complexity is the international organisation, which serves home and overseas markets, but has a centralised headquarters in its country of origin. The multinational organisation produces goods or services in relatively autonomous overseas subsidiaries. The global organisation operates worldwide through independent overseas divisions, which are co-ordinated rather than controlled by a central headquarters. Finally, the transnational organisation, first described by Bartlett and Ghoshal (1991). The transnational corporation operates simultaneously as an international, multinational and global organisation. Specialised units could be located anywhere in the world, and are managed as a seamless network, by footloose managers with a global mindset.

In 2001, there were estimated to be 63,000 TNCs, which had 800,000 foreign affiliates, and which controlled two-thirds of world trade. Of the top 100 non-financial TNCs, 91 were based in the US, the EU or Japan (Unctad 2001). Of the companies in the 2006 Fortune Global 500 (measured by turnover), 172 were based in the EU, 114 in the US, 70 in Japan and 20 in China (Fortune 2006).

Interbrand identifies its Best Global Brands each year. To qualify as a global brand, the brand must achieve more than a third of its sales outside its home country (which excludes Wal-Mart, most of whose sales are in the US). Interbrand's valuation is based on expected future earnings, rather than on current turnover or profit (Interbrand 2006). It is interesting that only one company (Toyota) appears in the top ten of both the Fortune and Interbrand lists. Whereas there are five oil companies in the Fortune top ten, there are none in Interbrand's.

Not all industries can be globalised. Clark (2005, p413) distinguishes four patterns of industry internationalisation, based on level of international trade in the industry's products, and degree of foreign direct investment.

- *Sheltered industries* supply a domestic market, and are not attractive to foreign investment. Typical examples would be hairdressing or railways.
- *Multidomestic industries* supply domestic markets, but may do this in a number of countries. Typical examples would be hotels or management consulting.
- *International industries* supply a world market, but are tied to one country by availability of raw materials (diamond mining or agriculture or by economies of scale (aerospace).
- *Global industries* have no national restrictions, and can truly be globalised – cars, oil, consumer electronics.

However, even global industries may still be forced to differentiate between national markets. This may be because:

- cars must be made either left or right hand drive, depending on local laws and regulations
- distribution channels may differ between national markets

- some markets are lead markets – they have a higher level of sophistication and acceptance of innovation
- differences in national culture may affect acceptability of products (Clark 2005, p429).

Perlmutter (1969), identified three major types of multinational companies:

- *Ethnocentric*, where each local subsidiary is expected to conform to the style and culture of the parent company, regardless of local conditions. Managers here are typically expatriates from the home country. This corresponds to Rollinson's international organisation.
- *Polycentric*, where each subsidiary is allowed to manage in its own way, and to develop its own culture. For example, IBM Ireland was allowed to recognise unions, although the IBM culture is generally anti-union (Marchington and Wilkinson 2008, p33). Managers in the local subsidiaries are likely to be nationals of that country, with few if any expatriates. This corresponds to Rollinson's multinational and global organisations.
- *Geocentric*, where local subsidiaries focus on worldwide objectives, making a unique contribution based on its local core competencies. Managers would be recruited on a global level, taking the best from anywhere in the world. Pucik (2007) quotes the example of ABB, where Percy Barnevik, the CEO, decided that the company needed about 500 hand-picked global managers – from a workforce of 200,000 – ready to move across countries, functions and businesses. The geocentric organisation corresponds to the transnational corporation.

Figure 6.1 Patterns of internationalisation

6.8 MULTINATIONALS AND BRANDS

Are multinationals and their brands too powerful? Foreign-owned multinationals employ one worker in every five in European manufacturing, and sell one euro in every four of manufactured goods in Europe (Venables 2005). Aisbett (2003) quoted the claim that 52 of the world's largest economic units are corporations, not states. However, supporters of globalisation like Legrain dispute this. They point out that this figure compares the turnover of corporations with the GDP of states. This leads to double or triple counting in the case of corporations. The correct comparison is with company value added (after deducting the cost of inputs). On this measure, there are only two corporations in the top 50 (Wal-Mart and Exxon), and 37 in the top 100. The US economy is 200 times bigger than Wal-Mart, Japan 100 times bigger, China 20 times bigger (Legrain 2003, pp139–140).

Corporations are also less powerful than nation-states. They cannot impose taxes or regulations, they cannot go to war, they cannot force people to buy their products, and, unlike states, they can go bust.

There are also limits to their mobility, although this tends to benefit their home country rather than the developing world. It is very rare for companies to move their headquarters from one country to another (although Ericsson did it in 1999, when it moved its corporate HQ from Sweden to London to avoid high Swedish taxes) (Legrain 2003, p159). Nokia was happy to stay in very high cost Finland until its takeover by Microsoft, and Lego in Denmark. On the other hand, the 'branch factory syndrome' seems to apply. When companies downsize, it always seems to be the branch factories rather than those near the headquarters which are closed down first.

Foreign direct investment (which creates multinationals) originates predominantly from developed countries (93% in 1998–2000), and also goes to other developed countries (78%). Of the FDI which goes to developing countries, the great bulk goes to China (the 2005 takeover of Rover by China's Nanjing Automotive, and the takeover of Corus in 2007 and Jaguar-Land Rover in 2008 by India's Tata are very much the exceptions – for now). Inward investment creates jobs in the host country, but can also force up wages there, which in the long run makes the host less competitive. One country which has avoided this vicious circle is Ireland, which has used the additional wealth brought in by high-tech multinationals to invest in its infrastructure and education, which makes it still attractive even at higher wage levels (Venables 2005), although its heavy reliance on inward investment also made it extremely vulnerable during the economic crisis of the late 2000s.

One clear counterweight to global corporations would be global trade unions. On 1 May 2007, the TGWU and Amicus merged to form the UK's biggest union, Unite, with 2 million members. Its joint general secretaries, Derek Simpson and Tony Woodley, writing in *The Guardian*, said: 'the challenges presented by world capitalism... cannot be met by any union that confines its operations within one country alone'. They announced an agreement to seek a merger with the United Steel Workers of the US and Canada, to form the first transatlantic union. 'Only a worldwide organising agenda has any long-term hope of levelling the playing field' (Simpson and Woodley 2007).

 GLOBAL EMPLOYMENT RIGHTS – THE CASE OF QATAR AIRWAYS

CASE STUDY 6.3

There are no globally-enforced employment rights. However, there are employment conventions monitored by the International Labour Organisation (ILO), the labour arm of the United Nations. One such is the Discrimination (Employment and Occupation) Convention, 1958 (No. 111), ratified by 172 countries, including Qatar (in the 1970s).

In 2014, the International Trade Union Confederation and the International Transport Workers' Federation complained to the ILO about non-observance of the Convention by state-owned Qatar Airways in respect of sexual discrimination. Eighty per cent of Qatar Airways cabin crew are women, and 90% are expatriates. They have a clause in their contracts which states 'The company reserves the right to automatically terminate your contract as a flying cabin crew member should you become pregnant.' Dubai-based Emirates Airlines has a similar clause, but says it will make every effort to find a ground-based job, while Abu-Dhabi-based Etihad said that a pregnant member of flight crew would be found a ground job. Similar clauses were scrapped by American airlines in the 1970s.

Until recently Qatar Airways also had a clause which said employees must 'obtain prior permission from the company in case [he or she] wishes to change marital status and get married'. In addition, there is a ban on female cabin crew being dropped off or picked up from work by men other than their brother, father or husband. Under Qatari law, any foreigner who is dismissed may be liable for financial penalties, and will be deported.

In response, the Qatar government, which bans all trade unions, said that a pregnant member of staff was open to apply for a ground job. This was not acceptable to the ILO, which said they should actively be helped to find alternative employment within the company. On the marriage clause, the government said that this clause had been dropped from new contracts, but admitted that half the staff were still on old contracts. On the ban on travel to work, the government said that this reflected Qatari social norms, but the ILO felt that as it only applied to women, it amounted to indirect sexual discrimination.

The ILO can rule against Qatar, but it has no way of enforcing this ruling. Akbar Al Baker, the chief executive of Qatar Airways, accused the organisation of having a 'vendetta' against both Qatar and its national airline. 'I don't give a damn about the ILO – I am there to run a successful airline. This is evidence of a vendetta they have against Qatar Airways and my country.' In discussion with the CEO of Qantas about employment relations problems, he is alleged to have said: 'Put the union leaders in jail.'

Sources: ILO (2015); Booth (2015); Topham (2015b); Lobel (2015)

CASE STUDY 6.4

TESCO IN THAILAND

Retailers in the developed world are increasingly facing saturated markets. Companies like Tesco and Wal-Mart already dominate their home markets, and prospects for further growth are limited. An obvious solution is to expand overseas.

However, retailing is much less globalised than other major industries. Of the world's top 250 retailers in 2006, 104 have no international operations at all. The most globalised retailer, the French supermarket group Carrefour, has stores in 29 countries (Economist 2006c). Turn this on its head, and Carrefour has no presence in over 80% of the world's countries.

Many retailers have had spectacular failures overseas. Wal-Mart pulled out of Germany in 2006, having previously failed in Indonesia; Marks & Spencer pulled out of continental Europe in 2001;

while IKEA abandoned Japan as early as the 1980s (Emmott et al 2002; Economist 2006c).

So what is the secret of success as a global retailer? The experience of Tesco in Thailand provides some clues.

To most people in the west, Thailand is little more than an exotic holiday location, but it is actually a significant player on the world stage, and is one of the 20 biggest world economies. Its population is 64 million, and its GDP per head (on a purchasing power parity basis) is slightly higher than that of Brazil or Turkey. The Thai economy on a PPP basis is one third the size of the UK's.

In the 1980s and 1990s, it was one of the Asian tiger economies, which enjoyed the kind of explosive growth experienced by China today. It received a severe setback in the late 1990s (the Asian financial crisis started in Thailand in 1997), but by 2000 it was back on the growth path, and in 2003 its growth rate of GDP was 6.9%. Literacy is high at well over 90%, which encourages the rapid dissemination of new ideas, inflation and unemployment is low, and its capital, Bangkok, is one of the major world conurbations (CIA 2007).

The Asian financial crisis provided an ideal opportunity for Western retailers to enter Thailand. During the crisis, the Thai baht collapsed in value by 25% against the dollar, making inward investment much cheaper. Among those retailers taking advantage of the opportunity was Tesco.

Tesco entered Thailand in 1998 by purchasing the Thai retailer Lotus. Expansion has been rapid. In February 2007, Tesco Lotus had 366 stores open – 57 hypermarkets, 17 Value stores, 23 Talad Lotus stores, and 269 Express stores. By 2008, 500 Express stores had been opened (Tesco Lotus 2007).

By 2006, Thailand had the third highest sales in the Tesco group (after the UK and South Korea), at just under £1bn a year (Fletcher 2006). Group sales in Asia grew by over 60% in 2006 (Datamonitor 2006). Information on profits from the Thai operation is not available, but as Tesco Lotus paid over 1bn baht (about £16m) in corporation tax in 2006, profits must be substantial. In 2007, the Tesco Lotus brand was launched to improve the company's image of being international, but with Thai culture. A new philosophy 'Rau Sai Jai Khun' (We Care) was created to communicate the company's feelings to customers, staff and the community (Tesco 2015).

Why has Tesco done so well in Thailand? The Tesco expansion was a classic example of glocalisation (Swyngedouw 2004). Throughout the process, Tesco was extremely sensitive to Thai conditions. Rather than starting with a green field operation, it took over Lotus, but was careful to retain the Lotus brand name and logo, which were well known in Thailand. It tailored its scale of operations by opening shopping malls, hypermarkets, supermarkets (Value stores) or convenience stores (Express stores) as appropriate to local demand. It even supported small 'Mom and Pop' competitors by selling them 'Club Packs' for resale (Tesco Lotus 2007).

Tesco sourced 97% in Thailand, and it also facilitated the export of Thai products worth over £100m a year to Tesco UK. The company also set up a charitable foundation, Tesco for Thais, which although small scale, was valuable in securing goodwill in Thailand.

Tesco gained from the open market policies espoused by the Thai prime minister Thaksin Shinawatra between 2001 and 2006. However, there are always losers in globalisation, and Thailand has been no exception. Between 1996 and 2001, the share of retail food sales in Thailand made through traditional markets fell from 75 to 50%, which has severely damaged the earnings of thousands of Thai market traders. Before he was overthrown by a military coup late in 2006, Thaksin was seriously considering placing curbs on foreign-owned retailers and giving greater support to small shopkeepers. These policies have been taken further by the military government, and this may clip even Tesco's wings in the future (*Economist* 2007a).

By 2015 Tesco Lotus was Tesco's second largest international business, serving more than 12 million customers every week in over 1,700 stores across Thailand. In December 2014, the Thai retail billionaire Dhanin Chearavanont is understood to have approached Tesco about a deal and, although he was rejected, the tycoon is considering another bid. Tesco Lotus is currently valued at around $10bn (Ruddick 2015).

This case study illustrates Perlmutter's model of globalisation. Tesco's approach was polycentric, with the whole operation driven by Thais. Ironically, after getting it right in Thailand, Tesco then got in wrong in the US. Its Fresh and Easy operation in California was ethnocentric, driven from the UK, and ignored a lot of the market research that the company had done on the ground. It was abandoned in 2012, at a loss of £1.5bn (Butler 2012).

6.9 THE GLOBALISATION DEBATE

Aisbett (2003) identifies four main areas of concern over globalisation:

1   An objection not to globalisation in principle, but to the way in which it is skewed in favour of developed countries. This is exemplified by the protectionist agricultural policies of the US and the EU.

2   Loss of sovereignty, to transnational corporations and to institutions like the IMF and the WTO.

3   Neo-liberal or 'Washington consensus' policies, as imposed by the IMF on debtor countries – privatisation, welfare cut-backs etc.

4   The rise of big corporations. Of the 100 biggest economic units in the world, 52 are corporations. They can expand or contract their activities in particular countries in order to maximise their overall profit.

However, Aisbett points out that the debate is no longer between supporters and opponents of globalisation. The anti-capitalist protest movements of the late 1990s have run out of steam, and the main arguments are now between enthusiastic and cautious globalisers. Even Oxfam has recognised that globalisation can have some benefits. A similar point is made by Jacobs (2001).

Aisbett identifies areas of agreement between the enthusiastic and cautious globalisers. These include:

● Trade is often a source of economic growth and growth is good for the poor (although the Green party argues that local production may be more efficient) (Lucas, 2001).
● The US and the EU should open their markets to the developing world.
● Safety nets should be provided for the losers from globalisation, and education, health and welfare in developing countries should be safeguarded.
● Income is an inadequate measure of poverty, and social factors should be taken into consideration.
● Excessive corporate power is a problem.
● Political reform is needed in many developing countries.

There are also still important areas of difference, outlined in Table 6.1.

Table 6.1 Alternative views on globalisation

Issue	Enthusiastic view	Cautious view
Attitudes to poverty	Globalisation in all its forms is good for the poor, and reducing poverty is what matters, even at the cost of increased inequality	Reducing inequality is equally important, and globalisation frequently increases it
Trade liberalisation	Trade liberalisation is always beneficial	Totally free trade will often have adverse social or environmental side-effects. Decisions should be taken on a case-by-case basis
Transnational corporations	Their activities should be encouraged as they provide jobs and bring in new technologies	Big corporations destroy indigenous producers, and the net effect may be negative

Issue	Enthusiastic view	Cautious view
Privatisation	Government provision of essential services in developing countries is invariably corrupt and/or inefficient, and therefore these services should be privatised	Only government provision of essential services can ensure that they are available to the poor
Competitiveness	Opening developing economies to foreign trade and investment improves competitiveness by destroying local monopolies	Opening developing economies to foreign trade destroys indigenous producers whether or not they were monopolies and further increases the power of the transnational corporations

CASE STUDY 6.5

WIN-WIN GLOBALISATION – DECAFFEINATED COFFEE

Costa Rica is a major producer of high-quality coffee. However, it does not have the facilities to meet the demand of some of its customers for decaffeinated coffee. It has solved this problem by sending coffee for decaffeination to Germany. The Germans then extract the pure caffeine, and send the decaffeinated coffee back to Costa Rica. They make no charge for the service, as they sell the pure caffeine to global companies like Coca-Cola.

Source: Information from the Doka Coffee Estate, Costa Rica, in November 2015

The high point of globalisation came in the 1990s, in the euphoria which followed the collapse of communism, and 'the end of history'. This era of full-blooded, red in tooth and claw globalisation may have already passed. The onward march of e-commerce, and the idea that the world had entered a 'new economic paradigm' of endless economic growth, was shattered by the dot.com crash in 2000, and the collapse of giant new economy corporations like Enron and WorldCom. Just as the economic confidence of the US was shaken, its sense of political and military invulnerability was shattered by the attacks of 11 September 2001.

Coupled with the US military response to 'the war on terror', there is a growing though implicit feeling that the war on terror will be lost unless the West wins the hearts and minds of the Third World. Hence the criticisms from both left and right of the aggressive neo-liberal policies of the IMF and the World Bank, and possibly a more caring approach to debt relief and aid.

At the same time there is a growing realisation that globalisation has not made the nation state redundant. The role of the nation state is to provide good governance. In an article previewing his book, *State Building*, Francis Fukuyama (who previously spoke of 'the end of history') quotes from the doyen of free-market economists, Milton Friedman, as saying that his advice to former communist countries ten years ago had been to concentrate on privatisation. Now he feels that he was wrong. 'It turns out that the rule of law is probably more basic than privatisation.' (Fukuyama, 2004).

6.10 GLOBALISATION, GROWTH AND POVERTY

The evidence appears to be indisputable that globalisation has led to higher growth in most of the developing world, particularly in China and East Asia. The Asian Tigers, particularly South Korea and Thailand, were early to liberalise their trade, and have experienced rapid growth. So has China, following its market reforms in the 1980s, and India, where Manmohan Singh, successively Finance Minister and Prime Minister, reduced protectionism.

Wolf (2005, p142) quotes World Bank figures from 2002 which suggest that the gains from globalisation have been widespread. In the 1980s less globalised countries had higher GDP per head than more globalised ones, while by 1997 the situation was reversed. Annual growth rates per head in the more globalised countries were 3.1%, in the less globalised ones only 0.5%. Further evidence came from growth of a global middle class (defined as an annual income of between $3,650 and $14,600 a year, at purchasing power parity and 1993 prices). In 1960, 64% of the global middle class lived in high income Western countries, and only 6% in Asia, the Middle East and North Africa. By 2000, only 17% lived in developed countries, and 51% in Asia, the Middle East and North Africa (Wolf 2005, p170). In terms of percentages, however, there is still a gap. While over 90% of people in the US and Europe in 2010 were middle class in terms of income, this falls to 31% in Central and South America, and to 4% in sub-Saharan Africa (Straw and Glennie 2012).

There is some evidence that multinationals in developing countries pay higher wages than local manufacturing employers, although the evidence is rather old, dating from 1994 (Emmott et al 2002). Multinationals in low income countries paid an average wage of $3,400, while local employers paid $1,700. The ratio of 2:1 between multinational and local wages was higher than that in high income countries, where the ratio was 1.4:1.

Strong as the evidence seems, there are some caveats. GDP per head is not the same as standard of living, and there were losers as well as winners in the globalising country. Winners tended to work in manufacturing, losers in agriculture and extractive industries. Workers in developing countries tend to be non-unionised, capital inflows are unstable, multinationals can move out very quickly, and the risk of financial crisis increases, as in Thailand in 1997 (*Economist* 2001, p16).

The proportion of people living in poverty (defined as $1.25 per day in 2005 prices) is projected by the UN to fall below 900 million by 2015 – representing a fall from 46% in 1990 to 15%. However, the overwhelming majority of this fall has come in China and India which will have cut poverty by 203 million and 368 million respectively between 2005 and 2015. There is also evidence that inequality has increased in globalising countries. As measured by the Gini coefficient, inequality has increased in China, India, Argentina, and the Russian Federation, while it has fallen slightly in Brazil and Indonesia, between the early 1990s and the late 2000s. (Straw and Glennie 2012). Income inequality in India has doubled over the past two decades, with the top 10% of wage-earners currently making 12 times more than the bottom 10%, compared to six times 20 years ago (BBC 2011b). As Legrain points out, globalisation is no guarantee of economic success. It won't help war-torn countries like Somalia or the Democratic Republic of Congo, it won't cure Aids and it won't stop crooked rulers salting money away in Switzerland (Legrain 2003, p52). But although not a sufficient cause for economic growth, it seems to be a necessary one.

> ## ? REFLECTIVE ACTIVITY 6.4
>
> **Why is Africa poor?**
>
> The United Nations Development Programme has two main approaches to the definition of national poverty. One approach calculates a Human Development Index for member states, based on an equation incorporating life expectancy, educational attainment and real income per head. The other categorises countries on the basis of their stage of economic and social

development. The poorest of these are labelled as Least Developed Countries (or, popularly, The Fourth World). These countries are characterised by extreme poverty, civil war or ethnic clashes, political corruption, and government based on dictatorship, warlordism or kleptocracy ('rule by thieves'). On both measures, Africa, particularly, sub-Saharan Africa, does extremely badly (UNDP 2006). Of the bottom 30 countries on the Human Development Index, all except Yemen are in Africa. Of the 50 countries defined as Least Developed, 34 are in Africa.

Question

Why do you think that Africa has not shared in the growing prosperity of the rest of the world?

6.11 GLOBALISATION AND THE LABOUR MARKET

Does globalisation help or harm workers in developed countries? As always, the evidence is mixed. Legrain (2003) argued that it is very hard to separate out the impact of globalisation from the impact of higher technology. Manufacturing has been declining for many years in all developed countries, while at the same time manufacturing jobs have been outsourced to third world countries. He suggests that most of the impact comes from technology rather than globalisation. He cites the example of Bethlehem Steel in the US, where the Sparrows Point plant in Maryland produces the same amount of steel as it did in the 1960s, but with 3,500 workers rather than 30,000 (Legrain 2003, p37). As he says, 'producing more with less is what economic growth is all about'.

Legrain makes an attempt to quantify the relative effects of globalisation and technology. Between 1990 and 2000, manufacturing's share of GDP fell by around 6%, while the manufacturing trade deficit worsened by only 0.4% of GDP (Legrain 2003, p40).

The impact on jobs has been disproportionately on unskilled workers. Third world countries have an abundance of unskilled workers, which suggests that it is jobs using unskilled workers which will be offshored from rich countries.

However, more recent work suggests that the impact of globalisation on rich country workers may be greater than previously realised. Globalisation is becoming more complex. Increasingly parts of production processes are being offshored, rather than the whole process. This is known as 'high resolution globalisation', 'trade in tasks' (*Economist* 2007b) or vertical disintegration (International Labour Review 2006). A good example is the Barbie Doll. The raw material (plastic and hair) comes from Taiwan and Japan. Assembly takes place in the Philippines, Indonesia and China. Moulds come from the US, as does the last coat of paint. Marketing and R&D is centred in the US.

The rich world's comparative advantage in high tech sectors is falling, as education levels in countries like China and India are rising rapidly. China and India produce as many graduate scientists and engineers as the US, EU and Japan combined (*Economist* 2006a). Increasingly, higher-skilled jobs are being offshored – in software, medical diagnostics, finance and business consulting.

These findings are supported by a CIPD report on *Offshoring and the Role of HR* in January 2006 (CIPD 2006b). A total of 589 organisations responded to a survey, covering 2.4 million employees. Of these, 14% had offshored at least one activity in the past 5 years, 7% are currently considering it, and 4% had decided against it. The most popular offshoring locations were India (53%) followed by China (27%) and Poland (18%). A wide range of functions were offshored:

Manufacturing and production	34% of those who have offshored
IT support	24%
IT development	22%
Call centres/customer services	22%
Financial, back office support	19%
Product development	18%
Accounts	16%

Fifteen per cent have brought back activities that were previously outsourced. The most common motives for outsourcing were cost reduction (86%), UK skills shortages (27%), to improve processes (21%), and involvement in a joint venture (21%). The biggest disadvantages were seen as: managerial control is more difficult (48%), associated job losses in the UK (44%), language problems (30%) and risk of disruption to supply (24%).

Most interesting was the type of job lost:

Skilled	29%
Semi-skilled	25%
Managerial	19%
Unskilled	15%
Graduate	8%

The report includes a case study of a telecommunications firm, which offshored 500 jobs to Delhi in 2004–5. It decided to employ these staff directly, rather than to outsource the operation, because it was felt that outsourcing might compromise quality of service and managerial control. Activities offshored included transactional processing for all operational areas, including order handling, part of engineering and sales support; processing of company payments and credit control; and IT support and development.

Motives for offshoring were to reduce costs; to take advantage of skilled Indian graduates; to exploit the differences in time zone; and to take advantage of less restrictive Indian employment law.

The company employed 4,100 staff across Europe, including 1,200 in the UK. Of these a total of 400 were made compulsorily redundant, with 100 of these redundancies in the UK (CIPD 2006b, pp7–8).

A report quoted in *The Economist* in 2013 measured the gains and losses in jobs caused by outsourcing in the US between 2000 and 2010. Gainers were transport equipment (95,000 jobs), machinery (50,000), metals and minerals (21,000), paper and printing (13,000) and automotive (6,000). Losers were wood and furniture (9,000), food and beverages (18,000), chemicals, plastics, petroleum and coal (84,000), textiles and clothing (284,000), computers and electronics (407,000) and other (70,000) (Booth 2013). Clearly losses heavily outweighed gains, but as a proportion of a US labour force of 155 million, the net figures are very small.

A relatively new development in outsourcing is microtasking or crowdsourcing, where jobs are broken down into small components, which are then carried out by large numbers of people over the internet. As the tasks can be performed anywhere on the world, pay rates are very low – typically $1–2 an hour – but this may well be more than many people can earn. For example, one of the leading crowdsourcing firms, CrowdFlower, places work in refugee camps in Kenya (Graham 2010; Islam 2015).

A report by McKinsey in 2003 suggested that financially offshoring was a win-win situation. They claimed that every $1 previously spent in the US and now offshored to India creates a benefit of $1.47. The lion's share of this ($1.14) went to the US in the form of cheaper services and greater export of US goods to India, while 33 cents accrued to India as new wages, extra profit and extra tax revenue (Finch 2003).

However, Simon Evenett, professor of trade and development at St Gallen University in Switzerland, argues that the peak of manufacturing offshoring has passed. One reason for this is the increase in the price of oil in the last ten years or so. With oil at around $100 a barrel, compared with $25 in the mid-1990s, there is a strong incentive to shorten supply chains to minimise transport costs (Stewart 2013). Perhaps the trend in future will be short-distance offshoring – the US to Mexico, or Germany to the Czech Republic. However, the price of oil collapsed in 2015 to around $50 a barrel, which may reverse this trend.

Changing attitudes to offshoring are epitomised by the US conglomerate GE. Its charismatic CEO, Jack Welch, said in 1998, 'Ideally you'd have every plant you own on a barge to move with currencies and changes in the economy.' His successor as CEO, Jeff Immelt, calls outsourcing 'yesterday's model' (*Economist* 2013d).

The threat of globalisation seems to be increasingly to wages, rather than jobs. Real wages in the US, Germany and Japan are all falling. The share of wages in GDP is the lowest for three decades, while profits are at all-time highs. In the US, the share of profits in GDP rose from 7% in 2001 to 13% in 2006 (*Economist* 2006b).

Globalisation has boosted profits in several ways. Firms have reduced their costs by offshoring, while the bargaining power of workers in developed countries has been weakened as firms can always threaten to offshore. The global capital–labour ratio has massively shifted against workers. In the last 20 years, China, India and the former Soviet Union have effectively joined the world market economy, doubling the world supply of workers from 1.5 billion to 3 billion. Economic theory says that this would raise the return to capital and lower that to labour, which is exactly what has happened. At the same time, incomes have become more unequal. The top 1% of workers in the US now receive 16% of GDP, rather than 8% in 1980.

Case Study 6.6 examines some of the impacts of globalisation on the UK labour market.

THE OFFSHORING OF CALL CENTRES

CASE STUDY 6.6

The call centre industry in the UK is large, employing 867,000 people, or 3% of the workforce, in 2004 (Shah, 2004), and this had grown to over a million by 2011 (Hudson 2011). It is also a new industry, having grown from almost nothing over the past 30 years. As a result, there has been considerable concern about the steady movement of call centre jobs, particularly in the financial services industry, to India, particularly to Mumbai and Bangalore. Opponents of globalisation see this as an example of the detrimental effect of globalisation on

UK employment, while supporters see it as a positive development, lowering costs for UK industry, and so increasing national prosperity.

Both are right. The short-term effect is that the UK is losing jobs. Call centres in the UK were frequently set up in areas of high unemployment, and the loss of these jobs is disproportionately felt. On the other hand, if outsourcing increases the profits of UK companies, this should free up resources for future investment. A certain short-term loss must thus be set against a possible long-term gain.

The typical Indian call centre goes to great lengths to make their operators acceptable to UK consumers. The call centres operate on UK rather than Indian time, and operators are expected to keep themselves informed about the English weather, and the latest plot twists in *Eastenders* (Warren 2007). However, there is some evidence that Indian call centres are less efficient than UK ones. One study claimed that UK operators answered 25% more calls per hour, resolved 17% more calls first time, and stayed with their company three times as long, although this is offset by average salaries in India at only 12% of the UK level (Clennell 2004). This would suggest that UK companies which are more concerned with the quality of their customer service than with minimising their short-term costs should think very seriously before they outsource to India.

There has also been considerable movement of the call centre industry away from India. One move is to other developing countries, including Bulgaria, South Africa, and, particularly, the Philippines, where the local accent is seen as more acceptable. By 2011 the Philippines was the world leader, with $7.6bn in voice service exports, compared with $7bn for India (Crabtree 2012). The other trend is the repatriation of call centre jobs from India back to the UK and the US. Both Barclays and Santander have moved many of their banking call centre jobs back to the UK. When the motorcycle manufacturer Harley-Davidson looked to outsource part of its IT call centre, the contract went to the Indian company Infosys, but in Milwaukee, not in India. This was the 18th office which Infosys had opened in the US (*Economist* 2013).

The long-run future of the call centre industry in the UK must lie with developing a more sophisticated knowledge-based, value-added service. Basic information giving services can be better performed in India, or over the Internet. The Indians are themselves moving up market into more sophisticated areas. Indian companies like Hinduja are offering advanced services that require professionals like dental workers, nurses, accountants, lawyers and mathematicians (Crabtree 2012).

6.12 GLOBALISATION AND THE RECESSION

Did globalisation cause the recession? Almost certainly not on its own, but certainly elements of globalisation contributed to the recession. A prime cause was the incorporation of China in the world economy from the mid-1990s onwards. Tens of millions of Chinese moved from the countryside into industrial jobs, and being part of a frugal culture, saved a high percentage of their incomes. These savings went into Chinese banks, who then invested the money in the US, where a lot of it found its way into the sub-prime mortgage market. US house prices boomed, but eventually the bubble burst in 2007 (*Economist* 2009a; Rosner 2013; Walden 2014).

A further linkage is the way in which sub-prime loans in the US were securitised and parcelled up into collateralised debt obligations, and then sold on as bonds to other financial institutions around the world. As noted in Chapter 4, by 2007 these were part of a syndicated debt iceberg worth $14tr, and the securities were so complex that no individual bank could adequately assess the individual risk which it was running – a risk compounded by the reckless way in which the lending agencies had given these bonds an AAA rating. Only globalisation, and the complex computerised linkages which it had enabled between financial institutions worldwide, made this possible.

More generally, globalisation had encouraged an increasing emphasis throughout the Western world, and particularly in the US and UK, on the importance of finance. This encouraged a 'master of the universe' feeling among the banks, a feeling that they were untouchable and could do no wrong. This made the banks reckless and prepared to bend the rules, as discussed in Chapter 9 in relation to the manipulation of interest rates by Barclays Bank.

Going further back, it could be argued that growing income and wealth inequality in the US and UK, which has been attributed at least in part to globalisation, was itself a contributing factor to the sub-prime mortgage crisis in the US. Many of the so-called 'ninja' borrowers in the sub-prime market ('no income, no job, no assets') were in this position because their wages had been held down by globalisation (see Section 6.11, *Globalisation and the Labour Market*).

More generally, the linkages created by globalisation mean that it is no longer possible for an individual country to insulate itself from the effects of the recession, as the Soviet Union and Nazi Germany could to a large extent in the 1930s. For several years China and India seemed to buck the trend, but eventually by 2012 even China became affected by the slow-down in demand for its exports. This then had a knock-on effect on those countries supplying China with raw materials, such as Brazil, Canada and Australia.

The portents for the future are worrying. Quantitative easing is pumping money into the housing market again, encouraged by the UK government, which is boosting demand for housing without increasing its supply. Eventually the current housing bubble will burst, or another crisis will develop, and this time round the world economies will be less well equipped to deal with it. With interest rates virtually at zero, there is no way that they can be cut further. Stephen King, chief economist at HSBC calls this the world's 'Titanic problem' – there are lots of icebergs out there, but very few lifeboats (Elliott 2015c).

Will the recession slow the process of globalisation? Certainly the depression of the 1930s did slow globalisation. Most countries abandoned free trade, one of the major tenets of globalisation, and introduced protectionism, as well as competitive devaluations. Such an effect is less likely with this recession, as all major trading nations, including China, are members of the World Trade Organization, and so tied by its anti-protectionism rules, which can be enforced by the WTO (Lin 2010). However, there are still worrying straws in the wind.

- The US in 2012 claimed that the Chinese telecoms company Huawei was a threat to US security because of its alleged close links with the Chinese Communist party and military – a claim indignantly denied by Huawei (Cellan-Jones 2012).
- Some countries are taking action to manage the free movement of capital. Brazil, for example, has used taxes on foreign exchange to stem the appreciation of the real (Stewart 2013).
- In 2012, Brazil imposed a quota on car imports from Mexico. As a result, Ford increased its output in Brazil by 20%.
- China launched investigations against Danone and Nestle for allegedly fixing the price of baby formula, which was widely seen as a protectionist move (*Economist* 2013a).
- In 2008 Iceland became the first industrial country for decades to introduce controls on the export of capital, in order to protect its failed banks (*Economist* 2013b).
- The American airline Delta complained about preferential loans given to Air India to buy Boeing aircraft, on the grounds that this export subsidy hurt Delta, which directly competed with Air India on some routes (*Economist* 2013c).
- In 2003, 60% of UK respondents to a Eurobarometer poll were in favour of globalisation, and 27% opposed. By 2014, this had hardened to 47% in favour, and 37% opposed (Eurobarometer 2014).
- In 2011 the Global Trade Alert report found that 194 new protectionist measures had been put in place since the G20 summit in Seoul in November 2010 – more than twice the number of market-opening measures that had been introduced during the same period (Evenett 2011).

- In May 2015 senior officials of FIFA, the governing body of world football, were arrested by the FBI for alleged bribery and corruption (Gibson and Gayle 2015).
- At the June 2015 meeting of the International Air Transport Association, the three global US airlines – Delta, US Airways and American – complained that their counterparts in the Gulf – Emirates, Etihad and Qatar – received $40bn in state subsidies. They argued that the Gulf airlines should be expelled from the Open Skies agreement that allowed free trade in aviation. Emirates retaliated by arguing that the American airlines had themselves received massive state subsidies, and that the Gulf airlines supported US jobs through their massive aircraft purchases from Boeing. Willie Walsh, chief executive of British Airways's parent company IAG, supported the Gulf airlines, and said that the American argument is 'a move back to protectionism' (Topham 2015a).

The result is what Ip describes as 'gated globalisation' – more state intervention, and more friction, as national self-interest trumps international co-operation (Ip 2013).

6.13 THE THIRD WAVE OF GLOBALISATION

The first wave of globalisation, in the period up to 1914, was dominated by the UK and characterised by free trade, while the relationship between the developed and undeveloped world was based on imperialism, with third world countries seen as sources of raw materials and as captive markets for the West. Although the UK seemed to be dominant, under the surface both Germany and the US were growing more rapidly than Britain.

The movement towards globalisation stalled between 1914 and 1945, with war, depression and competitive protectionism. The second wave, from the 1950s to 2007, was dominated by the US, with the relationship with the developing world based on outsourcing of manufacturing from the West to the East. Again, things were changing under the surface, with China and the other BRICS countries (Brazil, Russia, India, China and South Africa) gradually shifting from low-tech to high-tech manufacturing.

Straw and Glennie (2012) argue that we are now in a third wave of globalisation, which will be dominated by developing counties, particularly but not exclusively China. In 2009, China contributed 18% of global growth, compared to 14% from the US. The country is now the world's largest exporter of goods and the second largest importer. Between 2001 and 2010, the Growth 8 countries (those countries which contribute more than 1% to world GDP: China, India, Brazil, Russia, Korea, Mexico, Indonesia, and Turkey) contributed the same amount to the increase in world GDP as the G7.

Group 8 countries are no longer just passive recipients of outsourcing. In 2011 China had 46 of the Fortune 500 top companies, compared with nine in 2001. Group 8 firms are also investing heavily in the G7. Nanjing Automotive of China took over Rover in the UK in 2005, Tata of India owns Tetley Tea, Corus Steel and Jaguar-LandRover, while the Turkish company Beko is the market leader for refrigerators in the UK (Dombey 2012). The Chinese B2B e-commerce company Alibaba was valued at $168bn when it floated in the US in 2013 (Arthur 2014). China invested £11.7bn in Britain between 2005 and 2013, and is expected to invest £105bn in British infrastructure by 2025 (Plimmer and Hornby 2014).

Emerging economies are moving up the supply chain, and are eroding the comparative advantage that G7 countries have in high-tech manufacturing and services. The UK needs to become more adaptive, and to build on its comparative advantage in sectors such as aerospace, pharmaceuticals, financial services, education services and creative industries. At the same time, developed countries like the UK must increase innovation, investment, and the level and effective deployment of skills.

LENOVO – A THIRD WAVE GLOBAL COMPANY

Lenovo Group is a £21bn personal technology company, with sales in 160 countries. It is the largest PC producer in the world, having recently surpassed Dell and Hewlett Packard (HP), and is a serious competitor for Apple and Samsung in smartphones.

The company started as the New Technology Development Company in Beijing in 1984, as an offshoot of the Institute of Computing Technology at the Chinese Academy of Sciences. It was designated as a *guoyou minying* (state-owned, people managed) company, owned by a state body (the university), but with autonomy in management. After successful privatisation in the 1990s, the CAS remained as major shareholder.

In 1988 NTDC moved to Hong Kong and renamed itself Legend Computer Group. Legend produced low-level PCs for the Chinese market, and also developed sales and service networks for US PC manufacturers including Dell and HP. In the mid-1990s, the total size of the Chinese PC market was about a million units a year, compared with 21 million in the US and 5 million in Japan. Foreign manufacturers did not bother to export their latest models to China, which was seen as a poor market.

In 1996, Legend slashed its prices, and introduced the latest central processing unit from Intel. This quickly propelled it to market leader in China. By 1999 its market share in China was 27%, and it was the market leader in the Asia-Pacific region, ahead of IBM and Compaq. Its understanding of the local market illustrated the Chinese proverb, 'a powerful dragon would have a hard time defeating a local snake'.

In the late 1990s, Legend was successfully privatised, while retaining the goodwill of both the China Academy of Sciences and the Chinese government. Its listing on the Hong Kong stock market gave it good access to capital. In 2001, China joined the WTO, and the Chinese market became more competitive. When Legend's domestic share reached 30% it realised that it had to expand internationally. In 2003 it renamed itself Lenovo (as the Legend brand name was already taken in the West) and in 2004 it took the huge gamble of buying IBM's Thinkpad PC business for $1.75bn. This gave it a global brand, access to world-class R&D, and experienced international managers. Post-acquisition, seven out of 15 top managers were non-Chinese. An American, Stephen Ward from IBM, became CEO, quickly succeeded by William Amelio, formerly of Dell.

However, implementing the merger was fraught with difficulties. Integrating a much bigger business would have been difficult enough, but cultural differences made it even harder. Only one of the negotiating team sent to the US spoke English, and none had business experience outside Asia. The Americans were used to vigorous debate, while the Chinese deferred to authority. When Amelio left the company he complained about its 'yes, yes, yes' culture. The company was also hit hard by the Great Recession, which led to heavy losses.

In 2009 Yang Yuanqing took over as CEO. At the time of the IBM takeover, Yang spoke little English, so he moved his family to the IBM headquarters in North Carolina, and immersed himself in American culture. He cut the global workforce by 10%, and introduced his Protect and Attack strategy – protect the power bases in PCs and in China, and aggressively attack new products and markets. Yang bought back the smartphone business which his predecessor had sold, and later acquired the smartphone arm of Motorola, putting the company in direct competition with Apple and Samsung.

Part of the Protect and Attack strategy is to customise products for new markets. This involved local manufacture, with plants in India, Brazil and Mexico as well as China, the US and Japan. The strategy is to build up market share in the medium term, without worrying too much about profit.

Lenovo has now fully recovered from the Great Recession. It is firmly established as the world number 1 in PCs (a cash cow business), and is building up a strong position in star businesses such as smartphones. It has a turnover of $30bn, and sales in 160 countries. The company is now truly global. It has joint headquarters in Beijing and North Carolina, the official company language is English, the top management committee has nine members from six different countries. The company operates a bottom-up performance culture, and HR and reward practices are standardised worldwide.

Sources: *Economist* (2013f); Ahrens and Zhou (2013); Clark (2014); Evolving Globalisation (2014)

CASE STUDY 6.8

GLOBALISATION AND TAX AVOIDANCE

One unfortunate consequence of globalisation is that it facilitates tax avoidance (the perfectly legal exploitation of loopholes in the tax system, as distinct from illegal tax evasion). Globalised companies have considerable freedom to manipulate their accounts in order to declare most of their profits in low-tax countries, thus minimising their tax bills.

This problem was investigated by the UK House of Commons Public Accounts Committee in October 2012. They summoned representatives of three American-owned globalised corporations (Starbucks, the coffee shop firm, Amazon, the online retailer, and Google, the internet service provider). This case study will concentrate on Starbucks, which has always promoted itself as an ethical company.

The Committee found that Starbucks had made a loss for 14 of the 15 years it has been trading in the UK. They found this 'difficult to believe' as the company had 31% of the UK market, and it had reported to its shareholders that the UK business was successful and making profits. They identified three ways in which profits were manipulated to reduce UK tax:

- Starbucks UK pays a licence fee of 4.7% of turnover (recently reduced from 6%) for intellectual property (use of the trademark, etc) to the European headquarters in the Netherlands. Starbucks admitted that they had a confidential but 'special' tax deal with the Dutch government.
- The UK buys coffee from the Netherlands, including a mark-up, and the Dutch company then buys it from Switzerland, with a 20% mark-up, increasing profit in the Netherlands and Switzerland, which has a 'very competitive' tax rate.
- There is an inter-company loan between Starbucks US and Starbucks UK, at an interest rate which the Committee said was 'set at higher rate than any similar loan we have seen' (Parliament Publications 2012).

Starbucks responded with a statement from its Chairman and CEO, Howard Schultz, on 23 October. He pointed out that Starbucks UK had paid £160m in National Insurance, VAT and business rate over the last three years. He also said that Starbucks always adheres to local tax rules. In the US, local accounting rules stipulated that taxable income in regional markets be calculated before accounting for the impact of intercompany licence and interest payments.

On this basis, the UK made an accounting profit. In the UK, however, tax law requires that taxable income is calculated after accounting for licence and interest payments. Hence, no taxable profit in the UK, and no tax. Schultz concluded: 'We must do our best to strike a balance between profitability and social responsibility, and we will continue to strive to meet our own high ethical standards for how we...serve communities and operate in the countries where we do business.' (Starbucks 2012a).

Margaret Hodge, the Labour chairman of the Committee, was not impressed. The level of tax taken from multinational firms with large UK operations was 'outrageous and an insult to British businesses and individuals who pay their fair share' (BBC 2012b).

The Committee also pointed out that HM Revenue and Customs calculated the gap between tax actually collected, and that which would be collected if all individuals and companies complied with both the letter and the spirit of the tax law. In 2010–11 this was £32.2bn, barely down since 2004–5 (HMRC 2012). This represents half of the total UK education budget (Ashley 2012).

In response to the Committee hearings, which were widely publicised, a boycott of Starbucks was organised through social media (the Chief Secretary to the Treasury, Danny Alexander, admitted that he was boycotting Starbucks) (Syal and Wintour 2012). This seems to have had an effect, as on 3 December 2012 Starbucks announced that although it planned to continue the licences payments, it would no longer use them to reduce its UK tax liability, and on 6 December announced that for the next two tax years it would pay £10m a year to HRMC, whether or not it made a profit. This appears to be a reasonable, if not over-generous figure. Starbucks's main rival, Costa Coffee, is slightly bigger (40% of the branded coffee shop market, as against Starbucks's 31%), and paid corporation tax of £18m in 2011–12 (Pratley 2012; Starbucks 2012b).

A new development in 2014–15 was the Fair Tax Mark organisation, which gives accreditation to companies who pay a fair amount of tax. A fair tax means that a business pays the right amount of tax (not using tax havens or artificial transactions to avoid tax) in the right place (if a multinational company makes a profit in the UK it should be taxed in the UK, not shifted to a tax haven), and at the right time (Fair Tax 2015a). The first FTSE 100 company to obtain Fair Tax accreditation was the energy supplier SSE in January 2015. Their finance director, Gregor Alexander, said, 'Taxes are the way that every member of society makes a contribution to the cost of providing the public services we all rely on. That is why paying the right amount of tax matters and why SSE has a responsibility to make a fair contribution.' (Fair Tax 2015b).

? REFLECTIVE ACTIVITY 6.5

Globalisation and your organisation

What impact, if any, has globalisation had on your own organisation?

GLOBAL OR LOCAL HR?

In the September 2012 issue of *People Management*, Peter Reilly and Tony Williams examine the pros and cons of the 'one company' approach to HR in a globalised company (Reilly and Williams 2012).

They identify a number of advantages of the 'one company' centralised approach. These include:

- promotion of common values
- consistent treatment of staff
- export of good practice (including ethical issues like child labour, and regulation issues such as adherence to the requirements of the Sarbanes-Oxley Act)
- greater operational and cost control.

However, there are also downsides:

- stifling of innovation
- the centre gets out of touch
- ill-conceived policies are ignored or subverted, and HR tends to get the blame (One example they quote is of a US-Sri Lankan joint venture, where no employees were allowed to ride a motorcycle on company business, as insurance was too expensive. This completely ignored the fact that many Sri Lankans can afford a motorbike, but very few can afford a car.)
- organisations see the value of diversity at home, but often ignore it overseas.

Their conclusion is that a compromise is usually best – the 'connected company' approach. This should be based on cost-benefit analysis. Where the costs of a one company approach are high, but the benefits low, for example with local resourcing and employee relations, the local units should be given autonomy, but where the benefits outweigh the costs, for example with the HR information system, systems should be centralised. In the connected company, 'the goal of integration is retained...but within a model of devolved accountability to operating units to share/learn/reuse the common offerings in the light of their own particular needs' (Reilly and Williams 2012, p31). In addition, HR should always take into account cultural issues. As we saw in the previous section, the eastern approach to business is based on consensus. Any attempt to impose Anglo-Saxon-centralised command and control HR is unlikely to be successful. (See also Reflective Activity 6.6)

? REFLECTIVE ACTIVITY 6.6

Jaguar-Land Rover – a cultural football

Few companies have been through as many different international owners as Jaguar-Land Rover. Both Jaguar and Land Rover became part of British Leyland (BL) in 1968. In 1975 BL was nationalised, and in 1988 it was sold to British Aerospace (BAe). In practice Jaguar and Land Rover, along with the rest of the group, were managed by Honda under a strategic alliance with BAe. In 1994, the whole group was sold to BMW, which itself sold out to Ford in 2000. Finally, in 2008, Ford sold Jaguar and Land Rover to Tata. Land Rover has thus successively been under British (both private and public), Japanese, German, American and Indian management.

The Dutch guru Geert Hofstede has identified what he calls his cultural dimensions, which he says accurately describe national characters. His dimensions are:

- *Power Distance* (PD). The extent to which societies accept that power is and should be distributed unequally. Organisationally, high Power Distance will lead to hierarchical organisations with large wage differentials.
- *Individualism* (IDV). The degree to which individuals are integrated into groups. Collectivist societies with a low individualism score will have a high level of employment security and commitment to staff.
- *Masculinity/Femininity* (M/F). Masculine societies are assertive and competitive, with high levels of organisational conflict.
- *Uncertainty avoidance* (UA). The degree to which people feel comfortable in ambiguous situations. Low uncertainty avoidance is reflected in informal, unstructured organisations.
- *Long-term orientation* (LTO). In organisations this will be reflected in short-term profit maximisation, versus long-term growth.

The following table summarises those of Hofstede's findings which are relevant to Jaguar-Land Rover:

Country	PD	IDV	M/F	U	LTO
United Kingdom	Low	High	Medium	Low	Low
Japan	Medium	Low	High	High	High
Germany	Low	Medium	Medium	Medium	Low
United States	Low	High	Medium	Low	Low
India	High	Medium	Medium	Low	Medium

Source: Hofstede 2009

To some extent, the information in this table is reflected in attitudes to quality at Jaguar-Land Rover. Under British management, quality was a low priority – most of the time the group was struggling for survival. Honda brought in a high priority for quality, with the emphasis placed on the 'soft' aspects – total quality management, *kaizen* (continuous improvement), quality circles, just in time – and a realisation that the pay-off from quality would be long-term. BMW was also concerned with quality, with a shorter-term orientation and a more top-down approach, while Ford concentrated on 'hard' aspects of quality, such as Six Sigma. It is yet to be seen what Tata's approach will be, but evidence on Tata's management style suggests a high commitment to quality.

It is important to bear in mind that Hofstede's approach has been heavily criticised. One key criticism is that his basic research is very old, carried out between 1967 and 1973, and originally based solely on (mainly male) employees of IBM.

Question

What other criticisms can you make of Hofstede's approach, (a) in general and (b) in relation to Jaguar-Land Rover? (You will find Marchington and Wilkinson (2008) *Human Resource Management at Work*, 4th ed, pages 29–31 useful.)

MANAGEMENT IN THE G20 – JAPAN, INDIA AND SOUTH AFRICA

This case examines HR issues in three major members of the G20 – Japan, India and South Africa. The Seminar Activity for this Chapter examines the biggest and most dynamic of the G20 countries, China.

Japan

The best way to understand HR in Japan is through Japanese history. Until the mid-nineteenth century, Japan was a feudal society. Power was exercised through great land-owning families, the *daimyo*, (equivalent to the barons in feudal England). They were answerable to (and frequently rebelled against) the hereditary military dictator, the *shogun*, who was himself answerable, at least on paper, to the figurehead emperor, who was seen as divine. Under the *daimyo* were the *samurai*, a military caste comparable to knights in medieval Europe, whose role was to serve their lord for life, sacrificing their own lives if required, and who in return received lifetime support from their lord. The whole system was based on mutual obligation. The duty of the samurai was reinforced by the concepts of *gambare* (will to endure) and *gaman* (stoical acceptance of hardship). Although the *samurai*'s role was originally purely military, by the nineteenth century they also undertook many administrative roles on behalf of their lord. The rest of the population, the merchants and peasants, were of little account, and the *samurai* had the right to kill a peasant without legal redress.

The feudal system was formally abolished after the Meiji Restoration in the 1860s, when the emperor seized back power from the *shogun*, and embarked on a breakneck programme of modernisation, but the *samurai* system evolved seamlessly into the new Japan. Industrialisation was organised around huge industrial conglomerates, the *zaibatsu*, who in effect replaced the *daimyo*, while the samurai evolved into industrial managers. The *zaibatsu* were abolished by the Americans after 1945, but speedily re-emerged as *keiretsu*, who still dominate much of the Japanese economy – companies such as Mitsui and Mitsubishi.

Hangovers from the feudal system include:

- Lifetime employment – *nenko seido*. Male employees and managers in large corporations, particularly the *keiretsu*, stay with the same company for life, with little recruitment above entry level, and a promotion system based on seniority. Managers are predominantly generalists, who may well work in a number of specialisms during their career. There is little sense of a distinct HR progression.
- Loyalty to the company is paramount, and there is almost total identification of the employee with the company. This extends to industrial relations, where unions are organised on an enterprise basis, with much movement of executives between the company and the union.
- The culture of organisations is based on the concept of *wa* (harmony). Conflict is to be avoided wherever possible. This extends to decision-making within the organisation. New proposals are circulated throughout the organisation on formal cards (*ringi*), and each department adds its comments to the *ringi*. The aim is to reach mutual understanding (*nemawashi*). Decision-making is thus slow, but commitment to a decision, once taken, is strong.
- *Gambara* and *gamban* are still expected. Japanese managers work extremely long hours, and a recognised illness in Japan is *karoshi* (death through overwork).

- There is an emphasis on perfection (reflecting Japanese institutions such as the tea ceremony and calligraphy), hence the Japanese obsession with quality.
- Those outside the *nenko seido* system – workers in small companies, contract workers, women – have fewer rights and much inferior employment conditions.

The Japanese system has many strengths, but also some weaknesses. Conformity is all, and mavericks are not encouraged, as they threaten *wa*. A Japanese proverb says the protruding nail should be hammered down. It is also important to remember that the *nenko seido* system only ever applied to a minority of workers. Even within the *keiretsu*, lifetime employment only applied to 'salarymen'.

The system has also come under increasing pressure since the onset of the long recession in Japan in 1990. For the first time, large companies such as Sony and Nissan have made large-scale redundancies among core workers, not just contract workers, and the *ringi* decision-making system has largely been abandoned as too slow. However, the underlying commitment to *wa* remains (Hales 2001).

India

Three major influences have shaped the Indian approach to management – the legacy of the British, the legacy of Gandhi, and the legacy of Hindu Vedic philosophy.

- The British left a tradition of bureaucracy (the permit raj), which still permeates much of Indian management today.
- Gandhi left a preference for small-scale, village-based industry (symbolised by the spinning wheel), heavily protected by import tariffs and regulation. This is still seen as an ideal by many Indians, but in practice has been swept away by the economic reforms started by Manmohan Singh (see Seminar Activity 4).
- From the Hindu Vedic scriptures comes the concept of cosmic order, supported by common vision, universal brotherhood and equitable prosperity for all (Sharma and Talwar 2004). Business excellence can only be achieved through prosperity for all, or by taking care of all stakeholders. The ultimate good is the good of society, not personal wealth or self-esteem. As one of the Vedic hymns puts it, 'One should sacrifice the individual for the sale of family interest, family for the sake of village, village for the sake of nation, and abandon everything for defending higher values of life.' (Sharma and Talwar 2004). Modern Indian management gurus like C. K. Prahalad and Rakesh Khurana stress capitalism's ethical and societal obligations (Crainer and Dearlove 2005).
- The Vedic principles are clearly displayed in the philosophy of the leading Indian conglomerate Tata (although the Tata family are actually Parsees, not Hindus). The founder of the Tata group, Jamsetji Tata, said in 1868, 'In a free enterprise, the community is not just another stakeholder in business, but is in fact the very purpose of its existence.' (Branzei and Nadkarni 2008).

South Africa

The African concept of *ubuntu* has striking similarities with the Japanese concept of *wa*. *Ubuntu* can be defined as humaneness – a spirit of caring and community, harmony and hospitality, respect and responsiveness (Mangaliso 2001).

Ubuntu stresses the collective – the family, the clan, the community – an exact parallel with the Indian Vedic approach. Kinship and teamwork are key to the concept. As in China, age is equated with wisdom. *Ubuntu* permeates decision-making in South Africa. Just as with *nemawashi* in Japan, decision making is a slow process, considering all points of view, and the aim is to reach consensus.

One practical application of *ubuntu* comes in reactions to recession. The *ubuntu* approach will be to share the burden in a fair way – leading to pay cuts across the board rather than lay-offs.

What do these explorations of management and HR practices in the non-Western world tell us? What is striking is the similarity of approach across Japan, India and South Africa. Each culture stresses harmony, consensus, and community – a very different approach from the self-centred and profit-oriented approach of the West. There are clear parallels with the best practice of high-performance HRM (Marchington and Wilkinson 2008).

6.14 THE EUROPEAN UNION

6.14.1 THE HISTORICAL BACKGROUND TO THE EUROPEAN UNION

The origins of the European Union go back to the period just after the Second World War, when there was a strong desire in Continental Europe (particularly France and West Germany) to ensure that a further war would be impossible.

The founding states of the European Economic Community, set up by the Treaty of Rome in 1957, were France, West Germany, Italy, Belgium the Netherlands and Luxembourg. Britain declined an invitation to join, seeing its economic interests as lying much more with the US and the Commonwealth.

The UK, Ireland and Denmark joined on 1 January 1973, Greece on 1 January 1981, Spain and Portugal on 1 January 1986, and Sweden, Austria and Finland on 1 January 1995. The former East Germany automatically joined on German reunification in 1990. Norway twice negotiated entry, but on each occasion that was rejected by a referendum. Switzerland did not apply to join, citing its long-standing policy of strict neutrality (it was not even a member of the United Nations until 2002), but it has close economic relations with the EU, and is required to enforce many EU policies, as is Norway.

In 1976, the institution adopted the name European Community, and the Maastricht Treaty of 1992 adopted the name European Union from 1 January 1993.

Up to the end of the twentieth century, the EU was very much a Western European club. With the exception of Greece, Spain and Portugal, which had recent histories of Fascist rule, all the members were long-standing stable, prosperous, democratic countries. This changed fundamentally with the next enlargement, from 15 to 25 members on 1 May 2004. This came about with the accession of five post-Communist central European states (Poland, Hungary, The Czech republic, Slovakia and Slovenia), the three Baltic states of Estonia, Latvia and Lithuania, which had previously been republics within the USSR, and two small Mediterranean islands (Malta and Cyprus). Since 2004 three further Eastern European states, Bulgaria, Romania and Croatia, have joined.

6.14.2 THE AIMS OF THE EU

The European Union has a number of general aims. These include:

- upholding peace in Europe by integrating national economies
- increasing prosperity by developing a single market
- easing inequalities between people and regions
- pooling the energies of Member States for technological and industrial development
- developing an effective means of resolving political disputes
- implementing a Union-wide social policy

- implementing European Monetary Union
- assisting people of the third world.

These aims reflect a number of different perceptions concerning the future development of the Union (Morris and Willey 1996).

Single market ('European single market')

This sees the EU in economic terms, and concentrates on removal of national restrictions which limit the free movement of labour, capital, goods and services. In effect, the EU is seen as solely a free trade area, without a political dimension. Common political institutions should be minimal, and so should the structure of EU law, which should be limited to that necessary to ensuring that the single market functions effectively. The single market concept underpinned the early development of the European Community, and reached its fullest expression in the Single European Act 1986, which led to the setting up of the Single European Market in 1993. At least in theory, this ensured the free movement of labour, capital, goods and services. However, this does not fully work in practice. For example, the Schengen Agreement in 1990 eliminated internal border controls within the EU, meaning that travel within the EU was possible without a passport, but the agreement has never been implemented by the UK and Ireland.

Federalist ('United States of Europe')

Here the EU is seen as having the structure of a federal state like the USA or Germany – a central, or federal government which sets the general direction of policy, and local governments (states in the US, *Länder* in Germany, nation states in the EU) which are responsible for the practical administration of policy. Some political mechanism is needed at the centre to decide on overall policy, but this should be kept to a minimum. The function of EU law is to settle disputes between the central authority and the member states. Central to this perspective is the concept of subsidiarity, which says that as a matter of principle, decision-making in the EU should be taken at the lowest possible level.

Integrationist ('Europe')

The aim here is ultimately a long-term shift of power from member states to EU-wide institutions. The classic example of this is Economic and Monetary Union, which led to a single currency, the euro, and to control of EU monetary policy passing from member states to the European Central Bank. Subsidiarity may still apply, but the member states would only have those powers specifically delegated to them by the central government. EU law would not only settle disputes between member states and the centre, but would also directly impinge on EU citizens.

The issue of how far to move towards the integrationist model is central to an understanding of the crisis surrounding the euro.

?   REFLECTIVE ACTIVITY 6.7

Models of the EU

1   Which of the models of EU organisation (single market, federalist, integrationist) would best describe the view of the following political parties in the UK?

- Labour
- Conservative

6.14.3 THE INSTITUTIONS OF THE EU

Responsibility for achieving the aims of the EU rests with four institutions:

- The Commission
- The Council of Ministers
- The European Parliament
- The Court of Justice.

And two auxiliary bodies:

- The European Central Bank
- The Economic and Social Committee.

The Commission

The Commission is the executive of the EU. It is responsible both for proposing policy and legislation, and for implementing policy after it has been agreed. It is completely independent of member states, even though its members are appointed by the member states.

Before the 2004 enlargement, the Commission had 20 members, two each from France, Germany, the UK, Italy and Spain, and one from each of the other member states. Each Commissioner was responsible for an area of EU policy. The Commission is headed by a President, appointed by the Council of Ministers. The President is usually a powerful political figure in his own right. The President until October 2004 was Romano Prodi, ex-prime minister of Italy, and from late 2004, Jose Manuel Durao Barroso, ex-prime minister of Portugal. The current (2015) President is Jean-Claude Juncker, previously prime minister of Luxembourg. The Treaty of Nice in 2002 made provision for reform of the Commission after enlargement. Each member was to have one Commissioner, a major concession by the large member states, who lost one of their two Commissioners.

The responsibilities of the Commission are laid down by the various EU treaties (Rome, Maastricht, Amsterdam, Nice, etc.). They include:

- *Initiating legislation*. The Commission tables proposals to the Council of Ministers after wide-ranging consultation with interested parties.
- *Guardian of the treaties*. The Commission has to ensure that the treaties and EU legislation are properly implemented.
- *Implementing policy*. The Commission either directly implements policy itself, or supervises programmes administered by member states under the principle of subsidiarity, which we looked at earlier.

The commission is collectively answerable to the European Parliament, and can be removed by a vote of censure carried by a two-thirds majority – although there is no procedure for removing individual Commissioners. In early 1999, after a report which criticised the then President, Jacques Santer, and several individual Commissioners, and a series of debates in the European Parliament, the whole Commission resigned, and Santer was replaced by Romano Prodi.

The Council of Ministers

The Council is the final decision-making body of the EU. It consists of representatives of the governments of the member states. In practice, the Council is really a series of specialist bodies, dealing with particular areas of policy, and attended by the appropriate Ministers from the member states. When the Heads of State or Government meet, the Council is referred to as the European Council, which meets twice a year. Each member state in turn acts as President of the Council for six months. Council meetings are attended by the President of the Commission, who has a full right to take part in discussions, but who does not have a vote.

Until 1986, decisions in the Council of Ministers were taken by unanimity, which meant that each member state had an absolute veto. This was becoming unworkable, and would clearly become more so as more countries joined the EU. The Single European Act in 1986 introduced the concept of qualified majority voting (QMV), under which decisions in clearly specified areas could be taken by a majority vote. In practice, this gave the Big Four states a collective veto, but meant that they could not force a proposal through unless they obtained the support of several of the smaller states. From 2014 a new system of qualified majority voting is being phased in, of 55% of member states comprising 65% of EU citizens. This will remove the Big Four veto (CIPD 2014c).

The European Parliament

This is directly elected by all member states for five years. The most recent elections were in June 2014, with the next elections due in 2019. Its powers are mainly budgetary. It has the final say on all 'non-compulsory' spending (any spending which is not the inevitable consequence of EU legislation, making up 25% of the budget). It can also reject the budget in total, and did so in 1979 and 1984.

The Parliament has a right to debate all EU issues, and the Council can reject its views only by a unanimous vote. It cannot initiate legislation (the responsibility of the Commission), nor does it have the final say in passing law (the responsibility of the Council of Ministers), but it can reject measures which were passed by the Council of Ministers through QMV. In October 2004, it came very close to rejecting the whole of the new Commission proposed by the new President, José Manuel Barroso, because of the illiberal views held by the Italian nominee. The crisis was only defused at the last minute when Barroso withdrew his whole Commission for reconsideration, and the Italian government withdrew its nominee.

The European Court of Justice (ECJ)

The ECJ rules on the interpretation and application of EU rules, and on disputes between the Commission and member states. Its decisions apply directly in the member states. It consists of judges appointed by the member states. Findings are decided by a simple majority, and dissenting opinions are never published. Rulings are binding in all EU member countries, take precedence over all other legal decisions, and are not subject to appeal (Osborn 2004).

ECJ decisions have had a huge impact on UK employment law, in fields such as equal pay, discrimination, business transfers and working time, as illustrated in Case Study 6.11.

THE WORKING TIME DIRECTIVE AND JUNIOR DOCTORS

The European Working Time Directive was enacted into UK law as the Working Time Regulations from 1 October 1998. The Regulations call for:

- an average of 48 hours' working time each week, measured over a reference period of 26 weeks
- 11 hours continuous rest in 24 hours – ie no shift can exceed 13 hours
- 24 hours' continuous rest in 7 days, or 48 hours in 2 weeks – ie the maximum number of consecutive days of duty is 12
- a 20-minute break in work periods of over six hours
- 5.6 weeks' annual leave, pro-rata for part-time staff.

Individuals have the right to opt out of the 48-hour week provision, but cannot be forced to do so, and have the right to opt back in at any time. There is no opt-out from the rest and leave provisions.

Initially, junior doctors in training were exempt from the Regulations, although they applied to all other doctors and NHS workers. Junior doctors were notorious for working up to 100 hours a week, and often for being on duty for 24 hours or more continuously. The Regulations were extended to junior doctors in 2004, with a maximum average working week of 58 hours, reduced to 56 hours a week by August 2007, and to 48-hours a week from August 2009.

Until 2000, it was thought that when the Regulations were extended to junior doctors, their impact would be less serious because of the on-call system. On-call time was not normally regarded as working time, unless the doctor was actually called on. This was changed by the European Court of Justice in 2000 in the *SiMAP* judgement (*Sindicato de Medicos de Asestencia Publica v*

Conselleria de Sanidad y Consumo de la Generalidad Valenciana). The ECJ ruled that on-call time where the doctor is required to be on the premises counted as working time, even if the doctor was actually asleep for part of this time. For doctors on call but not required to be on the premises, working time only started when the doctor responded to a call.

This was confirmed in the Jaeger case in 2003 (*Landeshauptstadt Kiel v Jaeger*), which added the additional stipulation that if working hours were exceeded, a rest period should be taken immediately, not at a later date (NHS Employers 2009).

The NHS has recognised that there are particular problems with the 48-hour regulations in some hospitals, and a postponement of implementation (a derogation) was obtained from the EU covering specialities such as paediatrics and obstetrics in 38 trusts, permitting an average 52 hours a week until 2011 (Hope 2009). Opinion within the medical profession was divided. The strongest opposition came from the Royal College of Surgeons (Brockett 2009; House 2009). The surgeons put forward two main arguments against implementation of the 48 hour week:

- Continuity of care would be disrupted, as patients would be seen by more different junior doctors, which would make it more difficult to detect subtle changes in a patient's condition.
- More seriously, training would be disrupted. Surgeon training is still very much based on 'sitting by Nellie', observing consultants at work. A shorter working week would considerably cut the opportunities for this.

The NHS response to the surgeons' concerns on training is that medical education has changed. Greater use is being made of e-learning, simulation and skills labs, leading to less need for the 'sitting by Nellie' approach (NHS Employers 2009, p10).

Nurses were much more favourably inclined to the Regulations. When interviewed by the *Nursing Times*, Wendy Reid, the national clinical lead for the European Working Time Directive, said that it was important not just to tackle the problems of implementation by juggling the rotas of junior doctors. What was needed was a fundamental rethink of skills mix and a reduction of artificial barriers between roles. Many of the jobs carried out by junior doctors could be done as well, if not better, by nurses. She cited the Hospital@Night programme, whereby multidisciplinary teams were used to provide out-of-hours clinical cover. Many of these teams were led by nurses. 'Patients no longer care what your badge says,' she said (Ford 2009).

The main lessons to be drawn from this case are firstly that it is essential that HR thinks holistically outside the box when introducing a change as radical as this one. Merely reducing junior doctors' working hours is not enough. Working practices, training practices and skills mix all have to change as well.

The Economic and Social Committee

This is a consultative body made up of representatives of employers (UNICE – the Union of Industrial and Employers' Confederations of Europe – and CEEP – The European Centre of Enterprises with Public Participation), trade unions (ETUC – the European Trade Union Confederation), and special interest groups (collectively known as the 'social partners'). It must be formally consulted by the Commission on economic and social proposals.

The European Central Bank

The ECB was set up in 1999 to administer Economic and Monetary Union (EMU). It has sole responsibility for setting interest rates in the eurozone. It is headed by a President appointed by the Council of Ministers, and representatives from each member of EMU (which does not include the UK).

?   REFLECTIVE ACTIVITY 6.8

EU institutions and power

1   Why do you think that ultimate power in the EU lies with the Council of Ministers rather than the Commission?

2   You work for a FTSE-100 company. Your company is concerned about a possible change in EU social policy which could lead to legislation in the next few years. How can your company influence forthcoming EU decisions on this change?

6.15 EU ENLARGEMENT

The enlargement of the EU which took place on 1 May 2004, from 15 to 25 members, increased the population of the EU by 74 million, ranging from 38 million in Poland to 400,000 in Malta. This enlargement was qualitatively different from any which had gone before

- The sheer number of new entrants was larger than any before. This in itself put new strains on the EU's institutions, and increased pressure for speedy agreement on the Constitution.
- Some of the new entrants – Latvia, Lithuania and Slovakia for example – are far poorer than any previous entrant. GDP per head of the new entrants is about 15% of the old EU average.
- The biggest new entrant, Poland, has a massive and under-developed agricultural sector.
- There were fears in some quarters – which proved to be justified – that enlargement would release a flood of immigrants from the new to the old EU states.
- Eight of the new entrants are ex-communist, and three, the Baltic states, were once part of the USSR. Russia will inevitably feel threatened by this, particularly as an outlying part of its territory, Kaliningrad, is now completely surrounded by EU territory (Poland and Lithuania).
- One new entrant, Cyprus, is divided between an officially-recognised Greek state, which is in the EU, and a non-recognised Turkish state, which is not.
- Further expansion is inevitable. Bulgaria and Romania joined in 2007. These countries are even poorer than the 2004 entrants. The accession of Croatia followed in 2013. As of 2015, six more countries were candidates for membership – Iceland, Serbia, Montenegro, Macedonia, Albania and Turkey – although only Iceland was at an advanced stage of negotiation (BBC 2014a).

? REFLECTIVE ACTIVITY 6.9

Polish plumbers

On 1 May 2004, ten new members joined the EU. Eight of these, known as the A8, came from Central and Eastern Europe, the biggest of these being Poland, with a population of about 38.5 million. The UK already had a significant Polish minority, the descendants of the Free Poles who had fought on the Allied side in the war, and who had decided not to go back to a Communist Poland. In the 2001 census, there were nearly 61,000 people who had been born in Poland, with a third of these living in London (BBC nd). With their descendants, they made up a population of Polish ancestry of about a quarter of a million.

Under the EU rules on free movement, people from the A8 countries had the right to come to other EU countries, but this did not necessarily extend to the right to work. As part of the accession arrangements, the 15 'old' EU countries had the right to impose restrictions on work for A8 citizens for up to seven years. Only Sweden allowed A8 citizens an unrestricted right to work. The UK and Ireland granted them right to work, but no right to unemployment benefit until they had worked continuously for a year.

It was forecast at the time of accession that 13,000 A8 workers a year would come to the UK. However, this has proven to be a gross under-estimate. Denis MacShane, who was Europe minister at the time, claimed that the original figure was based on all 15 old EU members opening their doors to A8 workers (MacShane 2006).

Although it is clear that many more A8 workers, particularly Poles, are working in the UK than originally thought, nobody really knows how many. As Poles and other A8 citizens can enter the EU without visa, there is no way to telling how many of those who enter the country intend to work, and how many are just passing through. The Office for National Statistics carries out random interviews on arrivals to the UK and on this basis estimates that 56,000 Poles entered the UK to work in 2005. However, the Department of Work and Pensions says that 170,000 Poles applied for National Insurance numbers in 2005 (Doward and McKenna 2007).

The other main source of information on numbers is the Worker Registration Scheme (WRS), under which A8 workers are encouraged to register. This is not compulsory, is not required for the self-employed, and costs £75. There is also no requirement to deregister if a worker leaves the UK. In May 2005, the BBC reported that 176,000 had registered by March 2005. Of these, 82% were aged between 18 and 34, 96% were working full-time and a third may have been working illegally in the UK before accession and merely regularising their position. Poland was the biggest provider, with 56% of the total, followed by Lithuania with 15%, and Slovakia with 11% (BBC 2005a). This is not surprising, as Poland had by far the biggest population of the A8 countries, it had 20% unemployment, wages one-sixth of those in the UK, and a well-educated population, many of whom spoke English.

Some figures are also available from the Polish end of the migration. In 2004, the year of accession, there were fewer movements of Poles out of the country than in 2003 (27.2 million compared with 38.6 million) (Iglicka 2005). However, there is no way of telling how many of these were going out of Poland to work, or, perhaps, on day trips to Germany or the Czech Republic. What may be significant, however, is that the number of those leaving by air increased by 37% in 2004 to 1.89 million. Official emigration in 2004 was also lower than in 2003, and only 543 Poles officially emigrated to the UK, compared with 12,646 to Germany.

Rumours and urban myths abound of the number of Poles in the UK. There are said to be 10,000 in Slough, 15,000 in Boston, Lincolnshire, 3,000 in Crewe (Doward and McKenna 2007). According to the 2011 census, about 7,000 of Boston's population of 64,600 came from the A8 countries plus Romania, well below the 15,000 suggested. This has put considerable pressure on local infrastructure such as housing and schools, although it has also been pointed out that the local maternity unit would have closed but for the extra demand from eastern European births (Pidd 2012).

Remember also that despite the myths, most Polish and other A8 immigrants are not plumbers. Among the A8 immigrants, 24% work in distribution, hotels and restaurants, 21% in manufacturing, 14% in construction, and a significant but unstated proportion in agriculture and food processing (House of Lords 2008, p18).

The plain truth is nobody really has any idea how many Poles are working in Britain. Latest estimates are that up to 1m Poles may have left Poland, although they have not all come to the UK (Barrell et al 2007). If, say, a third have come to the UK, this makes about 400,000. It is thought that most Polish and other A8 workers come to the UK with every intention of going back to Poland, and, unlike other immigrant groups, going back is very easy and cheap – £10 on a Ryanair flight. When questioned by the Joseph Rowntree Foundation immediately after accession, only 6% said they intended to stay in the UK permanently. A year later, this had risen to 29% (Spencer et al 2007). In September 2007, 62% of those arriving in the previous 12 months said they intended to stay for less than one year (House of Lords 2008), although the experience of other immigrant groups suggests that more will stay than initially expected to.

With the onset of the recession in 2008, many Polish workers returned to Poland, which was the only country in the EU to experience positive economic growth in 2009. In the year to September 2009, 12,000 more Poles left the UK than entered (Pidd 2011). In May 2011, Germany also opened its borders to Polish workers, as the transition period agreed in 2004 came to an end. It is expected that up to 1m Poles may emigrate to Germany (Hall et al 2011).

The situation became clearer by 2011. The Office for National Statistics announced that the UK had 545,000 Polish-born residents in 2010, the biggest foreign-born national group (ONS 2011). Of these, 86% were of working age, 80% of these were in work, and unemployment was 5.5%. Corresponding figures for the UK as a whole were 60%, 70% and 7.8%. The 2011 Census figure for people born in Poland was 579,000 (BBC News 2012a).

1 What do you think is the likely economic and social impact of the influx of Polish and other A8 workers into the UK?

2 How can trade unions respond to the issues raised by the influx of Polish workers?

TURKEY AND THE EU

CASE STUDY 6.12

Turkey has been an associate member of the EU since 1963, and has sought full membership since that date. It was formally recognised as a candidate in 1999 (Lungesen 2004), and formal accession talks started in October 2005 (Akcapar and Chaibi 2006). However, accession talks were 'part-suspended' in December 2006 following a dispute about Turkish recognition of Cyprus (Tisdall 2007).

Should Turkey join the EU?

There are four requirements for new entrants to the EU, known as the Copenhagen Criteria.

- Each applicant must show that it is in sympathy with the fundamental ethos of the EU, by demonstrating that it practices liberty, democracy, respect for human rights and fundamental freedoms, and the rule of law.
- Each applicant must create a functioning market economy.
- Each applicant must comply with the body of EU laws and standards (the *acquis communitaire*) – which is 100,000 pages long!
- The applicant must be part of Europe.

Turkey does have a history of military coups, and a dubious human rights record in relation to its treatment of its Kurdish minority, but the country argues that it meets the criteria. It is a long-standing democratic country, and since the present government came to power in 2002, it has taken a number of steps to improve its human rights record. It has abolished the death penalty, released some Kurdish activists, and started TV broadcasts in Kurdish. Few dispute that it has a functioning market economy. Only

a small part of Turkey (Thrace) is technically within geographical Europe, with the rest (Anatolia) being in Asia, but Turkey has always seen itself as part of Europe. The geographical position of Turkey could be a problem, as it has frontiers with Iraq, Iran and Syria, but the former EU enlargement commissioner, Guenter Verheugen, saw this as an asset not a drawback. Membership would demonstrate to the Middle East that the EU could work with a Muslim country (Lungesen 2004). As the Portuguese foreign minister said about the negotiations with Turkey, this was a victory for Europe and a bitter defeat for Osama bin Laden. Turkish membership should increase Turkish prosperity and so, paradoxically, decrease rather than increase immigration from Turkey (Kirisci 2007).

There is some opposition to Turkish entry on the grounds that its 70 million predominantly Muslim population would upset the religious and cultural balance of the EU, but Turkey is constitutionally a secular state not an Islamic one, and to say that we don't want Muslims in Europe is an insult to the Muslim minorities in the UK, France, Germany and Spain. However, in April–May 2007 there was considerable unrest in Turkey over the election of a known Islamist as President, with the threat of a military coup to preserve secularism. The Islamist AKP party has strengthened its grip on power, and was heavily criticised in the EU over the suppression of environmentalist demonstrations in Istanbul in 2013 and its re-opening of hostilities with Kurdish separatists in 2016.

One argument against Turkish entry was that Turkey was too poor. However, this is difficult to support, as Turkey's GDP per head on a purchasing power parity basis is almost identical to that of Romania, which joined the EU in 2007 (CIA 2007). Another fear is an increased influx of Turkish workers into the EU, which already has 3 million Turkish-born workers. However, Turkey claims that by 2015 its economic growth will have reached a point where it will itself be a net importer of labour.

The strongest argument against Turkish entry is its sheer size. Its population is just smaller than that of Germany, but it is rising at 1% per annum, and will soon overtake Germany. The population of the EU 27 is probably already falling. By 2050, Turkey could make up between a fifth and a quarter of the total EU population. This is of particular concern to France and Germany, which see their power base being eroded.

In surveys in 2005, 35% of EU citizens supported Turkish entry, while 52% opposed it. If Turkish entry were approved, Austria would hold a referendum on the issue before agreeing to ratify the accession. Only 10% of Austrians support Turkish entry, which may be a historical folk memory of two sieges of Vienna by the Turkish Empire (Akcapar and Chaibi 2006).

Until recently, Turkish public opinion has been firmly in support of EU membership, but this is now waning, due to what the Turks see as the patronising approach of the EU. One Turkish commentator said, 'Europe is not ready for Turkish membership.' (Tisdall, 2007). As Islamism in Turkey grows, the Turks increasingly see their future as a big player in Islamic Central Asia and Middle East, rather than a smaller player in the predominantly Christian EU.

In October 2015, the EU appealed to Turkey for help in stemming the flow of refugees primarily, but not solely, from the civil war in Syria. Turkey's price for this appears to be financial help, Turkish access to the Schengen Agreement, allowing visa-free movement to the EU, and a re-opening of negotiations on Turkish membership of the EU (Morris 2015).

6.15.1 EU EMPLOYMENT POLICY

Employment policy in the UK is influenced by the EU at several different levels.

EU treaties

The treaties set out the competencies of the EU. The organisation is only allowed to act in areas set out in the treaties. The various treaties, culminating in the Lisbon Treaty of December 2009, have always been committed to improvements in working conditions. The right to equal pay for work of equal value was in the founding Treaty of Rome in 1957 (CIPD 2014c). National economic policies must be consistent with the EU's broad economic guidelines, which stress a high level of employment as a major objective. Employment policy was a key element of the Lisbon Strategy on EU competitiveness agreed in 2000. The Lisbon strategy was replaced by the Europe 2020 strategy on 17 June 2010. The Europe 2020 strategy aims to create jobs, and encourage 'green' economic growth and create an inclusive society. The strategy's main employment targets include:

- raise EU employment rate from 69% to 75%;
- reduce school drop-out rates to less than 10% (Civitas 2010).

The treaties stress a commitment to improved living and working conditions with a view to harmonisation (remember that one of the key EU principles is a level playing field between member states); social protection; dialogue between management and labour; development of HR with the aim of lasting high employment; and combating exclusion.

However, the treaties also stress that the EU should avoid placing excessive burdens on small- and medium-sized businesses.

An important element in the Lisbon Treaty was the incorporation of the Charter of Fundamental Rights, originally agreed in 2000, but never accepted by the UK. The Charter guarantees a number of individual rights, some of which relate to employment, but as part of the treaty negotiations, the UK and Poland were granted an opt-out from the Charter, joined at the last minute by the Czech Republic.

The Lisbon Treaty also lays down how decisions must be taken on employment matters. Unanimity is required for proposals that concern social protection and social security, and protection of workers' interests on termination of the employment contract. All other employment issues are subject to co-decision, which gives a significant role to the European Parliament and ensures that no one member state can exercise a veto.

EU directives

While the treaties deal with the principles of EU employment policy, details of implementation are enforced through EU directives. HR professionals will be familiar with most of them, including collective redundancies, TUPE, discrimination, equal pay, health and safety, information and consultation, atypical workers, pregnant workers, agency workers and working time. If the requirements of an EU directive set a lower standard than that already existing in national law, member states are not allowed to reduce their level of worker protection.

Social partner agreements

EU employment policy is also made by agreements between the social partners, the European Trade Union Confederation (ETUC), representing trade unions (including the TUC), and UNICE, representing employers (including the CBI). EU-level social partner agreements include parental leave and leave for family reasons, the protection of fixed-term, part-time and teleworkers, and workplace stress. The European Commission also encourages agreements made by sectoral social partners.

For further details, see the CIPD's *Employment Law: EU influence* factsheet, last revised in November 2014 (CIPD 2014c).

6.15.2 THE EURO AND THE EUROZONE CRISIS

The concept of the euro dates back to the Maastricht Treaty of 1992, which established the programme of Economic and Monetary Union (EMU), with the intention to create a single currency by 1999. Under EMU, all EU members agreed to keep their exchange rates within narrow bounds (the Exchange Rate Mechanism (ERM)), and to accept limits on their public spending and borrowing. The UK left the ERM in 1993. The spending limits were formalised in the Stability and Growth Pact in 1997, which said that all countries in the eurozone should keep their annual budget deficit below 3% of GDP, and their total public debt below 60% of GDP. If a country broke the rules for three consecutive years, it could be fined by the European Commission.

In 1998, eleven members agreed to fix their exchange rates and handed over their power to set interest rates to the European Central Bank. The UK, Sweden and Denmark refused to join, and Greece was not invited to join, because it did not qualify under EMU rules (it did join at the last minute in 2001). The twelve countries of the eurozone started to use the euro on 1 January 2002. Of the new members that joined the EU in 2004, Slovenia, Cyprus, Malta, Slovakia, Estonia, Latvia and Lithuania have adopted the euro. It is also the official currency in the statelets of Monaco, San Marino and the Vatican (James and Sonny, 2006, 2012).

The members of the eurozone had voluntarily surrendered two key tools of economic policy – the power to vary their exchange rate, and to vary their interest rates. This, and the last-minute decision to admit Greece, were to prove crucial weaknesses when the eurozone crisis started in 2008, and intensified from 2010. EMU also attempted to control fiscal policy through the Stability and Growth Pact, which was designed to control the spending of the weak southern European members. However, in 2003, both France and Germany broke the Pact, but avoided punishment by the Commission. Thereafter, the Pact was effectively dead, although a modified version, the Fiscal Treaty, was introduced in 2011. The UK and the Czech Republic refused to sign up to the Fiscal Treaty (James et al 2006, 2012).

The fundamental weakness of the eurozone was that the economies of its members were too diverse. At one extreme was Germany, extremely wealthy, with very high productivity, and a pathological aversion to inflation. At the other extreme was Greece, a poor country with low productivity, a tendency to inflation and poorly controlled public spending, and a reputation for tax evasion. For a time, the cracks were papered over. Eurozone interest rates were low, which stimulated runaway housing booms in Ireland and Spain, while Greece fudged its public borrowing to appear to stay within the Stability and Growth Pact. With the onset of the world recession in 2008, the weaknesses of the eurozone became all too apparent. The Irish and Portuguese governments were forced to ask the EU for financial bail-outs, but the weakest link, predictably, was Greece.

In February 2010 the EU instructed Greece to cut its public spending and raise its taxes to reduce its debt, and the eurozone agreed to lend Greece €80bn. In May 2010 the eurozone set up a more formal rescue fund, the European Financial Stability Facility, a temporary fund with resources of €440bn (increased to €800bn in March 2012), which made a second bail-out loan of €109bn to Greece). The crisis eased somewhat after a speech by Mario Draghi, the President of the ECB, in which he said the ECB was 'ready to do whatever it takes' to save the euro (Draghi 2012). Later in 2012, the eurozone agreed that the EFSF could lend direct to banks, rather than only to sovereign states. In November 2012, the Facility lent €37bn to four Spanish banks to finance restructuring (Tremlett 2012). The EFSF was replaced by the permanent European Stability Mechanism in 2013.

In order to qualify for bail-out loans, Greece has made savage cuts to its public spending, including pensions and health spending. Greece has found itself caught in the same trap as George Osborne in the UK – savage cuts in public spending increase the budget deficit rather than reduce it.

Meanwhile Greece moved closer to total collapse. Greek GDP had fallen by 25% by 2014, the biggest drop anywhere since the 1930s. Malaria has returned to Greece for the first time in 40 years, schools are cold because they cannot afford to buy heating oil, and politics seemed to be polarising between the far left and the neo-Nazi far right (Smith 2012).

By late 2014, the collapse in GDP seemed to have stabilised, but Greek opposition to austerity was growing. In January 2015, a general election was won by the hard left anti-austerity party Syriza with 35% of the votes, defeating the ruling centre-right coalition. The neo-Nazi Golden Dawn came third, but with only 6% of the votes. The centre-left PASOK, which had ruled Greece until 2012, was reduced to 4%.

Negotiations soon opened for a further bail-out, but opinion among other members of the eurozone had hardened. It appeared that Germany was ready to contemplate Greek withdrawal from the euro (so-called Grexit), and they were supported by Austria, Belgium, the Netherlands, Finland the Baltic states and Slovakia (BBC 2015c). Eventually a bail-out package was agreed by the Troika of the EU, the European Central Bank and the IMF. The Greek prime minister Alexis Tsipras rejected the deal, and called a referendum in Greece. On 5 July 2015, the terms of the bail-out were rejected by 61%.

Clearly Tsipras was expecting the Troika to soften its terms, but they hardened them instead. The Greek government then blinked first, and in August 2015 the Greek parliament accepted the package by 222 votes to 64. Thirty-two Syriza MPs voted against.

Tsipras then resigned and called new general elections for September, which Syriza won with a slightly reduced majority.

The terms of the bail-out were extremely tough. The scope of taxation was widened, with most exemptions from VAT ended, including the lower rate for the Greek islands, intended to compensate for the higher cost of living there, and corporation tax was increased. The pension age was increased, and concessions for the poorest pensioners removed, some employment rights were scrapped, and privatisation was extended, with many Greek public assets transferred to a 'trust fund' outside the control of the Greek government (Plummer 2015). There was to be no further debt relief, despite the opposition of the IMF, which felt that some debt relief was essential (BBC 2015d).

What can be done to cure the eurozone debt crisis? The normal approach for a country with control over its currency would be to devalue, thereby making its exports more competitive, which in the medium term will stimulate its economy, and also to cut its interest rates. Neither of these is available to Greece, as the European Central Bank controls the euro exchange rate and eurozone interest rates. The only approach available is 'internal devaluation' – making exports more competitive by forcing down wages and prices through public spending cuts. This may eventually work in Greece, but there are no signs that it is yet doing so. The only other remedies available to Greece are two doomsday solutions – leaving the euro, restoring the drachma, and then drastically devaluing; or defaulting on debt, as Argentina did in the late 1990s.

One solution open to the eurozone would be to write off at least some of the debts owed to it by Greece. Some very tentative steps were taken towards this in November 2012 as part of the third bail-out (Strupczweski and Breidhardt 2012), and it is favoured by the IMF, but this would be seen as a desperate last resort by the eurozone. Other euro countries, especially Germany, are worried about moral hazard – if they let Greece off, they would come under intense pressure to do the same for Ireland, Portugal, Spain, and possibly at a later date Italy.

Another medium-term solution involves Germany. Greece (and the other southern European economies) cannot compete with Germany. Internal devaluation tries to make countries like Greece more competitive, but an alternative approach would be to make Germany less competitive. This would involve deliberately creating inflation in Germany, but the Germans regard this prospect with horror, as there are folk memories of the hyperinflation which hit Germany in the early 1920s, and which contributed to the rise of Nazism. There is also a doomsday solution involving Germany, which is the mirror image of that facing Greece – that Germany should leave the euro, restore the mark, and then revalue. This might make economic sense, but is clearly politically impossible.

In the long term, the only viable solution is fiscal union, which would almost certainly also entail political union. A country like the UK has a single currency, the pound, and rich and poor areas. However, disparities between regions are less marked because the UK has a common taxation system. Poor areas in the UK pay less in taxation, particularly income tax and VAT, but receive more in public spending, such as unemployment benefit. To some extent the EU budget is redistributed from rich to poor countries, but to a much smaller extent. It is possible that in the long term the members of the eurozone might agree to common taxation, but it is inconceivable that the UK would agree.

It is instructive to consider how Iceland dealt with its financial crisis in 2008. Iceland's three biggest banks had become bloated and vastly over-extended, and were nine times as big as Iceland's total GDP. They collapsed in late 2008, but the Icelandic government refused to bail them out. This led to a fierce diplomatic row with the UK and the Netherlands. Icesave, a subsidiary of Landsbanki, one of the Icelandic banks, had aggressively marketed savings accounts in the UK and the Netherlands, which they promised had the same deposit protection as in the EU. When the crash came, Icesave reneged on this promise, and depositors had to be bailed out by the UK and Dutch governments. They sued the Icelandic government, but lost (Bowers 2013).

Iceland devalued by 60%, obtained help from the IMF, wrote off many internal debts, and cut spending and increased taxation, but in such a way that the burden fell most heavily on the rich, and the poor were protected. The Prime Minister was also put on trial for negligence, but was acquitted.

By 2012, the Icelandic banks had been restructured as three small domestic-only banks, money borrowed from the IMF was repaid, and the economy was well on the way to recovery (Olafsson 2012).

Parallels between Iceland and Greece, while not exact, are interesting. Iceland was a much wealthier country to start with, Icelanders (unlike Greeks) paid their taxes, and, most important, Iceland had control over its own economy. It was able to devalue, and to give priority to protecting its own citizens, rather than the banks and foreign creditors. Not surprisingly, there is considerable grassroots opposition to the possibility of Iceland joining the EU (the author's own observations in Iceland in June 2013).

The best source to keep up to date on the euro crisis is the BBC News website (www.bbc.co.uk/news/). A range of sources from this website are in the Bibliography. There is a blow-by-blow account of the final tortuous negotiations for the bail-out in July 2015, and the key roles played by the German chancellor Angela Merkel, the German finance minister, Wolfgang Schäuble, the head of the IMF, Christine Lagarde, and the Greek prime minister Alexis Tsipras, in Traynor (2015).

6.15.3 BREXIT

The UK Prime Minister, David Cameron, announced in 2013 that if re-elected, and after renegotiation with the EU, he would hold an in-out referendum on EU membership by the end of 2017. With the election of a Conservative government in May 2015, Brexit (British exit from the EU) became a live issue. As of late 2015, the date of the referendum was not known, nor were the likely results from renegotiation (Watt 2013; Parliament 2015). The only definite was the question to be asked. Originally the proposed question was 'Should the United Kingdom remain a member of the European Union? Yes or No', but the Electoral Commission felt that this would introduce the risk to bias towards 'Yes'. They proposed 'Should the United Kingdom remain a member of the European Union or leave the European Union?' The responses would be: 'Remain a member of the European Union' or: 'Leave the European Union'. This was accepted by the Government.

Technically leaving the EU would not be difficult. The other member states do not have to agree. All that is required is two years notice, but in practice disentangling the UK from the EU would be extremely complex (House of Commons Library 2013).

There is little agreement on the costs or benefits of UK membership of the EU, which makes any cost-benefit analysis of leaving almost impossible. At one extreme, UKIP claims that the EU costs the UK 5% of GPD (UKIP 2011). At the other extreme, the Department of Business, Innovation and Skills estimates an annual benefit of 6% of GDP (UK Government 2010).

The UK is a net contributor to the EU budget. In 2011, the UK paid £15bn gross, but after benefits this was reduced to £8bn, or £128 per head of population. This disguised considerable variation across the constituent countries of the UK. Scotland about broke even, while both Wales and Northern Ireland were net gainers. Depending on the post-Brexit relationship between the UK and the EU, not all net contributions would be avoided. Norway (not an EU member but a member of both the European Free Trade Area and the European Economic Area) pays £106 per head to the EU, and Switzerland (a member of EFTA) pays £53 a head (House of Commons Library 2013).

Cameron is playing his cards close to his chest, but in November 2015 he announced that he has four key demands:

1 An opt-out on the core EU aim of 'ever closer union' including boosting the powers of national parliaments, so groups of them can block proposed EU legislation.

2 To safeguard the interests of the UK as a country and specifically of the City of London outside the eurozone.

3 To curb internal EU immigration by cutting benefits, specifically restricting in-work benefits and access to social housing to immigrants from the EU to those who have worked in the country for four years.

4 To make the EU more streamlined and competitive (Adler 2015; BBC News 2015e).

In February 2016, broad agreement was reached on points 1, 2, and 4, and a compromise on point 3, whereby benefits would be curbed, but only for new immigrants. Cameron then announced that the referendum would be held on 23 June 2016.

Eurosceptics cannot agree on the kind of UK they would want after Brexit. Four different models have been put forward (Leonard 2015):

1 Singapore on steroids, as advocated by Douglas Carswell, the sole UKIP MP – a trading nation with a large financial sector, high levels of migration, a small state with low taxes.

2 Little England, advocated by Nigel Farage, the leader of UKIP, with restrictions on immigration and an emphasis on British sovereignty.

3 People's Republic of Britain, advocated by Jeremy Corbyn before he became leader of the Labour party in September 2015 (although he has since backed away from euroscepticism) – control of big business, and active industrial policy.

4 Bigger Switzerland – preserving the best elements of the EU, while shedding the worst, accepting free movement of labour, and most, but not all, EU regulations.

It is expected that if the UK left the EU, it would rejoin the European Free Trade Area, established in 1960 as a free trade alternative to the EU, and probably also the European Economic Area, an umbrella organisation including members of the EU and EFTA, excluding Switzerland, which would give the UK continuing access to the EU internal market.

 BREXIT AND EMPLOYMENT

CASE STUDY 6.13

Brexit would have a major impact on employment in the UK in at least two areas – immigration and the labour market, and employment law.

Immigration and the labour market

The impact of Brexit on immigration and the labour market would depend on the terms of exit which are negotiated by the British government. At one extreme would be a Norway-style exit, where the UK remains in the EEA, and thus accepts all the EU single market regulations, including free movement of labour from the EU. In this case immigration from the EU (and of UK nationals to the EU) would continue unchanged. In the case of a Switzerland-style withdrawal, where the UK was a member of EFTA but not of the EEA, some restrictions on free movement of labour could be negotiated with the EU. At the other extreme, the UK could leave without an agreement on the free movement of people, and could impose its own controls. These could mean extending rules on the immigration of people from outside the EU to EU nationals. This would probably restrict immigration to high-skilled workers through a points system (House of Commons Library 2013). The London Chamber of Commerce and Industry has warned that this could lead to a shortage of low-skilled workers (LCCI 2013).

The impact of restrictions on immigration from the EU would vary from sector to sector. The sectors with the highest levels of employment of non-UK EU-born individuals in 2012 were (ONS 2012b):

Hotel and food	9%
Manufacturing	7%
Business administration	7%
Transport and storage	7%
Arts and entertainment	6%
Financial and insurance	6%
Construction	6%
Professional, scientific and technical	6%
Overall percentage of workforce	5%

The sector with the lowest level of EU employment was public administration and defence (2%).

Employment law

The first point to note is that important parts of employment law are not derived from the EU. These include contracts of employment, the national minimum wage, unfair dismissal, and discrimination on grounds of sex, race and disability (although the law on discrimination on grounds of age, sexual orientation and religion is based on the EU Equal Treatment Framework Directive 2000) (CIPD 2014c). EU law is the basis of UK law on transfers of undertakings, working time, information and consultation, collective redundancy, paternity, maternity and parental leave, and atypical workers.

If Brexit was carried out through a Norway or a Switzerland method, it is likely that the UK would still have to comply with much of EU employment law. It is highly unlikely that France or Germany would agree to what they would see as 'social dumping' if the UK was exempted from EU employment law (Emmott 2015). In addition, UK law is inextricably bound up with EU law. European Court of Justice decisions have become part of UK legislation and case law.

Even within the EU, the UK has negotiated considerable exemptions from EU employment law. For example, the UK has held on to the individual opt-out from the 48-hour working time limit. In addition, the Conservative UK government does not appear to have a great appetite to change employment law (except for restriction of trade union rights). For example, the Conservative government has decided not to accept the Beecroft Report proposals on dismissal at will (see Chapter 3).

In conclusion it seems unlikely that Brexit would have an immediate and sweeping impact on existing employment law. On the other hand, the UK *could* be exempt from future EU employment law developments (depending on the terms of the exit negotiations).

? REFLECTIVE ACTIVITY 6.10

An in-out referendum

The UK Prime Minister, David Cameron, announced in 2013 that, if re-elected in 2015, he intends to renegotiate the UK's relationship with the European Union, leading to an in-out referendum by 2017 on whether the UK should leave the EU.

Question

What would be consequences for your own organisation if the UK left the EU?

6.16 THE EU AND OTHER REGIONAL BLOCS

The EU is not the only major regional trading group in the world. The North American Free Trade Agreement (NAFTA) covers the US, Canada and Mexico, while the Association of South East Asian Nations (ASEAN) includes the Asian Tiger states of Indonesia, Malaysia, the Philippines, Singapore and Thailand, as well as states including Vietnam and Myanmar, with China, India, Japan and Australia as Dialogue Partners. Both NAFTA and ASEAN are primarily free trade area agreements, as thus of much narrower scope than the EU.

All three encourage trade within their own area, and thus may indirectly discourage trade between the three blocs. Those of you who have read George Orwell's *1984* may see parallels with his three competing blocs of Eurasia, Eastasia and Oceania, who divided up the world between them!

In 2000, the so-called Triad of the US, the EU and Japan received 71% of total world inward direct investment, and was responsible for 82% of outward direct investment. (Williams, F 2001)

THE UK STEEL CRISIS 2015

CASE STUDY 6.14

The collapse of the UK steel industry in the autumn of 2015 illustrates many of the themes of this book: competition (Chapter 3), government policy (Chapter 4), regulation (Chapter 5), globalisation (Chapter 6), the European Union (Chapter 6), and China and India (Chapter 4).

The world steel industry has been transformed in the last 15 years. World production doubled in the 15 years to 2015, while China's annual output quintupled to 800m tonnes, nearly all of this for domestic use. EU steel output has fallen from 22% of world production in 2001 to 10% in 2015 (Davies and Neslen 2015).

China now makes half the world's steel, but as its economic growth slows, China has a steel glut. The OECD estimates that world capacity exceeds demand by up to

600m tonnes per year, with China accounting for over half of that. As a result, China is increasing its exports, at prices which are widely regarded as dumping. Other steel producers are being overwhelmed (*Economist* 2015e). In the UK, imports of Chinese steel have risen from 2% of UK demand in 2011 to 8% in 2015. More seriously, the price of slab steel fell by 45% in 2014–15 (West 2015).

The steel industry has several elements characteristic of intense competitive rivalry in Porter's Five Forces model (see Section 3.4.1). It has high fixed costs, which leads to a temptation to try to maintain output during a slump, leading to price wars. It has volatile demand. As a basic product, steel is very vulnerable to the investment cycle. It also has very high shut-down and clean-up costs. The tendency is thus to keep production going if possible, even at a loss, but if this is not possible, to mothball plants rather than scrapping them.

The industry in the UK has had a turbulent history. It has been nationalised twice, in the 1940s and the 1960s, and privatised twice, the second time in the 1980s, as British Steel. British Steel then merged with a Dutch firm to create Corus, which was taken over in 2007 by the Indian conglomerate Tata. Tata has since off-loaded several plants to other companies, notably the Thai steel maker SSI. The industry is thus a classic example of globalisation, both in terms of markets and of ownership.

The UK is a very small player in the world steel industry. In 2013, output was 12 million tonnes (Tovey 2015), less than 1% of world output. Employment in the industry is around 30,000, one-tenth of the number employed in 1971 (*Economist* 2015e). The UK steel industry is now smaller than that of Spain.

The crisis in the UK industry developed very quickly in the autumn of 2015. First SSI, the Thai owner of Redcar, went into liquidation with the loss of 2,200 jobs. Tata then announced plans to mothball plants in Scunthorpe and Motherwell, with the loss of another 1,200 jobs, and Caparo, a company founded in the 1960s by the Indian-born Labour peer Lord Paul, went into partial liquidation, with a threat

to a further 1,700 jobs (BBC 2015f). Within a matter of weeks, the steel industry had lost 5,000 jobs, nearly 20% of its total employment, with a knock-on threat to thousands more jobs.

The industry blamed a number of factors for the crisis. The biggest was China. There were calls for the EU to impose anti-dumping tariffs on Chinese steel, but unlike the US, the EU moves very slowly on trade matters (Davies and Neslen 2015). The industry also complained about the high cost of energy in the UK, at 9p per kilowatt hour, compared with 4p in France (Tovey 2015). The business secretary, Sajid Javid, promised to try to reduce energy costs, possibly by cutting back on environmental commitments, although this would need to be agreed with the EU. The government also promised to look at the burden of business rates on the industry (Hellier 2015).

Predictably, the free-market leaning *Economist* argued against state intervention to protect the industry. They argued that it would be wrong to protect a single declining industry, which has long ceased to be of strategic importance (*Economist* 2015e).

In March 2016, Tata announced that it was putting the whole of its UK steel operations up for sale, including its biggest plant, Port Talbot, which employed 5,500 workers and was allegedly losing £1 million a day (BBC 2016).

KEY LEARNING POINTS

- Since the mid-1940s, the world economic system has been regulated by three major international institutions: the IMF, the World Bank and GATT (now the World Trade Organization). All have been criticised by the Left as imposing capitalist norms on the developing world.
- Multinational corporations tend to have polycentric employment patterns, while transnational corporations have geocentric employment patterns.
- Globalisation has been characterised as having three main elements: the expansion of markets, the transformation of politics and the emergence of new social and political movements.
- The theory of comparative advantage and international specialisation underpins the concept of globalisation. Globalisation has also become more feasible with modern developments in communications, particularly air transport and the Internet.
- Aisbett (2003) identified four main areas of concern over globalisation: an objection not to globalisation in principle but to the way in which it is skewed

in favour of developed countries; loss of sovereignty to transnational corporations and to institutions like the IMF and the WTO; neo-liberal or 'Washington consensus' policies; and the rise of big corporations.

- Globalisation has almost certainly raised GDP in developing countries, while in developed countries it has held down inflation, but also real wages.
- Offshoring of jobs to developing countries increasingly affects skilled and professional jobs as well as the traditional call centre jobs.
- Globalisation may have contributed to the severity of the world recession from 2008 onwards.
- The Third Wave of globalisation will be led by developing countries, particularly China.
- The HR systems in Japan, China, India and South Africa share a desire for harmony, and a regard for stakeholders.
- The European Union's key aims have always been to maintain peace in Europe (particularly between France and Germany) and to enhance prosperity.
- Although there is general agreement on these over-riding aims, there are considerable differences of opinion about the future direction of the EU, epitomised by the Single Market, Federalist and Integrationist perspectives.
- The Commission is the executive of the EU, initiating and implementing policy; the Council of Ministers is the political decision-making body; the Parliament is mainly consultative; the European Court of Justice rules on the legal interpretation of the EU treaties and legislation.
- The EU expanded from 15 to 25 members in 2004, with the accession of mainly ex-communist countries from central Europe, and to 28, with the accession of Bulgaria, Romania and Croatia. The expansion in 2004 led to very large but initially unexpected immigration form the new members, particularly from Poland.
- The eurozone crisis is an almost certainly inevitable consequence of economic disparities between eurozone members.
- A referendum will be held in June 2016 on British membership of the EU (Brexit).

? REVIEW QUESTIONS

1. What are the main roles of the IMF, the World Bank and the WTO?
2. What are the major differences between multinational and transnational corporations?
3. What do you understand by ethnocentric, polycentric and geocentric patterns of employment?
4. What were the main reasons for the collapse of the Doha Round?
5. Do you agree that transnational corporations have too much power?
6. In what ways does globalisation (a) help and (b) damage the Third World?
7. What do you understand by the expressions *wa* and *ubuntu*?
8. What are the key elements of the Single Market, Federalist and Integrationist approaches to the EU?
9. What are the main roles of the European Parliament?
10. What are the three criteria for accession to the EU?

11 Why was there such a high level of immigration from Poland to the UK after 2004?

12 What are the causes of the Greek euro crisis?

13 Why is the restriction of in-work benefits for other members of the EU so contentious?

EXPLORE FURTHER

Further Reading

Books on the EU tend to be dry and fact-ridden, but two which are relatively readable are Neill Nugent (2006) *The government and politics of the European Union*, 6th edition, and Michelle Cini (ed.) (2007) *European Union politics*.

Micklethwait and Wooldridge's book *A Future Perfect: The Challenge and Hidden Promise of Globalization* (2000), is an easily readable though old (but positive) introduction to globalisation. More recent pro-globalisation books are Martin Wolf (2005) *Why globalization works*, and Philippe Legrain (2003) *Open World: the truth about globalisation*. Joseph Stiglitz's book *Globalization and its discontents* (2003), is fiercely critical of the role of the IMF. In 'Is continued globalization of the world economy inevitable?' *The International Economy*, Summer 2004, vol 18 issue 3, thirteen experts put forward their views on the future of globalisation.

For both the EU and globalisation, the way to keep up to date is read good quality newspapers regularly. The same general advice applies as to Chapter 2 – make sure you get a balance of left- and right-wing views.

Useful websites

The BBC news website (www.BBC.co.uk) often has useful background information. For a generally anti-globalisation perspective, check out websites like Oxfam (www.oxfam.org.uk) or ActionAid (www.actionaid.org.uk). The website of the think tank Civitas (www.civitas.org.uk) has a useful series of Factsheets on EU issues.

Audio and video material

The CIPD has two useful podcasts on globalisation – *Globalisation and HR* (Podcast 13, November 2007), and *The future of global HR* (Podcast 20, June 2008). The CIPD website also has a blog section which often has useful contributions on globalisation, the EU and HR implications. Two videos from Oxford Martin (part of Oxford University), are valuable. One, by Professor Ian Goldin, *Globalisation for development*, November 2012 (www.oxfordmartin-ox.ac.uk/videos/view/212), is a positive though critical view of globalisation, the other, by Pascal Lamy of the WTO, *Is Doha dead?*, September 2012, is a short discussion of the future of the Doha Round (www.oxfordmartin-ox.ac.uk/videos/view/201). Finally, a *Wall Street Journal* video, *Europe at the brink*, December 2011, gives an American perspective on the eurozone crisis (http://live.wsj.com/video/europe-at-the-brink—a-wsj-documentary).

HR IN CHINA

Management in China has been affected by two major factors – the influence of Confucianism and the influence of the Communist revolution.

Confucianism stresses harmony, respect, discipline and technical competence (Jacques 2009). This is reflected in a great respect for authority, particularly authority based on seniority and/or age. Chinese organisations are highly hierarchical, with considerable distance between managers and workers (no open-plan offices), and a high degree of formality (no first names, managers addressed by their name and job title – Engineer Wu, Accountant Liu, and so on) (Gamble 2003). However, this is slowly changing as managers accept that executives recognise that they must empower their employees and push responsibility further down in the organisation (Javidan and Lynton 2005).

Chinese desire for harmony is very similar to the Japanese concept of *wa*, although the latter is derived from Buddhism rather than from Confucianism. A desire for harmony is also derived from the Daoist religion, widespread at the village level in China. The concept of yin and yang – balanced opposites – is a Daoist concept.

Also important is the concept of face. Managers will see any personal reprimand or expression of disapproval as a loss of face, and a serious setback to their self-esteem, while a Western manager will treat a rebuke as just one of those things, quickly forgotten. Shame is commonly used as a disciplinary device in Chinese companies – withholding favour, leading the subordinate to feel shame and lose face.

After the revolution, the Communist party introduced the concept of the iron rice bowl (*tie fan wan*), whereby state-owned enterprises (SOEs), often owned by local authorities or the People's Liberation Army rather than directly by the state, were the mechanism through which welfare was delivered in China. They provided lifetime employment, housing, schooling, medical treatment and pensions, and literally protected their workers from cradle to grave. Since the reforms introduced by Deng Xiaoping 30 years ago, the iron rice bowl has slowly rusted away. Many SOEs have gone bust, while others have evolved into joint ventures with foreign companies, or Chinese private enterprise companies like Galanz. The Chinese welfare state has virtually vanished, and is now having to be slowly and expensively reintroduced. Urban workers with residence rights in cities now have access to basic state healthcare and pensions, but farmers and migrant workers usually do not. City-born workers receive a pension of around £200 per month at 60, while the rural pension is much lower (*Economist* 2015d).

Workers from the old SOEs have found it difficult to adjust to a more dynamic work environment, but up to now there has been an endless supply of new, young, usually female, workers from the provinces who have no pre-conceptions about work, but who have been brought up to respect authority and to conform. However, the Chinese population is rapidly ageing. In 2014, 16% of the population was aged 60 or over, and this will rise to a quarter by 2025. At the same time the supply of young workers will fall as a result of the one-child policy (abandoned in October 2015). Increasingly factories are having to take on older workers (*Economist* 2015).

Another crucial factor in the development of attitudes in contemporary China is the Cultural Revolution, which raged throughout China from the mid-1960s to the accession of Deng Xiaoping as supreme leader in 1979.

The Cultural Revolution was a deliberate attempt by Mao Zedong to overthrow Confucian ideas of respect for authority. All sources of authority were attacked, leading to chaos throughout China. Those seen as opposed to permanent revolution were attacked verbally, and ritually humiliated, and frequently physically attacked as well. Deng Xiaoping was beaten up, and exiled to run a small factory in the provinces, and his son was crippled for life. The Chinese people and their leaders now regard the Cultural Revolution period with horror, reinforcing the drive for stability and harmony. The Chinese leadership was also given a severe fright by the Tiananmen uprising in 1989, when China came within a whisker of suffering the same fate as the Communist regimes in Europe. The reaction of the leadership was to crack down on human rights, but at the same time to press ahead with economic reforms designed to increase the material prosperity of China, and to be very flexible on employment rights.

When the author was in China in October 2012, he found people surprisingly prepared to talk about what they perceived as the shortcomings of the country. These included the ending of the iron rice bowl, the growing inequality in China, the rocketing cost of housing in the big cites, and above all the endemic corruption. The Chinese government is attempting to tackle all these. Attempts to improve the welfare system were noted above, inequality is being tackled through a sharply progressive income tax system, and by a rising minimum wage. The state is building 10 million low-cost housing units a year, and strenuous efforts are being made to tackle corruption, with penalties including

execution. However, as always in China, the good intentions of the central government are often thwarted by resistance from grass-roots officials (Hessler 2011).

All enterprises employing more than 25 workers in China are required to have a trade union committee, with local unions affiliated to the All China Federation of Trade Unions, with 170 million members, which reports to the Chinese Communist Party. The trade union leader in an organisation is usually the HR manager. The Chinese constitution does not guarantee a right to strike, but strikes are not prohibited, and are common, especially in southern China. The 2007 Labour Contract Law requires employers to consult trade unions in the case of lay-offs, and provides that workers who have served two consecutive fixed term contracts of employment to move to an 'open-ended contract' with greater job security. China has a minimum wage, which increases by about 20% a year. The Communist party is happy to encourage higher wages, as it sees this as increasing domestic demand, and also as promoting harmony. The trade union system also allows the party to remain in touch with grass-roots feelings (Emmott 2011).

The Chinese education system and the one-child policy have both had an impact on management in Chinese companies. Traditionally, Chinese education has been rigid and formalistic. Memory and rote learning has been encouraged, and creativity discouraged. Anyone over about 30 was educated in this kind of system, and these people form the middle ranks of Chinese companies. However, the Chinese government has recognised that the economy needs to be more innovative, and not just to copy the West. The result is that creativity is now much more encouraged, at least in secondary and tertiary education. Chinese companies have been forced to develop responsiveness, improvisation, flexibility, and speed (Hout and Michael 2014).

There is also an official realisation of the importance of English, which is now the compulsory second language throughout the Chinese education system. Junior managers in their twenties have adequate English, and are more flexible than their superiors. The one-child policy has ensured that junior managers are more confident and less respectful of authority than their seniors. As only children, they have been brought up as 'little emperors', used to getting their own way (Connor 2013). They want to be trusted to take decisions, and they want a culture of honesty and openness (Connor 2010; Rush 2004; Meyer and Shen 2010).

There is a great shortage of good young managers in China, and a ferocious war for talent. One company hired 50 graduates, and after a year had held on to only one (Connor 2011). This has an impact on management development. Career development is important, but most important is status, title and who you work for (Watkins 2011). In the West, if a firm doesn't develop its managers, they leave. In China, if it does develop its managers, they leave. If a top manager goes, his senior staff are likely to follow him (Dragonfly Group 2015). It is significant that in China, most MBA students are top managers, rather than junior or middle managers.

The best HR leaders in China are developing the concept of the 'open family', which combines the values of openness (demanded by young managers), and family – the Confucian values of loyalty and service to the community (Connor 2010).

One factor unique to China (and to the overseas Chinese) is *guanxi*, or connections. This is a system of mutual obligation, whereby a favour made must be returned. This can over-ride loyalty to one's employer, and is second only in importance to loyalty to one's family. *Guanxi* can be used by management – doing favours for one's employees will create a reciprocal obligation – but on the other hand, it can be a danger to organisations. Vanhonacker quotes the example of a Chinese sales rep for a pharmaceutical company, who sold drugs on the side from local companies that compete with his foreign employer, but with which he had a *guanxi* obligation. Selling competitors' products is a way to pay back favours, fortify *guanxi* and make money (Vanhonacker 2004).

The CIPD's Next Generation HR Asia project (Connor 2010, 2011) identified characteristics and strengths of 'Next Generation' HR leaders in China:

- A sense of purpose, which combines a set of values and a vision for the future.
- Humble authority, a recognition that they can best influence the business through others.
- Insight into the needs of the organisation, which extends beyond HR. Good Chinese HR leaders are always business partners.
- Risk taking. Like everyone else in China, HR leaders are cautious but at the same time prepared to take risks.
- Fast implementation cycles. China is moving at a breakneck pace, and speed of implementation is often more important than excellence. Chinese companies favour flat, loose structures that allow them to jump on new opportunities and expand quickly (Hout and Michael 2014).

Question

What can the UK in general, and HR in the UK in particular, learn from China?

CHAPTER 7

Demographic and Social Trends

LEARNING OUTCOMES

When you have completed this chapter you should be able to understand, explain and critically evaluate:

- the key demographic statistics in a local, national, European and international setting
- the important effects produced by changes in demographic influences, especially those produced by world-wide migration
- how demography has major influences on businesses and government, who need to respond in a positive way
- the appropriateness of responses by businesses and government to take advantage of major demographic changes
- the major theories of social stratification and their application to the UK setting
- the nature and extent of social mobility in the UK
- the reasons for the slowing rate of social mobility in the UK and its effects
- the extent and nature of inequality and poverty in the UK
- the similarities and differences between equal opportunities and diversity.

7.1 DEMOGRAPHY

7.1.1 INTRODUCTION

Demography looks at populations – their sizes, characteristics and the way they change. It sounds like a dry and academic subject, but that is far from the truth. Population changes throughout the ages have been one of the major determining factors in economic development, political activity and social change. A growth in population can lead to a number of consequences. It can lead to wars, such as when the Roman Empire constantly fought with the barbarians in the search to extend its boundaries to secure more extensive food supplies for its growing population, or the sweeping hordes out of Mongolia and the Far East a few centuries later. It can also lead to extensive economic growth. It was only possible for the industrial revolution to get under way in the UK factories in the late eighteenth century with the growing supply of surplus labour from the countryside, following the enclosure movement and technological agricultural developments. China's rapid growth and industrialisation from the 1980s occurred for the same reason.

Nor would the vast choice of international food and restaurants we enjoy today have happened without the post-war migratory patterns, first from the new Commonwealth countries, followed by young entrepreneurs from all around the world.

Rapid movements in demography have occurred in recent years. Throughout history, the human race has been young, but now that is changing. In the next 50 years, both birth rates and death rates will continue to decline so fast that populations will age dramatically. For the first time in history, there will be more elderly people than young people, with the average age rising from 24 in 1950 to 29 in 2010 and projected to rise to 39 in 2050. In a growing number of countries, the populations will actually start to decline. It is, indeed, likely that the world population itself will peak around the middle of the century (Wallace 2001; United Nations 2015).

These changes will change economies and working habits, revolutionise pensions and healthcare provision and even alter some of the markets for goods and services.

7.1.2 POPULATION GROWTH

It has been estimated that in the year 1000, world population was around 300 million. It grew slowly over the next 750 years to 728 million in 1750. Over the next 250 years, there was a continuing spectacular growth, with a doubling of population to 1,500 million by 1900 and a further doubling to 3 billion by 1960. It has taken only 40 years for the population to double again to 6 billion by 2000 and grow again to over 7 billion by 2015.

The breakdown by continent of the growth from 1800 to 2010 is shown in Table 7.1.

Table 7.1 World population 1800 to 2015 (millions)

	1800	1850	1900	1950	1975	2000	2015
Asia	635	809	947	1,402	2,395	3,683	4,393
Africa	107	111	133	224	416	784	1,186
Europe	203	276	408	547	676	729	738
Latin America and Caribbean	24	38	74	166	322	519	634
North America	7	26	82	172	243	310	358
Oceania	2	2	6	13	21	30	39
World total	**972**	**1,262**	**1,650**	**2,524**	**4,073**	**6,055**	**7,349**

Source: United Nations (2015)

It can be seen that the growth has not been consistent across the world. Up until 1900, population increased rapidly in the developing world, but stayed relatively subdued in the poorer developing world. Since 1900, the bulk of the world population growth has been in the developing world, with an astonishing five-fold growth of population in Africa and Latin America since 1950. This has been accompanied by a rapid slowing in growth in the developed world, especially in Europe, with some countries showing an absolute decline in recent years. Germany, for example, had a loss of 1.5 million between 1987 and 2011 (Vasager 2013).

In the ex-communist countries, the population has already fallen from 311 million in 1992 to 280 million in 2015, with sharp falls over this period in the Ukraine (from 51 million to 37 million – over 25%) and Romania (from 23 million to 16 million). Further falls of over 10% are expected by 2025 in Russia, Georgia, Belarus and Bulgaria (United Nations 2015).

In the UK, as shown in Table 7.2, the spurt in population took place in the nineteenth century and has slowed considerably since 1900. Scotland's population has actually remained static since 2001. However, for the UK as a whole, there have been signs of a robust reversal of this trend in recent years with a steady growth developing, chiefly due to the net effect of migration.

The effects of the potato famine and lack of industrial development in Northern Ireland can be seen with an actual decline in population from 1851 to 1901 when vast numbers of young people left Ireland to go to the England mainland, America and the colonies. In more recent times, Ireland has reversed the general European trend with a considerable growth in population, reflecting a more buoyant agricultural and industrial economy arising principally from joining the European Union in 1973; greater economic opportunities have also halted mass migration abroad.

Table 7.2 UK population 1801 to 2014 (thousands)

	1801	1851	1901	1951	2001	2014
England	8,305	16,764	30,515	41,159	50,035	54,324
Wales	587	1,163	2,013	2,599	2,988	3,089
Scotland	1,608	2,889	4,472	5,096	5,258	5,389
Northern Ireland	*	1,443	1,237	1,371	1,701	1,826
Total	*	22,259	38,237	50,225	59,982	64,628

* not available
Source: National Statistical Office (2015)

7.1.3 DRIVERS OF POPULATION CHANGE

Taking the world as a whole, the only two factors controlling population change are the level of the *birth rate* and the level of the *death rate*. Within any particular country or region, another factor is important, namely the *migration in and out* of that country or region.

Birth rate

The *birth rate* is usually expressed in terms of the number of live births per 1,000 population. The fertility rate is the average number of births for each woman of child-bearing age. A rate of 2.1 is required to maintain the population over an extended period of time, excluding migration.

Table 7.3 Birth statistics – UK

	Actual births – annual average for decade (thousands)	Fertility rate
1900s	1,091	3.5
1930s	824	1.8
1950s	839	2.2
1960s	962	2.6
1970s	736	2.0
1980s	757	1.8
1990s	744	1.7
2000s	701	1.65
2014	748 (actual year)	1.94 (actual year)

Sources: Office for National Statistics, National Records of Scotland (2015)

During the twentieth century, the fertility rate peaked at 2.95 in 1964, while the lowest year for births was 1977 (657,000).

The birth rate is determined by:

- the number of women in the population who are of child-bearing age, and
- the proportion of this group of women who actually have children – this is called the 'fertility rate'.

It is clear from Table 7.3 that there was a steady drop in the birth rate in the UK from 1900 to the early 2000s, with the exception of a baby boom in the 1960s (plus a similar shorter boom in the period 1946–49). The birth rate mirrored the fertility rate, although the latter has had greater variations.

Having said this, there has been a reverse in the decline of births in the UK during the early 2000s and a steadily rising fertility rate. This has been due to a number of factors:

- Up until 2008, there was continuing economic affluence, providing the sense of economic security allowing family units to trade off the risks of the potential loss of income. However, since 2008, this economic security has rapidly dispersed without any immediate decline in the fertility rate.
- The influence of government policies to encourage working women through a raft of measures including enhanced maternity pay and new rights to apply to work flexibly.
- The influence of an increased migrant population, especially from the Indian sub-continent and some parts of Africa (such as Somalia), where larger families are the norm. By 2014, the number of live births had risen to 750,000, an increase of 50,000 over the average for the period 2000–09, with over 25% of the babies born to mothers who came from outside the UK, compared with 12% in 1990. The most common countries of origin of the mothers were Pakistan, Poland and India.

This trend has been in part responsible for a spurt in the UK population to over 64 million in 2014, an increase of over 500,000 per year over the previous five years. Another trend is that women are having children much later in life. The mean age of women having their first baby was 23.7 in 1970 but this had increased to 30.2 in 2014. An increasing number of women are childless. One in five women in their forties has no children compared with one in ten in the 1940s.

Table 7.4 compares the UK with other countries, showing that fertility is generally higher than the rest of Europe but lower than most developing countries, with estimates of the change in fertility in 2050.

Table 7.4 World fertility rates

	2010–15	Estimate 2050
UK	1.9	1.9
USA	1.9	1.9
Japan	1.4	1.7
Germany	1.4	1.6
Greece	1.3	1.6
China	1.6	1.7
Hong Kong	1.2	1.6
India	2.5	1.9
Pakistan	3.7	2.3
Brazil	1.8	1.7
Nigeria	5.7	3.6
Algeria	2.9	2.0
World	2.5	2.2

Source: United Nations (2015)

The suggested causes of the reduced fertility rate are as follows:

- Women are taking charge of their fertility. The widespread use of the contraceptive pill and other modern devices from the 1970s onwards allowed decisions to be taken on family planning, unheard of previously. Many women (and couples) have decided not to have families or to have just one child, often so that two careers can be pursued. This is connected with postponing starting a family until later. Having children usually brings a savage reduction in household income as one member, usually the mother, may stop working or go part-time. However, this attitude change can be restricted by strong cultural and religious attitudes, which currently prevail in predominantly Muslim countries.

- It is no longer necessary to have a large family as an insurance against obtaining care in older age. The extended family has generally declined in importance as the state has stepped in to provide or support services that have traditionally been carried out by family members.

- The cost of bringing up families has risen, especially in higher education, so the average expenditure on children has not fallen with the birth rate – it is simply a case of each child represents a larger financial investment, despite government financial incentives.

- In the wider world, children are no longer as useful as they once were. Fewer people live on farms where children can help out and child labour, although still an area of international concern, is far less prevalent and strong attempts have been made to eradicate this practice in recent years.

- About three-quarters of African countries are presently participating in various family planning programmes. Most governments encourage private planned parenthood associations to carry out various phases of the programmes. Governments often integrate family planning in their maternal and child health services by emphasising birth spacing for health reasons.

- In addition to active family planning programmes, many African governments have taken legal measures to reduce fertility. For example, some countries have raised the legal age for marriage. Others have outlawed polygamy. Some countries also now limit child allowances for government officials to no more than three or four children and some limit the number of maternity leaves.

The effect of population changes on Japan is shown in Case Study 7.1.

 JAPAN FACES CONTRACTION PAINS

CASE STUDY 7.1

Japan is getting old at an astonishing pace, a far cry from the position just after 1945. Then, the over-65s were around 5% of the population, well below the figure for the other major economies. In 2015, the elderly accounted for 33% of the population, due to the large post-war baby-boom generation and the fact that average life spans have increased from 50 in 1947 to 85.

The fertility rate fell below the 2.1 replacement level in 1970 and reached a low of 1.26 in 2005 before stabilising at 1.32 in 2007. In 2005, the actual population began to fall in absolute

terms with very little migration allowed to balance the picture. From 126 million in 2015, it is estimated that the population will drop to 95 million by 2050, with the elderly accounting for 40% of the total.

As the proportion of elderly citizens increases, so the number of young people declines. Around 16 million are currently in their twenties but, in the next ten years alone, this will drop to 13m. Recent graduates are already reaping the benefit with more job offers than labour available, so pushing up the price of graduate jobs. However, the flip side is that today's young graduate must support an ever-larger proportion of retirees. By 2030, there will be two employees for each retiree; by 2050, the ratio will fall to 1.5 employees per retiree. Most commentators regard this as unworkable, as do most graduates, the majority of whom are not paying the fixed portion of their state pension scheme, which indicates that they expect the scheme to be closed before they retire.

The biggest falls in population are taking place in the countryside, where younger villagers have been migrating to the towns since the 1970s. The hugely inefficient agricultural sector has been subsidised equally hugely for 50 years, backed by massive tariffs to keep out foreign rice and other products. While the economy grew strongly, Japanese society went along with supporting traditional agricultural cultures and values, but the young voted with their feet and joined emerging, innovative industries and services. Now the over-65s make up 40% of rural communities and 60% of all farmers, so many communities have become unviable.

In response, one small isolated hamlet, down to nine villagers all over 60, has contracted with an industrial waste company to sell their valley and all its farms so it will disappear under 150 feet of industrial ash. On a larger scale, Yubari, a former mining town on Hokkaido Island, has had a population fall from 100,000 to 13,000 since 1950 and has gone bankrupt through spending too much money trying to (unsuccessfully) promote the town's profile. Another town decided to actively shrink its physical environment, moving public institutions from the suburbs back into the centre of town and refusing permission for all additional dwellings outside a prescribed (and smaller) town boundary.

On the macroeconomic front, the Government has taken radical decisions over state pensions. Eligibility for the fixed part of the pension has risen from 60 to 65 in stages by 2014 and eligibility for the flexible (and larger) part will rise

to 65 by 2026. Most commentators regard this as not fast enough. Businesses have a cultural problem with a higher retirement age. Pay is based very much on seniority so employees staying longer in the workplace would cost the organisation much more money. However, because older employees are respected, it would be extremely difficult to impose pay cuts when employees stay on to a later retirement age.

If the retirement age is delayed until 65 or 70, it would go some way to solving the decline of the supply of labour. Japan already has one of the highest proportions of the elderly still in the workforce. This is not because Japanese simply like to work or do not feel a useful part of society otherwise. For many it is that they have to work to survive. Most of these jobs are 'down-shifting' into menial work, such as doing repairs and acting as a night-watchman, with wages that are mediocre.

However, a bigger influence would be to increase the participation rate of women, which was 63% in 2012, compared with 68% in the UK or the USA. Cultural problems are even greater here, with male chauvinism dominating offices, a work culture of long hours and a shortage of childcare facilities. Japan still, apparently, does not have an expression for 'work–life balance'. Large numbers of women permanently drop out of the labour market when they have children. As the average Japanese father does not help in the home (partly due to the long-hours culture), this engenders anxiety from the wife about extending the family. By the time their children have grown up, they then have caring responsibilities for their ageing parents, often living with them.

In 2002, the Japanese Government announced that every Japanese woman who gives birth is to receive the equivalent of £1,700 plus up to £15,000 worth of help with childcare. The fact that this initiative is likely to cost around £5bn indicates the degree of anxiety over the continuing decline in Japan's birth rate. So far, the effect seems to be marginal, even in the cities, as the attraction is limited of bringing up families in tiny Japanese apartments, where beds are folded up during the day and the father is not seen until late at night due to the long work-hours culture. The woman's duty continues to involve the tight supervision of children's education where tutoring for make-or-break exams is crucial and which also raises the cost of childcare. Women must also sign up for the whole wife-mother package – births outside marriage are rare.

A rapidly ageing population, supported by fewer and fewer working people, could keep Japan in a state of semi-permanent recession. It is estimated that if current trends continue, young people in 2025 will have to pay around 25% of their salary as a tax to simply keep pensions at

their current level. It remains to be seen whether the financial inducements, the availability of 'baby shops' to help women with childcare and 'grandmother networks' to support young families will make any difference or whether women will continue to wait until their aspirations in the workplace have been better satisfied.

As a postscript, a scandal erupted in 2011 when it was discovered that 230,000 listed centenarians in Japan could not be found. Many had died unreported; a surprisingly large number of families had lost track of them under the strain of modern urban life despite the fact that records indicated they were being cared for by their relatives.

Sources: Norton (2002); McNeill (2010); (Economist 2015a)

Death rate

As measured by deaths per 1,000 population, the UK rate has fallen from 23 in 1851 to 10.1 in 2013. The advances of medicine, reduced infant mortality and generally improved health, clean water supply and sanitation facilities have allowed life expectancy to increase, as shown in Table 7.5. The gap between male and female life expectancy was six years in 1990 but has narrowed since then to three years. This has been due to the decline in heavy and dangerous industrial work, the large reduction in smoking and the adoption by a good proportion of a healthier lifestyle. Women, on the other hand, are more likely to have had considerable working experience to juggle with family upbringing, leading to an increase in stress. It is expected that the gap will continue to reduce and even be eliminated over the next generation.

Table 7.5 UK life expectancy

	Male	Female
1901	48	52
1950	66	72
1990	72	78
2015	79	82

Source: Office of National Statistics (2015)

The UK life expectancy is around the European average, but some developed countries, such as Japan and Singapore, exceed our rates. So, as people live longer, the death rate falls. The actual number of deaths, however, has not fallen by the same proportion because the population has substantially increased over this period. In 1900, the number of UK deaths was 624,000 compared with 580,000 in 2014.

The picture is not rosy throughout the world. Although life expectancy in Europe averages 74 and in Asia it is 67, 28% of all countries have a life expectancy of less than 60.

The average for Africa is 50 and there are still sub-Saharan African countries where societies live with the appalling situation of life expectancy being less than 50, with the worst example – Sierra Leone – currently only 41 for women and as low as 39 for men. On top of poor health, there are numerous outbreaks of war and disease (especially HIV/AIDS and SARS), while poor living conditions are very common.

In developed countries, the main feature of a dropping death rate is the rapid ageing of the population with a rapid growth in the numbers over retirement age. In 2015, 12% of the world's population is aged over 60. By 2050, this is likely to have increased to 22%. This has considerable effects on social and economic patterns as will be shown later in the chapter.

Migration

The third factor determining population levels is the number of people migrating into or out of a country. Clearly, if more people enter a country than leave it, the population will rise. International migration has always been substantial. Man's original ancestors migrated out of Africa to populate the world and most of North and South America, Oceania and parts of Southern Africa have been colonised by migrants who have replaced the small indigenous populations.

It has been estimated that about 191 million people live outside their country of birth or citizenship (United Nations 2006). Political, social, economic and environmental upheavals have been the spur to large-scale movements. Religious dissension encouraged Puritan migration to America in the seventeenth and eighteenth centuries and persecution has forced Jewish populations to leave their homelands, be it Russia in the nineteenth century or Germany under the Nazis. Due to very poor economic and social prospects, the Irish migrated all over the world for 150 years, Chinese labour was used to build the American railroads and much of Dubai and Quatar's current building boom is being built using Nepalese and Indian skilled craftsmen. Britain eagerly recruited in the West Indies and the Indian subcontinent in the early post-war years to staff the health service and public transport when local labour was in short supply. At the same time, there was a substantial outflow of skilled labour to take up new lives in Australia, Canada, New Zealand and South Africa, often under 'assisted passages' incentives.

On a world scale, certain migration paths are especially important, as Dicken (2003) explains:

> ... there are massive movements across the Mexico–United States border and from parts of Asia to the United States. Australia has become an important focus of migration from South East Asia... and from countries around the Mediterranean to Germany. (p521)

In recent years, migrants have moved to richer countries because they are better organised. As Collier (2013) explains:

> A factory worker in Nigeria produces less than he would in New Zealand because the Society around him is dysfunctional: the power keeps failing, spare parts do not arrive in time and managers are busy battling bribe-hungry bureaucrats. When a rich country lets in immigrants, it is extending to them the benefits of good governance and the rule of law. (p24)

In general terms, the twentieth century has seen far more restrictions placed upon migrants by governments fearful of the economic and social consequences of mass immigration. Although immigration was never easy (both America and Australia veered towards operating a 'whites only' policy for decades), the latter half of the twentieth century has seen severe restrictions imposed by countries all over the world, exacerbated by fears of terrorism in the twenty-first century.

In the case of the UK, the Commonwealth Immigration Act in the mid-1950s imposed severe limitations on free entry for mostly ethnic would-be migrants and subsequent legislation tightened the regulations further. Commonwealth immigration dropped sharply from 150,000 per annum to less than 50,000 within a few years and has continued at roughly this rate until the 2000s.

Since the mid-1990s, the net inflow of migrants has escalated substantially, as shown in Table 7.6.

Table 7.6 UK net inflow of migrants (thousands)

1990	19
2001	190
2004	244
2006	200
2008	163
2011	220
2014	318

Source: Migration Observatory, University of Oxford (2015)

For much of the 1980s and 1990s, there was a rough balance between emigration, mostly to the 'old' Commonwealth (Australia, Canada, etc.) and America, and immigration (mostly from the 'new' Commonwealth – Indian subcontinent and Caribbean). During the 2000s, however, there was a substantial rise in migrants from the European Union A8 accession countries, especially Poland, and an increase from the 'new' Commonwealth, with the numbers from Africa also rising. 2008 showed a sudden reverse of this situation, with a large number of migrants returning home, including an estimated 50,000 Polish workers, and applications for work permits from the A8 countries halved in the three months to December 2008 compared with 2007, a drop of 24,000 (*People Management* 2009a). Additional barriers to immigration were introduced by the UK Government in 2006 with a revised points system reducing the number of potential applicants for work permits. However, this was only a temporary reduction as the 2014 figure shows.

The net figure for 2014 is made up of an inflow of 641,000 (of which 284,000 entered to work and 193,000 to study) and an outflow of 323,000.

Case Study 7.2 illustrates the effect on the labour market of the rise in migration from Eastern Europe.

CASE STUDY 7.2

MIGRATION FROM EASTERN EUROPE AND ITS EFFECT ON THE LABOUR MARKET

Philpott's (2007) research paper examined the effects of the migration from the countries that acceded to the EU in 2004 and on whom no restrictions on movement and work were placed by the UK Government. These were Poland, the Czech Republic, Estonia, Hungary, Latvia, Lithuania, Slovakia and Slovenia, the so-called A8 countries.

Level of migration

Nearly 580,000 migrants from the A8 countries registered for work between 2004 and 2006 (Home Office 2007) and a further 100,000 have been estimated to be working on a self-employed basis. Poland is the main source, with 579,000 resident in the UK in 2011. And the effect on the internal Polish labour market has been so great that Poland has had to ease its own restrictions on entry of labour from the Ukraine, Belarus and Russia to fill skilled vacancies and gaps in the seasonal agricultural market (Polska 2006).

This is way in excess of the official UK government forecast figure in 2003 of around 10,000 per year. Expectations have been massively exceeded due to the following factors:

- A large number of migrants were already working unofficially in the UK and their registration allowed their work to be 'legal'.
- Most of the A8 countries have high unemployment figures (20% in Poland, for example).
- Earnings in A8 countries are typically *six times lower* than in the UK.
- Working conditions, including health and safety provision, are often at a lower standard than in the UK.
- The arrival of cheap flights and coach travel has made the regular journeys cheaper and easier.
- The degree to which agency intervention would apply was greatly underestimated, especially in the building, agriculture and hospitality sectors.

On top of that, the freedom of entry from these countries has meant that an unspecified number have been able to settle permanently without restriction in most cases. Of that number, it is estimated that 380,000 have stayed on a permanent basis. However, this is only an estimate as there is no register of A8 migrants leaving the UK.

Nature of migrants, chosen work and pay levels

Most were young, with 80% under 35, while 80% had some form of qualification (mostly technical), although only 5% have degrees. Only 6% had dependants

arriving with them. Around 70% worked in low-paid, unqualified work, such as process operation/packing and in warehousing (40%), hospitality (18%) and farming (4%), while 6% work as care assistants and sales assistants. The average pay was between £4.50 and £5.99 an hour.

Good for economy?

The Government has spelled out the apparent benefits of this unprecedented migration. They identify fewer jobs unfilled, less inflationary pressures (which could fuel higher pay increases) and faster economic growth. The Ernst & Young ITEM club estimated that the activities of the migrants reduced interest rates by 0.5% and GDP was around 0.2% higher (ITEM Club 2006). The Bank of England concluded that the level of unemployment that can be sustained without raising inflation has been lowered as migrants take the low-paid jobs that often remain vacant (Blanchflower et al 2007). Moreover, responses by employers rated migrants higher than conventional employees in terms of productivity, reliability, attendance and quality of work (CIPD/KPMG 2005).

On the downside, however, there was some increased strain on the social infrastructure, notably housing, transport, hospitals and welfare. Overall, although the picture looked very positive, there was a contrary view from the House of Lords Economic Affairs Committee in 2008, which found no evidence of large-scale economic benefits and that immigration had a negative impact on the low-paid and training for young UK workers and contributed to high house prices.

Sources: Philpott (2007); McSmith (2007); Whitehead (2008); *People Management* (2013a)

You should note that statistics for migrants are notoriously unreliable. Although records of those entering the UK are regarded as accurate, at least in terms of actual numbers, those leaving the UK, due to the less arduous emigration procedures, are not as accurate. Much of the estimates are made up of samples from the International Passenger Surveys and other surveys of migrants' intentions, which many commentators regard as suspect. Figures for illegal immigrants are completely unknown, with the UK Government refusing to even make an estimate. An example of the unreliability of the migration estimates arose when the Home Secretary, Jacqui Smith, had to apologise to Parliament in 2007 for underestimating by 300,000 the number of foreign workers entering the UK in the ten years up to 2007 (Stewart 2007).

Between 2001 and 2014, the number of UK residents who were born abroad had risen from 4.3 million to 7.7 million (13% of the total population), with India (700,000), Poland (580,000) and Pakistan (480,000) being represented most heavily. The number of Poles has risen substantially from 60,000 in 2001, but those from the Republic of Ireland have dropped from 480,000 to 405,000. In London, those born abroad have risen to 40%, an increase of over 1 million. However, many parts of Wales and the north of England have less than 3% of the population in this category (Casciani 2012; Cooper et al 2014).

Comparing the statistics for those born abroad with Europe, the UK is twelfth overall but has the highest proportion of the larger countries (those with a population over 50 million).

On another front, there was a significant rise in asylum-seekers to the UK in the early 2000s, which peaked at 103,000 in 2002, but this figure rapidly fell to only 25,000 in 2015 (Home Office 2015). Government actions to speed up the system of dealing with applications has caused some reduction in applications but not eliminated the total. Only around 20% of asylum-seekers have their application accepted but many are able to stay in the UK while their appeal is heard, which can take many months.

Following the developing crisis in war-torn Syria in 2015, the UK government agreed to take around an additional 1000 more asylum seekers from that country but would not take part in the proposed EU-wide system of allocating 40,000 migrants,

The reasons for the increasing numbers of migrants include:

- Britain's economic performance since the mid-1990s has been very positive, better than most of Europe, up until the onset of the recession in 2008, from which it has recovered better than most EU countries. The job picture in the UK, especially in London, has been especially resilient.
- There is a strong culture of entrepreneurship, with open opportunities for small businesses to flourish, perhaps more so than in other parts of Europe, although not so strong as in America.
- There are established ethnic communities from all parts of the world, allowing greater ease of transition and community support.
- The number of low-paid unskilled jobs available is very high, especially in the hospitality, caring and building industries. Some are in the black economy, encouraging asylum-seekers and illegal immigrants. It is estimated that 87% of foreign-born UK residents are working (Cooper et al 2014).
- In the education field, there has been a huge growth in undergraduate and postgraduate courses taken up by international students, who are able to help their financing through part-time work.

On coming to power in 2010, the Conservative-led coalition vowed to reduce annual net immigration to below 100,000 by 2015. Actions included tightening visa controls, making it difficult to get entry for study (although an exception was made in 2013 for Indian students), for work and to join relatives in the UK (*Economist* 2013a). However, this policy has failed badly as overall numbers continue to rise.

Europe has been faced with a similar situation, although most countries show less hostility to migrants. While the UK's number of asylum-seekers represents 0.5% of the population, Sweden's 333,000 represents nearly 4%, while Austria's is 5%. Asylum-seekers to France are currently running around half the UK rate. During 2015, the EU faced a migration crisis as Greek, Turkish and most Balkan borders failed to contain the huge number of migrants fleeing from Syria, joined by large numbers from Afghanistan and elsewhere. It is estimated that over a million have followed this path. Despite the generous lead given by Germany and Sweden (where most of the migrants aim to live), there has been severe opposition from mainly Eastern European states to allowing an apparently unlimited number of migrants. The means and political will-power to control the large numbers are proving difficult to achieve.

7.1.4 ETHNICITY OF POPULATION

An inevitable development of the increase in migration has been a growth in the ethnic variation in most developed countries. In the UK, of 6.3 million who were born outside the UK, around 8% of the population, some 5 million are from ethnic minorities, nearly double the figure in the 1970s (Ellis 2009). In the 2011 census, the number of respondents who defined themselves as 'White British' fell from 88% in 2001 to 81%. Those of a mixed-ethnic background doubled to 1.2 million and the rate for children under 5 was 6% – a sign, if complex, of growing integration.

Ethnic populations have also become more widely spread. For example, in 2001, 80% of African populations lived in London, but in 2011 this had declined to 58% (*Economist* 2012a). The largest group are from the Indian subcontinent – around 55% of the total, while West Indians make up a further 15% (actually a declining proportion as many retire back to their countries of origin), with the remainder from Africa, Asia and the Middle East.

They have generally settled over the years in urban localities, with large congregations in inner east London boroughs and towns in the Midlands and the north of England. As a whole, they have a lower age profile with a much smaller percentage over 65, chiefly because migrants tend to be in lower age categories. Also, many migrants retire to their countries of origin.

Ethnicity of population is far greater in the United States, as shown in Case Study 7.3.

CASE STUDY 7.3

'LATINOS' ARE A MAJOR FORCE IN THE US ECONOMY

People of Hispanic origin (Latinos, as many prefer to be called) make up 12% of the US workforce today, but this will become at least 25% in 50 years' time due to their much larger families and current age profile. They originate from across Latin America, but predominantly Mexico, and their growth rate is 3% per annum, compared with 0.8% for the rest of America. As a group, they are a key catalyst for economic growth. In some of the larger cities, such as Los Angeles, they make up the majority of the under-18 age set. Their disposable income jumped 29% from 2001 to 2004, double the pace of the rest of the population, and they have a growing influence on all consumer patterns, especially food, clothes and entertainment.

The Latino boom brings a welcome charge to the economy at a time when other countries' population growth has slowed to a crawl. Without a steady supply of new workers and consumers, a greying US might see a long-term slowdown along the lines of ageing Japan.

Yet this demographic change produces potential problems. One of the major issues relates to language. With a huge Spanish-speaking minority, there could be pressures for recognition of an official second language, much as French is in Canada today. This could harm assimilation and encourage a form of separatism in states such as California, just like it has been a major cause of conflict in Quebec.

Another issue is the perception that large numbers of poorly educated, non-English speakers undermine the US economy. Although the steady influx of low-skilled workers helps keep America's gardens tended and floors cleaned, those workers also exert downward pressure on wages, causing friction with other groups of workers in this sector.

A case in point is Harris County in Texas, which includes the city of Houston, where the population increased by 21% during the 1990s. Forty-two per cent are of Hispanic origin and this ethnic group is responsible for 80% of the growth. There are no zoning laws in the county, so developers can build wherever they think

there is the demand. At the new 28,000-acre community of The Woodlands, a three-bedroom house costs around $130,000 (c.£90,000) compared with an equivalent house in San Francisco costing $700,000. The area is surrounded by woodland and crime is very low.

Rapid growth in this form may eventually cause environmental problems, but it greatly slows the pace at which America ages. The benefits of such migration were seen as so great by President Obama that he declared an extensive amnesty in 2014 for illegal immigrants, estimating that such action added as much as $200bn over 10 years.

Sources: *Business Week* (2004b); *Economist* (2006a); Stelzer (2014a)

Migration is a very emotive subject, bringing to the mix a number of political, economic, social and psychological issues. Broadly speaking, there are a set of reasons for encouraging migration and another set for discouraging it, as follows:

Encouraging migration

- We live in a global economy and we need to make the best use of all talents, from whatever the source.
- Migrants have energy and enthusiasm and a willingness to succeed. They have made a substantial effort to move from their home country and practice indicates that they are motivated to work hard.
- Most migrants are in the age group 18–40 and, in an ageing population, it is important to have a good source of younger labour.
- In countries where the population is static or declining, an alternative source of labour is essential. That explains why Germany in particular, recognized the need to accept as many as one million asylum-seekers and other migrants when border controls broke down in 2015.
- Migrants make up such a large proportion of the labour force, estimated at 10% (ONS 2015a), that the labour market would tighten dramatically if this source was reduced or eliminated. In fact, 15% of firms employ 10% or more migrants in their workforce (Smedley 2008).
- Migrants can fill the low-skill jobs that are currently difficult to fill – they prevent wage rates rising too high. At the same time, the country has high-skill jobs that are difficult to fill, especially in IT and many professions, and migrant are the major source of filling these posts.
- It is not unusual for migrant entrepreneurs to offer ethnic goods and services which expand the marketplace to the benefit of the consumer. Thai food and ethnic textiles are obvious examples.
- It is arguable that it is more beneficial for the UK economy for migrants to carry out work in the UK rather than that work to be outsourced to a migrant's home country.
- Why should migrants be prevented from benefiting from the UK's successful economy? After all, for 200 years, the UK benefited from running the economies of its colonies, so it is time for those benefits to be shared.

- Remittances from migrants back to their home country have been substantial and help to alleviate poverty. For some African countries, such as Kenya, they account for bigger flows of capital than aid or foreign investment (*Economist* 2009b).
- The Office for Budget Responsibility (Smith 2014) reported that existing high levels of migration work to reduce long-term indebtedness due to higher tax intake and education fees. They have estimated that public sector net debt by 2050 would be 40% under current levels but as high as 90% if migration was reduced to 100,000 per annum. Moreover, immigrant are less likely to claim state benefits or credits than natives (29% compared to 37%) (Dustmann and Frattini, cited in *Economist* 2014a).

Discouraging migration

- The UK is very densely populated and an inflow of immigrants leads to pressure on housing and jobs.
- Where there is a large source of low-skilled labour, it discourages employers from becoming more productive by automating production or innovating the services provided.
- Too much migration encourages the black economy, which reduces tax revenue and is associated with crime.
- The process of policing and administrating prospective migrants is very expensive and difficult to carry out efficiently and fairly.
- Migrants can be socially marginalised, staying in their own communities, retaining their own cultures and religions and not integrating effectively. This can create social problems and difficulties with the next generation.
- Excessive migration can cause security problems, with international conspiracies leading to terrorist activity (Nichiporuk 2000).
- Although young migrants may well contribute towards GDP growth, by the time they age, they will be net claimants, especially if they are joined by older relatives.

7.1.5 OTHER DEMOGRAPHIC CHANGES

Working population

You will have seen in Chapter 3 the outline changes in the UK employment structure. Table 7.7 shows the comparative statistics for 2006 and 2015.

Table 7.7 UK labour market 2006 and 2015 (thousands)

	Male		Female		Total	
	2006	2015	2006	2015	2006	2015
Employed	12,800	13,444	12,480	13,126	25,280	26,580
Self-employed	2,780	3,096	1,020	1,424	3,800	4,510
Total labour market	15,580	16,540	13,500	14,550	29,080	31,090
Part-time	1,600	2,180	5,700	6,180	7,300	8,360
Temporary					1,500	1,660
Unemployed					1,400 (4.8%)	1,820 (5.8%)
Economically active					30,480 (79%)	33,889 (78%)
Economically inactive					8,120 (21%)	9,558 (22%)

Source: ONS (2015)

Compared with the early 1990s, there has been a growth of around 4.5 million in the total working population, made up of a natural growth in the population (including the rise in migrant workers) and an increase in the participation level. The rate of employment for women has risen much more steeply than for men, with the women's total rising by more than 2 million over the last ten years (see Chapter 3 for a discussion on *The feminisation of work*).

From 1992 to 2007, there was a steady reduction in *unemployment*, which halved over the period and led to a more confident labour market, so the number of temporary employees declined. However, the recession starting in 2008 substantially altered this picture, with a rise of 1 million in unemployed over the four-year period. By 2012, the peak had been reached and the rate fell to below 6% by 2015.

Another factor which influenced the employment statistics was the number of adults claiming incapacity benefit (a proportion of which can be regarded as hidden unemployed), which rose to 2.6 million by 2008, an increase from 800,000 in 1983. In the following four years, both the Labour Government and the Coalition Government made strenuous efforts to tackle this high number with various reforms to the benefits system and it subsequently dropped marginally to 2.5 million by 2015. Over 1.2 million of these claimants had been in receipt of the benefit for more than five years.

The number of people self-employed increased substantially in the 1980s under the Thatcher period, when entrepreneurial activity was strongly encouraged. However, it remained steady in the early 2000s but the onset of the recession had an effect of encouraging a proportion of those losing their jobs to go self-employed, so increasing their numbers to over 4.5 million by 2015, representing 14% of the workforce.

The decline in the birth rate leading to an ageing population has already affected the size and nature of the potential working population, those within the age range 16 to 60 (female) or 65 (male). Table 7.8 shows this information starkly.

Table 7.8 UK working population – age distribution 1901 to 2026 (%)

	Under 16	16–24	25–44	45–64	Over 65
Males					
1901	34	20	28	15	4
1931	26	18	29	21	7
1961	25	14	27	25	9
1991	21	14	30	22	13
2001	21	11	31	23	13
2014	19	11	27	27	16
2026*	18	10	26	26	19
Females					
1901	31	20	28	15	6
1931	23	17	30	21	8
1961	22	13	25	26	14
1991	19	12	28	21	18
2001	20	10	29	23	18
2014	18	11	25	26	20
2026*	17	10	25	26	22

*forecast
Source: ONS (2015)

Table 7.8 shows that the younger male working population aged 16–44 has fallen from 48% of the population in 1901 to 39% in 2001 and is expected to decline further to 36% by 2026, with a similar picture for women. The age in the age group 16–24 has actually halved. On the other hand, there has been a considerable growth in the older employee groups. Not all pensioners are an immediate drain on the economy as many choose to work after retirement age. There are around a million in this category, a figure that has risen by 34% over the last ten years. However, they do face a degree of discrimination, as shown in Case Study 7.4.

CASE STUDY 7.4

AGE STEREOTYPES AND DISCRIMINATORY ATTITUDES TOWARDS OLDER WORKERS: AN EAST–WEST COMPARISON

This study compared age stereotypes among 567 respondents sampled in the UK and Hong Kong, and examined how these stereotypes were related to discriminatory attitudes at work. Compared with the Hong Kong sample, UK respondents saw older workers as more effective at work, but less adaptable to change. As expected, respondents' own age was predictive of positive age stereotypes, although for supervisors this relationship was moderated in the case of perceptions of work effectiveness. Stereotypical beliefs were found to significantly affect respondents' attitudes towards the training, promotion and retention of older workers, their willingness to work with older workers and their support for positive discrimination. Findings also suggest that anti-age discrimination policies in the respondent's organisation had a positive impact on beliefs about the adaptability of older workers and possibly also on attitudes towards providing them with training. Implications of the findings were discussed in light of the existing socio-political environment in the UK and Hong Kong.

Source: Chiu et al (2001)

Given that far more young people go on to further and higher education, with the government target of 50% attending some form of higher education, this reduces the younger working population even further.

?   REFLECTIVE ACTIVITY 7.1

A development in the working population in recent years has been the growth of what is known as 'atypical employment', which is not full-time 9 to 5 employment. It covers part-time, shiftwork, teleworking and a host of variable working arrangements. What are the driving forces for this growth?

Participation rates

People used to work until they reached pensionable age (many, of course, did not last that long, worn out by heavy industrial work or poor diets). As late as 1975, 84% of men aged 60–64 were 'economically active' in the UK, but this fell to 65% by 1995. This was chiefly the result of the recession in the early 1990s, where many older men lost their jobs and found it difficult to obtain alternative employment. Many were disabled and obtained disability benefits which are higher than unemployment benefits. Organisations also encouraged older employees to take early retirement, sometimes providing generous redundancy payments or enhanced pensions.

By the early 2000s, this position was changing. Participation rates for men 50 to 64 rose from 65% to 78% from 1995 to 2014 (ONS 2015) and for those over retirement age it has risen from 7.5% in 2000 to 12% in 2015 (ONS 2015), a total close to 1.5 million, including one gallant gentleman who was over 100 in 2015. This rise has been partly to do with the prosperous economy where many part-time jobs are available, especially in the service sector, and partly to do with the decline in pension prospects arising from the two stock market crashes in 2003 and 2008, where the value of personal pensions declined by as much as 50%.

For women, there has been a substantial increase in the participation rate, rising from 63% in 1979 to 75% in 2015. Women have developed their careers, continued at work while raising a family or returned to work much more quickly than in previous decades. They have also taken up new careers and skills through obtaining qualifications, many through some form of government initiatives. Other support has come through the strengthening of equal opportunity legislation, where the barriers to women's employment and development have been steadily removed.

The economically inactive can be regarded as a 'reserve army' that can be drawn on during periods of tight labour markets (Smallwood 2006). He explains that:

> There are huge economic benefits associated with a growing workforce, mirrored by the severe problems that arise when a country's population starts to decline. After all, gross domestic product growth over the longer term is the sum of the growth in the employed workforce and the rise in productivity of that workforce, so the faster the working population goes up, the faster the economy grows. Over the past decade, the growth in the working population has added well in excess of £50bn to GDP, and swelled the treasury's coffers by nearly half that. (Smallwood 2006, p6)

? REFLECTIVE ACTIVITY 7.2

Two organisations have just set up in an area of high unemployment and low participation, with the support of various government grants and loans. They are as follows:

Jones Supermarkets have set up a regional distribution centre to employ 450 staff in warehousing and logistics positions on 24/7 operations.

Williams Toys and Games have established a manufacturing and distribution centre to employ 200 staff. There is a seasonal element to the work so a number of staff will be working flexibly, including evening shifts and weekends for the busy autumn period. Most of the toys and games are imported finished or semi-finished, so the work is essentially unskilled and semi-skilled and involves a high element of packing and distribution.

Question

Given that setting up in the area will help reduce the unemployment rate, are there ways in which the organisations can help further improve the participation rate?

Sectoral employment

The number of people working in *manufacturing* has been declining since the 1950s, when it stood at over 6 million. Since 1993, however, there has been a particularly steep drop as work has migrated to the developing and emerging nations, especially China and India, so less than 3 million worked in manufacturing in the UK in 2015.

Table 7.9 Sectoral employment 2005 and 2015 (thousands)

Selected sectors	2015	2005
Manufacturing	2,634	3091
Construction	2,106	2220
Service sector total	28,143	25,410
Of which:		
Wholesale, retail	4,925	5,036
Financial services, information and communication	2,488	2,347
Hotels, catering	2,269	1,966
Education	2,935	2,566
Health	4,237	3,584
Public admin and defence	1,497	1,790

Source: ONS (2015)

Table 7.9 shows a number of trends: first, a reflection in the changing pattern of consumer demand, where we spend much more money on consumer and leisure activities – holidays, eating out, shopping and at the hairdressers. (In fact, the highest rate of growth of any individual job from 1990 to 2005 was hairdressing.) Second, there was increased expenditure by the Labour Government on health and education, as promised in their election manifestos, which has led to an increase in jobs in both sectors. Despite the recession and the change of government, there has been a continuing inexorable climb in the numbers employed in these two sectors.

There has been an increase in administration and IT jobs but a surprising small decline in wholesale and retail numbers, reflecting the degree of automation in this area in recent years.

Although numbers in the public sector grew during the Labour Government, the Coalition Government reduced public sector employment with the policy of encouraging private enterprise to replace numbers employed, a policy which had a modicum of success.

The manufacturing sector has continued to decline, if at a slower rate. It should be remembered that there was a labour force of over 7 million in 1980 in this sector. This is a Europe-wide trend, with the exception of Germany. France has a similar proportion of workers in manufacturing, with Spain's proportion only slightly larger.

?   REFLECTIVE ACTIVITY 7.3

Consider the scenario where the main manufacturing employer in a country town, employing 1,500 staff, announces it is closing down.

Questions

1   What are the implications for the local economy?

2   What are the overall implications for the UK of the decline in manufacturing employment?

Changes in geographical population location

A final aspect of demography is the internal movement of population within countries. For over 200 years there has been a steady movement away from the land and into the cities around the world as agriculture has become mechanised and farms consolidated. In the last hundred years or so, this movement has extended in certain countries to widespread geographical patterns. In Italy, it has been a mass movement from the poor, rural south to the more prosperous urban north. In the UK, the movement is in the opposite direction with a general move from the industrial areas, especially in the north, to the more balanced economies of the south and east.

The population of the north-eastern counties of England actually dropped in the 1990s and population increases in Yorkshire and Lancashire were quite small. On the other hand, counties in the south-east, such as Cambridgeshire, increased by 10% or more as an estimated 250,000 citizens moved from north to south (Brindle 1999).

7.2 TRENDS TO WATCH – AND THE FUTURE?

Until quite recent times, it was considered that if the world's population continued to increase at its current rate, such a growth would be completely unsustainable. Food and energy would run out, leading to the Malthusian nightmares of war, pestilence and disease, causing a decline in population to sustainable levels. Currently (late 2015), despite the continuing growth of world population, the prices of most food and raw materials have shown a substantial decline. Food has declined by 10% and metals by 15%. The world oil price has plunged by almost 50% from over $100 a barrel to less than $50. This has not been accompanied by poverty and starvation – quite the contrary as one measure has shown the proportion of world population in extreme poverty has fallen from 30% in 2000 to 10% in 2015 (Roser 2015). This would indicate that improved productivity in food cultivation and mineral/oil extraction has exceeded the increased demand from a growing population, which is very good news for the world's population.

Uncertainty prevails, however, as to whether these deflationary pressures are temporary or long-term. This is matched by the uncertainties over the future direction of world population growth. Economists have been divided as to the scenario at 2050, with some estimates of population at 10 billion and still growing and others indicating a more conservative outcome. Much depends on the movement of the fertility rate and whether the reduction occurring as society gets more prosperous is countered by cultural and religious tendencies towards retaining large families.

There is also a question mark over increasing life expectancy. It is still likely that we can all expect to live a little longer every decade, but AIDS is continuing to have a serious effect in sub-Saharan Africa and is spreading its tentacles into other areas, with some rapid growth in HIV in Eastern Europe, South America and the Far East. So the increase in life expectancy, although having in itself important consequences, may only marginally influence the long-term population, unless AIDS treatment improves substantially.

In the UK, the stabilisation of the fertility rate at around 1.9 will inevitably bring to an end the natural population growth, probably around 2035 or 2040, where it will peak at around 70 million, depending on migration assumptions, according to latest predictions. However, the Government Actuary's Department has reported that life expectancy is growing faster than previous predictions and should rise to 81 for men and 85 for women by 2030 (ONS 2015). If this occurs, the population will continue to grow for a little longer, although the average age of the population will rise.

However, there is no doubt that *the population will become older*. In 2030, 15 million will be over current pensionable age, compared with 11 million now. In 2007, the number of pensioners overtook the number of children. The average age is set to rise from 38.8 in 2000 to 42.6 in 2025.

To summarise, over the next 20 years, the world population will continue to grow rapidly, but this growth will then start to taper off. Populations in developed countries will become distinctly older and internationally diverse. An ageing world may bring a severe reduction in labour forces and greater pressure on the productive young. However, the number of older workers who will be in much greater health will increase substantially. Populations in developing countries will also age but from a very low base figure and will become internationally mobile.

7.3 IMPLICATIONS OF DEMOGRAPHIC PREDICTIONS

As indicated at the start of this chapter, demographic trends will have substantial implications across the world at local, national and international levels. We will examine these implications in outline for the following groups:

- implications for organisations, especially in the UK private sector
- implications for governments, especially the UK Government
- implications for international society.

7.3.1 IMPLICATIONS FOR ORGANISATIONS

A slowdown in population growth and an ageing population has effects both on the nature of the marketplace and on the sources of labour. The CIPD (2015a) have pointed out that 9.2 million over-50s will leave the workforce in the next 20 years, including 1.2 million in education alone and social work and caring professions will lose a high proportion of their labour force. Adaptations to their current business practices could take the following forms:

Sources of labour – with far fewer school-leavers and younger people generally, organisations will have to look elsewhere for labour, particularly if the economy reverts to growing steadily under the full employment conditions seen in the 16 years up to 2008. Alternative sources can involve moving away from the traditional full-time 9 to 5 job design and moving to a more flexible model where much greater use is made of part-time jobs, job-shares, flexible hours and working from home. These flexible modes can meet the working needs of those with caring responsibilities, principally (but not exclusively) women, and older people generally who are retired or semi-retired. Some retailers, such as B&Q and Tesco, have specifically targeted older potential staff, which has led not just to an easing of recruitment difficulties but to considerable customer satisfaction arising from the knowledge such staff bring to the job. As a spokesperson for Nationwide Building Society explained:

> Many customers prefer dealing with more maturity and experience and older workers tend to be more loyal and committed. (*Economist* 2004b)

Retailer ASDA offers a variety of flexible working practices, including 'Benidorm leave', where employees can take up to three months' unpaid leave in the winter to take an extended holiday. They also offer grandparents' leave and carers' leave together with a seasonal colleague's scheme which attracts older people to work ten weeks a year at the peak times. Store managers are encouraged to visit older people's clubs and these policies have resulted in the number of over-65 employees rising to 3,500 in 2006 (CIPD 2007).

Bridgend County Borough Council adopted, in the early 2000s, a number of policies centred on 'Age Positive' to combat a tight labour market and changing demography. These included allowing employees who work beyond retiring age to contribute to their pension, introducing a mentoring scheme that involves those coming up to retirement coaching younger employees in valuable skills and ignoring an employee's age when considering training and development opportunities (Persaud 2004). Wetherspoons have targeted mid-day working for older people looking for a few hours per week to match their busy periods which has partly contributed to the company having a turnover rate which is half of their competitors (DWP 2012).

A further example of a progressive approach to the employment of older employees is shown in Case Study 7.5.

CASE STUDY 7.5

ALLEVARD SPRINGS'S APPROACH TO EMPLOYING OLDER WORKERS

Allevard Springs specialises in the design and manufacture of coil suspension precision springs for the automotive industry. At its factory in the Rhondda Valley, Glamorgan, staff turnover is very low, with 83% of employees having worked in the plant for over five years.

Recruiting the right staff

The company has a positive view about employing older workers; there is no reference to age on application forms and recruitment decisions are based on a person's ability to carry out the job or task allocated to them and not on the basis of age.

Despite a high level of unemployment in the area, Perry Stephens, management services manager, says that:

There is a shortage of skilled maintenance people, which older people play an important part in filling. For example, the company currently has five 'super skilled' engineering technicians and two of them are over 60 and one is over 50 years of age.

The company's view is that employers can benefit enormously from having older people in their workforce, bringing with them skills learned during their working life coupled with a willingness to continue to learn. Perry continues: 'If somebody is capable of doing whatever job function is required, then age doesn't come into it.'

Keeping good staff

Perry says that although he is aware of the misconception that older people may take more time off work because of illness, this hasn't been his experience:

'I find that it's the exact opposite. There's quite a number of older people who haven't missed any time whatsoever, such as Paul, who's had one day off in over 20 years.'

Perry also finds that older employees are just as happy as their other employees to work the usual shift patterns; 'We've got quite a few people in their late fifties still doing the regular shifts: 6.00–2.00; 2.00–10.00; 10.00–6.00.'

Each individual's training and development needs are informed by annual staff appraisals. Again, age is irrelevant in this process, as is seniority. All staff, whether on the shop floor or in senior management, receive their appraisal.

Flexible retirement

The company's retirement age is 65 but it is happy for employees to work beyond that. Jane is one employee who is interested in this possibility, after joining the organisation at the age of 60.

Jane was recruited on a temporary basis to help the purchase ledger clerk when the factory's accounts department found itself shorthanded. She had lots of previous experience and was able to use all of the necessary software programs. When the accountant became aware of how skilled she was, she was asked to help with some other work.

Jane soon became a permanent employee and enjoys her role: 'Work keeps you active and keeps your mind alive, especially when you're learning new things. It also gives you a routine and you make friends too. It makes no difference whether you're young or older – working is a benefit to everybody.'

Other staff have retired and decided to return to the organisation – one for a further 15 months and another who is still enjoying work and plans to continue.

The business benefits for Allevard Springs of an age-diverse workforce include:

- low staff turnover – 83% of employees have worked in the plant for over five years
- recruiting from wider talent pool and retaining experience helps to fill skills shortages
- wide age spectrum makes for a relaxed, friendly culture.

Source: DWP (2011)

The CIPD (2015a) have suggested that equipping line managers with an understanding of older employees' needs and ensuring the over-50s are not forgotten in development plans would also enhance retention of staff.

It is unlikely that the offers of early retirement with enhanced pensions will be generous in the future. The UK Government has already moved away from funding such arrangements centrally, requiring each department or agency to bear the costs involved. This has already led to a substantial reduction in such offers and employees choosing early retirements currently have to fund this out of their own pension schemes, in most cases.

Given these factors, it is not surprising that a greater proportion of those over retirement age choose to continue to work, enhancing the participation rates of pensioners as detailed earlier. However, as in the example of Japanese older workers in Case Study 7.1, there is the danger of 'Balkanisation' of labour markets, where employees at both ends of the demographic market have poor job security, menial work and low pay (Roberts 2006).

Change in markets – as the patterns of population change, their consumer needs alter accordingly. With an ageing population, there will be a *decline* in demand for products for the young, such as baby foods and prams and, eventually, to products for teenagers and the age group 18–25. The brewing industry has seen a substantial decline in the demand for beer as the largest consumers have traditionally been those aged 18–25, a declining age group, although their drinking habits have also changed. Similarly, sales of teenage fashion goods – clothes, CDs, jewellery – have become sluggish in recent years. Although the per capita spending has increased as the general level of prosperity has risen, it does not make up for the reduced population in those age brackets.

On the other side, there are some sectors of industries which *gain* from an ageing population. The most dramatic is the travel and tourism industry as older people spend a higher proportion of their income on holidays than most other groups. For a number of cyclical reasons, they also have become a much wealthier segment of the community. Saga, floated on the stock market for close to £1bn in 2004, is a clear winner, providing a vast range of holidays – active and inactive – to a growing market, broadening their product range to insurance and other financial services. The cruise industry has also grown substantially.

On the financial front, it has been estimated that, worldwide, people over the age of 55 hold around 70% of the planet's wealth and there is a huge market here for service providers involved in investments, pensions and general financial security (Dyson 2013), as shown in Case Study 7.6.

CASE STUDY 7.6

WEALTH ADVICE FOR THE ELDERLY IN THE US

Examples of some of the services provided especially for older US citizens include:

- **Reverse mortgages** – in 2006, 76,000 US citizens took out mortgages where they receive a lump sum or a line of credit and do not pay any interest while the mortgage is running. All the fees and accumulated interest are paid off when the house is sold, usually (but not always) when the mortgagee dies. Currently, the federal government guarantees such mortgages, so that if a homeowner's debts are greater than the value of his home at the time of death, the estate will not have to make up the shortfall. This partly explains why the number of reverse mortgages taken out increased by 77% over the total for 2005. However, fees can be very high for this financial instrument (as much as 10%) and the mortgagees' heirs are not always happy by the way that the inheritance is eroded by high fees and interest payments.
- **Elder services group** – a product marketed by Wells Fargo and other providers to the banks' ageing and generally prosperous clientele, the bank will handle investments, pay regular bills, process insurance claims, arrange and monitor healthcare (including the high costs associated with surgery and treatment in the US)

and provide regular reports on the client's financial situation. Some go further and give advice on funeral arrangements, nursing homes, organise taxi contracts when eyesight fails and even deal with regular logistics for pills and other pharmaceutical products.
- **Wealth management** – an increasing number of providers are entering the market to handle investments for the elderly. Citigroup, for example, have built 17 regional 'planning centres' for its wealthy customers – mainly baby boomers on the edge of retirement with more than $5m in assets to invest. They bring together tax and trust lawyers, specialists in insurance, philanthropy and experts in small business sales so all the options are covered. Wachovia have developed a financial programme that allows them to focus on customers with a minimum of $250,000.

Due to the complexity of this financial area and the declining faculties of some of the clients, the providers are increasingly attempting to avoid the 'hard-selling' approach. A number, including HSBC bank, are using older or even semi-retired employees to carry out the sales negotiations so, hopefully, the claims for mis-selling are reduced.

Source: *Economist* (2007b)

? REFLECTIVE ACTIVITY 7.4

Summarise the effects of an ageing population on the tourism, retailing and banking industries.

Housing presents an interesting reflection of demographic changes. Although the population is now growing only slowly, the price of houses has risen substantially due, mostly, to a somewhat unexpected higher demand. This has come about because, as the fertility rate drops and the population ages, there is no corresponding drop in the number of households. Whereas young children live with their parents, older people live mostly in their own housing unit. Many stay in their own homes looking after themselves to the end, or nearly to the end, of their lives, assisted by a benefits system that encourages such behaviour. Add to this the increase in divorce, which often creates additional demand for housing, and the rise in students living away from home, perhaps the rise in house prices is not so unexpected. A winner here has been the construction companies that provide retirement homes in the UK, such as McCarthy and Stone.

Other clear winners in the demographic stakes are those who market *products specifically for the elderly*. There will be growing markets for mobility products and those aimed at improving healthcare, from pharmaceutical products to private hospitals. These include:

- 'Nutraceuticals', including vitamins, nutrients, minerals and herbal extracts, a market estimated to be worth $8bn in the USA alone. Nutritional scientists are working on a new array of food products that are scientifically designed to improve your health and longevity and which will have specific appeal to the middle-aged and elderly.
- There are more than 100 US bio-tech companies actively researching age-related disorders (Wallace 2001), such as the role of telomeres in cell ageing, which may keep skin young and elastic, and tissue engineering, which may offer the prospect of replacement parts for the body.
- Stannah lifts has become another household name, while magazines devoted to older readers (such as *Yours*) have substantially increased their circulations.

The same reasoning can be applied to the next age group down, call it 'middle-aged', where their demands for financial services (savings products, pensions) and some luxury products (Mercedes cars, boats and homes in the sun) have grown very strongly in recent years. Sales of prestige cars have held up surprisingly well in the UK since the recession started in 2008.

7.3.2 IMPLICATIONS FOR GOVERNMENTS, ESPECIALLY THE UK GOVERNMENT

For governments, the biggest potential difficulty arising from the ageing population is the increase in the *dependency ratio*. The dependency ratio calculation is the ratio of working-age population to the dependent population. The dependent population are children under 16 and older people over retirement age.

As the proportion of the population over retirement age increases, it puts a much greater strain on the working population, who need to fund the services for older people. As detailed above, there has been much greater reliance on the state for looking after older people. There is no doubt this strain will be with us soon, as shown in Figure 7.1.

Figure 7.1 shows the startling change in dependency that has occurred already and will get worse in the future. Currently just over four employees provide earned income to support one pensioner. This will decline to just over three by 2026, and to 2.8 by 2035. The position is worse for other countries. For Germany, the ratio will be less than three by the same year and it will reduce to around two by 2040. By 2050, the Japanese ratio will have deteriorated to an astonishing 1.3. with Italy and Spain close behind. For the world as a whole, the current figure of nine is likely to reduce to four by 2050 (*Economist* 2009a).

Figure 7.1 UK dependency ratio – ratio of 16–64-year-olds to over-65s

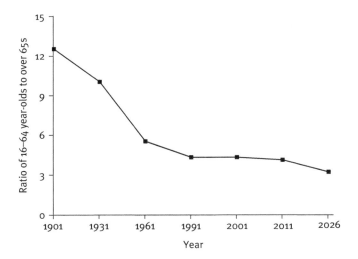

The problem for governments is how to raise the increased revenue required from what could be a dwindling source of working population. It has been estimated that, in the UK, each pensioner costs the Government around £10,000 per year, net of any tax receipts, through the old age pension, a variety of benefits (housing, disability, etc.) and the vast range of medical care (primary care, free prescriptions, hospital stays). Older people are much more prone to illness and therefore impose much greater costs on the health services. Sixty-five per cent of Department for Work and Pensions benefit expenditure goes to those over working age, equivalent to £100bn in 2010–11, or one-seventh of public expenditure. Continuing to provide state benefits and pensions at today's average would mean additional spending of £10bn a year for every additional 1 million people over working age (Parliamentary Business 2010).

It could be argued that some of the additional money required can be raised by savings on services to young people with reduced expenditure on maternity units and compulsory schooling, although any closure or reduction in services is met by solid resistance from the community. Because employees in their forties and fifties earn more than employees in their twenties, it is expected that increased tax revenue will go some way towards filling this gap. However, the problem with this argument is that the higher taxes to be extracted (or higher voluntary savings) by the young/middle-aged will reduce their purchasing power and thereby reduce GDP. This may produce an era of 'secular stagnation' (Summers 2014).

The problem is acute in the fire service and the police force. Their pension fund allows retirement after 30 years' service on two-thirds of annual salary and many others retire early on health grounds. This has produced the situation where Merseyside Fire and Rescue Service has 1,678 working staff but is paying the pensions of 1,691 retired staff, and a similar situation exists in police forces in Lincolnshire, Northern Ireland and the City of London, among others. Efforts have been made to reduce the huge costs involved and police and fire crews who have joined the service since 2006 will have to work for 35 years (Watts 2008).

The *pension implications* are tough for the UK and America, but at least there is reasonable private pension provision that is located in properly funded systems. This, however, is the exception compared with the rest of the world. For most of Europe and other developed countries, the proportion of pensions paid by the state is very much higher and this is funded as transfer payments under a pay as you go (PAYG) basis, that is, directly out of taxation income, rather than from an actual fund of money that has been invested. A major cause of the Greek Government's ongoing financial crisis from 2010 is the overgenerous, unfunded state pensions which the government is having to painfully address. As, incidentally, is Illinois state in America which has ignored US government funding standards over a number a years so the unfunded pension liability rose to over $100bn by 2014. The state is now known as 'America's Greece (Economist 2014b) and is facing equally painful options, one being state bankruptcy.

Table 7.10 shows the implications for selected countries in terms of the huge government expenditure necessary to pay the pensions as a proportion of their GDP (gross domestic product).

Table 7.10 Public pension expenditure as a percentage of GDP

	1995	2020*	2040*
UK	4.5	5.2	7.1
USA	4.1	5.2	7.2
The Netherlands	6.0	8.4	12.1
France	10.6	11.6	14.3
Sweden	11.8	13.9	14.9
Spain	10.0	11.3	16.8
Germany	11.1	12.3	18.4
Italy	13.3	15.3	21.4

* estimate
Source: ECOFIN (2006)

There are already substantial problems in France, Spain and Italy over the high levels of public sector borrowing. The European Union has attempted with little success to fine these countries as part of the Stability Pact arrangements made at the time of the establishment of the euro to prevent governments incurring excessive expenditure to buy themselves out of financial difficulties. Many commercial organisations are moving production out of these countries to the UK, Eastern Europe and the developing world to avoid existing high taxation rates. So how such pension liabilities can be met is sorely testing the economic advisors and central banks in these countries. This problem has been exacerbated by the greatly increased level of government debt incurred to bail the banks out of the financial crisis which began in 2007 and the resultant recession.

? REFLECTIVE ACTIVITY 7.5

Not all writers regard the pension liabilities as insurmountable or see the necessity of huge increases in taxation or reductions in benefit to solve the pensions problem. What do you consider to be the basis for their optimism?

A further problem arises from *irregular internal migration*. Those parts of the country that attract population are faced by considerable pressures on housing, transport and infrastructure services. For example, the housing shortages in London and the south-east of England have produced continuous shortages in essential public services, especially teachers and nurses, who cannot find affordable housing, especially in their early careers. Similar problems occur in the Milan and Turin areas of northern Italy. The governments are faced with planning dilemmas. If they allow housing on green belt land in and around London, it arouses massive opposition. If new roads are built to alleviate congestion, the traffic merely increases within a short time to clog up the system.

In some parts of the world, all of these difficulties gel into a bleak prognosis. In California, for example, the State Department of Finance has forecast a 75% increase in population to 60 million by 2050, making it a 'country masquerading as a state' (Kyser 2007). This will lead to a water and power catastrophe, decaying infrastructure, education funding gaps and huge state debt.

Finally, there are problems associated with the *skills base*. Little has changed since Jackson (1998) explained that:

> One reason why the market has been unable to absorb the... unemployed has been the increasing demand for employees with appropriate skills and capabilities. Gaining entry to the labour market has become more difficult as manual occupations have declined and as employers have become more selective about recruits to jobs in the service and quaternary sectors. Britain needs a better trained workforce if it is to meet the challenge from its competitors in Europe and overseas and the current skills gap means that many find themselves excluded from the opportunities of employment. (p125)

Options for governments

The only two ways that governments can approach a solution to the financial problems brought on by longevity and the ageing population is to either raise taxes or reduce benefits. Some countries have already taken bold steps, such as New Zealand abolishing the universal right to an old age pension and the UK Government is raising the age when women can claim the pension to 65 in the period 2010–20, and the state pension to 67 for both men and women by 2028. It was originally planned for this to occur in 2046, but the clear financial requirement caused the Coalition Government to rapidly bring this forward and thereby save £60bn. Auto-enrolment into pension schemes (where employees have to optout if they do not want to join) has been found to boost saving by 40% (Ellis, Munnell and Eschtruth 2014).

Other suggested benefit reductions are means-testing fuel allowances and reducing the age allowance in income tax. However, bold steps in reducing benefits can be very damaging politically and are not taken lightly. Certainly people can be encouraged to increase their savings for the future by making a larger contribution to their pension schemes, which is done by most governments. In Japan, this has been very successful and the Japanese are the highest savers in the world. (Incidentally, this high saving and reduced consumption has contributed towards a prolonged recession in Japan through most of the 1990s and 2000s.)

Some commentators believe it is likely that when the full effects of the higher dependency ratio reach the population as a whole, society will be much more affluent and willing to pay the additional costs as part of the understanding that a measure of the decency of a society is how they look after vulnerable groups, such as the elderly. This will have the effect of placing a greater emphasis on community care for the elderly (Bartlett and Peel 2005).

An alternative approach is to attempt to reverse the demographic trends and to encourage bigger families. This can be done by providing greater financial incentives (tax reliefs and maternity/child benefits) and by encouraging organisations to be more family-friendly so that women are able to combine motherhood and a job more easily. The Chinese Government is moving away from the 'One Child Policy' instituted in 1979, as shown in Case Study 7.7.

CASE STUDY 7.7

CHINA AND THE ONE CHILD POLICY

By 2050, China will have more than 438 million people over 60, with 100 million aged over 80. There will be just 1.6 working-age adults to support every person over 60, compared with 7.7 in 1975. One of the unexpected outcomes of the One Child Policy has been to encourage Chinese families to be great savers. This is because the One Child Policy created a surplus of men and has driven up the cost of marriage, as more men compete with fewer women. To keep up, families with sons have been holding off spending to create wealth that boosts their sons' marriage prospects. Economists have concluded that Chinese marriage-price inflation could account for as much as half of the increase in the country's household saving since 1990. It is estimated that the policy has prevented as many as 400 million births.

The spectre of an ageing population hangs heavy over Shanghai, where the proportion of working adults to retirees is low and threatens a major burden. Family planning authorities in the city are proactive in encouraging families with one child to have a second through extensive publicity and home visits, although financial incentives have not yet been introduced.

In 2013, the Chinese National Bureau of Statistics announced that the working-age population had shrunk by 3.45 million, chiefly as a result of the One Child Policy. The Chinese government announced in October 2015 that the policy will be loosened, or even abandoned but, despite this, the growing affluence and increased education is likely to balance the loosening effect and keep the fertility rate around 1.6. However, there are increasing signs that the reduction in the labour force is causing wages to rise and many goods to be less competitive, especially when compared with poorer Eastern economies, such as Vietnam. Academics argue whether the seemingly unending migration from the land to the cities is coming to a halt and that only further wage increases will encourage the flow to continue.

Sources: Coonan (2009); Dubner and Levitt (2009); *Economist* (2013b)

The problem is that such actions by governments, such as shown by Japan in Case Study 7.1, appear to have only a marginal effect on the indigenous population. Actions in similar forms by many governments in developed countries have done little to reverse the flagging fertility rate, with the exception of the UK and USA.

A drastic action could be to open the doors wider to migrants from developing countries. This makes a great deal of long-term economic sense but has a number of political obstacles to overcome in terms of the perceptions of migrants 'taking jobs' and the additional pressures on housing and transport.

One response to the overcrowding in some parts of a country has been to attempt to disperse government departments (as long ago as the early 1970s, the Department of National Savings was moved to Durham, for example) and to provide additional tax and benefit incentives to businesses to move to poorer regions, which is a major pillar in the European Union's economic policy.

The most drastic governmental action seen so far has been in Ulyanovsk, in Russia, where September 12 has been declared 'Conception Day' and couples that conceive under their 'Give Birth to a Patriot' programme can win cars, fridges or cash prizes (*Sunday Times* 2007).

Not everybody, however, insists that an ageing population is so great a problem. Mullan (2002) argues that demographic ageing has no determinate relationship to national economic activity and that modest levels of economic growth will be more than sufficient to create the wealth required to sustain the costs brought on by greater numbers of elderly dependants.

7.3.3 IMPLICATIONS FOR INTERNATIONAL SOCIETY

The global economy

The most worrying aspect of the current demographic changes is that the mature and ageing population appears to lead directly to reduced economic growth. Europe and Japan have seen the fastest decline in fertility rates and have also seen the slowest economic growth in the early twenty-first century. America, on the other hand, has had a milder decline and has managed to maintain a faster growth rate over the period. In the 'Tiger' economies – China, Korea, Taiwan – and on the Indian subcontinent, where fertility rates, although falling, still remain at or above replacement level, there is a much higher rate of economic growth.

The United Nations has projected that America, with its higher fertility rate and greater migration, will catch up Europe's population by 2040 (currently it is 100 million less) and exceed it by 40 million by 2050. The economic implications are far-reaching. The working population of Europe will start to decline in 2010 but, for America, the current steady growth in its workforce will even start to accelerate in 2025. This will result in the US economy growing twice as fast as that of Europe for the next 50 years. In 2000, America accounted for 23% of global gross domestic product (GDP) compared with Europe's 18%. By 2050, the United Nations estimates America's share will be 26% while Europe's will have shrunk to only 10%. By 2050, the American economy will be two and a half times as big as Europe's with all the additional political clout that this implies (United Nations 2015).

In reality, the only way this situation could be reversed would be by radically changing Europe's tight immigration controls, which is a very unlikely event, or if America's fertility rate dropped sharply, as it becomes a mature economy.

International migration of work

In the early 2000s, Barclays Bank and other financial institutions announced that they would be cutting their workforces and transferring chunks of their customer service and 'back-office' administration work to other countries, particularly India. The cost of carrying out this work in developing countries is just a fraction compared with UK costs and the workforces are young, educated, English-speaking and flexible in their approach to working hours and the nature of work. These decisions were made because the demographic changes, and the responses made by governments (India has invested heavily in English-speaking education), have made such countries good substitutes for UK labour.

This situation has been replicated around the globe. In America, work migration is an important political issue dividing the parties, while German unions had to respond in the early 2000s to threats to move industrial work in companies such as Volkswagen to Eastern Europe by agreeing to reduce hourly wages (see Case Study 7.8).

EXAMPLES OF GERMAN JOBS EXODUS

Lufthansa: European ticket sales based in Krakau, Poland. Aircraft engines serviced in Hungary, China and the Philippines.

Motorola: 600 engineering jobs moved to China. Repair work moved to Eastern Europe.

Deutsche Bank: Deutsche Software subsidiary moved to India with 4,000 jobs.

SAP, business software and systems: created 1,500 jobs in Bangalore, India and new 120-strong R&D centre in Shanghai.

Continental Tyres: three German factories closed – work transferred to three new factories in Romania, the Czech Republic and Slovakia.

The effect of transferring jobs can be dramatic on individual towns. In Wittenberge, in the former East Germany, the population has fallen by 50% as manufacturing jobs migrated after unification and other work failed to materialise, despite incentives. Around the area in abandoned sites, wolves and lynxes have returned for the first time in 100 years.

Source: Woodhead (2004); Pancevski (2013)

? REFLECTIVE ACTIVITY 7.6

In 2003, the South African Government placed a prohibition on UK companies recruiting qualified nurses to work in the NHS, viewing the exodus of skilled workers such as nurses as a matter of long-term disaster for the country. Do you agree with this viewpoint? Discuss the issue from both viewpoints.

World's resources

In the twentieth century, the inventiveness, organisational powers and application of technology from farmers, merchants, entrepreneurs and companies of all sizes allowed the tripling world population to be adequately provided for in terms of food, water and power. Not completely, of course, with intermittent famines and a growing imbalance between rich and poor countries. However, it had been considered unlikely that such expansion of resources could continue at this breakneck pace for another 100 years. The availability of additional water resources in the current developing countries is likely to be the stumbling block to the easy accommodation of an additional 4 billion people who required a high lifestyle.

The forecasts of a levelling-out of the population by mid-century could be regarded, therefore, as good news for everybody. The strains on space and exploitation of a limited land mass, especially where global warming appears to be reducing capacity, may now be much lessened, although these pressures are brought about not just by numbers of population but by their overall demands. A richer, more consuming population still has the capacity to wreak enormous damage on our planet's infrastructure.

7.4 SOCIAL TRENDS

7.4.1 INTRODUCTION

This section analyses recent trends in society and social/family structure in the UK. It considers social mobility and inequality, and the continuing existence of poverty in the

UK. This is followed by an examination of diversity in the UK, its desirability, associated difficulties and implications for management.

One of the key drivers of a democratic society is its emphasis on fairness. This applies not only in the political sense with universal franchise or in the legal sense with the application of the rule of law applying to everybody. It applies also to the equality of opportunity and a fair spread of wealth and income. These can be measured through social mobility and income and wealth measures, including the Gini coefficient.

7.4.2 SOCIAL MOBILITY

Social mobility can be thought of in absolute and relative terms. The former refers to processes of adjustment in the income or occupational structure of the economy, indicating the number or proportion that move from one social class to another. The latter, sometimes called social fluidity, is associated with an individual's *opportunities* for progression within the social hierarchy. Social mobility can also be thought of as intra-generational (chances for social progression within an individual's own lifetime) and inter-generational (a comparison of achieved social position with that of one's parents) (Nunn et al 2007).

Other dimensions are the absence of poverty and access to decent standards of health and education. Quality of life varies with social class, ethnic group, gender and locality (Aldridge 2004).

Until the Second World War, there was considerable absolute social mobility in Britain, but downward mobility was nearly as common as upward. Since the Second World War, upward absolute social mobility has considerably outweighed downward, with the trend increasing – it is much higher for men born in 1950–59 (the latest available figures) than for men born in 1920–29 (the first group to have reached maturity after the Second World War). The main reason for this upward mobility is that there is 'more room at the top'. In 1900, the middle class made up 18% of the population, while the working class made up 62%. By 2010, the middle class was 46% of the population and the working class 36%.

The main interest in research in this area is that social mobility is generally associated with higher economic growth. So a country that successfully promotes social mobility is more likely to increase the general standard of living and opportunities for prosperity for all of its population (Nunn et al 2007).

While the picture on absolute social mobility looks positive, the picture is very different when one looks at relative mobility. Because the middle class is bigger, this means that children of middle-class parents have less risk of falling down into the working class, that is, downward social mobility has fallen. The result has been that the chances of a working-class child making it to the middle class have changed little – it is estimated that a working-class child is 15 times less likely to make it into the middle class than a middle-class child is to stay in the middle class.

Most worryingly, there is some evidence that social mobility, however it is measured, is slowing down. This is best shown by figures on income. Studies have been made of the correlation between fathers' earnings and offspring's earnings. A correlation of zero would imply complete income mobility between generations, that is, that a father's income has no influence on his offspring's income, while a correlation of one would imply total immobility, that is, that an offspring's place in the income scale is exactly the same as his or her father's. For the UK correlations have been found of between 0.4 and 0.6 for sons' earnings, and between 0.45 and 0.7 for daughters. The higher the correlation, the less the income mobility and, by implication, the lower the level of social mobility.

Closer examination of the correlations shows two disturbing trends:

- Correlations are much higher in the UK than in countries such as Canada, Sweden or Finland.

● A comparison of those born in 1958 with those born in 1970 shows the correlations increasing – that is, social mobility in the UK is falling.

One study compared two sons both born in 1958 who left school in the 1970s. The parents of one earned twice as much as the parents of the other. By their early thirties, the son of the richer parents earned 17.5% more than the poorer son. For two comparable boys born in 1970 who left school in the 1980s, the income gap had widened to 25% (Blanden et al 2005).

In 2007, the educational charity the Sutton Trust researched the educational backgrounds of 500 leading figures in the law, politics, medicine, journalism and business. They found that over half had been educated in an independent school, although these only educate 7% of the population, and that this figure had barely changed over the past 20 years. In addition, 47% of the top 500 were Oxbridge educated (Sutton Trust 2007). A linked research report in 2010 found that social mobility had declined further, as shown in Case Study 7.9.

CASE STUDY 7.9

SOCIAL MOBILITY IN THE PROFESSIONS

This research report investigated the origins of those individuals entering into the top professions in the two British birth cohort studies. Sampling took place from two groups of 18,000 born in 1958 and 1970, identifying those who were working in the professions at age 33 and identifying their parents' income at birth.

Comparing the average family incomes in childhood of those working in the top professions indicates that those who go into professions come from families with incomes higher than average. More worryingly, this trend appears to have worsened for many of the professions considered for those born in 1970 compared with those born in 1958, with the gaps in family income between the top professions and the sample average increasing over time.

For example, those born in 1958 who went on to become doctors came from families with an income of 42% greater than average, but this had increased to 63% for those born in 1970. For accountants, the trend was even greater, with a figure rising from 1% to 40% between the two cohorts, while the figures for journalists/broadcasters rose from 5% to 42%. The only professions where this trend did not apply were teachers, academics and musicians.

The report investigated whether the ability (as measured by IQ) of those entering professions had risen over the period but found no significant difference.

Source: Macmillan (2010)

Since 2010, reports have indicated a more mixed picture. Bukodi et al (2014) have found that around 75% of individuals in their study born between 1946 and 1984 finished up in a different class compared to their fathers which indicated that social mobility was not in decline. However, the decline in opportunities in professional work and the competition for jobs has meant that many individuals from a middle-class background have found it difficult to maintain this status so the mobility is downward.

The factors that influence social mobility have been set out by Nunn et al (2007):

● *Social capital* – there is some evidence that traditional working-class social capital has declined, which may have weakened its assumed negative effects on social mobility, while other 'negative' forms of social capital have emerged, such as cultures of worklessness, anti-social behaviour and drug abuse. A lack of positive role models, peer pressure, poverty of ambition and risk aversion may serve as barriers to social mobility. By contrast, middle-class families tend to have access to a wider range of social networks that are more advantageous from the point of view of enabling upward mobility and protecting against downward mobility.

- *Cultural capital* – can also help middle-class families to confer social advantages on their children, increasing their potential to move upwards and protecting them from downward movement in the social hierarchy. A child with a professional father is still 20 times more likely to end up in a similarly privileged job than a child from than those born with a working-class father (Bukodi et al 2014).
- *Early years influences* – are seen as key to influencing later life chances. Convincing evidence shows that early experiences such as the quality of the home environment, family structure, pre-school care and relationships with caring adults produce a pattern of development in later life that is hard to reverse, even through schooling.
- *Education* – appears to be one of the most important factors influencing social mobility. However, there is considerable evidence that the introduction and expansion of universal education systems in the UK and Western Europe have not led to increasing levels of relative social mobility. This is due to a range of factors, including the ability of middle-class families to take advantage of educational opportunities. For example, when comparing individuals with identical education achievements, those who had a private education earn 7% more than then peers (Cattan et al 2014). This process is referred to as 'opportunity hoarding' by McKnight (2015) where a private education ensures better exam results and improved social and presentational skills.
- *Employment and labour market experiences* – recent decades have seen the emergence of important labour market trends with implications for social mobility. First, substantial levels of worklessness and long-term economic inactivity have emerged in some areas and/or among specific population groups. Second, research has identified the emergence of a prominent 'low-pay – no-pay' cycle for some groups. There is also evidence that specific groups face particular disadvantages in the labour market and that women who take career breaks often have difficulty re-entering the labour market in the same position and, therefore, frequently experience downward social mobility after having children.
- *Health and well-being* – ill-health results from social and environmental factors identified with lower socio-economic status, and ill-health and caring responsibilities can lead to declining socio-economic status.
- *Area-based influences* – localised environmental problems appear to combine with socio-economic disadvantage to produce negative area-based influences on potential for social mobility. For example, inequalities in access to private transport combined with poorer quality provision in some important public services in deprived areas may mean that lower socio-economic classes are unable to exercise effective choices over access to these services.

In January 2009, the Government published a white paper on social mobility (*New Opportunities: Fair Chances for the Future*). This identified the crucial role of education as a driver of social mobility. Research has shown that children on free school meals (a useful proxy for poverty) have only half the average child's chance of getting five good GCSE passes (Toynbee 2009). This is crucial, as five good GCSEs is the entry requirement for A-levels, and 95% of those with A-levels go on to higher education and the increased life chances that follow from this. The Government proposed paying bonuses of £10,000 to teachers working in the toughest schools, defined as the 500 'national challenge' schools where less than 30% achieve five good GCSE passes including maths and English, and a high proportion are eligible for free school meals (Sparrow 2009). The Government also proposed to invest £57m in an expanded nursery and childcare programme for 15% of the most disadvantaged families.

The white paper also announced plans to set up a cross-party panel chaired by the former health secretary Alan Milburn, a leading Blairite, to identify ways to increase the number of people from low-income backgrounds entering professional jobs. Milburn's panel produced *Fair Success to the Professions* in July 2009 (Milburn 2009a). He pointed to an increased opportunity for social mobility if entry to the professions could be widened, as 90% of the jobs likely to be created by 2020 would be professional and managerial. He updated the Sutton Trust figures in entry to the professions quoted previously and found that, if anything, the independent school bias was increasing. Only 7% of children attended private schools, but they made up 75% of judges, 70% of finance directors and a third of MPs. In nine out of 12 professions, including medicine and the law, the proportion coming from wealthy families was increasing (Jack 2009). Milburn also quoted evidence that of six (unnamed) European countries, the UK had the lowest rate of social mobility for men and the second lowest for women.

The report saw the key to social mobility as being in education. Private schools (and the best state schools) not only produced better-qualified children, but they also developed the soft skills of confidence, teamwork and interview skills through extra-curricular activities and mentoring. Later, privately educated children made full use of professional internship programmes, which were usually organised on the basis of 'who you know'. State school pupils had neither the aspirations, the skills nor the contacts to break into the charmed circle.

Milburn made a number of recommendations, including:

- university students to be recruited from wider social backgrounds
- no-fee degrees for students living at home
- professions to publish more details on the social background of their intakes
- better careers advice aimed at raising aspirations
- more extra-curricular activity for state school pupils (BBC 2009).

Milburn also stressed that it was not just the working class that was blocked from the professions. Writing in the *Observer*, he said, 'it will be more and more middle-class kids, not just working-class ones, who miss out', and 'we need a new focus, unleashing aspirations, not just beating poverty' (Milburn 2009b). Milburn was subsequently appointed as chair of the Social Mobility Commission set up in 2011 to monitor social mobility and reduce child poverty.

In response to the first recommendation, the Government created the Office of Fair Access (OFFA) in 2012 with substantial budget to run access programmes and encourage universities to link in with education establishments at all levels, not just sixth forms. For example, Nottingham Trent University holds 'family fun evenings' for 10- and 11-year-olds from poorer areas and their parents to introduce them to higher education (Harrison 2012).

7.4.3 INEQUALITY

Inequality in society can be measured in a number of ways, but the easiest methods are through distribution of income or distribution of wealth. There has been a renewed interest in this subject since the publication of Thomas Picketty's (2013) surprise world best-seller 'Capital in the 21st Century' which surveyed wealth inequality across the globe. The book's central thesis is that inequality is not an accident but rather a feature of capitalism that can be reversed only through state intervention. The book thus argues that unless capitalism is reformed, inequality will get worse and the very democratic order will be threatened.

Disposable Income distribution

Table 7.11 compares net income for 2000 and 2013/4. It shows that the top 10% of earners take home around 25% of all earnings, rising from £47,000 to £73,000) although this percentage has dropped over the period. This was chiefly due to the effects of the recession which began in 2008 when the high bonuses paid in the financial sector were scaled back rapidly and jobs hollowed out. The total bonuses for bankers, for example, did not exceed the 2007 level until 2015.

At the other end of the spectrum, the average income for the bottom 10% of earnings were very low, rising only to £9,000 in 2013/14 and chiefly made up of benefits.

Table 7.11 UK Income after tax and other deductions

Population	2000 net income		2013–14 net income		Net income % change
(deciles)	£'000	% of total income	£'000	% of total income	
Bottom 10%	6	3	9	3	0
20%	7	4	15	5	+25%
30%	9	5	18	6	+20%
40%	11	6	21	7	+16%
50%	14	8	25	8	–
60%	16	9	28	9	–
70%	19	11	34	11	–
80%	22	12	40	13	+8%
90%	28	16	49	16	–
Top 10%	47	26	73	23	11%
Mean net income	17		31		

Source: ONS (2014)

Wealth is much more difficult to measure and hence to compare across time. Measures rely to a much greater extent on disclosure and those with extreme wealth are less likely to be willing to give full disclosure on all their wealth, much of which may be transferred to low-tax locations. Recent measures have attempted to estimate wealth as a combination of four components and the total wealth in 2012 is shown in Table 7.12:

Table 7.12 UK total wealth

	£billions
Property wealth	3,528
Financial wealth	1,299
Physical wealth	1,102
Private pension wealth	3,586
Total	9,515

The value of private pensions for those on final salary schemes (defined benefit) has risen substantially as interest rates have fallen as a much bigger pot of money is required to pay out the guaranteed pension sums.

Wealth distribution

In the 1920s, the top 1% owned over 60% of marketable wealth (Abercrombie and Warde 2000). This had fallen to 43% by 1954 and this fell at a much faster rate to 19% by 2005 (ONS 2006a). The main reason for this was the spread of home ownership, from 20% just after the war to around 75% by 1995.

Table 7.13 Distribution of wealth (UK) (%)

Population	Total net wealth 2012 By decile of population £billions		Total net wealth 2005	Total net wealth 1995
(deciles)	£'000	% of total	% of total	% of total
Bottom 10%	20	0.2	-0.5	-0.6
20%	57	0.5	0.1	0
30%	126	1.3	1.6	0.3
40%	255	2.6	4.1	1.7
50%	495	5.1	6.1	4.5
60%	590	6.1	8.1	6.6
70%	850	8.8	10.5	9.9
80%	1,220	12.6	13.4	12.5
90%	1,840	19.1	18.9	19.7
Top 10%	4,230	43.5	37.7	46.2

*Adjusted for inflation
Source: Karagianaki (2011); ONS (2014)

It is clear from Table 7.13 that wealth inequality has become more complicated over this period. The top 10%, (the most difficult to measure) still own over 40% of UK wealth, even though this percentage fell from 46.2 in 1995 to 37.7 in 2005 but then rose again to 43.5 in 2012. This oscillation may simply be due to the difficulties in collecting accurate data and the figures may, in reality, be much larger overall.

For the top 50%, wealth ownership has dropped from 95% to around 90%, reflecting the additional wealth at the lower end of the scale as poorer groups have acquired more pension rights and the first generations of house buyers in the 1950s and 1960s now own their houses outright.

Inequality and the very wealthy

One area where there is little doubt over the trend of inequality is the percentage of wealth owned by the very rich. In 2015, there were 1844 billionaires in the world and 38,280 individuals with over £100m (Knight Frank 2015). The share of the top 0.1% was the same in 2007 as in 1937 (Milne 2007). Sixty-nine per cent of all land held by individuals is owned by 0.3% of the population (Dorling 2014). The number of UK bankers earning over 1m Euros per year rose to 2,700 in 2014, 12 times higher than any other country in the European Union and much greater than Germany (212) and France (177) (Goodway and Prynn 2013). Chief Executives of UK companies earn on average 183 times the rate of a full-time worker (although much of this pay is in the form of long-term share incentives which can be unpredictable).

This aspect of inequality has caused considerable social and political friction in recent years. Very great wealth has historically been created by talented individuals exploiting an exceptional invention, growing an industrial empire or by accumulating assets, especially land. However, from the mid-1980s onwards, a considerable number of large fortunes were won from the financial sector, especially forms of banking, such as hedge funds, equity funds and derivatives trading. These reached their peak in the years leading up to the financial crash of 2007–08, when many of the banking operations had to be bailed out by governments across the developed world. Although many of the bankers and traders lost their jobs, they kept all their winnings and were usually paid off in a handsome fashion, leading to the view that they won all ways round – when times were good, they received obscene pay, bonuses and profits; when times were bad, they received obscene compensation, paid for by the taxpayer. In addition, it was considered by many commentators that the work they did (especially speculating and selling complex financial instruments that the buyer did not understand) was, at best, of no social value and, at worst, fraudulent.

Atkinson (2015) has added to the debate by detailing the subtle ways that the very rich are able to influence government policy in order to protect their wealth, for example, by backing government moves to keep interest rates low and prioritising low taxes over investment in education and infrastructure at the expense of the poor.

Gini coefficient

A method used by statisticians to measure overall inequality is the Gini coefficient. This expresses income distribution on a scale of 0 to 100, with 0 representing total equality. The higher the figure, the more uneven the distribution. The Gini coefficient figures have changed, as shown in Table 7.14.

Table 7.14 UK Gini coefficient (before housing costs)

1961	1970	1979	1991	1997	2002	2008	2011	2013
26	26	25	34	33	36	36	34	33

Source: George and Wilding (1999); Clark (2004); IFS (2009); Cribb et al (2012); ONS (2014)

On the Gini figures, inequality was constant over the period 1961–79, widened greatly under the Thatcher Governments and widened a little more under New Labour. By 2013, somewhat surprisingly, there was a reduction back to the level of the late 1980s.

This has been due to the following causes:

- Earnings reduced across all component parts of the income distribution, with the pain being shared by all groups in the labour force, not just those becoming unemployed.
- The top earners suffered because of the increase in the top rate of tax from 40% to 50% (although this was reduced to 45% in 2013).
- The Government continued to raise rate benefits in line with inflation, leading to a higher increase in benefits than in earnings, a trend continued in April 2012 when benefits were raised by 5.2% while average earnings were less than 3%. This had the effect of increasing the income of the poor and hence narrowed the wealth gap. In 2015, the old age pension was increased by 2.5% despite inflation being negative at –0.1% due to an election promise to continue the existing uprating of benefits

system. (However, from 2013, the Chancellor changed course by pegging a number of benefits to 1% for three years for those out of work to try to avoid the situation where those on benefits, mostly in the lower groupings, increased their earnings more than those at work.)

Inequality in the UK is higher than in the rest of the European Union. The figure for the EU (15 members) was 31 in 2014, with France at 29 under a socialist government and Germany at 31. Inequality is much less in Scandinavia, where it averaged 25. However, on a world scale, the UK does not fare so badly. The Gini coefficient in the US was 41, China at 41, Brazil at 52 and South Africa at 62 (World Bank 2015).

It could be said that this spread merely reflects that society's take on equality. In America and China, greater emphasis tends to be placed on equality of opportunity, with the general philosophy that those who succeed do so, generally, through their own effort by grasping opportunities that arise. However in China, the general dissatisfaction with the gap between the rich, often corrupt officials and the general population has led to a strong initiative to combat social inequality in 2013, including raising the minimum wage to 40% of average urban wages, increasing taxes on the rich and raising expenditure on education, healthcare and public spending from 30% of the total 2009 budget to 38% by 2015 (*Economist* 2013c).

Europeans tend to be more egalitarian and wish to retain traditional cultures that have led to low income inequality. So they accept the state using a greater level of taxation.

High levels of inequality rarely lead to stable governments. Latin America, for example, has had the highest level of inequality in the twentieth century and also a history of unstable and impoverished states, although there are strong signs of a growing middle class, with the proportion of Latin Americans living in poverty dropping from 41% in 2000 to 28% in 2010 and two in five citizens upwardly mobile over that period (*Economist* 2012b).

However, the focus by many countries on redistribution of wealth by taxation and improving benefits has brought its own problems. High welfare-oriented economies reduce real poverty but also take away the self-help and entrepreneurial culture which may leave a sizeable underclass welfare-dependent at great expense to the community.

Finally, a number of reports attempt to demonstrate that rising inequality is costly to a country. For example, the OECD (2014) calculated that inequality in the UK cost 9% of GDP growth for the period 1990–2010 urging all countries to invest more money in education, especially for the disadvantaged.

7.4.4 CHANGES IN FAMILY STRUCTURE

The move to smaller families and a higher participation rate for women has led to changes in the structure of families and the role of family members. Table 7.15 shows the change in family structures from 2001 to 2014.

Table 7.15 Changing family structures

	2001	2014
Married couples/civil partner	72.4%	67.6%
Co-habiting couples	12.5%	16.0%
Same-sex couples/civil partnerships	0.3%	0.4%
Lone mother/father	14.8%	16.1%
Total number of families	17 million	18.6 million

Source: ONS (2015a)

Table 7.15 shows the continuing decline in the traditional married family. The number of co-habiting couples has risen by a third and the number of reported same-sex families has more than doubled, while lone mothers have risen to around one in seven of all families. Forty-seven per cent of all children were born out of wedlock in 2011, ten times the rate of 1911, where the figure was close to 4% (Hall 2012).

The decline in the popularity of marriage is influenced by a number of factors, including the fact that women have become more independent. Women have equal rights and have proven over time that they have the potential and ability to support themselves and find that it may be easier to deal with temporary relationships or to leave unhappy marriages. They are also more work-focused, thus giving them less time to cope with their relationship. Working to support a family while trying to stabilise finances can influence the likelihood of a stressful marriage. Also, with both partners working (in most cases), there is less 'family time', which makes raising children difficult. This often happens in the stage where couples are raising young children.

The number of marriages has declined substantially over the last 40 years, as shown in Figure 7.2.

Figure 7.2 Marriages in the UK

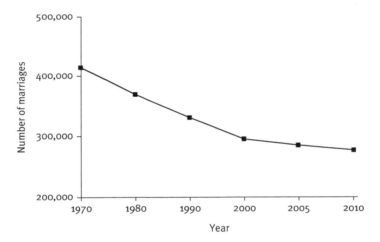

The mean age for men getting married was 36.5 and for women, 34.0, a substantial increase since 1990.

As a consequence of the decline in marriages, the number of UK divorces has fallen from 157,000 in 2001 to 118,140 in 2012.

Working women (especially those in full-time work) spend less time in domestic routines, which has led to a considerable growth in industries devoted to convenience foods, eating out and hired-in domestic help. Information from the ONS *Family Spending* (2009) survey shows that the proportion of income spent on eating out has increased by 50% over the period 1980 to 2009, although the recession and the growing cost of energy caused some reining-back of expenditure in this area.

The changes in the labour market have led to changes in the nature of society, as shown in an example from the 1980s in Case Study 7.10.

CHANGING SOCIETY IN SOUTH WALES

Doreen Massey carried out a survey of the implications of the massive closures of the steel and coal-mining industries in the early 1980s. She identified the difference between the former labour market, which was heavily male-dominated with a high proportion of manual and semi-skilled labour, and a new labour market that had grown up with economic restructuring. This was typified by new jobs in the electronics industries and high level of female employment. The previous labour market had created a patriarchal society that had remained relatively stable over many generations. The new market offered less stability and less security and led to changes in social patterns and family organisation.

Source: Massey (1984)

REFLECTIVE ACTIVITY 7.7

What actions can the Government take to mitigate the negative consequences of areas of declining manufacturing?

Other changes have involved the caring responsibilities for children becoming more shared between spouses, while there are many examples of active grandparents taking a substantial responsibility for day-to-day care of younger children.

On the other hand, there is the challenge of looking after older relatives, with around half living into their eighties and many into their nineties and beyond. In the past, many have lived in, making this an extended family, but, in Europe, this practice is declining, although it is still the norm in Japan. The need for a degree of personal privacy, the day-to-day medical and psychological challenges of coping with an elderly relative and the widespread growth in sheltered accommodation have been reasons for this trend.

Changes in family life are not just a UK phenomenon. In Europe, 40% of births were out of wedlock in 2013 compared with only 17% in 1990, with the figure for Scandinavian countries, Slovenia and Bulgaria rising to well over 50%. Only Greece had a rate of less than 10%. The European marriage rate collapsed from 7.9 per 1,000 people in 1970 to 4.0 per 1,000 in 2013, while the divorce rate doubled between 1970 and 2013 from 0.9 per 1,000 people to 2 per 1,000 (Eurostat 2015a). UK currently falls around the midway point in these measures, which is influenced by the traditional approach to marriage by the growing groups of immigrants.

7.4.5 POVERTY

Absolute poverty in the Ethiopian sense does not exist in the UK. A more useful definition is relative poverty, and this is inescapable in a society in which income is distributed unevenly.

The definition currently utilised in the EU is household income below 60% of median income (after housing costs) – approximately £15,000 a year in 2011. On this definition, poverty rose steadily throughout the Thatcher and Major years, reaching a peak of 13.9 million people (nearly a quarter of the population) in 1997, falling since to 12.4 million in 2004 and then rising again to 14 million (16% of the population) in 2011 (Clark 2004;

Eurostat 2012). The UK was around the European mid-point of poverty levels in 2011, around the same level as Germany, with the lowest being Iceland at 9% and the highest Bulgaria at 22%.

Poverty is particularly influenced by a number of factors:

- *Children* – not surprisingly, the percentage of households with children are around twice as likely to be under the poverty line as households without children. When New Labour came to power in 1997, one of its main objectives was to eliminate child poverty, which had grown from one in seven in 1979 to one in three in 1997. By 2003, they had reduced it to 2.6 million and this has further reduced to 2.3 million by 2011, over a million less than in 1998. One of the continuing difficulties has been the high level of poverty among lone-parent households. One in four of all children were in a lone-parent family and 72% of this group were classed as in poverty. Putnam (2015) has explained the strong connection between dining alone (a situation that is statistically more likely in a one-parent family) and educational and social advancement. An example of research into child poverty is shown in Case Study 7.11.
- *Gender* – despite 30 years of equal pay legislation, average female hourly earnings are still only around 86% of male earnings, and women on average work fewer hours than men. This particularly hits single-parent households headed by women (the vast majority).
- *Ethnicity* – whereas 20% of white households are in poverty, this figure is much higher for ethnic households. For Bangladeshi households, 70% are in poverty, and this compares with 50% for black African households, 30% for Indian and black Caribbean. However, after we take account of the fact that Indians on average have higher educational qualifications than whites, their 'like for like' earnings are lower. Reasons identified for this phenomenon include the high level of unemployment (25% of Bangladeshi and black Africans), the high proportion of lone-parent families, the higher average number of children and work carried out in low-skilled and part-time work (Kenway and Palmer 2007).

 CHILD POVERTY

CASE STUDY 7.11

The London University's Institute of Education researchers carried out a study of 14,000 7-year-olds in 2008. They found that despite governments having spent billions to eliminate child poverty since 1999:

- Almost one-fifth of 7-year-olds live in severe poverty – homes where the total income, including benefits, is less than £254 a week (this is an average among those surveyed). The average income for families in the study was £563 a week, say researchers.
- Almost three-quarters of children whose parents are of Pakistani or Bangladeshi origin live in poverty – homes where the total income for a

family with two children is under £330 a week. This is largely because of high unemployment rates for mothers and fathers, the researchers say.

- Just over half (51%) of black 7-year-olds and just over a quarter of white 7-year-olds live in poverty, with three-fifths from these groups in single-parent families. Seven-year-olds are most likely to live in poverty in the north-east (40%) and least likely in the south-west (22%). The figure for London was 36%. Just under 7% of 7-year-olds living in poverty do not have two pairs of all-weather shoes, according to parents. Just under 50% do not get pocket money.

- Just over half of mothers without any qualifications are in the poorest fifth, while 32% of fathers without qualifications are in this group. More than half of the mothers and fathers with postgraduate qualifications are in the top income group.
- The mothers of the 7-year-olds were asked to place their children's behaviour in one of three categories:

normal, borderline and/or serious behaviour problems. About 12% of children in single-parent families and 15% of children living with a step-parent were described as having serious behaviour difficulties. This is compared with 6% for children living with both of their birth parents.

Source: Shepherd (2010)

Poverty matters because it affects future life chances. Infant mortality rates are twice as high for unskilled manual groups as they are for professionals. Life expectancy for male professionals in 2005 was 80, and for female professionals 85, while for unskilled manual groups the corresponding figures were 73 and 78 (Womack 2007). The lower your income, the more likely you are to be a victim of burglary.

The percentage of children aged between 5 and 15 experiencing mental disorders is between two and three times higher for those living in households with an income of less than £100 a week than they are for those in households earning over £700 a week. Most poor children fail. Their depressed parents are unable to give them aspirations (Toynbee 2009).

Poverty persists across the generations. Of people whose families were poor when they were in their teens in the 1970s, 19% were poor in their early thirties, while where families were not poor in the 1970s, 10% were poor as adults. Dividing 19% by 10% shows that the odds of being poor as an adult were doubled if one's parents were poor. For teenagers in the 1980s, the odds of being poor were quadrupled when parents were poor (Blanden and Gibbons 2006).

The rising number of single-parent families and the dependence of many such families on the benefit system, which is especially strong in the UK, presents a further financial challenge to governments as well as implications on housing provision and, in certain areas, an effect on crime.

How easy is it to move out of poverty? The answer seems to be not easy, but not impossible. Evidence from the British Household Panel Survey shows that just over half of the individuals who were in the bottom quintile (lowest 20%) for income in 1991 were still there is 1996. In other words, half had escaped from dire poverty. Over a one-year timespan, 65% stayed in the bottom quintile, and of those who escaped, most stayed in the bottom two quintiles (that is, the bottom 40%) (Giddens 2006). McKnight (2000) found that the unemployed are most likely to gain employment in the lowest-paid sectors when they do find work, and that the lower-paid are more likely to become unemployed than the higher paid.

Child poverty could be ended, but at a cost. It would involve a massive increase in child tax credits, estimated at £30bn up to 2020. Barnard and Goulden (2006) point out that this only represents one year's economic growth. Money alone will not be enough. Considerable practical and emotional support in increasing the self-esteem of lone-parent families will also be needed, through the expansion of educational programmes such as Sure Start and employment programmes such as New Deal. Although Sure Start had an uncertain start providing limited overall benefits, by 2011, a research project found a good number of significant improvements arising out of the scheme, including more stimulating and less chaotic home environments (NESS 2010).

?   REFLECTIVE ACTIVITY 7.8

Poverty and inequality

In 2014 the average UK CEO earnings in the FTSE 100 companies was £4,700,000, taking into account bonuses and share options. The average UK wage was £26,500. This differential can be calculated at 185:1. In the USA, this differential is even higher – the 16,000 families making up the richest 0.01% control 11% of American wealth and the top 0.1% (160,000 families) own 22%, having declined to an average of 10% between 1940 and 1990. Now it is back to the same situation as in the 1930s where the richest 0.1% and the poorest 90% have the same share of wealth (Saez and Zucman 2014).

The differential of earnings and wealth is much lower in most European countries, especially in Scandinavia.

Questions

1   Consider what the impact of these differentials is likely to be on the motivation of employees in the UK and the USA.

2   Should the Government take any action to reduce this differential?

3   Why should social inequality matter to employers? What can they do about it?

4   What action should the Government take, if any, to try to reduce social inequality?

?   REFLECTIVE ACTIVITY 7.9

Social class

● 'There is no such thing as society' (Margaret Thatcher)
● 'The classless society' (John Major)
● 'We are all middle-class now' (anon).

Question

Explain each of these statements. Do you agree with any of them?

7.4.6 EQUAL OPPORTUNITIES AND DIVERSITY

The UK is a very diverse society: diverse in terms of race, sex, sexual orientation, religion, age, disability and life experience. Equality of opportunity is based on legislation and has as its main aim assimilation – that whatever a person's background, they should all have the opportunity to achieve the same outcomes. Diversity is much more about difference. The differences between the two are illustrated in Table 7.16.

Table 7.16 Comparing managing diversity with equal opportunity

Managing diversity	Equal opportunity
Is the concern of all employees, especially managers	Seen as an issue to do with human resource practitioners
Does not rely on positive action/affirmative action	Relies on positive action/affirmative action
Concentration on issues of movement within the organisation, the culture of the organisation and meeting business objectives	Less of an emphasis on culture change and meeting business objectives; premised more on moral and ethical objectives
Embraces a broad range of people – no one is excluded	Perceived as an issue for certain groups in the labour market such as women, ethnic minorities and people with disabilities
Ensures all employees maximise their potential and their contribution to the organisation	Concentration on issues of discrimination
Internally driven	Externally imposed
Aims for diversification	Aims for assimilation

In 2005 and 2006, the CIPD published three related Change Agenda documents on diversity, entitled *Managing Diversity, Measuring success* (CIPD 2006a), *Managing Diversity: Learning by doing* (Taylor et al 2005) and *Managing Diversity: Linking theory and practice to business performance* (Mulholland et al 2005). This was followed up by a set of directional cases in 2010 – Opening up Talent for Business success – Integrating Talent Management and Diversity (McCartney and Worman). These are invaluable in an understanding of diversity.

The CIPD defines diversity as 'valuing everyone as an individual – valuing people as employees, customers and clients' (CIPD 2008). Diversity is traditionally viewed as being concerned with categories of race, gender, ethnicity, age and disability, but true diversity is much wider than this. Anderson and Metcalfe (2003) identify three different types of workforce diversity:

- *social category diversity* – differences in demographic characteristics such as race and sex (the traditional definition)
- *informational diversity* – differences of knowledge, experience, functional background, etc
- *value diversity* – differences in personality and attitudes.

A need for diversity is being driven by economic and social change – a more culturally mixed society as a result of immigration, an ageing population, pressures of globalisation and the trend towards a 24/7 society. There are simply not enough white, English-born, young and middle-aged males to fill all the jobs. Managing diversity is seen as a much subtler process. Employees are not selected or promoted on the basis of ethnic or gender calculations but because of their individual and varied contribution that they can make to their job and the organisation.

There is clear evidence of a continuing inequality based on race and sex. The National Equality Panel (Hills 2010) found the following:

- White British pupils with GCSE results around or below the national median are less likely to go on to higher education than those from minority ethnic groups. Pakistani, black African and black Caribbean boys have results at the age of 16 well below the median in England.
- Compared with a white British Christian man with similar qualifications, age and occupation, Pakistani and Bangladeshi Muslim men and black African Christian men have an income that is 13–21% lower. Nearly half of Bangladeshi and Pakistani households are in poverty.
- Girls have better educational outcomes than boys at school and are more likely to enter higher education and achieve good degrees, but women's median hourly pay is 21% less than men's, although this difference has narrowed since the 1970s. In fact, median earnings differ by around 12% for full-time earners but the big difference is in part-time rates, where women form the large majority and are crowded into low-pay sectors, such as catering, caring and retailing.

7.4.7 THE BUSINESS CASE FOR DIVERSITY

Although the equal opportunity (EO) legislation of the 1970s had an immediate impact in eliminating the worst excesses of sexist and racist behaviour, most organisations introduced EO policies and practices chiefly out of fear of the legal sanctions rather than seeing the long-term benefits that such action would bring.

However, by the 1990s it began to be realised that substantial *demographic changes* were occurring which would inevitably lead to skills shortages over the following years. The birth rate had fallen dramatically in the 1970s and there was little sign of recovery in the next 20 years, so it was known that the number of 16–25-year-olds would take a sharp fall. If the traditional sources of labour (young, white, male, qualified, full-time employees) became much reduced, organisations realised that they would have to rethink their human resourcing policies and look for untapped sources of expertise. Job descriptions would need to become more flexible to accommodate part-time working; specifications would have to be altered to eliminate unnecessary requirements on height and lifting ability and broadened to envelop all sections of the community; working conditions and benefits would have to change to allow wheelchairs, language classes, career breaks and childcare facilities.

These changes in the work patterns were taken up by many employers, with females playing a larger part in business organisations. Interestingly enough, this played its part in the birth rate recovering somewhat in the 2000s, although it was also due partly to the increase in immigration to the UK of people of child-bearing age and to the generally prosperous period with low unemployment, which encouraged support for females to be able to retain their jobs and go back to work quickly, which became more the norm.

A second reason relates to the *changing nature of the workplace*. There was a sharp decline in industrial and manufacturing jobs in the 1980s and 1990s (over 2 million jobs were lost in this period) and this ran alongside a growth in the service sector. Whereas a large proportion of industrial jobs were held by men, the opposite was true for a majority of the service sector employment. One forecast is that 70% of all new jobs to be created up to 2020 are expected to be taken by women. Companies in this sector have a positive incentive to encourage the best applicants by providing career opportunities and a supporting environment for all staff.

The growing emphasis on *customer relations* in a competitive economy is another reason for focusing on wider opportunities. Active diversity management can open up new opportunities and improve market share by broadening the customer base. This has been seen particularly in the financial sector, where banks and building societies are focusing on diversity issues in the way they target their products and services. They are becoming much more user-friendly to women, taking on board the increasing spending power of the female professionals and they are also addressing the needs of ethnic minority businesses.

Customers, in effect, were increasingly looking through the front door of the companies they buy from. If they did not like what they see in terms of equality or social responsibility, they would not go through the door.

The Halifax Bank recognised this opportunity by specifically targeting the Chinese community in Manchester, which was substantially unrepresented in the bank's employees. The business benefits of having a group of Mandarin or Cantonese speakers in the branches led to an immediate increase in mortgage business of around 40% (Merrick 2001). JD Wetherspoon have deliberately spread their recruiting across all ages to reflect their customer base and now employs many staff over 70 and one over 90 (Syedain 2010). When HSBC recruited in the Birmingham area in the mid-2000s, 49% of their intake were from ethnic minorities to match the local community (CIPD 2005).

Conveying an image as a *good employer* also has repercussions on equality issues. Companies seen to have high ethical stances, with such policies as 'dignity at work' which prevent harassment and bullying, become more attractive to both customers and potential employees. It improves the employer brand. On the other hand, those seen as dominated by a white, male culture may not appear to provide the environment required. Moreover, in the case of equal pay, there is no greater demotivating force in the workplace than a sense of injustice over pay by a large section of the workforce. Internal equity, including fair pay and treatment for men, women and minority groups, is a vital part of the perception of 'fairness'.

All these reasons have encouraged organisations to raise their profile on equality issues.

Jones (2006) has examined the business case in detail. She identifies a number of benefits:

- *Marketing* – sales tend to increase when staffing reflects the organisation's customer base – Lloyds TSB reported a 30% increase in sales in branches where staffing was changed to reflect the ethnicity of customers.
- *HRI* – Rajan et al (2003) found that diversity led to higher staff motivation, higher retention and reduced recruitment costs. Diversity policies also made employees feel valued and respected, and this increased their sense of engagement.
- *Stakeholders* – diversity policies improve the organisation's image with its stakeholders.
- *Creativity and decision-making* – diverse organisations tend to be more creative. Diverse teams avoid the risk of group-think and tended to make better decisions. However, in some situations, homogeneous groups tended to perform better – where the main tasks were routine, and where the organisation was contracting rather than growing (Jones 2006; CIPD 2006a).

There is also a strong economic case for increasing women's participation in the workforce and increasing their equality and the inequality of other disadvantaged groups. In the developed world, the effect of gender gaps causes 15% loss in GDP (Cuberes and Teignier 2015). If the gender gaps in hours worked and productivity were bridged, Western Europe could increase their GDP by 25% (Woetzel et al 2015). The more disabled people who are integrated into a working situation, the lower the welfare benefits costs. Alesina et al (2015) calculated that GDP rises in countries where ethnic inequality falls. The wider the recruitment net is cast by all organisations, the more likely it is that hidden talent is found and utilised.

?   REFLECTIVE ACTIVITY 7.10

Binna Kandola and the business case

The psychologist and diversity expert Binna Kandola has said that: 'the search for the business case for diversity is an exercise in futility'. He argues that diversity is ultimately a moral issue and that what prevents diversity from moving forward is the bias and stereotyping that we all carry (Kandola 2009).

Do you agree?

If you are a CIPD member, you can read Kandola's articles on the People Management website.

7.4.8 MANAGING DIVERSITY

It is important to note that these benefits of diversity do not just happen. Diversity has to be managed effectively. Mulholland et al (2005) liken it to managing change. They quote the example of the turkey producer Bernard Matthews, who was suffering from a shortage of labour in rural Norfolk. This was tackled by bringing in immigrant labour from Portugal, which increased the proportion of Portuguese employees from 3% to 30% of the workforce. However, in order to make it work, Bernard Matthews developed local support networks, promoted local English language training and created partnerships with the Home Office, Norfolk Police and HSBC to facilitate integration of the new workforce.

Diversity strategies can operate at three different levels, and achievement of all three is necessary for an effective diversity policy (Jones 2006):

- *Representational diversity* – ensuring that the workforce is more representative of the population as a whole. The key here is recruitment.
- *Inclusive processes* – underlying processes – retention, progression, development, etc, must support representational diversity. Bernard Matthews clearly did this in the example quoted above.
- *Inclusive culture* – provide people with a culture where they feel respected. The attitudes of top management are critical here.

 DIVERSITY

CASE STUDY 7.12

The war against crime

The Metropolitan Police has set up a Cultural and Communities Resource Unit, headed by a (black) detective chief inspector, Keith Fraser. The unit maintains a database of the range of backgrounds, lifestyles and specialisms in the Met and the City of London Police. The unit has 800 people on its books and has located experts who have helped with 700 criminal enquiries all over the country. Examples of the work of the unit include:

- The murder of an elderly Bengali woman, where white officers were

getting no co-operation from the community. Bengali officers immediately got co-operation.
- A Chinese person had been missing in the north of England for two weeks. A Chinese policeman from London found him in a day and a half.
- Tamil officers are investigating violence between rival Tamil gangs.
- A voodoo expert helped interpret seemingly innocuous but actually sinister objects sent to a Bangladeshi man.

As Detective Chief Inspector Fraser says, 'The unit highlights the true meaning of diversity and the fantastic opportunities and benefits it gives policing.' (Cowan 2004).

Shariah mortgages

Islamic finance is regulated by *shariah* law. One of the main principles of *shariah* law is a prohibition on usury, the payment of interest. This makes a conventional Western mortgage impossible under *shariah* law. The solution developed by Islamic banks is a version of sale and lease-back. The customer in effect sells their house to the bank, pays rent (not interest) on it, and then at a later stage buys the house back from the bank. Interestingly, exactly the same process had developed in late medieval England to get round Christian prohibitions of usury. Unfortunately, under UK law this represented two property sales, each of which was liable to stamp duty. In the 2006 Budget,

Gordon Brown recognised this, and abolished the requirement for double stamp duty (Parker 2005).

Pearson

The publisher Pearson, which owns the *Financial Times*, came top of a 2009 survey of FTSE 350 companies, which measured both the quality of equal opportunities and diversity policies and the proportion of women on the board. The chief executive and the chief finance officer are both female. In 2003, 9% of its staff were from ethnic minorities, and by 2009 this figure had increased to 15%. This follows on from a five-year plan launched in 2002 to communicate diversity awareness to employees. It holds annual outreach programmes for students which help produce candidates for its internship scheme. The *Financial Times* is part of a scheme in Tower Hamlets which acts as a matchmaker between firms and ethnic minority jobseekers (Sunderland 2009).

An example of two different approaches by London boroughs to deal with integration is shown in Case Study 7.13.

CASE STUDY 7.13

ETHNIC INTEGRATION IN THE LONDON BOROUGHS OF NEWHAM AND TOWER HAMLETS

Newham, which includes the Olympic Park, is officially Britain's least-white borough, with only 16.7%, and a quarter of households having somebody who speaks English as a first language. To improve the rate of integration, Newham Council have taken a number of initiatives. Some are unsurprising, such as providing very cheap English-language classes. Some are more unexpected; at age five, each school child is provided with a (Western) musical instrument, to learn Western style of music, which they can keep if they finish their music course; ethnic-language newspapers have been removed from all the libraries; no grants are available for any ethnic-based

activity, from faith or religion. The council encourages street activities, as long as everybody is invited and nobody is excluded.

Tower Hamlets, the next door borough, on the other hand, where the demographics are very similar, has a mayor whose ruling council is 100% Bengali, although Bengalis only make up a third of the population. A considerable amount of funds go towards ethnic and faith-based activities, where lunch clubs and arts classes tend to be separate and segregated. Language teaching is subsidised for each ethnic group.

Source: Gilligan (2012)

WOMEN ON THE BOARD

In 2009, Co-operative Asset Management, a fund manager, carried out a survey of female representation on the boards of FTSE 350 companies, extensively reported in the *Observer*. They ranked companies on two measures:

- the sophistication of equal opportunities and diversity policies
- female representation on boards of directors.

Companies tended to score better on theory than on practice. Many had impressive-sounding policies, and 94% said they had an equal opportunities policy, but then failed to have women on their boards. Typical was Barclays, which scored 7.8 out of 10 for its policies, but zero for its board, which contained no women. Royal Bank of Scotland was even less diverse, as its board was not only all men, but also predominantly Scottish. This may in part explain the banking crisis. A separate survey showed that 89% of business executives thought that the banking culture encouraged excessive risk-taking, and 83% thought that this was fuelled by male machismo. The only company with a perfect score for both policies and practice was Pearson (see Case Study 7.13).

Overall, women held only 34 executive board seats out of 970. Most female directors were non-executives, and 130 companies (nearly half of the 297 companies that responded) had no women on the board. Of a total of 2,472 directorships, women held just under 10%.

Opinion is divided over whether diverse boards improve performance. One study suggests that women on the board do not improve financial performance, but could improve governance, while another study found that firms with more diverse boards had better financial performance. However, commonsense suggests that companies which do not have female directors are missing out on an important source of talent.

Suggestions to improve the gender balance include:

- Increase the availability of flexible working. At lower levels of management, where flexible working is generally available, the gender balance is relatively equal. However, higher up the organisation, flexible working is less likely to be available and this discriminates against women.
- Overcome a tendency for male bosses to recruit in their own image.
- Provide mentoring and networking opportunities for female executives.
- Use succession planning to identify and fast-track outstanding female candidates.
- Shareholder pressure – Co-operative Asset Management intends in future to consider diversity when it is assessing company governance.

Many of these ideas were taken up by the Davies Report (2011) commissioned by the Department for Business, Innovation and Skills. The report found that women only made up 12.5% of total FTSE 100 directors, and Lord Davies recommended that they should be aiming for a minimum of 25% female board member representation by 2015. As part of the report, Lord Davies and his panel state that companies should fully disclose the number of women sitting on their boards and working in their organisations as a whole, to drive up the numbers of women with top jobs in business.

The Coalition Government, however, rejected the concept of quotas, saying that 'women want and expect to reach the top on merit, not because of political correctness', and the best help the Government could provide was by attempting to reduce the cost of childcare and increasing its availability by providing increased grants to childcare providers and allowing parents on low incomes to recover part of their childcare costs.

By 2014, figures showed that the percentage of women on FTSE 100 boards had risen to a record 20.7% with four FTSE companies having four women on their boards. Lord Davies reported that: 'The rate of change that we have seen at the heart of our biggest companies over the last 3 years has been impressive. The voluntary approach is working and companies have got the message that better balanced boards bring real business benefits. We are finally seeing a culture change taking place at the heart of British business.' (Davies 2014).

A year later, the target of 25% was reached, although 260 out of the 286 female board members were Non-Executive director. A new target was set at 33% for 2020.

An attempt to introduce compulsory quotas of 40% representation on boards by the European Union failed in 2011 when the proposal was rejected by member states.

Sources: Sunderland (2009); Davies (2011); Hookham and Pancevski (2012). Davies (2014)

A fuller discussion of organisational strategy on flexible working is found in Chapter 10.

KEY LEARNING POINTS

- The major demographic trends across the world are a major decline in the birth rate, population ageing and increasing migration, both of people and jobs. These trends are strongest in the developed world, especially Europe.
- These trends are likely to continue to produce a reversal of world population expansion around 2050. Developed countries are likely to be faced by declining populations before that time unless they change policies and allow higher rates of migration.
- These demographic changes provide opportunities for organisations to move into new product and service areas. The reduction in the availability of younger labour means that organisations will need to reorganise work patterns to encourage greater participation from women, older people and other groups.
- Governments will increasingly be faced with the need for higher expenditure on pensions, benefits and health services as a result of demographic changes. At the same time, the higher dependency ratio is likely to necessitate higher levels of taxation to finance this expenditure. Initiatives to combat these difficulties can include encouraging larger families through incentives, reducing benefits and stimulating personal savings for pensions and health.
- It is likely that an ageing population will be a less productive one, providing challenges for the world economy and wealth creation. There has been a rapid transferring of jobs and services around the world as an outcome of globalisation.
- Throughout most of the twentieth century, social mobility in the UK was high, as the absolute size of the middle class rose considerably at the expense of the working class, but these trends have slowed in recent years.
- There are considerable inequalities in both income and wealth in the UK, and these inequalities have been widening in recent years.
- Inequality is closely related to relative poverty, which has persisted in the UK and which leads to an impairment of the life chances of the poor.
- Equal opportunities is about assimilation, while diversity is about celebrating difference.

- Diversity is of different types: social category diversity, informational diversity and value diversity: differences in personality and attitudes.
- In order to manage diversity, it is necessary to achieve representational diversity, inclusive processes and an inclusive culture. The attitudes of top management are critical.

REVIEW QUESTIONS

1   What have been the main changes in sectoral employment in the UK since 1992?

2   Provide five reasons why migration can provide benefits for an economy and set out five problems that migration can bring.

3   How can the UK Government handle the current crisis in pension provision due to the ageing population? What options does it have?

4   How is the 'participation ratio' measured and what has caused the rate to rise in the UK since the late 1990s?

5   What are the implications for organisations in terms of changing markets arising from demographic changes?

6   How can demographic changes affect HR activities and policies?

7   What is the difference between absolute and relative social mobility?

8   What is the Gini coefficient and what does it tell us about inequality in the UK?

9   Identify three main differences between equal opportunities and diversity.

10 Why is representational diversity only one element of a successful diversity strategy?

EXPLORE FURTHER

Further reading

The most readable and dynamic book source on demography remains Paul Wallace's *Agequake* (see References) while regular reports on all areas of UK demography can be found on the ONS website. Wider perspectives are given in books by Poston and Bouvier (2010) *Population and Society* (Cambridge), May (2012) *World Population Policies* (Springer) and Le Bras (2008) *The Nature of Demography* (Princeton University Press).

For a more international approach, see May (2012) *World Population Polices: their Origin, Evolution and Impact*, (Springer).

Social class and social mobility are discussed in any good sociology textbook. Recent research includes the CIPD (2013) report *Improving Social Mobility: Inside the HR profession and beyond*. Poverty and inequality are covered in Vic George and Paul Wilding (1999) *British Society and Social Welfare: Towards a sustainable society*. You should not fail to read commentaries on Thomas Picketty's book *Capital in the 21st Century* (2014) – the original is rather long! Excellent overviews of the evidence on social trends are given in two papers by Stephen Aldridge, an economist in the Prime Minister's Strategy Unit (formerly the Performance and Innovation Unit), listed in the References.

You should read the excellent CIPD factsheets relevant to this chapter, which are regularly updated, including subjects such as *The psychological contract, Work–life balance* and *Diversity,* together with the regular legal updating the CIPD website provides.

Useful websites

The Work Foundation (www.theworkfoundation.com) publishes several research reports on social topics. The journal *CentrePiece* (www.cep.lse.ac.uk/centrepiece), published by the Centre for Economic Performance at the London School of Economics, has useful articles with social themes.

SEMINAR ACTIVITY 7.1

IS EXECUTIVE PAY TOO HIGH?

There is much debate on the issue of whether high executive pay can be justified.

Arguments put forward to support such high levels include:

- Senior Executives are recruited in an International Labour market

A key argument has been the fact that the pool of talent for senior executive jobs is an international one as such people are generally willing in move to any country if the job and its rewards warrant such a move. To be able to persuade potential candidates from American and, to a lesser extent, other high salary countries, such as Switzerland, for non-US senior executive positions, the job has to carry US-style levels of reward or the size of the pool will be much reduced. Once the position has been filled at US reward levels, it then becomes difficult to fill it next time round at rates that are far below this level or the next incumbent may feel undervalued.

Salary levels for executives are highly transparent in most Western countries (due to regulatory processes) so, once the decision is made (and published) to pay the new CEO highly, then this process tends to trickle down the organisation. Other board members may

dislike such a huge gap with their CEO and, in any case, it is not unknown for the new CEO to bring on board new colleagues paid in the same way as himself (very occasionally 'herself'). Then executives further down the chain become aware of general reward rises and better performers will feel dismayed if they are not asked to join this attractive new culture. Within a comparatively short time, the organisation's executive pay as a whole is taken up a new notch, in line with 'international market rates'. Once there, it is very difficult to reduce.

This is good evidence to support the argument that the market for top executives is international. An example here is that of Dick Brown, an American, who was CEO for Cable and Wireless in 1997. He was offered a similar position at competitor AT&T at a much higher salary. Cable and Wireless managed to persuade him to stay by offering him a doubled salary and a high long-term earnings potential. Within two years, he had been headhunted to lead another US telecoms company.

- Shortage of Talent

An associated argument is that the required candidates for top positions are simply not around in sufficient numbers so the price of top talent has risen sharply. Most top international companies are very large and complex, often dealing with a vast product list, such as General Electric, or operating in some many countries, such as Nokia and Coca-Cola, or employing so many (Wal-Mart employed over 1.2 million in America alone in 2013 and around double that world-wide). So very high pay is required to find such people with the ability to take on such vast responsibilities and get them sufficiently motivated to be prepared to move anywhere and devote the whole of their time to carrying out their executive job.

The theoretical support here comes from Tournament theory. First put forward by Lazear and Rosen (1981), the basic framework of Tournament theory assumes that employees will compete in a 'knock-out' tournament to achieve promotion to the highest levels. The way to encourage huge commitment from employees at the lower levels is to make substantial prizes in the form of excessive salaries/benefits for those at the top. Employees are assumed to exert effort to increase the likelihood of securing the 'prize' and the effort expended depends on the differential in pay between the top and bottom, the number of competitors and the employees' perceived view on the possibility of them winning the prize. This theory goes some way to understand the huge pay rates for top sportspeople and celebrities in the arts and media.

In the commercial arena, however, it does not explain why more such people are not available to become top executives. In the international market place, where standards of business education around the world have risen substantially in the last 50 years, there should be far more, not less, available talent, especially when developing countries are taken into account. It would be expected that this rise in supply would act as a depressant on reward rates but it has not happened. The argument is that the quantity of

supply may have increased but the quality is uncertain. Just as the international market for football players (or football managers) has hugely widened in the last ten years, most organisations are not prepared to take too many risks and hence go for proven talent for their top performers, with the associated reward costs, to get quick and (perhaps) guaranteed results. Sometimes it works, but not always.

Also implied in this argument is the need to take on external candidates. If an organisation needs shaking up or setting out in a new directions, then external candidates with no baggage may be appropriate, but they generally cost more money, whatever the level of recruitment. At the most senior level, where they can be the most valuable in effecting change, they are very expensive indeed.

- Actually, senior executives are quite cheap.

An unusual argument is that the total reward costs for *executives that make a real difference to organisational performance* are not very high. The total pay for the eight executive board members for Tesco in 2009 was around £30–35m (depending on what costs you count, but including most employment costs). Given the profits in 2008–9 were over £3bn, they cost only around 1% of the profits they generated. The argument goes that they, therefore, give very good value for money. Perhaps if their salaries had been 20% less, then the profits may have been 50% less, who knows?

Even if you add on another 100 executives below this level, then this figure rises to no more than £60m and the costs only rise to 2%. The percentage in other organisations may average a little more, such as in banking or technology where employees may be more highly skilled but it is still a very small total cost.

- High pay reflects the level of risks taken by senior executives.

The risks referred to here are two fold. First, it is the ability to identify opportunities that may involve risk-taking (ie make substantial investments which may or may not bring a large return) and know how to deal effectively with them. This is part of a previous argument of paying for unique talent.

The second risk involved is the risk that the executive takes in working it that position. By taking up such a high profile position, the risks of failure are serious. If it does not work out as a success, then the executive loses a substantial salary which may not be possible to re-coup. Their reputation is also in the public eye, making the 'after-life' of failure quite difficult, as seems to be the case with the dismissed CEO of Royal Bank of Scotland (Fred Goodwin) and the two both chief executives of BP (Brown and Hayward) who both left under a cloud and with far less wealth than they would have expected.

- Executives' pay is heavily contingent on performance

A high proportion of executive pay is contingent upon performance, ranging from over 50% for the average CEO to around 30% for the executive just below board level. The argument is that the huge salaries are only paid when the organisation has performed really well. If the executive does not perform then the high rewards are not paid. This argument is supported by Kaplan (2008) whose research showed that the companies with CEOs in the top quintile of actual pay (in other words, the most highly paid, chiefly by performance pay) were the top-performing companies relative to their industry. Companies with CEOs in the bottom quintile of actual pay were the worst performing quintile relative to their industries. In other words, CEOs were clearly paid for performance and rightly so. He even went on to indicate that the evidence was that CEOs may be underpaid.

In theory, the argument that bonuses are strongly aligned to company performance appears to be a good one but is not watertight. There are numerous accounts of executive targets being insufficiently stretching or of targets being achieved through increased prices in limited competition areas, such as the water industry where executives received double-digit pay raises of nearly £1m while rising customers' bills well above inflation (Watts 2010). However, a recent development is that some major companies, including Land Securities, are inserting in executive contracts a clause to the effect that bonuses will be clawed back if it is found that executives had acted unlawfully, had acted with too much risk or others reasons were determined that strongly indicated the bonuses were not deserved (Churchard 2012b). For example, HSBC plans to claw back bonuses from executives, past and present, after an investigation by the US authorities revealed the bank had laundered cash for criminal organisations. The employer could recover millions of pounds in bonus awards from employees, reportedly including former chief executive Michael Geoghegan and Sandy Flockhart, a senior executive at the bank's Mexican operation (HSBC 2012).

- If you publish every detail of pay, you are bound to get pay inflation

One of the factors that make executive pay different from most other pay systems is the degree of regulation which compels the full details of directors' pay to be published by the companies. This is one of the reasons that so much research is published – because the data is so readily available. It is thought that transparency provides benefits for the shareholders who can hold directors to account.

Unfortunately, too much information can be a bad thing, as explained by Dymond and Murlis (2009):

'...because executives now know what other executives earn and what they earn it for (at least in part), pay levels have increased as these highly competitive individuals demand parity.'

Compensation committees, when taking decisions on pay rates, will have in front of them full data on executive pay elsewhere. No self-respecting committee will want to be seen paying below the median rate and most would like to be seen paying more. An influence here is that the committee will be made up of a number of non-executive directors who are executive directors elsewhere and therefore, cynics will say, may have a vested interest in inflationary increases.

● Senior executives can choose an even more remunerative career

One of the arguments that is little discussed concerns those individuals who, in fact, never become directors of large organisations but, instead, set up their own companies and become very rich. An organisation in the construction industry, well-known to the writer, was set up in the 1970s by a young entrepreneur and, despite many setbacks and rough patches, successfully grew the company to a turnover of £40m by 2014, employing 200 people, making £4m annually. He takes a return through salary and dividends of around £2m a year and his wealth is estimated at around £60m. He could possibly have worked his way up to a very senior position in the construction industry but he achieved his wealth much quicker and with much more satisfaction through being an entrepreneur.

The main point here is that countries need good senior executives to run their major industrial organisations. Britain needs good (home-grown) executive talent to build and develop our large and medium size operations so they can compete in the world. If potential talented individuals decide at an early age that they can achieve wealth in an alternative way, then the likelihood is that Britain as a whole is the loser. The argument, therefore, is that we must make being a senior executive attractive enough or they will choose an alternative, less vital path. Today, they are more likely to go into hedge funds or merchant banking and, given recent events, we can be less sure of the benefits those industries bring to the well-being of UK PLC.

Question

Discuss these arguments for high executive pay. Do they have merit? Put forward counter-arguments in favour of greater equality for each section.

Technology

LEARNING OUTCOMES

When you have completed this chapter you should be able to understand, explain and critically evaluate:

- the key technological developments in information technology and other fields
- the direct impact such changes have had on organisations
- how technology has influenced goods, services and the labour markets
- the ways that human resources can make use of technology to improve techniques and services
- the concept of knowledge management
- some of the reasons why technology has not always been seen as a beneficial influence.

8.1 INTRODUCTION

No one doubts that massive technological advances have changed the world, as set out in the discussion of the causes of globalisation in Chapter 6. The developments in information and communication technologies, biotechnology, energy supply and transportation have altered the world beyond recognition over the last 50 years. To put it more accurately, technological change enables massive changes to take place – changes in organisation, communication, products, marketing and distribution together with associated ways of managing people. The uniqueness of technology is that, once it has been invented, it cannot be 'un-invented'. Other resources can be used up (oil), can suddenly disappear (chief executives) or be replaced (buildings), but the technological knowledge will always survive. In fact, once one organisation uses that technology and gains competitive advantage, it needs to be adopted in some form by all the competitors to ensure survival.

The speed of technological advance is increasing, prompting even speedier changes in society. In fact, writing about examples is quite difficult because, by the time this book is printed, most of the examples will be out of date and the most influential changes of the next ten years are only known about by small cliques of researchers in multinational research and development labs and their counterparts in leading universities.

8.2 WHAT'S HAPPENING IN TECHNOLOGY?

8.2.1 PATTERNS OF TECHNOLOGICAL DEVELOPMENT

The common differentiation between man and other animals is the ability to design and use tools, so primitive technologies have been utilised for many thousands of years. However, the beginnings of the industrial revolution in the mid-seventeenth century saw the early stages of fundamental technological growth, where machines replaced hand operations.

Although technological invention appears to follow a continuous and unrelenting line, a pattern has been identified by, among others, Hall and Preston (1988). Named K-waves, after the Russian Kondratiev, who first developed the concept in the 1920s, a 50-year cycle for each wave has been identified, as shown in Table 8.1.

Table 8.1 Kondratiev's K-waves

K1	1770s to 1830s	Early mechanisation in textiles and water power with the construction of canals, which lead to the first large-scale factories and companies.
K2	1830s to 1880s	Invention of steam power used in railways and machines, which lead to vastly improved communications and location independent of water sources.
K3	1880s to 1930s	Inventions of electricity, steel, chemicals and synthetics creating new industries with reliable and powerful energy leading to very large-scale production and control (trusts and cartels) and opening up of transportation and communication through cars and aircraft. Technologies were integrated to create assembly line techniques.
K4	1930s to 1980s	Explosion of development of cars and aircraft together with petrochemicals and consumer durables. Controlled through integrated manufacturing processes and by multinational organisations.
K5	1980s to current	ICT developments producing ability to source and manufacture flexibly across the world, creating global brands, communicated by television, radio and Internet technologies. Robotics allows complex manufacturing and medical processes.

There can be much debate about the timing of these waves and the overlapping feature of new technologies, but an economic pattern emerges that shows four stages. First, the invention and diffusion of the technology produces prosperity, especially for the organisations leading the way. However, after a period, demand slackens or competitors catch up, leading to a recession, where new investment falls. After such a period, the third stage is that of outright depression, arising from reduced activity and restructuring with mass unemployment before the final stage, recovery, appears, when the economic conditions improve sufficiently for the next wave of technological development.

?   REFLECTIVE ACTIVITY 8.1

There is some evidence that the current technological cycle is swinging towards a down phase. Set out the reasons why this down phase might be occurring and also explain why the contrary may be true – that the current technological phase is gathering more steam.

8.2.2 TYPES OF TECHNOLOGICAL CHANGE

Freeman (1987) identified four different types of technological change:

1 *Incremental innovations* – these are small-scale changes made at a local level. For example, a quality circle might come up with a new way to calibrate existing equipment in a factory.

2 *Radical innovations* – they change the way things are done. For example, the development of semiconductors rather than valves in the 1960s changed the ways in which computers could operate.

3 *Changes of technology systems* – these often involve linking together two existing technological systems to form a new system. For example, multimedia entertainment systems bring together computer and TV technologies.

4 *Technology revolutions* – these occur about every 50 years or so and revolutionise our approach to technology. One was the development of the steam engine in the 1770s, another, the growth of the railways in the 1830s. The development of the computer in the 1940s and the creation of the worldwide web/Internet have been the latest two.

8.2.3 INFORMATION TECHNOLOGY

In all technological developments, it is in the field of information technology that the speed of development has been the greatest, as has the effect upon society. A stream of inventions has followed the arrival of the first commercial computer in the 1950s. In *hardware*, the integrated circuits have become increasingly powerful through the invention of optical chips and biochips paralleled by the improvements in data storage systems.

The variety of delivery devices – laptops, tablets, smart phones, etc, continue to expand while the price continues to decline, except for the top range products such as Apple phones. Ever more powerful laptops and tablets allow work to be carried out at any location and on the move.

In *software*, there is this massive ability to network information so it is available to multiple organisational users; to operate real-time systems so leisure activities, such as flights or theatre tickets can be booked electronically; in banking, money markets around the world are linked with instant access to information and market changes; programs can control tools to perform any task previously carried out by hand, such as cut, weld or burn; controls can be programmed into complex machinery which determines the output and the quality of the process.

All these developments have led to the computer being at the heart of business and, increasingly, private lives. Production, sales, distribution, finance, human resources, are all aided by computer systems which increase the speed of operation, while providing reliable operations, communications and storage. Data, in the form of intellectual property, can even be fed into a 3D printer, costing as little as £10,000, which can then produce a finished good, such as a toy. This is done by spraying successive layers of materials, such as polycarbonate or clay, forming an output far quicker and cheaper than starting with a lump of material and machining away the unwanted parts, so that objects like toys can be made as a small unit without the huge overheads of assembly lines. One of the suppliers to GE jet engines prints metal parts with such printers (*Economist* 2012a).

8.2.4 COMMUNICATION TECHNOLOGIES

Supporting the development in information technologies have been two major technological developments in communication. First, satellite communication, starting in the mid-1960s, has increased exponentially so that there are now over 100 geo-stationary satellites in orbit facilitating cheap and instantaneous communication and data transmission.

Second, the invention and development of optical fibre technology has provided a competitor in huge capacity handling at great speed. FLAG Europe-Asia, for example, is a 27,000 km system servicing half the world at lower and lower costs. An example (*Economist* 2000) is that the cost of transmitting the *Encyclopaedia Britannica* electronically from New York to Los Angeles was $187 in 1970. By 2000, the entire contents of the Library of Congress could be sent the same distance for less than $40.

Both these developments have led to the creation of mass markets, allowing consumers to be aware of the goods and services on offer. Even if incomes are low, the spread of multinational advertising and brand creation produces images that people can aspire to so that they become future consumers. Television has had the most dramatic effect because it makes no demands on a standard of literacy, unlike the printed word. The technological development improvements since its invention in the 1930s, which have consistently reduced the price and increased the quality and reliability, have had two effects on the mass markets. The first effect is direct, in that most television channels are commercial, so the products and services are directly communicated to the consumer. The second effect is more elliptical in that television programmes show styles of life that create the aspirational effect. This was most pronounced in Eastern Europe under communism where the nightly broadcasting of Western shows indicated clearly how far behind the communist economic model was compared with the West and contributed to its eventual collapse.

The swiftness of communication improves the effectiveness of markets. Producers and consumers widely use mobile phones to aid their business choices. Jensen (2007) researched the rapid spread of mobile phones among the Kerala fishermen off the Indian coast and found that they were able to land their catch in the markets which provided the best return. This reduced the overall price for consumers, provided more consistency of supply and prevented the widespread wastage which occurred when fish could not be sold. So a much more efficient market prevailed.

The most important example of the integration of communication and information technologies is the smartphone, where the portable package, available at an increasingly affordable price, provides web information and the ability to communicate by phone, text and email. 4G technology, launched in the UK in 2012, provides broadband Internet access to devices such as mobile phones and tablets at fast speeds and can be used for rich media, such as streaming videos.

8.2.5 TRANSPORTATION TECHNOLOGIES

The 'shrinking world' is a simplistic but accurate description of the rapid technological change since the 1940s, heralded by the invention of the jet engine and its development into the *commercial jet liner*. The time difference in travel by air compared with boat and train has been so substantial that it has created two linked mass markets. First, for the traveller, whether business or pleasure, for whom the swiftness and pleasure of the journey is joined to the associated activities it allows. Second, for the tourist, where the travelling is a means to take holidays in other countries and where a vast supporting infrastructure has been built up – hotels, holiday complexes, leisure activities. The break-up of the nationalised, non-competing flag-carrying airways has allowed the creation of a flood of low-cost carriers, bringing regular travel to the mass market. When linked to the online flight and accommodation booking systems, consumers have the ability to create their own holiday package at highly competitive rates, which has seen the demise of 50% of holiday tour companies.

Another less publicised change, but of considerable importance, has been the development of *containerisation* for the movement of freight across land and sea. It is such a simple and obvious development that it tends to be overlooked but it only started in 1956 and, before that time, loading and unloading cargo could be a slow, hazardous and wasteful activity (Levinson 2006). It was also associated with strong union presence in the ports of most developed countries, threatening strike action against developments that may reduce labour costs or employment. By the 1980s, the union power had been broken in both America and the UK and, today, the container can be 'stuffed' on the factory site, loaded and unloaded quickly by crane and enjoy protection against weather and theft throughout its journeys. In the 1960s, freight costs averaged 30% of total costs for imported goods; under containerisation, this has been reduced to 1%, a massive cost saving.

8.2.6 THE INTERNET

There has been an astonishingly rapid development of Internet technology since its origins in the US Defense Department in the mid-1970s and its commercial usage since the mid-1990s. It now affects all aspects of work and leisure at a steadily reducing cost that now puts its utilisation within the grasp of most citizens in the developed world and many in the developing world. Society communicates through emails, while hard-copy communications (such as letters) are used only in specific situations. Some organisations, such as easyJet, have attempted to become completely paper-free by scanning all the incoming post and insisting on all correspondence, internal and external, being carried out through emails. The Internet provides a huge range of information that is relatively simple for anybody to access. It facilitates buying and selling transactions to take place at the workstation.

We live in the age of the *'Internet of Things'*, the concept whereby smart devices (objects containing microchips that connect them to the internet) have become ubiquitous. For industry, machinery contains interlinked environmental sensors that provide real-time feedback on a variety of conditions to a distant central source which is then acted upon by intelligent software algorithms that process the data to improve productivity, quality and safe working. Any equipment failures are predicted long before they happen. Businesses are able to follow the progress of their products from factory to shop to end-consumer and the products are able to 'speak' to whoever handles them. Designer handbags can vouch for their own authenticity via embedded codes. Even such things as fizzy drinks and washing powders can be made 'smart' so that the manufacturer can detect when and how the products are used.

In 2014, 3.9 billion devices were connected to the internet. By 2020, companies are expected to spend over £300bn on internet-linked systems contributing over £10tr to the world economy (Raconteur 2015).

Examples are growing of 'smart' cities which connect infrastructure from roads to bins, lights to power networks to a digital grid, enabling the city to respond like a living organism to the needs of residents, as shown in Case Study 8.1.

CASE STUDY 8.1

BRISTOL – THE SMART CITY

Bristol has launched an experiment to become a 'smart city' to connect all manner of objects with each other and with individual's smart phones, backed by a super-fast, high-capacity fibre network. Elements of the experiment include:

- Water consumption, air quality, light, sound and temperature levels will be monitored in a series of 100 living home 'laboratories' to discover to reality of how individuals and families live. The results will provide data to suggest ways that behaviour can be

altered to save money and live more healthily. This will include sleep patterns that individuals are not aware of.

- 10,000 frail and elderly people re monitored by a control room which alerts the NHS, social services or their next-of-kin in case of a health scare such as a fall.
- Restaurants are involved in a scheme whereby prices are reduced at off-peak periods communicated to potential customers through a phone app.

- A 'Buxi' (bus-taxi hybrid) scheme is operating in one suburb that will adapt its route to combine the low cost of public transport with the flexibility of a taxi.
- Plans are being made to create a single control centre to combine a number of real time networks, such as traffic monitoring, accidents, vehicle licensing.
- Large savings will be made by fitting sensors to all 42,000 street lights which will alert a control centre when they blow, and direct maintenance staff to replace them.

Source: Hellen (2014)

? REFLECTIVE ACTIVITY 8.2

Not all organisations have been enthusiastic to implement online buying and selling. What holds them back from gaining advantages in this area?

A more recent arrival is the 'Cloud'. The cloud is the concept that the electronic information the consumer wants is stored and processed on computers somewhere else (in the 'cloud') and delivered to the consumer when and how they need it. The Internet becomes the operating system; online software runs in the computer's browser to create the files that are needed and these files are stored in remote data centres. Films can be streamed from the cloud directly onto netbooks, books streamed onto e-readers, music onto iPods and other imaginative applications appear daily (see Case Study 8.2). Software for our own device will not need to be upgraded because the software we use will be tested and constantly 'sprinkled' into the cloud by operators. No longer will there be a need to back up data or fear losing our laptop because no important data will be stored on the devices (Arlidge 2009).

As Nicholas Carr explained:

A hundred years ago, companies stopped generating their own power with steam engines and dynamos and plugged into the newly built electric grid. The cheap power pumped out by electric utilities didn't just change how businesses operate. It set off a chain reaction of economic and social transformations that brought the modern world into existence. Today, a similar revolution is under way. Hooked up to the Internet's global computing grid, massive information-processing plants have begun pumping data and software code into our homes and businesses. This time, it's computing that's turning into a utility. (Carr 2008, p12)

The difficulty faced by the communication industry is how to continue to obtain income from their services (books, newspapers, TV, music) now that they are not being sold in the traditional way. The transfer from individual consumer purchase to subscription services may not generate as much income.

The main concern for businesses and individuals is security. Signing up for cloud services inevitably means providing both personal information but also surrendering all our data to the cloud provider. A hacker can obtain access simply by knowing a password, rather than having to get access to a computer system and there have been numerous examples of data and pictures being stolen or damaged. Moreover, a fire at a data storage unit could destroy vast amounts of data.

More distant worries include the fact that the individual consumer's data can be mined to provide a purchasing profile which will be profitable for advertisers, who can target each consumer individually, and that one company will emerge as the giant of the industry and, in effect, own all the data – every email or document produced. Here, governments are currently discussing future regulatory environments to prevent monopolies emerging.

CASE STUDY 8.2

SHOPPING – SOFTWARE APPLICATIONS

One of the cloud-based applications offered in 2009 by Google was ShopSavvy, where the phone's camera becomes a barcode scanner which allows you to scan the barcode of a product you want to buy in one shop and data will be directed to your phone giving you a list of shops (with their locations) where it can be bought cheaper.

Facial-recognition software is being trialled in shop windows to identify features of shoppers and immediately present advertisements of items in the shop that may be of interest. For example, the camera (hidden within a digital display) may identify a teenage girl and the display will then advertise a new perfume endorsed by a popular pop singer; or it may advertise a hair dye when it identifies a more mature shopper. When the system becomes more sophisticated it may be able to identify likely clothes for the shopper or even headache tablets for those looking 'peaky' or holiday offers for those looking sad.

Sources: Arlidge (2009); Keers (2011)

8.2.7 WEB 2.0 AND SOCIAL MEDIA

Coined by Tim O'Reilly in 2004, Web 2.0 is a term which refers to the sociable and interactive aspects of the web which allow a user to discuss and share ideas. It is generally deemed a 'people-centric web as it stimulates networking and collaboration, including blogging and social networking'. Social networking sites are unique not just in the way that they allow individuals to meet strangers, but also that they allow users to articulate and make visible their round of social networks – with a public display of their connections through their list of 'friends'.

Facebook, the most prominent social networking site, is second only to the Google web search engine in terms of Internet traffic, with an estimated number of users worldwide approaching 1 billion and 26 million UK users. Twitter, a microblogging site begun only in 2007, had between 250 and 500 million users worldwide in 2012 (Bennett 2012). LinkedIn, essentially the business end of social networking, had a world-wide membership approaching 414 million, of which 10 million lived in the UK in 2015.

Organisations have made increasing use of social media in the fields of recruitment, communication, engagement and discipline, as explained later in the chapter.

Company involvement in social media touches on a number of ethical issues. These are, first, the subjects which are discussed on social media by employees and, second, the balance between the wider rights of individuals and the more specific explicit and implicit expectations of behaviour at work which could be upheld through employment law (Broughton et al 2011). In the first case, Valentine et al (2010) have found that dismissing a blogging employee is more likely to be considered ethical if the subject of the blog is work-related than if it is non-work-related. However, a key factor to be considered in both kinds of blogging is the 'moral intensity' of the content. The concept of moral intensity covers a range of factors, including the potential consequences of the comments made, for example the likelihood of an employee's comments harming the company and the scale of any harm.

8.2.8 BIOTECHNOLOGY AND MEDICAL TECHNOLOGIES

Biotechnology is the process of altering life forms, essentially through genetic modification. Arising from the fundamental discovery of the structure of DNA in 1953 by Crick and Watson, modification of biological processes allows such interventions as the introduction of new genes into organisms, breeding organisms to form new variants or treating organisms with new compounds.

One example of biotechnology is in the creation of genetically modified organisms (GMOs). Here, plants, animals and micro-organisms (bacteria, viruses) have had their genetic characteristics modified artificially in order to give them new properties. This could include a plant's resistance to a disease or an insect, the improvement of a food's quality or nutritional value or a plant's tolerance of a herbicide.

The implications for food production and medical advance are astounding. The biotechnology industry has promised a vast increase in food production which would be sufficient to eradicate all forms of under-nourishment world-wide. In medicine, applications promise the eventual eradication of genetic diseases, such as cystic fibrosis, as well as better understanding and treatment in common diseases and conditions, such as cancer and Alzheimer's disease. Governments around the world have co-operated in the massive genome project to map all human genes, which was successfully completed in 2004.

However, the outcomes in recent years have proved problematical. In food production, there has been considerable opposition to the acceptance of GM foods in many countries, especially the UK, to the extent that all UK trials of GM cereals were halted in 2004 and only restarted a few years later on a very limited basis under very strict controls. Many trials, however, have had to be abandoned due to protesters damaging the crops.

There have also been very few signs of long-lasting medical developments. In cystic fibrosis, for example, the discovery of the errant gene in 1984 has not led to any improved treatment, due to technical problems of gene therapy processes, and results in other treatments have been mixed, as shown in Case Study 8.3.

 GENE THERAPY

CASE STUDY 8.3

In 1999, Jesse Gelsinger, a 19-year-old with a rare liver disorder, participated in a voluntary clinical trial using gene therapy at the University of Pennsylvania. He died of complications from an inflammatory response shortly after receiving a dose of experimental adenovirus vector, a new device to direct the new gene to the appropriate location. His death dealt a blow to the confidence of scientists and halted all gene therapy trials in the US for some years and then only restarted for those diseases where no known cure was available.

In 2008, gene therapy was used in America to restore vision in patients with a rare and usually incurable form of blindness affecting around 6,000 people in the USA. The patients had a rare inherited disorder called Leber's congenital amaurosis, which begins eroding eyesight at birth and leaves them blind by their mid-twenties. Four of the six patients treated had much-improved eyesight. It is hoped that gene therapy may work particularly well with eye disorders because the immune system, which can reject the virus carrying the genes, isn't as active in the eye. And because it's easy to test vision, doctors know quickly whether the therapy works.

Sources: Subramanian (2004); Szabo (2008)

In medical research, there is a growing usage of 'Big Data' allied to open-source health aps as shown in Case study 8.4.

CASE STUDY 8.4

OPEN-SOURCE HEALTH APS

Information on people with chronic conditions, such as Parkinsons, diabetes or health disease, is often difficult to gather accurately as it relies on self-reporting. The use of mobile devices packed with sensors worn by patients can provide huge amount of accumulated individual data. They will record movement, exercise, heart rates, weight, blood-analysis, food intake, even the style of walking by the strength of an individual's tapping on the phone's screen.

Apple has produced a suite of software called ResearchKit which will make it possible to create scientific apps that work with its mobile devices easily and cheaply. It is 'open source' which means anybody can design data-collecting apps which take advantage of the features of these devices. They can customise them and share code encouraging innovation. It also streamlines informed consent as all the patient needs to do is to watch a video and answer questions. For the patient, it provides their own data on what is associated with bad days or, in the case of asthma, what may be triggering attacks.

The volume of data which will eventually be accumulated (with informed consent) will, when number-crunched, provide greater opportunities for breakthroughs in diagnosis and treatment.

Source: Economist (2015b)

8.2.9 ARTIFICIAL INTELLIGENCE (AI) AND ROBOTICS

Artificial intelligence is the science and engineering of making intelligent machines, especially intelligent computer programs. It is related to the similar task of using computers to understand human intelligence. AI is studied in overlapping fields of computer science, psychology, philosophy, neuroscience and engineering dealing with intelligent behaviour, learning and adaptation.

Research in AI is concerned with producing machines to automate tasks requiring intelligent behaviour. These are synthesised in what are called 'expert systems'. Examples include control, planning and scheduling, the ability to answer diagnostic and consumer questions, speech and facial recognition. A recent development has been the extension into computer vision, where tests have shown that computers can be trained to 'recognise' complex objects in photographs marginally better than humans can (*Economist* 2007a).

As such, the study of AI has also become an engineering discipline, focused on providing solutions to real-life problems, knowledge-mining and software applications, together with games. However, the world had to wait until 1977 for IBM's Deep Blue to beat the world chess champion, Garry Kasparov. One of the biggest difficulties with AI is that of 'comprehension'. Many devices have been created that can do amazing things, but critics of AI claim that no actual comprehension by the AI machine has taken place.

From the early days of computers, attempts have been made to replicate human activity, with the first industrial robot used by General Motors in 1961. Robots are utilised in four main ways:

1 *In place of humans* – the most common use has been in manufacturing, where robots have replaced humans in jobs that are dirty, dangerous and difficult. They work faster, to more reliable degrees of quality and can operate around the clock. The introduction of paint-spraying in car factories by robots reduced the labour force by 85% and improved the quality standards by 90%. Net-a-Porter, the retailer, operates a robot-only fulfilment factory in London (*People Management* 2013b). They are now seen in all manufacturing and agricultural environments, as examples show in Case Study 8.5. Another example is unmanned surveillance planes, both in the military and increasingly in civil surveillance, such as used in unauthorised migration watch on extended borders between the USA and Mexico and Russia and its neighbours.

CASE STUDY 8.5

INDUSTRIAL ROBOTS ARE RESHAPING MANUFACTURING AND AGRICULTURE

It would be tough to find a company seemingly more evocative of twentieth-century, 'old economy' America than Allied-Locke Industries. The family-owned-and-run manufacturing firm is headquartered about 100 miles due west of Chicago in rural Dixon, Illinois. No one walking onto Allied-Locke's low-light, high-decibel factory floor is going to mistake the place for the clean room at a semiconductor manufacturing plant. Allied's operations appear about as unglamorous and low-tech as one might expect at a maker of chains and sprockets – except, that is, for a smattering of robots.

Although the pervasive grease and grime make these computerised machines with their articulated arms look like they originally came with the place, the robots – all adorned with user-friendly female names like 'Heidi' – are relative newcomers at the 300-employee firm. In 2000, the company picked up four used robots (they formerly resided in a now-shuttered Caterpillar plant) for around $40,000 each to assist in the heated hardening of pins that help form the links in its chains.

Those four robots – along with seven more purchased since then for various tasks such as welding and loading – have allowed Allied-Locke to get more

production out of the same number of workers. And that has helped it avoid new hiring. That sort of situation represents the other face of the well-publicised issue of America's declining manufacturing employment. If American workers aren't losing jobs making Nike sneakers to Vietnamese workers, they are losing out to machines as companies look to increase productivity.

As the saying goes in manufacturing, 'automate or evaporate'. And robots represent the cutting edge of automation technology in the United States. While Japan is often thought of as most adept at the use of robots, America is now a top market for them. In 2003, North American manufacturing companies shelled out $877m for robots and the amount is rising by over 20% per annum.

Materials handling has remained the largest application for robots, followed by spot welding. The automotive industry is still the biggest robot user, ordering nearly two-thirds of robots sold across America.

Lettuce is California's main vegetable crop, growing $1.6bn worth in 2010, accounting for 70% of all lettuce grown in America. Thinning the crop has been a very costly labour-intensive task but a robot called 'Lettuce Bot' has been introduced, pulled by a tractor at two miles per hour and at 98% accuracy. It starts by taking a photo of the plants as it passes, which it compares to a database of more than a million different backdrops of soil and other plants to help it decide whether the plant is a weed or a young lettuce growing too close to another. If it is a weed, a nozzle at the back of the machine squirts it with concentrated fertiliser, which is more deadly than a pesticide, but acts as a feed to the remaining plants.

Similar machines are in the planning stage to plant tulips and other bulbs, harvest, trim and package mushrooms and to water and rotate heavy potted plants around nurseries.

Sources: Pethokoukis (2004); *Economist* (2012b)

2   *Doing jobs that humans find difficult* – robots can be miniaturised to work in very confined spaces where access for humans is difficult or impossible, such as drains. They have been designed to work in areas affected by earthquakes or tornados to help to identify the trapped and injured.

3   *To help humans perform better* – in the military, robots have been utilised for walking through minefields, deactivating unexploded bombs or clearing out hostile buildings.

Boston Dynamics have produced a legged robot which can travel at three miles per hour, climb steep terrains and carry up to 120lb in rough terrain impenetrable to wheeled or tracked vehicles. Robots designed to help soldiers on the battlefield have to be carried onto the battlefield by those soldiers. For that reason, robot builders try to design 'man-portable' designs. A man-portable robot can be carried by a single soldier, usually in a special backpack.

For civilians, robots are developing much more slowly in the field of household gadgets to cook, vacuum and clean buildings. Mitsubishi, for instance, have designed and marketed a one-metre tall humanoid Wakamaru robot, costing around £7,000, to act as a mechanical house-sitter and secretary. It can recognise up to 10 faces and understands 10,000 words and can be utilised to watch over homes while owners are away, alerting them to possible burglaries, record notes and appointments and remind their owners with well-timed announcements. It can even monitor the condition of a sick person.

Drones, famous for their military capacity for smart bombing and assassinations, are also being utilised for civilian purposes. At Luton Airport, a drone, navigated by lidar, is used to inspect the wings and fuselage of an Airbus A320 for damage by lightning or bird strike. It completes the job in 20 minutes compared to ten hours by engineers on moving platforms (Ford 2015).

The driverless car has come a stage further in recent years with a specially adapted Volkswagen Passat, costing £265,000, which is licensed in Berlin to drive itself from one specified address to another on public streets. It uses sophisticated GPS, two screen-mounted cameras, six lasers, a spinning Velodyne laser scanner on the roof and radar front and back. Also tested in Germany is a car controlled only by human thought, which works by isolating and identifying the electrical patterns that are given off when the 'driver' thinks about a given course of action, such as braking or turning a steering wheel (Conway 2011). Google's massive investment in self-driven cars reached the one million mile point in 2015, although this success was hindered by one car crashing into a bus in February 2016.

4   *Training for humans* – Case Study 8.6 demonstrates the benefits of using robots for simulation purposes.

MEDICAL SCHOOLS USE ROBOT BIRTH SIMULATOR FOR TRAINING

The American Institute of Medicine, an arm of the National Academy of Sciences, estimates that as many as 98,000 US patients die annually from preventable medical errors. By using a robot and analysing in detail what went wrong, these errors can be engineered out. Noelle is a lifelike, 'pregnant' robot used in increasing numbers of medical schools and hospital maternity wards.

The full-sized, blonde, pale mannequin is in demand because medicine is rapidly abandoning centuries-old training methods that use patients as guinea pigs, turning instead to high-tech simulations. It's better to make a mistake on a $20,000 robot than a live patient. The robot mannequins range in price from $3,200 to $20,000, the most expensive being the closest to approximating a live birth. She can be programmed for a variety of complications, can labour for hours and produce a breech baby or unexpectedly give birth in a matter of minutes.

She ultimately delivers a plastic doll that can change colours, from a healthy pink glow to the deadly blue of oxygen deficiency. The baby mannequin is wired to flash vital signs when hooked up to monitors. The computerised mannequins emit realistic pulse rates and can urinate and breathe.

A training session would involve a set of doctors and nurses tending to Noelle, who would be hooked up to standard delivery monitoring machines. However, in the corner would be an engineer from the manufacturer using his laptop to inflict all sorts of complications through wireless signals to the robot, which would override any pre-programmed instructions. The medical team would learn through their role-plays how to deal with all types of emergencies and the harm they inflict by making wrong decisions.

Source: Elias (2006)

8.3 IMPACT ON BUSINESS STRATEGY, GOODS AND SERVICES

The impact of new technology can be seen in two main developments: in business strategies and the method of operation, on the one hand; and in new products and services, on the other.

8.3.1 EFFECTS ON BUSINESS STRATEGIES AND OPERATIONS

The biggest effect is for organisations to have the ability to be *flexible* and to be *eager to change*. New developments put old technologies out of business quickly. For example, in the 1990s, only luxury cars had air conditioning; in the twenty-first century, few cars, except those at the very cheapest end, will sell without it. Given the extended period of design and development, manufacturers need to build in the ability to alter the standard product quickly and effectively to within a very tight budget. In reality, the product must combine extreme reliability that new technology has brought with design obsolescence to ensure the customer continues to purchase a company's new products.

Schumpeter (1976) identified the potential risks of not reacting quickly enough to major technological inventions as 'creative destruction', which can completely destroy the organisation. As an example, the arrival of digital technology in the early 2000s completely undermined Kodak's film and photographic paper operations. Although generally recognised as slow to react, they eventually produced their own digital equipment and provided innovations, such as self-service kiosks and an online printing service.

Associated with this trend is the need to *mass-customise* your products, perhaps something of a contradiction. Mass production is needed to produce the cost saving, but varieties are required to meet all the customers' varied needs. A good example in services is Compass PLC, which delivers thousands of catering contracts across the world, every one different but with some essential common sourcing, marketing and administration systems. The system becomes more complex but IT systems allow control and monitoring of every detail. The customised feature has altered manufacturing approaches to assembly lines, many of which have been abandoned in favour of *cell production systems*, where groups of multi-skilled employees work in teams to meet the differing production contracts, taking responsibility for quality, waste reduction and innovation.

The vast improvements in efficiencies in production, brought about through robotics and other IT processes, and the ability to manufacture on a global basis have led to a growing *decline in manufacturing in developed countries* as the technology has been transferred to developing countries, together with using the sources of cheap capital and labour. Examples have been given in Chapter 7 of outsourcing manufacturing from Germany to Eastern Europe and from UK call centres to India.

Technology has offered two additional *marketing opportunities*. Better knowledge of an organisation's customers through manipulation of a vast amount of purchasing data allows much closer targeting of their requirements, a process that retailers such as Homebase and Tesco have developed through loyalty cards (see Case Study 8.7). This quantity of information is only available to large organisations, but the second opportunity, the web, can be used by any sized business. In fact, the web has allowed many niche organisations to market, sell and distribute their products and services at low costs, many without the overheads of retail premises. Web-based business activity has expanded exponentially since the mid-1990s, especially business to business where sourcing can be fixed through web-based tendering or even a quasi-auctioning system. Web-marketing opportunities are a bonus for small firms by allowing them to access huge markets for specialised products.

 TESCO'S CLUBCARD

CASE STUDY 8.7

In 1995, Tesco launched their Clubcard and, by 2009, it had 16 million members (50% of households) providing complex information on each individual's shopping habits. Dunnhumby, its majority-owned marketing subsidiary, processes 100 baskets a second, equal to 6 million transactions per day. Each product has 45 pieces of data; it is judged, for example, on whether it is cheap or expensive, brand or own-brand, ethnic or traditional, exotic or basic. Non-food purchases have their own sets of classification. By their purchases, consumers are filtered by demographic,

socio-economic and lifestyle characteristics. It is possible to generate a map of how the individual thinks, works and shops. They can be classified across 10 categories – wealth, travel, promotions, green, time-poor, credit, living style, creature of habit, charities – and into sophisticated sub-groups, such as whether they are pet owners and whether they cook for themselves often or not at all.

A personality build-up can define a 'Mrs Pumpkin' who makes pennies work when she shops, mostly uses cash, has a steady repertoire of products but experiments with new ones, has increased her spending on eco-friendly items, is involved in charity-giving, is rarely away and likes using the promotions offered.

This information is integrated with information in the public domain from Electoral Rolls, Land Registry and the Office for National Statistics to generate a profile of the area.

This information helps Tesco to decide on major strategic moves, such as the launch of Express convenience stores and the 'Finest' range and also in micro-strategies such as which products should go on to the shelves at what times and what personal communications and offers should be made to customers. For example, if customers have stopped buying bread for a period, they must be

buying it elsewhere, so special cut-price bread vouchers are sent to them to entice them back. It is invaluable in launching specialised Clubcard clubs, such as a wine club and a mother and toddler club, which provide more direct marketing opportunities.

This personal information is then sold on to major suppliers who can use it to research and develop their product range according to shoppers' tastes and individual promotions. The information itself has been classed in such a way that it circumvents disclosure provisions in the Data Protection Act, so it is difficult for individuals to know what Tesco's personal information on them contains.

Sources: Tomlinson and Evans (2005); Davey (2009)

? REFLECTIVE ACTIVITY 8.3

It is evident that some forms of technological development provide organisations with a competitive advantage. One example is the invention by St Helens glassmaker Pilkingtons of the float glass process in the 1950s. This brought huge competitive advantages in both the quality of the sheet glass and the productivity levels. Apple's marketing of iTunes, where it was impossible for songs bought to be played on competitor's equipment, allowed Apple to capture 80% of the US and UK market in the first two years and gave them huge bargaining power with the major record companies.

Think of a further THREE examples of this process and explain why such an advantage was gained in this way.

8.3.2 SPECIFIC PRODUCTS

The implications arising from the recent rapid developments in information technology and communications for the marketplace are substantial. Here are just a few examples at the time of writing:

- Increasing offering by subscriptions of movies, music and television/radio programmes by operators such as Disney, Comcast and Rhapsody will mean that programming-on-demand will take the place of normal TV and radio schedules. The BBC has set up a subscription service for all its huge archive of programmes. This will allow the viewer to choose exactly which episodes of, say, *'Allo, 'Allo!* or a set of 1970s *Play for Today* they want to watch, when they want to watch them.
- Flat-screen, computerised smart TVs consistently drop in price and become essential furniture of the networked home, with 4G bandwidth to fill the high definition screens.

- Myriad websites compete with TV, music and video producers and distributors. Individuals can beam up their own productions onto the web and become their own publishers.

Although there is little disagreement that technology has increased living standards generally, recent criticisms extend to the disproportionate economic power that now accumulates around companies who 'own the fastest computers with the most access to everyone's information'. Lanier (2013) has explained that citizens donate extremely lucrative information – our interests, demographic predilections, buying habits, cyber-movements – in exchange for 'free' admission into social media networks. In the financial world, for example, digitisation has allowed banks to repackage the 'information' of a mortgage debt and sell it on as increasingly complex financial products, while excluding the indebted home-owner from a percentage of the profits. Lanier argues that the early Internet years have placed such stress on open access and knowledge-sharing that it has distracted people from demanding fairness and job security in an economy predicated on data flow. He has also identified the strain on middle-level jobs in many professions that are being destroyed, especially in the music, legal and communication industries. Even universities are at risk as they are 'Napsterised' by the free flow of online information.

Lanier's greatest worry is the huge increase in power in what he calls the 'Siren Servers' – Google, Apple, Amazon and a handful of other companies able to monopolise 'big data' and able to quickly buy out (and often stifle) creative new companies who may act as competitors. Without greater state intervention through higher regulation and taxation of their activities, the risk becomes greater of technology's job-creation going into reverse, leaving a huge and growing pool of unemployed labour.

8.4 EFFECTS ON LABOUR MARKETS AND HUMAN RESOURCES

Technology both eliminates jobs and creates them. The introduction of railways in the nineteenth century eliminated most jobs in the canal transport industry but created a substantial net increase in jobs in total – in the rail industry itself, in the suppliers to the industry and in the associated expansion of industry and commerce that fast rail transport provided.

The same is true in today's technological changes. The IT software industry has created a huge number of jobs around the world, while the outcomes of their labour have reduced jobs selectively in manufacturing, distribution and administration. As mentioned earlier, introducing robotics into paint-spraying operations in car production, for example, has reduced the labour requirements in this function by 85%. On the other hand, this technological change, among others, has reduced the price of the finished car to the extent that it is affordable to a greater mass market and employees in car manufacturing around the world continue to show a small overall increase.

It is the nature of the labour force that has changed with technological innovation. A polarisation has occurred with an increased demand for highly trained professional and technical employees and, at the same time, a reduced demand for low-skilled assembly and production operatives on the other. An even bigger decline has occurred in the demand for semi-skilled employees or those with traditional apprentice-served skills, most of which have been replaced by automation. This is also reflected geographically, with most of the employees in Silicon Valley and other high-tech clusters in America and Japan in the high-skills category, while the actual production of semiconductors, printers and other hardware is being carried out in East Asian countries and Mexico with largely low-skilled employees.

The perceived need for a reservoir of highly skilled employees has been the driving force for advanced countries, including the UK, to lay greater stress on achieving an increased percentage of the population to be qualified through higher education (the current target is 50%) or through an education programme of skills achievements. Doubts remain, however, as to the value to the student of many graduate courses that appear attractive and enjoyable, such as many media arts courses, but offer little hope of long-term careers.

8.4.1 INCREASE IN TEMPORARY LABOUR

Information technology can provide information in a more reliable form and at a much more rapid rate. This allows organisations to respond far quicker to variations in consumer demand which, in turn, requires the labour market to become far more flexible.

Employers have responded in their employment model by making much greater use of non-standard employment, such as part-time or temporary employees. Supermarkets, for example, use their sales data to forecast precisely the number of checkouts required every hour of the year and use part-time employees to resource the varying needs. The need for temporary staff for Christmas and holiday periods can also be precisely pinpointed through the accurate data provided. This allows them to reach their business target of queues no greater than one or two people.

Case Study 8.7 shows a micro example of this process.

CASE STUDY 8.8

LETTUCE LEAVES AND THE LABOUR MARKET

It has become clear in recent years that consumers are steadily reducing their purchases of whole lettuces and increasingly purchasing packages of prepared lettuce leaves in a variety of forms. For supermarkets, this has provided an excellent opportunity with Tesco PLC selling over £150m-worth a year, with a very high mark-up (as applies to most ready-prepared foods). But such packs have a very short shelf life, despite the chemical methods applied during their preparation. In addition, the purchase of such packs (often on impulse) varies very much in line with the weather.

Supermarket responses to this scenario are to assemble incredibly accurate information on purchasing trends, adjust for forecast weather conditions and put in their orders with a very short delivery time – usually no more than a day in advance, sometimes shorter. The suppliers, who are dealing with large orders they cannot afford to lose, in turn need to adjust their labour requirements flexibly. Most cannot afford to operate a system of on-call labour so they turn to labour service providers. One pack-house, for example, contracted in 2004 for 2.7 million hours of temporary labour for lettuce and other convenience salad packs. The providers, now known as 'gangmasters', have large groups of itinerant labour, mostly from overseas, who they call on a daily basis to meet heavily fluctuating demand in preparing lettuce packs and other highly seasonal goods.

Estimates of the immigrants (legal and otherwise) engaged in such work vary greatly, but it continues to rise by every report. Provista, a major player, recruits regularly from Eastern Europe, which goes some way to explain the increase of 70,000 in reported work permits from that area since the accession of a group of such countries in 2004.

Source: *Economist* (2004a)

The direct implications for human resource practitioners of new technologies can be seen in the fields of recruitment and selection, teleworking and call centres and in the way the human resource operation is structured.

8.4.2 TECHNOLOGY IN RECRUITMENT AND SELECTION

Recruitment has moved a long way in the last few years. Initially the changes reflected the need to attract talent from the Generation Y group, who were early adopters of new technology but, as the use of the Internet and 3G and later technologies become universal, companies cannot afford to depend only on the printed word for their recruitment activities. This applies especially where companies are looking to recruit from Generation Z (those born from 1990), who have never known life without the Internet. Web-based recruitment is attractive because the response can be far quicker (possible except when filling in online application forms) and it works out far cheaper, even when using generic websites. The advance of e-recruitment saved the NHS £100m from 2005 to 2008 with 95% of applications received online and 99% of shortlisting carried out online (Chubb 2008).

Company websites

All organisations include a career opportunity and job vacancy section on their website, and the company website came top of the effectiveness rating in a 2015 CIPD survey. Some are more sophisticated than others.

Whitbread developed a dedicated recruitment website in 2004 called www.run-a-restaurant.com. In its first four months, the site was searched 100,000 times, resulting in 1,300 applications, which allowed their brands Brewsters and Brewers Fayre to recruit more than 60% of their candidates directly and boosted the nine-day retention figure from 90% to 95%. It saved them a considerable sum of money.

Procter & Gamble has extended their web-based recruitment to devise a virtual career fair (Stevens 2010a). This six-hour event saw 1,200 people visit the fair, to view corporate videos and presentations and network with existing employees.

Marks & Spencer promotes online applications through its website. The process encourages unsuitable candidates to screen themselves out as soon as possible. It then assesses the remainder against a customised behavioural profile, using algorithms to check answers against a psychometric benchmark (Chenoweth 2014).

Generic websites

Sometimes called online job boards, there are a large number of Internet recruitment companies which can be divided into those which cover all areas, such as Monster and total jobs, and those which deal with only one sector, such as NHS Jobs. The CIPD reported that 33% of employees rated them as effective (CIPD 2010). All newspapers and magazines, including the CIPD, have developed their own online sites to run alongside the printed version.

CV scanning

Software has been developed which can scan CVs to see how closely they match the job specification in terms of experience, skills, qualifications and competences required.

Phone/iPhone application

Various systems have been devised to attract applicants through their mobile phones. Adidas have developed an iPhone application specifically to drive graduates to its recruitment site, which yielded 4,500 applications in the first year (Evans 2011). A second example, LV=, an insurance and pensions company which utilises interactive media, is shown in Case Study 8.9.

CASE STUDY 8.9

LV= RECRUITS VIA INTERACTIVE MEDIA

Bournemouth-based LV= has introduced a scheme based on a series of posters, each of which features a real staff member. Interested jobseekers are invited to take a photo of the poster using their mobile phone and send it to a quoted number. Image recognition software will process the request and the person will then receive a pre-recorded phone call from the employee in the poster, in which they talk about their experiences in the company. This unusual approach is to pass the message that the organisation is highly creative and that insurance is not a stuffy or dull career and to confirm that the people in the poster are real employees.

Source: Brockett (2010)

Social networking

Many employers are now using social media to directly recruit. The main serious site is LinkedIn, and 14% of employers rated them as effective in the 2010 CIPD survey. Most individuals who have joined such a site will ensure their pages are updated with a full review of their skills and experience, which can be easily viewed by employers. Global engineering company CH2M HILL has used the website to recruit 10% of their hires in 2010 and typically use the platform as a sourcing stream for highly skilled roles commanding salaries of £50,000-plus. LinkedIn has recently announced the launch of a 'recruiter tool' for employers, which includes an engine for users to refer contact for a job and a function for recruiters and managers to exchange and give feedback on candidate profiles (Stevens 2011). Another example is KPMG, which uses social networking sites to tell students about campus events and setting up online communities for interns. It also communicates through the platform of Second Life (Chynoweth 2007).

A more unlikely user is CERN, the world's largest particle physics laboratory in Switzerland, as detailed in Case Study 8.10.

CASE STUDY 8.10

CERN – SOCIAL MEDIA CAN TRANSFORM THE QUALITY OF RECRUITMENT

CERN recruits professionals in a wide diversity of fields, not just in physics and engineering, so it advertises all job vacancies on Twitter, LinkedIn and Facebook. It goes further than this, however, because the intention is to interact with the potential audience, such as candidates, and with those who may know others who could wish to apply. For example, they use Facebook to host a weekly question-and-answer session led by one of the CERN recruiters, while LinkedIn provides a forum for more specialised discussions. Since starting to use social media, CERN has seen the number of applications soar from 7,000 in 2008 to 24,000 in 2011, a far greater increase than can be explained by the recession. The range of communication media helps to clarify the requirement that appointments can only be made from one of the 20 states that fund the organisation.

Source: Cook (2012)

Automated telephone screening

Telephone screening is another new development. Here, an applicant calls a freephone number, day or night, and keys in their unique personal identification number, which automatically sets up a file for them on the company's HR system. During the interview, typically lasting 15 minutes, the candidate answers multiple-choice questions using their telephone keypad. The computer scores and weights their answers and automatically sends them an application form or schedules a face-to-face interview if they are successful. The system then sends the HR manager an interview schedule.

Initial testing

Large, well-known employers are often faced with a huge response for specific positions, especially in a graduate intake. Many have developed forms of online initial testing to reduce the number of applications to numbers they can handle without having to deal with each individually. Examples of this are John Lewis's Initial Situational Judgement test, detailed in Case Study 8.11, and L'Oreal's virtual business game, outlined in Case Study 8.12.

 JOHN LEWIS INITIAL SITUATIONAL JUDGEMENT TEST

CASE STUDY 8.11

John Lewis received 3,500 applicants for its retail management graduate scheme in 2010 and, given the general economic situation, more were expected in subsequent years. Dealing with this in-house proved an impossible drain on HR resources and it was calculated that to manually screen each application would cost £6.00 each, so outsourcing was an expensive option.

The company therefore devised an online test which presented 20 scenarios all based around situations that a branch manager might typically face, each with four possible solutions. Applicants were required to rate each solution on a five-point scale ranging from 'counterproductive' to 'very effective'. The answers are then automatically scored and those with the best scores progress to the next stage of the recruitment process.

To ensure an accurate assessment, a sample group of branch managers completed the test and their responses were analysed and used as a basis for the scoring system. A further benefit of the scheme is that it gives the applicant a semblance of a 'job preview' – an opportunity to understand the nature of the likely problems/issues that are faced in retail management.

The cost of this test was £4.50, so a saving of 25% was made through devising this test.

Source: IDS (2011)

 L'OREAL'S VIRTUAL BUSINESS GAME

CASE STUDY 8.12

L'Oreal introduced their online virtual business game 'Reveal' in 2010 as part of their graduate recruitment programme. Players move through the Reveal platform as avatar characters working on virtual projects and solving business tasks across various departments, including finance, sales, marketing and the supply chain. Participants are then assessed against what the company considers to be the best solutions for the problems posed. It is available in 10 languages as part of the firm's global graduate recruitment strategy. The game can be played anywhere and people receive very in-depth feedback as they go through the exercises and tasks.

The best players who achieve great results are invited for interview. It is a way of bypassing the more formal part of the recruitment procedure as the company has a strong indication of the candidate's strengths. It is seen as a way of attracting candidates to the organisation and gives something back to them.

Source: Stevens (2010b)

Developments in this area are so fast that other devices will, no doubt, have been put in place by the time you are reading this section, so you will need to keep up with your contemporary reading in this subject.

Difficulties in using technology in recruitment

Not all professionals are wholeheartedly behind these new recruitment techniques, believing that ethical and practical issues remain unanswered. These include:

- Online applications make unreasonable demands on the time of the applicants, especially graduates who will need to make multiple applications to get their first job. Often the candidate only hears that the position has been filled when the extended form has been completed.
- The applicants may not always want to be judged quite so quickly and mechanically. Unless they have bought into the computer processes (and IT staff probably have), they may prefer to apply to organisations with a more human face.
- Research by Microsoft (2010) has found that 40% of their sample of 1,000 employers have chosen not to hire a candidate as a result of a negative online profile. Over 60% of employers found no moral hazard in searching the web as part of a final check before offering a position.
- Online psychometric tests that are part of the application process are used to screen out 90% of the candidates, which 'smacks of organisational expediency', according to Dulewicz (2004).
- Organisations are aware that some candidates get friends to complete the form for them or try under several names for practice (Harry Potter is very common). Organisations that set tests and business games online run the risk of a team of friends (and maybe their accountant parents) working together to produce a high-level solution which will allow them all to progress their application.
- The judgements made by telephone may enter into the realms of discrimination, in terms of age particularly, and will encourage a form of stereotyping when the specification cannot be overridden, as it can if handled by humans.
- Applicants may not be prepared for telephone interviews with instant forced choice judgements to be made which cannot be reversed, unlike in an interview situation where, if a question is not understood, it can be repeated or explained in another way. Ernst & Young decided to drop their phone interviews in 2008 after just one year's operation as too many applicants were passing this stage and little was gained, while applicants and the organisation lost the face-to-face experience that built relationships (CIPD 2010).
- Sites do not keep their promises. A study by the consultancy The Driver Is (Welch 2003) found that only nine out of 33 companies who allowed jobseekers to register for emails alerting them when new jobs were posted had actually sent out alerts within three months of the candidate registering.
- A CIPD 2010 survey showed that only 3% of respondents rated social networking sites as the most effective way of recruiting.

Some organisations have attempted to overcome some of the above difficulties. Marks & Spencer has eliminated competency-based tests because they take up too much time and clear with candidates first whether they are prepared to work shifts, weekends, be mobile and are eligible to work in the UK. Only then do they utilise online tests in numeracy, verbal reasoning and a 'talent screener', which judges their motivation. Successful candidates then move to the final stage, which is an assessment centre. The organisation believes that the online process has improved the success rate overall from 27% to 37%.

A further example of automated short-listing is the use of equipment to *electronically read CVs* using OCR (optical character recognition) software. The system's artificial intelligence reads the texts and, by using search criteria such as qualifications, job titles and companies where the applicant has worked, will produce a ranking list of applicants against the mandatory and optional aspects of the person specification.

This system is quicker and more consistent than if it were carried out manually but will only be as efficient as the search engine and will certainly miss many potential candidates, let alone the difficulty the technology faces in trying to understand poor handwriting.

 REFLECTIVE ACTIVITY 8.4

What are the advantages and disadvantages to employers and employees of online recruitment?

8.4.3 SOCIAL NETWORKING – OTHER USES

Gifford (2014) identified a number of other uses, benefits and drivers to which social networking has been put by organisations. Although these functions could be (and mostly were) performed through the organisation's intranet, it has been found that the take-up has been greatly increased by creating an enterprise social network platform which harnessing the 'buzz' and 'low friction' approach inherent in such networks. Southeastern, for example, found that take-up was 100 times as great when they set up their 'Workmate' network which performed many of the benefits detailed below:

- *Employee voice.* Social media in general is an open, discursive and dynamic channel that draws employees into discussions about their organisations, and gated enterprise social networks provide a safe place for such online conversations. Social media can facilitate ad hoc communications and collaboration, as well as ongoing initiatives such as employee representation structures.
- *Corporate communications.* Because social media is a more engaging platform than more traditional communications tools such as static intranets, employers can use it to put out corporate messages, quickly gauge how these resonate and land with employees, and help ensure that those messages have been properly understood. For induction and general employee communication, organisations such as Beds and Bars (see Case Study 8.13) have created a form of internal social networking. Many organisations strongly encourage their managers to take part in social networking activities. In MITIE, all top managers are required to open Twitter and Facebook accounts as the HR director considered that, if managers do not know how to use social media, they will not know how to engage with their employees and supply chain partners. Initially there were mixed results but others used the sites creatively, such as the pest-control division which tweeted about Archie, their mouse-detection dog (Syedain 2012). Devon and Cornwall

Police regularly put out requests for information over offences on Twitter, as part of their platform to enable officers to engage with the public.

- *Employee relations.* One particular way employers can use social media as a channel for employee voice and corporate communications is to get to the bottom of collective employment issues. By engaging with their workforces in open, two-way (or multi-directional) dialogue, they can demonstrate they are being reasonable and strengthen the relationship with their workforces. Cape, a manufacturing company, used social media to prevent what was fast becoming an industrial dispute at a Lincolnshire site in 2011.

- *Shared purpose and workplace community.* Enterprise social networks can be used to build shared purpose in an organisation by celebrating good work, reinforcing the organisation's mission and values and helping people gain a better understanding of how their work fits in with those of colleagues. Bromford Housing utilises Yammer to encourage colleagues, celebrate good work and give moral support or advice to those facing challenges. 40% of their posts concern personal matters supporting employees' natural desire to network and build relationships.

- Having a better-networked organisation lies at the core of most uses of enterprise social networks, but is also of inherent value in itself, as it can enrich employees' working lives and strengthen their identification with the organisation. Having personal posts as well as professional is often seen to contribute to this.

- *Operational agility.* Enterprise social networks facilitate co-operation and sharing of real-time information, which can help organisations resolve operational issues and deal with customer queries swiftly and efficiently. For example, Marks & Spencer found a set of slippers to replace a mismatched pair sold to a customer in the summer sale by placing the request on Yammer when their computer records indicated they were completely out of stock.

- *Insight and innovation.* Enterprise social networks also help organisations deliver better services over the longer term, being valuable tools for drawing on employee insight and experience to make improvements. As well as enabling ideas to be fed 'upwards', they provide forums for ideas to be incubated and honed. This encourages engagement and recognition, replacing old-fashioned 'suggestion schemes'.

- *Advocacy of the organisation.* By permitting and encouraging staff to engage with customers through social media, employers can harness the commitment of these natural advocates. Such interaction can also reinforce the pride employees have in their organisations and contribute to their enjoyment of their job. Adnams, the brewer, positively encourages employees to interact with customers on social media.

- *Recruitment.* Social media can vastly increase the pool from which employers can recruit and make the process of hiring more efficient. This is likely to be of particular benefit in fast-paced job markets.

- *Learning and development.* While there will always be a place for face-to-face learning interventions, social media can transform many aspects of learning and development, being used to curate knowledge, locate experts and facilitate peer-to-peer support, support self-directed learning and help employees prepare for and embed learning from training courses. For example, Santa Fe group have created an Academy Online where employees can produce, share and comment on learning content.

- *Distributed leadership.* Enterprise social networks provide a vehicle for employees throughout the organisation to informally step forward as leaders, influence directly and contribute to the wider organisation. This can help the organisation identify leadership talent but can also inculcate distributed leadership, whereby employees are valued for the expertise and skills they can contribute at any one time, rather than the positions they hold.

In addition, for knowledge management, organisations, such as InterContinental Hotels Group, have used social networking technology to allow employees throughout the world to connect with each other to share learning and develop skills. This process is estimated to cost only 5% of the cost of a leadership programme.

To encourage greater diversity, some organisations have set up networks specifically for minority and gender groups which provide help and encouragement to members of those groups, raise awareness of the challenges faced by a particular group, help line managers to support them better and act as a forum for consultation with the business on policies and procedures.

CASE STUDY 8.13

BEDS AND BARS EMPLOYEE CONSOLE

Beds and Bars operates a large number of hostels, pubs and bars across Europe and its workforce is primarily young. 'One of the key challenges we face in the youth travel industry is communication with our employees,' says Duane Vanner, People Manager, UK. 'Using a medium they are familiar with, can understand and respond to is essential when it comes to efficient and cost-effective on-the-job training.'

In early 2008, it was decided to create an interactive HRM tool based on social networking technology. Staff now log into the console as part of their introduction to the company and staff members are given a profile which they can update online. Through the console, employees can instantly communicate with each other across Europe, access custom-made training videos, apply for places on a variety of training courses and access internal job listings. The development challenges faced included the heavy security required for the site and ensuring it was fully functional across all platforms, including mobile phones. Vanner says that project's goals – to increase employee involvement in company learning activities, provide accurate and accessible up-to-date training and increase product knowledge and awareness – have all been met.

Source: People Management (2009b)

Problems with using social networks

A number of employment issues have arisen regarding social networking.

The consensus among HR professionals and employment lawyers is that it is possible for employers to *discipline* those who make comments using social media sites. This is particularly the case where employee comments can be clearly considered defamatory and for criticising their organisation on their personal networking site, taking into account the fact that, in terms of the personal and temporary nature of such communications, this is far from uncommon. On occasions, it can be close to the boundaries of libel or deformation. In October 2008, 13 Virgin Atlantic crew members were dismissed following their participation in a discussion on Facebook during which it was alleged they brought the company into disrepute and insulted passengers. They had apparently criticised their company's health and safety standards and also called their passengers 'chavs'.

A more marginal case occurred in 2011, when an employee of BG plc was disciplined for uploading his CV onto his LinkedIn profile and registering an interest in 'career opportunities' because the company claimed that information on his CV was confidential and for breaching its conflicts-of-interest policy. The employee resigned, claiming constructive dismissal, and the two parties reached a confidential agreement so the issue of whether the employer was justified in its actions (especially complaining about the job-hunting aspects) was never known (Hodgkiss 2012).

On the other hand, however, a number of high-profile cases of employees being fired for usage of social media have resulted in the dismissals being overturned (Schoneboom

2011). One example was Joe Gordon, a Waterstone's employee who was dismissed in 2005 because of including some criticisms of his company in his satirical blog. He was offered reinstatement following a successful tribunal claim. Following such cases, many writers on employment law have argued that it is crucial for employers to have some kind of social media policy in place to determine what is acceptable and what is not. Such a policy would be intended to discourage employees from making certain kinds of adverse comments using social media and, in the event that employers find evidence of objectionable comments written by an employee, would make it easier from a legal point of view to take action against that employee (Broughton et al 2011).

Second, employees may engage in criticising other members of staff, including both colleagues and their own managers. This, in its extreme forms, can be regarded as cyber-bullying and the question arises as to whether the company should step in to stop extended and painful personal campaigns, under its duty of care responsibilities. If the organisation does not take appropriate disciplinary action against the posting of such information, it could be held vicariously liable for those comments and in breach of its duty of care owed to the employee about whom information was posted.

Third is the issue of whether employers should investigate potential employees' social networking sites to obtain a more detailed personal profile, including such areas as their drinking habits. However, there are potential dangers here for the employer, apart from the obvious risk of information from this source being unreliable. There is also the potential for a discrimination claim. An unsuccessful job applicant could bring such a claim if they feel that they were not successful in their job application because of a discriminatory perception of them by the prospective employer. For example, if a job candidate has a social networking profile that reveals their age, religious belief or sexual orientation and is invited to an interview and discovers that their profile was viewed by the prospective employer but they were not subsequently appointed (and they believed that they were the best candidate for the job), there is a chance that they may consider bringing a claim for discrimination.

Fourth, employees can spend a considerable time in the workplace on their social networking sites, generally referred to as 'cyberslacking'. In one study, employees admitted to at least one hour per week using the Internet and email for non-work-related purposes, of which Facebook and Twitter were two of the most used sites (Foster 2010). Some employers have decided to block such sites, including Portsmouth City Council in 2009, but other organisations have taken the view that this is draconian and that employees should be trusted in this area, as they are generally trusted with private phone calls and occasional personal web searches during working hours. Other organisations have become specific, including one which specifies allowing 'up to five brief emails a day' and another limiting employees to 'no more than 30 minutes a day use during break times'. In Foster's research, the views of employees are similarly broad. In response to the statement, 'I should be allowed unlimited access to email and Internet for personal use without restriction at work', there was an almost symmetrical response from strongly agree through to strongly disagree.

8.4.4 TELEWORKING

The development of the world-wide web and associated technological innovations has facilitated the process of working at a distance to the employee or main contractor. The process allows a variety of models, ranging from the ability to work one or two days at home with a laptop to being a fully-fledged teleworker hundreds of miles away where physical contact with the office site is restricted to an annual conference visit. As phones merge with computers, video calls will become far more common, with far-flung teams working on shared documents in virtual meetings.

Advantages of teleworking

- Productivity gains – employees working from home are often more productive. They get away from the frequent interruptions and distractions that pepper the working day. It is also in their interests to show they are more productive so the teleworking arrangement can continue.
- Employees can work out a work–life balance much more easily with more time spent at home. Caring responsibilities can be balanced with work to be completed, as long as the will and the self-discipline are present.
- Time-saving – for mobile teleworkers, the ability to complete tasks at remote locations, rather than returning to a central office, saves considerable time and expense. Time is saved on regular commuting to work.
- Reduced accommodation costs – most organisations sell teleworking to their boards through setting out the huge savings in accommodation costs, especially where these are in central city locations.

Difficulties that could arise

- Teleworking can be difficult to manage without the daily face-to-face contact. Managers often want quick answers to questions or a special task performed quickly. This is far more difficult with remote workers. Supervisors and managers need specialised training to manage the remote worker. Contact has to be regular but not too intrusive.
- Performance management systems need to be carefully devised. It has to be much more based on outputs and outcomes rather than traditional measures such as attendance. Regular meetings need to be held to discuss the employees' performance.
- Employees may not have the work distractions but they may have the home ones instead – children, other family members, friends, callers, etc, can all disrupt a steady work flow. Relationships with family members can suffer if the borders between work and home are not drawn tightly to everybody's satisfaction.
- Health and safety in the home needs to be carefully monitored.
- Dealing with confidential documents in the home setting has to be addressed.
- Some teleworkers feel too remote from the workplace. They miss the comradeship of the office and lose out on the regular gossip and social activities. There is also a general concern that teleworkers lose training and promotion opportunities because of their low visibility.

?   REFLECTIVE ACTIVITY 8.5

Research has shown that teleworkers often suffer from social isolation. Can you suggest ways that these effects can be mitigated?

8.4.5 CALL CENTRES

The invention and development of the automated call distribution (ACD) system, which both released the need for a switchboard operator and also provided detailed call information, has promoted the introduction of a growing number of call centres. According to Unison union, there were over 1 million employees working at 5,000 call centres in the UK in 2015, a number that is increasing despite the dispersal of many such jobs to the Indian subcontinent, where labour rates are cheaper.

Operators work with the required database to answer customer queries or process sales and service agreements, and most build in an interactive instruction guide for the employee to follow, which reduces the time and cost for training. The technology also allows management to monitor calls to identify process glitches, training needs and earnings through any incentive scheme. Call centres can take a distributed form, allowing calls to be channelled to teleworkers at distant locations, with the technology allowing access to all necessary data.

The implications for human resource practitioners are quite complex here, where there has been much debate about the high staff sickness and turnover, quality of job design and the ethical nature of the job requirements.

?   REFLECTIVE ACTIVITY 8.6

Call centres have some of the highest staff turnover rates (average over 40%) and absenteeism rates (over 6%) in any UK employment sector. Can you suggest why this has happened and what should be done about it?

8.4.6 EFFECT ON THE STRUCTURE OF HUMAN RESOURCE OPERATIONS

Sparrow et al (2004) and Reddington et al (2005) have set out some of the opportunities that technology has provided in facilitating new and developing human resource systems:

- *Shared services* – the system adopted by many large organisations, such as Standard Chartered Bank, Whitbread and HSBC, to extract the routine HR processes from operating units and place them in a central service, not necessarily anywhere near a head office. Activities include payroll, record-keeping (attendance, starters and leavers, pensions), the operation of recruitment, job advertising and short-listing together with advice on company HR systems and employment law. Technology allows the access to the databank of information held at the centre that can be drawn upon by local managers and video-conferencing arrangements for wider discussion of action on, say, a difficult disciplinary situation. Many shared services have access to a network of experts for areas such as reward and benefits or selection testing.
- The savings that are made by using this system involve the cutting back of duplication of HR support at each operating unit (averaging 20–40%), moving the work to low-cost locations, savings on purchasing of technology and services at one point rather than many and a near certainty that consistent decisions will be made, avoiding litigation in discrimination and other legal areas (Reilly 2000).
- *E-enablement of HR processes* – the ability to get HR information to and from, and support on to, line managers' desks without a formal HR intervention allows far more time for the HR department to focus on more strategic areas. The early stages of development here of access to policy documents and routine statistical processes has moved on to empowering line managers to take greater control of their HR responsibilities. They can access external information on pay and benefits, authorise pay increases, select the appropriate standardised terms and conditions to go in an offer letter, process key data on an individual's performance management and manage their staff and training budgets. Norwich Union (Parry et al 2007) had four key drivers when they introduced an HRIS self-service functionality in 2006:
  - *enabling line management* – encouraging managers to take more responsibility for managing their people through being able to access and maintain records
  - *improving and simplifying core processes* – providing real-time updates on core data, removing duplication and increasing online processing, increasing standardisation and economies of scale in administration

    ○ *adding value through HR expertise* – allowing HR resource to move from transactional to performance-enhancing activity, facilitating the introduction of new HR activities online, such as competencies and flexible benefits, encouraging individuals to take increased ownership of their own details and career management

    ○ *e-enablement of HR* – mirroring business practice.

● *Outsourcing of HR and shared services provision* – service centres and e-empowerment can be organised in-house or may be outsourced to firms that have the technological expertise to offer such services at low cost. For example, Arinso Corp have contracted with Shell to produce a shared services system utilised by over 100,000 employees across 45 countries (Glover 2004). HR departments may therefore be reduced in capacity, with interesting implications for career planning. The normal stepped climb up the organisation may instead become leaps between service providers and organisations, not unlike the current career path of senior management.

An example of shared services is shown in Case Study 8.14.

CASE STUDY 8.14

SHARED SERVICES ARE SUCCESSFUL IN SAVING MONEY AND MAINTAINING SERVICES

A Local Government Association (LGA) report in 2012 examined five shared services projects covering a range of co-operative arrangements between authorities, fire and rescue services and local NHS trusts. The report shed light on how efficiencies were being made by councils sharing back-office functions, including HR, IT and legal services. Savings are achieved through consolidating organisation structures, integrating information technology, reducing accommodation and improving procurement. The five projects had saved a total of £30m between them.

It found that there was typically a two-year 'payback period' before the set-up and integration costs were cancelled out and savings kicked in. Initial savings came from reducing headcount and duplication of staff, in staff changes. Afterwards, further savings came from improved use of IT, reduced need for

assets such as office space, and cultural change leading to better processes, the report said. Few problems were reported by the participants.

Although the savings were not sufficient to make up the 28% cut in the money councils receive from central government, measures such as the shared service arrangements currently in operation at more than 200 local authorities have helped to dampen the impact.

Local authorities have been much more successful in sharing services than central government departments have, despite being hit by greater proportional spending cuts, said the LGA. While shared services have traditionally focused on back-office functions, many local authorities are now looking at which front-line services can also be shared.

Source: LGA (2012)

8.5 KNOWLEDGE MANAGEMENT

So great is the speed of technological innovation and so dominant are the changes that it brings in the form of new products, services or the way we live and work, that commentators have expressed the view that we now live in the 'knowledge economy'. Furthermore:

A firm's competitive advantage depends more than anything on its knowledge, or, to be slightly more specific, on what it knows, how it uses what it knows and how fast it can know something new. (Prusack 1997)

Having the knowledge can be regarded as even more important than possessing the other means of production – land, buildings, labour and capital – because all the other sources are readily available in an advanced global society, while the right leading-edge knowledge is distinctly hard to obtain. Linked to this thinking is the concept of 'intellectual capital', which can be bought (and, if appropriate, stored securely) either through purchasing patents or intellectual property rights or through employing the highly skilled/intelligent employees/consultants who possess that capital (Stewart 2001).

This capital is not necessarily discoveries and processes that can be patented. Society is developing in such a way that services are becoming the dominant commodity over manufacturing. This means that skilled services in areas such as advertising, design, leisure and even sport can command very high fees – just look at the prices paid for the world's top 100 footballers, film stars or music performers. So wealth created in the economy is increasingly perceived as derived from knowledge and intangible assets (Storey and Quintas 2001).

? REFLECTIVE ACTIVITY 8.7

Knowledge value

Do you see knowledge as a source of competitive advantage in the marketplace? If so, how?

Because it is such an important asset, organisations are starting to assess their own collection of knowledge bases and ensure they are available for use. This is not just about sorting patents but analysing the knowledge gained through the experiences of their skilled staff. In HSBC, for example, a senior manager has been appointed to identify banking expertise among staff and ensure this knowledge is not lost when they retire or leave the organisation and to organise ways that critical knowledge can be shared across the organisation. Part of the role is to develop 'tacit knowledge', such as the intuitive approaches to problem-solving in a particular work context or vague ideas about a new product or service, into 'explicit knowledge' that can be written down and communicated (Stredwick and Ellis 2005).

Consideration must also be given to the development of what Hansen et al (1999) refer to as *codification* strategies, where knowledge is codified and stored in databases where it can be readily accessed and used by employees, and *personalisation* strategies, where knowledge is closely tied to the person who developed it and is shared mainly through direct person-to-person contacts. How to ensure the balance between these two approaches is crucial to the success of knowledge management. For example, if greater emphasis is given to personalisation, there needs to be formal encouragement of a highly developed process of social networking to allow informal opportunities to arise for knowledge-sharing outside of standard meetings. Many knowledge-based companies organise social events, even organise company holiday weekends, for this purpose.

In the human resources field, how knowledge workers are recruited, trained and motivated has come under much scrutiny in recent years. As a group, research has shown that they can be distinguished by their demand for greater autonomy in their work, by their intrinsic motivation and greater sense of task satisfaction and by their emphasis on career-progressing projects rather than immediate financial gratification (Scarborough and Carter 2007). The implication is that recruitment pays as much attention to skills and potential as to actual knowledge and that the performance management process is crucial to retention success.

8.6 TECHNOLOGY – THE DARKER SIDE

Although technological developments generally lead to improvements in standards of living, not all are seen as universally benign. For every five citizens that welcome new products, job opportunities, improved quality and variety of services, better healthcare and ease of transportation, a sixth will see a darker side with bleaker effects. For example, the migration online of book and record sales and the invention of the e-reader have devastated the number of book and record shops on the high street.

Examining three of the short case studies illustrated in this chapter shows further illustrations of the darker side of technology:

- *Gene therapy* (see Case Study 8.3) – in itself, this is a dispiriting case of unfulfilled expectations but there are further difficulties in this area. One of the success stories has been the development of devices to allow accurate screening for genetic disorders. This can be carried out at any age and even for unborn babies. The main benefit is that such disorders can be treated at an early stage so that the prognosis improves. However, this presents a number of problems. First of all, insurance companies (and employers who provide and pay for life insurance of their employees) are very interested in carrying out such tests before accepting insurance risk. For those citizens with no disorders and long life expectancy, life insurance costs would be cheap but pensions expensive. For those with a disorder, the opposite would apply, with life assurance virtually impossible to obtain. There is considerable debate currently as to whether such tests should be compulsory, the outcome of which would leave vulnerable citizens uninsurable and regarded as second-class. Alternatively, governments can attempt to force insurance companies to ignore the results of such tests and not apply prohibitive insurance costs. A second problem is the dilemma faced by the parents where pre-natal tests show up genetic disorders. It provides the opportunity for the birth to be aborted and some of the life-long pain averted, but such an irreversible decision is a very hard one to take and most parents (except those who already have one disabled child) choose to avoid taking such tests.
- *Lettuce leaves* (see Case Study 8.8) – there are a number of ethical and regulatory issues surrounding this case. First, it is becoming very difficult to challenge the power of the largest supermarkets in demanding such tight schedules on suppliers and, subsequently, their employees. In America, Walmart, with over 25% of the huge US market, virtually writes the rules with suppliers being unable to match their negotiating power. The situation in the UK is somewhat better, with a competing group of supermarkets matched against, in certain product areas, a similar group of large producers, but the growing dominance of Tesco is creating some worries for regulators. This issue is discussed further in Chapter 5 on regulation. The second issue is whether it is ethical for so much migratory labour, living in poor conditions, to provide fresh food for the community in the twenty-first century. It is hoped that they are protected in the UK by the National Minimum Wage, but many will slip through the net and the rules concerning deductions for accommodation are very complex with such situations being rarely investigated. Added to this are some safety issues, which were shown graphically by the death of 20 illegal Chinese immigrants working as cockle-pickers in

Morecambe Bay in 2003. Consumers may demand fresh produce at affordable prices, but these may come at indefensible cost.

- *Shared services* – there are experiences of 'one product fits all' which may not apply in fast-moving, customer-oriented businesses. The quality of the service provided by unqualified staff can be questionable with a background in call centre work rather than human resources. Many opportunities for seriously effective HR interventions and innovations can occur through regular discussions about routine issues, often in informal settings, which are far less likely to happen under formalised shared services environments. Moreover, services that are shared across countries run the risk of cultural confusion.

- *The rise of the Cyber-Bully* – the ubiquitous use of Facebook, Twitter and other social media has allowed bullying on line to grow rapidly. Here, anonymous insults and threats can cause extreme damage to a person's health and live-style which is very difficult to stop. A number of 'Celebrities' have stopped using social media after facing such an experience.

8.6.1 THE DARKER SIDE OF EMPLOYMENT

Alongside the potential problems faced by employees in call centres, teleworking and social networking sites, there has been much research into the inherent problems that new technology brings to the workplace, demonstrating its dialectical nature, where advances in one direction produce problems of their own (Martin 2005). These can take various forms, such as:

- *Lack of expected productivity increases* – Productivity has not increased as rapidly as expected in Western economies over the past 10 years, which may be related to the structure of the workforce. The industrial revolution brought workers together in factories whereas the internet atomises the workforce, encouraging employees towards self-employment, especially in support services. In the UK, 360,000 self-employed jobs have been created from 2010–2014, which is 40% of the total job creation. The vast majority of these were one-person businesses, often on lower pay. On the other hand, the number of self-employed having staff working for them (job-creating entrepreneurs) actually reduced over the period. Gordon (2013), found a similar phenomenon in America.

- *Too much information* – Technology brings economic progress as businesses and individuals have access to devices that improve communication. But now we have 'infobesity' — there's so much information out there that no one could harness it. The life cycle of products and companies will shorten, and risk assessment will play a growing role in decision-making. This is likely to lead to fewer numbers employed (Dobbs, Maiyka and Woetzel 2015).

- *De-skilling of manual work* – especially in industries such as house-building where pre-fabrication, using computer-controlled design and machine tools, has replaced many traditional skills. A major consequence in the UK has been the near collapse of trade training by large house-builders which, in turn, has led to severe shortages of servicing and maintenance trades, such as plumbers and electricians, where the market is dominated by small organisations. Even software work has been substantially automated and routinised. Other jobs have almost disappeared, including translators (Lanier 2013).

- *De-skilling of professional jobs* –lawyers, accountants and other skilled professions are facing a stiff challenge from algorithms used in 'deep learning'. Much of the revenue from professions comes from the high level of discovery work done by juniors. Deep learning does much of this work more profoundly and consistently through systems such as pattern recognition which can produce detailed answers to legal and financial questions (Baxter and Straw 2014).

- *Call-centres* have been roundly criticised as the new 'industrial sweatshops' with automatons working in psychic prisons on prepared scripts to finely tuned bonus schemes, leading to poor employee morale and depressive illnesses (see Case Study 8.15).

- *The ubiquitous presence and use of social networking sites* can have deleterious effect upon individual's health. Kross and Verduyn (2013) found that the more someone uses Facebook, the more dissatisfied they are with life. This is chiefly because the most common emotion aroused is envy. Employers should therefore beware of encouraging further usage in the workplace by using such sites as their chief communication vehicle.

- *Internet misuse can take a number of forms.* One that has proved costly is the spreading of false information via the Internet. Employers can be held vicariously liable for their employees' activities when using the Internet and are responsible if staff send email messages that breach confidentiality or are defamatory. In the case of *Western Provident v Norwich Union*, Norwich Union was forced to shell out £450,000 in damages and costs for slander and libel after Western Provident discovered damaging and untrue rumours circulating on Norwich Union's internal email system. They were about Western Provident being in financial difficulties and being investigated by the Department for Trade and Industry (Hall 2004).

- The *intrusion of surveillance* technology has presented dilemmas for employers who have the responsibility and opportunity to monitor employees to ensure no laws are being broken (such as downloading of pornography) but appreciate employees' fears and resentment at such a process taking place. Monitoring attendance (through card-swiping security systems) and performance (such as call centre systems detailed earlier) have become cheap and accurate but present challenges to employment cultures where employees' trust and independence of action are highly valued. Surveillance may focus employees' attention on organisational and strategic targets but also have the tendency to discourage innovation (Taylor 2004).

- A special *problem of e-business employment* is the lack of contact with the customer and a poor level of social interaction. This has led to higher levels of staff turnover than in conventional businesses (PricewaterhouseCoopers 2000). There has also been some sense of alienation related to virtual meetings, where the growth of video-conferencing has been surprisingly slow, although most evidence would support the view that the correct usage of mobile phones and emails has generally enhanced employees' social contact.

- Some commentators picture ICT in a tyrannical frame in the sense that it provides *more intensive work* through the huge amount of data it provides and the options available and it also *demands longer hours* at the work face through its additional ability to provide 24/7 coverage (Green 2002). However, not all research supports this view. In a CIPD-financed project, Nathan et al (2003) provided little evidence that ICT directly impacted on increased working hours. Employees were using more technology and they were working longer hours, but the causal relationship was not proven.

- Although many of the accident-driven jobs in traditional industries have been eliminated by automation, *new health problems* have emerged, both physical (repetitive strain injury, eyesight deterioration) and psychological (stress-related illnesses).

- Research has given an indication that technology can encourage *work presenteeism* (Churchard 2012a). The availability of information throughout the day and night has increased the difficulty for employees to 'switch off', and the need to be up and running encourages coming in to work despite being ill or, at least, checking emails and other information when ill at home.

Problems for society

Technology also presents problems for society to face, including examples such as:

- *Technology has reduced equality.* The successful technology entrepreneurs, especially those that originated, developed or have been bought up by the likes of Apple, Amazon, Google and Facebook, are immensely wealthy and technology has added large numbers to the list of billionaires. On the other hand, some of their employees, particularly those at Amazon, are working on minimum wages. Furthermore, technology has 'hollowed out' many industries, reducing the middle-earners substantially leading to an increase in the Gini coefficient (see Chapter 7).
- *Technology centres power into a few right-wing hands.* Keen (2015) describes the arrival of 'rapacious late capitalism' and 'secessionist fantasies' of Silicon Valley giants who build walled cities, blacked-out buses (Google), state-free islands (Paypal) and massive tax-avoidance schemes.
- *Technology reduces free expression.* Concerns have been expressed over the huge decline in newspaper advertising income as readers and advertisers turn to the Internet. This means that the disappearance of the independent free press becomes more likely, with the implication of fewer independent investigations in a democratic society. In America, income dropped from $63bn in 2000 to $19 billion in 2012. Most newspapers are searching for a new online model with full or partial pay walls but few are generating sufficient income. At the same time, the power of online advertisers to observe and follow individual buying habits has led to invasive micro-targeted advertisements popping up regularly and strongly reinforcing such habits. Their success has meant that the migration of advertising to the web has accelerated swiftly (Sullivan 2012).
- *Misuse/overuse of data.* Research has indicated that it is possible to identify important personality traits by analysing as few as 50 'tweets' and thereby accurately channel advertisements to individuals (*Economist* 2013d).

 SUICIDES AT FRANCE TELECOM

CASE STUDY 8.15

Over an 18-month period during 2008–09, 24 employees at France Telecom committed suicide following the implementation of a wide-ranging restructuring plan called 'Time to Move'. A sociologist, Monique Crinon, who interviewed a cross-section of staff, identified feelings of being undervalued and low self-esteem running through the company from top to bottom. One senior worker in her fifties was demoted to work in a call centre and reported that she had stepped back in time to an era where mainly young women staff were terrorised and controlled. Employees had to make several sales an hour from dictated scripts, had to ask permission to leave for toilet breaks and had to file a written explanation for going one minute over a lunch break. The teams were repeatedly broken up with staff being moved to other centres at two days' notice, leaving workers feeling isolated and feeling like failures in a bonus-driven system. In a similar case, a 51-year-old employee was moved from a back-office job to a call centre and eventually committed suicide by throwing himself off a motorway bridge in September 2009.

Less than a week later, the company suspended the restructuring and Louis-Pierre Wenes, deputy chief executive and the architect of the restructuring, resigned.

Sources: Chrisafis (2009); Investortoday (2009)

In labour market terms, a divide has developed between two major segments of employment – the knowledge-intensive organisations and the knowledge-routinised ones, called the 'hour-glass' model by Coyle and Quah (2004). Knowledge-intensive jobs use advanced and complex ICT skills and require high human capital levels. Employees work long and often unsociable hours but their jobs are often (but not always) associated with high pay, extensive training, career development and high personal and job satisfaction. Knowledge-routinised jobs, on the other hand, are lowly paid, require much lower levels of human capital and the routine ICT work provides much less personal satisfaction.

8.7 TRENDS TO WATCH – WHAT OF THE FUTURE?

8.7.1 'THE HORSE IS HERE TO STAY!'

Forecasting the effects of new technology is very tricky and many serious and well-respected forecasters have got their forecasts very wrong. In an excellent article by Smith (2004), which details truly awful forecasts, he quotes pioneers in the IT industry from whom we would have expected a clearer vision. For example, IBM forecast in 1952 that their worldwide sales of mainframe computers would be 52 and, 30 years later, had raised it to 200,000, roughly what they now ship a week. Even Bill Gates made gaffes, such as stating in 1981 that '640K should be enough for anybody'. Going further back, the president of Michigan Savings Bank advised people in 1901 against investing in the Ford Motor Company, quoting the statement at the top of this section.

There was a better performance by Kahn in his 1967 book *The Year 2000*, where he predicted computers, mobile phones, video recorders and satellite dishes. But he, like many forecasters since, seriously misjudged the effect of technology on working lives. Almost everybody has forecast that we would all be working far fewer hours (30 a week at most, according to Kahn), have much more holiday and retire very early. This was because technology would take away jobs, which it clearly does. What almost all futurologists failed to grasp is that, while some jobs disappear, more arise in their place. Production jobs have disappeared either through automation and robotics or to developing countries with cheaper wages. In their place have arisen industries that provide services – either business services, such as IT, financial services and all manner of consultancies, or those that provide personal services, such as leisure, health and beauty and personal finances. At the same time, services that used to operate for the few, such as hotels, eating out, travel and tourism, are now used by everybody in increasing numbers.

What is just as significant is that such new and developing industries are generally very labour intensive (automated hairdressing is still not with us), so technology has released employees from the grind of heavy production but provided instead the more sociable but equally routine (and absolutely vital) activities involved in such activities as 'housekeeping' in hotels and 'care working' in hospitals and old people's homes. This explains why the average working week has decreased only marginally in the last 25 years and why unemployment in flexible societies, such as the UK and America, remains very low.

Finally, a truly apocalyptic view of the effect of recent technologically change is expressed by Keen (2015) in *The Internet is not the Answer*, who explains that technology that was supposed to empower the masses is having the opposite effect, where there is vastly increased surveillance, invasion of privacy and exploitation of data. This has led to the establishment of immensely powerful monopolies, such as Amazon, massive manipulation of people's opinions on social networks (such as Facebook) and a future of 'non-taxpaying billionaires and beggars'.

KEY LEARNING POINTS

- Technological development can occur through incremental innovation, radical innovation, change in technological systems or technological revolution.
- 'Business intelligence' is a key concept where the aim is to transform large amounts of data, often scattered across the organisation, into the key information that drives informed decision-taking, and to deliver it in an easily read form through the computer screen to anybody where and when they need to know.
- Technological developments provide the capacity for organisations to be *flexible* and to be *eager to change*, in fields such as product design, advertising and marketing (especially on the web), customer relations and quality development.
- Technology has had a profound effect upon labour markets through facilitating novel flexible working practices, such as annualised hours, complex shift systems and multi-skilling, together with the development of sophisticated recruitment and selection processes.
- Human resource systems have been affected by the technological changes that allow systems of shared services, outsourcing and e-enablement of HR processes, especially recruitment and selection.
- Social media usage has increased substantially and many businesses encourage and integrate social networking processes into their core activities.
- It has been recognised in recent years that knowledge management is a vital process to ensure that organisations can collect, store and distribute key areas of knowledge that help create competitive advantage.
- Technological progress produces its own ethical dilemmas in areas such as gene therapy, consumer choice and outsourcing.

REVIEW QUESTIONS

1. In what ways does technology offer improved marketing opportunities?
2. Name five difficulties associated with the employment of teleworkers.
3. Provide four examples of how technology helps HR administration and management become more efficient.
4. What is the difference, according to Freeman, between a radical and an incremental innovation?
5. Give three examples of developments in communication technologies and their effect on markets.
6. Provide four examples of how technology can provide difficulties in the employment setting, as well as benefits.
7. What are the four main cycles of K-waves?
8. Give four examples of the use of technology in the recruitment and selection process.
9. What is the connection between technology and flexibility requirements?
10. What are 'shared services' in the HR setting, how are they facilitated by technology and what savings are made?

EXPLORE FURTHER

The best source of contemporary technology and its effects is the weekly *Economist*, which has a dedicated section on this subject. Two useful learned journals in this area are *New Technology, Work and Employment* (Blackwell Publishing) and *Work, Employment and Society* (Sage), which often deal with the effects of technology on working practices and human resources. Recent articles in the former include:

BARNES, S. (2012) The differential impact of ICT on employees. *New Technology, Work and Employment*. Vol 27, No 2. June. pp120–32.

WHEATLEY, D. (2012) Good to be home: time-use and satisfaction levels among home-based teleworkers. *New Technology, Work and Employment*. Vol 27, No 3. November. pp222–41.

And in the latter:

RUSSELL, B. (2012) Professional call centres, professional workers and the paradox of the algorithm: the case of tele-nursing. *Work, Employment and Society*. Vol 26, No 2. pp195–210.

Other valuable sources include:

MELE, N. (2014) *The End of Big: How the Digital Revolution makes David the New Goliath*. London: Picador.

WADHWA, M. and HARPER, A. (eds) (2015) *Technology, Innovation and Enterprise Transformation*. Hershey, PA: IGI-Global

SEMINAR ACTIVITY 8.1

HUMAN RESOURCE SYSTEMS AND TELEWORKING

Imagine that you are Head of Human Resources in an organisation that is planning to introduce teleworking on a large scale. Consider how your HR systems and practice systems should adapt to this new initiative.

CHAPTER 9

Ethics, Social Responsibility and Sustainability

LEARNING OUTCOMES

When you have completed this chapter, you should be able to understand, explain and critically evaluate:

- different approaches to ethics and ethical principles
- the problems involved in resolving ethical dilemmas
- whistleblowing
- the nature of professional ethics
- how far business ethics exist as something separate from general ethics
- values and codes of business ethics
- approaches to corporate governance
- the principles of risk management
- the principles and issues underlying corporate social responsibility
- the principles and issues underlying sustainable development
- the role of HR in sustaining corporate social responsibility and sustainability
- the role of the government in corporate social responsibility and sustainability
- corporate social responsibility and profit.

9.1 INTRODUCTION

This chapter examines the nature of ethics, and different approaches which can be taken to ethical problems. It discusses professional and business ethics, stakeholder theory, values, and codes of ethics. The second half of the chapter analyses corporate governance, corporate social responsibility (CSR) and sustainability, the role of businesses, HR and the government in promoting CSR, and the extent of compatibility between CSR and profit.

9.2 ETHICS

The theory of ethics can be extremely complex, and in order to be of use in a day-to-day work situation, it must be made practical. Here we immediately run up against a problem. To philosophers, ethics is about the theory of right and wrong, not about the practical application of those principles. This is the area of morals. Ethics involves the values that a person seeks to express in a certain situation, morals the way he or she sets out to achieve this (Billington (2003).

A wider definition of ethics is given by Connock and Johns (1995). This includes three elements:

- fairness
- deciding what is right and wrong
- the practices and rules which underpin responsible conduct between individuals and groups.

Billington lists five distinctive features of ethics (Billington 2003, pp20–5):

1   Nobody can avoid ethical decisions. We all make ethical decisions every day.

2   Other people are always involved in ethical decisions. There is no such thing as private morality.

3   Ethical decisions matter – they affect the lives of others.

4   Although ethics is about right and wrong, there are no definitive answers. The philosopher can put forward principles which should guide decisions, but the ultimate decision is always down to the individual.

5   Ethics is always about choice – a decision where the individual has no choice cannot be unethical.

?   REFLECTIVE ACTIVITY 9.1

Ethical choice

Can you think of any situations where an individual has no choice about what action they should take – in a work environment, or any other situation?

9.2.1 ETHICAL PRINCIPLES

Billington identifies three different approaches to ethics:

- *Absolutism*: Ethics are underpinned by absolute values, which apply in all societies and to all situations – the 10 Commandments. The problem here is that an absolutist might make decisions which could be seen as morally repugnant. For example, a pacifist who believes literally in the absolutist statement 'thou shalt not kill' would logically have found himself refusing to fight the evil of Nazism.
- *Relativism*: Ethics depend on the situation, and on the cultural mores prevalent at a particular time or place. Thus for example, racism in Victorian England, or child labour in present-day Pakistan must be seen as reflecting the mores of those societies; the 'when in Rome' principle. This approach has been criticised on two grounds – that it freezes the status quo and is therefore inherently conservative, and that in practice every major religion (Buddhism, Christianity, Confucianism, Hinduism, Judaism, Islam and Sikhism) subscribes to the absolutist Golden Rule (see Table 9.1) (Snell 1999).
- *Utilitarianism* – as Jeremy Bentham put it in the early nineteenth century, 'the good of the greatest number is the criterion of right or wrong' (Billington, 2003, pp35–40, 119). This begs the question, what does 'good' mean?

Archie Carroll widened out these principles into eleven ethical guidelines (Carroll 1990).

Table 9.1 Carroll's ethical guidelines

Name of principle	Description
Categorical imperative	You should not adopt principles of action unless they can be adopted by everyone else
Conventionalist ethic	Individuals should act to further their self-interest as long as they do not violate the law
Golden rule	Do unto others as you would have them do to you
Hedonistic ethic	If it feels good, do it
Disclosure rule	You should only take an action or decision if you are comfortable with it after asking yourself whether you would mind if all your associates, friends and family were aware of it
Intuition ethic	You do what your 'gut feeling' tells you is right
Means-end rule	You should act if the end justifies the means
Might-equals-right ethic	You should take whatever advantage you are powerful enough to take
Organisation ethic	Be loyal to your organisation
Professional ethic	Do only that which can be justified to your professional peers
Utilitarian principles	The greatest good of the greatest number

Source: adapted from Carroll (1990)

The three most popular among managers were the golden rule, the disclosure rule and the intuition ethic.

Cavanagh et al (1981) identified three basic ethical philosophies:

- utilitarianism – the greatest good of the greatest number
- individual rights
- social justice – ie collective rights.

Forsyth (1980) argued that ethical decision ideologies are based on two dimensions – idealism, the degree to which an individual believes that ethical behaviour always results in good outcomes, and relativism, the degree to which an individual believes that moral rules are situational. He constructed a two-by-two matrix based on these two dimensions (Figure 9.1).

Figure 9.1 Forsyth's ethical dimensions

Source: Based on Forsyth (1980)

- Situationists prefer to analyse each situation and to decide on appropriate moral behaviour based on this analysis.
- Subjectivists base their moral judgements on individual rather than universal principles.
- Absolutists believe in strict, universal moral codes.
- Exceptionists believe in universal moral rules as guides but are open to practical exceptions.

 REFLECTIVE ACTIVITY 9.2

Examining bodies and ethics

Edexcel is one of four major examination boards in England, Wales and Northern Ireland. It awards 1.5 million qualifications a year, which include GCSEs, A levels, BTEC qualifications, NVQs and GNVQs. Its annual turnover is £112m. The other major examination boards are AQA (turnover £128m) and OCR (turnover £77m), and WJEC, which mainly operates in Wales.

Edexcel was formed in 1996 as a result of a government-inspired merger between BTEC, a quango (quasi-autonomous non-governmental organisation), which specialised in vocational qualifications, and the University of London Examinations and Assessment Council, owned by London University, which specialised in GCSE and A level qualifications. At this stage Edexcel had charitable status.

Edexcel and the other exam boards are answerable in England to Ofqual, the regulator for the industry, and ultimately to the Department for Education, while WJEC is answerable to Ofqual and the Welsh government.

Running an examination board is a high-risk activity. GCSE and A level results are issued in a blaze of publicity each summer, and any mistakes made by the exam boards are picked up by the media in a blaze of adverse publicity. Exam boards always seem to get the blame, even for things which are not their own fault.

In 2003, Edexcel was taken over by the media giant Pearson, a FTSE 100 company with wide interests, including the *Financial Times*, and the publisher Pearson Education. Pearson already had interests in examination systems overseas, and saw it as its aim to 'globalise the marking process'. It is investing heavily in order to computerise the examination system, including online testing and marking.

Ken Boston, the chairman of the Qualifications and Curriculum Authority, said at the time of the takeover, 'I see no reason why we should blanch at private sector companies.' However, other commentators were less complacent. Martin Ward, deputy general secretary of the Secondary Heads Association, said, 'The entry of a commercial organisation... has the potential for less accountability', while Ted Wragg, emeritus professor of education at Exeter University, said, 'I feel alarmed about the future... People want to feel that an examination board is focused on standards, not profit.'

In 2011 scandal blew up when the *Daily Telegraph* secretly filmed a WJEC seminar for teachers, who had paid £200 a head to attend, where the attenders were told which questions pupils could expect in the forthcoming exams. The *Telegraph* also quoted a named examiner at a seminar telling teachers that a compulsory question in the examination 'goes in cycles.' He gave the subjects for the forthcoming exam, saying, 'We're cheating, we're telling you the cycle.' When told that this information was not in the course specification, the examiner was alleged to have said, 'No, because we're not allowed to tell you.' An Edexcel examiner was alleged to have told a seminar that its examinations were easy. This was denied by Edexcel, who said: 'we do not actively market our exams as easier.'

The Secretary of State, Michael Gove, called for an urgent investigation by Ofqual, and also raised the issue of whether there should be a single examining body. He said, 'The chief risk of market failure with qualifications is in regard to standards – the so-called 'race to the bottom.' Chris McGovern, chairman of the Campaign for Real Education, said: 'You wouldn't dream of having, say, different boards offering driving licences.'

Sources: Lewis (2002); Curtis (2004); BBC (2011c)

Question

Do you think that the public service role of Edexcel is incompatible with its private ownership?

CASE STUDY 9.1

THE ETHICS OF MPS' EXPENSES

The MPs' expenses scandal made headlines for weeks in the summer of 2009. The *Daily Telegraph* had obtained tip-offs from a whistleblower, which it drip-fed into the public arena. The result was to finish many political careers, and to throw the whole parliamentary system into disrepute.

Examples included Sir Peter Viggers's infamous duck island, Douglas Hogg's moat, Jacqui Smith's husband's 'adult' videos, Gordon Brown's cleaning bill and Cheryl Gillan's dog food.

Six different ethical categories can be identified:

1   *The silly but petty*: the dog food and the adult films

2   *The silly but outrageous*: the duck island and the moat

3   *The retrospectively punished*: MPs were allowed to claim cleaning expenses, with their reasonableness assessed by the Parliamentary Fees Office. However, when Sir Thomas Legg, the commons auditor, reported in October 2009, he retrospectively imposed a limit of £2,000 a year on cleaning, with the result that the Prime Minister, Gordon Brown, was required to repay over £10,000.

4   *Playing the system*: In one case an MP repaid a relatively small mortgage on his London home, and took out an extremely large mortgage on his constituency home. The mortgage interest on this was claimed as an expense.

5   *Tax avoidance*: The widespread practice of 'flipping' mortgages. Inland Revenue rules permit the proceeds of selling a designated first house to be free of capital gains tax, but the sale of a second house is liable to CGT. In one case, an MP designated her constituency home as her main residence for one month, so avoiding CGT.

6   *Fraud*: In one case (an MEP rather than an MP), the person involved claimed a secretarial allowance of £3,000 a month, but paid his assistant only £500. The result in this case was a prison sentence.

I feel that the ethical implications in these cases are different. In the first case, no real ethical principles are involved, although they could fall foul of the disclosure rule. The amount spent on dog food was petty, and Jacqui Smith claiming for the adult films was clearly a mistake.

In the second case, the MPs involved should have thought of the disclosure rule. The sums of money involved in each case (over £1,000) were excessive, and the MPs involved should have considered what public opinion would feel if these were made public.

The third case, retrospective punishment, raises more ethical issues for Sir Thomas Legg than for the MPs concerned. Retrospective punishment is generally viewed with disfavour by the UK legal system. As commentators pointed out at the time, £2,000 a year does not cover much cleaning in London if you pay the London living wage, National Insurance, holiday pay and so on.

The fourth case, playing the system, is, I feel, unethical, although it is not in any way illegal, and some would see it as acceptable. I think it falls foul of the golden rule, the disclosure rule and the professional ethics rule. The fifth case, tax avoidance, again is not illegal, but would generally be seen as unethical, and again is covered by the golden, disclosure and professional ethics rules. The final case is clearly unethical as well as criminal.

Two problems with the expenses system were:

- An unclear distinction between expenses and allowances. In some cases MPs received allowances, for example for communications, which implies a right to claim up to the full amount of the allowance, while other spendings were designated as expenses, where the right is only to be reimbursed for actual spending. This distinction was not always clearly made in the press.
- The system of allowing MPs to take out mortgages on designated second homes, and allowing mortgage interest on these second homes as an expense. This was justified on the grounds that most MPs needed a base in London as well as their constituency home. This not only permitted flipping, but also meant that even where there was no sharp practice, the MP would almost certainly make a capital gain (whether taxed or not) at public expense. It also raised the issues of cleaning and gardening, neither of which would have applied if an MP had been renting a serviced flat.

Eventually in November 2009 Sir Christopher Kelly, the chairman of the Committee on Standards in Public Life, produced a blueprint for a reformed system.

- MPs within commuting distance of London would no longer be able to claim for a second home. If they have to work late in Westminster, they could claim for an overnight hotel stay, capped at £125.
- Other MPs could claim for a second home, but must rent not buy, with rent capped at £1,250 a month.
- No more claims for cleaning, gardening or furnishing.
- Any capital gain on a state-funded mortgage should be 'surrendered to the taxpayer'.
- No communications allowance.
- A ban on MPs employing relatives, to be phased in over five years.

The issue of MPs' expenses is still a live one, as evidenced by the resignation from Parliament in November 2012 of ex-minister Denis MacShane.

Sources: Watt et al (2009); Watt and Stratton (2009); Stratton (2009); Summers (2009)

9.3 ETHICAL DILEMMAS

Managers face ethical dilemmas at work every day of their working lives. Some typical ones are examined in an Reflective Activity 9.3. On the basis of interviews with managers in Hong Kong, Snell identified a number of typical sources of dilemmas.

The four most common were policy or request by superior that is mistaken (25 per cent incidence); subordinates' perceived deceit, incompetence or disobedience (18 per cent); policy or request by superior that is ethically suspicious, exploitative or unfair (13 per cent) and conflicting instructions, decisions or directives from above (nine per cent) (Snell 1999).

Snell's interviews also suggested four possible responses arising from requests by a superior to do something they knew to be wrong (Snell 1999, p348):

- 'little potato' obedience (quiet, fearful, humble, deferential conformity)
- token obedience (following orders half-heartedly and semi-incompetently)
- undercover disobedience (only pretending to obey, and keeping disobedience hidden)
- open disobedience (conscientious objection)

Carroll's ethical guidelines can be used as a template for resolving ethical dilemmas:

- *Stage 1*

Rank each of Carroll's guidelines from 11 (most important to you) to 1 (least important to you).

- *Stage 2*

Consider your ethical dilemma against each of the guidelines. If you can justify the action under a criterion, put + in the next column, if you cannot justify action, put -.

- *Stage 3*

Score each criterion by taking its ranking and putting + or – in front of it.

- *Stage 4*

Add up the scores. If the figure is positive, for you the action is ethically justified; if negative, it is unjustified.

- *Stage 5*

If the overall score comes to 0, change the rank for your most important criterion to 12, and redo the sums.

Remember that this method can only tell you whether or not a particular action is ethically justifiable, not exactly what you should do about it.

An example of the scoring is shown in Table 9.2.

Table 9.2 Ethical scoring

	Rank	+/-	Score
You should not adopt principles of action unless they can be adopted by everyone else	9	-	-9
Individuals should act to further their self-interest as long as they do not violate the law	5	+	+5
Do unto others as you would have them do to you	11	-	-11
If it feels good, do it	2	-	-2
You should only take an action or decision if you are comfortable with it after asking yourself whether you would mind if all your associates, friends and family were aware of it	10	-	-10

	Rank	+/-	Score
You do what your 'gut feeling' tells you is right	6	-	-6
You should act if the end justifies the means	1	+	+1
You should take whatever advantage you are powerful enough to take	3	+	+3
Be loyal to your organisation	4	+	+4
Do only that which can be justified to your professional peers	8	-	-8
The greatest good of the greatest number	7	+	+7
Overall score			-26

In this case, the conclusion is quite clear, according to your values, you find this course of action ethically unacceptable, and should not do it.

? REFLECTIVE ACTIVITY 9.3

Ethical dilemmas

1　You are a personnel manager for a medium-sized company, and you are faced with what you see as a series of ethical dilemmas. Consider how you would approach each scenario, and what ethical principles you would apply.

Scenario 1 It is the custom in your industry for customers to be lavishly entertained. Your company gives each customer's sales manager a bottle of very good quality malt whisky on his or her birthday, his or her partner's birthday, and at Christmas. Your purchasing manager expects similar perks from his suppliers.

Scenario 2 Your organisation is undertaking a number of redundancies. You decide who is to be made redundant. The production manager asks you to add a particular worker to the list. This worker does not meet any of your criteria or redundancy, but he is well-known for not getting on with the production manager. You point out that if you sack this worker without justification, he will take you to an Employment Tribunal and will win a claim of unfair dismissal. The production manager's response is, 'Fine, it'll be worth it to get rid of him.'

Scenario 3 You are responsible for training, and you have used an old friend of yours to run a recent training programme. Your friend met all your criteria, and had adequate if not glowing references. However, the feedback from the programme is strongly negative. You are about to repeat the programme, and your friend has asked you if he/she will be given a repeat contract.

2　How far do you think Snell's identified responses to ethical dilemmas are likely to be universally valid, and how far do you think they reflect the culture of Hong Kong?

9.4 WHISTLEBLOWING

Whistleblowing describes a situation where an individual is so concerned about the behaviour of an organisation or of individuals within it that he or she feels constrained to raise this with a third party, who may be inside the organisation, but is normally outside.

De George (1999) argued that six conditions must apply before whistleblowing can be morally justified:

1   A product or policy of the organisation needs to have the potential for harm to members of society.
2   The employee should report all the facts to their immediate supervisor.
3   If the immediate supervisor does not act effectively, the concerned employee should take the matter higher in the company, exhausting all internal channels.
4   The employee should hold documentary evidence to support their charges.
5   The employee must believe that whistleblowing will lead to a change in the product or policy (ie don't sacrifice yourself pointlessly).
6   The employee must be acting in good faith without malice or vindictiveness.

9.5 THE PUBLIC INTEREST DISCLOSURE ACT 1998

The Public Interest Disclosure Act (PIDA) gives some protection to whistleblowers, although it does not give a right to whistleblow, as strict criteria are laid down which must be met. The Act also places the burden of proof on the complainant.

The disclosure must relate to a specified set of malpractices:

- a criminal offence
- failure to comply with a legal obligation
- a miscarriage of justice
- danger to health and safety
- damage to the environment
- deliberate concealment of any of the above.

Internal procedures can only be sidestepped (De George's steps 2 and 3) if:

- the employee reasonably believes they would be penalised by the employer for making the disclosure
- the employee is concerned that evidence would be concealed or destroyed
- the employee has previously disclosed essentially the same information to the employer.

If the whistleblowing case falls within the definitions of the PIDA, the employee will be entitled to compensation if he or she has been victimised or dismissed as a result of the Whistleblowing Act (Fisher and Lovell 2006).

9.6 PROFESSIONAL ETHICS

Thinking of words to describe a professional, you would probably come up with words like:

- qualified
- objective
- impartial
- honest
- competent
- accountable.

These words all imply ethical principles, and one main role of a profession is to set and maintain ethical standards for its members. Rosemary Harrison (2002, p139), stresses two aspects:

- qualified advice
- standing by the integrity of that advice.

This implies two ethical responsibilities:

- to the organisation for which one works, (organisational ethics) and
- to impartial integrity (an absolutist ethic, which lies at the heart of professional ethics).

Most professions lay down ethical standards for their members to follow through a Code of Ethics, and the Chartered Institute of Personnel and Development is no exception. Its *Code of Professional Conduct and Disciplinary Procedures* (2003c) can be downloaded from www.cipd.co.uk.

Lawton (1998, p88) suggests ten functions for a code of professional ethics:

1 To promote ethical, and deter unethical behaviour

2 To provide a set of standards against which to judge behaviour

3 To act as guidance to decision making

4 To establish rights and responsibilities

5 A statement indicating what the profession stands for

6 To create a contract between professionals and clients

7 To act as a statement of professional development

8 To legitimise professional norms and justification for sanctions

9 To enhance the status of the profession

10 A statement of professional conduct.

CASE STUDY 9.2

THE DISCIPLINARY POWERS OF THE CIPD

In an article in *Personnel Today* in October 2001, Paul Kearns argued that the CIPD should be prepared to 'strike off' negligent, incompetent or dishonest members, in the same way that the General Medical Council strikes off doctors, or the Law Society solicitors. He argued that this was essential for the CIPD to have credibility as a profession, particularly given its new Chartered status. The implication was that such a striking off should be public, and that a person who had been struck off should be prevented from practising the profession.

In response, the Secretary of the CIPD, Kristina Ingate, made three points. First, a comparison with professions such as medicine or the law is not appropriate. Personnel is not a statutory closed shop, unlike medicine or law, and CIPD membership is not a requirement to work in the personnel field. Secondly, the CIPD has a disciplinary procedure, and as a last resort, members in breach of its Code of Professional Conduct can be expelled from the Institute, although admittedly this is likely to be for misconduct rather than for incompetence. However, she urges caution. By its very nature personnel is about human relationships, frequently in stressful situations. As a result, a complaint about a personnel practitioner will frequently either be totally unwarranted, or in reality a complaint against the policies or practices of the employer, rather than the individual practitioner. Thirdly, CIPD members have high standards of both conduct and competence, and members are expected to keep their competence up to date through continuing professional development.

9.7 BUSINESS ETHICS

We have now moved some distance from our original concern with individual ethics. As we have seen, professions can impose ethics on their members. We now go one step further, and consider whether there is, or should be, a distinct field of study called business ethics – in other words, does a business, organisation or public body have any ethical responsibilities over and above the ethical responsibilities of the individuals who work for it?

Peter Drucker argues that ethics is by its very nature a code of individual behaviour. As a result, a business has no ethical responsibilities separate from those of every individual. An act which is not immoral or illegal if done by an individual cannot be immoral or illegal if done by a business. For example, if an individual pays money to an extortionist under threat of physical or material harm, that individual has in no way acted immorally or illegally. However, he quotes the case of the Lockheed aircraft company, which gave in to a Japanese airline which extorted money as a prerequisite for purchasing its L-1011 airliner, and was heavily criticised for doing so. He says, 'There was very little difference between Lockheed's paying the Japanese and the pedestrian in Central Park handing over his wallet to a mugger.' (Drucker 1990, p236).

It seems to me that Drucker's example is a poor one. The mugger can do the pedestrian a great deal of physical harm if he does not hand over his wallet. On the other hand, the airline could not positively harm Lockheed by not buying its plane. I would regard the Lockheed case not as extortion by the airline, but as bribery by Lockheed, and a clear case of breach of business ethics.

In contrast, Michael Hoffman argues that companies can be held morally responsible (Hoffman 1990, p250). Companies can be morally good or bad according to the consequences of their actions. They espouse values, and individuals coming into the corporation are subject to those values. These values are maintained and reinforced by the culture of the organisation. As a result, it is quite legitimate to talk of business ethics as separate from individual ethics.

？   REFLECTIVE ACTIVITY 9.4

The child labour dilemma

You are personnel manager for a UK clothing retailer. In addition to your personnel duties, you are also the company's Ethics Officer, responsible for implementing the Code of Ethics. One of your successful clothing lines is T-shirts, which are assembled in Pakistan and imported into the UK.

Opening your e-mails today, you find a report from one of your buyers of his recent visit to Pakistan. He reports that in a plant in Lahore, he has seen girls who look no older than ten, sweeping the floor between the rows of sewing machines the other women work on. Your code of ethics does not specifically mention child labour, but it does contain a clause about treating all workers, both directly employed and employed by suppliers, with dignity and respect.

Your first action is to e-mail Mansur Khan, your agent in Lahore, and to ask him to investigate. He reports back that working conditions aren't bad. The girls concerned are aged from eleven upwards, and are the daughters of female production workers. He also says that child labour below the age of 14 is illegal in Pakistan, but there is widespread evasion of the law, which is not generally enforced.

Your first reaction is to tell your Purchasing Department to insist that the supplier stops employing the children, or your contract with them will be cancelled. However, a friend then brings to your attention the view of the International Confederation of Free Trade Unions (ICFTU), which has called for clauses on labour standards to be incorporated into World Trade Organization (WTO) agreements, despite claims by developing countries that they could be used to prevent third-world goods competing against Western products.

The ICFTU is concerned by employers that pay low wages, use child labour, ignore health and safety standards and deny staff union representation. Some argue that free trade is exacerbating exploitation by allowing companies to relocate to wherever production costs are lowest, regardless of local employment standards. But NGOs and developing countries argue that if third-world countries are to compete in the global economy, they cannot afford to pay the same levels as Western employers, because their productivity levels are much lower. Developing countries should not be denied the competitive advantage they gain from cheaper wages (see Hussain-Khaliq (2004), which draws an interesting distinction between child labour and child work).

You are now thoroughly confused. Do you have the right to impose Western moral principles on the factory in Lahore, if there is a risk that as a result the girls and their mothers will lose their jobs?

You decide that the best way forward is to use Archie Carroll's ethical principles.

Question

Using in turn the golden rule, the disclosure rule, the intuition ethic and the utilitarian principle, think about what your response to this problem would be.

9.8 VALUES

Values underpin ethics, and the values of an organisation underpin its business ethics. Organisational values answer the question 'what do we stand for?' What are the key principles that matter to us? This is the second of three questions which organisations must ask themselves as they evolve their mission statement (see BITC 2000):

- What are we here to do? (purpose)
- What do we stand for? (values)
- What would we like to see ourselves become? (vision)

Values, as long as they are shared, help to bring together the people in an organisation, and get them working for a common aim (purpose and vision). Successful companies place a high emphasis on values, and share three characteristics (Deal and Kennedy 1990, p108):

- They stand for something.
- Management fine-tunes their values to conform to the environment of the organisation.
- The values are known and shared by everyone in the organisation, and are also known, understood and supported by key stakeholders.

A value-driven company is likely to be more consistent in its decision-making, to be single-minded, and not deflected from its long-term vision by short-term expediency. Its staff are also likely to be more committed and motivated, as long as they have ownership of the values. However, values can be counter-productive if top management behaviour is not consistent with their stated values. For example, one of the long-standing values of Marks & Spencer was support of suppliers, and the company lost a great deal of public sympathy when it axed long-standing suppliers in the UK in order to buy more cheaply abroad.

9.9 CODES OF ETHICS

One definition of a code of ethics is 'a written, distinct, formal document, which consists of moral standards which help guide employee or corporate behaviour' (Schwartz 2001, p27).

Codes can be of three different types (Brinkmann and Ims 2003, p266):

- *Educational* – aimed at increasing moral awareness and behaviour within the organisation
- *Regulatory* – detailed rules for behaviour, which recognise moral conflicts and help with resolving them
- *Aspirational* – laying down general values, and communicating ideals to individuals within the organisation.

Poor codes of ethics tend to be inward-looking, and to ignore external stakeholders, and they tend to be regulatory and over-detailed. Many companies do not make their codes of ethics available to external stakeholders, and some do not even make them easily available to their own staff (which would seem to make them totally counter-productive).

Good codes of ethics recognise the importance of relationships with all major stakeholders, both internal and external, and involve stakeholders in their preparation. They are also clearly communicated to all stakeholders, and training is provided to stakeholders in order to ensure that they are understood and effective.

Even a good code of ethics is no guarantee of ethical behaviour. The existence of codes of ethics did not prevent the scandalous collapse of Enron and WorldCom in the US, or the deliberate over-statement of oil reserves by Shell. Just as with values, top management must live the code of ethics at all times. If they do not, all respect for the organisation is likely to collapse.

Finally, an American survey in 1987 measured opinions on codes of ethics among American businesspeople. Respondents were asked to comment on a number of statements, with responses coded from 1 (strongly agree) to 4 (strongly disagree). The responses are shown in Table 9.3.

Table 9.3 Opinions on codes of ethics

	Mean response
Professionals consider codes as a useful aid when they want to refuse an unethical request impersonally	1.8
Codes raise the ethical level of the industry	2.1
A code helps managers in defining clearly the limits of acceptable conduct	1.9
In cases of severe competition, a code reduces the use of sharp practices	2.7
People violate codes whenever they think they can avoid detection	2.5
Codes are easy to enforce	3.3
Codes protect inefficient firms and retard the dynamic growth of the industry	3.3

9.10 CORPORATE GOVERNANCE

Corporate governance is concerned with two main questions:

- In whose interests should an organisation be run?
- How should these purposes be determined?

The two key issues in corporate governance are conflict of interest and accountability. Conflict of interest comes back to the agency issue we have already discussed. Managers are the agents of shareholders, but because of their control over key resources, particularly information, their power is greater than that of shareholders. How should this power be managed, and how should managers be held accountable to shareholders (and other stakeholders)?

CASE STUDY 9.3

CORPORATE GOVERNANCE IN THE VENETIAN REPUBLIC

The Venetian Republic dominated the Mediterranean for a thousand years, from its founding in the ninth century as a group of poor fishing villages, to its abolition by Napoleon in the early 1800s. Much of its success was due to its elaborate system of corporate governance.

The head of the Venetian Republic was the Doge, who was elected for life. However, his power was strictly limited. Each Doge on election signed a contract (*promissione*), which set out and limited his powers, and against which his performance was monitored each year. Over the centuries, these *promissioni* were progressively tightened. Weak or ineffective Doges were retired, and really bad ones ran the risk of assassination. Even after his death, the Doge was still subject to independent review. If he was found to have been a bad or ineffective ruler, his family could be fined.

Each Doge was assisted by four Ducal Counsellors, who were independently appointed by the State, not by the Doge himself. Their term of office was short (two or three years), which meant that they could not become too powerful. There were also a whole series of other state committees, which ensured that leadership experience was widely diffused, providing a wide pool of potential Doges or Ducal Counsellors.

Company law in the UK and US (the Anglo-Saxon model) supports the shareholder approach – companies must be run in the interests of their shareholders – although UK corporations do have legal responsibilities to other stakeholders. Other countries take a different approach to corporate governance. In Germany, companies have two-tier boards, a supervisory board and a management board (the Rhine model). The management board runs the company on a day-to-day basis, but is answerable to the supervisory board, which has shareholder, employee and third-party representatives on it, and which represents the interests of stakeholders (Farnham 1999, pp300–1).

Big business in Japan is organised through large integrated corporations called *keiretsu* (Mitsui, Mitsubishi, etc). These are both vertical, where manufacturers, suppliers and sub-contractors are members of the same *keiretsu*, and horizontal, where the *keiretsu* companies operate in different markets. Mitsubishi, for example, is involved in gas, chemicals, plastics, steel, aluminium, cement, butter, brewing and paper (Charkham 1994, p77).

Customers and suppliers are thus frequently within the same *keiretsu*, and relationships with them are thus much closer than in the West (as a corollary, customers and suppliers outside the *keiretsu* might find themselves much more harshly treated, leading the system open to charges of cronyism). Japanese society is also heavily based on the concepts of family, consensus and *wa* (harmony). This leads naturally to a heavy reliance on the stakeholder approach. The hierarchy of interests tends to be customers first, employees second, managers third, and shareholders last. The assumption was that managers and employees 'eat their rice out of the same pot', ie that differentials should be narrow. The controversy over excessive 'fat cat' rewards to top management which is so prevalent in the UK would have been impossible in Japan. However, because the stakeholder approach is supported by culture rather than law, it is vulnerable to changes in that culture, and has been shaken by the long recession in Japan over the last two decades.

In 1990, foreign institutional investors held 5% of shares in Japanese companies. By 2006, this had increased to 26%. These foreign investors want results now, not at some vague time in the future. Dore (2006) examined Japan's two most recent recoveries from recession, in 1986–1990, and 2001–2005. In the earlier period, wages rose by 19%, salaries and bonuses of directors by 22%, and dividends by only 2%. In the later period, the balance was totally different. Wages were down by 6%, directors' reward up by 97%, and dividends by 175%.

Each system has its strengths and weaknesses, as summarised in Table 9.4.

Table 9.4 Corporate governance systems

	Strengths	Weaknesses
Anglo-Saxon model	Dynamic and innovative Fluid capital investment	Volatile and unstable Short-termism Weak governance
Rhine model	Long-term strategy Stable capital investment	Lack of flexibility Conservatism
Japanese model	Very long-term strategy Stable capital investment	Financial speculation Crony governance Weak accountability

Source: adapted from Johnson et al (2011), p174

The conflict of interest and accountability questions are also tackled in different ways. In the US, the approach is one of compliance, where corporate governance regulations are laid down by law, and must be followed. Typical is the Sarbanes-Oxley Act of 2002, which followed the scandals in Enron and WorldCom. This states that all companies listed in the US must introduce codes of conduct, ethics policies and whistleblower hotlines. This also applies to foreign companies seeking a listing on the New York stock exchange. However, the key weakness of the compliance approach is that it does not internalise corporate governance in the culture of the corporation. As with other law, determined managers will find ways of obeying its letter, but thwarting its spirit. Enron had a code of ethics, and on paper abided by all legal requirements (Crane and Matten 2007).

The UK approach is to use voluntary codes of practice, but to force firms to issue explanations if they choose not to abide by them. The key to the UK approach is separation of powers. In 1992 the Cadbury Report called for separation of the roles of Chairman and CEO in listed companies. The CEO represented the executive managers, while the Chairman acted in the interests of shareholders. The supermarket chain Morrison's had a combined Chairman and CEO (Sir Ken Morrison, the founder), until it took over Safeway in 2003, but its explanation, that in effect it was a family business, was accepted by the Stock Exchange. Cadbury also called for the increased use of Non-Executive Directors (NEDs) on boards, who again would represent the interests of shareholders. This was strengthened by the Higgs Report in 2003, which called for NEDs to be a majority on boards, and for them to be independently appointed, to avoid charges of cronyism if they were selected through the 'old boy network' from among friends of the chairman or CEO (Fisher and Lovell 2006). Again the example of Enron illustrates the risk of cronyism. The vast majority of its directors were non-executive.

BANKS AND ETHICS: BARCLAYS BANK, LIBOR AND WILFUL BLINDNESS

Barclays Bank is one of the leading UK banks. During the banking crisis of 2008, it narrowly avoided being forced into a UK government rescue programme like Halifax Bank of Scotland and the Royal Bank of Scotland. However, evidence was produced in 2012 which suggested that Barclay's independent survival had been based on misleading, and possibly fraudulent, information.

The key to this is the obscure but very important interest rate, LIBOR (or London Inter-Bank Offered Rate). This is the rate of interest at which banks are prepared to lend money to each other, and it is set by the British Bankers Association based on information supplied by the banks. It is important in two main ways

Many other interest rates, including some mortgage rates, are based on LIBOR. If LIBOR rises, millions of borrowers will have to pay a higher rate of interest. If the interest rate figures submitted by an individual bank are above those submitted by other banks, this is interpreted by the financial markets as a sign of weakness and vulnerability at that bank.

In June 2012, the UK and US financial regulation authorities imposed a fine of £290m on Barclays for manipulation of LIBOR. This was based on two separate series of incidents. Between 2005 and 2008, Barclays filed artificially high interest rate figures, in an attempt to force up LIBOR, and boost its own profits. This was clearly fraudulent. In 2008–9, Barclays did the opposite, submitting artificially low figures to try to hide the extent to which it was under financial stress. This was successful, and Barclays avoided a UK government financial rescue. Barclays later claimed that the 2008–9 policy was based on a 'nod and a wink' from the Bank of England, strenuously denied by the latter.

The head of Barclays Capital, the financial trading arm of the bank responsible for the LIBOR submissions, was the American banker Bob Diamond, who in January 2011 became the CEO of the Barclays Group. When the fine on Barclays was announced, there was considerable pressure on Diamond to resign, but instead the sacrificial lamb was the Chairman, Marcus Agius, who offered his resignation, although he later agreed to stay on in the short term. Diamond initially refused to resign, saying that he had no idea that his traders were fiddling LIBOR, and only did so when put under intense pressure from Parliament, the Bank of England and the Financial Services Authority (FSA).

Gradually it became clear that LIBOR was not an isolated problem for Barclays. The FSA accused Barclays of having a 'gaming' culture, continually pushing at the boundaries of the regulatory rules, while the Governor of the Bank of England said Barclays had been 'sailing too close to the wind across a wide number of areas'. The FSA apparently expressed concern when Diamond was appointed as Chief Executive, and also about the bank's culture under Diamond.

What went wrong? Firstly it is important to note that Barclays is not an isolated case. Many other banks are under investigation for LIBOR-related offences, while both HSBC and Standard Chartered were heavily fined by the US authorities for regulatory offences in August 2012. Part of the problem was clearly caused by the 'cowboy' approach of Diamond, and in denying that he knew anything about the LIBOR fixing, Diamond was either a fool (if he didn't know, he should have done), or a villain (he knew, but pretended he didn't, and did nothing about it; interestingly, Rupert Murdoch claimed similar ignorance about phone-hacking – classic examples of wilful blindness), but the real problem is the culture of the banking industry, particularly in financial trading.

Peter Cummings, the banker whose corporate loans division left HBOS close to collapse was fined £500,000 in September 2012 and banned for life from the City. The FSA criticised his failure to 'exercise due skill, care and diligence by pursuing an aggressive expansion strategy within the corporate division, without suitable controls in place to manage the associated risks' between January 2006 and March 2008. It also said he failed to 'take reasonable care to ensure that the corporate division adequately and prudently managed high value transactions which showed signs of stress' in the run-up to the financial crisis (Independent 2012a).

The esoteric nature of the business encourages a cultish sense of loyalty to the team, and a concurrent feeling of contempt towards the rest of the world. Clients are 'punters', there to be manipulated. Rules are to be bent, and those who observe them are 'suckers' or 'wimps'. In such a culture, it is very difficult to be a whistleblower.

Anand, Ashforth and Joshi introduce the concept of a 'social cocoon' (Anand et al 2004). This is a micro culture created within a group where the norms may be very different from those valued by society or even the wider organisation (for example a bank dealing room). Membership in such a group is highly prized, and employees are more likely to accept and adopt the norms of the group. Newcomers are socialised into the norms of the group by veteran members.

Parallels can be drawn with the 'canteen culture' of the police, and with the culture of street gangs.

Investment banking is notorious for its huge (some would say obscene) bonuses, and at the same time for its insecurity. The weakest performers are regularly culled, and when a new team leader is appointed, he or she is likely to bring in their own team. Bankers find it very difficult to move to another industry, as their skills are highly specialised. Again, ultra-short-termism is encouraged, and whistleblowing discouraged (Luyendijk 2012). Parallels can be drawn with Premier League footballers.

In addition, banking has a cosy relationship with both politicians and regulators. Tony Blair was paid £2.5m a year by JP Morgan, while half of the Conservative party's funding comes from the finance industry. In 2008, there was a perception that banks were too big to fail, and they have received £12tr from the UK taxpayer (Chakraborrty 2012). When Paul Tucker was promoted to number two at the Bank of England, Bob Diamond emailed: 'Well done, man. I am really, really proud of you.' Tucker replied, 'You've been an absolute brick.' (*The Guardian* 2012b).

What can be done? One solution is to break the bonus culture – clearly an HR issue. Another is to separate investment (wholesale) from high street (retail) banking, so if an investment bank fails, it would not be at risk of dragging down a high street bank with it. This was done in the US through the Glass-Steagall Act, not repealed until 1999, while something similar has been proposed by the Vickers Report (the Independent Commission on Banking) in 2011. This proposed ring-fencing wholesale from retail banking. This was accepted by the Government, but will not be implemented until 2019! (Treanor 2012; Zingales 2012). A third solution is to discourage some of the most esoteric and socially useless derivatives trading through some kind of transactions or Tobin tax (see Activity 9.6). The bottom line is that trust must be restored to banking.

In August 2012 Barclays appointed its head of retail banking, Antony Jenkins, as CEO to succeed Bob Diamond. In a series of symbolic moves, he accepted a remuneration package half the amount of that paid to Diamond, said that 'many things will have to change at Barclays, including compensation, across the group', and announced that in future the bank's target would be a return on capital of 11.5%, rather than 13%, implying much lower risk (Kollewe 2012). He also consciously tried to make the bank more ethical, winning praise from, among others, the Archbishop of Canterbury. However, Jenkins was sacked in July 2015, and the bank announced new strategic objectives – double the share price in the next three years, be more aggressive in lending decisions, put more emphasis on Africa, and put more emphasis on the investment bank. In other words, a return to the policies which contributed to the banking crash in 2007–8! (*Observer* 2015)

HSBC: Switzerland, Stephen Green and tax evasion

HSBC was founded in 1865 on 'Scottish banking principles' of conservatism and lack of ostentation. Board members were instructed to fly economy. The core of the company was East Asia, hence the name Hong Kong and Shanghai Banking Corporation. It was run as a colonial operation, with control over particular countries given to International Officers, who were given a high degree of autonomy. They were typically white British males, with distinct similarities in class and attitudes to district officers in colonial Africa. Until 1989 they were not

allowed to marry without the chairman's permission until they were 30 (Pratley 2015b).

By the early 1990s, it was becoming clear that sooner or later Hong Kong would be handed back to China, and that it would be prudent to diversify geographically. In 1992, HSBC bought Midland Bank, one of the UK's 'big four' banks, establishing a new base in the UK.

In 1999, HSBC embarked on a spending spree that was to fatally transform its culture. It purchased Republic National Bank of New York and Safra Republic Holdings, both of which had a reputation for chasing high net worth customers, many of whom had something to hide. The two purchases became HSBC Private Bank (Suisse) SA. In 2002 it acquired the Mexican bank, Bital. It carried on with Bital's fast-paced growth and failed to implement many of the anti-money laundering checks required of banks with US operations. Paul Thurston, who was 'for 14 stressful months' in 2007 and 2008 the head of the Mexico bank, told Congress: 'Some of the things I found, frankly, took my breath away.'

Even odder was the acquisition in 2003, of Household Finance, a US sub-prime lender that had been accused of predatory practices. The idea was that HSBC could transform Household and adapt it to HSBC's prudent banking model. The Household boss, William Aldinger III, joined HSBC's board and became the highest paid director of a UK company. During the US sub-prime crisis Household collapsed, leading to huge write-offs. HSBC was referred to in the US as 'Highly Suspect British Company' (Pratley 2015c).

Despite Household, HSBC came through the banking crisis relatively unscathed and with a good reputation, helped by the personality of its chairman from 2003 to 2010, Stephen Green, an Anglican priest and author of *Good Value: Reflections on Money, Morality and an Uncertain World*, published in 2009. He had an apparently well-deserved reputation as an ethical banker. In 2010 he joined the Coalition government as a trade minister, and was made a peer (Garside et al 2015).

Things started to unravel for HSBC in 2012. It was accused by a US Senate committee of helping sanctions-busting by Iran, laundering money for Mexican drugs cartels, and refusing to cut off a Saudi bank suspected of having links to al-Qaida. HSBC was given a $1.9bn fine by the US authorities (*Independent* 2012b).

Meanwhile, a scandal closer to home was about to break in Switzerland. In 2007, a whistleblower, Herve Falciani, extracted client data on tax avoidance and evasion from inside HSBC Suisse. In 2008 he fled to France with the files. In early 2010, the French tax authorities released the files to their foreign counterparts, including Britain's HM Revenue and Customs. This was before Stephen Green was made a trade minister, and while he was still chairman of HSBC. In early 2013, Dave Hartnett, previously head of tax at HRMC, joined HSBC as a consultant, six months after his retirement.

In early 2015, the HSBC files were published by *The Guardian* and the BBC, and they made explosive reading. It appeared that not only did HSBC Suisse have dubious clients, but that in many cases there appeared to be evidence that the bank was conniving at tax evasion (*The Guardian* 2015a).

Belatedly HSBC is putting its house in order. Its Swiss business now has 70% fewer private banking customers than it did in 2007, and its global head count in risk and compliance has risen to 24,000 – a tenth of the workforce. Green's successor, Stuart Gulliver, has sold operations in countries where the bank accepted it doesn't stand a chance of implementing

'know-your-customer' rules – they include Colombia, Peru, Uruguay, Paraguay, Costa Rica, El Salvador and Honduras (*Economist* 2015c).

What went wrong at HSBC? The failure appears to be one of culture and size. In 1998 the bank had 25 million customers; by 2003 it had 110 million. Even if it had not made some highly dubious acquisitions, its old colonial style federal structure could no longer cope. Local officials in Mexico and Switzerland were given a free hand, with predictable results. Finally, some blame must attach to Stephen Green. From 2005, Green was chair of HSBC's Swiss supervisory company, HSBC Private Banking Holdings (Suisse) SA. In his book, Green wrote 'For companies, where does [corporate social] responsibility begin? With their boards, of course. There is no other task they have which is more important.' Fine words, but they do not seem to have been matched with actions (*The Guardian* 2015b).

Clearly the culture of banking has to change. Barclays has introduced a 'transform agenda' which involves measuring performance against Five Cs – customer and client, colleague, citizenship, conduct and company – and against the bank's official values of respect, integrity, service, excellence and stewardship. The Banking Standards Review Council sees part of the problem as the lack of professionalism in banking. Only 100,000 of the two million who work in the UK financial services industry have a professional qualification in banking. As we noted earlier in this chapter, one role of a professional body is to enforce ethical standards in their profession (Hazlehurst 2014).

Worryingly, a 2015 survey of financial executives in the US and UK by Notre Dame University and the US lawyers Labaton Sucharow suggests that ethical standards in banking may have deteriorated even further. Twenty-three per cent of respondents (28% in the UK) said it was likely that their colleagues had engaged in illegal or unethical behaviour, compared with 12% in 2012. When questioned about their own behaviour, 24% in the US and 32% in the UK said they would use (illegal) insider trading to make a guaranteed $10m if they knew they would get away with it. Nearly a third of respondents felt that the compensation and bonus schemes in force in their bank could encourage employees to indulge in illegal or unethical behaviour (Tenbrunsel and Thomas 2015).

9.11 CORPORATE SOCIAL RESPONSIBILITY

Corporate social responsibility (CSR) is the way in which an organisation expresses its values in behaviour towards stakeholders. The European Commission defines it as 'a concept whereby companies decide voluntarily to contribute to a better society and a cleaner environment' (European Commission 2001), while the DTI defines it as an organisation which recognises that its activities have a wider impact on society; takes account of the economic, social, environmental and human rights impacts of its activities, and works in partnership with other groups and organisations (DTI 2002).

Archie Carroll puts forward a four-part model of CSR (Carroll 1991).

1   Economic responsibilities: required by society
2   Legal responsibilities: required by society
3   Ethical responsibilities: expected by society
4   Philanthropic responsibilities: desired by society

Several key points come out of these definitions:

- CSR is voluntary. Mere compliance with legal requirements is not CSR. An organisation's CSR behaviour must go beyond the law.
- CSR is active. It involves behaviour, not just good intentions.
- CSR involves environmental as well as social responsibilities.
- CSR is often carried out in partnership with others.
- Although the European Commission only mentions companies, CSR extends to all organisations, public and private, profit-making and not-for-profit.

CSR can take a number of forms. These include:

- Community involvement, frequently in partnership with other organisations. This can include sponsorship of worthy bodies, or direct involvement of the organisation's employees in community activities. Sponsorship carries its own risks, however, if it turns out that the organisation is supporting unpopular causes. In 2014, Guinness withdrew its sponsorship from the New York City St Patrick's Day parade because LGBT (lesbian, gay, bisexual and transgender) groups were banned from the parade (although a compromise was reached for 2015) (Isidore 2015), while in 2015 several major sponsors withdrew sponsorship from the football governing body FIFA when it was involved in a corruption scandal (Rumsby 2015).
- Socially responsible investment, which can include ethical banking, and refusal by pension funds to invest in companies making, for example, armaments or cigarettes.
- Corporate governance, concerned with the behaviour of a company towards its shareholders, and including elements like the appointment and responsibilities of non-executive directors.
- Fair trade – buying goods produced by suppliers who are, for example, organic, or non-employers of children, or not based in human-rights abusing countries like Burma.
- Sustainability – acting in such a way as to assist the long-term survival of the planet.

EBOLA, ETHICS AND HUMAN RIGHTS

CASE STUDY 9.5

In 1976 scientists identified a new disease in Central Africa, which they named Ebola after a local river. The disease had some very particular characteristics. It had a very high death rate of up to 70%, and killed through extreme dehydration, internal and external bleeding and collapse of vital organs. It was not contagious – it was quite difficult to catch, as it could only be spread through contact with bodily fluids. Unlike measles or cholera, it was not air borne or water borne. In addition, there was no risk of infection until the victim displayed symptoms. However, it was extremely infectious. Only a handful of viral particles were required to infect a new victim, and the number of viral particles were at their maximum at the point of death. As a result, not only medical staff but also burial teams were at high risk.

Until 2014, there were a few isolated outbreaks of Ebola in Central Africa, particularly in the Democratic Republic of Congo, but these were easily contained and quickly petered out. This situation changed radically in 2014. The disease established a new base in West Africa. Starting in Guinea, Ebola spread rapidly to the neighbouring countries of Liberia and Sierra Leone, with a combined population of 20 million. By the time the disease started to peter out in February 2015, around 25,000 people had been infected, with at least 10,000 deaths. There had also been isolated cases in Senegal, Mali, Nigeria, the US and Spain (BBC 2015g; *Economist* 2014d).

Ebola raises a number of ethical and human rights issues.

Developing and testing of treatments and vaccines

Historically, there has been little incentive to develop a vaccine for Ebola, as the disease infects poor people in Africa, who would be unable to pay enough to make a vaccine profitable (*Economist* 2014e).

Several different experimental drugs were used on patients with Ebola in the US and Europe, and survival rates there were much higher than in Africa, but without rigorous scientific trials there was no way of telling whether this was because of the drug, or because of better supportive care (*Economist* 2014f).

The problem was that proper clinical trials require blind testing, with some patients receiving the new drug, and others a placebo with no clinical benefit. However, this raises the ethical issue that using a placebo could in effect condemn those patients to die. To get round this problem, it was decided that placebos would not be used, but that instead ring vaccination would be used – all contacts of an infected person would be vaccinated, half immediately and half after three weeks. The results were spectacular – none of those vaccinated immediately developed Ebola, and only 1% of those vaccinated after three weeks (Gallagher 2015).

Quarantine

Kaci Hickox is a nurse working in Sierra Leone who returned to the United States on 24 October. She clearly anticipated being screened for Ebola. Although she had no symptoms suggestive of infection, she was put into compulsory isolation by the State of New Jersey. Was this a breach of her human rights?

The UN's Siracusa principles outline the circumstances within which restriction of human rights are justified. In order for a restriction like compulsory quarantine to accord with the Siracusa principles:

1   It must be provided for, and carried out, in accordance with the law.

2   It must be in the interest of a legitimate objective of general interest.

3   It must be strictly necessary to achieve the objective, in a democratic society.

4   There should be no less-restrictive/intrusive means through which the same objective can be achieved.

5   The restriction must be based on scientific evidence, and not imposed arbitrarily or in a discriminatory way.

It is also vital that such restrictions be of limited duration, and subject to appeal and/or review.

Containment of the Ebola virus is a legitimate objective but the arguments for compulsory quarantining of asymptomatic health workers are dubious. The quarantine put in place by New Jersey appears to be unnecessary and not based on scientific evidence (Lander 2014).

Responses by the affected states

In many cases the responses of the governments of Sierra Leone, Liberia and Guinea to Ebola have infringed human rights. Quarantines have not been adequately monitored, making them ineffective from a public health perspective and disproportionately impacting people unable to evade the restrictions, including the elderly, the poor, and people with chronic illness or disability.

A Sierra Leonean journalist has been arrested after criticising the government's approach to Ebola. During senatorial elections in Liberia, queuing voters had to stand three feet apart and bring their own pens, restrictions that did little to encourage a high turnout. Security forces in all three counties have fired on protestors. Across the region, rulers are accused of trying to gain political advantage from the epidemic by directing international aid toward their support bases (*Economist* 2015f).

Response of the West

The response of Western counties to the epidemic was extremely slow, and more concerned with protecting themselves than with helping the affected countries. Six months separated the US Center for Disease Control's recognition of the outbreak in March and President Obama's call for international mobilisation in mid-September (Donnelly 2014). As Lawrence Gostin says, 'the perception persists that disease threats originate in the global South, requiring international law to prevent their spread to affluent regions' (Gostin 2014).

International airlines such as British Airways, Emirates, Air France and Kenya Airways stopped flying to Sierra Leone, Liberia and Guinea. This made it difficult to get health workers and aid to the affected areas. Aid sent by Japan had to be loaded in Accra in Ghana and sent 900 miles by road to Sierra Leone, because air transport was not available (*Economist* 2014g).

Sierra Leone struggled in its fight against Ebola because so many doctors and nurses have left for jobs in Britain and elsewhere in the West. The country only had just over 100 doctors before the epidemic, of whom at least ten have died of Ebola (Robinson 2014).

However, although the response of the West was slow, in the end it may have been decisive. The UK sent military and NHS medical volunteers to Sierra Leone, two of whom caught Ebola but survived after treatment in the UK. The US sent non-medical troops, who played a key role in building new treatment centres. The biggest contribution came from Cuba, which has always seen medical aid as a branch of soft diplomacy (Gomez 2014).

CSR has been criticised as often being little more than a PR stunt, designed to boost sales rather than to benefit society. This is particularly true of community involvement activities. This has been called 'cause-related marketing'. For example, Vodafone sponsors the England cricket team, but in return gets endless exposure of its logo on players' shirts during Test Matches. Tesco runs its Computers for Schools project, which supplies computers to schools, but only after customers have collected vouchers to verify their spend in Tesco stores. (For a spirited condemnation of cause-related marketing, see Monbiot (2001)).

Brammer, Millington and Pavelin (2006) analyse to what extent philanthropy is strategic. They define strategic philanthropy as the practice of giving corporate resources to address non-business community issues that also benefit the firm's strategic position and, ultimately, its bottom line (it is probably significant that one criterion for listing on the FTSE4Good stock market index is charitable giving of at least £50,000 a year). Strategic philanthropy can be seen as one end of a continuum, with altruistic philanthropy at the other. I think one criterion for altruistic philanthropy would be that the giving is to an unpopular cause (funding counselling for convicted paedophiles, for example). This is rare. Even the Co-op Bank, which together with the Body Shop is probably seen as one of the most ethical businesses in the UK, campaigns on issues generally seen as morally right, for example, against trade in conflict diamonds, or the use of cluster bombs. Early in 1999, Industrial Relations Services carried out a survey of ethics in the workplace (*IRS Employment Trends* 675, March 1999). The survey asked why organisations were involved in community activities. Respondents could choose as many of six responses as they chose. The results were:

		Per cent
1	Enhancement of corporate image	82
2	Moral obligation	62
3	Employee satisfaction	59
4	Develop staff potential	51
5	Promote the business	46
6	Improve profitability	15

Short-term profits (no 6) were mentioned by only a small minority of respondents, while long-term profitability (nos 1 and 5), employees (nos 3 and 4) and moral obligation (no 2) were seen as much more important. Perhaps community involvement is a rare example of a true win-win situation (see also Kelly 1999).

? REFLECTIVE ACTIVITY 9.5

Is your own organisation involved in the community?

Find out what community activities (if any) your own organisation is involved in. If possible, also try to find out why the organisation chose these particular activities. Was the primary motive short-term profits, long-term profits, employee benefit or moral obligation (or a mixture of several of these)?

FAIRTRADE

Fairtrade is one of the retail successes of the 2000s. Sales of Fairtrade coffee grew from £15.5m in 2000, to £65.8m in 2006, when it commanded 18% of the UK roast and ground coffee market. Similar rates of growth have been seen for tea, chocolate and cocoa, and bananas.

Fairtrade is a product labelling scheme, which acts as an independent guarantee that disadvantaged producers in the third world are getting a better deal. Its standards are set by an international certification body, Fair Trading Labelling Organisations International, and administered at a country level by national Fairtrade organisations. In the UK the administering body is the Fairtrade Foundation, a charity set up by Cafod, Oxfam, Christian Aid, Traidcraft Exchange and the World Development Movement.

The majority of coffee and cocoa is grown by small farmers, organised into co-operatives, while bananas and tea are usually produced on plantations. In the former case, it is the co-operative which is given Fairtrade certification, in the latter, it is the plantation, which guarantees minimum health and safety and environmental standards, and that no child or forced labour will be used. In return, producers are guaranteed a price which is sufficient to cover sustainable production, plus a premium which is invested in community development. For example, the minimum price paid for Fairtrade cocoa is $1600 a ton, plus $150 per ton premium, as long as the world (New York) price is below $1600. If the New York price rises above $1600 a ton, the Fairtrade price will be the New York price plus $150 premium. This means that producers are guaranteed a stable price, and they are insulated from market fluctuations, which in the case of primary products can be violent.

An example quoted on the Fairtrade website is the Juliana-Jaramillo group of banana farmers in the Dominican Republic. Until 1962, the Granada Food Company ran vast plantation estates in the area, providing housing, water supply and schools. In 1962, they pulled out and the infrastructure collapsed. Granada even took the zinc roofs off the estate houses. The government divided 15% of the estates among local farmers, giving each worker about 15 hectares each.

In 2000, Fairtrade introduced the local farmers to a UK-based company, Mack Multiples, and they worked together to improve the quality of their fruit and to develop sales to Sainsbury's. A local farmer, Alfredo Martinez, says that he is now guaranteed a minimum price, receives money weekly, and is making twice what he was before Fairtrade. Environmental standards have been improved, and education and health standards have been restored.

However, not everyone is so impressed with the Fairtrade achievement. Firstly, Fairtrade is not necessarily the same as ethical sourcing. For example, Marks & Spencer sells Fairtrade cotton clothing. This guarantees that the raw cotton was produced ethically, but not necessarily that the whole of the supply chain was ethical. In any case, Fairtrade cotton only makes up about 1% of that purchased by M&S each year.

Secondly, there is a feeling that Fairtrade is being exploited by large retailers. They see the Fairtrade label as a way to segment socially aware consumers, who are willing to pay a premium price for Fairtrade products. The result is that the main beneficiaries are the supermarket groups, rather than the Fairtrade producers.

Thirdly, major producers are also jumping on the Fairtrade bandwagon. The best known is Nestlé, whose Partner's Blend coffee has Fairtrade certification. This is seen as unacceptable by some ethical campaigners, who point to the long-standing claims that Nestlé unethically promotes its powdered milk compounds in third world countries.

Fourthly, Fairtrade has been criticised by some economists, particularly Americans, because it is seen as biased towards co-operatives and because it guarantees a minimum price. The rival US-backed scheme, Rainforest Alliance, does not guarantee a price, and has been described as 'Fairtrade lite' by its critics. This became a bone of contention in the attempted takeover of Cadbury by the US food conglomerate Kraft in 2009. Cadbury had obtained Fairtrade certification for its Dairy Milk chocolate, while Kraft had Rainforest Alliance certification for its Kenco coffee. Kraft argued that it opposed Fairtrade because it provides a subsidy that distorts the workings of the open market.

Finally, building on Kraft's point, some economists claim that Fairtrade, by guaranteeing a price above the world price, is in effect encouraging over-production. Fairtrade counters by saying that for all commodities, Fairtrade is only a small percentage of world output, and that the Fairtrade price gives farmers surplus income which encourages them to diversify.

In 2014, sales of Fairtrade products in the UK slipped for the first time, by 4%. This was largely a reflection of the general fall in grocery sales, and the switch towards cut-price retailers like Lidl and Aldi, which stock fewer Fairtrade products. However, more than 4,500 products are Fairtrade-certified, and the UK is one of the world's leading Fairtrade markets, with sales of £1.57bn in 2012.

On balance, like me, you may well think that Fairtrade benefits the third world and should be encouraged, but as with most things, the situation is not as simple as it appears at first sight.

Sources: Fairtrade Foundation website www.fairtrade.org.uk; Crane and Matten (2007); Murray (2006); *Economist* (2006d); Prosser (2007); Bowers (2009); Norton (2015)

9.12 SUSTAINABILITY

Sustainability is about our responsibility to the ultimate stakeholder: our own future, and the future of the planet. We are using up the resources of the earth and degrading the planet at an increasing rate, and this can only be at the expense of future generations. Sustainable development is 'development that meets the needs of the present without compromising the ability of future generations to meet their own needs' (Fisher and Lovell 2006, p21). This definition stresses that sustainability must be based on needs, not on wants. DesJardins (2007) quotes the formula I = PAT. Environmental impact (I), is the product of population (P), consumption per head or affluence (A), and technology (T). A sustainable society will limit its population growth, avoid excessive consumerism, and promote technology which reduces resource use. 'To operate sustainably, an organisation must... [be] supportive of the survival of the physical environment and also the communities and economies in which it operates' (*Accountability Primer: Sustainability* (nd), www.accountability.org.uk).

DesJardins quotes the example of Gold n'Plump Poultry in Minnesota, which processes 4 million pounds of chicken a week. Its waste water treatment plant produces large amounts of solid waste. Each week it sends 100,000lb of solid waste to Mississippi Topsoils, where it is combined with residential waste and sawdust to produce saleable compost. An opposite example is the UK's trade in gingerbread. Every year the UK imports 465 tonnes of gingerbread, while at the same time exporting 460 tonnes. This results in excessive use of resources in transportation, and increases the UK's carbon footprint, for no obvious benefit (Simms 2009).

At the macro level, we have the problem of global warming and the associated climate change, the result of the excess of greenhouse gases, particularly carbon dioxide, in the atmosphere, caused at least in part by our excessive burning of fossil fuel. This can only be tackled at global level (global social responsibility). The Kyoto Treaty in 1999 committed industrialised countries to large reductions in carbon emissions, but this effort was frustrated by the refusal of the Bush Administration to ratify the treaty. The UK is fully committed to the Kyoto principles, and has introduced a Climate Change Levy on polluting industries. In December 2015, world agreement was reached on actions to minimise the increase in global temperatures.

At a micro level, sustainability concerns us all, organisations and individuals alike. At an individual level, it is as basic as composting our garden waste, rather than sending it to landfill sites, and turning off our television sets at night, rather than leaving them on standby. At an organisational level, it can be about energy conservation, and also about the kind of activities highlighted in Case Study 9.7 and Reflective Activity 9.6.

CASE STUDY 9.7

PLASTIC BAGS – AN UNSUSTAINABLE OPTION?

Seventeen billion plastic carrier bags are used in the UK every year, 14 billion of which are given away by supermarkets. Only one in 200 of these are recycled. The rest go into landfill, weighing 100,000 tonnes, where they take up to 1,000 years to decompose. The vast majority of bags are made from oil derivatives. Most are non-degradable, a few are degradable – they break down when exposed to sunlight (but not in landfill) and a very few are biodegradable, made of corn starch, and do break down in landfill.

Several countries have taken action to control their use of plastic bags. In 2002, Bangladesh banned them outright, as they were causing flooding by blocking storm drainage channels during the monsoon. They are also banned in South Africa, and San Francisco is the first US city to impose a ban. Taiwan has banned plastic plates, cups and cutlery as well as plastic bags, leading to a 25% in its landfill.

Ireland took a different route, introducing a tax of 15 cents (about 10p) a bag in 2002. This cut plastic bag usage by at least 90%, although some small bags are exempt. Usage has slowly crept up again since 2002, leading to an increase in tax to 22 cents in July 2007.

The small town of Modbury in Devon became the first town in Europe to ban plastic bags in April 2007. None of the town's 43 traders, including the Co-op supermarket, issues plastic bags.

Individual stores have taken unilateral action. IKEA charges 10p a bag, and has seen plastic bag use fall by 97%. The discount stores Aldi and Lidl have always charged for bags.

Tesco, the heaviest bag user of all, with 4 billion bags issued each year – costing it £40m at 1p per bag – introduced a scheme in 2006 whereby customers received one 'green' Clubcard point, worth 1p, for each bag which they reused, whether or not the reused bag originally came from Tesco. This was intended to cut Tesco's usage by 25%, or 1 billion bags a year. Each bag saved saves Tesco 1p, so the only net cost to Tesco is when it pays out for other stores' bags. Tesco has also made all its bags degradable (but not biodegradable).

Tesco's move has been welcomed by the government, but criticised by Friends of the Earth as 'a very small step' and a 'greenwash', as it does nothing to cut the excessive amounts of food packaging used by Tesco and all other supermarkets, and because Tesco has chosen not to go biodegradable.

However, the plastic bag industry fought back. Barry Turner, the Chairman of the UK Carrier Bag Consortium, claims that although plastic bags are made from oil, they use by-products such as naphtha ethylene and propylene, which would otherwise have to be flared off. He also criticises the use of paper bags rather than plastic. Paper bags weigh more than plastic, are four times as expensive to produce, and most seriously, whereas plastic bags in landfill remain inert, paper bags decompose to release the greenhouse gases methane and CO_2.

Although the obvious response to Turner's claims is 'he would say that, wouldn't he', the situation is clearly more complex than at first sight. Perhaps the ideal solution is that advocated by Sainsbury's – the more extensive use of 'bags for life', more heavy duty bags which sell or 10p, which can be reused many times, and which the store guarantees to replace free when they wear out, whereupon Sainsbury's send the worn out bag for recycling.

In the UK the Scottish Parliament considered and rejected a tax of 10p a bag in 2006, and a MORI poll suggested that throughout the UK 63% would support a 10p tax. London has considering a ban, while the former Prime Minister, Gordon Brown, has said that he would like to see a total ban on single-use plastic bags.

Wales was the first UK country to bring in a tax, of 5p on all single use bags, plastic, paper or biodegradable, applicable to all retailers, and with the net proceeds going to charity. This came into force in October 2011 (Welsh Government 2012). Northern Ireland followed in April 2013 and Scotland in October 2014, where the tax led to an immediate drop of 90% in bag use (*The Herald* 2014). England finally introduced a 5p levy from October 2015, but paper bags are exempt, and so are small- and medium-sized retailers, a move criticised by the Commons Environmental Audit Select Committee (Harvey 2014).

Sources: Turner (2006); Finch and Allen (2006); Butler (2006); *Economist* (2007c); Barkham (2007); Aldred (2007); Wintour (2007); Hickman (2009); Welsh Government (2012); *The Herald* (2014); Harvey (2014).

? REFLECTIVE ACTIVITY 9.6

Tobin tax and global warming

What is a Tobin tax?

It is a transaction tax, originally proposed by the US economist James Tobin in the 1970s. It would impose a small levy of all financial transactions throughout the world. Tobin originally proposed a 1% tax, but what is now being suggested is much smaller – 0.05 or even 0.005%.

How much money would it raise?

The sums involved are enormous. The volume of financial transactions in the global economy is estimated to be nearly 75 times as big as global GDP, most of it in speculation on the derivatives markets, which are seen as of dubious real value. Adair Turner, sometime chairman of the Financial Services Authority, described some City activities as 'socially useless'. A 0.005% levy on foreign exchange trades alone would raise $30bn, while a study by the Austrian government suggested that a 0.05% levy on UK financial trades would raise $100bn a year (and $420bn worldwide), even if it led to a two-thirds fall in transactions.

Who would pay for the tax?

Like all output taxes, the cost would be shared between buyers and sellers – the financial speculators and the banks.

Who is in favour?

France and Germany have been in favour for some time, and Gordon Brown announced his conversion in November 2009. At present, the US and the IMF are opposed, although some economists close to the Obama administration are thought to be in favour.

What has this got to do with global warming?

In order to combat global warming, all economies must invest huge sums in greener energy technologies. The West can afford this, but the developing world, and India and China, cannot. Coal is the primary energy source in both India and China. A clean coal-fired power station is 50% more efficient (ie less polluting) than the average plant in India and China. Implementing clean coal technology would cost India up to $8bn a year. Gordon Brown has proposed that only half of the proceeds from a Tobin tax should be spent at home. The other half would finance economic development and climate change reduction in the developing world (the agreement on global warming reached in December 2015 has called for a $65bn fund in assist developing countries in combating global warming).

Where are we now?

In 2011, The European Commission proposed a Financial Transactions Tax (a variant of a Tobin tax). This was approved by the European Parliament in 2012 and the Council of Ministers in 2013 (with the UK abstaining). The tax was scheduled to start in eleven countries in 2014, but was postponed, and may now start in 2016.

The UK has become more lukewarm on the idea of a Tobin tax. In the 2015 General Election it was proposed only by the Green Party, The Communist Party, The Alliance Party in Northern Ireland, and Plaid Cymru.

Question

What do you think would be the practical obstacles to the implementation of a Tobin tax?

Sources: Elliott (2009); Mathiason and Treanor (2009); Inman (2013); Holley (2015); whoshallivotefor (2015)

CASE STUDY 9.8

COSTA RICA – A MODEL OF SUSTAINABLE DEVELOPMENT

Costa Rica is a small, seemingly unremarkable country in Central America. However, it is remarkable as the only country in the world to abolish its army, in 1949, following a short but bloody civil war. It decided to divert the money saved not to tax cuts, but to increased spending on education and health – as was said at the time, 'the army would be replaced by an army of teachers' (Ministerio de Cultura, Juventud y Deportes Costa Rica 2004). The country had already set up a socialised national health service in 1941 (well before the UK). The results have been spectacular. Public education to high school level is free and universal, and the literacy rate is 95%. Infant mortality rates and life expectancy are better than in the US (Seager 2009). The political system is stable and democratic, and the country has the lowest level of corruption in Latin America (except Chile) (Transparency International 2012).

Costa Rica also realised that its main national asset is its beautiful and varied countryside and its diverse and exotic wildlife, making it ideal for eco-tourism. Twenty-five per cent of its land area is in national parks and other protected areas, the highest in the world, and it is the only country in the world to have totally abolished hunting.

The New Economics Foundation's Happy Planet Index combines measures of a country's environmental footprint with the happiness of its citizens. On this measure in 2009 and 2012 Costa Rica is the best in the world (the UK is 74th, the US 114th) (Seager 2009). It is the only country in the world to meet all five of the UN Development Programme's criteria to measure environmental sustainability (UNDP 2011). The country generates 94% of its electricity from renewable sources (100% for the first three months of 2015, following heavy rainfall), and has decided not to exploit significant reserves of oil off its Caribbean coast (Tufft 2015).

Sources: As cited, plus the author's own experiences in Costa Rica February 2013 and November 2015

9.13 RISK MANAGEMENT

An important element of sustainability is risk management. Risk management is not necessarily about avoiding risk – it is about assessing risk, and ensuring that it is consistent with the strategy of the organisation, whether it is risk averse or risk seeking. On the whole, an organisation seeking sustainability will tend to be relatively risk averse.

Risk management is about answering several questions:

- What risks are we facing?
- What are the underlying causes of those risks?
- What is the likelihood of the risky event occurring?
- What is the outcome if the risky event does occur? Risk is measured by likelihood times outcome.
- What can be done about the risk? Possibilities include avoidance, reduction, retention or transfer.
- What decision is taken about the risk?
- How can the decision be tracked, monitored and reviewed?

Figure 9.2 An Ishikawa diagram

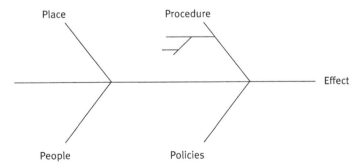

It is important to note that in identifying a risk, we must identify its causes rather than its symptoms. A technique for doing this is an Ishikawa, fishbone or cause-effect diagram (named after its inventor, Kaoru Ishikawa, a Japanese quality expert). This is frequently done in a group as a brainstorming exercise. An effect is identified, and then possible causes for this effect are brainstormed. These are then grouped into major categories, and the problem is further brainstormed to identify sub-causes, plotted as sub-bones on the skeleton diagram below. Categories commonly used for problems with a large HR element are the four Ps – place, procedure, people, policies.

Quantitatively, two risks (likelihood x outcome) might appear identical, but one may have a high likelihood (say 50%) and a low financial cost (say £10,000), and the other a low likelihood (say 0.1%) and a high financial cost (say £5m). Each would represent a risk of £5,000, but how they are treated is likely to be very different. In the first case, the risk may be ignored (ie retained within the organisation), while in the second case, it is likely that the risk will be transferred (through insurance).

The possible strategies for dealing with risk include:

- *Avoidance.* Here a risky activity is not performed at all. For example, after the terrorist attacks in London in July 2005, many Americans avoided all travel to the UK. In a business context, avoiding risk usually means also giving up the opportunity of profit, so except in extreme cases it is unlikely to be a viable strategy.
- *Reduction.* This involves the use of methods which reduce the severity of the loss or the likelihood of it occurring. An example here is the prohibition on the use of hand-held mobile phones while driving.
- *Retention.* Here the risk is accepted when it occurs. This will frequently be done where the risk is small, or where a very large organisation finds it cheaper to self-insure rather than pay insurance premiums to another organisation.
- *Transfer.* Here the risk is transferred to someone else, usually through an insurance contract, but also sometimes through outsourcing. This is commonly used for risks which have a low likelihood of occurrence, but which would be catastrophic if they did happen – for example, the second scenario discussed above, where the likelihood of occurrence was very low (0.1%), but the outcome very high (a loss of £5m). Here the risk is only £5000, but the organisation might be prepared to pay a higher insurance premium than this (say £10,000) to cover the risk.

Once a decision has been taken about how to manage a particular risk, this decision then has to be monitored and periodically reviewed, as the risk parameters may change over time.

? REFLECTIVE ACTIVITY 9.7

Risk in the NHS

The NHS has a model for assessing and managing risk (NHS Commissioning Board 2012). This involves two variables:

The likelihood that harm, loss or damage from the identified hazard will occur. This is scored between 1 and 5:

1 Rare – probably will never happen.

2 Unlikely – do not expect it to happen, but it is possible it may do so.

3 Possible – possibly may happen.

4 Likely – probable that it will happen.

5 Almost certain – likely to occur in the majority of cases.

The severity of the impact, again scored between 1 and 5

1 Insignificant or minor – no or slight impact.

2 Moderate – moderate impact.

3 Significant – significant impact.

4 Very significant – impact on NHS objectives covering several areas.

5 Major – impact on NHS objectives requiring radical review.

The two variables are then combined in a matrix to evaluate rating for the risk

	Very High (5)	C	D	E	E	E
	High (4)	C	C	D	E	E
Impact	Medium (3)	B	C	C	D	D
	Low (2)	A	B	B	C	C
	Very low (1)	A	A	A	A	A
		Rare (1)	Unlikely (2)	Possible (3)	Likely (4)	Almost certain (5)
				Likelihood		

Action to be taken varied according to the risk rating:

A: Acceptable level of risk – manage by routine controls
B: Acceptable level of risk – manage by routine controls
C: Acceptable level of risk – manage by monitoring and controls
D: Unacceptable level of risk which requires constant active monitoring and controls
E: Unacceptable level of risk which requires immediate corrective action

Question

One risk in the NHS is wrong site surgery, where surgery is carried out on the wrong patient, or on the right patient, but at the wrong site on the body. How would you classify the severity of this risk on the NHS risk severity matrix? Clearly this risk cannot be avoided, retained or transferred. How could it be reduced?

9.14 CORPORATE SOCIAL RESPONSIBILITY, SUSTAINABILITY AND HR

Carroll identifies four philosophies of organisational responsiveness to CSR (Carroll 1979):

1 *Reaction*: the company denies all responsibility for social issues, claiming that they are the responsibility of government (the Friedman approach).

2 *Defence*: the company accepts responsibility but fights it, doing the least that seems to be required (the tobacco industry?).

3 *Accommodation*: the company accepts responsibility and does what is expected of it (most major companies in the UK).

4 *Proaction*: the company does more than is expected (Body Shop, the Co-op Bank).

Who should be responsible for directing an organisation's policy on ethics and corporate social responsibility? There are three leading contenders, each reflecting a particular perception of ethics and CSR:

- *Marketing/PR*, if CSR is primarily seen as a marketing tool, and the key relationship being that with customers (defence).
- *The Company Secretary*, if CSR is primarily seen as a matter of regulation, and the key relationship being the corporate governance one with shareholders (accommodation).
- *HR*, if CSR is primarily seen as a cultural issue and about human behaviour, and the key relationship being that with all stakeholders (proaction).

The theory on ethics and CSR would strongly suggest that the policy can only be meaningful if it permeates all the activities of the organisation, and if everyone in the organisation truly internalises the policy, rather than merely paying lip-service to it. This would suggest that HR should be the lead department. However, of even greater importance is that, whichever department is in day-to-day charge, top management, in the form of the CEO, should at all times behave ethically him or herself. Just as quality has Total Quality Management, ethics/CSR requires Total Ethical Management.

So what in detail should be the role of HR in ethics/CSR?

- *Helping to identify the values of the organisation*. HR should have experience with values, and is well placed to canvass opinions on values across a wide range of stakeholders. Here HR has a clear strategic contribution to make.
- *Drawing up a code of ethics*. HR should be used to drafting policies, many of which themselves have a clear ethical content.
- *Behaving ethically in its own relationships with a key stakeholder, the organisation's own staff*. Here the concept of the 'psychological contract' (discussed in Chapter 3) is important. This defines the implicit deal between employer and employees, as distinct from the formal deal contained in the contract of employment. It is an understanding about what each side can expect from the other. This has two implications for HR in the context of ethics/CSR: the psychological contract should itself be an ethical one, and the concept of the psychological contract can be extended to relationships with other stakeholders.
- *Managing the culture of the organisation*. A culture which fully supports ethics does not just happen, it has to be nurtured, maintained and communicated.
- *Development*. If staff in an organisation are presented with a CSR policy and a code of ethics, it will mean nothing to them until they are thoroughly trained in what they mean and how they should be implemented. This presents HR with a crucial development role, at all levels of the organisation. Some help here comes from the DTI's online CSR Academy, launched in July 2004 (see 'CSR help is at hand', *Personnel Today*, 27 July 2004).
- *Maintaining the 'employer brand'*. Increasingly companies want brand values to be reflected in everything that the organisation does. An ethical brand value has clear marketing advantages and recruitment/retention advantages (see CIPD 2003c, p23).

There is some evidence in a recent CIPD survey that HR has a smaller role than it thinks in CSR. Eighty-six per cent of HR professionals agree that there is a vital role for HR in embedding corporate responsibility, but only 56% of non-HR managers agree with this (Gifford 2012). Clearly HR must not only champion CSR but also be seen to do so.

HR should also have a leading role in promoting and maintaining sustainability. It could take part in setting up an environmental policy, and in the development, training and communication that supports such a policy.

The policy could include:

- *Energy minimisation* – turning off lights and computers overnight and at weekends, lowering central heating temperatures to 19^0C, use of video-conferencing rather than energy-hungry face-to-face meetings.
- *Transport policy* – choosing less polluting company cars, subsidised parking for staff who car-share, public transport loans or subsidies, loaning bicycles to staff, etc. Boots has reduced staff car journeys by 20% through its green transport plan.
- *Flexible working and homeworking.* Flexible working can enable staff to avoid rush-hour congestion, so saving on energy, and also makes bicycle usage more attractive (Davies and Smith 2007).

The TUC has promoted a Green Workplaces Project, which helps to ensure trade union support for sustainability initiatives. A joint union-management environment group at Scottish Power found that a call centre site had 200 old-fashioned VDU screens, with high energy usage. Half of these were currently left on at night and at weekends. Switching to low-energy screens and PCs, and development of a 'switch it off' culture could help to save a third of the site's emissions of CO^2. Actual savings in 2006–7 were 5% (TUC 2007).

In January 2010, just before his death, the management guru C. K. Prahalad published an article in the *Harvard Business Review* entitled 'The Responsible Manager', which set out his views on the manager's social responsibilities. To summarise, these were:

- understand the importance of nonconformity
- display a commitment to learning and developing yourself
- develop the ability to put personal performance in perspective
- be ready to invest in developing other people
- learn to relate to those who are less fortunate
- be concerned about due process
- realise the importance of loyalty to organisation, profession, community, society, and, above all, family
- assume responsibility for outcomes as well as processes
- remember that you are part of a very privileged few
- expect to be judged by what you do and how well you do it – not by what you say you want to do
- be concerned about the problems of the poor and the disabled, accept human weaknesses, laugh at yourself – and avoid the temptation to play God. Leadership is about developing modesty, humility and humanity. (Prahalad 2010)

Not bad precepts for the person, the manager and the organisation!

9.15 CORPORATE SOCIAL RESPONSIBILITY AND THE GOVERNMENT

The government has two main roles in CSR. Firstly, the government is itself a major employer and a major purchaser and supplier of services. In this role, it can and should behave ethically just like any other organisation.

However, the government also has a role in the promotion of CSR (Cowe 2004). In March 2000, the first minister for corporate social responsibility was appointed, within the Department for Trade and Industry (now the Department for Business and Skills).

The main interest of the government has been in securing greater transparency. The Pensions Act of 2000 requires pension fund trustees to make a statement of investment principles, disclosing their policy on social, environmental and ethical issues. Its Company Law Review led to the introduction in 2005 of a requirement on all public companies to include an Operating and Financial Review in their annual report to shareholders. In addition, the government set up a new CSR Academy in 2004.

However, locating the responsibility for CSR within the DTI, and then the DBS, has inevitably led to an emphasis on the corporate governance aspects of CSR. Other departments clearly also have an involvement in CSR – the Department of Work and Pensions in pensions, the Department for International Development in trade and aid aspects of CSR, and the Environment Department in issues of pollution, sustainability and climate change. The involvement of the government is likely to increase.

It could be argued that governments should go further and follow a policy of governmental social responsibility. In Chapter 4 we looked at the difference between gross national product and standard of living. We could go further and distinguish standard of living and quality of life. The latter is dependent on factors such as easy access to high quality public services, a low level of crime, a sense of community (as argued by Robert Putnam in *Bowling Alone* (2000)), and a high degree of equality (as argued by Richard Wilkinson and Kate Pickett in *The Spirit Level* (2009)). See also Fox (2012). The New Economics Foundation's 'measure of domestic progress' (MDP) model subtracts social and environmental costs and resource depletion from GDP. By the new measure, the UK economy peaked in 1976. The divergence of the two measures has been especially stark in the past 30 years, with an 80% increase in GDP but a sharp fall in MDP – fuelled by rising social inequalities in the Thatcherite 1980s – which the Labour government failed to curb (Herbert 2004).

One government which takes its social responsibilities seriously as that of the small and remote Himalayan kingdom of Bhutan, as examined in Reflective Activity 9.8.

?   REFLECTIVE ACTIVITY 9.8

Gross national happiness

Bhutan is a small, poor Buddhist kingdom in the Himalayas, between India and China. In 1972 its then king, Jigme Singye Wangchuck, proposed the concept of *Dzongkha*, or Gross National Happiness.

His argument was based on the perceived difficulties with the universally used concept of Gross Domestic Product, a measure of the annual output of a country. This included output which did not add to wellbeing, such as defence, police and pollution clean-up, while it did not include other measures which did add to wellbeing such as volunteer work and unpaid domestic work. It also did not take account of income distribution. Thus, GDP was not a good indicator of standard of living, even if the latter was defined as purely economic.

In addition, some forms of economic development are uneconomic if measured on a cost-benefit basis, particularly as in many cases the benefits are private, accruing to individuals or corporations, while the costs are public, borne by the community as a whole.

The concept of Gross National Happiness signalled commitment to building an economy based on Bhutan's culture and its Buddhist spiritual values. It held that material and spiritual development occur side by side, and reinforce each other. Four principles underpinned the concept:

- promotion of sustainable development
- preservation and promotion of cultural values
- conservation of the natural environment
- establishment of good governance.

These were then operationalised into eight measures:

- physical, mental and spiritual health
- time balance
- social and community vitality
- cultural vitality
- education
- living standards
- good governance
- ecological vitality.

In 2007 Bhutan ranked eighth out of 178 countries in subjective wellbeing, and was the only country in the top 20 to have a very low GDP (Nelson 2011).

Questions

1   What are the difficulties in calculating Gross National Happiness?

2   Is Gross National Happiness a concept that is only relevant to a country such as Bhutan, which is small, isolated, little-involved in world trade, and with a high degree of reverence for its king and his ideas?

9.16 THE BOTTOM LINE

Do corporate social responsibility and ethical behaviour increase a company's profits? A series of studies suggests that they do.

Firstly, corporate social responsibility seems to benefit an organisation's reputation. In 2002, Business in the Community carried out a survey on what the public thought of corporate responsibility (BITC 2002). Business leaders in general are not trusted. Only 25% of respondents trusted them to tell the truth – only ahead of politicians and journalists, and well below doctors and teachers. This suggests that business has a lot of ground to make up. The public wants business to be responsible. Only 2% think that companies should maximise their profits, regardless of society or the environment. Eight times as many thought companies should make a major contribution to society, regardless of cost.

Responsible behaviour also affects people's purchases. Eighty-six per cent in 2002 thought it very or fairly important that the organisation shows a high degree of social responsibility, up from 68% in 1997. One in six people have actively boycotted a product on ethical grounds in previous years.

Is this evidence conclusive? No. It is suggestive, but little more. If you were interviewed by Business in the Community, you might have a shrewd idea of the kind of answers which the interviewer would like! It is also unfortunately true that there is often a gap between what people say they do, and what they actually do.

The second piece of evidence is a report written by the management consultants Arthur D Little in 2003, again for Business in the Community (BITC 2003), *The Business Case for Corporate Responsibility*). This identifies a number of benefits from CSR:

- It offers a means by which companies can build the trust of their stakeholders. This is supported by the American strategy guru Michael Porter, who is reported as saying that how a company is perceived by its stakeholders is becoming a source of competitive advantage (Golzen 2001).

- CSR offers more effective management of risk. CSR encourages firms to understand and empathise with society and the environment, and this makes it more likely that they will be proactive about social and environmental risk.
- CSR helps to attract and retain a talented and diverse workforce.
- CSR stimulates learning and innovation within organisations.
- CSR facilitates access to capital. Over half of analysts and two-thirds of investors believe that a company that emphasises CSR is attractive to investors.
- CSR improves competitiveness, market positioning and profitability. The report quotes from Collins and Porras's *Built to Last*, a pioneering study in the 1990s, which compared successful companies which had been in business for at least 50 years, with a control group who had been less successful. They found that a key characteristic of the successful 'visionary' companies was that they had a core purpose beyond making money (Collins and Porras 2000).

Is the Arthur D. Little evidence conclusive? It is certainly very strong. Although some of the findings are based on opinion, others are based on hard evidence of changes in behaviour.

The third study was carried out by the Institute of Business Ethics in 2003. This examined a sample of FTSE350 companies which were perceived as being ethical (they had had code of ethics in operation for at least five years, they scored highly on *Management Today*'s annual league table of 'most admired companies', and they were rated highly by the specialist ratings agency SERM on their 'socio-ethical risk management'). These ethical companies were compared with a control sample.

The ethical companies were found to score more highly on three measures of financial performance – market value added, economic value added and price/earning ratio. On a fourth measure, return on capital employed, they did less well until the stock market collapse of 2000, but have performed better since then, suggesting that their profits are more stable (Caulkin 2003a; Maitland 2003).

Is this evidence conclusive? Again, it is very strong, but unfortunately it is not conclusive. There is clearly a strong correlation between ethical behaviour and profits, but this does not prove that the ethical behaviour causes the profits. The link may be the other way round – profitable companies may be more likely to be ethical – or both may be the result of some unknown third factor.

A more theoretical approach was taken by Reitz, Wall and Love (1998). They concentrated on the relatively narrow area of business negotiation, and argued that taking an unethical stance in negotiation has four major costs:

- *Rigidity.* Unethical negotiators will tend to stick to the patterns of negotiation which have paid off in the past. They will thus trap themselves in a rigid bargaining position which can be matched and exploited by their opponents.
- *Damaged relationships.* If a bargaining partner feels that he has been manipulated through underhand tactics, he is likely to feel embittered and to seek revenge.
- *Sullied reputation.* Success in business frequently depends on reputation. If you get a reputation for cheating or other unethical behaviour, this will harm your future business prospects.
- *Lost opportunities.* Negotiation is about finding a win-win situation, whereby both sides gain. A reputation for sharp dealing may lead potential partners to avoid making concessions to you, for fear that you will not make concessions back.

Their conclusion is that ethical negotiation is not only morally desirable, it is also good business.

REFLECTIVE ACTIVITY 9.9

CSR and profits – the contrary view

A strong case against CSR has been made by David Henderson (Henderson 2001). He makes the following points:

1   CSR involves organisations in higher costs, and, in so far as it means that they may forego some activities seen as non-responsible, lower revenue. The result will be lower profits (although he admits that in some cases, this could be offset by gains as a result of enhanced reputation). This argument is supported by evidence that in 2003, the Dutch insurance company Aetna spent €20m in order to comply with the US Sarbanes-Oxley regulations, introduced after the Enron scandal (Targett 2004).

2   Some of the leading CSR companies have gone through spectacular collapses in profits. He cites the US jeans manufacturer Levi Strauss, but the same point could be made about Body Shop and Ben and Jerry's ice cream.

3   The CSR agenda is frequently set not by 'society', but non-governmental organisations (NGOS) like Greenpeace, which he sees as anti-capitalist pressure groups, and as unrepresentative of society as a whole.

Critically evaluate these arguments.

KEY LEARNING POINTS

- Three main approaches can be taken to ethics, and these lead to a larger number of ethical guidelines. The most commonly used of these are the golden rule, the disclosure rule and the intuition ethic.
- All managers face ethical dilemmas on a daily basis in their work.
- Professionals have an ethical responsibility both to their organisation and to impartial professional integrity.
- There is a considerable argument over whether a separate business ethic exists.
- Values underpin ethics, and an organisation's values underpin its business ethics.
- Codes of ethics, unless they are internalised in the organisation's culture, do not guarantee ethical behaviour.
- Corporate governance is concerned with issues of conflict of interest and accountability.
- Corporate social responsibility is the way in which an organisation expresses its values through its behaviour towards stakeholders.
- Sustainability or sustainable development is concerned with safeguarding the environment for future generations.
- Risk management is an important element of a sustainability strategy.
- HR has a key role to play in promoting CSR and sustainability.
- The government has an important role in promoting CSR and sustainability.
- Although the evidence is not totally conclusive, it appears extremely likely that there is a positive correlation between CSR and profit.

REVIEW QUESTIONS

1   Distinguish between the absolutist, relativist and utilitarian approaches to ethics.

2   Describe the golden rule, the disclosure rule and the intuition ethic.

3   According to De George, what conditions must apply before whistleblowing is morally justified?

4   Does an organisation have any ethical responsibilities over and above those of the individuals within it?

5   Define purpose, values and vision.

6   How useful are codes of ethics?

7   Define corporate governance.

8   What are the key features of corporate social responsibility?

9   Define sustainable development.

10 In the context of risk management, what do you understand by risk avoidance, risk reduction, risk retention and risk transfer?

11 What is the role of HR in supporting CSR and sustainable development?

12 What elements could be included in an environmental policy?

EXPLORE FURTHER

Further reading

Stephen Connock's and Ted Johns's *Ethical Leadership*, published by the CIPD in 1995, is a useful summary of ethical issues from an HR standpoint. The CIPD has published a useful Factsheet on *Corporate Social Responsibility* (revised in October 2015). It also published in February 2012 a collection of thought pieces, *Responsible and Sustainable Business: HR leading the way*. Excellent books on ethics are Colin Fisher and Alan Lovell's *Business Ethics and Values*, 2nd edition (2006), although this is rather heavy going, and Andrew Crane and Dirk Matten's *Business Ethics*, 2nd edition (2007). A 2011 *Harvard Business Review* article by Beard and Hornick (It's hard to be good, Vol 89 Issue 11, November 2011) profiles five 'good' companies.

Useful websites

A useful website is Business in the Community (www.bitc.org.uk), which contains a number of useful reports and case studies on ethics and CSR. The SHRM has two useful Effective Practice Guidelines: *Shaping an Ethical Workplace Culture* (2013) (http://www.shrm.org/about/foundation/Products/Documents9–13%20Ethics%20EPF%20FINAL.pdf) and *HRM's Role in Corporate and Environmental Sustainability* (2012) (http://www.shrm.org/about/foundation/Products/Documents9–13%20CSR%20EPF%20FINAL.pdf)

Audio and video material

The CIPD has a podcast (Podcast 65) entitled *Corporate Responsibility and HR*, published in April 2012, and another (Podcast 81) entitled *Changing Values and Culture in the City* (May 2013). There are two *Harvard Business Review* videos on youTube (www.youtube.com/user/HarvardBusiness), *Build a Strategy for Sustainability* and *A Brief History of Doing Well by Doing Good*. There is also a video entitled *Business Ethics*, designed for use with US high school students, which discusses a number of ethical dilemmas (www.youtube.com/watch?v=SDPsSyoZNlw). The SHRM has a video, *Ethics – the fabric of business*, which discusses Lockheed Martin (http://www.shrm.prg/about/foundation/products/pages/ethicsdvd.aspx)

RESPONSIBLE TOURISM

SEMINAR ACTIVITY 9.1

In 1999, Richards and Gladwin put forward their definition of a socially sustainable enterprise (Richards and Gladwin 1999).

'The characteristics of a socially sustainable enterprise are that it would:

1   return to communities where it operates – selling as much as it gains from them

2   meaningfully include stakeholders impacted on by its activities in associated planning and decision-making processes

3   ensure no reduction in, and actively promote, the observance of political and civil rights in the domains where it operates

4   widely spread economic opportunities and help to reduce or eliminate unjustified inequalities

5   directly or indirectly ensure no net loss of human capital within its workforces and operating communities

6   cause no net loss of direct and indirect productive employment

7   adequately satisfy the vital needs of its employees and operating communities

8   work to ensure the fulfilment of the basic needs of humanity prior to serving luxury wants.'

Explore Worldwide is a UK tour company, specialising in small group exploratory holidays. Its brochure stresses its commitment to sustainability.

Respecting our planet

Our commitment to Responsible Tourism

Explore's dedication to Responsible Tourism is the driving force behind our Environmental Policy. Far from being an abstract ideal for us, Responsible Tourism shapes all our major decisions – from the concept that 'Small Groups Leave Fewer Footprints' to the choice of local agents and suppliers.

Here are our guidelines in a nutshell:

● By operating in small groups, we minimise the impact on the local culture and resources, whilst blending in more easily.

● We issue our travellers with clear guidelines on responsible tourism. These cover a variety of issues from littler and waste disposal in remote areas, to begging and artefacts. We encourage customers to buy local crafts and support local skills, but never to buy products that exploit wildlife or harm the habitat.

● We use locally owned suppliers wherever viable to provide and run services. This ensures that the local economy benefits directly. We also expect local suppliers to meet our standards, with particular consideration for the environment.

● When recruiting Tour Leaders, we assess their environmental credentials and then train them to our own standards. They are also required to complete a Responsible Tourism Audit on each tour.

● Throughout a tour, the Leader will encourage the education of our customers on the social workings of a region. And part of their role is to make sure that the local communities benefit from our visit, ensuring that we will always be welcome.

Explore's passion for travel goes beyond the yearning for discovery. Ours is a reasoned, tried and tested approach to the enjoyment of a truly amazing plant.'

Source: *Explore Worldwide 2004–2005 Brochure* [reproduced with permission]

Note: Although this is an old source, Explore's policy has not changed significantly since 2004.

Questions

1   Critically evaluate Explore's Responsible Tourism policy against Richards and Gladwin's principles.

Mark Ellingham, the founder of the *Rough Guide* series, declared that 'binge flying' constitutes a threat to the global environment. 'If the travel industry [ignores] the effect that carbon emissions from flying are having on climate change, we are putting ourselves in a very similar position to the tobacco industry.'

Source: Hastings (2007)

2   Is overseas tourism unsustainable?

Ecotourism is the most rapidly growing sector within the world tourism industry. It is defined as tourism that sends people to relatively untouched parts of the world and that is sensitive to the impact on nature caused by humans.

3   What would you say are the pros and cons of ecotourism?

Strategic Management

10.1 INTRODUCTION

This chapter will analyse the nature of strategic management, and identify different models of strategy. It will analyse the stages of strategic decision making – analysis, choice and implementation. The last part of the chapter will concentrate on the nature and practice of change management.

10.2 WHAT IS STRATEGIC MANAGEMENT?

The origins of strategy are military, and concern the art of war. A *strategos* was a general in command of a Greek army. Quinn (1980) identifies three elements of strategy:

- Goals or objectives. What is to be achieved, and when it is to be achieved. Major goals which affect an organisation's overall direction are strategic goals.
- Policies are guidelines which set out the limits within which action should occur. Major policies are strategic policies.
- Programmes lay down the sequence of actions necessary to achieve objectives. They set out how objectives will be achieved within the limits set by policies.

In other words:

- Where do we want to get to?
- What actions should we take to get there?
- How can we carry out these actions?

The essence of a strategy is to build a position so strong that the organisation will achieve its objectives no matter what unforeseeable forces attack it (ie how can we win whatever the enemy does?). Effective strategies should:

- contain clear and decisive objectives – sub-goals may change in the heat of battle but the over-riding objective provides continuity over time
- maintain the initiative
- concentrate power at the right time and place
- have built-in flexibility so that one can use minimum resources to keep opponents at a disadvantage
- have committed and co-ordinated leadership
- involve correct timing and surprise
- make resources secure and prevent surprises from opponents.

Strategic decisions have a number of characteristics:

- They are concerned with the scope of an organisation's activities – the boundaries which an organisation sets to its activities.
- They are concerned with matching the activities of an organisation to its environment.
- They are concerned with matching the activities of an organisation to its resource capability.
- They often have resource implications for an organisation – if current resources do not permit a particular strategy, can the necessary resources be acquired?
- They affect operational decisions – a whole series of implementing sub-decisions must flow from the making of a strategic decision.
- They are affected by the values and expectations of those who have power in and around the organisation – its stakeholders.
- They affect the long-term direction of an organisation (Johnson et al 2011).

Strategy can be seen at several levels:

- corporate level, concerned with the overall scope of the operation, its financial performance, and the allocation of resources to different operations
- competitive or business unit level – how to compete within a particular market at the level of a Strategic Business Unit (SBU)
- operational level – how the different functions of the organisation contribute to the overall strategy. This level is often seen as tactical rather than in any real sense strategic, but it can equally be seen as the implementation stage of strategy.

Strategic management is about doing the right things. It is:

- ambiguous
- complex
- non-routine
- organisation-wide
- fundamental
- involving significant change
- environment- or expectations-driven.

Operational or tactical management is about doing things right. It is:

- routinised
- operationally specific

- involving small-scale change
- resource-driven.

10.3 MODELS OF STRATEGY

10.3.1 CORPORATE PLANNING

This was a product of the 1950s and 1960s, a period with a largely placid environment. Detailed corporate plans covering the whole organisation were drawn up by a central planning team and then agreed by top management. The details of the plan were extremely complex, as were the models used, but the planning process itself was relatively simple because the corporate future was expected to be a continuation of the past. The role of line management was to implement the plan. The main exponent of corporate planning was Igor Ansoff. There are clear parallels with the system of central planning as used to run the Soviet Union.

The strength of the corporate planning approach is its rigour, and the vital information which is collected in the course of drawing up the plan. However, it has a number of weaknesses. It is inflexible – the plan is too vast and complex to cope with rapid change in the environment. However, some of the best corporate planners – those at Shell – coped with this by developing a range of scenarios about the future environment. One of these forecast exactly the huge rise in oil prices which happened in 1973, with the result that Shell could react very quickly to the new situation.

Centralised corporate planning is also demotivating. Nobody owns the plan except for the planners – the line managers who have to implement it have no commitment to it. At worst, corporate planning was an academic exercise, and the plan was put away in a drawer and quietly forgotten.

Classical corporate planning in the Ansoff sense has probably gone for ever. The external environment is now too turbulent for the luxury of a comprehensive plan, while the rigid top-down hierarchical approach to management is also a thing of the past. Classical strategic management has had to adapt to a new world and has become the rational approach. Some elements of classical planning do survive, including the need for a rigorous analysis of the external environment and of internal capabilities. Strategic management is still about doing the right things, and as we will see later, still goes through the stages of analysis, choice and implementation. These three stages form the core of all the major textbooks on strategic management, particularly of Johnson and Scholes's *Exploring Corporate Strategy*, originally published in 1983, and now in its ninth edition, renamed *Exploring Strategy* (Johnson et al 2011), having sold millions of copies, and contributed to the education of generations of management students.

The rational planning school defines an objective in advance, describes where-we-are-now, and uses a prescriptive approach, in which 'the three core areas – strategic analysis, strategic development and strategy implementation – are linked together sequentially'. In addition, Chandler, who famously argued that organisational structure follows strategy, supposes that strategy is determined centrally and, then, implemented structurally.

Corporate planning must be distinguished from business planning. The latter is primarily operational rather than strategic, and is essential for every successful organisation. Mintzberg argues that strategy is not the consequence of planning, but its starting point (Mintzberg 1998c, p632).

Business planning has two key roles. One is the co-ordination of the business's resources, and the other is control of the use of those resources. A good example of the former role is project management, using techniques such as critical path analysis – what activities need to be carried out to achieve the objective, in what order must they be carried out, which activities can be carried out simultaneously, and which must be sequential, and so on. To take an HR example, a particular project might require particular skills among the workforce. How many workers need to be recruited or trained, how long will this take, and at what point in the project will these trained workers be needed?

One useful acronym for project management is SMEAC – Situation, Mission, Execution, Administration, Command.

- Situation: Relevant background information – 'why'
- Mission: Purpose of the action – 'what'
- Execution: 'How' the action/project is to be performed
- Administration and logistics: Systems for recording and managing information, and ensuring all materials and equipment are available when and where required
- Command and signals/communications: Communications methods to enable effective coordination. (businessballs 2011)

The second major element in business planning is control. The main technique here is budgeting. This is generally seen as an accounting technique, but it has much wider application, and overlaps with project management. Budgeting normally starts with the identification of a key budget factor, often a sales forecast. From this, we can develop a production budget – how many units need to be produced and when. This leads on to a materials budget and a labour budget – what raw materials and workers are needed to meet the production budget, and how much will they cost. This process carries on throughout the business, and culminates in a cash flow forecast and a forecast balance sheet and profit and loss account. This part of the budgeting process should ensure effective co-ordination of resources. The next, equally important, stage is budgetary control, where actual progress is measured against budget, and corrective action taken if necessary.

? REFLECTIVE ACTIVITY 10.1

Eisenhower and planning

'Plans are useless but planning is indispensable.' (Dwight Eisenhower). What did he mean by this and do you agree?

Bear in mind the words of the heavyweight boxing champion Mike Tyson – 'Everyone has a plan until they get punched in the mouth.'

10.3.2 EMERGENT STRATEGIC MANAGEMENT

The emergent approach to strategy formulation has been characterised by trial, experimentation, and discussion, ie, by a series of experimental approaches rather than a final objective. Emergent strategy is undertaken by an organisation that analyses its environment constantly and implements its strategy simultaneously. Emergent strategy, with its acknowledgement that uncertainty is here to stay, has the potential to address the current challenges of organisations and the corporations charged with their management (Carr et al 2004).

This model emphasises adaptability in the face of a turbulent environment. There is no rigid long-term plan, although there are long-term visions and values. Strategy becomes bottom-up, as line managers react to or anticipate changes in the environment. The organisation has to be very responsive to changes in the environment, which requires managers at all levels constantly to monitor the environment. The organisation becomes a learning organisation in the fullest sense of the term, as it is constantly scanning and learning from its environment. Strategy ceases to be a purely linear process, and now emerges through a process of experimentation and trial and error.

Leading exponents of the emergent strategic management concept are:

Tom Peters. *In Search of Excellence* in 1982 (Peters and Waterman 1982) stressed the importance of a number of attributes for excellence, which emphasised values, simplicity, quick reactions and understanding the customer:

- stick to the knitting
- close to the customer
- productivity through people
- autonomy and entrepreneurship
- hands on, value driven
- bias for action
- simple form, lean staff
- simultaneous loose-tight properties.

He followed this up with *Thriving on Chaos* in 1985 (Peters 1985), where he argued that the organisation should cope with chaos by becoming chaotic itself – being in a continual state of flux.

Michael Porter. Porter approached strategic management as an economist. He stressed the importance of the competitive position of an industry (the Five Forces) (1980), the nature of generic strategies, and the importance of the organisation's value chain in identifying its competitive advantage (1985).

Ralph Stacey. In *The Chaos Frontier* (1991) and *Strategic Management and Organisational Dynamics* (1993), he developed the application of chaos theory to strategic management. The environment facing organisations is one of chaos – multiple and ultimately unpredictable reactions follow from a single event. The further the forecaster looks into the future, the more outcomes become possible. As a result the organisation must be highly responsive and reactive. The role of top management is to develop and support creativity and innovation.

Gary Hamel and C. K. Prahalad. In *Competing for the Future* (1994), they stressed that the key role of management is to manage the organisation in such a way that it is flexible and able to respond to a changed environment. This means identifying and developing the core competencies of the organisation. We will return to this later. Hamel later developed the *10 principles of revolutionary strategy* (Hamel 1996):

1 *Strategic planning isn't strategic* – it assumed that the future will be more or less the same as the present.

2 *Strategy making must be subversive* – strategy is about breaking rules and assumptions.

3 *The bottleneck is at the top of the bottle* – top managers are the most resistant to change.

4 Revolutionaries exist in every company.

5 *Change is not the problem, engagement is* – senior managers fail to give people responsibility for managing change.

6 *Strategy making must be democratic* – senior managers must recognise that creativity is spread throughout an organisation.

7 *Anyone can be a strategy activist* – senior managers must see activists as positive, not as anarchists.

8 *Perspective is worth 50 IQ points* – organisations have to use all their knowledge to identify unconventional ideas.

9 *Top down and bottom up are not the alternatives* – both are necessary.

10 *You can't see the end from the beginning* – strategy can often throw up surprises.

The key is that organisations must be run as a hotbed of innovation. Of a thousand unconventional ideas, probably only ten have the power to transform a business, and there is no way to identify these ten in advance. The role of leadership is to enable this experimentation to happen. One way to do this is to define the values of the organisation within which experimentation can take place. Hamel quotes the example of Virgin, which has more than 150 different businesses, but all are united by the proposition that the brands will imply customer value, fun and funkiness. The result is willingness to think outside the box. He contrasts this with Coca-Cola, which has been notoriously slow to innovate. Hamel describes a meeting with its chairman, Roberto Goizueta. Hamel asked him what his dream was for Coca Cola, and Goizueta said, 'That anywhere in the world, if somebody turns on a tap, out comes Coca-Cola.' No outside the box (or outside the tap!) thinking here.

Secondly, Hamel identifies the true innovators as being heretics, lovers of novelty, and deeply empathetic with customers, and he stresses that all these things can be taught. This teaching is the role of top management.

For more on Hamel's ideas, see Bernhut (2001).

Chan Kim and Renee Mauborgne. Kim and Mauborgne have developed the concept of Blue Ocean thinking. A Blue Ocean is a strategic area where competition is minimised, and therefore full of opportunity This contrasts with Red Oceans, which are over-crowded, rivalry is intense, and competition is bloody. Blue Ocean strategy is all about finding strategic gaps, finding or creating market spaces which are not currently served. This might involve developing a totally new product or service, or, more likely, developing a new element to an existing product or service (Kim and Mauborgne 2004).

James Quinn. In *Strategies for Change: Logical Incrementalism* (1980), Quinn developed the concept of logical incrementalism, that strategy does not consist of a big bang, but rather of a series of small steps (incrementalism). Johnson et al (2011, pp405–6) identify four main elements of the Quinn model:

- *Environmental uncertainty.* Constant environmental scanning is needed.
- *General goals.* Over-precise objectives might stifle innovation.
- *Experimentation,* best bottom-up.
- *Co-ordinating emergent strategies.* This is the role of the leadership – facilitation rather than direction.

A parallel is the way in which Texas software company Trilogy manages its 'fast cycle' development and consulting work. Rather than step sequentially through phases of planning, design, and operation (as in an industrial process), Trilogy loops rapidly through each of these activities again and again, each time generating a prototype – a product, however rough, that can be experienced directly and to which makers and customers can react (Austin and Devin 2004).

The main danger with the incremental approach is strategic drift. By definition, incremental change is small change rather than transformational change. There is a tendency to experiment, but only within a very narrow range of possibilities. Organisations become victims of their past successes, but fail to pick up that they are drifting away from their environment, which is changing more rapidly than they are. Eventually, the only choices are transformational change or death. Grundy (2005) claims that Marks & Spencer was guilty of strategic drift in the years preceding Philip Green's bid for the company in 2004. He says that 'Managers often believe they have a resilient strategy... as long as they are engaging in incremental and deliberate strategies which on the surface appear necessary but in reality are not sufficient to deal with the problem.' (p206).

10.4 HENRY MINTZBERG AND STRATEGIC MANAGEMENT

One of the most trenchant critics of corporate planning has been the Canadian guru Henry Mintzberg. His writings include *The Rise and Fall of Strategic Planning* (1994). He argues that old-style corporate planning was all about left brain activity – numbers, linearity, analysis. Strategic management is right brain – ideas, patterns, relationships, intuition. He talks of crafting strategy, rather than planning strategy.

Mintzberg is famous for his *Five Ps of Strategy:*

- Strategy as a **plan** for action. Here the strategy is made in advance of the actions to which they apply, and it is applied consciously and purposefully. However, as we will see later, outcomes may not be as expected.
- Strategy as a **ploy**, a manoeuvre to outwit opponents.
- Strategy as a **pattern**. A pattern of behaviour becomes a strategy. If a particular course of action tends to lead to favourable results, a strategy emerges. The strategy is the result of events, rather than the cause of them. A variation on this he calls the umbrella strategy, where top management lays down broad principles, and line managers have autonomy to act within these principles. Here strategy is both planned and emergent.
- Strategy as **position**. Strategy here is about finding a niche in the market, a position which balances the pressures of the environment and the competition.
- Strategy as **perspective**. Here the strategy reflects how the organisation views the world and its place in it. A classic example is Hewlett-Packard's 'H-P way', where the whole approach of the organisation is based on engineering excellence and innovation. The important thing here is consistency in behaviour.

Planned strategies often require modification as they are implemented, as environmental or organisational factors change. It is very rare that a long-term strategic plan can be implemented over a period of years without modification. The intended strategy may not be realised in practice, and even if it is, it may not achieve the desired results.

Mintzberg stresses that there is not an either-or choice between rational and emergent approaches to strategy. They are opposite ends of a continuum. Depending on the nature of the environment, either may be appropriate. Harrington et al (2004) argue that the more dynamic the environment facing an organisation, the more appropriate an emergent approach will be, and vice versa.

10.5 WHITTINGTON, PROCESSES AND OUTCOMES

Whittington (2001), stresses that we must go beyond the deliberate corporate strategy–emergent strategy dichotomy. These are different processes, and we should also consider different outcomes, either pluralist or revenue-maximising. If we plot outcomes against processes, we get a two-by two matrix, as shown in Figure 10.1.

Figure 10.1 Whittington's matrix

Source: Based on Whittington (2001)

Whittington's matrix gives four possible combinations:

- *Classic* (deliberate process, revenue-maximising outcome). This is the model of top-down corporate planning.
- *Systemic* (deliberate process, pluralist outcome). The planning process is rational, but it also takes account of social, political and human factors.
- *Evolutionary* (emergent process, revenue-maximising outcome). This stresses flexibility in the pursuit of a single goal.
- *Processual* (emergent process, pluralist outcome). Strategy emerges through experimental bargaining about both processes and goals.

?   REFLECTIVE ACTIVITY 10.2

The big lie of strategic planning

Read the article 'The Big Lie of Strategic Planning' by Roger Martin in the *Harvard Business Review*, January/February 2014, Vol 92 Issue 1. This can be downloaded from the Online Journals section of the CIPD website, and can also be accessed from EBSCO, available online through most university or local authority libraries.

Questions

1   Summarise the criticisms which Martin makes of the strategic planning, emergent (Mintzberg) and core competence (Hamel and Prahalad) models.

2   Critically examine Martin's own customer-based model. To what extent do you think that it is applicable to the public or voluntary sectors?

10.6 THE ELEMENTS OF STRATEGIC MANAGEMENT

The analysis so far may seem extremely complex, but the important thing to remember is that the essence of strategic management is very simple. It consists of getting answers to four questions:

1   Where are we?

2   Where do we want to get to?

3   How can we get there?

4   What do we have to do to get there?

From this we can derive the three elements of strategic management:

- Strategic analysis – tackles the first two questions: what is our current position and where to do we want to go?
- Strategic choice – tackles the third question: how can we get there, ie what strategy should we choose?
- Strategic implementation – what do we have to do to implement our chosen strategy?

10.6.1 STRATEGIC ANALYSIS

Strategic analysis is concerned with the strategic position of the organisation. What are the key characteristics of the organisation, what changes are going on in the environment, and how will these affect the organisation and its activities? The aim is to form a view of the key influences on the present and future wellbeing of the organisation:

- Expectations of stakeholders, the culture of the organisation, and most important, the organisation's vision and values.
- The environment, as identified through a STEEPLE analysis. The main problem is to distil out of the complexity the key environmental impacts for the purposes of strategic choice.
- Resources. Strategic capability is about identifying strengths and weaknesses by considering the key resource areas of the business such as physical plant, management, finance, products, etc.

Classical corporate planning saw environmental analysis as the key element in strategic analysis, while emergent strategic management sees culture and values as most crucial.

Gap analysis

The extent to which there is a mismatch (a gap) between current strategy and the future environment is a measure of the strategic problem facing the organisation. As Figure 10.2 shows, over time the current strategy is likely to get more out of line with the environment, and a planning gap will grow.

Figure 10.2 Gap analysis

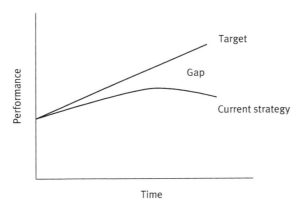

The organisation needs to choose a new strategy which will ensure that this gap is filled.

10.6.2 STRATEGIC CHOICE

Strategic choice involves three steps:

1 *Generation of strategic options.* Three levels of analysis are involved here – what fundamental or generic strategy should be followed; within this generic strategy, what strategic directions are needed; and then what methods of strategic direction are most appropriate?

2 *Evaluation of strategic options.* This involves testing options for suitability (do they fit the generic strategy, and will they provide the desired results); feasibility (are resources available or obtainable; and acceptability (do they fit the values of the stakeholders)?

3 *Selection of strategy* – either logically, using some kind of weighting criteria, or politically

10.6.3 STRATEGIC IMPLEMENTATION

Strategic implementation involves resource planning, organisational structure, systems, change management techniques, etc.

10.7 STRATEGIC ANALYSIS

10.7.1 VISION, MISSION, VALUES AND OBJECTIVES

Vision, mission, values and objectives are closely linked, and often confused. However, they are clearly distinguished by Peter Senge in *The Fifth Discipline* (1990).

- Vision is the *what* – the picture of the future we want to create, or the desired future state of the organisation (where do we want to get to?)
- Mission is the *why* – the over-riding purpose of the organisation, its scope and boundaries (what business are we in, why do we exist?)
- Values are the *how* – the underlying beliefs and ethical stance which drives how the business behaves (how are we going to behave while we are getting there?)
- Objectives operationalise all the other three – a precise statement of where we want to be and when, which turns the vision, mission and values into concrete quantifiable terms. It is frequently said that objectives should be SMART:
  - **S**tretching
  - **M**easurable
  - **A**chievable
  - **R**elevant
  - **T**ime limited

CASE STUDY 10.1

RADICAL DEMOTIVATION

A vision is intended to provide inspiration and guidance to employees. To be authentic they must drive the behaviour of the organisation's top leadership. Unfortunately, says the American academic E. L. Kersten, this frequently does not happen, and top management uses core values in order to control and manipulate staff through a technique which he calls Radical Demotivation (Kersten 2005).

Kersten suggests six guidelines which will ensure that core values lead to manipulation and control rather than inspiration and empowerment:

Guideline 1: The development of your company's core values should be outsourced to consultants. This will ensure that employees have no say in their formulation.

Guideline 2: Core values should not be anchored to any transcendent social

values. Avoid any suggestion that your organisation is about promoting public good. This will only make employees feel good about themselves. Instead go for vague but ultimately meaningless statements like 'quality products' or 'innovation'.

Guideline 3: Core values should be stated as ambiguously as possible. This follows on from Guideline 2. The more ambiguous the value, the less accountable can top management be if it violates it.

Guideline 4: Your values should be inconsistent with your strategic market focus. If your main strategic focus is low cost and maximum efficiency, put in a core value like 'we go the extra mile for our customers'. This means that whatever happens, it is always the fault of the employees.

Guideline 5: One or more values should be anchored to objectives over which the employee has little control. Similar to Guideline 4, this also passes the buck from top management to the employees

Guideline 6: At least one of your core values should be employee-oriented.

Something like 'above all, we value our employees'. The employees hope this is true, but as they find that it isn't, they will become increasingly cynical – radical demotivation.

CASE STUDY 10.2

A FAILURE OF VALUES

The Dow Chemical Company is a major US corporation, founded in 1897, and is the second biggest chemical company in the world. Its mission statement is 'To passionately create innovation for our stakeholders at the intersection of chemistry, biology, and physics' (Dow 2015).

Its 2015 values are stated to be

- integrity
- respect for people
- protecting our planet.

A key element of respect for people is 'Our communities are our neighbours; their acceptance of us is vital to our ability to operate'.

Unfortunately Dow has not always lived up to its stated values. From 1951 to 1975, Dow managed a nuclear weapons facility in the US. In 2008 it was ordered to pay compensation for environmental pollution at the site, although this was eventually reversed on appeal (*The Denver Post* 2010). Dow was also a major manufacturer of the defoliant Agent Orange, which was used by the US to destroy vegetation during the Vietnam war. This contained the carcinogen dioxin, responsible for thousands of cases of cancer and birth defects among the Vietnamese, as well as among American Vietnam veterans. In the 1980s Dow came to an out of court settlement with veterans' organisations which involved payment of up to $250m in compensation, but without any admission of liability (*New York Times* 2014).

Most serious was Dow's involvement in the Bhopal chemical disaster in 1984. A pesticide plant in Bhopal in central India,

operated by a subsidiary of the Union Carbide Company, exploded, causing around 5,000 deaths, and tens of thousands of long-term injuries and birth defects. Union Carbide was sued by the Government of India and agreed to an out-of-court settlement of US$ 470m in 1989. Union Carbide was then acquired by Dow in 2001, but Dow has refused to accept any further responsibility for the disaster, arguing that it had only bought shares in Union Carbide, and therefore was not legally liable for its actions. A Dow spokesperson said: 'What I can tell you is that Dow never owned or operated the former plant site in Bhopal.' However, Dow has accepted liability for Union Carbide's asbestos activities in the US, setting aside £$2.2bn for compensation. Some major institutional shareholders in Dow have suggested that if the company admitted liability for Bhopal, this would normalise its relationship with the Indian government, and enable it to expand its activities in the booming Indian chemical industry (Bermingham 2014).

Contrast Dow with the approach of the US pharmaceutical company Johnson & Johnson, which had as one of its leading products Tylenol, heavily sold as a painkiller, particularly for children. In 1982 someone replaced Tylenol capsules on sale in Chicago with cyanide capsules, and seven people died. The reaction of Johnson and Johnson's leadership was to go back to *Our Credo*, its expression of its values first written in 1943.

'We believe our first responsibility is to the doctors, nurses, and patients, to mothers and fathers and all others who use our products and services. In meeting their needs everything we do must be of high quality...' (Johnson & Johnson website)

All stocks were destroyed and the product was immediately withdrawn across the US, counselling and financial assistance were given to the victims' families, and after six months the product was relaunched with new triple safety tamper-resistant packaging.

What this case shows is that the higher an organisation's standards and values, the more serious are any shortcomings in failing to meet those standards. Johnson & Johnson 'walked the talk' where its stated values were concerned; Dow did not.

However, it seems that Johnson & Johnson is losing its ethical edge. It has experienced a number of recent scandals in the US. Erik Gordon of the University of Michigan blamed these failings on the current CEO, Bill Weldon, and his 'relentless focus on the bottom line'. Gordon says, 'The major function of the credo is like... wrapping yourself in the American flag. It is to distract people from what is going on.' (Knowledge@Wharton 2012)

What these cases show is that the higher an organisation's standards and values, the more serious are any shortcomings in failing to meet those standards.

CASE STUDY 10.3

THOMAS COOK AND ACTIONABLE BUSINESS PROMISE

In the early 1990s the UK travel agent and tour operator was seen as staid and conservative. Its main cash cow, the travellers cheque, was in decline, rapidly being replaced by credit cards and overseas automatic teller machines (ATMs). Thomas Cook then adopted the concept of the Actionable Business Promise. This has elements of vision, values and mission. It is a measurable statement of intent, which forms the basis for strategic decision making. It leads to a company-wide promise management architecture, which connects the promise to key functional and process activities. Finally, there is a process of promise affirmation, where the promise is continuously tested against stakeholder expectations and business reality.

In 1995 Thomas Cook developed a statement of intent for the business – 'to create the best and most profitable travel-driven service business in the world'. In itself there was nothing remarkable about this, but what is important is what happened next. The nine-member top management team worked through the statement to produce a common interpretation against which all the company's functions and activities would be measured. Each member of the team produced their own definition of each word in the statement, and these were debated until complete agreement was reached. The statement became the company's actionable business promise.

The statement was then shared with all executives, who were asked to illustrate how the statement would drive their day-to-day operational activities. As Paul Frederick, head of business transformation at the Thomas Cook Group, said, 'It was an intense process of developing a common organisation-wide definition for our strategy. Misalignment at the top would have produced a chain reaction of inconsistencies.'

All the company's core business processes were then redesigned to be consistent with the business promise. Functional activities were then realigned. For example, training was concentrated on customer service. Measurement was a key driver of alignment. New customer value enablers such as employee satisfaction were added to gauge the success of the newly-aligned core business processes.

Whereas the group's travel and service businesses were valued at $275m in 1995, they were sold in 2000 for $1.4bn.

What is really significant about the actionable business promise concept is the word 'actionable'. Unlike a mission or vision statement, which is often seen just as 'nice to have', the actionable business promise drives not only the group's strategy, but also its operations.

Source: Anderson (2005)

The mission and objectives of an organisation are constrained by four main factors (Johnson et al 2011):

- *Corporate governance:* External constraints on the organisation, set by company law; reports of investigations such as the Cadbury Report on non-executive directors or the Greenbury Report on directors' pay; regulatory bodies such as the Financial Services Authority, and targets and controls imposed by the government on public bodies (ie Best Value for local authorities).
- *Stakeholders:* Stakeholders can influence the organisation's strategic direction through their power and/or their interest.
- *Business ethics:* Ethics can impact on an organisation at three levels: general ethical policy; how the organisation interprets its corporate social responsibility when it formulates its strategy; and the ethical behaviour of individuals within the organisation. Clearly ethics is all about values, particularly the values of top management.
- *Culture:* Culture in organisations operates at three levels:

  1 Values, often written down as part of the mission statement, but often vague, like 'service to the community'.

  2 More specific beliefs, often expressed as policies.

  3 Taken for granted assumptions – the organisational paradigm – the 'way things are done here'. At grass roots level, these may often be in conflict with the values and beliefs officially expressed at a higher level. For example, the police force in the UK is totally committed to eradicating 'institutional racism', but at the level of 'canteen culture' there are still racist PCs.

10.7.2 THE MISSION STATEMENT

This is the most generalised statement of organisational purpose. It sets the direction of the organisation, and provides a benchmark against which policies can be evaluated.

An effective mission statement should achieve the following:

1   It should be visionary and long-term. It is meant to inspire and drive the organisation.

2   It should clarify the main intentions and aspirations of the organisation and the reasons why the organisation exists.

3   It should describe the organisation's main activities and the position it wishes to attain in its industry.

4   It should contain a statement of the key values of the organisation in relation to its stakeholders.

5   It should be taken seriously within the organisation.

6   It should be a focus for activity, which can serve as a continual guide, rather than a closed aim which can be fully achieved.

However, there are two great dangers with mission statements. The first is a risk that they can appear grandiose, or even ridiculous. Too many overblown mission statements have tended in the past to lead to the whole concept being treated with ridicule. Typical is the *Dilbert* website (www.dilbert.com), which contains a mission statement generator, which will produce randomly generated mission statements.

The other danger is that the mission statement may become set in concrete. The external environment may change in a way that renders the mission statement obsolete, and a hindrance rather than a help to strategy formulation.

CASE STUDY 10.4

KOMATSU – 'ENCIRCLE CATERPILLAR'

Komatsu produces earth-moving equipment, a sector where the market leader is the American company Caterpillar. In the 1960s Komatsu was a relatively small company, serving only the Japanese market, but when Yashinari Kawai became president in 1964, he announced the company's new mission statement – '*Maru C*' or 'encircle Caterpillar'. This was to be the driving force of the company's strategy for the next 20 years. Four themes built competitive advantage – protecting the home market against Caterpillar, reducing costs while maintaining quality, developing an international presence, and moving into new markets and products.

By the 1980s, Komatsu was the world's second-largest producer of earth-moving equipment, although it had failed to overtake Caterpillar. Unfortunately, while Komatsu had been focusing all its attention and energy on Caterpillar, it had ignored over-the-horizon changes in the environment. Demand for basic earth-moving equipment was falling, and new competitors in different but related industries were becoming an (unseen) threat.

Fortunately, the new company president, Tetsuya Katada, spotted the danger in time. He decided that the company's emphasis should be as a 'total technology enterprise', with the new mission statement 'Growth, Global, Groupwide'. Komatsu's sales decline was reversed, thanks entirely to an explosive growth in its non-construction equipment business, particularly industrial robots and semi-conductors.

Source: Hamel and Prahalad (1989)

? **REFLECTIVE ACTIVITY 10.3**

The WEA (Northern Ireland)

The Workers Educational Association (WEA) in Northern Ireland publishes its Mission Statement and WEA Values on its website (www.wea-ni.com), as follows:

The WEA Mission Statement

We will make learning accessible to all men and women, especially those removed from the educational experience. As well as offering opportunities to individuals we will assist those who wish to work collectively for the benefit of their communities and for the good of society as a whole.

The Value Base of the WEA

The WEA has been a catalyst for social change since it began in Belfast in 1910. The following values underpin our commitment to social change:

- Social inclusion – we make special efforts to reach those most removed from the learning experience.
- Voluntarism – we provide opportunities for people to volunteer to work both individually and collectively for the betterment of our society.
- Active citizenship – we equip people to play a full role in the social, economic, cultural and political life of our society.
- Building alliances – we work closely with others to improve opportunities for learning.
- Sharing experience – we share good practice to promote mutual learning.
- Equality – we promote equality of opportunity through learning.

[Reproduced with permission]

Question

Evaluate the WEA mission statement against the six characteristics of an effective mission statement listed in section 10.7.2.

10.7.3 RESOURCE ANALYSIS

Resource analysis is internal to the organisation. It is concerned with the strengths and weaknesses parts of SWOT analysis, and measures the efficiency and effectiveness of an organisation's resources, and their degree of fit with the external opportunities and threats also identified through SWOT. Ideally strengths should support opportunities, and be able to counteract threats. Resources should be seen in the widest sense, to include the organisation's competitive position, as identified through techniques such as Five Forces and portfolio analysis. However, SWOT analysis has severe limitations. The most important of these is that is subjective – different analysts will identify totally different strengths and weaknesses. Stevenson (1989) found no consensus among the managers in the companies he studied on the strengths and weaknesses of their companies. Higher level managers tended to be more optimistic about the balance of strengths and weaknesses than lower level managers.

Prahalad and Hamel (1990) identify the concept of the core competences of the organisation – those factors which give the organisation its key competitive advantages. Unlike resources, which are tangible, tradeable, and easily replicable, competences are based on the accumulated knowledge and skills of the organisation, are unique to it, and difficult to copy. They are based on people rather than things. Examples are the way in which Dell Computer builds all computers individually to order, or the reputation of Body Shop as an ethical crusader. Other analyses have suggested that the crucial competence needed by all organisations is the ability to be nimble, flexible and responsive to rapid and unpredictable changes in the external environment. The core competence model is very closely connected with the resource-based model of strategic HR.

Core competences can be based on:

- *Cost efficiency*: Many advantages based on cost efficiency are not really core competencies, as they can relatively easily be copied by other organisations. One which may lead to a core competence is cost efficiency based on experience – the more experience an organisation has, the lower its costs tend to be.
- *Value added*: Is the organisation more effective than the competition? In the early stages of the quality movement in the 1970s and 1980s, quality could be a core competence. Now it is a given – it is expected of all organisations and it does not in itself give a competitive advantage. Value added is more likely to be experienced by the customer through service than through the product itself – Dell does not necessarily sell a better computer, but it gives the customer a flexible computer configured to his or her requirements.
- *Managing linkages, between different stages of production, or through alliances with other organisations*: For example the low-cost airlines like easyJet and Ryanair pioneered the use of internet-based ticket booking systems and paperless tickets, giving them both a cost and an effectiveness advantage, as well as allowing a very flexible pricing system. They also offer web links to suppliers of hotels and car hire.
- *Robustness*: How easy is it to ensure that the competences are difficult to copy?

Johnson et al (2011) have developed the VRIN model as a way of assessing the strength of core competences:

- *V – value*
  Core competences are of value when they provide potential competitive advantage at a cost that allows an organisation to achieve acceptable level of return. The key components here are taking advantage of opportunities and neutralising threats; value to customers, providing potential competitive advantage, and cost.
- *R – rarity*
  Rare competences are those possessed uniquely by one or a few organisations. However, rarity may not last.
- *I – inimitability*
  Those competences that competitors find difficult to imitate or obtain. This is based on superior performance and linked capabilities.
- *N – non-substitutability*
  To what extent can competitors substitute other core competences for ours?

Teece (2007) has introduced the concept of dynamic capabilities – an organisation's ability to renew and recreate its strategic capabilities to meet the needs of changing environments. He suggests there are three types of dynamic capabilities: those concerned with sensing opportunities and threats, those concerned with seizing opportunities, and those concerned with re-configuring the capabilities of the organisation. There are clear parallels here with Hamel's concept of permanent revolution.

If it can develop a number of core competences, an organisation can greatly strengthen its strategic position. However, there is the danger that over time the core competences may no longer match the external environment. As computing becomes based on mobile phones rather than PCs and laptops, Dell's core competence may prove to be a weakness rather than a strength.

? REFLECTIVE ACTIVITY 10.4

Wonga – a business model under pressure

A payday loan is a short-term loan which provides credit until 'payday' when it will, in theory, be paid back. Payday loans can be applied for either in person at a specialised high street store, for example the Money Shop, or online with companies such as Wonga. In 2012, the government estimated the size of the payday loan market at £1–2bn, with a typical APR (annual percentage rate of interest) of 2500%. Other forms of high cost credit are pawnbrokers, with a similar size of market, but a much lower APR of around 100%, and home collected credit, a much older form of lending, with a market size of £4bn and a typical APR of 3–400% (House of Commons 2014).

Wonga was founded in 2007, and has grown rapidly to become the market leader in payday loans. At its peak in 2013, it made 3.7 million loans in the UK to one million customers, with a total value of £1.1bn. (BBC 2015h). The business solely operates online, and is based on highly sophisticated credit assessment algorithms. It charged 1% a day on loans initially of up to £400, for up to 30 days. It claims to reject 70% of applicants, and that its typical customer is a 'tech-savvy young professional' (Murray-West 2011). The Business Innovation and Skills Select Committee on Debt Management disagreed. In evidence, one economist defined the payday loan market as two very different segments – people who need money quickly, who intend to repay, and who will be in a position to repay, and people who lack control of their finances and who take out debt to purchase something they want at short notice without an ability to repay. The payday loan companies claim that most of their customers are of the first type, but this is not borne out by evidence. The Citizens Advice Bureau found that of those who had taken out a payday loan, 60% regretted the decision, 48% believed the loan has made their financial situation worse; and only 13% believed their payday loan had a positive impact on their finances (House of Commons 2012).

Over the years criticism of Wonga mounted.

- Loans were frequently rolled over several times if clients could not repay, and costs mounted alarmingly.
- The company used continuous payment authorities, which allowed it to take money from customers' bank accounts without notice.
- Its advertising, using cuddly puppets, was criticised for being aimed at children.
- It sent out fake letters purporting to come from solicitors to put pressure on late repayers – it apologised for this in 2014 and agreed to pay compensation of £2.6m to 45,000 customers (BBC 2015h).
- Critics argued that despite the vetting procedures, many loans went to people who had no prospect of being able to repay.

Matters came to a head in 2013, when the newly-appointed Archbishop of Canterbury, Justin Welby, announced that he wanted to 'compete Wonga out of existence' by encouraging the growth of credit unions (a form of social lending based on mutual principles). Wonga responded by publishing its Ten Commitments. These included that it welcomes competition, would 'always help customers in financial difficulty' and that it would never charge interest at an annual percentage rate running into the thousands (Openwonga 2013).

Wonga acquired a new chairman, Andy Haste, in the summer of 2014, and he immediately took action. He suspended the controversial puppet advertisements, announced that he wanted to restore Wonga's reputation, and said that in the short term Wonga would be smaller and less profitable. He said: 'We know it will take time to repair our reputation.' He also wrote off debts worth £220m from more than 300,000 customers, owing to a failure to assess properly whether those borrowers could repay. Lending volumes fell to £732m in 2014, from £1.1bn in 2013. It made 2.5 million loans in the UK in 2014, compared with 3.7 million in 2013, while total customer numbers in the UK fell from about one million to 575,000. The company went from a profit of £39.7m in 2013 to a loss of £37.3m in 2014, almost exactly equal to its cost of debt write-offs. (BBC 2015h).

The mounting criticism from stakeholders led the Financial Conduct Authority to tighten controls on the industry, which came into force in January 2015. Interest and fees will be capped at 0.8% a day, while the total cost of a loan would be limited to 100% of the original sum. Default fees would be capped at £15 (Rankin 2014). In addition, customers would face stricter affordability checks, and lenders would no longer be allowed to roll over a loan more than twice, nor attempt to reclaim payment from a borrower's account more than twice.

What went wrong? Wonga grew too fast, and as a result became careless. It cut corners in its procedures, and did not appreciate the strength of public discontent which was building up about its practices.

Question

Can Wonga survive and flourish in the new environment?

10.8 STRATEGIC CHOICE

10.8.1 GENERIC STRATEGIES

The concept of generic strategy was introduced by Michael Porter (1985). He identified possible strategies as being:

- *Cost leadership.* An organisation will succeed if it can achieve lower costs than its competitors, but sell its products at or near the industry average price.
- *Differentiation.* An organisation will succeed if it can produce a differentiated product which commands a premium price, but at the same time keep its costs to the industry average.
- *Focus.* An organisation will succeed if it concentrates on a niche market, in which it can achieve either cost focus or differentiation focus.

Porter argued that depending on the circumstances any of the three generic strategies could be viable, but that a mixed or hybrid strategy, combining two of the generic strategies, was highly unlikely to be viable.

Porter's model is now a quarter of a century old, and it was developed a long time before the rise of the Internet and e-commerce. However, a study by Kim, Nam and Stimpert (2004) found that at least in the case of B2C (business to consumer) e-commerce, Porter's model still held, with one important exception.

The characteristics of B2C seem to make cost leadership an attractive strategy. E-commerce has very low entry barriers, strategic initiatives and pricing are transparent and can easily be copied by competitors, and there are increasing returns to scale. It therefore makes sense to opt for low prices in order to build up market share quickly. However, although cost leadership was a good entry strategy, it was less effective in the medium term. Because of the ease of market entry, it was all too easy to get into a cost-cutting and ultimately unprofitable price war.

Differentiation was also an effective strategy. Although price was the most important factor for low-value items, for higher value ones like computers, furniture and cars brand was more important, and so was the level of service. A superior level of service was some protection against the entry of low-cost competitors. Amazon was successful because of its enormous stock list, quick delivery, and added value services like personalised recommendations. Focus was also effective. A niche market was a cheap way to enter, and an easy way to develop and deliver value to the customer.

In their empirical research, Kim et al made two interesting findings. One was that despite Porter, the most effective strategy was a hybrid cost leadership-differentiation one, such as that pursued by Amazon. The second was that hybrid 'clicks and mortar' companies, with both a high street and an internet presence, were more effective than 'pure play' e-commerce companies. Clicks and mortar companies often had an established brand reputation, and also could offer additional services, such as the ability to return goods bought online to a local store.

Case Studies 10.5 and 10.6 illustrate the application of two of Porter's generic strategies.

CASE STUDY 10.5

RYANAIR – A SUCCESSFUL FOCUSED COST LEADER

In 1991, Ryanair was a small, unsuccessful Irish airline, when its newly-appointed CEO, Michael O'Leary, went to America to meet Herbert Kelleher, Southwest Airlines' founder. The low cost carrier had transformed the economics of air travel in the US. From Kelleher, O'Leary learned the importance of cost control, through the use of one type of plane, point to point flights only, and elimination of all frills (*Business Week* 2006).

Since then, Ryanair has pushed the Southwest business model even further, and has become the biggest and most profitable low cost airline in Europe. Its success is based on three pillars – cut costs to the minimum ('nail down costs'), 'give nothing, sell everything', and efficiency.

Cost cutting

- Ryanair flies only one type of plane – the Boeing 737–800. This enables economies of scale in pilot training and maintenance.
- Ryanair's seat density on the 737 is 189, 15% more than other airlines.
- Ryanair places its orders for aircraft in a counter-cyclical fashion, taking advantage of weak demand to wring better prices out of Boeing. For example, it placed a very big order in the immediate aftermath of 9/11. In 2007, it was rumoured by the *Financial Times* to be selling some of its planes secondhand for more than it had paid for them (Done 2007).

- The company's planes are stripped of all non-essentials – seats do not recline, there are no window blinds, and no seat-back pockets. This shaves several hundred thousand dollars off the cost of each plane.
- Like other low-cost airlines, Ryanair does not use travel agents, thus saving up to 15% commission, but it has gone further than its rivals in promoting booking over the Internet, which minimises handling costs. By 2007, 98% of bookings were made over the Internet.
- Ryanair does not use air bridges at airports – passengers must walk to the plane. This saves on airport charges.
- Ryanair is notorious for using secondary, but very cheap, airports. These are often some way from the city which they nominally serve. Copenhagen-Malmo is actually in Sweden, not Denmark, and Frankfurt-Hahn is 140 km from Frankfurt. As easyJet repeatedly points out, this means that Ryanair's low fares are deceptive, as further transport costs are needed to reach the final destination. The secondary airports used are desperate for Ryanair's business, and are prepared to offer extremely good terms.
- Advertising on planes is widespread, as well as liveries which attack other airlines.
- Extensive use is made of Eastern European (particularly Polish) cabin crew.

● Aircrew are worked hard. Ryanair pilots fly 887 hours a year, close to the legal maximum of 900. EasyJet pilots fly 780 hours a year (Felsted 2003).

As a result of its rigorous cost-cutting programme, Ryanair's costs are two-thirds of those of easyJet, 60% of UK holiday charter airlines, and half that of full service carriers (Thompson 2005).

Charges

● Ryanair is notorious for charging its staff for perks normally seen as free: crew must pay for their own uniforms, they must pay for water drunk on flights, and they are banned from recharging their mobiles on company power sockets.
● Like other low-cost airlines, passengers are charged for refreshments on flights.
● Ryanair was the first airline to introduce a charge for baggage. This has the effect of raising revenue, and also of cutting the number of bags carried, so lowering baggage handling costs by an estimated £20m a year (*Air Transport World* 2006a). By 2009 the charge was £15 per bag per way.
● In September 2007 it introduced a charge for checking-in at the airport, which could only be avoided by checking-in online (Milmo 2007). By 2009, it was also charging for checking-in online. It also charges £5 per person per flight for payment using a credit or debit card.
● In 2002, Ryanair was heavily criticised when it refused to provide wheelchairs for disabled passengers at Stansted. A court ruling in 2004 judged that the responsibility for disabled passengers was shared between the airport and the airline. Ryanair's response was to place a 33p surcharge on all its ticket prices, which raised far more revenue for Ryanair than the costs which it was claimed to cover (Starmer-Smith, 2006).

In 2009, easyJet made £511m from baggage fees, insurance, early boarding and credit card fees – a fifth of its total revenue. Both the total and the proportion will be at least comparable for Ryanair (Milmo 2009).

Ryanair has made few friends. On the other hand, millions of travellers like its low fares. The airline is also unquestionably good at what it does.

Efficiency

As Ryanair gleefully points out on its website, the airline is extremely efficient. It claims:

● the best on-time record in Europe (91% on time arrivals in 2003, compared with 83% for British Airways and 82% for easyJet)
● the lowest level of cancellations
● fewest lost bags – 0.6 bags per 1,000 passengers in 2003, compared with BA's 14.2) (Ryanair 2003).

Results

Ryanair's model seems to be successful. In 2005, it had the fourth highest operating profit in Europe (behind BA, Air France-KLM and Lufthansa), and the 12th highest in the world, the 11th highest net profit in the world, and the 15th highest number of passengers carried (*Air Transport World* 2006b). In August 2005, for the first time it carried more passengers than the entire worldwide BA network (Ryanair 2007).

Suddenly, in the autumn of 2013 Michael O'Leary underwent a drastic transformation. Out went the old snarling Rottweiler, famous for comments such as 'you're not getting a refund so **** off', and in came the new cuddly kitten, saying 'I want to be loved by my customers' (Parker and Smyth 2013).

Two factors drove this dramatic turnaround. One was a report from the consumer organisation Which? voting Ryanair the worst UK brand for customer service (Griffith 2013a). Normally O'Leary would have shrugged this off, but it coincided with the first profit warning in the airline's history. Ryanair brought in a series of measures aimed at boosting its customer service – the ability to reserve a particular seat, lower prices for hold luggage, lower charges for forgetting to print off a boarding pass (Griffith 2013b). O'Leary also decided to back off as the public face of Ryanair – 'I'm getting in the way of the brand stuff' (Parker and Smyth 2013). To court business passengers, the airline also announced that it was to fly to more primary airports.

The new strategy was only a partial success. Profits for 2014 were down by 8%, the first ever fall (Ryanair 2014), and in a 2014 survey by Siegel and Gale on how brands make people's lives simpler, Ryanair came 114th out of 120 in the UK. As one aim of Ryanair's reforms was to make their website easier to use, this was not a comforting finding, particularly as their arch-rivals easyJet and British Airways came in at 62nd and 56th respectively (Siegel and Gale 2014).

More fundamentally, there is considerable doubt as to whether Ryanair's culture will be able to sustain an emphasis on customer service. In terms of Douglas McGregor's Theory X and Theory Y views of management (McGregor 1960), Ryanair is firmly Theory X, with a strong emphasis on authoritarian control, and very little autonomy allowed to staff. This is an ideal culture for cost leadership, but not appropriate for customer service, which requires much more flexibility and empowerment of staff (Theory Y). Ironically, Southwest Airlines, O'Leary's original model for Ryanair, is a Theory Y organisation, based on commitment, problem-solving, mutual respect and fun (Nortilli and Wong 2014).

In the short term, the switch to a new friendly Ryanair seems to have paid off. Profits for 2015 were up 66% to £623m, although this must be seen in the context of low fuel prices and a surge in profits across the global aviation industry (Topham 2015c).

CASE STUDY 10.6

NORTHERN ROCK: A FAILED FOCUSED DIFFERENTIATOR

Over a weekend in the middle of September 2007, the UK experienced the first serious run on a bank for a century. Hundreds of people queued for hours outside the branches of Northern Rock, desperate to withdraw their savings before the bank collapsed. How had a previously well-respected bank come to such a pass?

Northern Rock was a typical building society – taking in deposits from its members, and lending these out as mortgages. It was safe, solid and respectable. Its share of the national mortgage market was 2%. It was also very popular in the north-east because it had been very sympathetic to miners in mortgage arrears during the mining strike of the early 1980s.

In 1997, it demutualised, forming Northern Rock plc, and its status changed from a building society to a bank. As a public company its priorities changed. Rather than providing a service for its members, its priority was now to make profits for its shareholders. Within months, it showed a new face when it was criticised by the Office of Fair Trading of being 'cavalier' for unilaterally changing the terms offered to its depositors (Hughes and Tighe 2007).

Unlike some of the other demutualised ex-building societies, Northern Rock did not attempt to develop general banking services, but continued to specialise in mortgages. However, it was faced with problems in expanding in this area. Firstly, it only had 79 branches, mainly concentrated in the relatively impoverished north-east. This limited its ability to raise funds from depositors (known as retail funds). By comparison, the leading building society, Nationwide, had over 700 branches, and the big high street banks had thousands.

Northern Rock tackled this problem by raising funds through the interbank market, from other financial institutions (known as wholesale funds). As a building society, it would have been limited by law from raising more than 50% of its funds from the wholesale market, but no such restrictions applied to banks (BBC2 2007). At its peak in the early autumn of 2007, Northern Rock raised more than three-quarters of its funds from the wholesale market, on terms ranging from overnight to three months.

Wholesale borrowing is generally regarded as more risky and volatile than retail borrowing. Although retail depositors can in theory withdraw many of their funds on demand, in practice they are highly unlikely to do so. On the other hand, other banks will move their money elsewhere if they think they can get a better return. Northern Rock's reliance on wholesale funds was described by one experienced banker as akin to overtaking a queue of traffic on the outside of a bend – 'everyone knows it works (for a time), but only fools or the inexperienced would attempt it' (Croggon 2007).

Even when Northern Rock obtained more funds, it still had to persuade people to take out more of its mortgages. It did this through aggressive lending policies. It became known as the bank which would lend even if you had a patchy credit record. It was also prepared to lend more than other banks or building societies. In 2002, it introduced its Together loan, which allowed a borrower to borrow up to 125% of a property's valuation, or six times annual income. As other lenders were not prepared to lend more than four times income, borrowers flocked to Northern Rock.

Massive expansion continued throughout the first half of 2007, at a time when increasing warnings were being issued of the frothy state of the UK housing market, and of a worrying level of consumer debt. In the first half of 2007, Northern Rock took a 25% share of the new mortgage market, making it the biggest mortgage provider. (Collinson and Seager 2007).

With hindsight, it was clear that Northern Rock was over-trading, and taking unacceptable risks. In June 2007 it was forced to issue a profits warning, and its shares started to fall. Its strategy was described by Professor Willem Buiter, one of the founder members of the Bank of England's Monetary Policy Committee, as 'an extremely aggressive and high-risk strategy' (Duncan and Webster 2007).

Northern Rock might still have got away with it had it not been caught up in the backlash from a separate but related financial crisis, the sub-prime crisis in the US. Here, US financial institutions had pursued a Northern Rock-style strategy of aggressive lending to poor credit risks (the sub-prime market), eventually leading to a collapse of the US housing market in the summer of 2007. One consequence of this was a freezing-up of the interbank lending market in the UK, as well as the US. This meant that Northern Rock, which continually needed to roll over its wholesale borrowing, faced a liquidity crisis.

The crisis for Northern Rock came to a head on Thursday 13 September, when the bank applied to the Bank of England for emergency assistance (known as 'lender of last resort'). On Friday 14 September the Bank of England agreed to lend virtually unlimited funds to Northern Rock, but at a penal rate of interest, believed to be 7%.

This should have been the end of the crisis, but Northern Rock retail depositors interpreted this as a sign that the bank was about to fail, and a run on the Bank's cash started and quickly accelerated. Bank deposits were guaranteed, but only up to a maximum of £35,000, and only up to 90%. On Friday and Saturday, a sum estimated to be between £2bn and £3bn was withdrawn from Northern Rock branches. Eventually, to stop the run, the Chancellor, Alistair Darling, announced on Monday 16 September that the government would guarantee all deposits in Northern Rock, without limit. The immediate crisis was over, but the troubles of Northern Rock then became part of the general financial crisis of 2008–10. Northern Rock was nationalised, and the deposit guarantee was raised to 100% of £50,000.

The Government split Northern Rock into two businesses, Northern Rock Bank (the 'good bank') and Northern Rock Asset Management (the 'bad bank' which held the toxic mortgages). The former was sold to Virgin Money in 2012 and rebranded as Virgin Money. The latter remains in state hands.

This case illustrates several important points. One is that Northern Rock's strategy differentiated it from the rest of the mortgage industry, but only at the price of unacceptably high risk. Secondly, the case demonstrates the nature of moral hazard. The Bank of England was reluctant to intervene at an earlier stage in the crisis because of the risk of moral hazard – that in effect a rescue would reward Northern Rock for its reckless behaviour, and might encourage other institutions to be reckless in the future. Eventually, the Bank of England had no choice, and was forced to intervene to safeguard the stability of the whole banking system, as there was a risk that the panic might spread to other institutions. The bail-out safeguarded not only Northern Rock's depositors, who were innocent victims, but also the bank's management and shareholders, who should have known better (Davies 2007).

Porter's generic strategy concept has been further developed by Bowman (1996), who proposes the strategy clock, based on a combination of price and perceived added value. He identified eight possible strategies:

- *Low price/low added value* – not likely to be feasible in the long term unless the organisation operates in a protected niche.
- *Low price/standard added value* – equates to Porter's cost leadership.
- *Low price/high added value (hybrid)* – the strategy pursued by Japanese companies in the 1970s and 1980s, when they were gaining a foothold in European markets.
- *Standard price/high added value (differentiation)* – this would be a sensible strategy as a progression from the hybrid strategy.
- *High price/high added value (focused differentiation)* – likely to be a niche strategy, similar to Porter's differentiation focus.
- *High price/standard added value* – not a long-term viable strategy; why should customers pay more if they are not gaining added value?
- *High price/low added value* – only feasible for a monopoly in a market which is not contestable.
- *Standard price/low added value* – not viable in the long term; what is in it for the customer?

10.9 SELECTION OF STRATEGIES

This is concerned not with what strategies should be chosen, but how they should be chosen. Johnson et al (2011) propose four models:

10.9.1 FORMAL EVALUATION

Here the choice is based solely on analytical techniques. The decision process is impersonal and rational, and appears to be objective. This avoids the risk of taking decisions solely on gut feeling, but it should be remembered that a lot of the analytical techniques are themselves in practice subjective.

10.9.2 ENFORCED CHOICE

Here choice is imposed on the organisation from outside. This may be because of the dominant influence of an external stakeholder – for example, a supplier to Marks & Spencer has very little control over its own strategy. However, in the long term, even a firm in this situation does have some strategic choice – to widen its customer base, for example.

10.9.3 LEARNING FROM EXPERIENCE

The emphasis here is on incremental change on pilot basis with operating units, and then the application of the experience learned from this throughout the organisation. This method is increasingly used by government, which trials new policy initiatives through a pilot study before going for a national launch, and by many manufacturers, who test market new products before attempting a national launch. It is similar to Quinn's concept of logical incrementalism, which we discussed earlier. The advantage is that it pushes responsibility for strategic development down the organisation, but there is the possible disadvantage that there is never a fundamental strategic rethink – the organisation can suffer from strategic drift.

10.9.4 COMMAND

Here the dominant stakeholder (who may be the CEO, the biggest shareholder, or a government department) selects the strategic direction, and imposes it on the organisation. This has been the experience of the National Health Service, which has had fundamental strategic change imposed on it by successive governments at regular intervals.

10.9.5 EVALUATION OF STRATEGIES

Possible strategies should be evaluated on three levels, suitability, acceptability and feasibility.

Suitability

Is this a strategy which will produce a sound fit between the organisation and its environment?

- Will it exploit opportunities in the environment and avoid or neutralise threats?
- Will it capitalise on the organisation's strengths and core competences and avoid or neutralise weaknesses?

Various analytical techniques can be used to help answer these questions:
Life cycle analysis
The consultants Arthur D. Little have identified the life cycle/portfolio matrix (see Johnson and Scholes 1997). Here the strategies which should be adopted depend on the stage of the product/industry life cycle (embryonic, growing, mature or ageing), and the competitive position of the organisation (dominant, strong, favourable, tenable or weak). For example, the prescribed strategies for a strong firm in a growing industry are: fast grow, catch-up, attain cost leadership or differentiation. For a weak firm in an embryonic industry they are: find niche, catch-up or grow with industry. The model is open to criticism, as the definitions used are subjective (what is a favourable position in one environment may be a weak one in another), and because, like all models, it ignores all variables except those actually built into the model (stage of maturity and competitive position). For example, it ignores speed of technological development.

Portfolio analysis

We discussed the Boston Matrix in Chapter 3. Briefly, this categorises product lines on a matrix of market share and market growth rate, as:

- *Cash cows:* Low market growth, high market share
- *Stars:* High market growth, high market share
- *Question marks:* High market growth, low market share
- *Dogs:* Low market growth, low market share.

Here the preferred strategic options would be to attempt to balance the portfolio between stars and cash cows. Stars are profitable, but they do not generate much cash, while cash cows may be less profitable but are highly cash-generative. Hence use cash cows to finance stars. As with the life cycle model, this is superficially attractive, but again it ignores other variables.

Value chain analysis

Value chain analysis is yet another model developed by Michael Porter. He says that the activities of an organisation should be seen as a sequence of primary events:

- inbound logistics, deliveries, storage, etc
- operations
- outbound logistics (warehousing, wholesalers, deliveries, etc)
- marketing and sales
- service,

  while underpinning all of these were support activities:

- the firm's infrastructure
- human resource management
- technology
- procurement (purchasing, raising capital, recruitment).

All of these serve to add value for the organisation and form the value chain. The greater the synergies between the various elements, the greater the added value. Conversely, the whole value chain is only as strong as its weakest link. The aim of strategy should therefore be to strengthen the value chain as a whole, by building on existing strengths, or correcting weaknesses.

For example, the primary part of the chain might be strong, but the organisation might have problems caused by high turnover of staff. The strategic choice here would be to concentrate on improving staff turnover using HR techniques. Alternatively, the product might be strong, but its reputation is let down by poor after-sales service. After digging deeper, it might be discovered that the IT systems supporting service are inadequate.

The strength of the value chain technique is that it forces an analysis of how the organisation actually functions, and it avoids over-concentration on some of the more obvious strategic possibilities like merger or takeover. The weakness is that it is exclusively inward-looking. It should be combined with a rigorous analysis of fit with the environment.

Acceptability

Strategies have to be acceptable to internal and external stakeholders. This can be assessed in three ways: return, risk and stakeholder reaction.

Return can be assessed using a range of standard accounting techniques, including profitability analysis (discounted cash flow, etc), shareholder value analysis (looking at the overall increase in value for the shareholder, using techniques such as Economic Value Added, or cost benefit analysis (looking at non-financial as well as financial factors).

Risk can be assessed using techniques including the following.

- Break-even analysis – if the break-even point for the new strategy is a very high percentage of capacity, the project is highly risky.
- Ratio analysis – if the new strategy will result in very low levels of liquidity, as measured by standard ratios, it is high risk.
- Sensitivity analysis – how sensitive is the profit of the project to a shortfall in any of the key financial variables?
- Stakeholder reactions can be assessed using techniques such as stakeholder modelling (discussed in Chapter 9). Stakeholders may well have strong views on risk, and these should be taken into account.

CASE STUDY 10.7

STAKEHOLDER ACCEPTABILITY

An acceptable strategy – Ben & Jerry's and Unilever

Ben & Jerry's ice cream was one of the leading lights of the ethical business movement. It was not only concerned to trade ethically, it also wanted to change the world. It donated heavily to radical causes, and was deeply involved in the anti-globalisation movement. These values were fully supported by its staff and customers, both key stakeholders.

In April 2000, Ben & Jerry's was taken over by the strait-laced Anglo-Dutch conglomerate Unilever, a classic representative of the globalisation that Ben & Jerry's had opposed. Although it had a good ethical reputation, Unilever was in no sense radical. Ben Cohen, the joint founder of Ben & Jerry's, forecast that the takeover would lead to the destruction of the company.

However, when Unilever appointed a 25-year Unilever man, Yves Couette, to run Ben & Jerry's, he was given the license to be a 'grain of sand in the eye' of Unilever. He abandoned his suit and tie, and followed a deliberate policy of empowerment and delegation. Tough profit targets were set, but Couette pointed out to staff that this would mean that more money would be donated to charity through the Ben & Jerry Foundation, which would continue to have a free hand to support any charity or movement which it chose. Ben & Jerry's was given licence to modify

Unilever programmes. In the case of employee performance evaluation, Ben and Jerry's added social mission to the performance goals (Kiger 2005).

An unacceptable strategy – Marconi

Throughout the 1980s and 1990s, GEC was seen as a safe, rather stolid company, dominated by the safety-first philosophy of its long-time chairman, Arnold (Lord) Weinstock. The company prospered in household electrical goods and defence electronics, and built up a bank balance of several billion pounds. It appealed to risk-averse shareholders.

In the late 1990s, new management, headed by George Simpson, decided on a radical new strategy. The defence electronics business was sold to British Aerospace, most of the domestic electric businesses (Hotpoint, etc), were sold, and the company, now renamed Marconi, began a dash for growth in the exciting new world of internet electronics. The rationale was that Marconi would benefit from the dot.com boom which was raging at the time.

Unfortunately, the purchases were made right at the peak of the dot.com bubble, and when the bubble burst, many of the new acquisitions were effectively worthless. Marconi's share price plummeted, and when the company eventually went through a financial restructuring, shareholders effectively lost all their money.

Like all shareholders, the Marconi shareholders should have realised that any share investment is by its very nature risky, but they could legitimately argue that they had originally bought their shares in GEC precisely because it was seen as a low-risk company (Birkinshaw 2004).

Feasibility

Strategies have to be feasible in terms of resource availability. Techniques to measure this include:

- *Funds flow analysis* – what is the implication for future cash flows? If sufficient cash is not currently available, can it be acquired on reasonable terms?
- *Break even analysis* – what is the break even point given the present cost structure? If the break even point is too high, can the cost structure be improved?
- *Resource deployment analysis* – what are the key resources and competences required for each strategy, does the organisation already possess them, if not, can it reasonably acquire them?

CASE STUDY 10.8

STRATEGIC FIT AT STARBUCKS

Starbucks is one of the leading players in the growing coffee shop segment in the UK, with 30% of the market, and is also a leading global player, operating in 50 countries, with more than 17,000 company-operated or licensed shops.

In 2014 Dudovskiy analysed the ability of Starbucks in the UK to capitalise on opportunities and minimise threats. Specifically, he identified opportunities as new product development, applying technology to increase the level of operational efficiency, and increasing the range of its target customers, and felt that Starbucks had suitable strengths to capitalise on all of these. Threats were more serious. Spending in coffee shops is discretionary, and may be squeezed as consumer spending remains subdued.

More serious is the tax avoidance scandal that was examined in Case Study 6.8.

Dudovskiy also analysed how well Starbucks was performing against its critical success factors (CSFs). The company scored highly on shop design, through a welcoming atmosphere, and providing free WiFi; on customer service, supported by empowered staff; and on customer loyalty reward programmes. It was less successful on quality of products, where consumers have voted its closest competitor, Costa, as being of higher quality; and on corporate social responsibility, where the company has been compromised by the tax avoidance scandal.

Source: Dudovskiy (2014)

10.9.6 STRATEGIC OPTION SCREENING

Several methods can be used to screen options to see whether they meet criteria on suitability, acceptability and feasibility. These include:

Ranking

Here options are assessed against key factors in the environment, resources and stakeholder expectations, and a score (or ranking) established for each option. To take a very simple example, assume that a company has two strategic options, A and B, and two success criteria, profitability and stakeholder acceptability. It has established that it regards profitability as more important, and has given this a weighting of 70. Stakeholder acceptability has a weighting of 30 (producing a total weighting of 100).

Strategy A scores 50 out of 70 for profitability, but only 10 out of 30 for stakeholder acceptability. Strategy B scores less well on profitability, scoring 30 out of 70, but it scores 20 out of 30 for stakeholder acceptability.

This gives a total score for strategy A of 60/100 (50 + 10), and a total score for strategy B of 50/100 (30 + 20). Strategy A is thus the preferred option.

Decision trees

Here options are progressively eliminated by testing them against various criteria. For example, a company has two decision criteria, high growth (most important) and low cost (less important). It is considering four strategies:

- Strategy W   high growth, high cost
- Strategy X   high growth, low cost
- Strategy Y   low growth, low cost
- Strategy Z   low growth, high cost.

The first decision step would eliminate strategies Y and Z, because they are low growth, leaving W and X. The next decision step would eliminate W, leaving X as the preferred strategy.

Scenario planning

Here the options are evaluated against various scenarios for the future. For example, if the organisation thinks that the most likely future for UK exchange rate is stability, this would favour a policy of manufacturing in the UK. If the most likely scenario is seen as a rising pound, this would favour manufacturing overseas.

?   REFLECTIVE ACTIVITY 10.5

Strategic evaluation

A risk-averse firm with a strong current financial position, but little access to long-term capital, has decided that it must adopt a policy of unrelated diversification, in order to reduce its dependence on a declining industry. It has evaluated a number of areas for diversification, and decided on the appropriate industry to enter. It is now considering the best way to enter the new market.

Its options are:

A   Develop and manufacture a new product

B   Manufacture an existing product under licence

C   Set up a joint venture with a firm that already has expertise in this field

D   Buy out a firm already in the industry

E   Market under their brand name an existing Taiwanese product not currently imported into the UK.

They have established the following criteria, and weighted them as follows:

		Weighting
(a)	Low risk	40
(b)	Speedy entry into the market	20
(c)	Low capital cost	20
(d)	Profitability	15
(e)	Short payback period	5

Questions

1 Discuss the advantages and disadvantages of each method of entry.

2 Using your own judgement, assign scores to each strategy and rank them.

10.10 STRATEGIC IMPLEMENTATION

The final stage in the strategy process is implementation – having decided on the chosen strategy, how is it put into practice? Frequently this will be the most difficult phase of the whole process. It involves a key competency of all managers – the ability to manage change.

10.10.1 INCREMENTAL AND TRANSFORMATIONAL CHANGE

Most of the writers on strategic implementation distinguish between incremental and transformational change, although their terminology varies. Johnson et al (2011) see strategic change on a two-by-two matrix, type of change and extent of change. A small change is incremental, a large change transformational. Each is of two types, dependent on whether the change is proactive or reactive. Proactive incremental change is tuning, reactive incremental change adaptation, while transformational change is divided into planned and forced change.

Walton (1999) defines transformational change as change which results in entirely new behaviour on the part of organisational members. He sees transformational change as in its very nature strategic. However, drawing on the work of Quinn on logical incrementalism, he sees incremental change as a possible route to strategic change. He also identifies transitional change, the process of carrying out change.

Porter (1999) concentrates on the outcome rather than the process. Changes such as the introduction of re-engineering or Total Quality Management are transformational, but they are not strategic. He sees them as improving operational effectiveness rather than changing the strategic position of the organisation. They are about doing better the same things as the competition are doing. Operational effectiveness is about running the same race faster, strategy is about running a different race.

10.10.2 MODELS OF CHANGE

The classic model of change was identified by Lewin in the 1950s and developed by Schein in the 1980s (Armstrong 1999; Walton 1999). They identified three stages in change management:

- *Unfreezing* – creating a readiness for change, through creation of a sense of anxiety about the present situation. The sequence here is to enable those involved to be convinced of the need for change.

- *Movement* – taking action that will encourage the desired new behaviour patterns. This involves doing things differently, based on access to new information, and identifying with new role models.
- *Refreezing* – embedding the new ways of working into the organisation.

Lewin also developed the concept of force field analysis – analysing the restraining and driving forces within the organisation which oppose or support the proposed change, and then taking steps to encourage the driving forces and decrease the restraining forces.

Beer took a different approach. He argued that the approach which tries to change attitudes in order to change behaviour is flawed. He argued that change should be approached in an opposite way – put people in new roles which require new behaviours, and this will change their attitudes. This is similar to the theory of cognitive dissonance which we discussed in Chapter 9 in relation to ethics. Beer proposed a six-stage model of change (CIPD 2004):

1 Mobilise commitment to change through joint analysis of problems.

2 Develop a shared vision.

3 Foster consensus and commitment to the shared vision.

4 Spread the word about the change.

5 Institutionalise the change through formal policies.

6 Monitor and adjust as needed.

The Lewin and Beer models both come out of relatively placid environments. They have been criticised for their assumption that it is possible to plan an orderly transition from one static state to another static state (Burnes 1996). In a more dynamic and chaotic environment like that experienced at present, a more continuous and open-ended change process is more appropriate. They also assume that a 'one size fits all' model of change is appropriate, whereas a more modern perspective would be to take a contingency approach and to argue that each organisation has a unique relationship with its environment. Its approach to change should reflect this.

The emergent approach to change as put forward by Burnes and Shaw (CIPD 2004), stresses that change is not linear – it is not a movement from state A to state B – it is continuous and messy. Just like its environment, an organisation is in a continuous state of flux, and the forces for change emerge as the organisation engages with its environment. Change in this model is bottom-up rather than top-down, and it emerges through experimentation. What is important is to ensure that the organisation is responsive to change, and the best way of doing this is to ensure that the organisation is a learning organisation.

McCann (2004) relates change directly to the changing nature of the environment. In a placid environment, change is likely to be episodic, ie low-level and easily managed. Here the objective is to control change. Organisations cope with this by building some slack into their systems, which can act as a buffer in periods of change. As the environment grew more turbulent, change became continuous. Here the objective is to embrace change, by building agility into the organisation and removing barriers to change. Finally, in a very turbulent environment, shocks such as 9/11, the credit crunch or the swine flu pandemic will lead to disruptive change. To cope with this the organisation must prepare for change, by planning for contingencies and assuring a capacity for recovery and renewal.

Nadler and Tushman take a different approach with their congruence model (Nadler and Tushman 1980; Buggy 2005). Their model explores the links between strategy and performance. In order for strategy to be converted into effective performance, four elements have to be in congruence – people, culture, organisation and work (critical tasks) as shown in Figure 10.3.

Figure 10.3 Congruence model

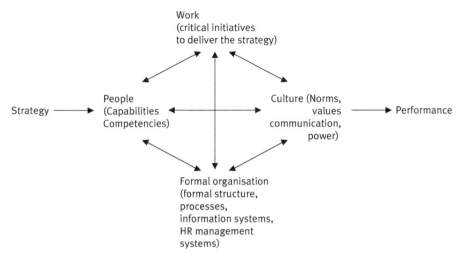

Source: adapted from Buggy (2005)

Points of congruence or incongruence should be identified – for example, is the work being done by the right people? (Work and People), do the formal and informal structures work co-operatively or do they compete? (Formal organisation and Culture). Points of congruence should be strengthened, and points of incongruence resolved. You may spot similarities with two models which we previously examined – Lewin's Force Field Analysis model (this chapter) and Thompson's E-V-R Congruence model (Chapter 1).

10.10.3 OPEN SYSTEMS

The open systems school is primarily interested in seeing organisations in their entirety, and therefore takes an holistic view rather than a particular perspective. This is reflected in its approach to change. Burke (1980) suggested this is informed by three factors:

- Sub-systems are interdependent. Therefore account must be taken of the dependence of other parts of the organisation.
- Training, as a mechanism for change, is unlikely to succeed on its own. This is because it concentrates on the individual and not on the organisational level. Burke argues that 'there is scant evidence that attempting to change the individual will in turn change the organisation'.
- For success, organisations need to tap into and direct the energy and talent of their workforce. This involves the removal of barriers and the promotion of positive reinforcement. Given that change is likely to require altering such things as norms, reward systems and work structures, the approach must therefore be at an organisational level, rather than an individual or group perspective.

Open systems approaches have attracted much research and interest but some shortcomings have been identified. Butler (1985) argued that social systems are so complex that sorting out all the cause and effect relationships may be impossible, while Beach (1980) argued that open systems theory runs the risk of being abstract rather than operationally useful.

10.10.4 MANAGING CHANGE

Kotter (1995) proposes an eight-step plan for transformation.

1   Establishing a sense of urgency – realising that change is needed.

2   Forming a powerful guiding coalition – a powerful and influential group of change leaders is needed.

3   Creating a vision – what will things be like after the change is achieved?

4   Communicating the vision.

5   Empowering others to act on the vision.

6   Planning for and creating short-term wins – a long change process that appears to be getting nowhere can be demotivating. Building in some short-term wins can improve morale.

7   Consolidating improvements and producing still more change.

8   Institutionalising new approaches – similar to Lewin's refreezing process.

Bridges and Mitchell (2000) identify three stages in a change programme:

1   Saying goodbye – letting go of the way that things used to be.

2   Shifting into neutral – the in-between stage when nothing seems to be happening, but everyone is in a stressful state of limbo. In the case of a major merger, this phase might take two years.

3   Moving forward – when people have to behave in a new way.

They describe seven steps in managing transition:

1   Describe the change and why it must happen – in one minute or less.

2   Make sure that the details of the change are planned carefully and that someone is responsible for each detail.

3   Understand who is going to have to let go of what.

4   Make sure that people are helped to let go of the past.

5   Help people through the neutral zone with communication, stressing the '4 Ps':

- The purpose – why we have to do this
- The picture – what it will look and feel like when we get there
- The plan – how we will get there
- The part – what each person needs to do.

6   Create temporary solutions to the temporary problems found in the neutral zone.

7   Help people launch the new beginning.

MOSES IN THE WILDERNESS

CASE STUDY 10.9

Bridges and Mitchell discuss the change management techniques used by Moses on his way to the Promised Land.

Magnify the plagues: Moses had to convince a key stakeholder (Pharaoh) that change was needed – that he had to let the Jews go. He did this through creating problems for Pharaoh – the

seven plagues. The worse the current situation seems, the greater the impetus for change.

Mark the ending: After the Jews crossed the Red Sea, there was (literally) no going back.

Deal with the 'murmuring': Don't be surprised when people lose confidence in the neutral zone. Moses faced lots of whingeing. He dealt with it by talking to people about their concerns.

Build up change champions: Moses and his lieutenant Joshua appointed a new cadre of judges to champion the change.

Capitalise on creative opportunities: It was in the Wilderness, not in the Promised Land, that the Ten Commandments were handed down.

Resist the urge to rush ahead: Not much seems to be happening in the neutral zone, but it is where the true transformation takes place. Moses was in the Wilderness for forty years!

Different stages need different leadership styles: Moses was an ideal leader for the neutral zone, but the Promised Land required a new type of leadership, provided by the conqueror of Jericho, Joshua.

10.11 RESISTANCE TO CHANGE

Pugh (1978) sees organisational change as a paradox. Situations and problems which cry out most strongly for change are the very ones which resist change most stubbornly. Individuals perceive change as a threat and react like rabbits caught in the headlights of a car – they go rigid.

Resistance to change can be better understood if you view organisations as a coalition of interest groups in tension. The organisation is a particular balance of forces which has been hammered out over time. Any change which threatens the current balance will encounter resistance. Combine this with psychological resistance from rigid people under threat, and it is easy to see how managing change is difficult. Organisations are ultrastable – they run like mad to stay in the same place.

As a consequence, real organisational change often:

- comes about much too late
- is a response to a threat posed by situations of considerable failure
- is made with insufficient thought and little consideration of alternatives
- is in order to live to fight another day.

At a more immediate level, change is most likely to be acceptable by individuals or departments who are basically successful in their tasks but who are currently experiencing difficulties. They will have the two basic ingredients of *confidence in their ability* and *motivation to change*. The next most likely to change are the successful. They will have the confidence but might not have the motivation. The least likely to understand and accept change are the unsuccessful.

An effective manager:

- anticipates the need for change
- diagnoses the nature of the change that is required and carefully considers alternatives
- manages the change process over a period of time so that it is effective and accepted.

Pugh has six rules for managing change effectively:

1 Work hard at establishing the need for change.

2 Don't only think about the change, think through it. This means thinking about the effects the change will have on individuals in terms of their jobs, status, prestige and so on.

3 Initiate change through informal discussions to get feedback and participation.

4 Positively encourage those concerned to give their objections.

5   Be prepared to change yourself.

6   Monitor the change and reinforce it.

Resistance to change can be of two types:

1   Resistance to the content of change – ie opposition to the specific nature of the change.

2   Resistance to the process of change – ie opposition to how to the change is introduced.

Each might be a perfectly rational response to change, however inconvenient to management.

Armstrong (1999) identifies eight reasons why individuals might resist change:

1   The shock of the new – people tend to be conservative, and they do not want to move too far from their comfort zones. To this I would add regret for the passing of the old.

2   Economic fears – threats to wages or job security.

3   Inconvenience.

4   Uncertainty.

5   Symbolic fears – the loss of a symbol, like a car parking space, may suggest that bigger and more threatening changes are on the way.

6   Threats to interpersonal relationships.

7   Threat to status or skill – a change may be seen as deskilling.

8   Competence fears – concern about the ability to cope or acquire new skills.

On the other hand, Woodward and Hendry (2004), in a survey of financial service organisations in the City of London, found that while change put pressure on employees a majority saw change as a part of organisational life and felt positive about it.

10.12 THE ROLE OF HR IN CHANGE MANAGEMENT

The crucial role of HR in change management can be clearly identified using Beer's model of change. HR intervention is crucial at each stage of the model, as follows:

1   *Mobilise commitment to change through joint analysis of problems*: HR should play a leading role in benchmarking and other environment-scanning techniques, and so help to spot the need for change. HR staff are likely to be the organisers of the teams and workshops who are involved in problem identification and analysis. Underpinning this should be a learning organisation, in which HR should be a prime driver.

2   *Develop a shared vision*: This involves an understanding of the culture of the organisation, and the ability to support and direct the visions which underpin the culture.

3   *Foster consensus and commitment to the shared vision*: It is essential that those affected by the change should feel that they have ownership of it. Developing and supporting ownership is a key HR skill, as is the fostering and supporting of change champions.

4   *Spread the word about the change*: Here, as noted by McCarthy (2004), communication is key. McCarthy stresses that this should involve communication *with*, rather than communication *at*, those involved. He suggests the concept of 'conversation' as being appropriate here.

5   *Institutionalise the change through formal policies*: This may well include the development of new HR policies on recruitment, reward and development. It is crucial that the reward system supports the new ways of doing things, for example.

6   *Monitor and adjust as needed*: HR policy will need to be proactive after the change process is apparently completed. Development policies should be responsive to the need for any new competencies which become apparent.

Armstrong (1999) identifies a number of 'guidelines for change management', in most of which the role of HR is key. These include:

- commitment and visionary leadership from the top
- understanding the culture
- development of temperament and leadership skills at all levels which support change
- an environment conducive to change – a learning organisation
- full participation of those involved, so that they can own the change
- the reward system should recognise success in achieving change
- a willingness to learn from failure – a support culture rather than a blame culture
- support for change agents
- protection of those adversely affected by change.

Ridgeway and Wallace (1994) discuss the role of HR in managing a common strategic change – a takeover. Here matching the culture of the predator and the target are key. They quote from Furnham and Gunter (1993) on how such a match should be identified. It would involve:

- identifying the culture of the acquiring company
- deciding on any changes needed to ensure that culture supports the proposed strategy
- identifying potential acquisitions and their cultures
- isolating likely changes to those cultures
- designing a format for assessing other cultures
- establishing criteria by which to identify suitable acquisitions.

Crucial here is establishing how the senior management of the target company will fit with the acquirer's culture, and what senior staff gaps will be exposed.

The HR department of the acquiring company will also be responsible for ensuring that the procedures and systems of the two companies are compatible, or can be made compatible, including any industrial relations implications. During the takeover process, the HR department also needs to manage communication. This will involve close liaison with PR, as employees of the target company will get a lot of their information about the takeover via the media.

?   REFLECTIVE ACTIVITY 10.6

Pearmount College

Pearmount College is a medium-sized further education college in the town of Hetherleigh (population 75,000). In many ways it is a typical FE college. In its Ofsted inspections, most aspects are rated as satisfactory (grade 3, the middle of the five grades available). A third of its courses are rated as above average, a third as below average. However, Pearmount is not typical in that it is a tertiary college. Unlike most FE colleges, it is responsible for all post-16 education in Hetherleigh. This gives the college a particular social responsibility. As the only post-16 provider, it cannot be selective in its recruitment policy. It is expected to provide educational opportunities for all of the post-16 population in the town.

There are four main types of post-16 providers, all of which compete to score highly in government league tables. These are school sixth forms, which are often selective, sixth form colleges, which are almost always selective, tertiary colleges, which are normally non-selective, and ordinary FE colleges, which tend to offer mainly vocational courses rather than A levels. The main league table competition is between sixth forms, sixth form colleges and tertiary colleges, and concentrates on A level results. Sixth form colleges tend to score more highly than school sixth firms and tertiary colleges. A recent Ofsted inspection of Pearmount noted that its A level results were at the FE college average, but below the average for sixth form colleges. It also criticised teaching as unimaginative, although it said that some vocational provision was excellent.

Post-16 education is funded by the Education Funding Agency, under government guidance. Government funding policy is to concentrate on three main target areas – full-time 16–19 education, adult basic literacy and numeracy skills, and adult level 2 qualifications (broadly GCSE grade A-C level). FE and tertiary colleges have responded to this by withdrawing from adult education, unless it fits into the funding priorities, or is fully funded by employers. Pearmount is typical in this. Over the last decade it has withdrawn from many advanced vocational and professional part-time programmes, and concentrated much more on full-time 16–19 programmes. The other continuing pressure from the EFA is to drive up the quality of further education provision, with the threat of withdrawing funding from courses within the priority areas which are deemed to be of low quality.

Jim Merryweather was appointed as the new principal of Pearmount College in September 2014, following the retirement of his predecessor, who had taken an active role in the town. Within a month of taking up his post, he produced a new teaching and learning strategy for the College. This stressed individual daily targets for students, with daily assessment and measurement of achievement; all assignment work to be completed in college; and fortnightly reports to parents on progress and attendance. His aim was to make the College one of the best sixth forms in the country.

Although there was some concern that the new strategy seemed to focus solely on full-time 16–19 students, it was broadly welcomed by teaching staff, and rapid progress was made in its implementation.

However, Jim also faced the problem that many of his staff were ageing, while others, who mainly taught vocational programmes for adults, were seeing much of their workload disappearing. Clearly the college staffing needed to be restructured. One way to do this could have been an early retirement programme, but what often happens in these programmes is that the people opting to take early retirement are the very people who you do not want to lose. Another option could have been a programme of retraining and redeployment.

Jim's solution was to propose a radical restructuring, which was announced just before the Easter holidays in April 2015. A new staffing structure was proposed, with more higher-paid posts, but also some low-level posts with a salary ceiling well below that previously available to lecturers. All members of staff were expected to reapply for posts under the new structure, with the clear expectation that some would be unsuccessful.

In addition, holidays were reduced, and the normal working week was increased to 37 hours, all of which could in theory be spent teaching. The working week was also extended to five and a half days, and staff could be requested to work on Saturdays. Staff would no longer be entitled to overtime or time off in lieu.

The reaction of staff was one of horror, particularly as the new posts were advertised internally immediately, although the proposals came under the 90-day consultation period for major redundancies. Teaching staff held a number of one-day strikes, were fully supported by their union and the students union, and also attracted a lot of support within the town.

By the end of the summer term in 2015, half the teaching staff had been made redundant, had found new posts, or had taken early retirement. There was severe concern that College staffing would be inadequate to meet demand in 2015–16, and also that the adverse publicity would dissuade many potential students from attending the College.

10.13 STRATEGIC LEADERSHIP

10.13.1 WHAT DO STRATEGIC LEADERS DO?

In this Section we examine the practical things which strategic leaders do to contribute to the success of the chosen strategy(ies) of the organisation.

10.13.2 WHAT BUSINESS ARE WE IN?

One of the first tasks of a leader is to define what business we are in. Defining a business too narrowly could lead to stagnation, while defining it too widely may lead to imprecision and drift.

In 2001, Hornby, the model railway company, was in trouble. Shareholders wanted to sell the company, but nobody wanted to buy it. The company was seen as staid and old-fashioned. Seventy per cent of its sales were to adult hobbyists, and 30% to children, and marketing was heavily based on nostalgia for a vanished world of stream railways. After the failure of the attempt to sell the company, new management was brought in, and Frank Martin became chief executive. He was horrified to find that the old management had just turned down the licence to make a Hogwarts Express set to tie in with Harry Potter, and he quickly reversed the decision (Teather 2007).

What business is Hornby in? The old management felt that it was a hobby business, and should not be interested in products, like Hogwarts, aimed at children. Martin took the view that this was short-sighted. The hobbyist market was ageing, and unless a new segment of customers was attracted, the business would eventually die. Under his leadership, licensing of media tie-in properties has become an integral part of the business. This seems to have been the right strategic decision, as the share price is now eight times higher than when he first joined the business.

10.13.3 DEVELOPING VISION AND SHAPING VALUES

The strategic leader determines or is associated with an overall vision that motivates others, helps create the shared beliefs within which people can work together more effectively, and shapes more detailed strategy developed by others in an organisation.

The Unilever chief executive Paul Polman epitomises value-driven leadership. He stresses how Unilever tries to gain the trust of its customers with respect to sustainability, and notes the importance of having personal values aligned with those of one's employer. He has driven Unilever's 'sustainable living plan', launched in 2010. This has three objectives, to be achieved by 2020: to cut the environmental impact of Unilever's products in half, to source sustainably all its agricultural supplies, and to improve the health and wellbeing of a billion people worldwide. (Bird 2010; Saunders 2011).

10.13.4 ENCOURAGING LEARNING

The learning organisation is an organisation that is capable of continual regeneration from the variety of knowledge, experience and skills that encourages questioning and challenge. Watkins and Marsick (1993) identify seven dimensions of the learning organisation:

1   Create continuous learning opportunities.

2   Promote dialogue and enquiry.

3 Promote collaboration and team learning.

4 Empower people towards a collective vision.

5 Establish systems to capture and share learning.

6 Connect the organisation to its environment.

7 Provide strategic leadership for learning.

The aim of top management should be to facilitate rather than direct strategy development by building pluralistic organisations, where knowledge is readily shared and experimentation is the norm.

10.13.5 RESOLVING DILEMMAS

Chief executives most often work in a pressure-cooker atmosphere where two kinds of tension are present. The first kind is the natural tension that exists among top teams, in which talented, driven people who have to work together are also competing with one another for results, power, and stature. The other kind is performance tension: the stress caused by three pairs of important objectives that, in many companies, come into conflict on a daily basis. These are profitability versus growth, the short term versus the long term, and the success of the organisation as a whole versus that of its individual parts. The most successful chief executives are the ones who get these tensions right (Favaro and Joni 2010).

10.13.6 MANAGING POLITICAL PROCESSES

Strategies develop as the outcome of bargaining and negotiation among powerful interest groups. Top management must understand the configuration of power within the organisation. Control over the allocation of resources is a useful asset for overcoming possible resistance. Another ploy is to build alliances with sympathisers, and marginalisation of those resistant to change. However, powerful groups in the organisation may regard this as a threat to their own power.

10.13.7 STAKEHOLDER RELATIONSHIPS

The previous section has dealt with the management of internal stakeholder groups. However, possibly an even more important task of the CEO is to manage relationships with external stakeholders. In many cases this may involve educating key stakeholders on the need for change. Paul Polman of Unilever provides a good example of this. He is convinced that the pursuit of short-term maximisation of shareholder value has led to widespread addiction to artificial highs, and ultimately to the financial crash of 2008–9.

In line with his commitment to long-termism, Polman has abandoned earnings forecasts and quarterly financial reports to the City. When this was announced, the share price dropped 10%. Although painful in the short term, in the long term this moved the Unilever shareholder base nearer to Polman's ideal, as it will have been those shareholders who sought short-term maximisation who sold out (Saunders 2011).

10.13.8 LEADING STRATEGIC CHANGE

Leadership is the process of influencing an organisation in its efforts towards achieving an aim or goal. This involves envisioning future strategy, aligning the organisation to deliver that strategy, and embodying change.

10.13.9 NINE ROLES OF STRATEGIC LEADERSHIP

In 2003, Loren Appelbaum and Matthew Paese identified nine roles of strategic leadership (Appelbaum and Paese 2003):

1 *Navigator*: Analyses large amounts of sometimes conflicting information. They understand why things happen and which factors really matter in the overall scheme of things.

2 *Strategist*: Focuses on creating a plan for the future. Strategists make decisions that drive the organisation towards its goals.

3 *Entrepreneur*: Always alert for creative and novel ideas. Able to develop ideas that have never been thought of.

4 *Mobiliser*: Gains support and resources they need to accomplish goals.

5 *Talent advocate*: Ensures the organisation has people with potential to meet present and future organisational needs.

6 *Captivator*: Builds upon an established foundation of trust to instil people with feelings of excitement and belonging.

7 *Global thinker*: Understands and accepts international cultural differences, and behaves in a way that accommodates people's varying perspectives.

8 *Change driver*: Focuses on continuous improvement. Identifies ideas for change and becomes the force driving the change home.

9 *Enterprise guardian*: Makes decisions that are good for the shareholder, even if the decisions cause pain to individuals or the organisation.

There is no one best style of strategic leadership. Successful strategic leaders adjust their style to the context they face – situational leadership.

10.13.10 THEORY E AND THEORY O

Beer and Nohria (2000) distinguish between Theory E and Theory O as approaches to managing change.

Theory E is top-down, pursues economic value, and emphasises structures and systems, and financial incentives. It can be characterised as a 'hard' approach to change. There are clear parallels to the traditional approach to strategic planning.

Theory O is bottom up as well as top down, based on developing organisational capability, culture change, participation and experiment. It is a 'soft' approach and has parallels with emergent planning.

However, Beer and Nohria also stress that combinations are possible:

- Start with Theory E and move on to Theory O – ie a hard approach to shock the organisation into facing up to change, and then a soft approach to actually getting the change through.
- Using both approaches simultaneously.
- Combining direction from the top with participation from below.
- Using incentives to reinforce rather than to drive change.

10.13.11 STYLES OF CHANGE LEADERSHIP

Johnson et al (2011, pp473–5) identify a number of styles of change leadership within the generic approaches.

- *Education*: persuading others of the need for and means of strategic change. This approach is long-term, but ultimately involves a willingness to change throughout the organisation.

- *Collaboration*: the involvement of those affected by strategic change in setting the change agenda. However, a negotiated agenda for change may be a compromise that satisfies nobody. If it does not satisfy key stakeholders, it may not work.
- *Participation*: the strategic leader retains co-ordination of and authority over processes of change but delegation of elements of the change process. This can help to build commitment, but runs the risk that employees may see it as manipulation.

The first three styles here are all examples of Theory O.

- *Direction*: The use of personal managerial authority to establish a clear strategy and how change will occur. Change is sold to subordinates who must implement it. This can provide fast change, but there is a risk of either passive or even active resistance.
- *Coercion*: The imposition of change or the using of edicts about change. This may be necessary in a crisis, but is very unlikely to be effective at other times.

These last two styles are examples of Theory E.

Style of leadership is partly a function of the personality of the leader, but great leaders can adapt their style to different contexts (situational leadership).

- *Time and scope*: Education or collaboration is suitable for incremental change, while control or directive approaches may be more suitable for transformational change.
- *Capability and readiness for change.*
- *Power*: A hierarchical organisation will tend to favour a directive style, while a networked or learning organisation will favour collaboration and participation.

They stress that the styles are not mutually exclusive. Styles can and often should change sequentially, while different styles may simultaneously be suitable for different stakeholders.

? REFLECTIVE ACTIVITY 10.7

BP and the Gulf of Mexico disaster

In the spring of 2010, a BP deep water oil rig in the Gulf of Mexico exploded, killing 11 people and injuring a further 17. This was bad enough, but the disaster then continued for a further six months, leaking 5 million barrels of crude oil into the Gulf, polluting beaches, and destroying the local inshore fishing industry.

Dealing with the disaster was the responsibility of BP's CEO, Tony Hayward, a trained geologist. His immediate handling of the disaster was seen as very complacent. He played down the scale of the disaster at all opportunities. *The Observer* (Wachman 2010) accused him of 'aloofness, wry smiles and stiff upper lip'. He was reported as saying that the amount of oil which had leaked was 'relatively tiny' compared with the 'very big ocean', while he also said during one tour of the Gulf, 'I want my life back.' He was also seen on a yacht at Cowes in July, not perhaps the most tactful way to take no doubt much needed relaxation (Webb 2010). In October he resigned as BP CEO, and was replaced by an American from Mississippi, Bob Dudley.

Reflecting back on the crisis later, Hayward said 'If I had a degree in acting from RADA rather than a degree in geology I may have done better.' He admitted that BP had virtually no contingency plans to deal with the crisis, because there had never been a serious deep water accident before. 'The equipment to contain and disperse on the seabed. . . had never been designed or built. It simply did not exist.' (Macalister 2010). BP was forced to make up its response as it went along, making it look 'fumbling and incompetent'.

Clearly Hayward was at fault for attempting to justify himself too much. The only sensible response in such a situation is to apologise immediately, profusely and frequently. However, there were some mitigating factors:

- BP was not the only company at fault. Halliburton, the US contractor infamous for its close association with ex-Vice President Dick Cheney, botched the cementing job on sealing off the well, while the rig operator Transocean had switched off fire alarms on the rig because of false alarms. The US oil regulator, MMS, also appeared to have been lax.
- The US media, and even to some extent President Obama, was determined to vilify BP. The company was always described as 'British Petroleum', to emphasise its foreignness, although it had changed its name to BP many years earlier. Half of BP's business and 40% of its shareholders are in the US. If anything, it is a US company which happens to be headquartered in London. By 2015, the disaster had cost BP an estimated $42bn, enough to run the NHS for three months, and more than the sanctions levied on Russia for invading Ukraine. As *The Economist* says, '[the penalties] feed the perception that [the US] legal system poses as serious a political risk to multinationals as anything they might encounter in emerging markets' (*Economist* 2015).
- Evidence has emerged that perhaps Hayward was right when he played down the extent of the disaster. In June, the Americans suggested that the slick might even reach Europe (Clark 2010), but by August, only a quarter of the leaked oil had not been dispersed, and by October, 93% of the Gulf fisheries were reopened.

Question

Critically examine the leadership style of Tony Hayward, and the management culture of BP.

Ridgeway and Wallace (1994) identify a number of competencies required for effective change leadership. These are:

- intellectual skills: intellectually curious and able to handle ambiguity
- influencing skills: assertive, proactive and energetic
- counselling and people skills: sensitive, flexible and adaptable, with a high tolerance of pressure.

While this list is solid, I think that it misses the true essence of change leadership. A good change leader must above all be driven by a vision of the future, and be able to inspire others with that vision. This involves a high sense of values, exceptional communication abilities, a sense of inspiration, and the ability to empower others with the vision. All of these qualities are illustrated in Case Study 10.10.

CASE STUDY 10.10

NELSON MANDELA

Nelson Mandela is almost universally recognised as the last, and one of the greatest, inspirational leaders of the twentieth century. His career illustrates the characteristics of a brilliant change leader.

Mandela was born in 1918, a member of a chiefly clan in the Xhosa tribe. He trained as a lawyer, and was drawn at an early age into the struggle against white domination through his membership of the African National Congress. The political struggle intensified in the 1950s after the election of the white supremacist National Party government, and the establishment of the apartheid system of racial segregation.

In the early 1960s, Mandela was on trial for his life. His statement from the dock in his trial put forward his vision: 'I have fought against white domination. I have fought against black domination. I have cherished the ideal of a democratic and free society in which all persons live together in harmony and with equal opportunities. It is an ideal which I hope to live for and to achieve. But, if needs be, it is an ideal for which I am prepared to die.'

Mandela was sentenced to life imprisonment on Robben Island, where he was to remain for 27 years. For much of this he was under a hard labour regime. A telling incident from his imprisonment throws more light on his vision. A particularly tough prison governor imposed a brutal regime on the prisoners, but when he was transferred, he wished Mandela and the other ANC leaders the best for the future. To Mandela, this illustrated the possibility of redemption. The man was brutal not because he had a brutal nature, but because he was conditioned by a brutal system. Like the Catholic Church, Mandela distinguished between the sin and the sinner. From this came his concept of redemption and reconciliation, which was to be a driving force of his presidency.

By the mid-1980s, another key player had entered the scene – F W De Klerk, the new National party leader. De Klerk recognised that the apartheid system must go, and that a settlement must be negotiated with the ANC. In Bridge's terms, this marked the end of the old system, and a move into the neutral transition zone. After lengthy negotiations, Mandela was released from prison in 1990. A new constitution was negotiated, leading to democratic elections in 1994, and the election of Mandela as the first democratic president of South Africa.

Mandela now faced his most severe test as a leader – how to hold the new South Africa together, and forge a new multiracial democratic state. He faced threats on all sides. A right-wing Afrikaner element was threatening civil war, and there was also an undeclared civil war between the ANC and the Zulu Inkatha Freedom Party. The Zulus were the largest tribe in South Africa, and resented the power held by the Xhosa Mandela.

Mandela's approach was to use symbolic acts of reconciliation. He visited the widow of the architect of apartheid, Hendrik Verwoerd. He also presented the rugby world cup to the victorious South African team wearing a South African rugby shirt. Rugby is an Afrikaner sport in South Africa, with almost totally white support. This action helped to reconcile the Afrikaner community to the new South Africa. He also pursued reconciliation with the Zulus. The Inkatha Freedom Party leader, Mangosuthu Buthelezi, was made minister for home affairs, and number three in the government, after Mandela and the vice-president Thabo Mbeki.

Mandela also used the idea of redemption through the Truth and Reconciliation Commission, which he launched with Archbishop Desmond Tutu. The idea here was that perpetrators of political crime could confess their involvement, and receive public absolution. Mandela insisted that this should apply as much to members of the ANC as to the agents of the apartheid regime.

Mandela's last great act of leadership was to recognise that by the end of his term as president in 1999, the transition phase had ended, and that South Africa was into the new beginning. Even his greatest admirers would not call Mandela a great administrator, and he recognised that a new type of more structured leadership was now needed. He therefore retired, leaving the way for Thabo Mbeki, a less charismatic but more structured politician, to succeed him.

When the sculptor Rodin was asked how he would sculpt an elephant, his reply was that he would start with a very large block of stone, and then remove everything which was not elephant.

Mandela had a similar vision. Everything which was not part of his vision of a democratic, multicultural South Africa was irrelevant, including bitterness, revenge and recriminations.

KEY LEARNING POINTS

- Quinn identifies three elements of strategy – goals, policies and programmes.
- Strategy can be analysed at several levels – corporate, business unit and operational.
- Approaches to strategy are connected with the nature of the environment. In the 1950s and 1960s, a placid environment encouraged the rational, logical corporate planning approach, while a more turbulent environment since the 1970s encouraged the more contingent, experimental strategic management approach.
- The leading exponent of the corporate planning approach was Igor Ansoff, while the leading exponents of the strategic management approach are Tom Peters, Michael Porter, Ralph Stacey, Gary Hamel and C K Prahalad, James Quinn, and Henry Mintzberg.
- It is important to distinguish between intended strategy and realised strategy.
- Strategic analysis is concerned with the strategic position of the organisation. What are the key characteristics of the organisation? What changes are going on in the environment, and how will these affect the organisation and its activities? This involves an analysis of the expectations of stakeholders, the culture of the organisation, the organisation's vision and values; the environment, as identified through a STEEPLE analysis; and the key resource areas of the business.
- The extent to which there is a mismatch (a gap) between current strategy and the future environment is a measure of the strategic problem facing the organisation.
- Vision, mission, values and objectives are closely linked, and often confused.
- The mission and objectives of the organisation are constrained by corporate governance, stakeholders, business ethics and culture.
- The mission statement provides a benchmark against which policies can be evaluated.
- Resource analysis is internal to the organisation. It is concerned with the strengths and weaknesses parts of SWOT analysis, and measures the efficiency and effectiveness of an organisation's resources.
- Prahalad and Hamel identify the concept of the core competences of the organisation – those factors which give the organisation its key competitive advantages.
- The concept of generic strategy was introduced by Michael Porter, and developed by Cliff Bowman.
- Possible strategies should be evaluated on three levels, suitability, acceptability and feasibility.
- There are two main models of strategic HR – the best practice and the best fit models.

- Transformational change is change which results in entirely new behaviour on the part of organisational members, and is in its very nature strategic.
- Bridges and Mitchell identify three stages in a change programme: saying goodbye, shifting into neutral and moving forward.
- Resistance to change can be rational, and must be managed. This is one of the key functions of HR in change management.
- The critical role of a change leader is to be inspirational and visionary.

REVIEW QUESTIONS

1 Explain what Quinn means by his three elements of strategy.

2 Why is the corporate planning approach inappropriate for a turbulent environment?

3 What is the role of gap analysis in strategic planning?

4 What are the differences between vision, mission, values and objectives?

5 What do you understand by the expression 'core competence'?

6 Explain the concept of generic strategy as developed by Michael Porter.

7 How can a proposed strategy be evaluated?

8 What are Pugh's six rules for managing change?

9 Why might individuals resist change?

10 What are the six stages in Beer's change model?

11 What are the key requirements for transformational leadership?

EXPLORE FURTHER

Further reading

The leading UK text on strategic management is Gerry Johnson and Kevan Scholes, *Exploring Corporate Strategy*. A new edition (the ninth) was published in 2011 (with Richard Whittington). Other valuable strategic management texts are John Thompson with Frank Martin, *Strategic Management: Awareness and change*, 5th edition (2005), Robert Clark, *Contemporary Strategy Analysis*, 5th edition (2005), and Bernard Burnes, *Managing Change; A strategic approach to organisational dynamics*, 4th edition (2004). *Academy of Management Executive* May 2002 (Vol 16 Issue 2) devotes virtually the whole issue to a discussion of Michael Porter's *Competitive Strategy*.

Useful websites

QuickMBA (www.quickmba.com/strategy/generic.shtml) has some useful articles on strategic issues, including one on Porter's generic strategies, which discusses fits between generic strategies and Porter's five forces. Knowledge@Wharton (www. knowledge.wharton.upenn.edu/category.cfm?cid=7), published by the Wharton Business School at the University of Pennsylvania, has useful strategic case study articles.

Audio and video material

The CIPD has produced a number of useful podcasts – Podcast 92 (July 2014), *What we're about – keeping true to your business's founding principles*, Podcast 56 (July 2011), *The importance of creating and sustaining a sense of shared purpose within organisations*, Podcast 32 (July 2009), *Building leadership capability for change: an interview with Gary Hamel*, and a double podcast, 31 parts 1 and 2 (May-June 2009) on *Making change happen*. YouTube has a video, Michael Porter on Competitiveness (youtube.com/watch?v=y51_cnpP99U).

THE UK BEER INDUSTRY

SEMINAR ACTIVITY 10.1

Introduction

The UK beer industry forms a fascinating case study. The structure of the industry is unlike that of the rest of British industry. Until the late 1990s, it was also very insular, with little contact with either European or world trends in the beer industry. In the last 15 years it has changed from almost exclusively UK ownership to a situation where most of the industry is owned by European or American companies. It is also an industry which has experienced enormous changes in its structure and product range over the last 40 years, and which was thrown into turmoil by government-inspired change since 1989.

In the rest of Europe (with the exception of the Irish Republic and Belgium) beer means lager – a pasteurised product which is light in texture and colour, and drunk cold. In the UK, lager has a large and growing share of the market, but beer in the UK also means ale and stout.

The beer industry in the UK was unusual before 1989 in being heavily vertically integrated. Some brewers controlled their own sources of raw materials, including malt and hops, and in some cases water, but much more important was forward integration. Much beer is draught beer, sold through pubs and clubs, known as the on-trade. The remainder is sold in bottle or can through off-licences and increasingly supermarkets, known as the off-trade. The off-trade, particularly beer sold through supermarkets, has

considerably increased its share of the market in recent years.

Of approximately 78,000 public houses in the UK in 1989, 46,000 were owned by brewers, including 34,000 owned by the big six companies. These were known as tied houses, because they were tied to the brewer, and obliged to sell his products, which may include spirits, wines and soft drinks as well as beer.

About 70% of tied houses were tenanted, with the other 30% being managed by employees of the brewery. Tenants pay rent, and take a margin on all goods and services sold. Traditionally, rents were pegged below market levels, but in return the tenant was obliged to buy his beer from the brewer at a price set by him.

Other public houses were free houses, which were owner-occupied, and normally could buy their beer from wherever they chose. However, in some cases a loan tie system operated. Here the brewer made a low interest loan to the publican, who in turn was obliged to sell the brewer's products.

The industry has been marked by a very considerable number of mergers, which reduced the number of companies from around 350 in 1950 to 64 in 1989. The structure of the industry was firmly established by the mid-1960s, when the Big Six brewers (Bass, Allied, Whitbread, Watney, Scottish and Newcastle and Courage) controlled 67% of production. By 1989 that had increased to 75%. In addition, as noted above, they owned nearly half the public houses.

Trends in the industry

Beer production in the UK peaked in the late 1970s, and has declined gently thereafter. Consumption has followed the same pattern. Beer consumption per head peaked in 1979 and by 2007 had fallen by over 20%. Over the same period, wine consumption has risen by two and a half times. In 1979 beer represented 60% of alcohol drunk, while by 2007 this had fallen to 40% (Institute of Alcohol Studies 2010).

Both imports and exports are historically of minor importance in the industry, mainly due to the cost of transporting a product which is mainly water. Beer which appears to be foreign is usually brewed in the UK under licence. However, in recent years the most rapidly growing segment of the market has been premium lager, much of which is imported from Europe.

The product mix decisively shifted in the period from 1960 to 1990. In 1960, 99% of all beer consumed was ale, while by 1990 lager had overtaken ale, and made up 51% of all sales. This has risen to 74% in 2010. Standard lager has a 40% share, and premium lager 34%. The main forces behind this seem to have been that the British acquired a taste for lager on European holidays; lager was seen as a young person's drink, and also as a drink that was acceptable to both sexes; its taste and quality were totally predictable, and national brands of lager were heavily promoted by the brewers.

Another long-term trend in the market has been the success of real ale. By the early 1970s, although most beer sold was still ale, it was overwhelmingly a pasteurised 'dead' product. Real ale, or cask-conditioned ale is by contrast a 'live' product, with the result that although its quality is much higher, it is more difficult to serve and does not keep as long as pasteurised beer. In the early 1970s, it appeared that real ale was likely to disappear from the market. It was then rescued by the activities of the Campaign for Real Ale (CAMRA), a classic example of an interest pressure group. Thanks to CAMRA's efforts, real ale revived and thrived. It is relatively easy to set up a real ale micro-brewery. Many free houses have done this, and you can more or less do it in your garden shed. Micro-breweries also have favourable tax treatment.

The Big Six brewers consolidated their dominant market position during the 1970s and 1980s through takeovers. They were also themselves in some cases the victims of takeovers. Watney was taken over by Grand Metropolitan, at the time predominantly a hotels group, but later a component of the wine and spirits conglomerate Diageo, while Courage passed to the Australian brewer Fosters. The third member of the Big Six to be involved in a merger was Allied, which merged with the food group J Lyons to form Allied Lyons.

The overall structure of the industry was analysed by the Monopolies and Mergers Commission in 1989. They identified over 200 brewing companies, classified as:

- six national brewers (Allied, Bass, Courage, Grand Met, S&N and Whitbread) who had 75% of UK beer production
- 11 regional brewers, such as Greene King and Wolverhampton and Dudley, who had 11% of beer production
- 41 local brewers, such as Adnams, who had 6% of beer production
- three brewers without tied estate (Carlsberg, Guinness and Northern Clubs Federation) who had 8% of beer production
- 160 other brewers, mainly very small and local, with less than 1% of beer production.

One key trend of the 1980s and 1990s was the growing internationalisation and homogenisation of the drinks industry. Throughout Europe, including the UK, the trend was towards lighter drinks, including lager rather than ale, light spirits like Malibu and Baileys rather than traditional spirits like gin or rum; wine, fruit juices, mineral water and colas.

Pubs became less of a male, beer-drinking stronghold. More pub drinking was done by women, who were more likely to drink lighter, less alcoholic drinks, and pubs became more of a family place to eat as well as to drink, although to some extent this trend was inhibited in the UK by the restrictive licensing laws. These in theory prohibited children under the age of 14 from entering bars. Increasingly the traditional pub was replaced by theme pubs (Irish-style bars, etc) and pub-restaurants.

An impact of the recessions at the beginning of the 1980s and 1990s was to encourage a trend towards drinking at home, rather than in pubs. This was assisted by a trend towards canned lagers rather than bottled beers, increasingly sold through supermarkets, usually at a price considerably below that charged in pubs.

The on-trade was also hit by demographic trends. The key pub drinking segment is the 18–25 age group, but from a peak of 23% of the adult population in the early 1980s, this age group fell to a trough of 14% in 1995.

In 1987, the Office of Fair Trading referred the brewing industry to the Monopolies and Mergers Commission (MMC) for investigation as a potential complex monopoly. This was legally possible although the biggest firm in the industry, Bass, only had a 22% share of the market, below the single firm monopoly threshold of 25%. Of particular concern was the way in which the price of beer was rising more rapidly than the general rate of inflation, and the potentially anti-competitive effects of the tied house system. The MMC carried out a painstaking investigation of the industry, and reported in 1989.

The MMC found that a complex monopoly did indeed exist, and that it acted against the public interest in three main ways:

- prices had been rising too rapidly
- consumer choice was restricted because one brewer usually did not allow another brewer's beer to be sold in his pubs
- the tenant's bargaining position was critically weaker than the landlord's (the brewer).

The MMC's particular concern was with the Big Six national brewers, and their recommendations were mainly aimed at this group. After negotiation these recommendations became the Beer Orders.

The Beer Orders specified that:

- no brewer should own more than 2,000 pubs, plus 50% of the excess number owned over 2,000. This meant that the Big Six brewers had to dispose of 11,000 pubs. None of the regional brewers owned more than 2,000 pubs
- tenants of pubs owned by brewers with more than 2,000 pubs (but not managers) to be allowed to stock a 'guest' beer (a beer brewed by a third party)
- the loan tie should be abolished.

The clear intention was that competition in the industry should be considerably increased, by limiting the impact of the tied house system, and by opening up opportunities for smaller brewers to get a foothold in the tied houses through the guest beer concept. The hope was that many, if not most, of the pubs sold by the Big Six would be sold to their tenants, and become free houses. Events were to show, however, that the brewers were ingenious in circumventing the spirit of the Beer Orders, while obeying its letter.

Trends in the industry since 1989

Production and consumption in the UK has continued to decline since 1989. In the 1990s, overall sales fell by 9%. Two major factors influencing the level of sales are the weather, with hot summers boosting sales, and major sporting events, particularly the football World Cup. Within this overall declining market, the trend towards lager has continued, with the biggest growth coming in imported premium continental lager.

The trend towards a growth in the off-trade at the expense of the on-trade (pubs and clubs) has continued. The off-trade grew from 20% in 1989 to around a third in 2000, 40% by 2006, and 49% in 2010. Supermarkets account for 28% of business. This trend has been assisted by technological developments which have enabled canned beer to be served with a head similar to that of draught beer – the so-called 'widget', a miniature nitrogen gas cartridge built into the can. The purchasing power of the big supermarkets is as significant in beer as in other grocery products. It was reported in the summer of 1993 that Tesco was able to import Stella Artois lager from Belgium at a price which undercut Whitbread, then the UK distributor, by 25%. The supermarkets also followed an aggressive pricing policy on beer, which saw its store price halve between 1998 and 2002. This policy was financed by a cut in the price which was paid to the brewers, described by Scottish and Newcastle as 'a blood bath'.

A further trend has come about as a result of the introduction of the European Single Market in January 1993. UK residents can now import alcoholic drinks from EU countries without limit, as long as the article has paid duty in an EU country, and it is to be consumed by the importer him or herself. Importing for resale is a criminal offence, but very difficult to prove.

Licensing laws are being liberalised. All-day opening is possible, between the hours of 11am and 11pm. A children's certificate scheme, allowing under-14s to be admitted, came into force in January 1995. The Licensing Act of 2003 allows pubs to alter their opening hours to suit local demand. This may mean that some pubs will choose to operate on a 24-hour basis.

The reaction of the brewing industry to the Beer Orders and other changes in the environment has been a massive restructuring. This started in October 1990 with a merger of the brewing interests of Courage and Grand Metropolitan. Under the deal, Courage acquired Grand Met's breweries, which it had originally obtained when it took over Watneys, and Grand Met ceased brewing entirely. In return Courage and Grand Met set up a joint company called Inntrepreneur, managed by Grand Met, which took over nearly all Courage's pubs and many of Grand Met's. This was the first appearance of the phenomenon which was to dominate the industry, the giant pubco, a company which ran pubs but did not brew.

In January 1993 came the launch of Carslberg-Tetley, a joint venture of Allied Lyons, the European seventh biggest brewer, and the Danish company Carlsberg, the European number three. Carlsberg already brewed lager in the UK, and because it had no tied estate, had built up its strength in the off-trade. Allied was strong on the on-trade, but weak on the off-trade. The deal was investigated and cleared by the MMC. Allied Lyons then merged with the wine and spirits company Domecq, and became Allied Domecq. The new company took the strategic decision to pull out of brewing. In 1996, Bass tried to acquire Allied's interest in Carlsberg-Tetley, but was blocked by the MMC. Carlsberg then bought out the Allied interest, but maintained the Carlsberg-Tetley name. Its Tetley Bitter is the best-selling cask ale in the UK.

Bass, the market leader, pursued a consolidation strategy, rationalising its production by closing three of its twelve breweries. The company sold 2,700 pubs to comply with the Beer Orders, many of them to new pubcos who agreed to take their beer from Bass. Whitbread, the long-standing number three in the industry, steadily lost ground, and fell to number five. In 1995, Scottish and Newcastle acquired Courage, immediately taking it to number one in the market.

By the late 1990s, the Big Six had shrunk to four – Bass, S&N, Carlsberg-Tetley and Whitbread. They were soon to shrink further when in quick succession the Belgian brewer Interbrew, maker of Stella Artois, acquired the brewing interests of first Whitbread and then Bass.

In addition, S&N moved into a leading position in Europe with the acquisition of Brasseries Kronenbourg, the number one beer brand in France, from the French food conglomerate Danone. Interbrew was then forced to sell off many of the brewing interests which it had acquired from Bass. These were purchased by the American number two, Molson Coors, while Interbrew retained ownership of the Bass brand. The American number one, and the biggest brewer in the world, Anheuser-Busch, brewed a small amount of Budweiser in the UK, but was not a leading player in the UK market. The series of mergers resulted in a market dominated by Scottish and Newcastle, InBev, and Molson Coors. S&N had a UK market share of 27% in 2006, Molson Coors 20%, and InBev (formed by the merger of Interbrew and the Brazilian company AmBev in 2004) 19% (*Economist* 2004d). Bass renamed itself Six Continents, and later demerged into two companies, Intercontinental Hotels, which concentrated on hotels, and Mitchells and Butlers, a pubco (Kew and Stredwick 2008).

In 2008, Scottish & Newcastle was acquired jointly by Heineken and Carlsberg. Heineken took S&N UK, while Carlsberg took most of the interests outside the UK, including Kronenbourg. By 2010, market shares in the UK were: Heineken 30.0%, Molson-Coors 21.9%, Anheuser-Busch InBev (the result of a merger in 2008), 19.8%, and others 28.2%. The global market was not quite so concentrated, with the leading three players (Anheuser-Busch InBev, SAB Miller and Heineken) having a 41.1% market share (Datamonitor 2011a, 2011b). The world growth areas are seen as Africa and Asia, especially China. AB InBev expects to generate 6% of its profits from China by 2021 (currently 1%, while SAB Miller expects to up profits there from 2 to 19% (Neville 2012).

In September 2015 it was announced that AB InBev had made a takeover approach to SAB Miller. This would produce a giant, with a 32% share of the global been market, and, possibly more important, 58% of global profits. The merger would have some global synergy. Although both are strong in Europe and North America, AB InBev dominates South America, and SAB Miller Africa (Holodny 2015).

A leading trend in the industry is the growth of pubcos. Pubcos basically see ownership of pubs as a property investment. Unlike breweries they have not been in the business long-term. They derive their income from two sources. One is the rents derived from tenants, the other is the modern version of the tied system, whereby the pubco could insist that beer was only bought from them, usually at inflated prices. The Small Business, Enterprise and Employment Act 2015 give tenants tied to the large pub companies the opportunity to opt for a rent-only deal, allowing them to buy their supplies of drinks on the open market at competitive prices. This clearly benefits both pub tenants and pub customers, but it also gives pubcos a greater incentive to sell off pubs, which are in any case in long-term decline, as increasingly people prefer to drink at home at much lower prices, with no risk of falling foul of drink driving laws (CAMRA 2015).

CAMRA reports that pubs in the UK are closing at a rate of 29 week. In 2014 1,722 pubs closed, with nearly a third of the closures were in London and south-east England. Many of these closures were for residential redevelopment, but there were also many cases which involved exploitation of a loophole in the planning laws. Because a pub is a retail establishment, it could be converted into another retail establishment, such as a supermarket, without planning permission. Nearly 200 pubs were converted into supermarkets in 2012–13, with more than half of these going to Tesco (CAMRA 2014). This loophole was blocked in 2015, when it was established that pubs designated by their local community as an Asset of Community Value (ACV) could not be converted without planning permission Pidd (2015). Six hundred pubs have been nominated as ACVs as at spring 2015.

Adnams plc

Adnams is a medium-sized real ale brewer based at Southwold in Suffolk. As well as brewing, it also has a pub estate, runs hotels and cook shops, imports and distributes wine, and operates a distillery.

Suffolk is a stronghold of real ale. The largest regional brewer, Greene King, is based in Bury St Edmunds, while the local brewer Mauldon, is based in Sudbury. Adnams stresses its East Anglian roots. It is the largest employer in Southwold. Casks of Adnams ale used to be delivered to the pubs of Southwold by horse and dray until September 2006, when the distribution centre was moved to a new location two miles outside the town. Adnams's most recent advertising campaign has the slogan: 'Beer from the Coast'.

The Sole Bay Brewery in Southwold was purchased in 1872 by George and Ernest Adnams. George left to emigrate to South Africa in 1880, and, as the company website puts it, 'was eventually eaten by a crocodile'. The company was incorporated in 1890, and has remained independent since then, The Adnams family was joined in 1902 by Pierse Loftus and his brother Jack, and Adnams still has members of each family on the board, with Jonathan Adnams as chairman and Simon Loftus as a non-executive director.

The company has a complicated corporate structure, which means that control is held by the Adnams and Loftus families through A (voting) shares, although these represent a small percentage of the total share capital. This arrangement runs counter to the best principles of corporate government, and has been criticised by one major holder of B (non-voting) shares. To compensate B shareholders, they receive a higher level of dividend than the A shares.

In his Chairman's Statement in 2011, Jonathan Adnams was critical of the government's escalator beer duty, increasing by more than inflation each year. He also criticised the tax subsidies given to microbreweries, worth on average £200,000 a year, and not available to Adnams (Adnams 2011a).

Adnams's profits peaked before the recession in 2007 at £4.2m, they then slumped to £1.5m in 2008, and had recovered to £3.3m in 2011, and £3.8m by 2014. The biggest driver of beer business success in 2011 was the market for drinking at home. Having had a tough 2010, this business made a major move forward in 2011. Over 20% of beer is now sold in bottles, cans and mini-casks.

Adnams opened a distillery in Southwold towards the end of 2010, which had a very promising first year of operation. The volumes sold have inevitably been small, but they are made at premium prices, and have exceeded expectations. The company started with vodka, gin and liqueurs, and sold its first single malt whisky in 2013, after maturing it in wood for the required three years. In 2013, Adnams won the best gin award at the International Wine and Spirit Competition, and followed this with the best vodka award in 2014, the first time this had been awarded outside Russia, Poland and France (Adnams 2014).

Adnams has long held to a values-led approach. To quote from the Adnams Values Statement (2011b):

● 'We're committed to managing the environmental impact of our operations, treating our employees well and having fun while we're at it.
● At Adnams we want to make sure that our impact on society is a positive one, expressing the company's values in ways which combine social and business benefits with long-term

sustainable success. We work for the long-term, looking beyond immediate success to a sustainable future.

- We deal with people openly and honestly, building strong, supportive relationships.
- We expect commitment to these values, and aim to translate them into everyday realities.
- We value our place in the community, and work to enhance the quality of local life.
- We take pride in all that we do, aiming to be a beacon to inspire others.'

In the 2014 Values Statement, Adnams's values were summarised as sustainability, diversity, fulfilment, quality, environment, integrity and commitment (2014b).

Another aspect of the values approach is staff remuneration. 'We make no claims to be high payers, but we do seek to provide a good range of benefits and we have stood clear of the gross pay inequality that has been seen in some other places. The ratio of our highest salary to our average salary is a relatively modest 8.8 times.' (Adnams 2011a).

Adnams's strategy is a differentiation one, based on the following:

- A strong identification with East Anglia in general, and Southwold in particular. As Southwold is an up-market seaside resort, this reinforces other elements of the strategy.
- Concentration on the premium sector of the real ale market. The company produces a limited range of beers, supplemented by special brews, which are either seasonal or commemorate particular events.

- Increasing emphasis on the off-trade, beer sold to drink at home. Premium real ale (unlike standard lager) is not subject to heavy price cuts in supermarkets.
- Brand extension, with the brand being stretched to include pubs and hotels, wine merchanting, upmarket cook shops, and now spirits.
- Sustainability. Adnams launched a carbon neutral beer in 2008 – its Adnams East Green product is produced for Tesco supermarkets. Adnams also opened a new brewery in Southwold in 2008, which it described as the first brewery in the UK to include a full energy recovery plant, and also switching to lightweight bottles in 2007 (Datamonitor 2009). It also operates an anaerobic digester, which feeds biomethane into the National Grid. The approach is moving on from 'doing the right thing' to being a 'restorative organisation' (Adnams 2014a).

Questions

1   Analyse key drivers of change in the UK beer industry since the 1980s, and identify opportunities and threats facing the industry in 2015.

2   Critically evaluate, using appropriate techniques, the following elements of Adnams's strategy:

- local identification
- the distillery
- sustainability.

CHAPTER 11

HR Delivery, Strategy and Performance

LEARNING OUTCOMES

When you have completed this chapter, you should be able to understand, explain and critically evaluate:

- the forces shaping the HR agenda
- models of HR delivery
- the links between HR and performance
- efficiency and effectiveness
- models of HR – best practice and best fit
- horizontal and vertical alignment
- HR practices and competitive strategy
- Miles and Snow and employment systems
- the resource-based view.

11.1 THE FORCES SHAPING THE HR AGENDA

The CIPD *HR Outlook Winter 2012–2013* (2013f) asked both HR leaders and business leaders (at or near board level), what challenges facing their organisation 'kept them awake at night'. Both groups identified the same five leading challenges, but in a different order. The leading challenges from an HR perspective were:

	HR leaders	**Business leaders**
Leadership capability	41%	18%
Economic uncertainty	28%	22%
Ensuring you have the skills and talents you need	27%	18%
Delivering on priorities with a limited budget	23%	25%
Managing the cost base	21%	20%

Key priorities for the next three years were seen as:

	HR leaders	**Business leaders**
Cost management	64%	57%
Increased customer focus	40%	33%

	HR leaders	Business leaders
Productivity	37%	33%
Growing domestic markets	36%	34%
Organisational flexibility	31%	30%
Innovation	24%	26%
New technology	24%	25%
Increased global presence	24%	22%

?   REFLECTIVE ACTIVITY 11.1

Forces driving the HR agenda

What do you think are the main forces driving HR in your own organisation, or one with which you are familiar?

11.1.1 MODELS OF HR DELIVERY

Chapter 2 touched briefly on some of the models of HR delivery. In this section, we will take this analysis further, and discuss three models: those of Tyson and Fell, Storey and Caldwell, and Ulrich.

The Tyson and Fell model

Using the analogy of a building site, Fell and Tyson (1986), identify three roles for HR (or the personnel function as it was then). These were:

- Clerk of the works – routine admin and clerical support to line managers
- Contracts manager – implementing procedures, administering industrial relations, and general trouble-shooting
- Architect – integrating HR into the broader business strategy.

This model formed the basis for Ulrich's three-legged stool model, which we will be discussing later in this chapter.

The Storey and Caldwell model

This model, originally developed by Storey (1992), and refined by Caldwell (2003), uses a two-by-two matrix map, with its dimensions the extent to which HR is strategic or operational, and the extent to which it is high or low profile.

- The internal contractor is responsible for negotiation with trade unions (if relevant), or with external sub-contractors, and also for service level agreements with other departments (as with Tyson and Fell's contracts manager).
- The service provider responds to routine operational requests from line managers (Tyson and Fell's clerk of the works).
- The change agent develops the HR culture, and works closely with top management on integrating HR into strategy (Tyson and Fell's architect).
- The adviser also works closely with management, but in a behind-the-scenes way, not necessarily as part of the management team. Caldwell found that this was the most common role.

Figure 11.1 The Storey and Caldwell model

Source: Adapted from Marchington and Wilkinson (2008)

Ulrich's HR roles

Dave Ulrich has contributed two models to the discussion. First, we look at his role of HR model, and later we will examine his three-legged stool model. Ulrich identifies five separate HR roles (Ulrich 2005).

- *Functional expert.* These are specialists, who can assist managers to make more effective people decisions. They may specialise in traditional HR areas like recruitment or reward, but they may also specialise in areas not always seen as part of core HR, like organisational development or business ethics. The main purpose of this role is to improve efficiency, and so add value to the organisation. If they do their job well, it will raise the status of HR in the organisation.
- *Human capital developer.* This role concentrates on helping people to develop, through training, career development, coaching or team building.
- *Employee advocate.* HR acts as a voice for employees in representing them to management and in enhancing their commitment and engagement. Ulrich sees this as a key role, harking back to the old welfare concept of personnel, but many in HR see it as of less importance.
- *Strategic partner.* HR acts as a partner to line managers in strategy formation and execution. This is an amalgam of Storey and Caldwell's change agent and adviser roles. We will examine the strategic or business partner role in more detail later.
- *HR leader.* Their role is to integrate the HR department, and to ensure that it functions efficiently and effectively.

?   REFLECTIVE ACTIVITY 11.2

Ulrich's roles of HR model

1   Can you spot anything which is missing from Ulrich's model?

2   Can an individual choose to specialise in one of Ulrich's five roles? Can an HR department?

Ulrich's three-legged stool model

The three legged stool model comprises shared service centres together with business partners and centres of expertise (Ulrich 1997).

Administrative tasks form the core of shared services activities, often in conjunction with a call centre and intranet. These tasks, previously performed locally by divisions or business units, are re-engineered, streamlined and centralised. This has the advantage of offering cost benefits through the economies of scale such a model provides. Savings can be considerable. In 2013, Derbyshire, Nottinghamshire and Leicestershire police forces set up a joint HR service centre, which was expected to save £900,000 – 41% of their total spend on HR administration (IDS 2013). Four shared service models are common:

- an in-house function
- an in-house function which also offers services on the open market to other organisations
- a unit offering HR services for a number of employees in a network – a number of local schools, for example
- an outsourced unit.

A variation on the shared service model is employee self-service (ESS) or manager self-service (MSS) systems. These are comprehensive HR information systems that enable non-HR employees and managers to undertake a number of HR-related activities themselves via a portal or intranet, without the need for any external intervention. For example, in an ESS system, individuals may be able to update their own personal details when their circumstances alter, while in an MSS system, managers might review absence records for all their staff.

CASE STUDY 11.1

SHARED SERVICE CENTRES IN CENTRAL GOVERNMENT

Shared services in the civil service have a mixed history. The Home Office shared service centre has been very successful. To date the Home Office's shared services drive has yielded over £41m in total savings and involves the delivery of HR, finance and procurement to 80% of potential users in the Home Office and their arms-length bodies. This included the integration of the Criminal Records Bureau (600 employees) and the Identity and Passport Service (4500 employees) HR services in 2010 (CBI 2012).

On the other hand, the Department for Transport shared service centre was a disaster. When the House of Commons Public Accounts Committee investigated the DfT in 2008, it was scathing. 'There are three ways in which implementation can fail: through delay in introducing planned developments; increased cost; or

by providing poorer services. The Department for Transport has suffered all three in implementing its shared services project...' The Department initially estimated that it would cost £55m to set up the Programme and that the benefits over the first 10 years would be £112m, yielding a net benefit of £57m. Current forecasts show that the Programme will cost £121m, benefits over the first 10 years will be £40m and the net cost to the Department will be £81m. Users of the system have little confidence in its abilities and the Department's performance indicators show a very poor and variable level of performance for the whole of the first year of operations. In some cases the service is worse than that previously provided.' (House of Commons Public Accounts Committee 2008).

Many organisations have for some time tried to develop relationships with key business units. In the Ulrich model this role is described as a business partner. These individuals are expected to work together with other managers on strategic development, organisational design and change management. This has three elements (Marchington and Wilkinson 2008):

- playing devil's advocate by asking difficult questions
- helping to craft strategies
- developing strategic skills in the management team.

When Ulrich originally developed the concept of the business partner, he saw this as including partnering by HR with both top and line management. Here we will look at strategic business partnering, which is solely concerned with top management. The CIPD Factsheet, *HR Business Partnering* (2014e), defines business partnering as a 'process whereby HR professionals work closely with business leaders and/or line managers to achieve shared organisational objectives. This means that the HR business partner becomes embedded within the business'. Business partners can take many forms. The role can even vary in the same organisation. At the Ministry of Defence, there are at least three types of business partner: single job-holders covering a whole business unit or area; people providing support at a similar level but in specialisms such as learning and development; and those who provide operational and even administrative support that can't easily be swept up into shared services (Arkin 2007).

In order to be a successful strategic business partner the HR professional needs to be 'business savvy'. This has three elements:

- business savvy – a deep appreciation of what makes the business successful
- context savvy – an understanding of the external environment of the business
- organisation savvy – a deep understanding of people, culture, leadership and change.

The successful strategic business partner has skills which are not necessarily learnt on a professional HR course:

- influencing and political skills
- strategic thinking
- ability to deliver results to achieve targets
- leadership
- business knowledge.

Peter Goodge (2004), says that there are five key elements to becoming a successful strategic partner.

1 Learn the business – HR aims to improve the use of human resources, business partners aim to improve the business.

2 Build great relationships, using political skills.

3 Build diverse relationships.

4 Be at the leading edge of HR.

5 Build credibility.

One major weakness of the strategic business partner model is that it does not happen in practice. One survey found that although 65% of HR directors called themselves strategic partners, they spent only 15% of their time on strategic work. They spent more of their time on operational issues (*People Management* 2011).

HR leaders also had very different perspectives on their strategic value to top management. When asked 'to what extent do you agree that the HR director is a trusted adviser to the CEO?', 74% of HR directors agreed, while only 15% disagreed. Only 41% of

CEOs agreed, while 24% disagreed (CIPD 2013a). That was echoed by research from consultancy CEB in 2014, which showed three out of four senior HR leaders expect their business partners to be strategic partners, but fewer than one-fifth of managers feel that's happening (Stevens 2015).

The third leg of the stool is Centres of Expertise with capability in such areas as resourcing, employee relations, reward and training, giving professional support to business partners, often developing detailed policy for corporate HR and acting as a reference point for shared services agents dealing with complex issues raised by clients.

The three-legged stool model has been heavily criticised by Reilly (2000). He argues that splitting HR creates a silo culture, with boundary disputes between the three legs. Accountability is not always clearly defined. Who is responsible for delivery in line with service level agreements? Reilly argues that service centres contribute most to meeting agreed targets, but the main interface with managers is with the business partner. Managers are frustrated because they no longer have a 'one stop shop' for HR advice, and unscrupulous managers can shop around the legs of the stool until they get the answer they want. It is nobody's job to provide operational, as distinct from strategic, support to managers, leaving what he describes as a 'Polo mint' type hole at the centre of the organisation. Other critics have pointed out that the three-legged stool model is not suitable for medium-sized organisations, which only need HR generalists.

These criticisms were tackled by Ulrich in 2008 (Ulrich, Younger and Brockbank 2008). He argued that his model was never intended to be prescriptive. He envisaged three types of organisations, with different HR requirements:

- small and medium-sized businesses, where HR is delivered by generalists
- holding companies, where HR is delivered by generalists within subsidiary companies, while the corporate centre's HR requirements are minimal
- diversified businesses, where the three-legged stool model is most relevant.

Ulrich et al also expanded the original three legs to five, in an attempt to meet the Polo mint criticism:

- service centres
- centres of expertise
- embedded HR (the old business partners)
- corporate HR, working with top management on corporate initiatives
- operational executors dealing with day to day HR problems, so filling the Polo mint hole.

Surveys have shown that a minority of organisations operate a three-legged stool system. In 2009, Lancaster University found that 64% of organisations had business partners, 35% HR service centres and 38% centres of expertise (Hird et al 2009). In 2013 the CIPD found that 28% of organisations used a three-legged stool model, while 41% had a single central HR team (CIPD 2013a). IDS (2013) found that just over half of organisations had a single central HR team.

11.2 DEVOLUTION OF HR TO LINE MANAGERS

There is frequently an underlying tension between HR and line managers.

- The line manager regards HR as out of touch with business realities, pushing through policies like work–life balance which they feel may conflict with their business goals.
- The line manager sees HR as constraining their authority to take decisions.
- They see HR as unresponsive and slow to act.
- They see HR as idealistic, pushing policies which are fine in theory but hard to put into effect (Marchington and Wilkinson 2008).

One solution to these tensions is to encourage line managers to take on more responsibility themselves for HR activities, although this responsibility is normally shared with HR, often through a business partner role. This should increase the line's ownership of these activities.

There are several problems involved in any delegation of HR to line managers. These include:

- *Lack of HR skills and competencies among line managers.* Their views on HR issues are likely to be based on gut instinct or prejudice. As a result they must be prepared to accept guidance from their HR partner and/or undertake more training themselves.
- *Disdain for HR work.* Some line managers think that HR is easy, and are resistant to advice. They are likely to be particularly hostile to the softer areas of HR, like employee engagement, which they may well see as pandering to employees.
- *Lack of time.* Line managers may feel that they are being given HR responsibilities on top of their normal functional duties, and so may give HR issues low priority.
- *Inconsistency.* Line managers may take an inconsistent approach to issues such as discipline or dismissals. This is important, as there are legal requirements, and it is essential in order to stay within the law that procedures are followed.

There is some evidence that the impact of HR professionals on line managers may be decreasing (Churchard 2011). In a survey quoted by Churchard, the percentage of line managers who recognised HR's influence on the business was down from 69% in 2010 to 56% in 2011. At the same time the number who agreed that HR adds value to the business was down from 68% to 59%. However, 87% of HR professionals feel that they add value. Just as with strategic business partners, HR has a higher opinion of itself than its internal customers have of it.

A more serious criticism of the devolution of HR to the line is put forward by Francis (2005). She makes the point that as HR tasks are devolved to line management, HR is freed up for a more strategic business partner role, which HR professionals see as attractive. Transactional, day-to-day HR is devolved either to the line or to service centres. The result is that the employee champion role of HR is downgraded, and not seen as a viable career move. Employees as a result will lose confidence in HR as their advocate. As Harry Donaldson, Scottish regional secretary of the GMB union, is quoted as saying in Francis's article, 'Employees will question whether their employer really cares about them. The role of employee champion will become the sole preserve of trade unions.'

A similar point is made by Whiteley (2013). He argues that many HR business partners have become captured by the finance department, and have aligned so firmly with the business partnering that they have deleted all notion of the people. To be a full HR business partner means understanding more fully the contribution of staff and their ability, and not being slave to expense-reduction tactics. Employee engagement has been sacrificed. To survive in a lean economy, businesses need to harness the commitment of their employees, not alienate them.

11.3 HR AND PERFORMANCE

11.3.1 EFFICIENCY AND EFFECTIVENESS

Performance depends on both efficiency and effectiveness. Efficiency is a measure of economy in the use of resources. Broadly, it is measured as outputs divided by inputs. It involves avoiding waste, avoiding over-manning, increasing labour productivity, generally 'doing things right'.

Effectiveness is a measure of how far an organisation achieves its goals. It is about 'doing the right thing'. Both are important, but as you will see from the matrix below, ultimately effectiveness is more important.

Figure 11.2 Efficiency and effectiveness

	Effective	Ineffective
Efficient	Organisation succeeds at minimum cost	Organisation controls costs, but does not succeed
Inefficient	Organisation succeeds but at high cost	Organisation fails

? REFLECTIVE ACTIVITY 11.3

Efficiency and effectiveness

- You are responsible for induction within your organisation. Suggest one efficiency and one effectiveness measure for your work.
- Can you think of a process (not necessarily in HR) which is both efficient and effective?

11.3.2 OPENING THE 'BLACK BOX'

Although there may be considerable doubt concerning the actual role HR should perform and how it should be done, human resource professionals established a place at the senior management table by the early 1990s through their ability to identify and solve practical problems in fields such as recruitment, employee relations and training. HR professionals and researchers then turned their attention to interpreting and reinforcing the maxim that 'people make the difference'.

Researchers have attempted to identify whether adopting HR practices can make an observable difference in practice to organisational performance in measurable terms. If it can be proven that the adoption of human resource systems, policies and procedures leads to higher performance, then this will reinforce the claim that HR has to a seat on the top table and a co-responsibility for strategic initiatives. This has often been referred to as 'opening the black box'.

In attempting to examine the impact of HR practices on organisational performance, a number of researchers have discovered some impressive and direct impacts and influences. This is referred to by Ramsey et al (2000) as the 'high road' approach to management, in which organisations choose to compete primarily on quality and rely especially on human resource development and employee contributions to succeed in this.

Much of this research has been carried out in America, with the best-known researcher being Mark Huselid (1995). He carried out in-depth surveys in top companies, matching the nature of the HR practices against performance measures, such as growth, productivity and profits. Using market value as the key indicator, he found that organisations with significantly above-average scores on using HR practices provided an extra market value per employee of between $10,000 and $40,000. He also found that the introduction of such practices led to an immediate impact (Guest 1998).

In the UK, a CIPD-financed project by the University of Sheffield's Institute of Work Psychology (West and Patterson 1998) concluded that HR practices are not only critical to business performance but also have a greater importance than an emphasis on quality, technology and R&D in terms of influence on bottom line profits. For example, effective HR practices were found to account for 19% of the variation in profitability and 18% in productivity, while R&D accounted for only 8%. This led them to conclude that the most important area managers should emphasise is the management of people.

Some of these findings have arisen from broad surveys across sectors and others from selected industries. Thompson (2000), for example, investigated 400 UK aerospace companies and concluded that high performing organisations, as measured by value added per employee, tend to use a wider range of innovative HR practices covering a higher proportion of employees. The greatest differentials between higher and lower performing organisations (as measured by value added per employee) was in the use of two way communication systems, broader job gradings and employees being responsible for their own quality.

A more detailed survey of such studies can be found in Marchington and Wilkinson (2008).

11.4 THE ROLE OF HUMAN RESOURCES IN RAISING PERFORMANCE

It therefore appears evident from research detailed above that human resources can make a sizeable contribution towards raising organisational performance. There are two major viewpoints as to how this can be done:

- Firstly, a number of projects have been set up to examine what makes up a truly exceptional collection of HR practices, often called 'bundles' that raises performance in the organisation.
- Secondly, there has been a considerable debate, one that is still very much alive, as to whether such a collection of practices (called 'best practices') will work in every situation, or whether the context and nature of the organisation puts different demands upon the practices to be operated (called 'best fit'). A third model is the resource-based model, which has close links to the core competence model.

11.4.1 BEST PRACTICE APPROACH – 'BUNDLES' OF HR PRACTICES

At the same time that researchers were attempting to prove conclusively that successful and effective HR practices improved the bottom line performance, it became clear that a differentiation needed to be made between such practices: in effect, that some worked better than others and, more critically, that although individual practices may be relatively unsuccessful, when brought together in a 'bundle' their combined outcome was much greater than their individual contribution. A number of writers have formulated these bundles into what they call a system of 'High Performance' or 'High Commitment', indicating that using the full set will inevitably lead to improved organisational improvement. It is emphasised by all the researchers that these bundles have to be coherent and integrated to have their full effect.

The *level of commitment* shown by employees is seen as key to high performance. Without such a commitment, employees will not be prepared to develop their skills and competencies, take on board the enhanced responsibilities for quality, work organisation and problem solving and 'go the extra mile' to come up with improvements and innovations or improve the customer's experience. That is why a number of researchers use the level of commitment as a key reflection of organisational success from a people management viewpoint.

For Purcell et al (2003), a committed employee will use discretionary behaviour in that the employee can give co-operation, effort and initiative because they want to, arising out of the fact that they like their job and feel motivated by the systems in place, especially the HR ones.

Researchers have found that a high level of commitment comes about from the implementation of the following HR practices:

Employee involvement

The thinking here is that it is impossible to gain the employees' trust if they do not both have the essential business information available to management and that they have at least the opportunity to be consulted on important issues that may affect their jobs and the way they are carried out. This passes the message that employees are treated as mature, intelligent beings, not just 'hands' or 'labour' who leave their brains in their lockers. The process of involvement can include briefing groups, staff surveys, focus groups or more sophisticated systems such as quality circles or recognition schemes. It can also extend to financial involvement through employee share-ownership. Marchington (2001) points out from his research that these practices are very popular with employees (80–85% of employees involved in such practices want them to continue), although he adds the disillusioning caveat that some employees enjoy working with them because it is 'better than working' or 'gives me a half hour off work'.

Employee voice

Millward et al (2000), by using the data from the 1998 Workplace Employee Relations Survey (WERS), have shown the close association between positive responses in attitude surveys and direct voice arrangement. A 'voice' for the employees does not have to be through a formal trade union and it is certainly not just ensuring there is a formal grievance procedure. The importance of this practice is that the employer recognises the importance of employee group viewpoints and suggestions and that the employee does not feel isolated so important issues can be raised in a formal (or informal) setting without the employee themselves having to, in effect, raise their heads above the parapet.

There has been a greater emphasis in recent years on the concept of '*employee engagement*' which combines the better features of involvement and employee voice (see Seminar Activity 11).

Harmonisation of terms and conditions

'Everybody works for the same team' is a common form of encouragement from senior management but falls on deaf ears if there is a clear manifestation of differing benefits at varying levels in the organisation. When Japanese companies began setting up satellite operations in the UK in the late 1970s and early 1980s, one of the surprises to commentators was the degree of egalitarian symbols on display.

In Nissan in Sunderland, for example, there was one canteen serving everybody and it was frequented by all staff including senior management; everybody was on the same level of holiday entitlement and wore the same overalls. Employees respected the equality and it fed the belief in the 'one company' ethos leading in turn to effective teamworking at all levels (Wickens 1987).

Employment security

The 'jobs for life' culture evident some 30 to 40 years ago no longer exists. Rather, it never really existed in the first place, except in pockets of the public services, such as prisons and the post office. Employees may have had a clear, well-trodden career pathway set out, but the precise directions, both geographically and occupationally, may have worked out very differently to expectations and preferences. In the last 20 years, the global and business environmental changes have caused such changes in employment that the pathway has become one made up of crazy paving and employees have to lay it themselves!

So how can any business promise employment security? The theorists indicate that the security is of a different dimension. There may be short-term guarantees of employment, such as 12 months or of the life of a large-scale contract or, more usually, it is the cultural imperative of the organisation that redundancies will only take place as a very last resort. Internal transfers, skills re-training, short-time working will all be alternatives to try to extend the employee's contract as long as possible to get over difficult times. It is, in effect, the opposite of the tough employer's 'hire and fire' short-term employment policy. It keeps to the HRM thinking that the employee is a critical asset, not a cost to be reduced.

Alongside these practices to encourage commitment, there are a group of practices that integrate with the organisation's business strategy:

Sophisticated recruitment and selection

Sophistication is essentially the combination of recognising the importance of bringing into the organisation the right people with the right skills and personality (having a strategic approach to human resource planning) and carrying out careful and detailed recruitment and selection procedures. These procedures especially refer to using psychological tests and structured interviews that match people effectively to the organisational culture, to the job and the team requirements.

Extensive training and development

It is clearly not enough to select the right people. In a swiftly changing world, employees need to constantly learn new jobs, which involves developing their skills and knowledge. They must also be prepared for enlargement of their jobs and to be ready for promotion opportunities. The emphasis switches in a subtle way from the organisation organising training courses to the organisation encouraging employees (individually or in groups) to undertake learning experiences, which can take many forms. The 'ideal' form of this item in the bundle is of employees undertaking self-directed life-long learning with the framework of a 'learning organisation'.

Self-managed teams

The practice of allowing teams to have greater control over their work is a relatively recent one, although theorists, such as Mayo and his colleagues at the Hawthorne production plant in America in the 1930s, have been advocating it throughout the twentieth century. It is linked closely to involvement and, in a fully-fledged system, team members are involved in decisions concerning work rotas, breaks, changes in production processes, leave and sickness arrangements. Moreover, they are encouraged to think about and promote local improvements on an individual and team basis. It involves reducing the power and day-to-day authority of local management, but, at the same time, retains their accountability. The research has shown that, when it works well, it is closely associated with high productivity and overall performance.

Extensive systems of flexibility

If constant and rapid change is the norm, then successful organisations need a workforce that is flexible enough to respond quickly to the required changes. They need to be multi-skilled, willing to work hours that suit the customer and willing to switch jobs and locations when necessary. The organisation also needs to have in place facilities to increase and reduce the employee numbers when required through systems of annualised hours or use of temporary and short-term contracts or by outsourcing work.

Performance pay

The emphasis on high performance outcomes inevitably has meant that pay systems are geared to reflect the level of performance. Employees' pay at all levels is contingent; in other words, it has an element that varies depending on the success of the outcomes. Examples of these systems can include bonus schemes for production employees and call centre staff, incentive systems for sales and service staff and executive bonuses for directors. Commitment should be encouraged by aligning the pay of employees with organisational performance.

Given that a bundle of HR practices leads to improved performance, then it follows that using this bundle is the best thing to do. In theory, it becomes a set of 'best practices' which can be universally applied.

The CIPD Shaping the Future project (Evans 2008) identified a number of enablers and barriers to high performance. Enablers included:

- shared purpose
- clear strategy
- strong leadership
- performance management that is lean and mean but not destructively so.

Barriers included:

- lack of clarity in performance management
- middle managers, who may not be good leaders.

HR could be either an enabler, if it took up the opportunity to make a strategic contribution, or a barrier, if it is isolated from the rest of the business.

? REFLECTIVE ACTIVITY 11.4

NHS workers and best practice HR

Recent research in the NHS asked 200 workers at a range of levels to indicate how they saw HR practices fitting together. Three sets of practices were generally seen as combined together. These were:

- professional development, through appraisal, training and career development
- employee contribution, through communication, teamworking and employee involvement and participation
- the employee deal, through recruitment, pay, non-monetary rewards, work-life balance and employment security.

Question

Do you agree with these combinations of HR practices? Would you put other combinations together?

Source: adapted from Marchington and Wilkinson (2008)

When reading the previous section it may have occurred to you that there does not appear to be much consensus as to what HR practices make up the full set. Each item of research comes up with a different set of best practices, some of which overlap with other research but each has a special leaning. Angela Baron of the CIPD suggests that the term high performance does little more than describe an approach to managing organisations that aims to stimulate discretionary effort and utilise skills. As she says, is this any different to good HR? She also doubts how widespread the approach actually is. A 2008 survey by the UK Commission on Employment and Skills found that just under a third of UK organisations take a high performance approach, but as she says, this may be because they were not sure what the term meant but thought it sounded like a good thing (Baron 2011). On the other hand, a report quoted in *People Management* in June 2012 suggests half of staff are not aware of their organisation's HR polices (*People Management* 2012).

In America, Bosalie and Dietz (2003) have reviewed 10 years of research in this area and have found little that recommends a common approach with the practices reported more extensively being training and development, participation and empowerment, performance pay and information sharing through involvement.

On the other hand a 2012 study by the Boston Consulting Group and the World Federation of People Management Associations (Strack et al 2012) found that companies highly skilled in core HR practices experienced up to 3.5 times the revenue growth and up to 2.1 times the profit margin compared with less skilled companies. In particular, high performance companies

- build stronger leaders
- do more to attract, develop and retain talented people
- treat and track performance with transparency.

However, a closer reading of the report shows that BCG were examining each best practice in isolation, they were not evaluating a package of best practices.

There is also doubt about the universality of the best practice approach – will it lead to better performance in all organisations, regardless of the environment in which they operate? Purcell has stated that this claim leads us 'down a utopian cul-de-sac' (Purcell 2003, p36).

Marchington and Grugulis (2000) suggest that best practice (high commitment HR) is more likely when:

- employers are able to take a long-term perspective
- labour costs are a low proportion of total costs
- knowledge workers can be rewarded for using their discretion
- firms and workers are in a strong market position.

This package would seem to fit perfectly with a high-tech Silicon Valley company such as Hewlett Packard in the 1990s, but the struggles which HP has had in the 2000s suggest that even here the link may be transitory.

? REFLECTIVE ACTIVITY 11.5

Nike and best practice

In the late 2000s the sportswear company Nike developed an HR training programme to strengthen HR in its contract manufacturers. Eight factories in Vietnam and eight in southern China were involved in 2008–9.

Each factory completed an employee satisfaction survey to better understand the top issues facing workers, and to measure trust and respect in the factory. Factories brought their survey results to the HR training sessions so that they could apply the insights of their workers to the creation of action plans and HR best practice.

Training modules included hiring practices, worker training and development, worker empowerment and retention, worker-management communication, compensation, performance management, and building a strong HR function. The factories also established a learning community to promote ongoing learning and sharing of practices.

Following the training, the factories implemented their specific action plans. One set goals was to reduce the number of workers reporting dissatisfaction with the behaviour and attitude of their direct supervisor from 15 to 5%. Another set goals to increase the technical skill levels of the workers.

Comments on the programme included:

- 'The HRM workshop was able to highlight the importance of having a strong HR system.'
- 'If HR is strong, we use effective processes to recruit the right people and develop them with a foreseeable career path.'
- 'The HR tools we received are helping us follow our projects closely.'
- 'HRM created a community where each factory set out the boundary of its own experience and knowledge. In return, each factory received many good practices.' (Nike 2010).

Question

To what extent do you think that this case study provides evidence to support the best practice model?

CASE STUDY 11.2

L'OREAL AND THE TALENT ADVANTAGE

L'Oreal is the world leader in beauty products. The linchpin of its growth strategy is building 'talent advantage' – a strategic approach to developing its talent portfolio and allocating resources:

1   incentivising leaders to identify and develop talent in their teams

2   motivating talent to move to strategic high-growth areas by linking career development opportunities to those areas

3   appointing talent managers in crucial markets to reinforce local recruitment, and promote the employer brand

4   establishing talent incubators to feed the talent pipeline

5   enhancing career visibility and leadership expectations by establishing clear, uniform definitions of talent and performance standards.

11.5 BEST FIT APPROACH

Because the extensive research reveals such a varied set of bundles and performances, considerable doubt has been shed on whether the application of the set of bundles or best practices will lead inevitably to improved performance. Many writers, therefore, have taken an alternative view that there is no 'holy grail' of practices which will magically improve organisational performance. What works well in one organisation may fail dismally in another where the context may be totally different. In a private sector organisation (a manufacturing company, for example), you may well expect performance pay to be widespread and to form the bulwark of performance management and motivation systems; however, in the voluntary sector, (a hospice charity, for example), it is highly unlikely that any of the staff would work under a performance pay scheme. The context, the vision, the values – they are so different.

Huselid himself comes down firmly on the side of a range of possible bundles, based on the reasoning that sustained competitive advantage depends partly on being able to develop arrangements that are hard to imitate (the resource-based concept). If the 'holy grail' was quite distinctive, then every organisation would immediately adopt it and the competitive advantage would be lost.

Thompson (2000), similarly, is reticent in recommending wholesale adoption of the innovative HR practices associated with high performing aerospace companies: 'That is probably too simplistic a message' (p19). Marchington and Grugulis (2000) adopt the same viewpoint: 'Best practice, it seems, is problematic... there are times when they appear to be contradictory messages.' (p1121).

How do you know which HR practices an organisation should adopt? Only by a combination of knowing and understanding the true nature and strengths of the organisation, so you can eliminate those practices that have little chance of success, and then by experiment.

In the knowledge-intensive firms, the best fit of practices have been found to be the kind that develop intellectual and social capital needed in order to acquire business and manager customer relationships. Here, the crucial aspect is the development of knowledge-sharing processes, not just the knowledge and skills of the workforce (Swart et al 2003).

Purcell's (1999) distinct preference for 'best fit' has led him to urge a much greater emphasis on sharing employee knowledge throughout the organisation. If organisations have unique circumstances that require unique sets of HRM practices, then it is vital that the knowledge and understanding of both circumstances and practices are held in common by all employees. With Peter Boxall, he argued that best practice HR is much more likely where the production system is capital-intensive or high-tech. Firms characterised by intense, cost-based competition, such as supermarkets, typically adopt a low-skill model of HR (Boxall and Purcell 2008). An example of a highly successful company whose HR practices could not be further from the best practice model is Ryanair, which was extensively discussed in Chapter 10.

Although there appears to be extensive evidence of HR practices adding to organisational improvement, there are a number of critics who doubt the close association. The greatest is Legge (2001) whose scepticism has been consistent and vociferous for many years. She points out the vagueness of definition of the 'best practice', such as performance pay, and the appropriateness of the measures used for organisational success. She also doubts whether the use of the practices actually influence the performance (the lack of causality).

There have also been studies that demonstrate that HRM practices can lead to a deterioration in working life. Danford et al (2004) researched the high performance HR practices introduced in an aerospace company but found some major negative impacts on the employees, such as substantial downsizing, a superficial implementation of empowerment and a lack of trust between the parties.

Best fit HR has also been linked to the life cycle model. For example, an organisation in the start-up stage will concentrate in its recruitment on obtaining the best workers to fill gaps, in the growth stage it is more concerned with succession issues, in maturity in maintaining its workforce, and in decline in managing downsizing (Farnham 2010; Kochan and Barocci 1985).

11.5.1 HORIZONTAL AND VERTICAL ALIGNMENT

One plausible model in the best fit tradition is that of horizontal and vertical alignment, most fully developed by Gratton and Truss (2003). This envisages HR in three dimensions:

- *vertical*: an alignment between organisational goals and strategy on the one hand, and HR policy on the other

- *horizontal*: an alignment between different HR policies so that they are consistent with each other
- *action or implementation*: how are the HR polices actually applied? Gratton and Truss see two dimensions to this: the experiences by employees of HR policies, and the behaviours and values of the managers as they are implementing policy.

Taking the first two dimensions – vertical and horizontal – we can envisage the possible combinations on a two by two matrix, as shown in Figure 11.3.

Figure 11.3 The horizontal-vertical alignment model

Source: adapted from Gratton and Truss (2003)

If we add the third dimension, action, we then have eight possible combinations rather than four. The four combinations given above are consistent with strong action.

- *Tactics driven* – weak horizontal alignment, weak vertical alignment, strong action. Here the HR function is primarily administrative, concerned with day to day issues, with limited relationship to the overall aims and objectives of the business or to each other.
- *Process driven* – weak vertical alignment, strong horizontal alignment, strong action. This combination occurs in organisations where the HR team has weak business or strategic skills but excellent HR process skills, coupled with the capability to translate these skills into practice.
- *Strategy driven* – strong vertical alignment, weak horizontal alignment, strong action. Here, the overall strategy drives HR, often through the performance-management processes. However, the HR policies do not necessarily reinforce each other.
- *Strategy and process driven* – strong vertical alignment, strong horizontal alignment, strong action. The 'ideal type' but difficult to achieve and hard to sustain.

Sitting behind each of the 'strong action' combinations is a corresponding 'weak action' combination.

- *Mere tactics speak* – weak vertical alignment, weak horizontal alignment, weak action. This type of organisation is purely reactive, and likely to stagger from crisis to crisis.
- *Mere process speak* – weak vertical alignment, strong horizontal alignment, weak action. The HR function has a strong, integrated set of HR policy goals but they are disconnected from the overall objectives and inadequately put into effect.

- *Mere strategy speak* – strong vertical alignment, weak horizontal alignment, weak action. The people strategy is clearly articulated but is not translated into a coherent set of HR policies nor implemented by line managers. Fine words, but nothing happens.
- *Mere rhetoric* – strong vertical alignment, strong horizontal alignment, weak action. Here, there is a strongly articulated people strategy that is linked into the business strategy and also demonstrates strong internal HR policy linkages, but the whole is not put into action in the day-to-day behaviour of managers nor reflected in the experiences of employees. As with mere strategy speak, nothing happens.

CASE STUDY 11.3

CHELSEA AND WESTMINSTER HOSPITAL

Chelsea and Westminster Hospital is one of the organisations which Gratton and Truss studied over a ten-year period. At the start of the study in 1993–94, the situation was 'mere tactics speak'. The incoming HR director was faced with a situation where only 27% of employees thought the HR department had a clear overall strategy guiding its activities. There were few formalised HR policies, and no systematic attempts had been made to link them to each other or to the hospital's goals. The hospital was failing to recruit and retain the individuals it needed, morale was poor and patient care needs were not always being met.

The first priority of the new HR director was to establish the credibility of the department by improving service delivery, moving the hospital from mere tactics speak to tactics driven. The next phase was to examine in detail the HR policies and practices within the hospital and to ensure that they were mutually reinforcing, and this was largely completed by 2000. However, vertical alignment remained weak. The business goals of any hospital are always complex, partly because of the conflicting interests of major stakeholders. Without a clear overall strategic goal, it was difficult for HR to establish strong vertical integration, and throughout the study it remained process driven. However, this was an enormous improvement on the situation in 1993.

Source: Based on Gratton and Truss 2003

? REFLECTIVE ACTIVITY 11.6

Horizontal and vertical alignment

Where would you position your own organisation (or an organisation with which you are familiar) on Gratton and Truss's three-dimensional model (vertical alignment, horizontal alignment and action)? What actions would you propose to strengthen any weaknesses which you have identified?

11.6 CRITICISMS OF THE BEST FIT MODEL

Just as with the best practice model, best fit has been heavily criticised:

- Just as with best practice, it is heavily prescriptive. It assumes that a particular set of HR practices will be suitable for an organisation with a particular strategic configuration, or a particular stage in the life cycle.

- It is over-simplified. Organisations are unlikely to be solely prospectors, or solely defenders. For different products or services, they could be either. It is also often difficult to identify exactly where an organisation is on its life cycle. It will tend to lurch from one stage to another, and perhaps even back again (Boxall and Purcell 2008).
- It is static. As organisations change their strategy in response to changes in the external environment, are they going to change their HR policies as well?
- Some organisations have no strategy beyond day-to-day survival. What are their best fit policies?

Both the best practice and the best fit models share the assumption that managers are free to choose the HR policies that they wish to adopt. However, a study from the University of Bath suggests that environmental factors heavily constrain the choices available to managers. The network of stakeholders to which an organisation belongs (clients, suppliers, alliance partners, etc) can have an important influence on the extent to which managers are allowed to exercise choice over their HR policies (Kinnie 2005).

Can the best practice and best fit models be reconciled? One way of doing so is that put forward by Boxall and Purcell (2008). They argue that the surface level of HR – that which determines day-to-day action – is likely to be based on best fit, while the underlying level, reflecting values and principles, could well be based on best practice principles. A parallel can be drawn with the absolutist and relativist models of ethics discussed in Chapter 9. When a majority of organisations in a branch of industry has adopted a successful HR practice, other firms can avoid competitive disadvantage only by implementing this practice as well. There is nothing to be gained, but a lot to be lost.

11.7 COMPETITIVE STRATEGY AND HR PRACTICES – PORTER, SCHULER AND JACKSON

Michael Porter argued in *Competitive Advantage: Creating and sustaining superior performance* (1985) that firms need to choose between three fundamental approaches to gaining competitive advantage:

- cost reduction
- quality enhancement
- innovation.

The HR implications of these strategies were examined by Schuler and Jackson (1987). Firms pursuing a cost reduction strategy concentrate on tight controls, minimisation of overheads and economies of scale. The emphasis is on quantity rather than quality. They will pursue cost reduction through increased use of part-time and temporary employees, outsourcing (including offshoring to low-wage countries), low wages (at or close to minimum wage levels), minimal levels of training and development, explicit job descriptions that allow little room for ambiguity, narrowly defined career paths, and short-term, results-oriented performance appraisals. There is usually little employee involvement, and unions are likely to be discouraged. An extreme example of a cost reduction strategy is that pursued by some gangmasters, who sometimes employ illegal immigrant labour at below minimum wage levels, and with little or no consideration for health and safety. After the Morecambe Bay tragedy in 2004, when 23 illegal Chinese immigrant cockle-pickers were drowned, the Gangmasters Licensing Authority was set up to regulate employment in agriculture, fishing (including cockle-picking) and food processing, but in 2009 Oxfam reported that gangmasters had subsequently moved into the less regulated construction, hospitality and care sectors, where there were still reports of workers being paid as little as £50 for a 49 hour week (Oxfam 2009).

Firms pursuing a quality enhancement strategy are likely to be much more attractive to work for. Their employment practices are very close to the high commitment HR model, emphasising sophisticated methods of recruitment and selection, and extensive and long-term training and development. There will be high levels of employee involvement and empowerment, and there is likely to be a high degree of job security. Pay is competitive and there is likely to be a concern for work-life balance. Unions are common, and there is likely to be a partnership approach to industrial relations. HR has a key role in supporting the organisation's culture. Quality enhancing firms are also likely to be concerned with the HR practices at their suppliers. It is vital to the success of the quality enhancement strategy that suppliers buy into it. A classic example is the Japanese-owned segment of the car industry

With an innovation strategy, people are managed in order to work *differently* (unlike either the cost reduction strategy, where they are encouraged to work *harder,* or the quality strategy, where they are encouraged to work *smarter*). The emphasis is on informality, flexibility and problem solving. The HR implications are:

- an emphasis on creativity
- long-term focus
- high level of co-operative, interdependent behaviour
- moderate degree of concern for both quality and quantity
- a high degree of risk-taking
- personal and self-development, rather than employer-directed T&D
- a high degree of ambiguity and unpredictability
- an emphasis on individuality, with little demand for unions
- an emphasis on profit-sharing, rather than high wages.

A classic example of long-term successful implementation of an innovation strategy is the American company 3M, which is discussed in Case Study 11.4.

 INNOVATION AT 3M

CASE STUDY 11.4

One of the most innovative companies over the past 80 years has been 3M – an abrasives manufacturer that broke its own mould by inventing masking tape in 1925, and which has carried on producing highly innovative new products ever since, from the audio tape to Post-It sticky notes. Its latest new idea is Post-it Picture Paper, which marries the Post-It technology to photographic paper, allowing users to print out pictures from their computer straight on to Post-Its.

How does 3M do it? The secret is bottom-up innovation. Someone in the labs, or manufacturing or marketing comes up with a new idea. When he has convinced his supervisor that he's on to something interesting, he will be set up with a small budget and told to get on with it. Harry Heltzer, who developed the idea that became Scotchlite, for adhesive reflective road marking, and later reflective signs, eventually went on to become president of 3M (Grant 2008).

To facilitate the innovation process, 3M has had a long-running policy which permits all research or marketing employees to spend up to 15% of their (and the company's) time on their own projects. In addition, the company operates two career ladders, which make it possible for a technical person to move as high as vice-president without having to take on a managerial role. The result, for years 3M was number one on Boston Consulting Group's Most Innovative Companies list, and it was praised in Jim Collins's and Jerry Porras's best-seller *Built to Last* in 1994.

Larry Wendling, 3M's vice-president of corporate research, identified 'the seven habits of highly successful corporations':

- From the chief executive down, the company must be committed to innovation.
- The corporate culture must be actively maintained.

- Innovation is impossible without a broad base of technology – 3M is a leader in 42 different technologies.
- Networking, both formal and informal. The scientists themselves run an annual symposium for all 9,700 R&D personnel, where ideas and ongoing projects are shared.
- Set individual expectations and reward employees for outstanding work. Hundreds of employees –selected by their peers – are honoured for scientific achievement every year.
- Quantify efforts. 3M carefully tracks its spending to see whether its R&D money is spent wisely.
- Research must be tied to the customer (Arndt 2006).

However, in the late 1990s the dream started to go sour. At a company which had prided itself on earning one-third of its revenue from products invented in the previous five years, the proportion had fallen to a quarter, and by the late 1990s, the company's share price was stagnating.

In 2000, 3M appointed James McNerney as its new CEO. McNerney was the first outsider ever to head the 100-year old company. He came from General Electric, where he had been a disciple of the legendary Jack Welch. His mission – to bring discipline to 3M. He sacked 8,000 workers (11% of the total) and imported GE's Six Sigma programme, a world-renowned statistical quality control technique. The basis of Six Sigma was to reduce variability, and so lower cost. The two main Six Sigma tools were DMAIC (define, measure, analyse, improve, control), and, more critical for 3M, Design for Six Sigma or DFSS, which aimed to systemise the new product development process. DFSS stressed constant review, and quick results. The result was that incremental improvement took precedence over blue-sky research. Traditionally, 3M had allowed researchers years to tinker with new ideas. The consensus within the company was that a new product like Post-It would have been impossible under a Six Sigma regime.

The results of the McNerney regime were predictable. The share price shot up, and so did short-term profits, but innovation stagnated. From number 1 on the Most Innovative Company list in 2004, 3M fell to second in 2005, third in 2006 and seventh in 2007.

In 2005, McNerney left to head Boeing, and was succeeded by George Buckley, a scientist who quietly proceeded to reverse many of his predecessor's reforms. He said, 'Perhaps one of the mistakes we made as a company – it's one of the dangers of Six Sigma – is that when you value sameness more than you value creativity, I think you potentially undermine the heart and soul of a company like 3M' (Hindo 2007). He has exempted the research scientists from DFSS, and increased the R&D budget by 20%. As one 3M executive said, 'We feel we can dream again'.

11.7.1 MILES AND SNOW AND EMPLOYMENT SYSTEMS

Miles and Snow (1978), suggest four main ways in which organisations can cope with and manage their environments. These involve an interaction between the organisation's strategy, its culture, and its environment. They can be:

- *Defenders*: They operate in generally placid environments. They do not actively search for new opportunities, but concentrate on maximising the efficiency of their existing operations. They are very vulnerable to a sudden shift in their environment.
- *Prospectors*: They are attracted to turbulent environments. They are constantly experimenting with novel responses to the environment. They thrive on change and uncertainty, but pay little attention to efficiency. They are decentralised and promote creativity and innovation. They are thus vulnerable if the environment settles down.

- *Analysers*: They are successful poachers. They watch competitors for new ideas, and adopt the successful ones. Their approach to the environment is therefore second-hand, and they let the prospectors make the mistakes. A classic example of the analyser strategy is the video-recorder war. Sony pioneered the industry with the Betamax format, but was eventually defeated by Matsushita and its VHS format. Analysers are seeking at the same time to maintain their shares in existing markets, and to exploit new opportunities. They can be seen as a hybrid between defenders and prospectors. One variant of the model distinguishes analysers with or without innovation.
- *Reactors*: They make adjustments to their strategy when forced to do so by environmental pressures. Unlike the defenders, they are prepared to change, but they are even more market followers than the analysers. They are not prepared for change, and do little planning. Miles and Snow see this strategy (or lack of it) as basically a failure mode.

Organisations must recognise that a strategy which suited them very well in the past may no longer be appropriate if the nature of the environment which faces them has changed. For example, big national airlines, which were highly bureaucratic and cost efficient, were highly successful in the tightly regulated environments of the 1960s and 1970s, but were hard hit by more agile budget airlines (Southwest in the US, Ryanair and easyJet in the UK) as the airline market was deregulated and became more turbulent.

In appropriate types of environment, each of the defender, prospector and analyser strategies can be successful, but the reactor strategy is unlikely to be successful in the long term.

Many later scholars have tested the validity of Miles and Snow's model, and generally have confirmed their findings. For example:

- Shortell and Zajac (1990) found that defenders are the first type of organisation to adopt new production technologies; analysers the first to adopt new management systems, and prospectors the first to develop new products.
- Gimenez (1999) found that among Brazilian small and medium enterprises, reactors were the least successful in terms of increasing their turnovers.
- Peng, Tan and Tong (2004) found that in China, state-owned firms followed defender strategies, privately owned firms prospector strategies and foreign owned forms analyser strategies.

Delery and Doty (1998) extended Miles and Snow's analysis, and looked at the degree of fit between the organisational models and HR systems. They concentrated on the defender and prospector models (they see analyser model as a middle of the road system, with elements of both defender and prospector).

They argued that the defender organisation concentrated on efficiency, on producing existing products in a better way, rather than developing new ones, and that this could be best supported by what they described as an internal employment system, which stressed:

- internal career opportunities and recruitment, with well-defined career ladders
- extensive formal training, with a high level of socialisation within the organisation
- behaviour-based appraisal, largely used for developmental purposes
- transparent pay structures based on hierarchy and seniority; little profit-sharing
- employment security
- a high degree of employee participation, with unions likely to be recognised
- highly defined jobs
- a well-established HR function, with considerable influence.

The prospector organisation constantly searches for new products and markets. The emphasis is on being new rather than being efficient. This is best supported by what they call a market-type employment system, which stressed:

- hiring from outside rather than developing insiders, with little use of career ladders
- little formal training, and only based on short-term needs
- results-based appraisals, with little tolerance for failure
- incentive-based pay systems
- very little employment security
- little employment voice, with unions tolerated at best
- loose and flexible job definitions
- limited role for HR.

A defender organisation is thus likely to attract someone looking for a long-term career, but not for excitement, while working for a prospector organisation is likely to be a lot more stimulating, but much more short-term (see also Marchington and Wilkinson 2008, pp152–3).

Delery and Doly attempted to test their hypotheses empirically through an analysis of the US banking industry, but their findings were not particularly strong. They only examined one role within the banks, that of loan officer. They obtained questionnaire results from 216 banks, but only a minority of these fitted either the market or the internal employment models. Two-thirds were middle of the road in their employment policies. They found that banks that implemented a prospector strategy 'reaped higher return from more results-oriented appraisals and lower levels of employee participation than did banks that relied on a defender strategy' (p826). However, although the theory suggested that internal career paths were more consistent with a defender strategy, their empirical research found the opposite. In general, they found that in the banking industry, 'the closer a bank's employment system resembled the market-type system, the higher its performance' (p827).

? REFLECTIVE ACTIVITY 11.7

The Miles and Snow model

Amazon is the most successful e-commerce company in the world. By market capitalisation it is the biggest retailer in the world, having recently passed Wal-Mart. Yet Amazon has been criticised for years for its oppressive HR policies, culminating in an influential article in the *New York Times* in August 2015.

Amazon is in effect two companies – the high-level IT company, based in Seattle, devoted to developing new innovative services, and the distribution company, based in warehouses throughout the world, including the UK. Criticism came first about conditions in the warehouses. In Pennsylvania in 2011, workers were expected to continue working in 100° heat, but were not allowed to open the loading bay doors, in case of theft. The company did, however, station ambulances to pick up workers who collapsed from heat exhaustion! The company uses electronic monitoring to ensure that pickers in the warehouse do not slack on the job.

All of this may not differ much from other low-skill, repetitive workplaces, but similar pressures seem to apply in the more high-skilled, innovative parts of the organisation. Very long hours are expected, and people who cannot cope with the pressure are dispensed with. Appraisal is continuous, and employees are encouraged to report anonymously on each other. Recruitment policy is described as 'purposeful Darwinism', where large numbers are recruited in order to make sure the organisation employs the stars of the future. Those who do not make the grade will leave. Only the strongest survive. As Jeff Bezos, the founder of Amazon, put it in 1997, 'you can work long, hard or smart, but at Amazon.com you can't choose two out of three'. One ex-employee told the *New York Times*: 'The joke in the office was that when it came to work–life balance, work came first, life came second, and trying to find the balance came last.'

Sources: Edwards (2013); Heskett (2015); Kantor and Streitfeld (2015); Daisey (2015)

Questions

1   How well do you think that Miles and Snow's model can be applied to Amazon?

2   'The Miles and Snow model is essentially only relevant to the private sector'. Do you agree?

3   Which, if any, of Miles and Snow's categories best fits your own organisation?

Burton et al (2004) examine the degree of fit between Miles and Snow's categories and a firm's organisational climate – its degree of trust, morale, conflict, reward fairness, leader credibility, resistance to change and scapegoating. They distinguish four types of climate:

- the group climate
- the developmental climate
- the rational goal climate
- the internal process climate.

The group climate is concentrated on internal focus with high trust and morale. The developmental climate is more externally oriented, also with high trust and morale – and low resistance to change. The rational goal climate is externally oriented to succeed, but with lower trust and morale, and low resistance to change. And, the internal process climate is more mechanical with a high resistance to change.

An internal process climate and a group climate, both being focused inwardly, are not very adaptive to the needs of a prospector or analyser-with-innovation strategy. In contrast, the developmental climate is too experimental for the efficiency focus of the defender strategy.

The internal process climate is rules-oriented and inwardly focused, well suited for a defender strategy where the focus on process is important, but such a climate does not change or adapt quickly, and is not necessarily aligned with the organisation's strategy. It makes for a particularly severe misfit with innovative strategies and for prospectors.

COKE VS PEPSI

CASE STUDY 11.5

Few rivalries are more intense than that between Coke and Pepsi. The two companies are head-on competitors in the soft beverages market, with core products that are the most recognised trademarks in the world. The crucial difference is that Coke is 70 years older, and its strategy is based on defending its market leadership. In Miles and Snow's terms, it is a defender. In contrast, Pepsi is a prospector, aiming to fill gaps in niche markets that Coke has not exploited.

Their culture and HR practices are consistent with these differences in strategy. Coke requires a commitment to its tradition, strong brand and culture. It recruits college graduates at entry level and gradually promotes 'suitable' candidates from within. The culture is one of intensive training, strong job security and seniority-based remuneration. Every CEO of Coke so far has been a career Coke manager.

Pepsi has a very different HRM policy. Pepsi hires employees with work experience, encourages individualism, rewards personal achievement, and rapidly promotes. It is obsessed by its mission of 'beating' Coke. Pepsi employees have less job security and are less likely to stay than their Coke counterparts. The advantage for Pepsi is a continuous flow of talent through the organisation and the ability to adapt quickly.

Both Coke and Pepsi are high-performance organisations. Neither system is superior to the other. Each has high consistency between strategy and culture, and the HR systems that have been created to support these (Hiltrop 2005).

? REFLECTIVE ACTIVITY 11.8

Mechanistic and organic organisations

Mary Jo Hatch (1997) distinguishes between mechanistic and organic organisations. Mechanistic organisations specialise in routine activities with strictly demarcated lines of authority and responsibility. Tasks are highly specialised. Organic organisations have less specialisation. They are less formalised and hierarchical than mechanistic organisations, and use lateral communication.

Question

What parallels can you see between the analyses of Hatch and Miles and Snow?

11.8 THE RESOURCE-BASED VIEW

The resource-based view of HR has much in common with Prahalad and Hamel's (1990) core competence theory. Prahalad and Hamel argue that core competences are those factors which give an organisation its competitive advantage. As discussed in Chapter 10, the effectiveness of core competences can be assessed through the VRIN model:

V – value
R – rarity
I – inimitability
N – non-substitutability.

The Resource Based View (RBV) of HR applies the core competence model to people factors within the organisation. How many times have you heard the phrase 'people are our greatest asset'? RBV is linked to the human capital approach, where people are seen as an asset to the organisation.

When we look at the relationship between strategy and HR it is clear that while best fit is an outside-in model, where the mix of HR practices is influenced by the external environment, mediated through the chosen strategy, RBV is inside-out. The external environment is seen as too volatile and unpredictable on which to base a viable strategy, so the strategy is chosen to fit with the organisation's (HR) core competences.

There is some debate about whether the RBV should be concerned just with managers and others with decision making ability in the organisation, or whether it should be concerned with all employees. Marchington and Wilkinson (2008) stress the latter. Another debate is about whether the RBV relates to people, HR practices and processes, or both. Boxall (1998) distinguishes between 'human capital advantage', based on employee skill, and 'organisational process advantage' such as learning and co-operation and the HR policies which support them. Together these form 'human resource advantage' – employing better people *and* using better HR processes.

The Final Report of the CIPD's *Shaping the Future* project (Miller 2011) identified eight themes important for sustainable organisational performance:

- alignment – the fit between the values, behaviours and objectives of stakeholders, and the organisation's purpose
- shared purpose – within the organisation
- leadership
- locus of engagement
- assessment and evaluation
- balancing long- and short-term horizons
- agility
- capability-building.

From this the Report drew ten insights for HR leaders:

1 The organisational change response needs to be truly agile and enduring, not a knee-jerk reaction.

2 It's a fine balance between alignment and flexibility. Avoid over-alignment.

3 Shared purpose can only be achieved by finding the human connection beyond profit or short-term efficiency.

4 Collaborative leadership brings sustainability.

5 Middle management have a valuable transforming and translating role, but are often by-passed.

6 An over-focus on today's needs is talent tunnel vision.

7 Truly understanding employees' locus of engagement can avoid the risk of over-attachment and under-performance.

8 Perceptions of unfairness undermine employee engagement.

9 Process-heavy organisations are often insight-light.

10 Leaders don't always know best about the long-term vision.

 NHS DUMFRIES AND GALLOWAY: DYNAMIC DELIVERY IN DIFFICULT TIMES

CASE STUDY 11.6

NHS Dumfries and Galloway serves 149,000 people in southern Scotland, and employs 5,000 people. In the late 2000s it launched its Delivery Dynamic Improvement (DDI) programme. The aim of the programme was to equip managers and clinical leaders with the knowledge and skills to enable them to build shared responsibility for dynamic continuous improvement in services provided to patients, as proposed in the Darzi Report.

Issues identified included:

- *Organisational purpose*. Most employees engaged with the core purpose of improving healthcare in the region and tackling health inequalities.

- *Cross-functional working*. DDI encouraged cross-functional working, knowledge-sharing, ownership and innovation across teams and professional boundaries. This was seen as a key enabler of sustainable performance.

- *Employees*. They were high quality, committed, and passionate about patient care.

- *Communication*. Generally positive, possible to feed views upwards.

- *Career progression and talent development*. Viewed as potential enabler of performance.

The Trust identified enablers to performance:

- a sense of purpose that allows staff to engage with the community through a person-centred approach
- improvements in cross-functional working and communication
- knowledge-sharing.

Threats to performance were:

- *internal*: disconnected middle management; a feeling that 'this is how we've always done things', and that we're pretty good already

- *external*: the coalition government's deficit reduction programme, which aims to reduce the Trust's costs by 4% through robust vacancy management, review of fixed term contracts, etc; pressure on public sector pay and pensions (Miller 2011).

It could be argued that this case illustrates either best practice or resource-based HR. In the last resort, it does not matter which it is. If it works, the label is irrelevant. As the Chinese leader Deng Xiaoping said, 'It doesn't matter whether a cat is black or white so long as it catches mice.'

Like the best practice and best fit models, RBV can be criticised. Firstly, where did the key resource or the core competence come from in the first place? It is very unlikely that it emerged fully formed, it is much more likely that it evolved over time, and that it did so through interaction with the environment. Business cannot be purely inside-out, totally ignoring the environment. The environment is there, it matters, and it imposes constraints.

Secondly, key resources are not for ever. As we saw with the EVR model in Chapter 1, resources and the environment can get out of alignment over time, as the environment changes. In the early 1990s, British Airways pursued a policy of building on the strengths of its staff through empowerment. The then group managing director, Bob Ayling, was quoted in 1993 as saying: 'I would like to create an environment where there is genuine communication of information, discussion of ideas and acceptance of decisions taken. What I am aiming to create is a company where the management are responsive to an intelligent workforce.' (Harrison 1993). However, by the late 1990s, and increasingly since, with the rise of Virgin Atlantic and the budget airlines Ryanair and easyJet, BA has been forced into successive rounds of cost cutting, and the empowerment environment has been replaced by one of mutual suspicion. At the other end of the airline industry, Ryanair has been hugely successful through a programme of ruthless cost-cutting, and a willingness to ignore anyone who gets in their way. For staff this has meant a determined anti-union policy (unlike BA which has strong unions). However, Ryanair is ultimately dependent on discretionary spending. Even at very low fares, no-one has to take a Ryanair flight, and as the recession drags on, Ryanair's environment is turning more and more hostile.

In the last resort, it could be argued that the only key resource that really matters is that of extreme flexibility in the face of a potentially chaotic environment, and to achieve this flexibility the organisation must be a learning organisation.

We have now gone full circle. We stand by the model put forward in Chapter 1, that there is a two-way relationship between HR and the environment, and we feel that the best fit model is the most appropriate way to understand this relationship.

KEY LEARNING POINTS

- Ulrich's three-legged stool model is an important model of HR practice.
- Effectiveness is ultimately more important to HR success than efficiency.
- There are three major models of strategic HR – the best practice, best fit and resource-based models.

REVIEW QUESTIONS

1. What do you understand by Ulrich's three-legged stool model? To what extent do you think that it is implemented in practice?

2. What is the difference between efficiency and effectiveness?

3. What HR practices are normally identified as part of a High Performance Workplace?

4. Explain horizontal, vertical and action alignment in the Gratton and Truss model.

5. In what situations is the best fit model more appropriate that the best practice model?

6. What are the links between the core competence and the resource based view of HR?

EXPLORE FURTHER

Further reading

Dave Ulrich has a useful *People Management* article on his roles of HR model (Role Call, 16 June 2005). The Final Report of the CIPD Project on Shaping the Future, Jill Miller, *Sustainable Organisational Performance: What really makes the difference* (2011) is useful. John Walton's *Strategic Human Resource Development* (1999) is useful for the HR contribution to strategic management, while Mick Marchington and Adrian Wilkinson's *Human Resource Management at Work* (2008) and David Farnham's *Human Resource Management in Context: Strategy, insights and solutions* (2010) are excellent on the best practice, best fit and resource based models of HR. The SHRM Effective Practice Guidelines pamphlet, *Human Resource Strategy: Adapting to the age of globalisation* (2008), is useful (http://www.shrm.org/about/foundation/Products/Documents/HR%20strategy%20EPG-%20Funal%20Online.pdf)

Useful websites

Ivythesis has a useful article on best practice versus best fit approaches to strategic HRM, which draws heavily on the work of Armstrong, and includes a case study on Intel in Ireland (http://www.ivythesis.typepad.com/term_paper_topics/2010/11/best-practice-vs-best-fit-approach-to-strategic-human-resource-management.html)

Audio and video material

The CIPD has produced a useful podcast – Podcast 30 (April 2009), *Building sustainable high performance*. Other relevant CIPD podcasts are Podcast 77 (April 2013), *Analytics: How HR can influence strategy through data*, and Podcasts 96 and 98, (December 2014 and February 2015), *HR's Role in Business Partnerships Parts 1 and 2*. The SHRM has a video entitled *HR in Alignment – How HR strategy is aligned with the overall business strategy to drive business results* (http://www.shrm.org/about/foundation/products/pages/hrinalignmentdvd.aspx)

SEMINAR ACTIVITY 11.1

MODELS OF HR

The three major models of HR – best practice, best fit and resource-based – have been extensively discussed in this chapter. Using the material here, in Chapter 3 and 4 of Marchington and Wilkinson's *Human Resource Management at Work*, and in the following case studies, critically examine the three models.

Case Study 1

Japanese multinationals in the UK

Doeringer, Lorenz and Terkla (2003) discussed the extent to which Japanese high performance work practices were used in Japanese-owned manufacturing plants in the UK, the US and France. In this case study we will look mainly at the evidence for the UK.

The authors investigated the extent to which Japanese manufacturing transplants used four practices which they saw as typical of High Performance Work Systems – job rotation, quality circles, self-managing teams and employee responsibility for quality control. They found that 66% of plants surveyed in the UK used at least one of these practices, but only 2% used all four. By far the most common practice used in the UK was employee responsibility for quality control, used by 60% of respondents. None of the other three practices was used by more than 20%. Results were comparable in France, but the US made more use of quality circles and self-managed teams.

The typical pattern for a Japanese transplant is that senior management will be Japanese, with long experience of operating high performance work systems in Japan. However, HR will usually be the responsibility of Western managers, hired because of their familiarity with local industrial relations practices. Their role is to design hybrid HR systems that adapt Japanese practices to local conditions.

High adopters of Japanese practices (using three or more of the techniques) have made a significant move towards partnership arrangements, with employee involvement in decision making, high investment in training, opportunities for the career advancement of shopfloor workers, and long-term employment guarantees.

The central obstacles to the greater adoption of high performance practices were lack of skills and training, and status. Employees with formal technical qualifications were reluctant to work directly alongside production workers in the same team.

A producer of photocopiers and fax machines had used Japanese supervisors and team leaders as teachers and technical trouble-shooters. When they were replaced by British supervisors, the company found that the new supervisors lacked the knowledge to teach and troubleshoot across the whole range of assembly jobs. Operators had little problem-solving experience or ability, and the new supervisors did not have the skills to train them. The result was that operators lacked the ability to take an effective part in quality circles and continuous improvement (*kaizen*), and these initiatives failed.

Case Study 2

The Bosman case and the football transfer system

Before 1995, a professional footballer could only move to another club with the agreement of his current club, even if his contract with the current club had ended. The buying club had to purchase the player from his current club, through the payment of a transfer fee, unless a free transfer was agreed. The latter was only common in the case of a player nearing the end of his career. The current club could prevent a transfer, even if the player was out of contract.

Jean-Marc Bosman, a Belgian footballer with RFC Liege, wanted to be transferred to the French club Dunkerque. Liege refused without the payment of a transfer fee, which Dunkerque was unwilling to pay. Bosman claimed that as an EU citizen, he had the right of freedom of movement within the EU, and that the existing transfer system prevented him from exercising this right.

The European Court of Justice found in his favour in 1995. As a result, transfer fees for out of contract players were illegal where a player was moving between one EU country and another. In

effect, an out-of-contract player would always move on a free transfer.

The implications of the case for the structure of the football industry have been far-reaching:

- Small clubs have been hard hit. Previously, they recruited young talent, with the hope that the player would develop, and could then be transferred to a bigger club for a large profit. After Bosman, they could only benefit from player development if they signed the young player on a long contract. This was very high risk, because if the player did not develop as hoped, they would be stuck with paying his wages until the end of the contract.
- To protect their investments in star players, bigger clubs also signed them on longer contracts. This meant that if a club were relegated, they would be forced to continue to pay star wages which they could no longer afford in a lower division. When Leeds were relegated from the Premier League, they were forced to sell their star players like Jonathan Woodgate at cut-price rates, just to get their salaries off the payroll.
- Player power was vastly increased. Star players either had the security of a long contract, or they could hold out for much high wages when negotiating the renewal of a contract. Alternatively, when their contract ended, they could move elsewhere, and demand a high signing-on fee (often running into the millions) from their new club.

Sources: Pearson (nd); Fordyce (2005)

Case Study 3

Engaging for success

In the summer of 2009, David MacLeod and Nita Clarke produced a report for the Department of Business, Innovation and Skills on employee engagement (MacLeod and Clarke 2009). Their brief was 'to take an in-depth look at employee engagement [one of the key components of the High Performance Workplace], and to report on its potential benefits for companies, organisations and individual employees' (p3).

Employee engagement proved elusive to define. The report found more than 50 definitions, including the useful 'you know it when you see it'. Eventually, building on the work of David Guest, the report defined employee engagement as 'a workplace approach designed to ensure that employees are committed to their organisation's goals and values, motivated to contribute to organisational success, and at the same time to enhance their own sense of well-being. Engaged organisations have strong and authentic values, with clear evidence of trust and fairness based on mutual respect, where two-way promises and commitments – between employers and staff – are understood, and are fulfilled' (p9).

The report found a strong correlation between high levels of employee engagement and measures of performance:

- Highly engaged organisations averaged 18% higher productivity and 12% higher profitability than those with low engagement.
- Fifty-nine per cent of engaged employees say that their job brings out their most creative ideas compared with 3% of disengaged employees.
- Engaged employees take an average of 2.69 sick days a year, the disengaged 6.19 days.

- Engaged employees are 87% less likely to leave the organisation than the disengaged.
- Seventy-eight per cent of engaged employees would recommend their company's products or services, as against 13% of the disengaged.

The flip side is that disengagement costs money. While 30% of workers were engaged, 20% were disengaged, and there is some evidence that this figure may be rising (p15). Between 1992 and 2001, the proportion saying they had a great deal of discretion over how to do their job fell from 57 to 43%. Forty-two per cent would refuse to recommend their organisation as an employer to family or friends. Gallup suggested that in 2008 the cost of disengagement to the UK economy was between £59.4 and £64.7bn (p17).

The report quotes many case studies. One concerns the construction equipment company JCB, which was hard hit by the recession in the construction industry in 2008. On October 2008 it proposed a shorter working week to the union, GMB, in order to avoid over 300 redundancies. Running up to the ballot, JCB held face-to-face sessions with employees to explain the background to the business situation and the steps that were being taken in response to it. As a result, employees understood the rationale behind the company's proposals and decisions. The union ballot voted two to one in favour of the shorter working week, although this meant a pay cut.

References

ABERCROMBIE, N. and WARDE, A. (2000) *Contemporary British society*. 3rd edition. Cambridge: Polity Press.

Accountability Primer: Sustainability. (nd) Available at: www.accountability.org.uk.

ACTION AID. (2006) *Confronting the contradictions: time for action on education*. London: ActionAid.

ADNAMS. (2011a) *Annual report 2011* [online]. Available at: www.adnams.co.uk [Accessed 20 August 2012]

ADNAMS. (2011b) Value statement [online]. Available at: www.adnams.co.uk [Accessed 20 August 2012]

ADNAMS. (2014a) Annual report 2014 [online]. Available at: www.adnams.co.uk [Accessed 20 April 2015]

ADNAMS. (2014b) Value statement [online]. Available at: www.adnams.co.uk [Accessed 20 April 2015]

AHMED, K. (2015) Banking and the failure of policing [online]. Available at: www.bbc.co.uk/news/business-34869083 [Accessed 25 February 2016]

AHRENS, N and ZHOU, Y. (2013) China's competitiveness: myth, reality and lessons for the United States and Japan. Washington, DC: Center for Strategic and International Studies Available at: http://csis.org/files/publication/130129_competitiveness_lenovo_casestudy_web.pdf [Accessed 21 June 2015]

Air Transport World. (2006a) Ryanair: ryanair.com. July.

Air Transport World. (2006b) The world's top 25 airlines. July.

AISBETT, E. (2003) Globalization, poverty and inequality: are the criticisms vague, vested or valid? *NBER Pre-conference on Globalization, Poverty and Inequality*, October.

AKCAPAR, B and CHAIBI, D. (2006) Turkey EU accession: the long road from Ankara to Brussels. *Yale Journal of International Affairs*. Winter-Spring 2006.

AKERLOF, G. (1970) The market for lemons: quality uncertainty and the market mechanism. *Quarterly Journal of Economics*. Vol 84, August.

ALDRED, J, (2007) Q&A: Plastic bags. *The Guardian*, 13 November.

ALDRIDGE, S. (2001) *Social mobility: a discussion paper*. London: Cabinet Office, Performance and Innovation Unit.

ALDRIDGE, S. (2004) *Life chances and social mobility: an overview of the evidence*. London: Cabinet Office, Prime Minister's Strategy Unit.

ALESINA, A., MICHALOPOULOS, S. and PAPAIOANNOU, E. (2015) Ethnic inequality. *Journal of Political Economy*. October.

ALLISON, G. (1971) *Essence of decisions: explaining the Cuban Missile Crisis*. New York: Little Brown and Company.

AMBURGEY, T. and DACIN, T. (1994) As the left foot follows the right? The dynamics of strategic and structural change. *Academy of Management Journal*, Vol 37 No 6

ANAND, V., ASHFORTH, B. and JOSHI, M. (2004) Business as usual: the acceptance and perpetuation of corruption in organizations. *Academy of Management Executive*. Vol 18, No 2, May.

ANDERSON, C. (2005) Narrowing the credibility gap, or, managing the art of the promise. *Ivey Business Journal*, July-August.

ANDERSON, T. and METCALFE, H. (2003) *Diversity: stacking up the evidence*. London: Chartered Institute of Personnel and Development.

ANDERTON, A. (2006) *Economics*. 4th ed. Harlow: Pearson.

ANSOFF, I. (1987) *Corporate strategy*. London: Penguin.

ANTHONY, A. (2015) Joseph Stiglitz: 'GDP per capita in the UK than it was before the crisis. That is not a success'. *The Observer*. 24 May.

APPELBAUM, L. and PAESE, M. (2003) What senior leaders do: the nine roles of strategic leadership [online]. *Development Dimensions International*. Available at: www. ddiworld.com/products-solutions/listing/strategic-leadership-experience/white-papers-monographs [Accessed 18 July 2012]

ARGENTI, J. (1993) *Your organisation, what is it for? Challenging traditional organisational aims*. Maidenhead: McGraw-Hill.

ARKIN, A. (2002) The package to India. *People Management*. 24 January. pp34–6.

ARKIN, A. (2007) Street smart. *People Management*, 5 April.

ARKIN, A. (2011) Is engagement working? *People Management*. November. pp22–7.

ARLIDGE, J. (2009) Are our heads in the cloud? *Sunday Times*. Magazine. 9 August. pp42–5.

ARMSTRONG, M. (1999) *Managing activities*. London: CIPD.

ARNDT, M. (2007) 3M's Seven Pillars of innovation. *BusinessWeek*. 10 May.

ARTHUR, C. (2014) The Chinese technology companies poised to dominate the world. *The Guardian*. 3 June.

ARTICLE 13 and CBI. (2007) Dwr Cymru Welsh Water. *CBI-CSR Case Studies*. September.

ASHLEY, J. (2012) Firms must pay their fair share of tax – this is war. *The Guardian*, 3 December.

ATKINSON, J. (1984) Manpower strategies for flexible organisations. *Personnel Management*. August.

ATKINSON, A. (2015) *Inequality: what can be done?* Boston, MA: Harvard University Press.

AUSTIN, R. and DEVIN, L. (2004) Successful innovation through artful process. *Leader to Leader*. Spring.

BAIRD, R. (2001) Britain's immigrants overstep line as numbers surge to 135,000 a year. *Express.* 16 November.

BAKER, R. (2009) Tesco extends double points offer as market share dips. *Marketing Week.* 20 August.

BANK OF ENGLAND. (2003) *Remit for the Monetary Policy Committee of the Bank of England and the new inflation target* [online]. Available at: www.bankofengland.co.uk [Accessed 8 February 2016]

BANK OF ENGLAND. (2004a) *The labour market* [online]. Available at: www.bankofengland.co.uk/targettwopointzero [Accessed 8 February 2016]

BANK OF ENGLAND. (2004b) *How do interest rates affect inflation?* [online]. Available at: www.bankofengland.co.uk/targettwopointzero [Accessed 8 February 2016]

BANK OF ENGLAND. (2007a) *Treasury Committee Inquiry into the Monetary Policy Committee of the Bank of England: ten years on. The Bank of England's submission regarding the economic context* [online]. Available at: www.bankofengland.co.uk [Accessed 8 February 2016]

BANK OF ENGLAND. (2007b) *Governor's open letter to the Chancellor of the Exchequer,* 16 April [online]. Available at: www.bankofengland.co.uk [Accessed 8 February 2016]

BARBER, B. (1998) Speech to the New Labour and the Labour Movement Conference, 19/20 June.

BARKHAM, P. (2007) World asks town that banned the plastic bag: how can we do it too? *The Guardian,* 12 May.

BARNARD, H. and GOULDEN, C. (2006) *What will it take to end child poverty? Firing on all cylinders.* York: Joseph Rowntree Foundation.

BARNEY, J. (1991) Firm resources and sustained competitive advantage. *Journal of Management.* Vol 17, No 1.

BARTLETT, C and GHOSHAL, S. (1991) *Managing across borders.* Boston, MA: Harvard Business School Press.

BARTLETT, H. and PEEL, N. (2005) Healthy ageing in the community. In: G. ANDREWS and D. PHILLIPS (eds) *Ageing and place.* London: Routledge.

BARON, A. (2010) What's the future for workforce planning? *Impact* 33. October.

BARON, A. (2011) *Is there such a thing as high performance working?* Reward blog. London:

Chartered Institute of Personnel and Development.

BARRELL, R., FITZGERALD, J. and RILEY, R. (2007) *EU enlargement and migration: assessing the macroeconomic impacts.* London: National Institute for Economic and Social Research.

BARRETT, C. and SHUBBER, K. (2015), City Link collapse reveals sector's systemic problems. *The Financial Times.* 4 January.

BATTERSBY, J. (1999) Nelson Mandela's moral legacy. *Christian Science Monitor.* 10 May.

BATTY, D. (2009) Timeline: the Baby P case. *The Guardian.* 22 May.

BATTY, D. and WEAVER, M. (2006) Q&A: private finance initiative. *The Guardian.* 3 May.

BAXTER, M. and STRAW, J. (2014) *iDisrupted.* New York: New Generation Publishing.

BBC. (nd) Born abroad: immigration map of the UK [online]. Available at: http://news. bbc.co.uk/1/shared/spl/hi/uk/05/born_abroad/html/overview.stm [Accessed 8 February 2016]

BBC. (2005a) New workers 'not hitting wages' [online]. Available at: http://news.bbc.co. uk/1/hi/uk/4582667.stm [Accessed 24 April 2007]

BBC. (2005b) Q&A: Common Agricultural Policy. 2 February 2005 [online]. Available at: http://www.news.bbc.co.uk [Accessed 24 June 2007]

BBC. (2009) Glass ceiling blocking top jobs [online]. July. Available at: http://news.bbc.co. uk/1/hi/8160052.stm [Accessed 25 February 2016]

BBC. (2011a) China overtakes Japan as world's second-biggest economy [online]. BBC News. 14 February. Available at: http://www.bbc.co.uk/news/business-12427321 [Accessed 11 November 2015]

BBC. (2011b) India income inequality doubles in 20 years, says OECD [online]. 7 December 2011. Available at: http://www.bbc.co.uk/news/world-asia-india-16064321 [Accessed 15 June 2015]

BBC. (2011c) Government calls for 'fundamental reform' of exam system [online]. 8 December. Available at: http://www.bbc.co.uk/news/education-16098331 [Accessed 25 February 2016]

BBC. (2012a) London 2012: Nick Buckles regrets taking contract [online]. 12 July. Available at: http://www.bbc.co.uk/news/uk-18866153 [Accessed 21 July 2012]

BBC. (2012b) Starbucks 'planning changes to tax policy' [online]. 3 December. Available at: http://www.bbc.co.uk/news/business-2058098 [Accessed 3 December 2012]

BBC. (2012c) What could happen next if Greece leaves the eurozone? [online]. 18 June. Available at: http://www.bbc.co.uk/news/business-18074674 [Accessed 28 November 2012]

BBC. (2012d) Eurozone crisis explained [online]. 19 June. Available at: http://www.bbc.co. uk/news/business-16290598 [Accessed 28 November 2012]

BBC. (2012e) Who's afraid of the euro crisis? [online]. 23 August. Available at: http:// www.bbc.co.uk/news/business-18284747 [Accessed 28 November 2012]

BBC. (2012f) EU summit: all but two leaders sign fiscal treaty [online]. 2 March. Available at: http://www.bbc.co.uk/news/business-17230760 [Accessed 28 November 2012]

BBC. (2012g) Q&A: EU fiscal treaty to control eurozone budgets [online]. 2 March. Available at: http://www.bbc.co.uk/news/business-16057252 [Accessed 28 November 2012]

BBC (2012h) At-a-glance: census 2011 findings [online]. 11 December. Available at: http://www.bbc.c.uk/news/uk-20677321 [Accessed 28 December 2012].

BBC. (2013a) Rentokil sells City Link for £1 to Better Capital [online]. 29 April. Available at: http://www.bbc.co.uk/news/business-22335092 [Accessed 18 January 2015]

BBC. (2013b) Q&A: NHS 111 [online]. 29 July. Available at: http://www.bbc.co.uk/news/health-22370621 [Accessed 27 December 2014]

BBC. (2014a) EU enlargement: the next seven [online]. 2 September. Available at: http://www.bbc.co.uk/news/world-europe-11283616 [Accessed 4 October 2015]

BBC. (2014b) Miliband attacks Sports Direct over zero-hours contracts [online]. 15 November. Available at http://www.bbc.co.uk/news/uk-30066568 [Accessed 30 May 2015]

BBC. (2015a) Sajid Javid: no fresh look at easier dismissals [online]. 24 May. Available at: http://www.bbc.co.uk/news/uk-politics-32864785 [Accessed 29 May 2015]

BBC. (2015b) China to end one child policy and allow two [online]. BBC News. 29 October. Available at: http://www.bbc.co.uk/news/world-asia-34665539 [Accessed 11 November 2015]

BBC. (2015c) Greek debt crisis; where do other eurozone countries stand? [online]. 8 July. Available at: http://www.bbc.co.uk/news/world-europe-33408466 [Accessed 12 October 2015]

BBC. (2015d) Greece debt crisis: IMF attacks EU over bailout terms [online]. 15 July. Available at: http://www.bbc.co.uk/news/business-33531845 [Accessed 12 October 2015]

BBC. (2015e) David Cameron sets out EU reform goals [online]. 11 November. Available at: http://www.bbc.co.uk/news/uk-politics-34770875 [Accessed 11 November 2015]

BBC. (2015f) Caparo Steel goes into partial administration [online]. 19 October. Available at: http://www.bbc.co.uk/news/business-34574982 [Accessed 13 November 2015]

BBC. (2015g) Ebola: mapping the outbreak [online]. BBC News Africa, 10 February. Available at: http://www.bbc.co.uk/news-world-africa-287550 [Accessed 8 May 2015]

BBC. (2015h) Payday lender Wonga reports £37.3m loss for 2014 [online]. 21 April. Available at: http://www.bbc.co.uk/news/business-32392544 [Accessed 23 April 2015]

BBC. (2015i) ECB unveils massive QE boost for eurozone [online]. 22 January. Available at http://www.bbc.co.uk/news/business-30933515 [Accessed 8 February 2015]

BBC. (2016) Tata steel jobs: David Cameron says there are 'no guarantees' on steel crisis [online]. 31 March. Available at http://www/bbc.co.uk/news/politics - 35930904 [Accessed 31 March 2016]

BBC2. (2007) *Working Lunch*. 19 September.

BEACH, S.D. (1980) *Personnel*. London: Macmillan.

BEARD, A. and HORNICK, R. (2011) It's hard to be good. *Harvard Business Review*, Vol 89 No 11. November.

BEATSON, M. (2015) Productivity – your doorstep checklist. *CIPD Blog*. 5 May. London: CIPD. Available at: www.cipd.co.uk/.../productivity-your-doorstep-checklist.aspx [Accessed 2 November 2015]

BEECROFT, A. (2011) *Report on Employment Law*. London: Department of Business, Innovation and Skills. November.

BEER, M. and NOHRIA, N. (2000) Cracking the code of change. *Harvard Business Review*. May-June. Vol 78, No 3.

BELL, A. (2015) How Damart turned internal challenges into award-winning service [online]. Available at: https://instituteofcustomerservice.com/membership/case-studies/how-damart-turned-internal-challenges-into-award-winning-service [Accessed 8 February 2016]

BENATI, L. (2006), *UK monetary regimes and stylised macroeconomic facts*. Bank of England Working Paper no 290. Available at: www.bankofengland.co.uk/research/Pages/workingpapers/2006/wp290.aspx [Accessed 25 February 2016]

BENNETT, S. (2012) *Twitter on track for 500 million total users by end of 2012* [online]. Available at: http://www.adweek.com/socialtimes/twitter-active-total-users/459139 [Accessed 8 February 2016]

BENTHAM, M. (2013) Boost for PM on migration as influx falls by one third. *Evening Standard*. 28 February. p4.

BERMINGHAM, F. (2014) Exclusive: 30 years on from Bhopal gas tragedy, Dow Chemical shareholders demand justice. *International Business Times UK*. 19 November.

BERNHUT, S. (2001) Leading the revolution: Gary Hamel. *Ivey Business Journal*. July.

BERSIN, J. (2015) *A modern HR operating model: the world has changed*. In: CIPD (2015) *Changing HR operating models*, pp 5-7. London: CIPD.

BETTIS, R. (1991) Strategic management and the strait-jacket: an editorial essay. *Organization Science*. Vol 2 No 3.

BILLINGTON, R. (2003) *Living philosophy: an introduction to moral thought*. 3rd ed. London: Routledge.

BION, W.R. (1961) *Experiences in groups: and other papers*. London: Tavistock (reprinted 1989, Routledge).

BIRD, A. (2010) Leading through values: An interview with Paul Polman of Unilever. *McKinsey Quarterly*. Issue 1.

BIRKINSHAW, J. (2004) The destruction of Marconi. *Business Strategy Review*. Spring. Vol 15 Issue 1.

BLACK, J. and HOPPER, M. (2011) *Breaking up is hard to do*. London: London School of Economics.

BLACKHURST, C. (2015) Where now for trade unions? *Work*. Summer.

BLAKE, R. and MOUTON, J. (1964) *The managerial grid: the key to leadership excellence*. Houston, TX: Gulf Publishing Co.

BLANCHFLOWER, D. (2015). Austerity has failed and Labour shadow chancellor John McDonnell is right that the Bank of England needs a new mandate. *City AM*. 29 September. http://www.cityam.com/225381/why-bank-england-boe-needs-new-mandate-jeremy-corbyn-john-mcdonnell [accessed 27 October 2015]

BLANCHFLOWER, D., SALEHEEN, J. and SHADFORTH, C. (2007) *The impact of the recent migration from Eastern Europe on the UK economy.* Bank of England Working Paper. London: Bank of England.

BLANDEN, J. and GIBBONS, S. (2006) Cycles of disadvantage. *CentrePiece.* Summer.

BLANDEN, J., GREGG, P. and MACHIN, S. (2005) Social mobility in Britain: low and falling. *CentrePiece.* Spring.

BLYTH. M. (2012). The last days of pushing on a string. *Harvard Business Review.* August.

BOONE, P. (2005) Effective intervention: making aid work. *CentrePiece.* Winter.

BOOTH, R. (2009a) Welcome to Barnet, the Tory test-pilot of no-frills government. *The Guardian.* 27 August.

BOOTH, R. (2009b) Tory-controlled borough of Barnet adopts budget airline model. *The Guardian*, 27 August.

BOOTH, R. (2009c) The Ryanair pricing model that could be a route to budget care in Barnet. *The Guardian.* 27 August.

BOOTH, R. (2010) Barnet's 'easyCouncil' finds it hard to cut with £1.5m spent, £1.4m saved. *The Guardian.* 26 October.

BOOTH, R (2015) Qatar Airways urged to scrap policy allowing it to sack pregnant cabin crew. *The Guardian.* 16 June.

BOOTH, T. (2013) Here, there and everywhere. *The Economist.* 19 January.

BOROUGHS, A. (2015) The future is centres of expertise. In, CIPD (ed.) *Changing HR Operating Models.* London: CIPD. pp8-11

BOROUGHS, D. (1999) Proving that one man can make a difference. *US News and World Report.* 24 May.

BOSALIE, P. and DIETZ, G. (2003) *Commonalities and contradictions in research on HRM and performance.* Paper presented at the Academy of Management Conference, Seattle. August.

BOSELEY, S. (2015a) Costly drugs cause harm on balance, health experts say. *The Guardian.* 19 February.

BOSELEY, S. (2015b) Ebola: the race to find a cure. *The Guardian.* 17 February.

BOWCOTT, O. (2004) Transcript reveals doctor's pleas for dying teenager. *The Guardian.* 18 October.

BOWCOTT, O. (2009a) Social work vacancies as high as 39 per cent. *The Guardian.* 17 June.

BOWCOTT, O. (2009b) Baby P council looks to US for social workers. *The Guardian.* 3 October.

BOWCOTT, O. (2009c) Hospital condemned over cleanliness gave itself top marks. *The Guardian.* 28 November.

BOWERS, S. (2009) Kraft chews on a sweeter deal for Cadbury. *The Observer*. 8 November.

BOWERS, S (2013) Iceland rises from the ashes of banking collapse. *The Observer*. 6 October.

BOWMAN, C. and FAULKNER, D. (1996) *Competitive and corporate strategy*. Homewood, IL: Irwin.

BOXALL, P. (1998) Achieving competitive advantage through human resource strategy: towards a theory of industry dynamics. *Human Resource Management Review*, Vol 8 No 8.

BOXALL, P. and PURCELL, J. (2000) Strategic human resources management: where have we come from and where are we going? *International Journal of Management Reviews*. Vol 2, No 2.

BOXALL, P. and PURCELL, J. (2008) *Strategy and human resource management*. 2nd ed. Basingstoke: Palgrave-Macmillan.

BRAMMER, S.J., MILLINGTON, A. and PAVELIN, S. (2006) Is philanthropy strategic? *Business Ethics: A European Review*. Vol 15, No 3.

BRANZEI, O and NADKARNI, A. (2008) The Tata Way: evolving and executing sustainable business strategies, *Ivey Business Journal*, March-April.

BRIGGS, P. (2009) *Northern Tanzania*. 2nd ed. Chalfont St Peter: Bradt.

BRINDLE, D. (1999) Northerners heed south's siren call. *The Guardian*. 27 August. p3.

BRINDLE, D. (2009) Ministers back plan for a national social work college. *The Guardian*. 29 July.

BRINER, R. (2001) Why family-friendly practices can also be performance-friendly. *People Management*. 8 November

BRINER, R. and CONWAY, N. (2001) *Understanding psychological contracts at work: a critical evaluation of theory and research*. Oxford: Oxford University Press.

BRIDGES, W. (1995) Breaking with the past. *Human Resources*. September-October.

BRIDGES, W. and MITCHELL, S. (2000) Leading transition: a new model for change. *Leader to Leader* 16. Spring.

BRINKLEY, I. (2013) *Flexibility or insecurity? Exploring the rise in zero hours contracts*. London: Work Foundation.

BRINKMANN, J. and IMS, K. (2003) Good intentions aside: drafting a functionalist look at codes of ethics. *Business Ethics: A European Review*. Vol 12, No 3.

BROCKETT, J. (2009) Working time rules are harming patients, say surgeons. *People Management*, 12 October.

BROCKETT, J. (2010) LV= recruits via interactive media. *People Management*. 17 June. p14.

BROOKS, I. and WEATHERSTON, J. (2004) *The business environment*. 3rd edition. London: FT Prentice Hall.

BROUGHTON, A., HIGGINS, T., HICKS, B. and COX, A. (2011) *Workplaces and social networking.* London: ACAS.

BROWN, D. (2003) A capital idea. *People Management.* 26 June. pp42–6.

BROWN, K. (2001) Standard that has delivered. *The Financial Times.* 30 October.

BUGGY, C. (2005) Recipe for making training stick. *Professional Manager.* May.

BUKODI, E., GOLDTHORPE, J., WALLER, L. and KUHA, J. (2014) The mobility problem in Britain: new findings from the analysis of birth cohort data. *The British Journal of Sociology.* Vol 66, No 1. pp 93–117.

BURGESS, J. (2009) The budget airline model won't work for councils. *The Guardian.* 2 September.

BURKE, A., van STEL, A. and THURIK, R. (2010) Blue Ocean vs Five Forces. *Harvard Business Review.* Vol 88, Issue 5. May.

BURKE, W. (1980) *Organisation development.* Toronto: Little, Brown and Co.

BURNES, B. (2004) *Managing change: a strategic approach to organisational dynamics* 4nd ed. London, Pitman

BURROUGHS, A. (2015) *Ulrich comes of age – a study of the impact of the Ulrich Model.* Available at: http://www.orion-partners.com/study-ulrich-comes-age [Accessed 15 January 2015].

BURTON, R. M. and OBEL, B. (1998), *Strategic organizational diagnosis and design: developing theory for application.* Boston, MA: Kluwer.

BURTON, R. M, LAURIDSEN, J. and OBEL, B. (2004) The impact of organisational climate and strategic fit on firm performance. *Human Resource Management.* Vol 43, No 1.

BUSINESSBALLS. (2011) SMEAC. Available at: http://www.businessballs.com/acronyms.htm#SMEAC-acronyms [Accessed 10 April 2015]

BITC. (nd) Stakeholder engagement case study: Anglian Water. Business in the Community. Available at: http://www.bitc.org.uk/sites/default/files/anglian_water_stakeholder_case_study.pdf [Accessed 10 January 2015]

BITC. (2000) Putting your heart into it: purpose and values. Report of the Business Impact Task Force 2000. Business in the Community. Available at: http://www.bitc.org.uk [Accessed 27 September 2004]

BITC. (2002) The public's view of corporate responsibility. Business in the Community. Available at: http://www.bitc.org.uk [Accessed 27 September 2004]

BITC. (2003) The business case for corporate responsibility. Business in the Community. http://www.butc.org.uk [Accessed 27 September 2004]

BUSINESS WEEK. (2004a) Wireless. 21 June. pp62–5.

BUSINESS WEEK. (2004b) America's Bebe Boom. 15 March. pp50–2

BUSINESS WEEK. (2006) Walmart with wings. 27 November

BUTLER, S. (2006) Would you like a bag with that, Madam? *The Times.* 7 October.

BUTLER, S. (2012) Fresh, but not so easy. *The Observer.* 9 December.

BUTLER, S. (2015a) Sports Direct faces multimillion-pound claim from zero-hours contract workers. *The Guardian.* 3 February.

BUTLER, S. (2015b) Aldi overtakes Waitrose to become UK's sixth-largest supermarket chain. *The Guardian.* 8 April.

BUTLER, S. (2015c) Tesco: six challenges in store for Matt Davies. *The Guardian.* 11 May.

BUTLER, S. (2015d) Tesco beyond Britain: how supermarket is faring abroad. *The Guardian.* 22 April.

BUTLER, S. (2015e) Tesco voted worst for observing guidelines on supplier dealings. *The Guardian.* 23 June.

BUTLER, S. and FARRELL, S. (2015a) Tesco reports record £6.4 billion loss. *The Guardian.* 22 April.

BUTLER, S. and FARRELL, S. (2015b) Upturn on the way, chief insists after record £6.4bn loss. *The Guardian.* 23 April.

BUTLER, V.G. (1985) *Organisation and management.* London: Prentice Hall.

CABLE, V. (2009) *The Storm: the world economic crisis and what it means.* London: Atlantic Books.

CABLE, V. (2012) *Statement by Vince Cable on the Beecroft Employment Law Report.* London: Department of Business, Innovation and Skills.

CALDWELL, R. (2003). The changing roles of personnel managers: old ambiguities, new uncertainties. *Journal of Management Studies.* Vol 40, No 4.

CAMRA. (2014) *CAMRA research shows expanding supermarket chains are calling last orders on hundreds of pubs.* Campaign for Real Ale press release. 6 February. Available at: http://www.camra.org.uk/press-releases [Accessed 20 April 2015]

CAMRA. (2015) *Three in a row for CAMRA campaigners as new laws are enacted to help pubs.* Campaign for Real Ale press release. 9 April. Available at: http://www.camra.org.uk/press-releases [Accessed 20 April 2015]

CAPELLI, P. (2008) *Talent on demand: managing talent in an age observing of uncertainty.* Cambridge, MA: Harvard Business School Press.

CARR, A., DURANT, R. and DOWNS, A. (2004) Emergent strategy development, abduction, and pragmatism: new lessons for corporations. *Human Systems Management.* Vol 23. March.

CARR, N. (2008) *The big switch – rewiring the world from Edison to Google.* New York: Norton.

CARROLL, A. B. (1979) A three dimensional model of corporate social performance. *Academy of Management Review,* 4.

CARROLL, A. B. (1990), Principles of business ethics: their role in decision making and an initial consensus. *Management Review.* Vol 28, No 8.

CARROLL, A. B. (1991) The pyramid of corporate social responsibility: towards the moral management of organizational stakeholders. *Business Horizons.* July–August.

CARTWRIGHT, S. and COOPER, S. (1997) *Managing workplace stress.* London: Sage.

CARVEL, J. (2003a) Marriage and family divorced as 41% of children reared in alternative ways. *Guardian.* 8 May.

CARVEL, J. (2003b) Blair puts NHS out to tender. *The Guardian.* 14 May.

CARVEL, J. (2007) The figure that shows it pays to be a man. *The Guardian.* 5 September.

CARVEL, J. (2009) Government pledges £58m to recruiting top quality social workers following Baby P case. *The Guardian.* 6 May.

CASCIANI, D. (2012) Census shows rise in foreign-born [online]. Available at: www.bbc. co.uk/news/uk-20681551 [Accessed 27 February 2016]

CASCIO, W. F. and WYNN, P. (2004) Managing a downsizing process. *Human Resource Management.* Vol 43.

CATTAN, S., CRAWFORD, C. and DEARDEN, L. (2014). *Economic effects of pre-school education and quality.* Institute of Fiscal Studies. November.

CAULKIN, S. (2003a) Wanted: one kick in the pants. *The Observer.* 18 May.

CAULKIN, S. (2003b) Ethics and profits do mix. *The Observer.* 20 April.

CAVANAGH, G., MOBERG, D. and VELASQUEZ, M. (1981) The ethics of organizational politics. *Academy of Management Review.* Vol 3.

CBI. (2005) *CBI response to Leitch Review of Skills.* London: Confederation of British Industry.

CBI. (2012) *A problem shared.* Available at: http://www.cbi.org.uk/media/1534060/ 20011906_a_problem_shared_pdf [Accessed 31 January 2015]

CELLAN-JONES, R (2012) Huawei hits back over US 'security threat' claim [online]. BBC News. 4 December. Available at: http://www.bbc.co.uk/news/technology-2059477 [Accessed 6 December 2012]

CENTRE FOR WORKFORCE INTELLIGENCE. (2012) *Workforce risks and opportunities: social workers.* Centre for Workforce Intelligence. March.

CHANDLER, A. E. (1962) *Strategy and structure: chapters in the history of the American enterprise.* Cambridge, MA: MIT Press.

CHAKRABORRTY, A. (2012) You've been bankered. *The Guardian.* 3 July.

CHARKHAM, J. (1994) *Keeping good company: a study of corporate governance in five countries.* Oxford: Oxford University Press.

CIA. (2007) *CIA World Factbook* [online]. Available at: https://www.cia.gov/library/ publications/the-world-factbook [Accessed 18 April 2007]

CIA. (2009) *CIA World Factbook* [online]. Available at: http://www.cia.gov/library/ publications/theworld-factbook/fields/2172.html [Accessed 29 October 2009]

CIA. (2012) *The World Factbook* [online]. Available at: http;//www.cia.gov/library/publications/the-world-factbook [Accessed 1 July 2012]

CIPD. (2003a) Managing the psychological contract. Factsheet. London: Chartered Institute of Personnel and Development.

CIPD. (2003b) *Work–life balance*. Factsheet. London: Chartered Institute of Personnel and Development.

CIPD. (2003c) *Code of professional conduct and disciplinary procedures*. London: Chartered Institute of Personnel and Development.

CIPD. (2004) *Frequently asked questions: parental rights and other family-friendly provisions*. London: Chartered Institute of Personnel and Development.

CIPD. (2005) *Managing diversity: people make the difference at work – but everyone is different*. London: Chartered Institute of Personnel and Development.

CIPD. (2006a) *Managing diversity, measuring success*. Change agenda. London: Chartered Institute of Personnel and Development.

CIPD. (2006b) *Offshoring and the role of HR*. Survey report. January. London: Chartered Institute of Personnel and Development.

CIPD. (2007) *Age and recruitment*. London: Chartered Institute of Personnel and Development.

CIPD. (2008) *Diversity: an overview*. Factsheet. London: Chartered Institute of Personnel and Development.

CIPD. (2009a) *The internship charter*. London: Chartered Institute of Personnel and Development.

CIPD. (2009b) *HR outsourcing and the HR function: threat or opportunity?* Survey report. London: Chartered Institute of Personnel and Development.

CIPD. (2009c) *Employee outlook: job seeking in a recession*. London: Chartered Institute of Personnel and Development.

CIPD. (2009d) *Talent management: an overview*. Factsheet. London: Chartered Institute of Personnel and Development.

CIPD. (2009e) *Managing redundancy, parts 1 and 2*. Podcast 29. London: Chartered Institute of Personnel and Development.

CIPD. (2009f) *EU employment policy*. Worksheet. London: Chartered Institute of Personnel and Development.

CIPD. (2009g) *Shared purpose and sustainable organisational performance*. Research insight. London: Chartered Institute of Personnel and Development.

CIPD. (2010) *Resourcing and talent planning*. Survey report. London: Chartered Institute of Personnel and Development.

CIPD. (2011) *Corporate responsibility*. London: Chartered Institute of Personnel and Development.

CIPD. (2012a) Business savvy: giving HR the edge [online]. London: Chartered Institute of Personnel and Development. Available at: http://www.cipd.co.uk/hr-resources/research/business-savvy-giving-hr-edge.aspx [Accessed 27 March 2013].

CIPD. (2012b) *Dealing with dismissal and compensated no-fault dismissal for microbusinesses: submission to BIS.* London: Chartered Institute of Personnel and Development.

CIPD. (2012c) *Responsible and sustainable business: HR leading the way.* London: Chartered Institute of Personnel and Development.

CIPD. (2013a) *Organising HR for partnering success.* London: Chartered Institute of Personnel and Development.

CIPD. (2013b) PESTLE analysis [online]. Factsheet. London: Chartered Institute of Personnel and Development. Available at: http://www.cipd.co.uk/hr-resources/factsheets/pestle-analysis.aspx [Accessed 1 January 2015]

CIPD. (2013c) SWOT Analysis [online]. Factsheet. London: Chartered Institute of Personnel and Development. Available at: www.cipd.co.uk/hr-resources/factsheets/swot-analysis.aspx [Accessed 1 January 2015]

CIPD. (2013d) Megatrends. London: Chartered Institute of Personnel and Development.

CIPD. (2013e) Zero-hours contracts: myth and reality. Research Report. London: Chartered Institute of Personnel and Development.

CIPD. (2013f) HR outlook, Winter 2012–2013. Available at: www.cipd.co.uk/hr-resources/survey-reports/hr-outlook-winter-2012-13-leader-perspectives.aspx [Accessed 27 September 2014]

CIPD. (2014a) *The psychological contract.* Factsheet. London: Chartered Institute of Personnel and Development.

CIPD (2014b) *HR outsourcing* [online]. Factsheet. London: Chartered Institute of Personnel and Development. Available at: www.cipd.co.uk/hr-resources/factsheets/hr-outsourcing.aspx [Accessed 1 January 2015]

CIPD. (2014c) *Employment law: EU influence.* Factsheet. November. London: Chartered Institute of Personnel and Development.

CIPD. (2014d) *Change Management.* Factsheet. London: Chartered Institute of Personnel and Development.

CIPD. (2014e) *HR business partnering.* Factsheet. London: Chartered Institute of Personnel and Development. Available at: http://www.cipd.co.uk/hr-resources/factsheets/hr-business-partnering.aspx [Accessed 22 February 2016]

CIPD (2015a) *Avoiding the demographic crunch: labour supply and the ageing workforce.* Chartered Institute of Personnel and Development.

CIPD. (2015b) *Flexible working.* Factsheet. London: Chartered Institute of Personnel and Development.

CIPD. (2015c) *Talent management.* Factsheet. London: Chartered Institute of Personnel and Development.

CIPD. (2015d) *Zero hours contracts*. Factsheet. London: Chartered Institute of Personnel and Development.

CIPD/ACAS. (2009) *How to manage your workforce in a recession*. London: Chartered Institute of Personnel and Development.

CIPD/KPMG. (2005) *Labour market outlook*. Summer/Autumn quarterly survey report. London: Chartered Institute of Personnel and Development.

CHENOWETH, C. (2014) Get me 50,000 people. *People Management*, September. pp32–36.

CHERNACK, T. J. and KASSHANNA, B. K. (2007) The use and misuse of SWOT analysis and implications for HRD professionals. *Human Resource Development International*. Vol 10, No 4. December.

CHILD, J. (2005) *Organization: contemporary principles and practice*. Oxford: Blackwell.

CHIU, W., CHAN, A., SNAPE, E. and REDMAN, T. (2001) Age stereotypes and discriminatory attitudes towards older workers: an East–West comparison. *Human Relations*. Vol 54, No 5. pp629–61.

CHOO, C. W. (2001) Environmental scanning as information seeking and organizational learning. *Information Research*. Vol 7, Issue 1. Available at: http://InformationR.net/ir/7-1/paper112.html [Accessed 8 February 2016]

CHRISAFIS, A. (2009) Stress and worker suicides mean the future's not bright at Orange. *The Guardian*. 19 September. p9.

CHRISTY, R. and CHRISTY G. (2009) The strategic context. In: RAYNER, C. and ADAM-SMITH, D. (eds). *Managing and leading people*. 2nd ed. London: Chartered Institute of Personnel and Development.

CHU, B. (2011) George Osborne's outer fringes. *The Independent*. 8 August.

CHUBB, L. (2008) Outsourcing recruitment would free up HR to focus on other priorities. *People Management*. 29 May. p9.

CHURCHARD, C. (2009a) 'Survivor syndrome' hits UK workforce. *People Management*. 7 August.

CHURCHARD, C. (2009b) Honda staff vote for 3% pay cut to save jobs. *People Management*. 16 June.

CHURCHARD, C. (2009c) Voluntary measures will secure BA's future, says HR chief. *People Management*. 17 July.

CHURCHARD, C. (2011) Fewer managers recognise HR's influence on business. *People Management*. 19 January.

CHURCHARD, C. (2012a) Technology encourages work presenteeism. *People Management*. 1 February. Available at: http://www.peoplemanagement.co.uk/pm/articles/2012/02/technology-encourages-work-presenteeism-claibms-research.htm [Accessed 8 February 2016]

CHURCHARD, C. (2012b) Bonus clawback proposed at Land Securities. People Management. July 9.

CHYNOWETH, C. (2007) War games. *People Management*. 3 October. p13.

CHYNOWETH, C. (2014) We wanted to end accidents – so we put on a show. *People Management*. August. pp20–21.

CISCO. (2010) *The evolving Internet: a look ahead to 2025 by Cisco and the Monitor Group's Global Business Network*. Available at: http://newsroom.cisco.com/dlls/2010/prod_0825106.html [Accessed 15 January 2015]

CITY LINK. (2014a) *Press release: City Link plans ahead to beat last year's successful peak performance*. 11 November. Available at: http://www.city-link.co.uk [Accessed 18 January 2015]

CITY LINK. (2014b) Press release: City Link gears up for peak 2014. 7 September. Available at: http://www.city-link.co.uk [Accessed 18 January 2015]

CIVITAS (2010) EU facts: the EU 2020 strategy. Available at: http://www.civitas.org.uk/eufacts/FSECON/EC12.htm [Accessed 28 December 2012]

CLANCY, C. (2009) The labour market and the economy. *Economic and Labour Market Review*. February.

CLARK, A. (2010) BP's behaviour was shameful. But it wasn't the only one to blame for the gulf disaster. *The Observer*. 31 October.

CLARK, D. (2004) Unto him that hath. *The Guardian*. 6 August.

CLARK, P. (2014). *Case study: the rapid growth of Lenovo*. OSC IB Blogs. Available at: http://blogs.osc-ib.com/2014/08/ib-teacher-blogs-dp_busman-case-study-the-rapid-growth-of-lenovo/ [Accessed 22 June 2015]

CLARK, R. (2005) *Contemporary strategy analysis*. 5th ed. Oxford: Blackwell.

CLARKE, S and DALEY, C. (2010) *The eurozone crisis*. Civitas. Available at: http://www.civitas.org.uk/eufacts/ [Accessed 1 December 2012]

CLEMENT, B. (2001) Honda workers vote for union recognition. *The Independent*. 11 December.

CLEGG, S., KORNBERGER, M. and PITSIS, T. (2008) *Managing and organizations*. 2nd edition. London: Sage.

CLENNELL, A. (2004) Call centre switches jobs back from India to Britain. *The Independent*. 23 January.

CLOSE THE GAP. (2007) *Case study: modern apprenticeships*. Glasgow: Close the Gap. Available at: http://www.closethegap.org.uk/content/resources/GBACaseStudy.pdf [Accessed 6 November 2015]

CLOVER, C. (2003) Members 'suspect voting system in National Trust' *Daily Telegraph*. 24 April.

CMI. (2006) *National management salary survey*. London: Chartered Management Institute.

CMI. (2007) *National management salary survey*. London: Chartered Management Institute.

CMI. (2009) *National management salary survey.* London: Chartered Management Institute.

CMI. (2014) *National management salary survey.* London: Chartered Management Institute.

COBWEB INFORMATION LTD. (2013) *Courier and parcel services: UK market synopsis.* SYN010. May. Available at: http://buty.gov.uk/CHHpHandler.ashx?id=15461&p=0 [Accessed 18 January 2015]

COHEN, R and KENNEDY, P. (2007) *Global sociology.* 2nd ed. Basingstoke: Palgrave Macmillan.

COLES, S. (2009) Are we still feeling the Five Forces? *Long Range Planning.* November.

COLLIER, P. (2013) *Exodus: how migration is changing our world.* London: Oxford University Press.

COLLINS, C. and PORRAS, J. (2000) *Built to last: successful habits of visionary companies.* 3rd ed. London: Random House.

COLLINSON, P. and SEAGER, A. (2007) Northern Rock crisis: call to City grandees that threw lifeline to drowning bank. *The Guardian.* 15 September.

COMMUNITIES AND LOCAL GOVERNMENT COMMITTEE (2011) Regeneration report. London: The Stationery Office.

COMMUNITY INTEREST COMPANIES ASSOCIATION. (2012) What is a CIC? Available at: http://www.cicassociation.org.uk/about/what-is-a-cic [Accessed 18 November 2012]

COMPETITION COMMISSION. (2003) *Extended warranties on domestic electrical goods: a report on the supply of extended warranties on domestic electrical goods within the UK.* Available at: http://webarchive.nationalarchives.gov.uk/+/http:/www.competition-commission.org.uk/rep_pub/reports/2003/485xwars.htm [Accessed 8 February 2016]

COMPETITION COMMISSION. (2007) *Groceries market investigation: emerging thinking.* 23 January. Available at: http://webarchive.nationalarchives.gov.uk/20140402142426/http://www.competition-commission.org.uk/inquiries/ref2006/grocery/pdf/emerging_thinking.pdf [Accessed 8 February 2016]

CONNOCK, S. and JOHNS, T. (1995) *Ethical leadership.* London: Chartered Institute of Personnel and Development. CONNOR, J. (2010) *The growth option: turbo-charging HR's impact in Asia.* Bridge/CIPD Next Generation HR Asia, December.

CONNOR, J. (2011) Eastern time. *People Management.* 21 January.

CONNOR, S. (2013) One child policy: China's army of little emperors. *The Independent.* 10 January.

CONTRACTOR, F. and LORANGE, P. (1998) Why should firms cooperate? The strategy and economics basis for cooperative ventures. In: CONTRACTOR, F. and LORANGE, P. (eds) *Cooperative strategies in international business.* New York: Lexington Books.

CONWAY, N. and BRINER, R. (2005) *Understanding the psychological contract at work.* Oxford: Oxford University Press.

CONWAY, G. (2011) No hands, no feet; I'm think-driving now. *Sunday Times*. In-Gear. 3 April. pp4–5.

COOK, A. (2012) Social media can transform the quality of recruitment. *People Management*. October. p49.

COONAN, C. (2009) China relaxes one-child rule to beat pension crisis. *The Independent*. 25 July. p18.

COOPER, J., CAMPBELL, S., PATEL, D. and SIMMONS, J. (2014) The reason for migration and labour market characteristics of UK resident born abroad. Occasional Paper 110. London: Home Office.

CORNELIUS, P., VAN DE PUTTE, A. and ROMANI, M. (2005), Three decades of scenario planning at Shell. California Management Review. Vol 48, No 1. Fall.

CORRUPT THE BRAND. (2012) Quotes and thoughts from the National Trust Going Local strategy. Available at: http://corruptthebrand.blogspot.co.uk/2012/09/quotes-and-thoughts-from-going-local.html [Accessed 25 January 2015]

COWAN, R. (2004) Met harnesses its diversity in the war against crime. *The Guardian*. 2 December.

COWE, R. (2004) Commanding heights. *The Guardian*. 8 November.

COYLE, D. and QUAH, D. (2004) *Getting the measure of the new economy*. London: The Work Foundation.

CRABTREE, J. (2012) India's call centres make move upmarket. *The Financial Times*. 25 June.

CRAINER, S. and DEARLOVE, D. (2003) Windfall economics. *Business Strategy Review*. Vol 14, Issue 4. Winter.

CRAINER, S. and DEARLOVE, D. (2005) Indian think. *Business Strategy Review*. Winter.

CRANE, A. and MATTEN, D. (2007) *Business ethics: Managing corporate citizenship and sustainability in the age of globalization*. 2nd ed. Oxford: Oxford University Press.

CRAVEN, N. (2015) Shares in Sports Direct jump and Mike Ashley handed £96 million windfall after Tory win kills off zero-hours reforms. *Mail on Sunday*. 10 May.

CRIBB, J., DISNEY, R. and SIBIETA, L. (2014) *The public sector workforce: past, present and future*. London: Institute for Fiscal Studies.

CRIBB, J., JOYCE, R. and PHILLIPS, D. (2012) Living standards, poverty and inequality in the UK. London: IFS. Available at: http://www.ifs.org.uk/comms/comm124/pdf [Accessed 8 February 2016]

CROGGON, P. (2007) Letter to the editor. The Times. 17 September.

CRUM, C. (2011) Yahoo revenue drop attributed to Microsoft seal. WebProNews. 19 October. Available at: www.webpronews.com/yahoo-earnings-2011-10 [Accessed 28 June 2012]

CUBERES, D. and TEIGNIER, M. (2015) *Aggregate effects of gender gaps in the labour market*. Paris: OECD.

CULLINAN, G., LE ROUX, T. and WEDDIGEN, R. (2004) When to walk away from the deal. *Harvard Business Review*. Vol 82, No 4.

CURWEN, P. (1997) *Restructuring telecommunications: a study of Europe in a global context*. London: Macmillan.

CURTIS, P. (2004) Market graders. *The Guardian*. 17 August.

DAILY TELEGRAPH. (2006) 2600 travel jobs axed as consumers book flights on Internet. 16 December.

DAILY TELEGRAPH. (2010) The cuts will strengthen Britain's economy by allowing the private sector to generate more jobs. Letter to the Editor. 18 October.

DAISEY, M. (2015) Amazon's brutal work culture will stay: bottom lines matter more than people. *The Guardian*. 22 August.

DALKEN, F. (2014) *Are Porter's Five Competitive Forces still applicable? A critical examination concerning the relevance for today's business*. University of Twente: The Netherlands.

DANESHKHU. S. (2007a) The quest for improved productivity. *The Financial Times*. 22 May.

DANESHKHU, S. (2007b) Output still trails other large countries. *The Financial Times*. 26 June.

DANFORD, A., RICHARDSON, M., STEWART, P., TAILBY, S. and UPCHURCH, M. (2004) High performance work systems and workplace partnership: a case study of aerospace workers. *New Technology, Work and Employment*. Vol 19, No 1. pp14–29.

D'ARCY, C. and KELLY, G. (2015) *Analysing the National Living Wage*. Resolution Foundation. July. Available at: http://www.resolutionfoundation.org./wp-content/uploads/2015/07/RF-National-Living-Wage-briefing.pdf [Accessed 3 October 2015]

DATAMONITOR. (2006) *Tesco plc Company Profile*. May. London: Datamonitor.

DATAMONITOR. (2009) *Adnams case study: overcoming the poor performance of the recessionary UK beer market*. London: Datamonitor.

DATAMONITOR (2011a) *The UK beer industry*. London: Datamonitor. DATAMONITOR (2011b) *The global beer industry*. London: Datamonitor.

DAVEY, J. (2009) Every little bit of data helps Tesco rule detail. *Sunday Times*. Business. 4 October. p7.

DAVIES, G. (2007) The roots of moral hazard. *The Guardian*. 15 September.

DAVIES, G. and SMITH, H. (2007) Natural resources. *People Management*. 8 March.

DAVIES, M. (2011) *Independent review of women on boards*. London: Department for Business, Innovation and Skills.

DAVIES, M. (2014) *Women on boards: three years on*. Department for Industry, Innovation and Skills.

DAVIES, R. and NESLEN, A. (2015) UK steel crisis: EU leaders vow 'full and speedy response' to halt cheap imports. *The Guardian*. 9 November.

DAY, G. and SCHOEMAKER, P. (2005) Scanning the periphery. *Harvard Business Review.* Vol 83, No 11. November.

DEAL, J. (1976) Pricing policies for new products. *Harvard Business Review.* Vol 54, Issue Nov/Dec (first published November 1950).

DEAL, T. and KENNEDY, A. (1990), Values; the core of the culture. In: CAMPBELL, A. and TAWADEY, K. (eds) *Mission and business philosophy.* Oxford: Butterworth-Heinemann.

DEAN, J. (1976) Pricing policies for new products. *Harvard Business Review.* Vol 54,

Nov/Dec (first published November 1950).

DE GEORGE, R. T. (1999) *Business Ethics.* 5th ed. Upper Saddle River, NJ: Prentice Hall.

DE GRAUWE, P. (2001) Competitiveness and compassion. *The Financial Times.* 8 November.

DE JONQUIERES, H. (2003) How enlightened international co-operation turned into a show case for indecision. *Financial Times.* 31 March.

DELERY, J. and DOTY, H. (1996) Modes of theorizing in strategic human resource management: tests of universalistic contingency, and configurational performance predictions. *Academy of Management Journal.* Vol 39, No 4.

DEMING, W. (1986) *Out of crisis: quality, productivity and competitive position.* Cambridge: Cambridge University Press.

DENVER POST. (2010) Appeals court tosses jury award in Rocky Flats case. 4 September.

DEPARTMENT FOR BUSINESS, INNOVATION AND SKILLS/NATIONAL STATISTICS. (2014) *Trade union membership 2013: statistical bulletin.* London: Department for Business, Innovation and Skills/National Statistics. Available at: http://www.gov.uk/government/uploads/attachment_data/file/313768/bis-14-p77-trade-union-membership-statistical-bulletin-2013.pdf [Accessed 30 May 2015]

DEPARTMENT FOR BUSINESS, INNOVATION AND SKILLS. (2015) Growth dashboard. London: DBIS. Available at: www.gov.uk/government/uploads/system/uploads/attachment_data/file/396740/bis-15-4-growthdashboard.pdf [Accessed 31 May 2015]

DEPARTMENT FOR INNOVATION, UNIVERSITIES AND SKILLS. (2007) *World class skills: implementing the Leitch Review of Skills in England.* Cm 7181. London: The Stationery Office.

DEPARTMENT OF TRADE AND INDUSTRY (1998) *Building the knowledge driven economy.* Available at: http://webarchive.nationalarchives.gov.uk/+/http:/www.dti.gov.uk/comp/competitive/prs_n2.htm [Accessed 29 August 2004]

DEPARTMENT OF TRADE AND INDUSTRY. (2001) *Opportunity for all in a world of change.* Available at: http://www.dti.gov.uk/opportunity for all [Accessed 29 August 2004]

DEPARTMENT OF TRADE AND INDUSTRY. (2002*) Business and society: corporate social responsibility.* London: Department for Trade and Industry.

DEPARTMENT OF WORK AND PENSIONS. (2011) *Allevard Springs case study*. Available at: https://www.gov.uk/government/uploads/system/uploads/attachment_data/file/142752/employing-older-workers-case-studies.pdf [Accessed 27 February 2016]

DEPARTMENT OF WORK AND PENSIONS. (2012) Wetherspoons case study. Available at: https://www.gov.uk/government/uploads/system/uploads/attachment_data/file/142752/employing-older-workers-case-studies.pdf [Accessed 27 February 2016]

DESJARDINS, J. (2007) *Business, ethics and the environment*. Upper Saddle River, NJ: Pearson/Prentice Hall.

DE VITA, E. (2009) Fast track India. *Management Today*, August.

DEY, I. and SMITH, D. (2009) Mr Darling's exceedingly poor fudge. *Sunday Times Business*. 12 July. p7.

DICKEN, P. (2003) *Global shift*. London: Sage.

DILBERT website (www.dilbert.com)

DILLOW, C. (2011) The wage squeeze. *Investors Chronicle*. 26 January.

DIRECTGOV. (2010) *Statutory guarantee pay*. Available at: http://www.direct.gov.uk/en/Employment/Understandingyourworkstatus/Temporarylayoff/DG_177591 [Accessed 12 April 2010]

DIXON, M. (1978) *Financial Times*. 2 November. p38.

DOBBS, R., MAIYKA, J. and WOETZEL, J. (2015) *No ordinary disruption*. PublicAffairs: New York.

DOERINGER, P, LORENZ, E. and TERKLA, D. (2003) The adoption and diffusion of high performance management lessons from Japanese multinationals in the West. *Cambridge Journal of Economics*. Vol 27.

DOLTON, P. (2001) *The labour market for teachers: a policy perspective*. London: Office of Manpower Economics.

DOMBEY, D. (2012) Turkey's Beko claims UK market top spot. *The Financial Times*. 6 December.

DONE, K. (2007) Ryanair orders 27 Boeing jets. *The Financial Times*. 31 May.

DONNELLY, P. (2014) Ebola and human rights: insights from experts. *Health and Human Rights Journal*. 20 November.

DORE, R. (2006) Japan's shareholder revolution. *CentrePiece*. Winter 2006/07.

DORLING, D., RIGBY, J., WHEELER, B., BALLAS, D., THOMAS, B., FAHMY, E., GORDON, D. and LUPTON, R. (2007) *Poverty, wealth and place in Britain 1968 to 2005*. York: Policy Press for the Joseph Rowntree Foundation.

DORLING, D. (2014) *All that is solid: the great housing disaster*. London: Allen Lane.

DOW CHEMICAL COMPANY (2015) www.dow.com [Accessed 17 April 2015]

DOWARD, J. (2003) Future imperfect as longer lifespan looms. The Observer. 28 December. p9.

DOWARD, J. (2009) Banana price war in supermarkets brings fear to the developing world. The Observer. 11 October.

DOWARD, J. and MCKENNA, H. (2007) Immigration figures 'are false'. The Observer. 29 April.

DOWNES, L. (1997) Technosynthesis: beyond Porter. Context. Available at http://www.contextmag.com/archives/199712/technosynthesis.asp [Accessed 28 June 2012]

DRACA, M. and DICKENS, R. (2005) The employment effects of the October 2003 increase in the National Minimum Wage. *CEP Discussion Paper*, June

DRAGHI, M. (2012) Speech by Mario Draghi, President of the ECB, 26 July. Available at: http://www.ecb.int/press/key/date/2012/html/sp120726.eu.html [Accessed 4 February 2013]

DRAGONFLY GROUP. (2015) Human resource issues in China. Dragonfly Group. Available at: http://www.dragonflygroup.com/index.php?option=com_content&view= article&id=69%3Ahuman-resource-issues-in-china-&catid=2%3Aother-articles&Itemid= 29&lang=en&56f721d951010f6f334c9b0c71b23b90=b [Accessed 10 October 2015]

DRUCKER, P. (1981) *Managing in turbulent times*. London: Pan Books.

DRUCKER, P. (1990) What is 'business ethics? In: CAMPBELL, A. and TAWADY, K. (eds)*Mission and business philosophy*. Oxford: Butterworth-Heinemann.

DUBNER, S. and LEVITT, S. (2009) www.Freakonomics.blogs [Accessed 5 December 2009].

DUDOVSKIY, J. (2012) *Ryanair: Porter's Five Forces Analysis*. Available at: http://research-methodology.net/ryanair-porters-five-forces-analysis/ [Accessed 30 May 2015]

DUDOVSKIY, J. (2014). Starbucks strategic fit analysis. Available at: http://research-methodology.net/starbucks-strategic-fit-analysis/ [Accessed 30 May 2015]

DUKE, S. and PANCEVSKI, B. (2015) Brussels hammers the tech giants. *Sunday Times Business*. April 19. p5.

DULEWICZ, V. (2004) Give full details. *People Management*. 26 February. p23.

DUNCAN, G. and WEBSTER, P. (2007) MPC founding member comes out swinging against Bank's bailout decision. *The Times*. 15 September.

DUSSAUGE, P. and GARRETTE, B. (1999). *Cooperative strategy: competing successfully through strategic alliances*. Chichester: John Wiley.

DYER, J., KALE, P. and SINGH, H. (2004) When to ally and when to acquire. *Harvard Business Review*. Vol 82, No 7/8. July/August.

DYMOND, J. and MURLIS, H. (2009) Executive rewards. In: CORBY, S., PALMER, S. and LINDOP, E. (eds) *Re-thinking reward*. Basingstoke: Palgrave Macmillan.

DYSON, R. (2013) Older, wiser – and how you could get wealthier. *Daily Telegraph*. 20 July. Y2.

EASYJET. (2007) easyJet web site. www.easyjet.com [Accessed June-July 2007]

EASYJET. (2015) easyJet web site. www.easyjet.com [Accessed May-June 2015]

ECB (2004) *Objective of monetary policy*. European Central Bank. Available at: www.ecb. int

ECOFIN. (2006) *The impact of ageing on public expenditure: projections for the EU25 member states on pension, health care, long-term care, education and unemployment, 2004–2050*. Brussels: ECOFIN.

ECONOMIST. (2000) Communication advances. *The Economist* 23 September. p24.

ECONOMIST. (2001) Globalisation and its critics. *The Economist*. 26 September.

ECONOMIST. (2003a) The big easy: economics and reality. *The Economist*. 3 May.

ECONOMIST. (2003b) The Doha squabble, *The Economist*. 29 March.

ECONOMIST. (2004a) Salad days. *The Economist*. 6 November.

ECONOMIST. (2004b) Return of the wrinklies. *The Economist*. 17 January.

ECONOMIST. (2004c) Debt threat. *The Economist*. 24 April.

ECONOMIST. (2004d) An awful lot of brewing in Brazil. *The Economist*. 6 March.

ECONOMIST. (2005) From Lisbon to Brussels. *The Economist*. 19 March.

ECONOMIST. (2006a) Now we are 300,000,000. *The Economist*. 14 October.

ECONOMIST. (2006b) In the twilight of Doha. *The Economist*. 29 July.

ECONOMIST. (2006c) Trouble at till. *The Economist*. 4 November.

ECONOMIST. (2006d) Voting with your trolley. *The Economist*. 9 December.

ECONOMIST. (2007a) Easy on the eyes. *The Economist*. 7 April.

ECONOMIST. (2007b) From cheque books to checking pulses. *The Economist*. 14 April.

ECONOMIST. (2007c) Plastics of evil. *The Economist*. 31 March.

ECONOMIST. (2008) Skunkworks. *The Economist*. 25 August.

ECONOMIST. (2009a) The people crunch. *The Economist*. 17 January.

ECONOMIST. (2009b) Go forth and multiply a lot less. *The Economist*. 31 October.

ECONOMIST. *(2011)* The next big bet. *The Economist*. 30 September.

ECONOMIST. (2012a) The London effect. *The Economist*. 15 December.

ECONOMIST. (2012b) The expanding middle. The Economist. 10 November.

ECONOMIST. (2012c) The new maker rules. *The Economist*. 24 November.

ECONOMIST. (2012d) March of the Lettuce Bot. *The Economist*. 1 December.

ECONOMIST. (2013a) An unwelcoming nation. *The Economist*. 2 February. p26.

ECONOMIST. (2013b) Peak toil. *The Economist*. 26 January.

ECONOMIST. (2013c) A house divided. *The Economist*. 9 February.

ECONOMIST. (2013d) No hiding place. *The Economist.* 25 May.

ECONOMIST. (2013e) Welcome home. *The Economist.* 19 January.

ECONOMIST. (2013f) From guard shack to global giant. *The Economist.* 12 January.

ECONOMIST. (2013g) The next big thing. *The Economist.* 8 January.

ECONOMIST. (2014a) What have the immigrants ever done for us. *The Economist.* 8 November.

ECONOMIST (2014b) America's Greece? *The Economist.* 20 December.

ECONOMIST. (2014c) An honest living. *The Economist.* 8 May.

ECONOMIST. (2014d) The war on Ebola; The epidemic in West Africa. *The Economist.* 18 October.

ECONOMIST. (2014e) Giving it a shot: vaccine-makers and Ebola. *The Economist.* 1 November.

ECONOMIST. (2014f) Unchained malady. *The Economist.* 15 November.

ECONOMIST. (2014g) Unintended consequences: Ebola. *The Economist.* 6 September.

ECONOMIST. (2015a) Breaking the baby strike. *The Economist.* July 25.

ECONOMIST. (2015b) Kitted out. *The Economist.* 14 March.

ECONOMIST. (2015c). Bargain basement. *The Economist.* 14 March.

ECONOMIST. (2015d) Bang goes retirement. *The Economist.* 18 April.

ECONOMIST. (2015e) Steeled for worse. *The Economist.* 24 October.

ECONOMIST. (2015f) After the passing: Ebola's legacy. *The Economist.* 3 January,

ECONOMIST. (2015g) Hiding Sir's black cash. *The Economist.* 14 February.

ECONOMIST. (2015h) A costly mistake. *The Economist.* 2 July.

EDGECLIFFE-JOHNSON, A. (2006) How upstarts continue to upset. *The Financial Times.* 15 August.

EDWARDS, C. (2004) Five-star strategy. *People Management.* 8 April. pp34–5.

EDWARDS, J. (2013) Brutal conditions in Amazon's warehouses threaten to ruin the company's image. *Business Insider.* 5 August.

ELECTRICITY ASSOCIATION. (1998) *Electricity industry review.* London: HMSO.

ELIAS, P. (2006) *Robot birth simulator used in med schools.* Associated Press. Available at: www.livescience.com/topics/robots [Accessed 8 February 2016]

ELLIOTT, L. (2004a) What the WTO needs is a new Reformation. *The Guardian.* 2 August.

ELLIOTT, L. (2004b) The outlook is not so Nice when hidden hazards are exposed. *The Guardian.* 18 October.

ELLIOTT, L. (2009) Brown is right: rich western banks must pay for developing nations to go green. *The Guardian.* 9 November.

ELLIOTT, L. (2012) Why more jobs may reflect hard times for workers. *The Guardian.* 3 December.

ELLIOTT, L. (2015a) Is Jeremy Corbyn's policy of 'quantitative easing for people feasible? *The Guardian.* 14 August.

ELLIOTT, L. (2015b) Will George Osborne's productivity plan help make Britain a world-beater? *The Guardian.* 25 May.

ELLIOTT, L. (2015c) Financial crisis fixes leave policymakers short of ammo for next recession. *The Guardian.* 1 June.

ELLIOTT, L. and CONNOLLY, K. (2007) In 2005, G8 pledged $50bn for Africa. Now the reality. *The Guardian.* 25 April.

ELLIOTT, L. and STEWART, H. (2011) IMF warns that world risks sliding into a 1930s-style slump. *The Guardian.* 15 December.

ELLIS, A. (2009) UK resident population by country of birth. *Population Trends* 135. Spring. London: ONS.

ELLIS, C., MUNNELL, A. and ESCHTRUTH, A. (2014) *Falling short: the coming retirement crisis and what to do about it.* Oxford: Oxford University Press.

EMMOTT, B., CROOK, C. and MICKLETHWAIT, J. (2002) *Globalisation: making sense of an integrating world.* London: *The Economist*/Profile Books.

EMMOTT, M. (2011) What's the future for employment relations in China? *Impact* 35. May.

EMMOTT, M. (2015) The impact of 'Brexit' on employment law. CIPD public policy blog. 10 August. Available at: http://cipd.co.uk/blogs/cipdbloggers/b/policy_at_work/archives/2015/08/10/the-impact-of-brexit-on-employment-law.aspx [Accessed 10 October 2015]

ENRIA, A. (2015) Banking regulation. European Banking Authority website.

ENTERPRISE. (2009) Case study: customer contact centre with the mod housing contract. Available at: http://www.enterprise.plc.uk/_common/download/brochures/MoD%20%28MHS%29%20-%20Customer%20Contact%20Centre.pdf [Accessed 27 March 2013]

EUROBAROMETER. (2014) *Public opinion in the European Union.* Eurobarometer 82. Autumn. Brussels: European Commission.

EUROPEAN COMMISSION. (2001) *Promoting a European framework for corporate social responsibility*

EUROPEAN COMMISSION. (2014) *Eurobarometer 82 Public opinion in the European Union.* Available at http://ec.europa.eu/public-opinion/archives/eb/eb82/eb82_first_en.pdf [Accessed 7 June 2015]

EUROPEAN UNION. (2004) European performance in competitiveness and innovation. Available at: http://www.europa.eu.int [Accessed 18 September 2004]

EUROSTAT. (2012) *Poverty and social exclusion in the European Union*. Available at: epp. eurostat.ec.europa.eu/cache/ITY_PUBLIC/3-08022012-AP/EN/3-08022012-APEN.PDF

EUROSTAT. (2015a) *Marriage and divorce statistics*. Available at: http://ec.europa.eu/eurostat/statistics-explained/index.php/Marriage_and_divorce_statistics [Accessed 27 February 2016]

EUROSTAT. (2015b) Gini coefficient of disposable income. Available at http://ec.europa. eu/eurostat/tgm/table.do?tab=table&language=en&pcode=tessi190 [Accessed 27 February 2016]

EVANS, C. (2008) Enablers and barriers to high performance working: insights from the first Shaping the Future Café event. London: Chartered Institute of Personnel and Development.

EVANS, J. (2011) Wider appeal. People Management. May. pp47–50.

EVENETT, S. (ed) (2011) Resolve falters as global prospects worsen: The 9th GTA Report. London: Centre for Economic Policy Research/Global Trade Alert. Available at http://www.globaltradealert.org/sites/default/files/GTA9.pdf [Accessed 15 June 2015]

EVOLVING GLOBALISATION. (2014) *Challenges in international business: a case study of Lenovo*. Norwich. Forum for Sustainable Development, University of East Anglia. Available at: http://evolving-globalisation-org/2014/03/17/sixth-post-title/ [Accessed 21 June 2015]

EXPLORE WORLDWIDE. (2004) 2004-2005 Brochure. Available at: http://www.explore. co.uk [Accessed 24 September 3004]

FAIR TAX MARK. (2015a) Fair Tax: what is it? Available at: http://www.fairtaxmark.net/what-is-it/ [Accessed 18 February 2015]

FAIR TAX MARK. (2015b) *Fair Tax: SSE*. Available at: http://www/fairtaxmark.net/sse/ [Accessed 18 February 2015]

FAMILY-FRIENDLY WORKING HOURS TASKFORCE. (2010) *Flexible working: working for families, working for business*. London: Chartered Institute for Personnel and Development.

FARNHAM, D. (1999) *Managing in a business context*. London: Chartered Institute for Personnel and Development.

FARNHAM, D. (2010) *Human resource management in context*. London: Chartered Institute of Personnel and Development.

FARRELL, S. (2015) Five lines of attack for embattled Tesco to start fighting back. *The Guardian*. 18 April.

FAVARO, K. and JONI, S. (2010) Getting tensions right: How CEOs can turn conflict, dissent, and disagreement into a powerful tool for driving performance. *Strategy + Business*. Autumn. No 60.

FAYOL, H. (1916/1949) *General and industrial management*. London: Pitman.

FEDERAL RESERVE (2004) *Frequently Asked Questions: Monetary Policy*, www. federalreserve.gov)

FELSTED, A. (2003) The Dublin-based airline has become a leading force in European aviation. *Financial Times*. 4 November.

FELSTED, A. (2012a) Tesco, every little revamp helps. *The Financial Times*. 7 March

FELSTED, A. (2012b) Tesco to focus on smaller stores. *The Financial Times*. 12 April

FELSTED, A. (2012c) Tesco rating cut as it reveals recovery plan. *The Financial Times*. 21 April.

FELSTED, A. (2012d) Clarke puts a brave face on Tesco sales slip. *The Financial Times*. 12 June.

FIELDER, F. (1967) *A theory of leadership effectiveness*. New York: McGraw Hill.

FINANCIAL CONDUCT AUTHORITY. (2015) Monthly PPI payouts. October. http://fca.org.uk/consumers/financial-services-products/insurance/payment-protection-insurance/ppi-compensation-refunds [Accessed 4 November 2015]

FINCH, J. (2003) In India, it's service with a compulsory smile. The Guardian. 17 November.

FINCH, J. (2009a) Morrisons beats rivals with bumper Christmas sales. The Guardian. 23 January.

FINCH, J. (2009b) Supermarkets: big four fight back in discount food feud. The Guardian. 25 July.

FINCH, J. (2012) Barclays: six things we learned. The Guardian. 5 July.

FINCH, J. and ALLEN, K. (2006) Tesco offers carrot to reduce use of plastic carrier bags. The Guardian. 5 August.

FIRST CHOICE (2007) www.firstchoiceholidaysplc.com [Accessed 3 August 2007]

FISHER, C. and LOVELL, A. (2006) *Business ethics and values: individual, corporate and international perspectives*. 2nd ed. Harlow: FT/Prentice Hall.

FISHER, L. (2005) Ricardo Semler won't take control. *strategy + business*. Winter.

FLETCHER, R. (2006) Thailand junta warns Tesco over expansion. *Daily Telegraph*. 28 September.

FOOD AND DRINK EUROPE (2003) Flexible pricing strategy keeps shoppers happy. Available at: http://www.foodanddrinkeurope.com/Retail/Flexible-pricing. 11 December. [Accessed 3 July 2012]

FORD, J. (2014) A new approach is needed for British dealmaking. The Financial Times. 11 June.

FORD, J. (2015) Easyjet announces plan to use drones for aircraft inspection. The Engineer. 12 June.

FORD, S. (2009), Working Time Directive tsar says the 48 hour week is good for nursing. Nursing Times. 2 June.

FORDYCE, T. (2005) 10 years since Bosman. BBC Sport. Available at: http://www.news.bbc.co.uk/sport1/hi/football [Accessed 14 October 2009]

FORMAN, F. N. and BALDWIN, N. D. J (1999) *Mastering British politics.* 4th ed. Basingstoke: Macmillan.

FORSYTH, D. R. (1980) A taxonomy of ethical ideologies. *Journal of Personality and Social Psychology.* Vol 39, No 1. July.

FORTUNE (2006) *Fortune Global 500.* Available at: http://www.money.cnn.com/ magazines/fortune/global 500) [Accessed 8 May 2007]

FOSTER, S. (2010) *In light of the increasingly integral role of the internet in the workplace, how do HR professionals best approach the monitoring and policing of its usage?* Unpublished Master's dissertation. University of Bedfordshire.

FOX, J. (2012) The economics of well-being. *Harvard Business Review.* Vol 90, No 1/2. January/February,

FRANCIS, H. (2005) Slippery slope. *People Management.* 30 June.

FRATERMAN, E. (2009) The case for customer satisfaction. Available at: http://www. customerfocusconsult.com [Accessed 27 February 2016]

FREEMAN, C. (1987) *Technology policy and economic performance: lessons from Japan.* London: Pinter Publishers.

FRENCH, W.L. and BELL, C.H. (1984) *Organization development.* Englewood Cliffs, NJ: Prentice Hall. FRIEDMAN, M. (1962) *Capitalism and freedom.* Chicago, IL: Chicago University Press.

FRIEDMAN, M. (1970a) *The counter-revolution in monetary theory.* London: Institute of Economic Affairs.

FRIEDMAN, M. (1970b) The social responsibility of business is to increase its profits. *New York Times Magazine.* 13 September.

FUKUYAMA, F. (1992) *The end of history and the last man.* New York: Avon Books.

FUKUYAMA, F. (2004) Bring back the state. *The Observer.* 4 July.

FULLFACT. (2015) Zero hour contracts facts. Available at: https://fullfact.org/factcheck/ economy/zero-hour-contracts-facts-41165 [Accessed 30 May 2015]

FURLONG, A. and CARTMEL, F. (2001) Capitalism without classes. In: GIDDENS, A. (ed.) *Sociology: introductory readings.* Revised ed. Cambridge: Polity.

FURNHAM, A. and GUNTER, B. (1993) *Corporate assessment.* London: Routledge.

GALL, G. (2001) ISTC wins in recognition vote. *People Management.* 22 November.

GALLAGHER, J. (2015) Ebola vaccine is 'potential game-changer'. *BBC News.* 31 July. Available at: http://www.bbc.co.uk/news/health-33733711 [accessed 5 August 2015]

GALLIE, D. (2000) The labour force. In: HALSEY, A.H. and WEBB, J. (eds) *Twentieth century British social trends.* Basingstoke: Macmillan.

GAMBLE, J. (2003) Transferring human resource practices from the United Kingdom to China: the limits and potential for convergence. *International Journal of Human Resource Management.* Vol 14, Issue 3.

GARSIDE, J., LEIGH, D., BALL, J. and PEGG, D. (2015) The boss: banker, peer, minister, priest. *The Guardian.* 10 February.

GAVETTI, G. (2011) The new psychology of strategic leadership. *Harvard Business Review.* Vol 89, No 7/8. July/August.

GEARY, J. and DOBBINS, A. (2001) Teamworking: a new dynamic in the pursuit of management control. *Human Resource Management Journal.* Vol 11, No 1. pp2–23.

GELMAN, V. (2011) *Russia's crony capitalism: the swing of the pendulum.* Open Democracy. Available at: http://www.opendemocracy.net/od-russia/vladimir-gelman/russia%E2%80%99s-crony-capitalism-swing-of-pendulum [Accessed 28 May 2015]

GEORGE, V. and WILDING, P. (1999) *British society and social welfare: towards a sustainable society.* Basingstoke: Macmillan.

GHEMAWAT, P. (2003) The forgotten strategy, *Harvard Business Review.* Vol 81, No 11. November.

GHOSHAL, S. (2000) Value creation. *Executive Excellence.* November. Vol 17, Issue 11.

GIBBS, S. (2015) Samsung back on top as world's biggest smartphone manufacturer. *The Guardian.* 29 April.

GIBSON, O. and GAYLE, D. (2015) Fifa officials arrested on corruption charges as World Cup inquiry launched. *The Guardian.* 27 May.

GIDDENS, A. (2006) *Sociology.* 5th edition. Cambridge: Polity.

GIFFORD, J. (2012) HR's role in corporate responsibility: still not convinced? *Impact.* Vol 41. December.

GIFFORD, J. (2014) Putting social media to work. Available at: http://www.cipd.co.uk/binaries/6545%20Social%20media%20research%20report%20(WEB).pdf [Accessed 27 February 2016]

GILBERT, H. (2015) Aldi overtakes Tesco in valuable brands survey. The Grocer. 27 May.

GILES, C. (2007) Productivity loses steam under Labour. The Financial Times. 23 January.

GILES, C. (2014) Pros and cons of raising UK minimum wage. The Financial Times. 7 January.

GILES, C. (2015) Solving UK's productivity puzzle is key to government finances. The Financial Times. 19 April.

GILLESPIE, A. (2000) Dell Computers. Business Review. September.

GILLIGAN, A. (2012) If someone asks, I'm British, end of story. Daily Telegraph. 15 December. p31.

GIMENEZ, F. (1999) Miles and Snow's strategy model in the context of small firms. Available at: http://www.baer.uca.edu/research/icbs/1999 [Accessed 3 November 2009]

GIUGLIANO, F. (2015) Weighing up four theories on the UK's productivity gap. *The Financial Times.* 19 April.

GLOVER, C. (2004) Tomorrow's world. *People Management.* 26 February. pp40–41.

GODLEY & CO. (2015) Chancellor George Osborne's fiscal charter approved after intense Commons debate. 15 October. Available at: http://www.godley.co.uk/news/business-news/archive/article/2015/October/chancellor-george-osbornes-fiscal-charter-approved-after-intense-commons-debate [Accessed 23 October 2015]

GOLZEN, G. (2001) What's the big idea? *Global HR.* September.

GOMEZ, E. (2014) Cuba's health diplomacy in the age of Ebola. *BBC News.* 14 November. Available at: http://www.bbc.co.uk/news/world-latin-america [Accessed 18 February 2015]

GOODGE, P. (2004) How to...build a career as an HR partner. *People Management.* 30 June.

GOODWAY, N. and PRYNN, J. (2013) Bankers' bonus culture lives on as millionaires' club tops 2,700. *The Independent.* 30 November. p12.

GOOLD, M. and CAMPBELL, A. (2002) *Designing effective organizations.* New York: Jossey-Bass.

GORDON, R. (2013) Is economic growth over? Faltering innovation confronts the six headwinds. Available at: http://www.nber.org/papers/w18315 [Accessed 27 February 2016]

GOSTIN, L.O. (2014) *Global health law.* Cambridge, MA: Harvard University Press. p179.

GOURLAY, S., ALFES, K., BULL, E., BARON, A., PETROV, G. and GEORGELLIS, Y. (2012) *Emotional or transactional engagement – does it matter?* CIPD/Kingston University Research Report. London: Chartered Institute of Personnel and Development.

GOYAL, A. and JHA, A. (2004) Dictatorship, democracy and institutions: macro policy in China and India. *Economic and Political Weekly (India).* 16 October.

GRAHAM, F. (2010). Crowdsourcing work: labour on demand or digital sweatshop? *BBC News.* 22 October. Available at: http://www.bbc.co.uk/news/business-11600902 [Accessed 24 September 2015]

GRANT, R. (2008) *Contemporary strategy analysis.* 6th ed. Oxford: Blackwell.

GRATTON, L. and TRUSS, C. (2003). The three-dimensional people strategy: Putting human resources policies into action. *Academy of Management Executive.* Vol 17, No 3.

GRAY, J. (1995) *Falsedawn.* London: Granta.

GREATER LONDON AUTHORITY (2011) *A Fairer London: The 2011 Living Wage in London.* London: GLA.

GREEN, C. (2015) Number of workers on zero-hours contracts has risen by more than 110,000, statistics show. *The Independent.* 25 February.

GREEN, F. (2002) *Why has work effort become more intense? Conjectures and evidence about effort-based technical change and other stories.* University of Kent Discussion Papers in Economics. July.

GRIFFIN, E., FINNEY, L., HENNESSY, J. and BOURY, D. (2009) *Maximising the value of HR business partnering.* Horsham: Roffey Park Institute.

GRIFFITH, G. (2013a) Ryanair gets thumbs down for customer service. *Management Today News.* 19 September http://www.managementtoday.co.uk/news/1212600/ryanair-gets-thumbs-down-customer-service/ [Accessed 13 October 2015]

GRIFFITH, G. (2013b) Ryanair in extra hand luggage allowance shocker. *Management Today News*. 25 October http://www.managementtoday.co.uk/news/1218301/Ryanair-extra-hand-luggage-allowance-shocker/ [Accessed 13 October 2015]

GRIFFITHS, J. (2012) Taking care of business. *People Management*. 25 September.

GRIMSHAW, D., WARD, K., RUBERY, J. and BEYNON, H. (2001) Organisations and the transformation of the internal labour market. *Work, Employment and Society*. Vol 15, Issue 1.

GRUNDY, T. (2005), Business strategy re-engineering and the bid battle for Marks and Spencer. *Strategic Change*, Vol 14.

THE GUARDIAN (2003a) Duisenberg decorated but still dithering. 10 May.

THE GUARDIAN (2003b) Accountability vacuum. 3 May.

THE GUARDIAN. (2012a) Tesco loses more market share. *The Guardian*. 24 April.

THE GUARDIAN. (2012b) Leading Article Libor scandal: gunfight on Threadneedle Street. *The Guardian*. 18 July.

THE GUARDIAN (2015a) From leak to global fallout. *The Guardian*. 12 February.

THE GUARDIAN (2015b) Tax dodging was systematic. The response from the bank and the politicians is anything but. *The Guardian*. 10 February.

GUEST, D. (1998) Combine harvest. *People Management*. 29 October. pp64–6.

GUEST, D. and CONWAY, N. (2002) *Pressure at work and the psychological contract*. London: Chartered Institute of Personnel and Development.

HALES, C. (2001) *Managing through organization*. 2nd ed. London: Business Press/ Thomson Learning.

HALL, A., DAY, M. and FREEMAN, C. (2011) Germany braces itself for invasion of Polish workers as it follows EU immigration rules. *Daily Telegraph*. 1 May.

HALL, C. and LINDZEY, G. (1978) *Theories of personality*. New York: Wiley.

HALL, D. and SAIAS, M. (1980) Strategy follows structure! *Strategic Management Journal*. Vol 1.

HALL, J. (2012) Tenfold increase in illegitimate babies in century since Titanic, ONS says. *Daily Telegraph*. 11 April.

HALL, L. (2004) Where to draw the line. *Personnel Today*. 1 June.

HALL, P. and PRESTON, P. (1988) *The carrier wave: new information technology and the geography of innovation*. London: Unwin Hyman.

HALL, S and HENRY, S. (2006) An independent Bank of England: is that enough? *National Institute Economic Review*. April.

HAMEL, G. (1996) Strategy as revolution. *Harvard Business Review*. July–August.

HAMEL, G. and PRAHALAD, C.K. (1994) *Competing for the future*. Boston, MA: Harvard Business School Press.

HAMMER, M. and CHAMPY, J. (1993) *Re-engineering the corporation.* London: Nicholas Brealey.

HANDY, C. (1991) *Inside organizations.* London: BBC.

HANLON, M. (2013) Stretch out, the human crush is almost over. *Sunday Times.* News Review. 20 January. p4.

HANSEN, M. and VON OETINGER, B. (2001) Introducing T-shaped managers. *Harvard Business Review.* Vol 79, No 3. March.

HANSEN, N., NOHRIA, N. and TIERNEY, T. (1999) What's your strategy for managing knowledge? *Harvard Business Review.* March–April. pp106–16.

HAO, N. (2012) Wuhan's development picking up steam. *China Business Weekly.* 15 October.

HARDING, R. (2004) Social enterprise: the new economic engine. *Business Strategy Review.* Winter.

HARRINGTON, R., LEMAK, D., REED, R. and KENDALL, K. (2004) A question of fit: the links between environment, strategy formulation and performance. *Journal of Business Management.* Vol 10, No 1. Spring.

HARRIS, J. (2012) Outsource to easyCouncil? Not in our name. *The Guardian.* 12 November.

HARRISON, A. (2012) Social mobility: universities need to do more says Alan Milburn. Available at: www.bbc.co.uk/news/education-19990126 [Accessed 22 October 2012].

HARRISON, M. (1993) Getting a grip on the flying shop. *Independent.* 22 November.

HARRISON, R. (2002) *Learning and development.* 3rd ed. London: Chartered Institute of Development.

HARVEY, F. (2014) A plastic bag charge will work – so long as we get it right. *The Guardian.* 7 February.

HASTINGS, M. (2007) Binge flying is just the beginning. The only way to stop this is a severe tax. *The Guardian.* 7 May.

HATCH, M J. (1997). *Organisation Theory: Modern Symbolic and Postmodern Perspectives.* Oxford, Oxford University Press

HAZLEHURST, J. (2014) Is banking beyond hope? *Work.* Winter 2014

HEALTH AND SAFETY EXECUTIVE (HSE). (2006) *2005/6 survey of self-reported work-related illnesses.* London: Health and Safety Executive.

HSE (2014) *Annual statistics.* Health and Safety Executive. Available at: http://www.hse.gov.uk/statistics/overall/hssh1415.pdf [Accessed 24 February 2016]

HSE (2015) Fatal Accidents 1995 to 2014. Available at: http://www.hse.gov.uk/statistics/fatals.htm [Accessed 27 February 2016]

HEDLUND, G. (1994) A model of knowledge management and the N-Form Corporation. *Strategic Management Journal.* Vol. 15.

HEFFERNAN, M. (2012) *Wilful blindness*. London: Simon & Schuster.

HELLEN, N. (2014) Bristol taps away to be the first smart city. *Sunday Times*. December 21. p18.

HELLIER, D. (2015) Government promises support for British steel producers. *The Guardian*. 16 October.

HELLOWELL, M. (2006) Alive and kicking. *Public Finance*. 17 November.

HENCKE, D. (2004) Big players lobbying for piece of the action. *The Guardian*. 27 October.

HENDERSON, D. (2001) *Misguided virtue: false notions of corporate social responsibility*. The Institute of Economic Affairs. London: IEA.

HENNESSY, J. (2009) Take your partners and advance. *People Management*. 29 January. p26.

THE HERALD. 2014 Plastic bag use down 90% as 5p fee introduced. 21 November http://m.heraldscotland.com/news/13190548. Plastic_bag_use_down_90__as_5p_fee_introduced/ [Accessed 16 January 2016]

HERBERT, I. (2004) When national happiness peaked. *The Independent*. 17 March.

HERRIOT, P. (1998) The role of the HR function in building a new proposition for staff. In: SPARROW, P. and MARCHINGTON, M. (eds) *Human resource management: the new agenda*. London: Financial Times/Pitman.

HERSEY, P. and BLANCHARD, K.H. (1977) *Management of organizational behavior: utilizing human resources*. 3rd edition. Englewood Cliffs, NJ: Prentice Hall.

HESKETT, J. (2015) What's wrong with Amazon's low-retention HR strategy? *Harvard Business School Working Knowledge*. 2 September. Available at: http://hbswk.hbs.edu/item/is-something-wrong-with-amazon-s-low-retention-hr-strategy [Accessed 2 October 2015]

HESSLER, P. (2011) Country driving. New York: Harper.

HEWDEN website. Available at www.hewden.co.uk [Accessed 10 January 2015]

HEYWOOD, A. (2008) Essentials of UK politics. Basingstoke: Palgrave Macmillan.

HF HOLIDAYS. www.hfholidays.co.uk [Accessed 14 July 2007]

HICKMAN, L. (2009) Do we really need to ban the bag? *The Guardian*. 11 August.

HILL, T. (1991) *Production and operations management: text and cases*. London: Prentice Hall.

HILL, T. and WESTBROOK, R. (1997) SWOT analysis: it's time for a product recall. *Long Range Planning*. Vol 30, No 1.

HILLS, J. (2010) *Report of the National Equality Panel*. London: Government Equality Office.

HILTON, I. (2004) A rampaging market, but a long way from global power. *The Guardian*. 13 November.

HILTROP, J. (2005) Creating HR capability in high performance organizations. *Strategic Change.* Vol 14. May.

HINDO, B. (2007) At 3M, a struggle between efficiency and creativity. *BusinessWeek.* 11 June.

HIRD, M., MARSH, C. and SPARROW, P. (2009). *HR delivery systems: re-engineered or over-engineered?* CPHR White Paper 09/05, Lancaster University. Available at: http://www.lancaster.ac.uk/media/lancaster-university/content-assets/documents/lums/cphr/hrdeliverysystems.pdf [Accessed 28 January 2015]

HIRSCHLER, B. and BERKROT, B. (2014) Pfizer walks away from $118 billion AstraZeneca takeover fight. *Reuters.* 26 May.

HIRST, J. (2005) The awkward age. *Public Finance.* 14 January.

HISCOTT, G. (2004) Big chains strengthen hold on Britain's shoppers. *The Independent.* 10 August.

HM REVENUE AND CUSTOMS (2012) *Measuring tax gaps 2012: tax gap estimates for 2010-11.*

HMSO. (2009) *New opportunities: fair chances for the future.* White Paper. London: HMSO.

H M TREASURY. (2006) *PFI: strengthening long-term partnerships.* London: HM Treasury. May.

H M TREASURY. (2007) *Chancellor of the Exchequer's reply to the Governor of the Bank of England.* London: HM Treasury. 17 April. Available at: www.hm-treasury.gov.uk [Accessed 6 June 2007]

H M TREASURY. (2010) *Budget Report.* London: HM Treasury.

HODGKISS, K. (2012) CV posting on LinkedIn. *People Management.* February. p20.

HODGKIN, P. (2007) Gift rap. *The Guardian.* 5 September.

HOFFMAN, M. (1990) What is necessary for corporate moral excellence?. In: CAMPBELL, A. and TAWADY, K. (eds) *Mission and business philosophy.* Oxford: Butterworth-Heinemann.

HOFSTEDE, G. (2009) *Geert Hofstede cultural* dimensions. Available at: www.geeet-hofstede.com/hofstede [Accessed 14 October 2009]

HOLIDAYBREAK. (2007) www.holidaybreak.co.uk [Accessed 14 July 2007]

HOLLEY, E. (2015) Resurrected Financial Transactions Tax poses threat to EU markets. Banking Technology. 4 February. Available at: http://www.bankingtech.com/276812/resurrecxted-financial-transaction-tax-poses-threat-to-eu-markets/ [Accessed 11 May 2015]

HOLMES, C. and MAYHEW, K. (2012) The changing shape of the UK job market *and its implications for the bottom half of earners.* London: Resolution Foundation.

HOLODNY, E. (2015) A Budweiser-Miller brewing company would be a monster. *Business Insider.* 16 September http://uk.businessinsider.com/sabmiller-ab-inbev-would-dominate-the-beer-market-2015-9?r=US&IR=T [Accessed 30 October 2015]

HOME OFFICE. (2007) Accession monitoring report. February.

HOME OFFICE. (2015) Asylum. Available at: https://www.gov.uk/government/publications/immigration-statistics-april-to-june-2015/summary [Accessed 8 February 2016]

HOOKHAM, M. and PANCEVSKI, B. (2012) Minister for women rejects quotas for female bosses. *Sunday Times.*11 November. p6.

HOPE, J. (2009) EU ban limiting doctors to 48 hour working week lifted over public health concerns. *Mail Online.* 16 October [Accessed 7 December]

HOPE, K. (2005) Hierarchy raises engagement at LSC. *People Management.* 14 July.

HOULDER, V. (2003) Dark cloud of suspicion hangs over National Trust. *Financial Times.* 26 April.

HOUSE, J. (2009) Calling time on doctors' working hours. *The Lancet.* 13 June.

HOUSE, J. D. and MCGRATH, K. (2004) Innovative governance and development in the new Ireland: Social Partnership and the integrated approach. *Governance.* Vol 17, No 1.

HOUSE OF COMMONS (2014) Payday loans Business Innovation and Skills Committee. http://www.publications.parliament.uk/pa/cm201314/cmselect/cmbis/789/789.pdf [Accessed 27 November 2015]

HOUSE OF COMMONS PUBLIC ACCOUNTS COMMITTEE (2008) *Shared services in the Department for Transport and its agencies* (Contains Parliamentary information licensed under the Open Parliament Licence v3.0.)

HOUSE OF LORDS. (2008) *The economic impact of immigration: Vol I: Report (HL Paper 82- I).* London: House of Lords Select Committee on Economic Affairs. April.

HOUT, T. and GHEMAWAT, P. (2010) China vs the world: whose technology is it? *Harvard Business Review.* Vol 88, No 12. December.

HOUT, T. and MICHAEL, D. (2014) A Chinese approach to management. *Harvard Business Review.* September. Vol 92, Issue 9.

HOYOS, C. (2006) Opec vows to defend minimum $60 for oil. *The Financial Times.* 20 October.

HRMGUIDE (2005) BT-Accenture contract renewed. Available at: www.hrmguide.co.uk/general/bt-accenture [Accessed 2 July 2012]

HUDSON, A. (2011) Are call centres the factories of the 21st century? BBC News. 10 March. Available at: http://www.bbc.co.uk/news/magazine-12691704 [Accessed 14 June 2015]

HUDSON, B. (2009) Captives of bureaucracy. *Community Care.* 9 April.

HUGHES, C. and TIGHE, C. (2007) Impregnable self-belief takes a battering. *The Financial Times.* 15 September.

HUNT, J. (1979) *Managing people at work.* London: Pan Books.

HUSELID, M. (1995) The impact of human resource management practices on turnover, productivity and corporate financial performance. *Academy of Management Journal.* Vol 38. pp400–22.

HUSSAIN-KHALIQ, S. (2004) Eliminating child labour from the Sialkot soccer ball industry: two industry-led approaches. *Journal of Corporate Citizenship.* Issue 13. Spring.

HUTTON, W. (1995) *The state we're in: why Britain is in crisis and how to overcome it.* London: Vintage.

HUTTON, W. (2004) We must dare to be dynamic. *The Observer.* 7 November.

HUTTON, W. (2007) *The writing on the wall.* London: Little Brown.

HUTTON, W. (2012) The American election is really a battle for the future of capitalism. *The Observer.* 22 July.

HUTTON, W. (2015) *How good we can be: ending the mercenary society and building a great country.* London: Little Brown.

HYMAN, R. (1987) Strategy or structure: capital, labour and control. *Work, Employment and Society.* Vol 1 Issue 1.

IFS. (2009) Have the poor got poorer under Labour? *IFS Observations.* October. London: Institute for Fiscal Studies.

IGLICKA, K. (2005) The impact of the EU enlargement on migratory movements in Poland, Centrum Stosunkow Miedzynarodowych (Center for International Relations, Warsaw). October. Available at: http://www.csm.org.pl [Accessed 30 May 2007]

INSTITUTE OF ALCOHOL STUDIES. (2010) *IAS Factsheet: Alcohol consumption in the UK.* Available at: www.ias.org.uk/resources/factsheets/consumption-uk.pdf [Accessed 20 August 2012]

INSTITUTE OF DEVELOPMENT STUDIES. (2011) *Recruitment John Lewis Partnership.* IDS Study 941. May. pp27–8.

INSTITUTE OF DEVELOPMENT STUDIES. (2004) The Royal Bank of Scotland group. *HR Studies Update.* Vol 769. March. pp14–17.

INSTITUTE OF DEVELOPMENT STUDIES. (2013) *The three-legged model of HR.* Available at: https://ids.thomsonreuters.com/hr-in-practice/features-analysis/three-legged-model-hr [Accessed 31 January 2015]

THE INDEPENDENT. (2010) Asda to take over Netto stores. *The Independent.* 27 May.

THE INDEPENDENT. (2012a) Banker who broke HBOS is fined £500,000. *The Independent.* 13 September

THE INDEPENDENT. (2012b), Accused: HSBC in the dock. *The Independent.* 18 July

INFOQUEST. (2002) *Annual business survey.* Los Angeles: Infoquest.

INKPEN, A and ROSS, J. (2001) Why do some strategic alliances persist beyond their useful life? *California Management Review.* Fall.

INMAN, P. (2013) EU approves financial transactions tax for 11 eurozone countries. *The Guardian.* 29 January.

INSTITUTE OF LEADERSHIP AND MANAGEMENT. (2013) *Flexible working: goodbye nine to five*. London: ILM.

INTERNATIONAL LABOUR ORGANISATION. (2015) Governing Body 324th Session, June. Geneva: ILO. Available at: www.ilo.org/wcmsp5/groups/public/—/ed_norm/—/relconf/documents/meetingdocument/wcms_376576.pdf [Accessed 26 June 2015]

INSTITUTE FOR SOCIAL AND ECONOMIC RESEARCH. (2002) Class matters. *ISER Newsletter*. October. London: ISER.

INSTITUTE FOR PUBLIC POLICY RESEARCH. (2001) *Building better partnerships*. June. London: IPPR.

INTERBRAND. (2006) *Interbrand best global brands 2006*. Available at: www.interbrand.com [Accessed 18 June 2007]

INTERNATIONAL ECONOMY. (2004) Is continued globalization of the world economy inevitable? *The International Economy*. Summer. Vol 18, Issue 3.

INTERNATIONAL LABOUR REVIEW. (2006) The internationalization of employment: a challenge to fair globalisation? *International Labour Review*. Spring-Summer.

INVESTORTODAY. (2009) Boss at suicide firm France Telecom asks to go. 5 October. Available at: http://www.investortoday.co.uk/news_features/Boss-at-suicide-firm-France-Telecom-asks-to-go [Accessed 27 February 2016]

IP, G. (2013) The gated globe. *The Economist*. 12 October.

IRS. (1999) *IRS Employment Trends* 675. March.

IRS. (2002) Court of Appeal guidelines for stress at work cases. *Employment Law Review 748*. 25 March.

IRS. (2003) Rewarding performance: Sainsbury's new bonus scheme. *Employment Review 784. Pay and Benefits*. 19 September.

IRS. (2004) Employment Review 792. *Pay and Benefits*. 23 January.

ISIDORE, C. (2015) Guinness returns to sponsor NY's St. Patrick's Day parade. CNN Money. 2 March. Available at: http://money.cnn.com/2015/03/02/news/companies/guinness-parade-sponsorship/index.html/ [Accessed 6 Februaey 2016]

ISLAM, G. (2015) Is capitalism as we know it beginning to collapse? *Work*. Winter.

ITEM Club. (2006) *Spring forecast*. London: Ernst & Young.

JACK, I. (2009) Onwards and endlessly upwards. *Guardian*. 25 July.

JACKSON, H. (2009) Obituary: Robert McNamara. *The Guardian*. 6 July

JACKSON, S. (1998) *Britain's population*. London: Routledge.

JACOBS, M. (2001) Bridging the global divide, *The Observer*. 11 November.

JACQUES, M. (2009) *When China rules the world*. London, Allen Lane

JAMES, W, BUTTER, B and SONNY, A. (2006, 2012) *Stability and growth pact.* Civitas. Last updated April 2012. Available at: http://www.civitas.org.uk/eufacts/FSECON/EC10.htm [Accessed 1 December 2012]

JAMES, W. and SONNY, A. (2006, 2012) *The Euro: economic and monetary union.* Civitas. last updated April 2012. Available at: http://www.civitas.org.uk/eufacts/FSECON/EC4.htm [Accessed 1 December 2012]

JAVIDAN, M. and LYNTON, N. (2005) The changing face of the Chinese executive. *Harvard Business Review.* December. Vol 83, Issue 12.

JEFFERIES, T. (2015) What happened to Thatcher's share ownership dream? It's nowhere near as common as the ex-Tory PM hoped 30 years ago – but does it matter? *This is Money.* 9 October. Available at: http://www.thisismoney.co.uk/money/investing/article-3265284/What-happened-Margaret-Thatcher-s-share-ownership-dream.html [Accessed 1 November 2015]

JENSEN, R. (2007) The digital provide: information technology, market performance and welfare in the south Indian fisheries sector. *Quarterly Journal of Economics.* August.

JOHNSON & JOHNSON website. (nd) www.jnj.com/connect/about-jnj/jnj-credo [Accessed 25 February 2011]

JOHNSON, G. and SCHOLES, K. (1997) *Exploring corporate strategy.* 4th edition. Hemel Hempstead: Prentice-Hall.

JOHNSON, G., WHITTINGTON, R. and SCHOLES, K. (2011) *Exploring strategy.* 9th ed. Harlow: The Financial Times/Prentice Hall.

JONES, A. (2006) *Rising to the challenge of diversity.* London: Work Foundation.

JONES, K. (2013) *The road less travelled? Improving the apprenticeship pathway for young people.* The Work Foundation. Available at: http://www.theworkfoundation.com/DownloadPublication/Report/344_Apprenticeship%20policy%20paper%20FINAL.pdf [Accessed 6 November 2015]

JOYCE, P. and WOODS, A. (1996) *Essential strategic management: from modernism to pragmatism.* Oxford: Butterworth-Heinemann.

JURAN, J. (1988) *Quality control handbook.* New York: McGraw Hill.

KAFKA, F. (1964) *The trial.* New York: Secker.

KAHN, H. (1967) *The year 2000.* Basingstoke: Macmillan.

KANDOLA, B. (2009) Under the skin. *People Management.* 30 July.

KANTOR, J. and STREITFELD, D. (2015) Inside Amazon: wrestling big ideas in a bruising workplace, *The New York Times.* 15 August.

KAPLAN, S. (2008) Are U.S. CEOs overpaid? *Academy of Management Perspectives.* Vol 22. pp5–20.

KARAGIANAKI, E. (2011) *The impact of inheritance on the distribution of wealth: evidence from the UK.* Paper 148. LSE Centre for Analysis of Social Exclusion.

KAY, J. (2002) The balance sheet. *Prospect.* July.

KAY, J. (2003) *The truth about markets*. London: Allen Lane/The Penguin Press.

KEARNS, P. and INGATE, K. (2001) Should the CIPD strike off poor practitioners? *Personnel Today*. 23 October.

KEEGAN, W. (2004a) Erm, there's a danger in paradise. *The Observer*. 17 October.

KEEGAN, W. (2004b) Keeping an eye on the competition. *The Observer*. 31 October.

KEEGAN, W. (2015) Who needs a 'long-term economic plan' when the oil price is falling like this? *The Observer*. 25 January.

KEEN, A. (2015) *The Internet is not the Answer*. New York: Atlantic Monthly Press.

KEERS, S. (2011) The ads that see you coming. *Sunday Times*. In-gear. 3 April. pp24–5.

KELLY, E. (1999) Corporate citizenship costs more than cash. *Professional Manager*. January. KENT, K. (2009) Employment changes over 30 years. *Economics and Labour Market Review*. Vol 3 No 2

KENWAY, P. and PALMER, G. (2007) *Poverty among ethnic groups*. York: Joseph Rowntree Foundation.

KERSTEN, E. (2005) Core values, devalued. *Workforce Management*. June.

KEW, J. and STREDWICK, J. (2008) *Business environment*. 2nd edition. London: Chartered Institute of Personnel and Development.

KEYNOTE (2006) Activity holidays.

KEYNOTE (2014) Activity holidays.

KHANNA, T., SONG, J., and LEE, K. (2011) The paradox of Samsung's rise. *Harvard Business Review*. July/August. Vol 89, Issue 7/8.

KIGER, P. (2005) Corporate crunch. *Workforce Management*, April

KIM, C. and MAUBORGNE, R. (2001) How to earn commitment. *The Financial Times*. 22 October.

KIM, C. and MAUBORGNE, R. (2004) Blue Ocean Strategy. *Harvard Business Review*. Vol 82, No 10. October.

KIM, C. and MAUBORGNE, R. (2014) Blue Ocean Leadership. *Harvard Business Review*. Vol 92, Issue 5. May.

KIM, J. (2012) Samsung risks following Sony and IBM's slide. BBC News. 8 March. Available at: http://www.bbc.co.uk/news/technology-15991487 [Accessed 15 June 2015]

KIM, K., NAM, D. and STIMPERT, J. (2004) Testing the applicability of Porter's generic strategies in the digital age: a study of Korean cyber malls. *Journal of Business Strategies*. Vol 21, No 1.

KIM, M. (2015) The woes of Jay Y: can the Galaxy S6 save Samsung's crown prince? *The Guardian*. 20 April.

KIMBERLEY, J. and CRAIG, E. (2001) Work as a life experience. *Financial Times*. 5 November.

KING, M. (2007) *The MPC ten years on: a speech to the Society of Business Economists.* 2 May. Available at: http://www.bankofengland.co.uk/archive/Documents/historicpubs/speeches/2007/speech309.pdf [Accessed 27 February 2016]

KINNIE, N. (2005) How much freedom do managers have to make strategic HR decisions? *People Management.* 2 June.

KIRISCI, K. (2007) Turkey in the EU: a win-win scenario. In: FRASER, M. (ed), *European Union: the next fifty years.* London: FT Business.

KIRKPATRICK, I. and ACKROYD, S. (2003) Transforming the professional archetype? The new managerialism in UK social services. *Public Management Review.* Vol 5, Issue 4.

KNIGHT FRANK. (2015) *The wealth report.* Available at: http://www.knightfrank.com/wealthreport [Accessed 27 February 2016]

KNIGHT, L. (2012) Eurozone's long reform wishlist. BBC News. 26 June. Available at: http://www.bbc.co.uk/news/business-18560234 [Accessed 28 November 2012]

KNOWLEDGE@WHARTON. (2012) Patients versus profits at Johnson & Johnson: has the company lost its way? 15 February. Available at: http://www.knowledge@wharton.upenn.edu/article.cfm?articleid=2943 [Accessed 28 August 2012]

KOCH, A.J. (2000) SWOT does not need to be recalled, it needs to be enhanced. Available at: http://www.westga.edu/bquest/2001/swot2.htm [Accessed 4 October 2012]

KOCHAN, T. and BAROCCI, T. (1985) *Human resource management and industrial relations.* Boston, MA: Little Brown.

KOLLEWE, J. (2012) Scandal-hit Barclays turns to safe pair of hands. *The Guardian.* 31 August.

KOTTER, J. (1996) *Leading change.* Boston, MA: Harvard Business Press.

KROSS. E. and VERDUYN, P. (2013) Facebook use predicts decline in subjective well-being in young adults. Available at: http://journals.plos.org/plosone/article?id=10.1371/journal.pone.0069841 [Accessed 27 February 2016]

KÜBLER-ROSS, E. (1969) *On death and dying.* New York: Macmillan.

KURTZ, S. (2004) The end of marriage in Scandinavia. *Weekly Standard.* Vol 9. p20.

KYSER, J. (2007) 60 million Californians by mid-century. *Los Angeles Times.* July 10.

LABOUR MARKET TRENDS. (2009) December. London: Office of National Statistics.

LANDER, F. (2014) Human rights and Ebola: the issue of quarantine. *Translational Global Health'* 5 November. Available at: http://blogs.plos.org/globalhealth/2014/11/ebola_and_human_rights [Accessed 18 February 2015]

LANIER, J. (2013) *Who owns the future?* London: Allen Lane.

LANSLEY, S. (2009a) *Life in the middle.* London: Trades Union Congress.

LANSLEY, S. (2009b) *Unfair to middling.* London: Trades Union Congress.

LAWRENCE, F. (2013) 111 helpline has fundamental flaws say critics. *The Guardian.* 30 July.

LAWTON, A. (1998) *Ethical management for the public services*. Buckingham: Open University Press.

LAWTON, A. and ROSE, A. (1994) *Organisation and management in the public sector*. Harlow: FT/Prentice Hall.

LAZEAR, S. and ROSEN, S. (1981) Rank order tournaments as optimum labor contract. *Journal of Political Economy*. Volume 89. pp841–864.

LEGG, R. (2005) Breach of trust. *The Guardian*. 14 September.

LEGGE, K. (1978) *Power, innovation and problem-solving in personnel management*. London: McGraw-Hill.

LEGGE, K. (2001) Silver bullet or spent round? Assessing the meaning of the 'high commitment management/performance relationship. In STOREY, J. (ed.) *Human resource management: a critical text*. London: Thomson Learning.

LEGRAIN, P. (2003) *Open world: the truth about globalization*. New ed. London: Abacus.

LEITCH, LORD. (2006) *Leitch review of skills: Prosperity for all in the global economy – world class skills*. London: HM Treasury.

LENNAN, D. (2001) Cartel crooks belong in jail. *The Financial Times*. 2 November.

LEONARD, M. (2015) What would a UK outside the EU look like? *The Guardian*. 5 October.

LEVINSON, M. (2006) *The box: how the shipping container made the world smaller and the world economy bigger*. Princeton, NJ: Princeton University.

LEWIN, K. (1943) Defining the 'field at a given time'. *Psychological Review*. Vol 50.

LEWIN, K. (1958) Group decisions and social changes. In: SWANSON, G.E., NEWCOMB, T.M. and HARTLEY, E.L. (eds) *Readings in social psychology*. New York: Holt, Rinehart and Winston.

LEWIS, G. (2015) Having a union rep can boost job quality, research finds. *People Management*. 13 March.

LEWIS, J. (2002) Testing time. *Personnel Today*. 9 April.

LI, F. (2012) Hubei's capital poised to grow. *China Business Weekly*. 15 October.

LIN, J. (2010) Globalization: after the recession. *The Times of India*. 6 January.

LIPSEY, R. and CHRYSTAL, A. (1999) *Principles of economics*. 9th ed. Oxford: Oxford University Press.

LIVING WAGE FOUNDATION. (2014) *New 2015 Living Wage Rates announced*. 3 November. London: Living Wage Foundation.

LOBEL, M. (2015) Qatar Airways raps ILO 'vendetta'. *BBC News*. 17 June. Available at: http://www.bbc.co.uk/news/business-33164931 [Accessed 26 June 2015]

LOCAL GOVERNMENT ASSOCIATION. (2012) *The services shared: costs spared*. London: LGA.

LOCKWOOD, B. and REDOANO, M. (2005) *The CSGR Globalisation Index: an introductory guide.* Centre for the Study of Globalisation and Regionalisation Working Paper 155/04. Warwick: CSGR.

LONDON CHAMBER OF COMMERCE AND INDUSTRY. (2013) *Help or hindrance? The value of EU membership to London business.* April. London: LCCI.

LORD, R. (1990) A measure of corporate success. *The Times.* 30 July.

LSC (2008) *National employers skills survey 2007: key findings.* London: Learning and Skills Council.

LUCAS, C. (2001) Doha spells disaster for development. *The Observer.* 18 November.

LUCAS, E. (2006) Red fades to grey. *Economist.* 27 May. p46.

LUCAS, E. (2009) Businesses that 'put back' are bucking the trend. *Professional Manager.* September.

LUNGESEN, D. (2004) Turkey's unrequited EU love'. *BBC News.* Available at: www.news. bbc.co.uk. [Accessed 30 June 2007]

LUYENDIJK, J. (2012) Banking: high risk culture. *The Guardian.* 29 June.

LYNCH, R. (2006) *Corporate strategy.* 4th ed. Harlow: FT/Prentice Hall.

MACALISTER, T. (2010) BP thought gulf oil spill 'simply could not happen', says ex-boss. *The Guardian.* 11 November.

MACCORMAIC, R. (2008) Twenty years of social partnership agreements. *Irish Times.* 4 August.

MACLEOD, D. and CLARKE, N. (2009) *Engaging for success.* London: Department for Business, Innovation and Skills. Available at: www.bis.gov.uk/macleod-review [Accessed 27 March 2013].

MACMILLAN, I. (1978) *Strategy formulation: political concepts.* St Paul, MN: West Publishing Company.

MACMILLAN, L. (2010) *Social mobility in the professions.* Bristol: Centre for Market and Public Organisations.

MACSHANE, D. (2006) Immigration: don't close our borders. *The Economist (US).* 30 October.

MADELEY, J. (2001) No end to shackles. *The Observer.* 21 January.

MAGNUS, G. (2011) Give Marx a chance to save the world. *Bloomberg View.* 29 August. Available at: www.bloomberg.com/news/2011-08-29/give-marx-a-chance-to-save-the-world-economy-commentary-by-george-magnus-html [Accessed 6 November 2012]

MAHONY, C. (2007) Under new ownership. *People Management.* 12 July.

MAITLAND, A. (2003) Profits from the righteous path. *The Financial Times.* 3 April.

MALTBY, P. (2003) *Public interest companies: fad or permanent fixture?* London: Institute for Public Policy Research.

MANGALISO, M. (2001) Building competitive advantage from *ubuntu:* management lessons from South Africa. *Academy of Management Executive.* August.

MANNING, A. (2003) *Monopsony in Motion: Imperfect Competition in Labour Markets.* Princeton NJ: Princeton University Press.

MANNING, A. and PETROLONGO, B. (2005) The part-time pay penalty. *Centrepiece.* December.

MARCHINGTON, M. (2001) Employee involvement at work. In: STOREY, J. (ed.) *Human resource management: a critical text.* London: Thomson Learning.

MARCHINGTON, M. and GRUGULIS, I. (2000) 'Best practice' human resource management: perfect opportunity or dangerous illusion? *International Journal of Human Resource Management.* Vol 11, No 6. pp1104–24.

MARCHINGTON, M. and WILKINSON, A. (2008) *Human resource management at work.* London: Chartered Institute of Personnel and Development.

MARKETING. (2004) Trouble strikes the travel agent. 23 June.

MARTIN, C and MILAS, C. (2013) IPPR policy brief. A very large gamble: evidence on quantitative easing in the US and UK. University of Bath. Available at: http://opus.bath.ac.uk/45323/ [Accessed 31 October 2015]

MARTIN, G. (2005) *Technology and people management.* London: Chartered Institute of Personnel and Development.

MARTIN, N. and SIMS, J. (1956) Power tactics. *Harvard Business Review.* Nov–Dec. p25.

MARTIN, S. and PARKER, D. (1997) *The impact of privatisation: ownership and corporate performance in the UK.* London: Routledge.

MARX, K. (1867, 2004) *Capital: a critique of political economy.* Harmondsworth: Penguin.

MASLOW, A.H. (1943) A theory of human motivation. *Psychology Review.* Vol 50. pp370–96.

MASON, P. (2012) Eurozone crisis: will the ECB's bond plan work?, *BBC News.* 30 July. Available at: http://www.bbc.co.uk/news/business-19044341 [Accessed 28 November 2012]

MASSEY, D. (1984) *Spatial divisions of labour: social structures and the geography of production.* Basingstoke: Macmillan.

MATHIASON, N. (2003) Debt duties. *The Observer.* 20 April.

MATHIASON, N. (2004) Casino bill derailed by bitter split in Cabinet. *The Observer.* 24 October.

MATHIASON, N. (2009) Recruitment firm Hays to appeal against £30 million price-fixing fine. *Guardian.* 30 September. p12.

MATHIASON, N. and TREANOR, J. (2009) Brown in secret push to sell 'Tobin tax' to City. *The Guardian,* 10 November.

MAYHEW, K and KEEP, E. (2014) *Industrial strategy and the future of skills policy – the high road to sustainable growth*. Research Insight. London: Chartered Institute of Personnel and Development.

MAYO, E. (1933) *Human problems of an industrialised society*. New York: Harpers.

MCAFEE, R. and TE VELDE, V. (2005) *Dynamic pricing in the airline industry*. Los Angeles, CA: California Institute of Technology.

MCCANN, J. (2004) Organizational effectiveness: changing concepts for changing environments. *Human Resource Planning*. Vol 27, Issue 1.

MCCARTHY, B. (2004) How to manage organisational change. *People Management*. 9 December.

MCCARTHY, T. (2009) BA staff shows blitz spirit. *People Management*. 30 July.

MCCARTNEY, C. (2009) *Fighting back through talent innovation*. London: Chartered

Institute of Personnel and Development.

MCCARTNEY, C. and WORMAN, D. (2010) *Opening up talent for business success – integrating talent management and diversity*. London: Chartered Institute of Personnel and Development.

MCCLANAHAN, P. (2013) Why the WTO agreement in Bali has finally helped developing countries. *The Guardian*. 6 December.

MCCURRY, J. (2009) Deflation stalks Japan as jobless figure hits peak. *The Guardian*. 29 August.

MCGREGOR, D. (1960) *The human side of enterprise*. New York: McGraw-Hill.

MCKEE, G. (2003) Managing human nature: leadership lessons from Venice. *Leader to Leader*. April.

MCKIE, R, (2015) Cancer drugs fund is 'waste of NHS cash'. *The Observer*. 11 January

MCKNIGHT, A. (2000) *Earnings inequality and earnings mobility 1977–1996: the impact of mobility on long-term inequality*. Employment Relations Research Series No 8. London: Department for Trade and Industry.

MCKNIGHT, A. (2105) *Downward mobility, opportunity hoarding and the glass floor*. London: Social Mobility and Child Poverty Commission.

MCNEILL, D. (2010) Mystery of Japan's 230,000 missing centenarians. *Independent*. 9 September.

MCSMITH, A. (2007) Figures show number of eastern Europeans in Britain exaggerated. *Independent*. 20 January. p24.

MEADWAY, J. (2014) *The UK's productivity puzzle*. New Economics Foundation. 24 January. Available at: http://www.neweconomics.org/blog/entry/the-uks-productivity-puzzle [Accessed 4 November 2015]

MEADWAY, J. (2015) Taxpayers spend £11 billion to top up low wages paid by UK companies. *The Guardian*. 20 April.

MEREDITH, R. (2007) *The elephant and the dragon: the rise of India and China and what it means for all of us.* New York: Norton.

MERRICK, N. (2001) Minority interest. *People Management.* 8 November. pp52–3.

METCALF, D. (2007) Why has the British National Minimum Wage had little or no impact on employment? *CEP Discussion Paper.* April.

MEYER, E. and SHEN E. Y. (2010) China myths, China facts. *Harvard Business Review.* Vol 88, Issue 1/2. January/February.

MICKLETHWAIT, J and WOOLDRIDGE, A. (2000) *A future perfect: the challenge and hidden promise of globalization.* London: Heinemann. p7.

MICROSOFT. (2010) HR managers snoop online. *People Management.* 11 February. p15.

MIGRATION OBSERVATORY, UNIVERSITY OF OXFORD. (2015) *The impact of migration on UK population growth.* Oxford: Migration Observatory.

MILBURN, A. (2004) *Inequality, mobility and opportunity: the politics of aspiration.* Speech to the Institute for Public Policy Research. 9 November.

MILBURN, A. (2009a) *Fair success to the professions.* London: HMSO.

MILBURN, A. (2009b) The UK is an unequal society in which class background too often determines life chances. *The Observer.* 19 July.

MILES, R. E. and SNOW, C. C. (1978) *Organizational strategy, structure and process.* Maidenhead: McGraw-Hill

MILLER, J. (2011) *Shaping the future, final report. Organisational performance: what really makes the difference.* London: Chartered Institute of Personnel and Development.

MILLER, S. (1999) Council pays £67,000 for stress injury. *The Guardian.* 6 July. p4.

MILLWARD, N., BRYSON, A. and FORTH, J. (2000) *All change at work: British industrial relations, 1980 to 1998 as portrayed by the Workplace Industrial Relations Survey series.* London: Routledge.

MILMO, D. (2007) Ryanair introduces £4 check in fee as latest surcharge to slash costs. *The Guardian.* 25 August.

MILMO, D. (2009) EasyJet warns of tough winter ahead after profits decline by £80m. *The Guardian.* 18 November.

MILMO, D. (2011) Ryanair snubs Boeing by announcing jet design pact with China's Comac. *The Guardian.* 20 June.

MILNE, S. (2007) You can't say it's a problem and then do nothing about it. *The Guardian.* 16 August.

MINISTERIO DE CULTURA, JUVENTUD Y DEPORTES. (2004) *Abolicion del Ejercito en Costa Rica.* San Jose, Costa Rica.

MINTZBERG, H. (1994) *The rise and fall of strategic planning.* Hemel Hempstead: Prentice Hall.

MINTZBERG, H. (1998a) The structuring of organisations. In: MINTZBERG, H., QUINN, J. B., and GHOSHAL, S. (eds) *The strategy process*. Hemel Hempstead: Prentice Hall Europe.

MINTZBERG, H. (1998b) The machine organization. In: MINTZBERG, H., QUINN, J. B. and GHOSHAL, S. (eds) *The strategy process*. Revised European edition. Hemel Hempstead: Prentice Hall.

MINTZBERG, H. (1998c) Five Ps for Strategy. In: MINTZBERG, H., QUINN, J. B. and GHOSHAL, S. (eds) *The strategy process*. Revised European edition. Hemel Hempstead: Prentice Hall.

MINTZBERG, H. and WATERS, J. (1985) Of strategies deliberate and emergent. *Strategic Management Journal*. Vol 6.

MONAGHAN, A. (2014). UK £50bn better off thanks to quantitative easing, says economist. *The Guardian* 17 April

MONBIOT, G. (2001) Superstores brand us to ensure we belong to them. *The Guardian*. 31 July.

MONBIOT, G. (2007) If Britain wants to help Africa's poor, it must stop acting like an emperor. *The Guardian*. 17 April.

MOORE, J. (2012) Tesco certainly has big issues, but critics must be mad to say it's in a real crisis. *The Independent*. 19 April.

MOORE, K. (2011) Porter or Mintzberg: whose view of strategy is the most relevant today? *Forbes*. 28 March.

MORETON, S. (2006) Are 'professional' HR practices compatible with volunteer management? London: Attend.

MORGAN, G. (1986) *Images of organisations*. Beverly Hills, CA: Sage Publications.

MORRIS, C. (2015) Migrant crisis: EU and Turkey form plan. BBC News. 16 October. http://www.bbc.co.uk/news/world-europe-34546876 [Accessed 19 October 2015]

MORRIS, H. and WILLEY, B. (1996) *The Corporate Environment*. London: Pitman. pp197–9.

MOULDS, J. (2013) Bank of England handed new remit in Osborne's Budget. *The Guardian*. 20 March.

MULHOLLAND, H. (2009) We will follow example of efficient Tory councils, says Osborne. *The Guardian*. 10 September.

MULHOLLAND, G., ÖZBILGIN, M. and WORMAN, D. (2005) *Managing diversity: linking theory and practice to business performance*. London: Chartered Institute of Personnel and Development.

MULLAN, P. (2002) *The imaginary time bomb*. London: I B Tauris.

MULLINS, L. (2007) *Management and organizational behaviour*. London: Pitman.

MULVEY, S. (2003) The EU law that rules our lives. *BBC News Online*. Available at: Available at: http//www.news.bbc.co.uk [Accessed 18 October 2004]

MURRAY, S. (2006) Fair trade products: confusions reigns over labelling. *Financial Times*. 12 June.

MURRAY-WEST, R. (2011) SponsoredWonga's interest rate of 4,200pc? It's not an automatic red card. *Daily Telegraph*. 19 September.

NADLER, D. and TUSHMAN, M. (1980) A model for diagnosing organizational behaviour: applying a congruence perspective. *Organizational Dynamics*. Autumn.

NAGLE, T. and HOLDEN, R. (2002) *The strategy and tactics of pricing*. London: Prentice Hall.

NARAYANAN, D. (2014) The world belongs to India. *Work*. Winter.

NATHAN, M. (2000) The paradoxical nature of crisis. *Review of Business*. Vol 21, No 3.4.

NATHAN, M., CARPENTER, G. and ROBERTS, S. (2003) *Getting by, not getting on, technology in UK workplaces*. London: The Work Foundation.

NATIONAL AUDIT OFFICE. (2009) Ministry of Defence service families accommodation. Available at: http://www.nao.org.uk/report/ministry-of-defence-service-families-accommodation/ [Accessed 27 March 2013]

NATIONAL EVALUATION OF SURE START SCHEMES. (2010) The impact of Sure Start schemes on 5 year olds and their families. London: NESS. November.

NATIONAL INSTITUTE FOR HEALTH AND CARE EXCELLENCE (2009) Promoting Well-Being at Work. London: NICE. November.

NATIONAL INSTITUTE FOR HEALTH AND CARE EXCELLENCE (2013) How NICE measures value for money on relation to public health interventions. London: NICE.

NATIONAL RECORDS OF SCOTLAND (2015) *Population data*. Available at http://www.nrscotland.gov.uk/statistics-and-data/statistics/statistics-by-theme/population [Accessed 25 February 2010]

NATIONAL STATISTICAL OFFICE. (2015) www.ons.gov.uk

NATIONAL TRUST. (2006) *Annual report and financial statements 2005-6*. Swindon: National Trust.

NATIONAL TRUST. (2010) *Going local*. Swindon: National Trust. NATIONAL TRUST. (2012a) Economic case for planning reforms debunked. February. Available at: http://www.nationaltrust.org.uk/article-13563986 [Accessed 27 September 2012]

NATIONAL TRUST. (2012b) Dame Helen Ghosh new Director-General. August. Available at: http://www.nationaltrust.org.uk/article-13563983 [Accessed 27 September 2012]

NATIONAL TRUST. (2014) *Annual report and financial statements 2013-14*. Swindon: National Trust.

NEEDLE, D. (2004) *Business in context*. London: Thomson.

NELSON, D. (2011) Bhutan's Gross National Happiness index. *The Daily Telegraph*. 2 March.

NELSON, P. (2001) Does IIP still make the grade? *Personnel Today*. 13 November.

NESS. (2010) *The impact of Sure Start schemes on 5 year olds and their families.* London: National Evaluation of Sure Start Schemes. November.

NETWORK RESEARCH. (2013) *UK parcel delivery research.* April. Available at: http://courier-direct.co.uk/news/wp-content/uploads/2013/03/UK-Parcel-Delivery-Research-May-2013.pdf [Accessed 18 January 2015]

NEVILLE, S. (2012) Bitter battle as brewers jostle for their place at the bars of Asia and Africa. *The Guardian.* 4 September.

NEVILLE, S. (2015) Sports Direct responsible for fifth of all zero hour contracts in retail sector. *The Independent.* 30 March.

NEWMAN, M, (2009) Social work degrees difficult to fail, MPs told. *Times Higher Education.* 6 August.

NEW YORK TIMES (2014) Retroreport: the dark shadow of Agent Orange. Available at: http://www.youtube.com/watch?v=uzvTB0mOS0w [Accessed 17 April 2015]

NHS COMMISSIONING BOARD (2012) Risk management strategy and policy. Available at: http://www.england.mhs.uk/wp-content/uploads/2012/11/risk-man-strat.pdf [Accessed 15 January 2015]

NHS EMPLOYERS. (2009) Working Time Directive: frequently asked questions for Employer Implementation Teams. September.

NICHIPORUK, B. (2000) *The security dynamics of demographic factors.* Westport, CT: Rand Publishing.

NIKE. (2010) Case Study: HRM in practice FY08/09. Available at: www.nikebiz.com/crreport/content/workers-and-factories/3-12-0-case-study-hrm-in-practice.php [Accessed 5 September 2012]

NORMAN, P. (2001) Are your secrets safe: knowledge protection in strategic alliances. *Business Horizons.* Vol 44, No 6. November-December.

NORTHAMPTONSHIRE TELEGRAPH (2008) Rabbit caused water contamination at Pitsford. *Northamptonshire Telegraph.* 14 July.

NORTILLI, A. and WONG, K. (2014) A case analysis of the organisational behaviour of Ryanair and its impact. *Journal of Contemporary Management.* Vol 3 Issue 4

NORTON, C. (2002) Japan bribes mothers in bid for baby boom. *Sunday Times.* 15 September.

NORTON, S. (2015) Fairtrade Fortnight 2015: 20 years on and sales are slipping, have we forgotten about ethical eating? *The Independent.* 4 March.

NUGENT, N. (2006) *The Government and Politics of the European Union.* 6th ed. Basingstoke: Palgrave Macmillan.

NUNN, A., JOHNSON, S., MONRO, S., BICKERSTAFFE, T. and KELSEY, S. (2007) *Factors influencing social mobility.* Report 450. London: Department for Work and Pensions.

OBSERVER (2014) Brutal competition batters supermarkets the world over. *The Observer.* 5 October.

OBSERVER. (2015) Jenkins went without Canterbury's blessing. Now Barclays goes back to gung-ho banking. *The Observer.* 12 July

OECD (2014) *An overview of growing income inequalities in OECD countries.* Available at: http://www.oecd.org/social/inequality-and-poverty.htm

OFFICE FOR BUDGET RESPONSIBILITY (OBR). (2010) *Budget Forecast June 2010.* Available at: http://.budgetresponsibility.org.uk/wordpress/docs/junebudget.annexe.pdf [Accessed 27 October 2015]

OFFICE FOR BUDGET RESPONSIBILITY (OBR). (2015) *Economic and fiscal outlook March 2015.* Available at: http://budgetresponsibility.org.uk/economic-fiscal-outlook-march-2015/ [Accessed 27 October 2015]

OHMAE, K. (1990). *The borderless world.* Glasgow: Collins.

OLAFSSON, S. (2012) *The Icelandic way out of the crisis.* Working Paper no. 1: 2012. Social Research Centre, University of Iceland.

ONS. (2000) *Social trends.* London: HMSO.

ONS. (2005) *Time use survey* [refers to 2003]. London: Office for

National Statistics.

ONS. (2006a) Distribution of wealth in the UK. *Social Trends.* Table s. 26. London: ONS.

ONS. (2006b) *Labour market trends.* December. pp32–3.

ONS. (2007) *16% of UK population are over the age of 65.* Available at: www.statistics.gov.uk/cci/nugget.asp?ID=949

ONS. (2009) *Family spending.* Available at:

http://www.ons.gov.uk/ons/rel/family-spending/family-spending/2009-edition/index.html [Accessed 25 February 2016]

ONS. (2011) *Family data.* Available at: www.ons.gov.uk/ons/rel/wellbeing/measuring-national-well-being/households-and-families/art—households-and-families.html#tab-Families

ONS. (2012a) *Population data.* Available at: www.ons.gov.uk/ons/taxonomy/index.html?nscl=Population

ONS. (2012b) *Labour market statistics.* January. Available at: www.uk/ons/rel/lms/labour-market-statistics/january-2012/index/html [Accessed 1 February 2013]

ONS. (2012c) *Labour force survey.* October-December.

ONS. (2013) *Labour market statistics.* January. Available at: www.uk/ons/rel/lms/labour-market-statistics/january-2013/index/html, [Accessed 1 February 2013]

ONS. (2014) *Wealth and income data.* Available at: http://www.ons.gov.uk/ons/rel/was/wealth-in-great-britain-wave-2/2008-2010–part-2-/report–chapter-3–financial-wealth.html#tab-Household-net-financial-wealth

ONS. (2015a) *Families and households 2014.* Available at: http://www.ons.gov.uk/ons/dcp171778_393133.pdf

ONS. (2015b) *UK trade December 2014.* Available at: www.ons.gov.uk/ons/rel/uk-trade/december-2014/stb-uk-trade–december-2014.html [Accessed 21 October 2015]

ONS. (2015c) *Population data.* Available at http://www.ons.gov.uk/ons/rel/pop-estimate/population-estimates-for-uk–england-and-wales–scotland-and-northern-ireland/mid-2014/index.html [Accessed 25 February 2016]

OPENWONGA. (2013) *Ten commitments.* Available at: http://www.openwonga.com

ORTON, M. and ROWLINGSON, K. (2007) *Public attitudes to economic inequality.* York: Joseph Rowntree Foundation.

OSBORN, A. (2003) State's golden share in BAA is illegal. *The Guardian.* 14 May.

OSBORNE, G. (2011) Britain is leading the way out of this crisis. *Daily Telegraph.* 7 August.

OSBORNE, H. (2014) Wonga looks beyond payday to try out longer loans. *The Guardian.* 26 March.

OXFAM. (2009) Turning the tide: how best to protect workers employed by gangmasters, five years after Morecambe Bay. Oxford: Oxfam.

PALMÅS, K. (2005) The UK Public Interest Company: the idea, its origins, and its relevance for Sweden. *CbiS discussion paper 1.* Göteborg University, Sweden.

PANCEVSKI, B. (2013) Ghost towns haunt Merkel as pole looms. *Sunday Times.* August 4. p24.

PARKER, A. and SMYTH, J. (2013) The mouthy airline chief who annoyed too many passengers. *The Financial Times.* 9 November.

PARKER, M. (2005) Global scramble to jump aboard the bandwagon. *The Times.* 26 April.

PARKHE, A. (2001) Interfirm diversity in global alliances. *Business Horizons.* Vol 44, No 6. November-December.

PARLIAMENT. (2015) Statement on Europe renegotiation 10 November. Available at: http://www.parliament.uk/business/news/2015/november/statement-on-europe-renegotiation-10-November-2015/ [Accessed 20 February 2016]

PARLIAMENT PUBLICATIONS. (2012) *Public Accounts Committee, Tax avoidance by multinational companies.* 3 December. Available at: http://www.publications.parliament.uk/pa/cm/201213/cmselect/cmpubacc/716/71605.htm [Accessed 3 December 2012]

PARLIAMENTARY BUSINESS. (2010) *Briefing paper.* Available at: www.parliament.uk/business/publications/research/key-issues-for-the-new-parliament/value-for-money-in-public-services/the-ageing-population/

PARRY, E., TYSON, S., SELBIE, D. and LEIGHTON, R. (2007) *HR and technology: impact and advantages.* London: Chartered Institute of Personnel and Development.

PEACHEY, K. (2015) Will Wonga and other payday lenders survive? *BBC News.* 22 April. Available at: http://www.bbc.co.uk/news/business-32394286 [Accessed 23 April 2015]

PEACOCK, L. (2007) Location beats pay as a top factor in attracting people to work in UK call centres. *Personnel Today.* 14 May.

PEARCE, F. (2002) We need more babies. *Sunday Times*. 17 March.

PEARSON, G. (nd) University of Liverpool FIH Factsheet: the Bosman case, EU law and the transfer system. Available at: http://www.liv.ac.uk/footballindustry/bosman.html [Accessed 14 October 2009]

PENG, M. W, TAN, J. and TONG, T. W. (2004) Ownership types and strategic groups in emerging economies. *Journal of Management Studies*. Vol 41, Issue 7. November.

PENNYCOOK, M., CORY, G. and ALEKESON, V. (2013) *A matter of time: the rise of zero-hours contracts*. London: Resolution Foundation.

PEOPLE MANAGEMENT. (2004) Royal Mail recruits excluded groups. *People Management*. 28 October.

PEOPLE MANAGEMENT. (2009a) A8 requests down. *People Management*. 12 March.

PEOPLE MANAGEMENT. (2009b) Beds and Bars employee console. *People Management*. 24 September.

PEOPLE MANAGEMENT. (2009c) British Airways staff asked to work for free. *People Management*. 16 June.

PEOPLE MANAGEMENT. (2011) HR directors spend only 15% of their time on strategic work. *People Management*. 24 January.

PEOPLE MANAGEMENT. (2012) Half of staff not aware of HR policies, figures show. *People Management*. 8 June.

PEOPLE MANAGEMENT. (2013a) They come over here, they take our jobs, that we probably didn't want anyway. *People Management*. January.

PEOPLE MANAGEMENT. (2013b) No sick pay, no back chat. *People Management*. June.

PEOPLE MANAGEMENT (2015) If you're good enough, we will find you. *People Management*. May.

PERLMUTTER, H V. (1969) The tortuous evolution of the multinational corporation. *Columbia Journal of World Business*. 4.

PERSAUD, J. (2004) Carry on working. *People Management*. 29 July. *Personnel Today* (2004) CSR help is at hand. *Personnel Today*. 27 July.

PESTON, R. (2015a) Weep for falling productivity. *BBC News*. 1 April. Available at: http://www.bbc.co.uk/news/business-32146712 [Accessed 1 November 2015]

PESTON, R. (2015b) China slowdown forces devaluation. *BBC News*. 11 August. Available at: http://www.bbc.co.uk/news/business-33858870 [Accessed 11 November 2015]

PETER, L. (2012), Q&A: Eurozone integration deal. 29 June. Available at: http://www.bbc.co.uk/news/business-18607756 [Accessed 28 November 2012]

PETERS, T. (1985) *Thriving on chaos*. New York: Knopf.

PETERS, T. and WATERMAN, R. (1982) *In Search of Excellence*. New York: Harper & Row.

PETHOKOUKIS, J. (2004) Meet your new co-worker. *Money and Business*. 3 July.

PETTINGER, J. (2012a) UK National Debt. *UK Economics*. 22 October. Available at: http://www.economicshelp.org/blog/category/uk-economy/ [Accessed 3 November 2012]

PETTINGER, J. (2012b) How the budget deficit was cut by 25%? *UK Economics*. 23 October. Available at: http://www.economicshelp.org/blog/category/economics/ [Accessed 3 November 2012]

PFEFFER, J. (1981) *Power and organisations*. Boston, MA: Pitman.

PHILLIPS, A W H. (1958) The relationship between unemployment and the rate of change of money wage rates in the UK 1861-1957. *Economica*. Vol 25, No 2.

PHILPOTT, J. (2002a) HRH – a work audit. *CIPD Perspectives*. Summer. London: Chartered Institute of Personnel and Development.

PHILPOTT, J. (2002b) Productivity and people management. *Perspectives*. Spring. London: Chartered Institute of Personnel and Development.

PHILPOTT, J. (2003) Europe. *Perspectives*. Summer. London: Chartered Institute of Personnel and Development.

PHILPOTT, J. (2007) Britain's Eastern European migrant workforce. *Impact*. Vol 19. May.

PHILPOTT, J. (2009a) The cost to employers of redundancy. *Impact* 26. February.

PHILPOTT, J. (2009b) Labour cost savings from alternatives to redundancy. *Impact* 27. May.

PHILPOTT, J. (2012) Counting the cost of the jobs recession. *Impact* 39. July.

PHILPOTT, J and DAVIES, G. (2006), No turning back? *People Management*. 14 September.

PICKARD, J. (2004a) One step beyond. *People Management*. 30 June.

PICKARD, J. (2004b) Should I stay or should I go? *People Management*. 25 March

PICKARD, J. (2006) Cable & Wireless calls time on outsourced HR. *People Management*. 26 October.

PICKARD, J. (2009a) Employee branding. *People Management*. 5 November.

PICKARD, J. (2009b) BP and Hewitt renew HR outsourcing deal. *People Management*. 12 February.

PICKETTY, T. (2014) *Capital in the 21st century*. Cambridge, MA: Belknap Press.

PIDD, H. (2009) Honda's Swindon factory reopens. *The Guardian*. 1 June.

PIDD, H. (2012) I stand in the school playground and all I hear is Polish. *The Guardian*. 12 December.

PIDD, H. (2015) Why Otley's pubs may be saved from last orders. *The Guardian*. 10 May.

PLIMMER, G. and HORNBY, L. (2014) China set to invest £105bn in UK infrastructure by 2025. *Financial Times*. 27 October.

PLUMMER, R (2015), Greece debt crisis: what's the deal? *BBC News*. 13 July. Available at: www.bbc.co.uk/news/business-33505555 [Accessed 12 October 2015]

POLLACK, C. (1997) European Union policies. In: LEWINGTON, I. (ed.) *Utility regulation*. Bath: Centre for the Study of Regulated Industries and Privatisation International.

POLSKA. (2006) *Economic ministry*. Poland. Available at: http://www.poland.gov.pl [Accessed 12 November 2006].

POOLE, E. (2015) *Capitalism's toxic assumptions*. London: Featherstone Education.

POOLER, M. (2015) Lidl move to pay its UK staff a 'living wage' to cost £9m. *Financial Times*. 18 September,

PORTER, M, E. (1980) *Competitive strategy*. New York: Free Press.

PORTER, M. (1985) *Competitive advantage: creating and sustaining superior performance*. New York: Free Press.

PORTER, M. (1999) *On competition*. New York: The Free Press.

PORTER, M. (2008) The five competitive forces that shape strategy. *Harvard Business Review*. Vol 86, Issue 1. January.

PORTER, M and KETELS, C. (2003) UK competitiveness: moving to the next stage. *DTI Economics Paper No 3*. DTI/ESRC. May.

PRAHALAD, C. K. (2010) The responsible manager. *Harvard Business Review*. Vol 88, No 1/2. January/February.

PRAHALAD, C. K. and HAMEL, G. (1989) Strategic Intent. *Harvard Business Review*. Vol 67, No 6. June.

PRAHALAD, C. K. and HAMEL, G. (1990) The core competence of the corporation. *Harvard Business Review*. Vol 70, Issue 5-6. May-June.

PRATLEY, N. (2012) Row exposes timidity of the taxman. *The Guardian*. 7 December.

PRATLEY, N. (2013) Online shopping: supermarkets eating themselves. *The Guardian*. 5 January.

PRATLEY, N (2015a) Good news in store. *The Guardian*. 30 September.

PRATLEY, P. (2015b) Prudent bank that became a goliath and lost touch. *The Guardian*. 10 February.

PRATLEY, P. (2015c) Its critics labelled it the Highly Suspect British Company – how right they were. *The Guardian*. 14 February.

PRICEWATERHOUSECOOPERS. (2000) *HR in e-commerce survey*. London: PricewaterhouseCoopers.

PROBY, W. (2005) Out of the country house and into the back to back. *The Guardian*. 15 September. *PROFESSIONAL MANAGER*. (2001) Focused females forge ahead. *Professional Manager*. November.

PROSSER, D. (2007) Fairtrade is booming – but is it still a fair deal? *Independent*. 24 February.

PRUSACK, L. (1997) *Knowledge in organisations*. London: Butterworth-Heinemann.

PUCIK, V. (2007) Reframing global mindset. In: SCHULER, R. and JACKSON, S. (eds) *Strategic Human Resource Management*. 2nd ed, Oxford: Blackwell.

PUGH, D.S. (1978) Understanding and managing organizational change. *London Business School Journal*. Vol 3, No 2. pp29–34.

PUGH, D., HICKSON, D. and HININGS, C. (1971) *Writers on organisations*. London: Penguin.

PURCELL, J. (1999) Best practice and best fit: chimera or cul-de-sac? *Human Resource Management Journal*. Vol 9, No 3.

PURCELL, J. (2005) *Business strategies and human resource management: uneasy bedfellows or strategic partners?* University of Bath Working Papers 2005, p16. Available at: www.bath.ac.uk/management/research/pdf/2005-16.pdf [Accessed 5 September 2012]

PURCELL, J. and AHLSTRAND, B. (1994) *Human resource management in the multi-divisional company*. Oxford: Oxford University Press.

PURCELL, J., KINNIE, N. and HUTCHINSON, S. (2003) Open minded. *People Management*. 15 May.

PURVIS, A. (2004) Why supermarkets are getting richer and richer. *The Observer*. 25 June.

PUTNAM, R. (2000) *Bowling alone*. New York: Simon & Schuster.

PUTNAM, R. (2015) *Our kids: the American dream in crisis*. Simon & Schuster.

PYM, H. (2014) Winter pressure – how helpful is NHS 111? *BBC News*. 16 December. Available at: http://www.bbc.co.uk/news/health-30507648 [Accessed 27 December 2014]

QUINN, J. (1980) *Strategies for change: logical incrementalism*. Homewood, IL: Irwin.

RACONTEUR (2015) http://www.raconteur.net [Accessed 12 July 2015]

RAFTER, M. (2005) Adventures in outsourcing. *Workforce*. June.

RAJAN, A., MARTIN, B. and LATHAM, J. (2003) *Harnessing workforce diversity to raise the bottom line*. London: Resource Group Centre.

RAMBLERS HOLIDAYS. (2007) http://www.ramblersholidays.co.uk [Accessed 14 July 2007]

RAMESH, R. (2013) The health service could keel over in 2016. *The Guardian*. 7 August.

RAMSEY, H., SCHOLARIOS, D. and HARLEY, B. (2000) Employees and high performance work systems: testing inside the black box. *British Journal of Industrial Relations*. Vol 38, No 4.

RANKIN, J. (2014) New payday loan rules to cap fees, total cost and default charges. *The Guardian*. 11 November

RAWNSLEY, A. and HELM, T. (2015) John McDonnell: It was a difficult appointment... we knew we were going to be hit by a tsunami. *The Observer*. 20 September.

REDDINGTON, M., WILLIAMSON, M. and WITHERS, M. (2005) *Transforming HR: Creating value through people*. London: Elsevier.

REILLY, P. (2000) *HR shared services and the realignment of HR*. Institute of Employment Studies Report 368. Brighton: IES.

REILLY, P. and WILLIAMS, T. (2012) One way to go? *People Management*. September.

REITZ, J., WALL, J. and LOVE, M. S. (1998) Ethics in negotiation: oil and water or good lubrication? *Business Horizons*. May–June.

RESOLUTION FOUNDATION. (2012) *Gaining from growth: the final report of the Commission on Living Standards*. London: Resolution Foundation.

RETAIL WEEK. (2009) Co-op reports record full-year profits. 6 May.

RICHARDS, D. and GLADWIN, T. (1999) Sustainability metrics for the Business Enterprise. *Environmental Quality Management*. Spring.

RICK, J., HILLAGE, S., HONEY, S. and PERRYMEN, S. (1997) *Stress: big issue, but what are the problems?* Institute of Employment Studies Report 311. July.

RIDGEWAY, C. and WALLACE, B. (1994) *Empowering change: the role of people management*. London: Chartered Institute of Personnel and Development.

ROBERTS, I. (2006) Taking age out of the workforce. *Work, Employment and Society*. Vol 20, No 1. pp67–86.

ROBERTS, K. (2001) *Class in modern Britain*. Basingstoke: Palgrave.

ROBINSON, D. and HAYDAY, S. (2009) *The engaging manager*. Report 470. Brighton: Institute for Employment Studies. November.

ROBINSON, J. (2014) Sierra Leone struggling in fight against Ebola because so many doctors and nurses have left to find jobs in Britain, report claims. *MailOnline*. 18 December. Available at: http://www.dailymail.co.uk/news/article-2878800/Sierra-Leone-struggling-fight-against-ebola-doctors-nurses-left-jobs-Britain-report-claims.html [Accessed 18 February 2015]

ROCHE, W., TEAGUE, P., COUGHLAN, A and FAHY, M, (2011) *Human resources in the recession: managing and representing people at work in Ireland*. Dublin: Labour Relations Commission.

ROGERS, S. (2012) Bobby Kennedy on GDP: 'measures everything except that which is worthwhile'. *The Guardian*. 24 May.

ROLLINSON, D. (2008), *Organisational behaviour and analysis*. 4th ed. Harlow: Pearson.

ROSAMUND, B. (2005) Globalization, the ambivalence of European integration and the possibilities for a post-disciplinary EU studies. *Innovation: the European Journal of Social Science Research*. Vol 18, No 1.

ROSER, M. (2015) World poverty. Available at: http://ourworldindata.org/data/growth-and-distribution-of-prosperity/world-poverty [Accessed 27 February 2016]

ROSNER, H. (2013) What really spurred the Great Recession? Kellogg Insight. Kellogg School of Management, Northwestern University. Available at: http://insightkelloggnorthwestern.edu/article/what_really_spurred_the_great-recession [Accessed 9 June 2015]

ROSSELSON, R. (2012) Pay ratios. *Ethical Consumer*. Issue 135. March-April.

ROUSSEAU, D. (2004) Psychological contracts in the workplace: understanding the ties that motivate. *Academy of Management Executive*. Vol 18, No 1. February.

RUCCI, A. (1997) Should HR survive? A profession at the crossroads. *Human Resource Management*. Vol 36, No 1. pp169–73.

RUDDICK, G. (2015) Thai billionaire Dhanin Chearavanont keen on Tesco Lotus deal. *Daily Telegraph*. 9 February.

RUDIGER, K. (2008) *The UK and India: the other 'special relationship'?* The Work Foundation Provocation Series. Vol 4, Number 3.

RUIGROK, W. (2004) A tale of strategic and governance errors. *European Business Forum*. No 17. Spring.

RUMSBY, B (2015) Fifa loses three key sponsors as Castrol, Continental and Johnson & Johnson sever ties with world governing body. *Daily Telegraph*. 22 January.

RUNDBLAD, G., HUNTER, P., KNAPTON, O. and VAN HERWEGEN, J. (2011) *Improving communication on Cryptosporidium and 'Boil Water' notices: Lessons from Pitsford*. Drinking Water Inspectorate. Available at: http://dwi.defra.gov.uk/research-completed-research/reports/dwi70-2-244.pdf [Accessed 10 January 2015]

RUSH, S. (2004) Leading in China: a conversation with Elizabeth Weldon, *Leadership in Action*, Vol 24 No 2, May/June

RYANAIR. (2003) *Economy and Mobility: the Ryanair Business Model*. Available at: http://www.ryanair.com [Accessed 18 July 2007]

RYANAIR. (2007) http://www.ryanair.com/site/EN/about [Accessed 18 July 2007]

RYANAIR. (2014) Annual report. Available at: http://www.ryanair.com [Accessed 22 April 2015]

RYLE, S. (2002) Banana war leaves the Caribbean a casualty. *The Observer*. 24 November.

SAEZ, E. and ZUCMAN, G. (2014) Wealth inequality in the USA since 1913. London: London School of Economics.

SAMUEL, M. (2009) Celebrities back social work in government recruitment push. *Community Care*. 1 September.

SANDS, S. (2004) Don't let them send you to Nebraska. *Daily Telegraph*. 14 August.

SAUNDERS, A. (2011) The MT interview: Paul Polman. *Management Today*. March.

SAWFORD, A. (2009) How Whitehall betrayed social workers. *The Guardian*. 12 March.

SCARBOROUGH, H. and CARTER, C. (2007) *Investigating knowledge management*. London: Chartered Institute of Personnel and Development.

SCHEIN, E. (1980) *Organisational psychology*. Englewoods Cliffs, NJ: Prentice Hall.

SCHLESINGER, L., KIEFER, C. and BROWN, P. (2012) New Project: don't analyse – act. *Harvard Business Review*. Vol 90, No 3. March.

SCHOLTE, J A. (200) *Globalization: a critical introduction*. Basingstoke: Palgrave.

SCHONEBOOM, A. (2011) Sleeping giants? Fired work bloggers and labour organisation. *New Technology, Work and Employment.* Vol 26, No 1.

SCHULER, R. and JACKSON, S. (1987) Linking competitive strategies with human resource management practices. *Academy of Management Executive.* Vol 1, No 3.

SCHUMPETER, J. (1976) *Capitalism, socialism and democracy.* London: George Allen & Unwin.

SCHUTZ, W. (1966) *The interpersonal underworld: FIRO – a three dimensional theory of interpersonal behavior.* Palo Alto, CA: Science and Behavior Books.

SCHWARTZ, M. S. (2001) A code of ethics for corporate codes of ethics. *Journal of Business Ethics.* Vol 41.

SCHWARTZ, P. (2003) *Inevitable surprises: think ahead in times of turbulence.* New York: Gotham Books.

SCOTT. A. (2009) HSE raps health trust for 'failing' on stress. *People Management.* 26 February. p9.

SCOTT, M. (2004) A burning issue for recruits. *The Financial Times.* 18 October.

SCOTT, W. R. (1987) *Organizations: rational, natural and open systems.* Englewood Cliffs, NJ: Prentice Hall.

SEAGER, A. (2009) Costa Rica is world's greenest, happiest country. *The Guardian.* 4 July.

SEARJEANT, G. (2007) Bank Governor hits back at criticism over inflation. *The Times.* 25 April.

SEGAL-HORN, S. (2002). Global firms – heroes or villains? How and why companies globalize. *European Business Journal.* Vol 14, Issue 1.

SEMLER, R. (1993) *Maverick!* London: Arrow.

SENGE, P. (1990) *The Fifth Discipline.* London: Century Business.

SEXTON, R. (2012) *The Exploration of Economics.* Sixth edition. Cincinnati, OH: South-Western College.

SEXTON, R. and FORTURA, P. (2005) *Exploring economics.* Scarborough, Ontario: Nelson.

SHAH, S. (2004) India 'losing ground to UK in battle of the call centres'. *The Independent.* 10 April.

SHARMA, A. K. and TALWAR, B. (2004) Business excellence enshrined in Vedic (Hindu) philosophy. *Singapore Management Review.* Vol 26, Issue 1.

SHAYLOR, A. (2015) We know what the future looks like. *Work.* Spring. pp33–35.

SHEPHERD, J. (2010) Child poverty study shows fifth of UK youngsters severely affected. *The Guardian.* 15 October. p23.

SHORTELL, S. M. and ZAJAC, E. (1990) Perceptual and archival measures of Miles and Snow's strategic types: the role of strategic orientation. *Academy of Management Journal.* Vol 33, No 4. December.

SIEGEL AND GALE. (2014) *Simplicity Index UK.* Available at: http://simplicityindex.com/2014/region/united-kingdom/ [Accessed 22 April 2015]

SIMMS, A. (2009) Questions for a new world. *The Guardian,* 17 November.

SIMPSON, D and WOODLEY, T. (2007) Organisation and solidarity across frontiers are the future, *The Guardian.* 1 May.

SKAPINKER, M. (2004). The psychology of consumption. *The Financial Times.* 31 March

SLACK, N., CHAMBERS, L. and JOHNSTON, R. (2007) *Operations management.* 5th edition. London: FT Prentice Hall.

SLYWOTSKY, A and NADLER, D. (2004) The Strategy is the Structure. *Harvard Business Review.* Vol 82 No 2 February

SMALLWOOD, C. (2003) People power rings changes. *Sunday Times.* 10 August.

SMALLWOOD, C. (2006) 'Reserve army' can defuse demographic time bomb. *Sunday Times.* 20 August.

SMEDLEY, T. (2008) And now for the good news. *People Management.* 6 March. pp25–30.

SMITH, A. (1776/1982) *The wealth of nations.* Harmondsworth: Penguin.

SMITH, D. (2004) Prophet warning. *People Management.* 23 December.

SMITH, D. (2007a) We still have a grip on inflation, says Bank. *The Sunday Times.* 22 April.

SMITH, D. (2007b) *The dragon and the elephant: China, India and the new world order.* London: Profile.

SMITH, D. (2014) Sticky problems of being a honeypot for migrants. *Sunday Times.* August 3. Business, p4.

SMITH, H. (2012) Greeks take an axe to the forests to stave off a bitter winter. *The Guardian.* 29 November.

SNELL, R. (1999) Managing ethically. In: FULOP, L. and LINSTEAD, S. (eds) *Management: a critical text.* Basingstoke: Macmillan.

SOCIAL TRENDS. (2004) Chapter 13: Lifestyles and social participation. Vol 34. London: Her Majesty's Stationery Office.

SOCIAL TRENDS. (2006) London. Her Majesty's Stationery Office.

SPARROW, A. (2009) Gordon Brown launches package of measures to boost social mobility. *Guardian.* 13 January.

SPARROW, P., BREWSTER, C. and HARRIS, H. (2004) *Globalizing human resource management.* London: Routledge.

SPENCER, S., RUHS, M., ANDERSON, B. and ROGALY, B. (2007) *Migrants' lives beyond the workplace: the experiences of Central and East Europeans in the UK.* Joseph Rowntree Foundation.

STACEY, R. (1991) *The chaos frontier: creative strategic control for business.* Oxford, Butterworth-Heinemann.

STACEY, R. (1993) *Strategic management and organisational dynamics.* Harlow: Pearson Education.

STARBUCKS. (2012a) Setting the record straight on Starbucks UK taxes and profitability. Blog posted by Howard Schultz. 23 October. Available at: http://starbucks.co.uk/blog/setting-the-record-straight-on-starbucks-uk-taxes-and-profitability [Accessed 3 December 2012]

STARBUCKS. (2012b) An open letter from Starbucks Coffee Company U. Press advertisement. 7 December.

STARMER-SMITH, C. (2006) Disabled groups attack 33p Ryanair levy. *Daily Telegraph.* 13 May.

STEADMAN, K., WOOD, M. and SILVESTER, H. (2015) Health and well-being at work. London: Health and Safety Executive.

STEELE, J. (2001) Food for thought: Amartya Sen. *The Guardian.* 31 March.

STELZER, I. (2014a) Migrant amnesty fuels growth – and a political row. *Sunday Times.* 30 November. Business section. p4.

STELZER, I. (2014b) Fear of change puts Europe in conflict with US tech giants. *Sunday Times.* December 7. Business section. p4.

STEVENS, C. (2015) Are HR business partners a dying breed? *People Management.* 26 January.

STEVENS, M. (2010a) Proctor and Gamble goes virtual to lure graduates. *People Management.* 22 April. p9.

STEVENS, M. (2010b) L'Oreal's recruitment gets a virtual makeover. *People Management.* 3 June. p10.

STEVENS, M. (2011) Social media. *People Management.* July. pp10–11.

STEVENSON, H. H. (1989) Defining corporate strengths and weaknesses. In: BOWMAN, C. and ASCH, D. (eds) *Readings in strategic management.* Basingstoke: Macmillan.

STEWART, E. (2007) Apology over wrong migration statistics from Home Secretary. *The Guardian.* 30 October.

STEWART, H. (2009) Union says yes to Honda pay cut. *The Guardian.* 22 June.

STEWART, H. and BOFFEY, D. (2011) George Osborne plan isn't working, say top UK economists. *The Observer.* 5 June.

STEWART, H. (2013) WTO faces struggle to remain relevant as cult of globalisation fade. *The Observer.* 13 January.

STEWART, T. (2001) *The wealth of knowledge: intellectual capital in the 21st century organisation*. London: Nicholas Brealey.

STIGLITZ, J. (2003) *Globalization and its discontents*. New ed. London: Penguin.

STOREY, J. (1992) *Developments in the management of human resources*. London: Blackwell.

STOREY, J. and QUINTAS, P. (2001) Knowledge management and HRM. In: STOREY, J. (ed.) *Human resource management: a critical text*. London: Thomson Learning.

STORR, F. (2009) *Humberside TEC, a learning company*. Available at: www.trojanmice.com/articles/becoming.htm

STRACK, R. CAYE, J-M. VON DER LINDEN, C. QUIROS, H.Y. and HAEN, P. (2012) *From capability to profitability: realizing the value of people management*. Boston Consulting Group/World Federation of People Management Associations.

STRATTON, A. (2009) MPs' expenses: Christopher Kelly outlines reforms. *The Guardian*. 4 November.

STRATTON, A. (2010) Labour's plan for the first 'John Lewis' council. *The Guardian*. 18 February.

STRAW, W and GLENNIE, A. (2012) *The third wave of globalisation*. London: Institute for Public Policy Research.

STREDWICK, J. (1997) *Cases in reward management*. London: Kogan Page.

STREDWICK, J. and ELLIS, S. (2005) *Flexible working practices*. London: Chartered Institute of Personnel and Development.

STRUPCZWESKI, J and BREIDHARDT, A. (2012) Eurozone, IMF secure deal on long-term Greek debt. *Reuters*. 26 November. Available at: http://www.reuters.com/article/2012/11/26/eurogroup-greece [Accessed 1 December 2012]

SUBRAMANIAN, S. (2004) *Biotechnology and society*. Available at: http://www.chennaionline.com [Accessed 24 November].

SULL, D. (2005) Dynamic partners. *Business Strategy Review*. Summer.

SULLIVAN, A. (2012) Small and smart, the saplings that will rise after the press forest fire. *Sunday Times*. 16 December. p24.

SUMMERS, D. (2009) British ex-MEP Tom Wise faces jail after £36,000 expenses scam. *The Guardian*. 5 November

SUMMERS, L. (2014) US economic prospect: secular stagnation, hysteresis and the zero lower bound. *Business Economics*. Vol 49.

SUNDAY TIMES. (2007) Russians told: have a baby and win a fridge. 19 August. p23.

SUNDERLAND, R. (2009) Women still face a steep climb to the top table. *Observer*. 23 August.

SUTTON TRUST. (2007) *The educational backgrounds of 500 leading figures*. London: The Sutton Trust.

SWANN, C. (2004) Sixty years on, and still contentious. *The Financial Times.* 29 May.

SWART, J., KINNIE, N. and PURCELL, J. (2003) *People and performance in knowledge-intensive firms.* London: Chartered Institute of Personnel and Development.

SWEENEY, P and CHIANG, L (2012) China approves $157 billion infrastructure spending. Reuters. 7 September. Available at: http://www.in.reuters.com/article/china-economy-idINL6E8K7JBJ20120907 [Accessed 20 February 2016]

SWYNGEDOUW, E. (2004) Globalisation or glocalisation? Networks, territories and rescaling, *Cambridge Review of International Affairs.* Vol 17, No 1. April.

SYAL, R and WINTOUR, P. (2012) MPs go to war over tax as Starbucks smells the coffee. *The Guardian.* 3 December.

SYED, M. (2015) How to blame less and learn more. *The Guardian.* 3 October.

SYEDAIN, H. (2009) Mutual benefit. *People Management.* 5 November.

SYEDAIN, H. (2010) A new era for age. *People Management.* 14 January.

SYEDAIN, H. (2012) On my agenda. *People Management.* June.

SZABO, L. (2008) Gene therapy takes a step forward. *USA Today.* Available at: usatoday30.usatoday.com/tech/science/2008-04-28-gene-therapy_N.htm

TANZANIA NATIONAL PARKS. (2009) *Tariffs November 2009.* Available at http://www.tanzaniaparks.com/parkfees/Tariffs-New-Dec11 [Accessed 1 July 2012]

TARGETT, S. (2004) Is good governance good value? *Financial Times.* 17 April.

TAYLOR, F. (1947) *Scientific management.* New York: Harper and Row.

TAYLOR, R. (2004) *Skills and innovation in modern Britain.* ESRC Future of Work Programme Seminar Series. Swindon: Economic and Social Research Council.

TAYLOR, S. (2008) *People resourcing.* 4th edition. London: Chartered Institute of Personnel and Development.

TAYLOR, W., PIASECKA, A. and WORMAN, D. (2005) *Managing diversity: learning by doing.* London: Chartered Institute of Personnel and Development.

TEATHER, D. (2007) Model executive puts Hornby back on track. *The Guardian.* 21 December.

TEECE, D. (2007) Explicating dynamic capabilities: the nature and microfoundations of (sustainable) enterprise performance. *Sustainable Management Journal.* Vol 28. August.

TENBRUNSEL, A. and THOMAS, J. (2015) *The street, the bull and the crisis.* Notre Dame University/Labaton Sucharow. Available at: http://www.secwhistlebloweradvocate.com/LitereatureRetrieve.aspx?ID=224757 [Accessed 21 May 2015]

TESCO website. (2015) http://www.tesco.com [Accessed 22 June 2015]

TESCO LOTUS. (2007) Tesco Lotus Key Facts. February 2007. Available at: http://www.tescolotus.net/company/keyfacts.asp [Accessed 27 April 2007]

THE WEEK. (2015) Average UK income passes pre-crash peak. *The Week.* 28 October.

THOMAS, K. (1976) Conflict and conflict management. In DUNETTE, M. D. (ed.) *Handbook of industrial and organisational psychology.* New York: Rand McNally.

THOMAS, T. (2009) Tesco eyes loyalty value with Clubcard relaunch. *Marketing.* 13 May.

THOMPSON, J. (2012) Supermarket giant says Christmas was disappointing and warns that growth in year ahead will be minimal. *The Independent.* 13 January.

THOMPSON, J. with MARTIN, F. (2005) *Strategic management: awareness and change.* London: Thomson.

THOMPSON, M. (2000) *The competitive challenge: final report: the bottom line benefits of strategic human resource management.* London: Society of British Aerospace Companies.

THOMPSON, M. (2005) *Strategic management: awareness and change.* 5th ed. London: Thomson.

THUROW, L. (1999) *Creating wealth.* London: Nicholas Brealey. p xv.

TIMES 100 BUSINESS CASE STUDIES. (2012) *Edition 16: Tarmac: Competitive advantage* through diversity. Available at http://businesscasestudies.co.uk/companies/ [Accessed 23 January 2015]

TIMES 100 BUSINESS CASE STUDIES. (2013) *Edition 17: Logica: Using skills to respond to* the external environment. Available at: http://businesscasestudies.co.uk/companies/ [Accessed 23 January 2015]

TIMES 100 BUSINESS CASE STUDIES. (2014a) *Edition 18: Hewden: securing a market-leading future through SWOT analysis.* Available at: http://businesscasestudies.co.uk/ companies [Accessed 23 January 2015]

TIMES 100 BUSINESS CASE STUDIES. (2014b) Edition 18: Capco: organisational structure in an innovative environment. Available at: http://businesscasestudies.co.uk/ companies/ [Accessed 23 January 2015]

TIPLER, C. (2011) The National Trust strategy for 2020. 'Going local': evaluating the impact on properties and stakeholders, unpublished MSc dissertation, University of Portsmouth (abstract only). Available at: www.eprints.prt.ac.uk/6092 [Accessed 25 January 2015]

TISDALL, S. (2007), Confident Turkey looks east, not west. *The Guardian.* 26 March.

TOMLINSON, H. (2001) Stop me and buy a Ben & Jerry's. *The Independent on Sunday.* 9 December.

TOMLINSON, H. and EVANS, R. (2009) Tesco stocks up on inside knowledge of shoppers'

lives. *The Guardian.* 20 September. p12.

TOMLINSON, M. (2004) *14-19 Curriculum and qualifications reform.* London: Department for Education and Science.

TOPHAM, G. (2015a) US and Gulf on brink of commercial air war. *The Guardian.* 13 June.

TOPHAM, G. (2015b) Glass ceiling in the sky: Qatar Airways problem with pregnant cabin crew. *The Guardian.* 19 June.

TOPHAM, G. (2015c) How fewer rules, more profit and being nice paid off for Ryanair. *The Observer*. 31 May.

TOVEY, A. (2015) The 'perfect storm' that has brought Britain's steel industry to its knees. *The Daily Telegraph*. 19 October.

TOYNBEE, P. (2009) Harman's law is Labour's biggest idea for 11 years. *The Guardian*. 13 January.

TRADING ECONOMICS. (2015) India GDP growth. Available at: http://www.tradingeconomics.com/india-gdp-growth [Accessed 11 November 2015]

TRANSPARENCY INTERNATIONAL. (2006) *Corruption perceptions index*. Available at: http://www.transparency.org/policy_research

TRANSPARENCY INTERNATIONAL. (2012) Corruption Perception Index 2012. www.transparency.org/cpi2012/results [Accessed 23 February 2012]

TRAVERS, T. (2009) Osborne shows he is a true blue. *The Guardian*. 10 September.

TRAVIS, A. (2010) David Cameron's empty immigration promise. *The Guardian*. 26 March.

TRAYNOR, I. (2015) Three days to save the euro. *The Guardian*. 22 October.

TREANOR, J. (2012) Vickers criticises government for watering down reform proposals. *The Guardian*. 15 June.

TREANOR, J. et al (2012) Chief banking regulator: 'Barclays had culture of gaming – and of gaming us'. *The Guardian*. 17 July.

TREMLETT, G. (2012) Bailout forces Bankia and other failed Spanish banks to make big cuts, *The Guardian*. 29 November.

TRIGGLE, N. (2015) Cuts to cancer treatments announced. *BBC News*. 12 January. Available at: www.bbc.co.uk/news/health-30787132 [Accessed 30 January 2015]

TUC. (2007) *Green workplaces project 2006-7: Objectives and outcomes report*. London: TUC.

TUC. (2008) *After Leitch: implementing skills and training policies: TUC submission to the Innovation, Universities and Skills Committee Inquiry*. London: TUC.

TUCKMAN, B. (1965) Developmental sequence in small groups. *Psychological Bulletin*. Vol 63. pp384–99.

TUFFT, B. (2015) Costa Rica goes 75 days powering itself using only renewable energy. *The Independent on Sunday*. 22 March.

TURNER, B. (2006) Plastic bags are much the lesser evil. *The Grocer*. 11 February.

TURNER, J., O'CATHAIN, A., KNOWLES, E., NICHOLL, J., TOSH, J., SAMPSON, F., COLEMAN, P. and COSTER, J. (2012) *Evaluation of NHS 111 pilot sites: final report*. Sheffield: University of Sheffield.

TURNER, P. (2010) From manpower planning to capacity planning – why we need workforce planning. In: CIPD (ed) *Reflections on workforce planning*. London: Chartered Institute of Personnel and Development.

TYSON, T, FELL F and TYSON, S (1986). *Evaluating the personnel function*. London, Hutchinson

UK GOVERNMENT. (2010) *Literature review – economic costs and benefits of EU membership*. Available at: http://www.gov.uk/government/uploads/attachment_data/file/220969/foi_eumembership_literaturereview.pdf [accessed 20 February 2016]

UK GOVERNMENT (2015a) *The future of apprenticeships in England*. Available at: https://www.gov.uk/government/uploads/system/uploads/attachment_data/file/447413/BIS-15-355-guidance-for-trailblazers-standards-to-starts-July-2015.pdf [Accessed 6 November 2015].

UK GOVERNMENT (2015b) *Summer Budget 2015*. Available at: http://www.gov.uk/.../topical-events/budget-july-2015 [Accessed 6 November 2015].

UKIP. (2011) *How much does the European Union cost Britain?* Available at: http://www.ukipmeps.org/uploads/file/cost_of_the_EU_25_5_11.pdf [Accessed 20 February 2016]

ULRICH, D. (1997) *Human resource champions: the next agenda for adding value and delivering results*. Boston, MA: Harvard Business School Press.

ULRICH, D. (1998) *Human resource champions: the next agenda for adding value and delivering results*. Boston, MA: Harvard Business School Press.

ULRICH, D. (2005) Role call. *People Management*. 16 June.

ULRICH, D. and BROCKBANK, W. (2009) The Business Partner Model. 10 years on: lessons learned. *Human Resource Management*. January.

ULRICH, D., YOUNGER, J. and BROCKBANK, W. (2008) The twenty-first century HR organization. *Human Resource Management*. Vol 42, No 4.

UNCTAD. (2001). *Transnational corporations and foreign affiliates*. Geneva: UNCTAD.

UN DEVELOPMENT PROGRAMME. (2006) *Human development report*. New York: UNDP.

UN DEVELOPMENT PROGRAMME. (2011) *Human development report*. New York: UNDP.

UNITE. (2013) Research uncovers growing zero hour subclass of insecure employment. Available at: http://www.unitetheunion.org/news/research-uncovers-growing-zero-hours-subclass-of-insecure-employment/ [Accessed 30 May 2015]

UNITED NATIONS. (2005) *Report on world fertility rates at 2003*. New York: United Nations.

UNITED NATIONS. (2006) *State of world population*. Available at: www.UNFPA.org/swp/2006

UNITED NATIONS. (2015) *World population prospects*. New York: Department of Economics and Social Affairs. Available at: http://esa.un.org/unpd/wpp/Publications/Files/Key_Findings_WPP_2015.pdf [Accessed 27 February 2016]

UNIVERSITY OF HULL BUSINESS SCHOOL. (2007) *Case study: Humberside Training and Enterprise Council*. Available at: Itsy.co.uk/sisn/orange/humber.doc [Accessed 27 March 2013]

US DEPARTMENT OF COMMERCE. (nd) http://www.ouedu/deptcomm/dodjcc [Accessed 25 February 2011]

VALENTINE, S., FLEISCHMANN, G., SPRAGUE, R. and GODKIN, L. (2010) Exploring the ethicality of firing employees who blog. *Human Resource Management.* Vol 49, No 1. pp87–108.

VALERO, A and ROLAND, I. (2015). *Productivity and business policies.* Centre for Economic Performance. March. Available at: http://cep.lse.ac.uk/pubs/download/ea021.pdf [Accessed 2 November 2015]

VANHONACKER, W. (2004) When good *guanxi* turns bad. *Harvard Business Review.* Vol 82, Issue 4.

VASAGER, J. (2013) Census highlights a divided Germany. *Daily Telegraph.* 1 June. p21.

VENABLES, T. (2005) Multinationals: heroes or villains of the global economy? *CentrePiece.* Spring.

VIDAL, J. (2007) Broader horizons. *The Guardian.* 25 July.

WACHMAN, R. (2010) When disaster strikes our corporate giants, sorry does seem to be the hardest word. *The Observer.* 26 December.

WAINWRIGHT, M. (1994) Mistakes led to chemical plant deaths. *The Guardian.* 21 June. p8.

WAKEAM, J. (2003) The five factors of a strategic alliance. *Ivey Business Journal.* May/June.

WAKEFIELD, J. (2014) Whodunnit? The mystery of the Sony Pictures hack. *BBC News.* 18 December. Available at: http://www.bbc.co.uk/news/technology-305350361 [Accessed 18 January 2015]

WAKELING, A. (2014) Give and take? Unravelling the true nature of zero-hours contracts. *Acas Policy Discussion Papers.* May. London: Acas.

WALDEN, M. (2014) *Globalization and the recession.* Cals News Center, North Carolina State University. Available at: http://www.cals.ncsu.edu/agcomm/news-center/economic-perspective/globalization-and-the-recession/ [Accessed 9 June 2015]

WALKER, A. (2012a) Q&A: European Stability Mechanism. BBC News. 8 October. Available at: http://www.bbc.co.uk/news/business-19870747 [Accessed 28 November 2012]

WALKER, A. (2012b) Eurozone: a very overcast outlook. BBC News. 15 November. Available at: http://www.bbc.co.uk/news/business-20344506 [Accessed 28 November 2012]

WALKER, R. (1990) Analysing the business portfolio in Black and Decker Europe. In: TAYLOR, B. and HARRISON, J. (eds) *The manager's casebook of business strategy.* Oxford: Butterworth-Heinemann.

WALLACE, P. (2001) *Agequake.* London: Nicholas Brealey.

WALL STREET JOURNAL. (2011) Corporate profit's share of pie most in 60 years. *Wall Street Journal.* 29 July.

WALSH, J. (2001) A happy reunion. *People Management*. 8 November.

WALTON, J. (1999) *Strategic human resource development*. London: FT/Prentice Hall.

WAPLES, J. (2009) *Sunday Times Business*. 4 October.

WARD, S. (2000) Brown to gamble on 'spend more' call'. *The Guardian*. 10 November.

WARNER, J. (2003) Network Rail spends away, but is it really value for money? *The Independent*. 8 May.

WARNER, J. (2007) Governor's letter should not be seen as a non-event. Rather, it highlights policy failings. *The Independent*. 18 April.

WARNER, M and WITZEL, M. (2003) *Managing in virtual organizations*. London: Routledge.

WARREN, E. (2007) Stars of India. *People Management*. 22 February.

WATERBRIEFING (2015) Southern Water accepts Ofwat final determination on AMP6 plan. Available at: http://waterbriefing.org/home/company-news/item/10406-southern-water-accepts-ofwat-final-determination-on-amp6-plan [Accessed 27 February 2016]

WATERS, R and MENN, J. (2009) Microsoft and Yahoo on defensive. *The Financial Times*. 31 July.

WATKINS, G. (2011) Perspectives on Asia: globalization and the war for talent. *Benefits and Compensation International*. Vol 41, No 3. October.

WATKINS, J. (2003) Wellness beats output slump. *People Management*. 18 December. p12.

WATKINS, K. E. and MARSICK, V. J. (1993) *Sculpting the learning organisation: lessons in the art and science of systemic change*. San Francisco, CA: Jossey-Bass.

WATT, N. (2009) Tory leader ditches referendum and backs away from EU 'bust-up'. *The Guardian*. 5 November.

WATT, N. (2013) Cameron to pledge in-out vote on EU. *The Guardian*. 23 January.

WATT, N. and STRATTON, A. (2009) Anger and anarchy among MPs at extent of Legg's demands. *The Guardian*. 14 October.

WATT, N., TAYLOR, M., MCVEIGH, K., TOPPING, A., SIDDIQUE, H. and STURCKE, J. (2009) MPs' expenses: what the latest information reveals about key figures. *The Guardian*. 18 June.

WATTS, R. (2008) Retired staff outstrip serving firemen. *Sunday Times*. 26 October.

WEAVER, M. (2001) Labour chooses third way to improve failing services. *The Guardian*. 22 October.

WEAVER, M. (2015) Economist defends 'Corbynomics' after Chris Leslie's criticism. *The Guardian*. 3 August.

WEBB, T. (2010) I needed RADA degree in acting, says ex-BP chief. *The Guardian*. 9 November.

WEBER, M. (1925) *Economy and society*. Oxford: Oxford University Press.

WEBER, M. (1964) *The theory of economic and social organization*. New York: Free Press.

WEIHRICH, H. (1982) The TOWS matrix: a tool for situational analysis. *Journal of Long Range Planning*. Vol 15, No 2.

WEISS, R. and MEHROTRA, A. (2001) Dynamic pricing and the future of e-commerce: an economic and legal analysis. *Virginia Journal of Law and Technology*. Vol 1. Summer.

WELCH, J. (2003) In the hiring line. *People Management*. 26 June. pp30–31.

WELDON, D. (2012) Profits before pay. *BBC Radio 4 Analysis*. 26 February. Available at: http://www.bbc.co/iplayer/episode/b)1c7nd5/Analysis_Profits_Before-Pay   [Accessed   7 November 2012]

WELSH GOVERNMENT. (2014) Single use carrier bags. 6 May http://gov.wales/topics/environmentcountryside/epq/waste_recycling/substance/carrierbags/?lang=en   [Accessed 13 January 2016]

WEST, K (2015) British steel industry buckles under the weight of cheap Chinese product. *The Guardian*. 28 September.

WEST, M. and PATTERSON, M. (1998) Profitable personnel. *People Management*. 8 January. pp28–31.

WHEATCROFT, P. (2004) Supermarkets take a convenient route. *The Times*. 17 August.

WHELAN, J. (2015) Business partnering, making it work. *Progress*. Issue 3. pp12–13. E-magazine, Corporate Research Forum. Available at: http://crforum.co.uk/research-and-resources/progress-issue-3-business-partner-making-it-work/ [Accessed 24 February 2016]

WHITEHEAD, T. (2008) Benefits of migrant labour 'overstated'. *Daily Telegraph*. 1 April. p14.

WHITELEY, P. (2013) Is HR ditching employee engagement when cutting staff costs? *Personnel Today*. 27 March.

WHITTINGTON, R. (2001) *What is strategy – and does it matter?* 2nd ed. London: Thomson.

WHITTINGTON, R and MAYER, M. (2000) *The European corporation: strategy, structure and social science*. Oxford: Oxford University Press.

WHOSHALLIVOTEFOR. (2015) http://www.whoshallvotefor.com/quiz/discuss/world/284 [Accessed 11 May 2015]

WHYTE, P. (2013) £28m profit by Holidaybreak. *Travel Trade Gazette*. 28 August.

WICKENS, P. (1987) *The road to Nissan: flexibility, quality, teamwork*. Basingstoke: Macmillan.

WILBY, P. (2013) The NHS will fail us so long as we look on it as a market. *The Guardian*. 8 August.

WILEMAN, A. (2007) India rising. *Management Today*. July.

WILKINSON, R. AND PICKETT, K. (2009) *The spirit level*. Harmondsworth: Penguin.

WILLIAMS, F. (2001) Global foreign investment flows 'set to fall to 40%'. *The Financial Times.* 19 September.

WILLIAMS, R. (2001) Under pressure, under pressure, under pressure. *Business Review.* September.

WILLOW, C. (2011) The wage squeeze. *Investors Chronicle.* 26 January.

WILSON, I. (2000) *The new rules of corporate conduct.* Westport CT: Quorum Books.

WINTOUR, P. (2007) Brown sets tough targets for reducing carbon. *The Guardian.* 20 November.

WINTOUR, P. (2015) Anti-austerity unpopular with voters, finds inquiry into Labour's election loss. *The Guardian.* 12 August.

WOETZEL, J. et al (2015) *How advancing women's equality can add £12 trillion to global growth.* Mckinsey Global Institute.

WOLF, M. (2005) *Why globalization works.* New Haven, CT: Yale Nota Bene.

WOMACK, S. (2007) How occupation affects life expectancy. *Daily Telegraph.* 25 October.

WOOD, P. (1995) The four pillars of human resource management; are they connected? *Human Resource Management Journal.* Vol 5, No 5.

WOOD, Z. (2012) Tesco calls time on megastores after profit warning shock. *The Observer.* 15 January.

WOODHEAD, M. (2004) Exodus heralds end of Schoder's IT dream. *Sunday Times.* 17 November.

WOODS, N. (2000) *The political economy of globalization.* Basingstoke: Macmillan. pp3–7.

WOODS, N. (2007) Power shift: do we need better global economic institutions? *Institute of Public Policy Research.* January.

WOODWARD, W. (2003) School firms' forte is 'lobbying for work'. *Guardian.* 5 May.

WOODWARD, S. and HENDRY, C. (2004) Leading and coping with change. *Journal of Change Management.* Vol 4, No 2. June.

WORKERS' EDUCATIONAL ASSOCIATION (WEA) IN NORTHERN IRELAND (nd). *Mission statement and WEA values.* Available at: http://www.wea-ni.com [Accessed 27 February 2016]

WORLD BANK. (2000) *Beyond economic growth: meeting the challenges of global development.* Geneva: World Bank. Available at: www.worldbank.org/depweb/beyond/beyondco/beg_04.pdf

WORLD BANK (2015) Gini Index. Available at: http://data.worldbank.org/indicator/SI.POV.GINI [Accessed 27 February 2016]

WORTHINGTON, I. and BRITTON, C. (2006) *The Business Environment.* 5th ed. Harlow: FT/Prentice Hall.

YATES, T. (2015) Corbyn's QE for the people jeopardises the Bank of England's independence. *The Guardian.* 22 September.

YOUNG, M. (1958) *The rise of the meritocracy.* Harmondsworth: Penguin.

YUEH, L. (2015) The end of an era for China. *BBC News.* 15 April. Available at: http://www.bbc.co.uk/news/business-32315208 [Accessed 11 November 2015]

ZHANG, Z. (2012) Economic powerhouse rising in Central China. *China Business Weekly.* 15 October.

ZHELTOUKHOVA, K. (2014) *HR: getting smart about agile working.* London: Chartered Institute of Personnel and Development.

ZINGALES, L. (2012) Why I was won over by Glass-Steagall. *The Financial Times.* 10 June.

Index